D0571714

WORK AND SOCIETY

WORK AND SOCIETY

EDWARD GROSS

THE STATE COLLEGE OF WASHINGTON

THE THOMAS Y. CROWELL COMPANY · NEW YORK

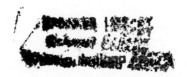

TO FLORENCE, DAVID, AND DEBBY

ACKNOWLEDGMENTS

Acknowledgment is gratefully made to the following agents, authors, and publishers who have granted permission to reprint excerpts from copyrighted publications.

American Catholic Sociological Review for excerpts from E. C. Hughes' "Principles and Rationalizations in Race Relations," *American Catholic Sociological Review*, **8**:3–11, 1947.

Brandt & Brandt for excerpts from George Orwell's *Down and Out in Paris and London,* New York: Harcourt, Brace and Company. Copyright © 1933 by George Orwell.

Canadian Citizenship Council for excerpts from its publication *The Problems of Race* (1944).

Richard Centers for the table from his article "Occupational Mobility of Urban Occupational Strata," *American Sociological Review,* **13**:197–203, 1948.

Columbia University Press for excerpts from:

D. V. Kennedy's *Union Policy and Incentive Wage Methods* (New York: Columbia University Press, 1945).

The National Manpower Council's report *Womanpower* (New York: Columbia University Press, 1957).

The Free Press for excerpts from:

E. C. and H. M. Hughes' *Where Peoples Meet* (Glencoe, Ill.: The Free Press, 1952).

S. M. Lipset *et al., Union Democracy* (Glencoe, Ill.: The Free Press, 1956).

Talcott Parsons' "Revised Analytical Approach to the Theory of Social Stratification" in R. Bendix and S. M. Lipset (eds.), *Class Status and Power* (Glencoe, Ill.: The Free Press, 1953).

Natalie Rogof's *Recent Trends in Occupational Mobility* (Glencoe, Ill.: The Free Press, 1953).

Harcourt, Brace and Company, Inc., for excerpts from *Men at Work* by Stuart Chase, copyright, 1941, 1943, 1944, 1945, by Stuart Chase. Reprinted by permission of Harcourt, Brace and Company, Inc.

Harper & Brothers for excerpts from:

E. C. Hughes' "Work and the Self" in J. H. Rohrer and M. Sherif (eds.), *Social Psychology at the Crossroads* (New York: Harper & Brothers, 1951).

G. E. Simpson and J. M. Yinger's *Racial and Cultural Minorities* (New York: Harper & Brothers, 1951).

Charles R. Walker's *Steel Town* (New York: Harper & Brothers, 1950).

W. F. White *et al., Money and Motivation* (New York: Harper & Brothers, 1955).

Harvard University Press for excerpts from:

C. M. Arensberg and S. T. Kimball's *Family and Community in Ireland,* Cambridge, Mass.: Harvard University Press, Copyright, 1940, by the President and Fellows of Harvard College;

F. J. Roethlisberger and W. J. Dickson's *Management and the Worker,* Copyright, 1939, Cambridge, Mass.: Harvard University Press, Copyright, 1939, by the President and Fellows of Harvard College;

L. Ulman's *The Rise of the National Trade Union,* Cambridge, Mass.: Harvard University Press, Copyright, 1956, by the President and Fellows of Harvard College; and

C. R. Walker and R. H. Guest's *The Man on the Assembly Line,* Cambridge, Mass.: Harvard University Press, Copyright, 1952, by the President and Fellows of Harvard College.

McGraw-Hill Book Co., Inc., for excerpts from A. Davis' "The Motivation of the Under-Privileged Worker," in W. F. Whyte (ed.), *Industry and Society,* New York: McGraw-Hill Book Co., Inc., 1946.

The National Council of the Churches of Christ for excerpts from E. E. Lowry's *Migrants of the Crops: They Starve That We May Eat,* 1938 (OP).

The National Opinion Research Center for excerpts from Paul K. Hatt and Cecil C. North's "Jobs and Occupations: A Popular Evaluation," *Opinion News,* 9:3–13, Sept. 1, 1947.

Harold Ober Associates for excerpts from Pearl S. Buck's *Fighting Angel.* Copyright © 1936 by Pearl S. Buck. Reprinted by permission of Harold Ober Associates Incorporated.

Random House for excerpts from Ely S. Chinoy's *Automobile Workers and the American Dream,* New York: Random House, 1955.

Donald Roy for excerpts from "Work Satisfaction and Social Reward in Quota Achievement," *American Sociological Review,* 18:507–514, 1953.

Rural Sociology for excerpts from C. P. Loomis' "Visiting Patterns and Miscegenation at Oxapampa, Peru," *Rural Sociology,* 9:68, 1944.

The Russell Sage Foundation for excerpts from L. Sharp's "Steel Axes for Stone Age Australians," in E. H. Specer (ed.), *Human Problems in Technological Change,* New York: Russell Sage, 1952.

The Society for Applied Anthropology for excerpts from:

O. Collins *et al.,* "Restrictions of Output and Social Cleavage in Industry," *Applied Anthropology* 5:1–14, Summer, 1946; and

M. Dalton's "The Industrial Rate-Buster: A Characterization," *Applied Anthropology,* 7:5–15, Winter, 1948.

United Steelworkers of America for excerpts from the *Agreement Between Carnegie-Illinois Steel Corporation and the United Steelworkers of America, CIO,* March 13, 1945, Philadelphia.

University of California Press for excerpts from Lloyd H. Fisher's *The Harvest Labor Market,* 1953.

University of Chicago Press for excerpts from:

M. Dalton's "Worker Response and Social Background," *Journal of Political Economy,* 55:326–327, 1947;

T. Parsons' "An Analytical Approach to the Theory of Social Stratification," *American Journal of Sociology,* 45:841–862, 1940.

D. Roy's "Efficiency and the 'Fix,'" *American Journal of Sociology,* **60**:263–267, 1954; and

D. Roy's "Quota Restriction and Goldbricking in a Machine Shop," *American Journal of Sociology,* **57**:429–438, 1952.

University of Minnesota Press for excerpts from Theodore Caplow's *The Sociology of Work,* Minneapolis: University of Minnesota Press, 1954.

John Wiley & Sons, Inc., for excerpts from:

R. Bendix's *Work and Authority in Industry,* copyright, 1956, John Wiley & Sons, Inc.; and

A. B. Hollingshead's *Elmtown's Youth,* copyright, 1949, John Wiley & Sons, Inc.

Yale University Press for excerpts from David Riesman *et al., The Lonely Crowd,* New Haven: Yale University Press, 1950.

PREFACE

The central assumption of this book is this: in order to understand any type of work, we must look at work comparatively. We understand factory workers better if we compare them with farmers, and we understand American farmers better if we also study Irish farmers. It follows from this assumption that we must limit ourselves to what we *know*, reliably, from research findings. I followed this course as closely as I was able and it produced two effects: (1) Since we know a good deal more about some subjects than others, some discussions, occupational mobility, for instance, are longer than others, such as occupational personality. While this is not as satisfying as a "balanced" treatment might be, I have not felt that the student would be any the poorer, and in fact that he might be encouraged by these gaps to raise questions in class, and best of all, perhaps, to plan to do some research himself to help fill them. (2) There is a relative scarcity of research on white-collar workers (though there is a good deal of sophisticated discussion), governmental organizations, military organizations, the transportation industry, and on other work organizations. The great bulk of research has been in the study of occupations, especially the professions, and of the factory, and our discussion in this book reflects this state of affairs. In addition, I have brought together materials based on research carried on by students of agricultural life and have made extensive use of the one outstanding study of the restaurant—that by William Foote Whyte.

There is an important bias—if it may be called that—throughout the book: I have paid most attention to findings that admit of wide generalizability. Consequently, although most of the material is drawn from American sources, I have not considered a finding any the more valuable because it happened to shed light on a peculiarly American problem. Nor have I considered another finding of less importance because there was no obvious American parallel. Further, my concern has not been only with the immediate and the timely. The AFL and CIO merged in 1955, and, as John L. Lewis once did, one of them may have "disaffiliated" by the time this book comes off the presses. If research is done on this merged group, that research will be worth examining, but we are not under obligation to report the fact of merger itself except, of course, as it may relate to research. The medieval guild may not shed much light on the operation of the union local but that does not make it any the less valuable as an occupational organization in its own right. As Everett C. Hughes once pointed out, our task as scientists is not that of bringing in the latest news.

But the major attempt to view findings in a broad context is achieved through a conceptual framework. I develop this framework, bit by bit, through the examination of cross-cultural research materials from Dobu and Eire—but that is simply a pedagogical device. As a simple count of name references would show, this framework derives from the work of Everett C. Hughes on the professions. The major concepts—the institutional system, the status and authority system, the career, and the work group—and many of the minor concepts are his. My contribution has been, essentially, that of showing how these concepts may be used in the study of all occupations, the farm, the restaurant and factory, and, I believe, anywhere where research can be carried out. In putting forth this theory, I have no axe to grind. I do not wish to make a case for "conflict of interest" approaches, "human relations" approaches, or any others. The test of a theory is how many important, valid hypotheses it generates, not how much heat it does.

More broadly, I have tried to carve out "man as worker" as a legitimate theoretical area within sociology, rather than to see it as a convenient research category or as "applied" sociology. The distinction between pure and applied sociology has not helped our understanding of work much and, instead, has produced wasteful intellectual conflict. One of the values of the study of work relations is that it forces the researcher into contact with actual workers. If, as a consequence, a finding should prove of value to the worker, his boss, or his union's business agent, so much the better. Yet because a piece of research admits of no possible application in the real world (and I find it difficult to imagine this), that does not, it seems to me, make it any the better or worse than the other finding. But whatever may be done with research findings, research of *any* kind requires theoretical guidance. We are at the point where we should be able to move a little beyond the "exploratory" study which adds its theory after the findings are in. This book is intended for courses with such names as industrial sociology, industry and the community, and sociology of occupations and its draws also on important contributions from the related fields of industrial psychology, business administration, and labor economics. It is a strong tribute to our conceptual framework that it pulls together this great mass of research findings in a meaningful manner and provides clues for what seem to be the most fruitful next steps.

The emphasis on research findings has necessarily made me highly conscious of the size of the intellectual debt I owe to others. But certain persons stand out in my mind. First is Everett C. Hughes for reasons I have already indicated. To William Foote Whyte I owe my empirical interest. His was a major influence in teaching me to carry on research myself as well as to appraise the research of others. Through his guidance as well as through the example he set by his own research, he convinced me that the study of work was a challenge worth pursuing for a lifetime. My interest in comparative analysis in general (and in Dobu in particular) I owe to C. W. M. Hart. Happily, since he is an anthropologist, he forced me continually to be on guard to avoid the provincialism that reduces the value of some of our research. It is difficult to pin down precisely the areas in which William F. Ogburn and the late Louis Wirth affected my thinking in this book. Their influence was broad and will be evident throughout. Herbert Blumer also made important impressions on my research concerns and has been an influence in the continuing task of separating out the immediate from the important.

To Arnold M. Rose I am particularly grateful for his careful and critical reading of the manuscript. My special thanks to Murray A. Straus and to J. B. Montague who read critically parts of the manuscript and to Martin Jay and Ruth Crowe for major assistance in the preparation of the indexes.

CONTENTS

PART FOUR

TWO MAJOR PROBLEMS:
UNIONS AND RACES AT WORK

PART ONE

THE WORLD OF WORK

CHAPTER ONE

THE AREA OF STUDY

WHY STUDY WORK?

When one thinks of the many pressing problems that besiege our world today, problems centering about war and peace and our very survival, certainly one of the first questions that one would wish answered is why we should give our attention to such a pedestrian, obvious thing as the everyday work that we all do. And the first answer is that it is precisely because work is an obvious thing that we must give our attention to it. A distinguished sociologist, Louis Wirth, was fond of saying: "If you wish to understand a man, find out what he takes for granted." In other words, examine those things about him that he regards as so obvious as not to be worth discussing, for it is these things that will be found to be closest to his innermost self. That is why he takes them for granted and raises no question about them. At times, sociology has had a reputation as a wastebasket science: it took for its subject matter whatever the other social sciences were not interested in studying. It was preoccupied with such matters as crime, prostitution, poverty—with the seamy side of life. The sociologist became the person who was interested in the queer, the unusual, the bizarre. But it is now clear that sociology deals with research into matters lying at the very center of human social life—the family, the church, the government, the city, the labor union. Our excursion into the study of work represents one of the main segments of this broad interest in the totality of man's social life.

For after all, the average man spends about one-third of his entire life as a worker; the housewife spends even more. And if we add to this the time spent in preparation, and the time the worker spends off the job worrying about his job or preparing for a better one, then surely a very large portion of his life is given over to work. And when one looks at the great volume of effort that has gone into the study of such matters as crime, race relations, population and the like, one would certainly admit that work is at least as important as those areas.

Work provides us, further, with one of the major bonds through which we are united with our fellows. A few people work alone—the lonely artist struggling in a rat-infested garret for contact with the infinite comes to mind. But most persons work in association with others on some common endeavor. Sometimes the resulting organization may be very complex. In medicine, the doctor finds himself caught up in a vast network of organizations which includes medical schools, medical societies, health insurance societies, state licensing bodies, hospitals, X-ray laboratories, and so on. Or the organization may be of the sort found in modern, large-scale industry, or government, or commercialized recreation, or education. And it is through our membership in such work organizations that we are provided with a fundamental index of status and self-respect. A hundred years ago, in rural America, when two strangers met, the first question was likely to be: "Where are you from?" And the answer meant something. When the newcomer mentioned a given town, or said "From the hill country," the other was then able to place him in his scale of values. He could make a shrewd estimation of the man's probable wealth and previous work experience. If it happened that they were both from the same area, then the next question was sure to be about each other's names. Again, in a period of stable residence, where one family lived on the same farm for generations, a name meant something. The family had a reputation—good or bad—and to be known as one of the Hatfields was very different from being known as one of the McCoys.

But under modern conditions of mobility, migration, the reduction in size of family, and urbanization, neither of the above two questions is likely to have much meaning. Place of birth is likely to be different from the place in which one was brought up, which in turn may be different from where one was educated, and that different in turn from where one takes a job. To be told the names of any of these places is to be told very little about the man. The name of his family is likely to be even less revealing. The question now that is likely to come up very early in conversation is: "What do you do?" and when that question is asked, we know that what it meant is what kind of *work* do you do. The answer one gets enables one to place the man at least approximately. Depending on his answer, we can estimate how much his income is, whether he is likely to be married or not, the size of his family, where he lives, where he works, how he spends his leisure time, what clubs he belongs to. And from our estimates of these things, we in turn make a judgment as to how we should behave toward him—whether we should accord him respect, tolerance, or contempt, whether we should seek his help, or offer him help, whether we want him as a friend or not. Indeed, it is precisely because place of origin and name have become unreliable as indices of status, that occupation becomes so important to us. At the same time, because we do make judgments about a man on the basis of his occupation, it becomes very important that these judgments be accurate. And in brief, that is what this book is about: Knowing what a man does for a living, what conclusions can one draw about him, and with what degree of accuracy.

WHAT IS WORK?

The term "work" is by no means easy to define precisely. If one asks the layman, he will answer: "It's what I do to earn a living" or "What I do to be able to pay my rent, or send my boy to college." This kind of answer refers to the purpose of work, but it does not tell us what work itself is. A wag once defined work as something you do when you would rather be doing something else. While obviously facetious, that approach implies that work has associated with it a quality of irksomeness or drudgery, and many persons would agree with that statement.[1] Yet not all work is irksome. Many persons enjoy their work tremendously, and to some it is synonymous with life itself. The notion that work is drudgery is undoubtedly tied up with religious ideas of working by the sweat of one's brow as a punishment for original sin. Indeed, work is employed as a punishment in many of our prisons. Such considerations as these are relevant to understanding people's conception of work, but they do not help us very much in defining it.[2]

Work may be looked at from several points of view. Among those

[1] This widely held view of work has been aptly described in Riesman (36) as follows: . . . it (work) is thought of as alien to man—it is a sort of disciplined salvage operation, rescuing a useful social product from chaos and the disorders of man's innate laziness. The same era . . . that saw the most astounding increase in man's mastery over nature took it as axiomatic, echoing a series of writers from Malthus to Sumner and Freud, that people had to be driven to work by economic necessity. Today, knowing more about the nature of man and of work, we still nevertheless tend to accept the psychological premise that work and productivity are disciplines exerted against the grain of man's nature.

[2] For an historical discussion of culturally defined conceptions of the nature of work, see Tilgher (45).

sciences concerned with it, the most important are physics, biology, medicine, psychology, economics, and sociology.

THE PHYSICIST'S CONCEPTION OF WORK

The physicist approaches work operationally (5, Ch. 1; 27): that is, in terms of the technique used to measure work. He defines it as Force multiplied by Distance and expresses the result in foot-pounds or ergs. If one lifts five pounds through two feet, one is said to have done ten foot-pounds of work. This definition serves the physicist admirably in *measuring* work, but does not tell us what he is measuring. A thorough operationalist would consider that question unimportant. The best statement we could get would be to the effect that work is "what happens" when force moves through distance. We thus get little help from the physicist. It should be noted that the physicist's definition is perfectly general: humans do work, but the same measuring device may be applied to beavers building dams, or to a crane lifting a steel rail off the ground.

THE BIOLOGIST'S APPROACH TO WORK

To the biologist, work involves the movement of muscles, or some activity of the nervous system. Here, there is some restriction of interest from the broad approach of the physicist, for the concern is only with living things. The biologist will note that when people work, there are various chemical reactions in the body and manifold cell activities. Fatigue is accompanied by the production of lactic acid in the muscles. We see then that the biologist does not define work for us. He asks us to tell him when someone is working. If such a person is identified, then the biologist stands ready to inform us what the physiological accompaniments of work are. Similarly, the doctor stands ready to advise on the limits of the human mechanism in the performance of work. Out of this interest has grown the field of Industrial Hygiene,[3] one of the earliest subjects of interest to students of factory life. It was recognized that such matters as accidents, poisonous dusts, and absenteeism due to illness and fatigue were matters of serious import to the conduct of any industrial activity, and the far-sighted industry today will usually have a medical staff for its employees.[4]

But while no one would wish to deny the importance of the biological aspects of work, we see that we do not get any help on a definition of work. We learn what the *effects* or *accompaniments* of work are,

[3] See (11, 18, 22, 40, 42).
[4] The significance of work stress has also become a major object of interest in psychosomatic medicine. See (7, 41).

provided we have already decided what work is. Further, these biological effects also accompany non-work activities; in fact, they are synonymous with activity itself. What the biologist and doctor do is apply generalized knowledge to the special case of activities that, for some reason, are called "work," for reasons of efficiency or from humanitarian motives.

THE PSYCHOLOGIST'S APPROACH TO WORK

It is with the psychologist that we encounter the first serious attempt to define work. The psychologist looks upon work as a *task* or series of tasks. By a task is meant a problem or something that is *to be done*. The field of Industrial Psychology addresses itself to the question of the relationship between the individual and the task. The typical procedure of the Industrial Psychologist is first to look at the defined task and then to analyze it into its components. For example, consider the task of operating a sewing machine in a clothing factory. The psychologist will note that its successful operation requires a certain intelligence, a certain eye-hand coordination, a certain minimal reaction time. At the same time, he will note that efficient work requires a certain intensity of lighting, a certain kind of chair. Allowance will be made for fatigue with the recommendation of certain rest periods. The next step is the drawing up of a series of tests in order to assess the worker's ability to perform the task. These will be tests of intelligence, of eye-hand coordination, reaction time, and whatever else the psychologist has decided is essential for the efficient performance of the task with minimum harm to the individual. On the basis of the results of those tests, the psychologist will decide that a given person can or cannot perform the task.[5]

The success with which the industrial psychologist can do his work is dependent on his ability to break the task down into its component skills and on the relevance of those skills to the successful performance of the job. Some of the greatest work of the industrial psychologists has been in the classical crafts, stimulated by such work as Gilbreth's [6] in time-and-motion studies of bricklaying. But such studies are today largely of academic interest. One may be able to show a worker how he can work more efficiently, but whether he will respond to this appeal is something else again. Here such matters as tradition, the good

---

[5] Cf. (6, 31, 44, 47).

[6] See Gilbreth (12a). Gilbreth was not himself an industrial psychologist, but his work, and especially that of his teacher, F. W. Taylor, were important influences on the development of industrial psychology. Also see (47, pp. 9 ff).

opinion of his fellows, antagonism to the boss, union controls, and other matters about which we will have much to say are likely to be of paramount importance. Psychologists have also attempted to grapple with these matters in their studies of motivation (48).

But of greater significance is the effect of mechanization on skills. Increasingly, the skills formerly required of the worker are being built into the machine, so that the worker becomes a machine-tender with very few skills being required except those of staying awake, or being alert—skills that most people may be assumed to have. The goal of many an industrial designer is to design machines that will require almost no human assistance. The result is to remove whatever original contribution the worker might make, and therefore what remains becomes highly boring. One result is that industrial psychologists have been decreasingly concerned with fitting the worker to the job—almost anyone *can* do the job. Rather, the concern has been shifting to preventing boredom, increasing satisfaction, and raising "morale." [7] As the problem of the relation between the individual and the job decreases in significance, it is replaced by the problem of the relation between the individual and his work group and by the problem of reconciling worker values with management values. No management (who, after all, pays the wage bill) is pleased to continue wage payments to a work group whose sense of group solidarity may be high but whose productivity is low. As industrial psychologists pay more attention to problems such as these,[8] their research comes to overlap that of the sociologist.

THE ECONOMIST'S VIEW OF WORK

Economics may be defined as the study of the relation between resources and effort. Man, like all living things, must make use of the resources of the world in order to live, and it takes effort to find these resources and change them into usable form. Those problems obviously involve production and distribution. The economist is concerned with determining *how much* effort it requires to get and transform resources; that is, with cost. Cost in turn involves power, transportation, manufacturing, distribution, sales, and so on. One part of this cost is the effort put out by humans, and the economist calls that effort *labor*.

The economist, therefore, sees work as labor, as one cost among others which arises because it is necessary, unavoidable. Why? Obviously for the production and distribution of goods and services. Therefore, the

---

[7] A term variously defined but referring, usually, to a set of feelings which helps a group to achieve its goals. See (3, pp. 208 ff. and *passim*).

[8] See (9; 23, pp. 86–89; 24, pp. 145–71; 48, Pts. 3, 4).

economist is not interested in work as such but in the *purposes* of work,[9] in what is to be accomplished by it, and what its products are worth. It is this viewpoint that the layman takes when he thinks of work. It is a *means* to some other end. This explains, too, why this approach is concerned with efficiency. Obviously, if something is a means, then one hopes to make that means as rationally oriented as possible to the achievement of one's goal. This approach tells us little about work as such, except that it is likely to have a purpose outside itself. However, even that is not always true since for some persons work becomes an end in itself and its own reward.

The economist himself, insofar as he has been interested in the study of work, has expressed this interest in areas such as labor economics. Of more immediate concern to us has been the adoption of the economist's approach in the field of business administration as exemplified in the areas of industrial and personnel management.[10] The emphasis in the latter areas has tended to be on workers as elements in the total cost picture, and on efficient management.[11] As is usually the case in applied areas, the approach has tended to be case or clinically oriented, with data drawn from the experience of particular businessmen, managers, or labor union men. At the same time, students of industrial or personnel management have shown a penchant for "principles" so as to render the results of their investigations in rule-of-thumb fashion to the businessman. For example, in industrial management, or what used to be called "scientific" management, it is common to speak of the "span of control." The general question is: How many men should a supervisor have under him so as to be able to supervise them adequately? W. E. Parker and R. W. Kleemeier (34, pp. 250–251) make the following statement:

[9] This point of view is well expressed in Alfred Marshall's (28, p. 65) widely used definition of labor (adapted from Jevons): ". . . any exertion of mind or body undergone partly or wholly with a view to some good other than the pleasure derived directly from the work." Presumably, then, if a man engaged in some activity purely for the pleasure of the activity itself, it would not be called "labor." Marshall himself expresses dissatisfaction with the definition, but feels that some such approach is needed at least for what he calls *productive* labor.

[10] The student interested in these areas should see, for historical perspective, the following: (1, 13, 14, 21, 25, 31, 43).

[11] Pigors and Myers (35, pp. 6–7), quote with strong approval Thomas G. Spates' definition of personnel administration, which is as follows: "Personnel administration is a code of the ways of organizing and treating individuals at work so that they will get the greatest possible realization of their intrinsic abilities, thus attaining maximum efficiency for themselves and their group, and thereby giving to the enterprise of which they are a part its determining competitive advantage and its optimum results."

For most work it has been found that no supervisor can effectively manage more than ten to fifteen workers. It is humanly impossible for the supervisor to know them intimately enough and to consider all the cross relationships in his group if he has more than this number. Fayol, the great French industrial engineer, computed the interrelationships present when there are ten subordinates. He found that there were 6,133 direct and group relationships when a supervisor had ten subordinates. Obviously, this is entirely too many for any supervisor to keep in mind each time he gives an order.

James C. Worthy (49, pp. 169–79), in criticizing this notion, comments that successful Sears, Roebuck organizations ". . . often deliberately give each key executive so many subordinates that it is impossible for him to exercise too close supervision over their activities." Under those conditions, those under him are likely to work at a much higher rate of efficiency and to have higher morale, as well. Gardner and Moore (12, p. 208) comment further on the mathematics of span of control reasoning:

. . . such reasoning, though mathematically correct, bears no relation to the realities of human relations.

The effect of such thinking, they point out, is to produce a "tall" organization (one with many supervisory levels) whether such an organization is needed or not. It produces a system of very close checking of subordinates which leads to a great waste of time for most activities. When, for any reason, a department must be expanded, the foreman or department head, unless he gets immediate assistance, is lost.[12]

Yet it was from just such attempts to explore some of the accepted "principles" of scientific management by the Harvard Graduate School of Business Administration at the Western Electric plant near Chicago, that there emerged the first major piece of research in the field of Industrial Sociology, about which we will have much to say later (24,37, 38). Of all fields, that of business administration has tended to work closest with sociology until it is often difficult to distinguish between the contributions of the two.

---

[12] Gardner and Moore (12, p. 211) note a large number of other problems created by span-of-control limitations on supervisors, of which two problems deserve special mention: a tendency for the subordinate to be overconcerned with what his supervisor thinks of him, and a tendency to "buck" decisions up the line.

For a reassessment of this widely used principle by one of the first to apply it to business organizations, see Urwick (46).

THE SOCIOLOGIST'S APPROACH TO WORK

Sociology is concerned with man's social life. Consequently, the sociologist is interested in work insofar as it involves some form of social organization. The focus therefore is on what are called *work relationships.* A work relationship is one in which persons perform activities which are designed to achieve objectives usually defined by others. The activities that they perform are called "work." For example, a factory work crew performs activities to reach objectives set forth by foremen, supervisors, or others; the factory as a whole performs activity to reach objectives set forth by boards of directors or indirectly by society at large in the form of customers; the doctor is one of an organized group who performs activities to reach objectives defined by his colleagues, his patients, the state, and others.

Our definition stated that the worker performs activities to reach objectives *usually* set forth by others. The word "usually" requires comment, because there are two apparent exceptions to the definition. The first is that occasionally an individual or group will define an objective for itself. A group of men may be walking through a forest, come across a log in their way, and then, without comment, combine efforts to push it out of the way. While it may not be denied that such situations do arise, they are usually brief, not very important, and rarely account for much of the time of the participants. The other apparent exception is provided by the fact that a major determinant of the objectives of persons is the culture of the society within which they live. These objectives may consist of a certain rate of production, a certain quality of services, a certain amount of money, and so on. However, culture never operates in isolation from people, but instead through surrogates; so that, in the last analysis, the persons who determine one's objectives may usually be located somewhere. It may be seen, then, that neither of these apparent exceptions turns out in practice to be very significant.

Work relationships may be examined from two complementary points of view. First, one may focus attention on a given *type of work* and consider the manner in which social relationships among practitioners of the type of work (or related practitioners) are defined. A type of work is ordinarily referred to as an *occupation.* And second, one may focus attention on the manner in which different occupations are related within a given *work organization,* such as the factory. To illustrate: One may regard doctors as an object of study and consider the relationships of doctors to one another, to related practitioners, such as dentists, opticians, psychiatrists, X-ray technicians, and to their patients. Or, one may look at the hospital as a work organization and consider the manner in which the various practitioners or specialists who are found in the hospital are related to one another *by* and *through* the hospital. That is, one considers the relationship to each other of supervisors, doctors, nurses, anaesthetists, radiologists, interns, nurses' aides and attendants, maintenance staffs, office and administrative staffs, boards of trustees, social workers, and so on.

These two ways of looking at work relationships—occupations and work organizations—correspond to two areas of study in sociology. The first is usually referred to as the Sociology of Occupations and Professions (7),[13] and the second is often called by the dubious name, Industrial Sociology—dubious because it is too limiting and because it suggests that the area is nothing more than an application of sociological knowledge to industry.[14] While both areas are recognized, they are usually dealt with separately without recognition of the very close relationship between them. An occupation is almost always practiced within a work organization and a work organization is nothing more than an organization of occupations.

When we look at *occupations,* we are interested in answers to the following kinds of questions: how is the occupation related to other occupations and to other parts of the society; how is payment made, such as wages, salaries, fees, etc.; what privileges, rights, and duties attach to different specialties; how does one enter the occupation; how does the occupation control its members; what determines success in the occupation; what is the relation between the occupation and the personality of a practitioner; and who control the occupation and how do such persons maintain their control. We are also interested in the manner in which the occupation represents itself to the outside world, in the form of professional associations or societies, through advertising and in other ways, and the legal and other controls that society imposes on it in turn.

By contrast, when we look at a *work organization,* we are interested in a different set of matters. In line with our definition of work, we conceive of a work organization as one having definite or prescribed objectives. In our society, there are at least two types of such organizations: those engaged in part time or as a hobby, and those engaged in full time. Usually this reduces to a distinction between activities on which one is not dependent for a living, and those on which one is. It is customary to restrict the term "work" only to the latter, and yet, surely persons who participate, say, in a Community Chest drive during their free evenings are working. Similarly, club activities and other social-

[13] For an assessment of research in this field, see Lastrucci (26).
[14] See (4, 17, 19, 20, 30, 32, 33).

recreational pursuits often have a good deal of work associated with them. The factor of pleasure is not relevant in this context. Indeed, any attempt to deal with work in the light of pleasure or its absence is liable to grave subjectivity.

The limitation imposed—that the organization shall have definite or prescribed objectives—requires comment. In a sense, all organizations have objectives. The objective may have been changed over time such that the original objective (perhaps unstated or unrecognized) is lost in antiquity, or the organization may have only a vague purpose, such as "fellowship." We restrict the concept "work organization" only to those organizations wherein the objective is *clear* and where it is *formalized*. This may take place as a consequence of the organization's position in society, such that there is a social demand for its services, or it may take place by virtue of the authority of certain persons who own or control the organization. When objectives are clearly enunciated, then the organization perforce requires that relationships within the organization shall be defined so as to achieve those obectives. Work organizations thus become control bodies so far as their membership is concerned.

Accordingly, it may be seen that work organizations in our society would include governmental staffs, schools, universities, restaurants, farms, business offices, armies, churches, hospitals, and factories. They would not ordinarily include families, gangs, social cliques, and similar organizations. However, non-work organizations may become work organizations on specific occasions, a possibility best illustrated by the family in many parts of the world, or in the case of the family-business in Western society. And, indeed, any organization has an element of work in it to the extent that activities are directed or controlled in the service of a stated or recognized objective.

THE SCIENTIFIC STUDY OF WORK RELATIONSHIPS

Having described our area, it is important to point out certain problems we shall encounter in studying it. Some of these problems are peculiar to the sociology of work; others are common to all the social sciences. The problems may be classified as dealing with: method, the relation of scientific findings to folk knowledge, and the application of findings to solve practical problems.

1. METHODOLOGICAL PROBLEMS

In studying man as a worker, we find our subject is fundamentally different from that which the biologist or astronomer, say, study. Humans are aware they are being studied and may color their responses or behavior accordingly. By contrast, the biologist does not have to be concerned that the microbe will behave differently in the laboratory from the way it behaves in its natural habitat. The stars go on their way whether astronomers look at them or not. But humans may "fake" responses, be kind to the investigator without actually telling him anything, or simply refuse to respond. The student of the sociology of work is continually faced with this problem since he can rarely reproduce real working conditions in the laboratory. Instead, he is usually conducting his research in actual factories or other work situations where he is literally on someone else's property to which he has been admitted, probably grudgingly, until he proves his worth. As such he is a stranger whose behavior, in spite of his assurances, is always suspect. Occasionally the researcher meets the attitude expressed (with unusual frankness) by an Air Force sergeant in a study of the "gripes" of servicemen (16):

I've seen you boys come and go for years. I've filled out so many questionnaires asking me for my gripes and opinions that I'm bored with them, and I've never seen 10 cents' worth of good come out of any of them. What are they sending you guys around for anyhow? They know what we need out here. Maybe they don't know everything, but they know the main things. And don't tell me they haven't got the money. They're paying *you,* aren't they? I'll give you a statement for your book, and maybe you won't like it. They ought to take the money they pay you and use it to put in a decent pool table in the day room. You can quote me on that.

When such resistance occurs, unusual skill is required in structuring the role of the researcher and in devising special, often indirect research techniques.

2. SCIENCE AND FOLK KNOWLEDGE

Those who are apologetic for the fact that the social sciences are not as advanced as the physical sciences will often offer the defense of youth. Yet, as Louis Wirth once pointed out, the problem the social sciences face is not that they are so young but rather that they are so old. Men have thought about themselves since the dawn of history and have expressed their conclusions in the form of political philosophies, systems of religious ethics, and thousands of proverbs and sayings. With time, these beliefs have passed into the thinking of people and come to be taken for granted. This situation creates a dilemma for the social scientist: if one of his findings goes contrary to a piece of folk knowledge, it may be rejected as absurd; but if he confirms a piece of folk knowledge, he is simply "belaboring the obvious." The former possibility is not so serious, for mankind will give up a belief if the proofs to the contrary are weighty enough; the latter possibility is very difficult to deal with. Thus, the Western Electric studies (23) showed that employees responded to a test program not because of anything in the program itself but rather because for the first time the company, by instituting the program, showed that it was interested in the welfare of its workers. Gilson (15), in reviewing the study, makes the standard comment that there is nothing surprising about this discovery, we knew it all before, and surely one should not have had to spend research funds to uncover this obvious fact. It *was* obvious in one sense. It was obvious in that it had become part of our folklore, but it had *never been tested* scientifically, and it is quite possible that the test might have shown the obvious belief to be false. The history of science is full of such cases. It is obvious to anyone with normal eyesight that the earth is flat; all we need do is look out the window to confirm it.

The student of the sociology of work may meet this problem when he attempts to gather data from working subjects. In most work situations—whether mills or doctors' offices—much of the work goes by routine. The researcher is thus forever "discovering" what is everyday routine to the worker. To some workers, he is merely nosy; to others, he is interested in unimportant matters. In a study of the writer's of the clique organization of an industrial office, it was found that members of cliques and often leaders of them either denied the existence of cliques or dismissed them as "natural." The behavior of workers is, of course, natural—as natural as the beating of the heart or making love. That fact does not make such behavior any the less interesting or worthy of examination.

3. THE APPLICATION OF FINDINGS

As we mentioned above, much of the research reported on in this volume was conducted in real working situations. In most cases, this has meant subsidization by management (occasionally by unions) and the consequent expectation that the findings should be "practical." This situation has forced the researcher to try, in each case, to solve two problems. First there is the problem of converting a research finding into a recommendation for action. Whether this is possible depends in large part on the skill and experience of the researcher in the arts of communication. The researcher is a scientist and cannot take over the job of foreman or superintendent. These jobs require administrative skills which most researchers do not possess. The best that most researchers can do is to so present their findings that they may be *taken into account* in any administrative decision. This means, usually, "translating" the findings from the jargon and technical language to lay language. Sometimes, in certain kinds of research, the researcher may be able to anticipate the effects of several alternative courses of action and those findings may be very useful in decision-making. But it is the administrator and not the researcher who must make the decision.

The second problem in the application of findings is that of taking sides. With management's paying the research bill, the researcher is in continuous danger of being identified by workers as pro-management rather than as an objective scientist. Bell (2) has accused those who conducted the Western Electric studies of being guilty of a "cow sociology" in which the worker is treated as a resource for management to be made more satisfied with his work with the object of increasing productivity. Without discussing the merits of that particular criticism,[15] it may be stated that this type of criticism is not widely applicable and rests on a misunderstanding. The industrial researcher is not working on *either* "management problems" or "labor problems" but on sociological problems. For example, considerable research [16] has dealt with informal leadership in the work situation; that is, the manner in which persons of power influence their fellow workers. If a representative of management becomes aware of this research, he may use it in a variety of ways. He may decide that informal leaders are a threat to his own authority and have them discharged or shifted to another department. Or he might try to influence the informal leaders to adopt management goals to the end of greater efficiency. A union leader might use the same research findings to choose persons to be groomed for union stewardship positions.

By itself, then, a research finding is not automatically biased in favor of any particular interest group. But in spite of this fact, the danger to which we have pointed remains. Often, the research findings are not made generally accessible and only management has the opportunity to act upon them. It may even ignore or suppress them. The same may occur when a labor union or government agency subsidizes a study. Some researchers have tried to avoid the problem by using funds provided by philanthropic foundations. Others have tried to reproduce working conditions in the classroom or laboratory,[17] with some degree of success. None of these represents completely satisfactory solutions, for at some time the research findings, however secured, will be applied in real situations. The researcher must decide whether he wishes to assume no responsibility for how his findings are used, or whether he wishes to assume the risks of being "identified" with one side or the other in order

[15] It is at least partly tenable if one uses the writings of Elton Mayo (one of the research leaders) as one's major example. Mayo often speaks of industrial conflicts as being due to misunderstandings and lack of knowledge. See Mayo (29, Ch. 1).

[16] See pp. 517–528.

[17] This is, of course, not the only reason for studying work behavior under laboratory conditions. A major reason is the desire to try to control relevant variables.

to be able to work in real situations and, perhaps, partially control the application of his findings.

CHAPTER REFERENCES

1. Alford, L. P. and Beatty, H. R., *Principles of Industrial Management,* New York: Ronald, 1951.
2. Bell, D., "Adjusting Men to Machines," *Commentary,* 3:79–88, 1947.
3. Blumer, H., in Lee, A. M. (ed.), *New Outline of the Principles of Sociology,* New York: Barnes and Noble, 1946.
4. ———, "Sociological Theory in Industrial Relations," *American Sociological Review,* 12:271–278, 1947.
5. Bridgman, P. W., *The Logic of Modern Physics,* New York: Macmillan, 1927.
6. Burtt, H. E., *Psychology and Industrial Efficiency,* New York: Appleton, 1929.
7. Caplow, T., *The Sociology of Work,* Minneapolis: University of Minnesota Press, 1954.
8. Carr-Saunders, A. M. and Wilson, P. A., *The Professions,* Oxford: Clarendon, 1933.
9. Child, I. L., "Morale: A Bibliographic Review," *Psychological Bulletin,* 38:393–420, 1941.
10. Dunbar, H. F., *Mind and Body: Psychosomatic Medicine,* New York: Random House, 1955.
11. Fleming, A. J.; D'Alonzo, C. A.; and Zapp, J. A. (eds.), *Modern Occupational Medicine,* Philadelphia: Lea and Febiger, 1954.
12. Gardner, B. B. and Moore, D. G., *Human Relations in Industry,* Homewood, Ill.: Irwin, 1952.
12a. Gilbreth, F. B., *Brick Laying System,* New York: Clerk, 1911.
13. ———, *Primer of Scientific Management,* New York: Van Nostrand, 1914.
14. Gilbreth, L., *Psychology of Management,* New York: Sturgis and Walton, 1914.
15. Gilson, M. B., Book Review, *American Journal of Sociology,* 46:98–101, 1940.
16. Gross, E., "Social Science Techniques: A Problem of Power and Responsibility," *The Scientific Monthly,* 83:242–247, 1956.
17. ———, "Some Suggestions for the Legitimation of Industrial Studies in Sociology," *Social Forces,* 33:233–239, 1955.
18. Hamilton, A. and Hardy, H. L., *Industrial Toxicology,* New York: Hoeber, 1949.
19. Hart, C. W. M., "Industrial Relations Research and Social Theory," *Canadian Journal of Economics and Political Science,* 15:53–73, 1949.
20. Homans, G. C., "The Strategy of Industrial Sociology," *American Journal of Sociology,* 54:330–337, 1949.
21. Hoxie, R. F., *Scientific Management and Labor,* New York: Appleton, 1915.

22. Johnstone, R. T., *Occupational Medicine and Industrial Hygiene,* St. Louis: Mosby, 1948.
23. Kahn, R. L., "An Analysis of Supervisory Practices and Components of Morale," in Guetzkow, H. (ed.), *Groups, Leadership, and Men,* Pittsburgh: Carnegie Press, 1951.
24. Katz, D., "Morale and Motivation in Industry," in Dennis, W. (ed.), *Current Trends in Industrial Psychology,* Pittsburgh: University of Pittsburgh Press, 1949, pp. 145–171.
25. Knowles, W. H., *Personnel Management,* New York: American Book Co., 1955.
26. Lastrucci, C. L., "The Status and Significance of Occupational Research," *American Sociological Review,* 11:78–84, 1946.
27. Lindsay, R. B., "Critique of Operationalism in Physics," *Philosophy of Science,* 4:456–470, 1937.
28. Marshall, A., *Principles of Economics,* London: Macmillan, 1907, Vol. 1.
29. Mayo, E., *The Social Problems of an Industrial Civilization,* Cambridge: Harvard University Press, 1945.
30. Mills, C. W., "The Contribution of Sociology to Studies of Industrial Relations," *Proc. Industrial Relations Research Assn.,* pp. 199–222, 1948.
31. Moore, H., *Psychology for Business and Industry,* New York: McGraw-Hill, 1942.
32. Moore, W. E., "Current Issues in Industrial Sociology," *American Sociological Review,* 12:651–657, 1947.
33. ——— *et al.,* "Industrial Sociology: Status and Prospects," *American Sociological Review,* 13:382–400, 1948.
34. Parker, W. E. and Kleemeier, R. W., *Human Relations in Supervision,* New York: McGraw-Hill, 1951.
35. Pigors, P. and Myers, C. A., *Personnel Administration,* New York: McGraw-Hill, 1951.
36. Riesman, D.; Glazer, N.; and Denny, R., *The Lonely Crowd,* New Haven: Yale University Press, 1950.
37. Roethlisberger, F. J., *Management and Morale,* Cambridge: Harvard University Press, 1952.
38. ——— and Dickson, W. J., *Management and the Worker,* Cambridge: Harvard University Press, 1940.
39. Rose, A. M., *Sociology: The Study of Human Relations,* New York: Knopf, 1956.
40. Sappington, C. O., *Essentials of Industrial Health,* Philadelphia: Lippincott, 1943.
41. Selye, H., *The Physiology and Pathology of Exposure to Stress,* Montreal: Acta, 1950.
42. Stern, B. J., *Medicine in Industry,* New York: The Commonwealth Fund, 1946.
43. Taylor, F. W., *Principles of Scientific Management,* New York: Harper, 1911.
44. Tiffin, J., *Industrial Psychology,* New York: Prentice-Hall, 1942.

45. Tilgher, A., *Work: What It Has Meant to Men Through the Ages*, New York: Harcourt, Brace, 1930.
46. Urwick, L. F., "The Manager's Span of Control," *Harvard Business Review*, 34:39–47, 1956.
47. Viteles, M. S., *Industrial Psychology*, New York: Norton, 1932.
48. ———, *Motivation and Morale in Industry*, New York: Norton, 1953.
49. Worthy, James C., "Organizational Structure and Employe Morale," *American Sociological Review*, 15:169–179, 1950.

CHAPTER TWO

WORK IN OTHER SOCIETIES:
AN APPROACH TO ANALYSIS

The world of work in modern Western society is highly complex. In order to understand it, we need a set of questions or categories—a conceptual framework—which will tell us what to look for and pay attention to.

We shall adopt a device which is common in sociology: we shall look for clues to the framework by examining work relations in societies *less complex* than our own. We do so for two reasons: (1) Because the organization of those societies is simpler [1] than ours, we are enabled to see relationships that would be obscure in our own society; (2) Since we are not members of the other societies, we can be more objective about them. We are not so likely to take behavior or customs for granted as we do in the society in which we grew up.

We shall first examine a relatively simple society—that of Dobu. Attention will then shift to the society of rural Ireland—much more complex than that of Dobu, but much simpler than our own. From these two societies we will be able to draw conclusions which will enable us to set forth a conceptual framework for understanding work in our own society.

---

[1] In recent years, owing to the results of more intensive research, anthropologists have tended to deemphasize this aspect of other societies: the societies have turned out to be much more complex than at first thought. But important differences in complexity remain, at least in the area of work organization.

THE SOCIAL SYSTEM OF DOBU [2]

Dobu is a small Melanesian island near New Guinea. The major work activity of the Dobuans revolves about the growing of yams, the main article of diet.[3] This work, which is the major responsibility of the men (though women assist), consists of two activities: (1) planting the yams, and (2) magical practices. The magic, it is hoped, will induce yam seeds from other persons' gardens to come into one's own.

A second segment of the social system of Dobu is that of residence. Most preliterate societies have a hard-and-fast rule about where a couple lives after marriage. The cohabitants of a village often regard each other as brothers and sisters and must, therefore, marry outside this local group. Normally, the newly-married pair lives either in the area of the bridegroom's people (patrilocal residence) or in the area of the bride's people (matrilocal residence). The question of where one lives after marriage is a vital one because, depending on whether one has patrilocal or matrilocal residence, one family loses. If the man goes to live at his bride's village, then his parents lose him and all of his children, they lose the prestige that may attach to having a large family, or they lose the help that he and his family would perform around the house or in making a living. And the same loss is suffered by the woman's family if she goes to live in her husband's village. In Dobu this problem is solved by a unique system of *bilocal* residence. After marriage, the newly married couple settles down first in the bride's village for a year and then moves to the groom's village for a year. The couple alternates back and forth in this manner every year. When children are born, they move back and forth with their parents, but after the onset of adolescence, children no longer move with their parents but settle down in one village. This is the child's *own* village, and is defined by where he owns property. Since the child inherits property through his mother, this means that he settles down in his mother's village. This point leads us to the next aspect of the social system of Dobu, that of land ownership.

In a village, different families work different plots of land. Those who own land are known as the "Owners of the Village" (hereafter called "Owners") and are those who are related in the female line.

---

[2] Different facets of Dobuan social life have been dealt with in (3, 4, 6). The description presented here draws on Fortune's treatment but is necessarily telescoped. The writer has drawn also from personal conversations with Dr. R. F. Fortune and C. W. M. Hart.

[3] The most important other activity of Dobuan men is participation in the Kula—the exchange of armshells and necklaces—with other islanders in the region. This activity is not primarily economic, though much trading goes on incidental to it.

There may be four such groups in a village. First will be the old women of the village who own land there and their brothers who had the same mother and therefore inherited land from the same person. The second category of Owners are the children, both male and female, of these old women, but not the children of their brothers (who will own land in *their* mother's village). The third category will be composed of the children of the females in the second category, and a fourth may be composed of the children of the females in the third category.

In addition to the Owners, there is a second group of persons resident in a village at a given time, who do not own land there. These are those who, for that year, are not in their own villages. They would include the husbands of female Owners and the wives of brothers of female Owners. These are referred to as "Those-resulting-from-marriage." The Owners and Those-resulting-from-marriage form two classes with widely differing rights and privileges.

The class system is simple enough: the Owners have most of the privileges and Those-resulting-from-marriage have almost none. A man in his wife's village may find himself maltreated with vehemence by his mother-in-law and her fellow Owners. He is forced to work in her yam garden and must bear her insults, and even those of his own wife.[4] From this treatment, he has no satisfactory recourse. If he puts up resistance, he finds he is in a village in which he is a stranger and his mother-in-law's (and wife's) kin will unite to assist her. Little remains for him but to leave in a huff or threaten suicide. Further, since villages practice black magic against each other, he is *always* under suspicion as a dangerous sorcerer.

Women are also maltreated on alternate years when they are not in their own villages but not so badly as are the men. The reason is that women's magic is considered stronger than men's magic. The final picture that presents itself, then, is one of men leading unhappy lives in alternate years.

Two questions are raised by the discussion thus far: why do men get married at all, and why is women's magic considered stronger than men's magic? The answers are closely related.

Adolescent boys do not, generally, wish to get married. The boy-member of the perambulating family soon appreciates the unhappy plight of his father and would like to avoid it. Yet all boys *do* end up married, a fact which may be explained, obviously, by the greater strength of women's magic.

---

[4] Fortune (4) tells us that a husband is especially concerned about his wife's sexual fidelity when she is in her own village. Though she is among her "brothers," sexual encounters occur often, though marriage is tabooed. If the husband objects, her kin are quick to insult, attack, or even eject the man from the village.

The sequence of events is as follows. It will be recalled that Owners in the same generation in a village regard themselves as brothers and sisters—an extension of the incest taboo to include the entire village. When a boy reaches adolescence, he is told he must be removed from temptation by sleeping outside of his village. Only two alternatives exist: [5] the Dobuan bush, which is full of dangerous spirits, and other villages, in which he is not welcome. As a consequence, the Dobuan adolescent boy wanders aimlessly, rejected by his kinfolk, terrified by the shadowy sights and odd sounds of the bush, as night falls.

Eventually his wandering brings him to the outskirts of a strange village where, perhaps, a girl notices him. He appeals to her—explaining his unhappy plight—and if she is impressed (and likes him), she may permit him to stay with her in her hut for the night. There, in a special portion of the hut reserved for her nubile daughter by her mother, she feeds him and keeps him hidden until just before daybreak when he sneaks out and rushes back to his own village.

The next night he does not wander. The process is repeated a number of times but with each recurrence the danger of detection (and forced marriage) obviously increases. If the boy is strongly determined not to marry, he will try to find other girls. But as time goes on, he is likely to find a girl to whom he feels especially attracted, and, also, he becomes ". . . weary of the rigorous regime of late roving nights and early morning risings."

One morning, the young man oversleeps. Should he now try to escape, he finds he is too late (4, p. 22):

The mother of the girl gets up before the young pair and steps out on to the house platform. There she sits calmly blocking up the exit with her body . . . Everyone (the villagers and others living nearby) circles around and stares. Into this glare of curious publicity the youth and the girl descend at last from the house and sit side by side on a mat on the ground. The spectators remain and do nothing but stare for half an hour or so. This staring ceremony makes the engagement . . . Finally, the starers disperse. The girl's mother, now formally the youth's mother-in-law, places a digging-stick (for yams) into the youth's hand and says, "Go, make a garden. . . ."

After this engagement, marriage is unavoidable and so begins the young man's yearly trek back and forth and his labor for his wife's people.

It is now clear why men conclude that women's magic is stronger

[5] Boys may also sleep in the house of a divorced man who is temporarily without a wife. But such houses are rare.

than men's magic. He sees, first, that women, particularly the old women in the village, have authority, and second, reluctant males wake up and find themselves married. It should be remembered that a man also has magic. This is inherited from his mother's brother and is used to entice yam seeds from other people's yam gardens into his own. But this practice does not work well, for the Dobuan male normally gets a poor yield. Consequently, his magic turns out to be ineffective. Not only does he not succeed in getting yams to move from other people's gardens to his own but not even all his own yam seeds produce yams, meaning that someone else has been more successful than himself.

The Dobuan explains all this by saying: Yam seeds are young yams, and, just like young men, they wander, and, in the same manner as young men, end up by being caught by young female yams in someone else's garden. Thus female magic is shown to be stronger than male magic at all points.

We have now gone over certain of the major segments of the social system of Dobu. Its major features are summarized in Figure 1.

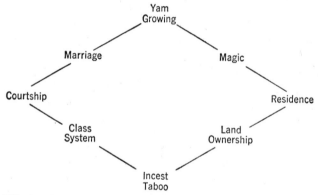

FIG. 1.

MAJOR ELEMENTS IN THE SOCIAL SYSTEM OF DOBU

CONCLUSIONS FROM DOBUAN ANALYSIS

There are five propositions or generalizations about work relationships that may be derived from the Dobuan material presented here.

1. *Work normally involves authority relationships.* In some respects this is a restatement of our definition of work relationships, in which we made work coincident with the setting of objectives for the worker by

someone else. (See p. 11.) Specifically, authority connotes an organized, legitimate relationship between two people in which one person has the right to influence the behavior of another. This process is seen quite obviously in the power that the man's mother-in-law, and women in general, have over the Dobuan male.

2. *Work normally involves a division of labor.* In Dobu, it took two forms: a sexual division of labor (only men grew yams), and the assignment of control over this labor (a sort of "managerial control") to older women.

It will be seen that all of the elements pictured in Figure 1 are connected with one another. If one were to describe any one element in isolation, it would sound ridiculous or be dismissed as an oddity. For example, if one were to describe yam-growing in Dobu, one would say that Dobuans spent alternate years trying to entice yam-seeds from other gardens into their own. If one stopped there, it would simply sound odd or silly. But if one moved on next to the incest taboo and pointed out that it meant that young men are forced to wander at night, and if one moved from that to a description of courtship (the short period which the young man spends with the young lady), and if one moved from that to marriage, which the young man deplores, and finally, to the magical beliefs of Dobuans, then yam-growing makes sense. For one would then point out that yam seeds wander and get caught just as young men do, since women's magic is stronger than men's.

3. It turns out then, and this is our third proposition, that *work is not an isolated activity, but is tied up with the whole social system.* This is true in Dobu, but it is also true in our own society. In our society, it is customary to think of work as something that is done from nine to five, after which the individual can relax and "be himself." Actually it is never an isolated segment of life. Rather, each worker brings to the work situation all of the culture of the larger society in which he participates. He brings with him a race, an educational level, experience, a religion, social class, family, and sex. If he is a Negro, then that makes a difference. If one gives the Negro psychological tests and interviews and then concludes that he *can* do the job, that alone may mean very little. Among Dobuans there is an attitude that yam-growing requires magic. Without it, one would not get any yams. In our society there is an attitude that certain jobs should be performed by white men alone. Since both are work attitudes, perhaps the Dobuan may help in understanding our attitude.

Many would take the view that magic will not add one jot to the yam-yield in Dobu or anywhere else. It might help give the farmer self-confidence but would not "really" affect the yam-yield. If this is true, removal of the magic should not have very harmful consequences. Yet, if a Westerner who felt sorry for Dobuan men were to arrange for the services of Western agricultural experts, what might happen? Most likely, the yam-yield would greatly increase. The Dobuan male would interpret this event as a great victory for men's magic and, as a consequence, would lose his fear of women's magic. Once he lost this fear, he would no longer be terrified by his mother-in-law, and quite possibly, might refuse to work for her at all. Furthermore, marriage itself only occurs because of women's magic. After the brief courtship (if it continued to take place at all in the same way) the young man might simply refuse to marry his benefactress.

Elderly women would not then have young men to work their gardens for them and one would have an old-age dependency problem on one's hands. Also, since many of the young ladies whom the young men refused to marry would probably be pregnant, there would be a second problem of unmarried mothers. By this time, one would probably have banished the agricultural expert and sent for a plane-load of social workers. But worse still might occur. Once men refused to marry, the system of dual residence after marriage would become meaningless and the class system would vanish with it. In short, the whole society and culture would be violently shaken to its foundations.[6]

Magic, then, is not extraneous to work in Dobu. Nor is the attitude in our society that certain jobs should be performed by whites (or Negroes, or women) only. One finds universally a feeling that a job should be carried out *only* by persons who are felt to have the "right" characteristics or features. With every job there go pragmatic and mythical components in varying proportions. The Dobuan uses magic, but no one would be so stupid as to forget to push the yam-seed into the ground. In our society, even an ardent racist who is trying to prevent the admission of Negroes to a labor union would not (nowadays) claim that Negroes were *incapable* of performing industrial jobs. Instead, he might try to appeal to fears of being underbid by Negro labor, which could be entirely mythical. It may be concluded, therefore, that there are two questions one must ask of the job applicant: can he do the job *and* will the group accept him. The latter question may turn out to be decisive.[7]

[6] The above is, of course, fanciful. But the large amount of research available on the effects of technological innovations in "underdeveloped" societies suggests that our description is entirely plausible. See Ch. 16.

[7] The above discussion should not, of course, be construed as a defense of the *status quo* in race relations. If a group rejects Negroes, one may refuse to hire Negroes, *or* one may try to change the group's attitudes. One cannot, however, *ignore* the attitude.

4. These considerations lead us to our fourth generalization about work: *work is tied up with attitudes of right and wrong.* Surrounding work, there are always conceptions of who the proper persons are, how the work should be performed, how new persons should be admitted, and how those considered unfit for membership shall be excluded.

5. There is, finally, a fifth proposition. Nothing was said above about particular individuals. Of course individual differences exist in Dobu as they do everywhere: each man's magic differs slightly from each other man's, as does each one's height and weight. A discussion of these differences would not have contributed materially to our discussion. Individual Dobuans come and go; *the culture and society remain.* This fact is not, however, obvious to the casual observer. Such an observer might report that a particular Dobuan male hated his mother-in-law. He might note further that he hated her because she was mean to him. Undoubtedly, degrees of hatred and degrees of meanness would be observable, but the important fact is that *some* hatred and meanness is found whenever a Dobuan male works for his mother-in-law. And if one looked further, one would finally discover that mothers-in-law are mean in Dobu because they can *afford* to be, for their magic is stronger than men's magic. In other words, to understand why one individual hates another, one has to examine the entire culture and social structure.

Similarly, in, say, a factory in our own society, it is common to encounter "individualistic" explanations for puzzling behavior. When workers are asked to explain such behavior on the part of some worker, they are likely to reply: "Oh, he's a queer duck" or "He's just that way." We would have to study the whole social structure and subculture of the factory, especially the workers' ideas of right and wrong, to understand why this particular individual is regarded as a "queer duck."

One might discover that the person in question was a rate-buster— one who violates the work group's conception of what constitutes a day's work and, instead, produces at top speed. Such a person is regarded with venom and attempts are made to control him and to embarrass him as much as possible.[8] If the man in question were a rate-buster, then it would have turned out that he was regarded as "queer" because he repeatedly violated an accepted value of the work group.

In sum, if one asks why Dobuan men hate their mothers-in-law, all one can answer is that the culture makes it inevitable. If one asks why workers hate rate-busters, all one can answer is that the subculture of the work group treats rate-busting as a threat to group welfare. Our fifth proposition, then, is that *individual behavior may be understood*

---

[8] The motives are complex. See pp. 517–558.

in terms of the total social structure and culture surrounding the work situation.[9]

Our five work generalizations may be restated serially for convenience of reference:

1. Work normally involves authority relationships.
2. Work normally involves a division of labor.
3. Work is tied up with the entire social system.
4. Work is surrounded by conceptions of right and wrong.
5. The behavior of the worker is to be understood in terms of the social system and culture within which the worker moves.

These generalizations are not proven by the Dobuan material. We have presented that material because it is simple enough to enable one to observe the plausibility of the generalizations. A very considerable portion of our analysis of the world of work will revolve about these propositions. We shall see that they are found in our own society and may be used to provide fundamental insights into work behavior in our society.

We proceed next to examine a second society, that of rural Ireland. We will have two objectives. First, we will wish to see whether the five generalizations stated above are found to hold in the case of a considerably more complex society, and second, we will wish to see whether the five generalizations are *adequate* for explaining or understanding work in that society. Then, through the examination of the Irish material—in which we will see a society considerably more like our own than Dobu—we will be enabled to draw up a conceptual framework for the analysis of work in our society.

THE SOCIAL SYSTEM OF RURAL IRELAND [10]

The study was carried out in the early 1930's in County Clare in southwest Eire. Eire is predominantly rural with the population concentrated on small farms, and it is the small farms that form the primary object for research. However, these are not subsistence farms. The small farmers, who are concentrated in the southwest, raise milch cattle or calves and sell the calves to large farmers at periodic fairs. The large farmers, in turn, fatten the cattle for the British beef market. But calves are not the small farmer's only product: he also raises vegetables and

---

[9] We do not, of course, imply that the social structure and culture will provide a *complete* explanation of individual behavior.

[10] The discussion is drawn from (1 and 2). All statistics quoted are from the census of 1926, the most recent available at the time of the study. Although the present tense is used, conditions are those of twenty years ago.

other animals both for sale and for his own use. His farm is, therefore, more diversified, and the swings of the business cycle do not hit him directly.

It is obvious that there are large economic and social differences between small and large farmers, and the small farmer will try to marry his daughter to the son of a large farmer (if one can be found). Consequently, since the small farm tends to be located in the west and the large farm toward the east, women, along with cattle, tend to move east. Having located the small farm in the country as a whole, we turn to the farm itself.

THE FAMILY FARM

The small farm is a family business operated without hired labor. Work activities follow a highly predictable yearly round. The seasonal rhythm of work reaches its lowest pitch in the winter when the farmer spends his time doing odd jobs and repairs and feeding his animals. Work comes to a standstill for Christmas. This is the period of the great religious ceremonies and is also the time for visiting, dancing, and other informal social activities. We observe immediately one of our work generalizations—the relatedness of work to other parts of society and culture. It is hardly a coincidence (and not peculiar to Eire) that the period of maximal religious and informal participation is the period of minimal work demands.

Shortly after the Christmas period, the farmer lays in his seeds and cleans his ditches. He spends his time in the evenings conversing with his neighbors about the coming planting. Both new and traditional experience with reference to seed and cattle are discussed back and forth. On February 1—St. Brigid's Day—spring officially begins. In February and March the gardens are prepared, potatoes are planted, and the fields made ready for cattle. March and April make up the period of calving and milk production. They are also the period of the spring cattle fairs and the time when the farmer plants turnips and mangels.

In May, turf-cutting begins.[11] It is the first activity in which the family cooperates as a unit, with one member of the family breaking up the turf, other members of the family breaking it up still further, others loading it into wagons and hauling it back to the farmyard. In late July and early August there occurs the most important harvest of the year, haymaking. The harvest is important because it provides the supply of fodder for the animals and especially for the income-producing cattle. Haymaking calls forth the united effort of the whole family be-

---

[11] Turf—a type of fuel similar to peat—is found near the surface.

cause it is a race against time and rain. It is called, appropriately, "saving the hay."

In August and September other crops will be harvested, particularly rye and oats. In October and November turnips and mangels are pulled and stored. This is also the period of the autumn fairs. Then the soil is turned, the gardens are plowed, and winter is here again.

In examining this work rhythm, we are made aware of the applicability of another of our work generalizations—the presence of a division of labor. In County Clare it is based not only on sex and age (as in Dobu) but also on family status. These distinctions may be conveniently discussed in terms of family roles.

The male head of the family is the husband, father, and owner of the farm. He has the controlling role and directs activities, subject to customary restrictions. It is his responsibility to look after the cattle and it is he who sells them at the fair and disposes of the income that he secures from their sale. However, this is performed in the interest of the family. If he secures a poor price or if he does a poor bargaining job, then his wife will certainly let him know her opinion of him as a provider. The produce is considered to be the man's, but he must divide the income neatly between the needs of the household and the needs of the farm. The family have a right to expect that he will look after their welfare.

The wife is in charge of the house and the area around it (the haggard) where the small animals are kept and a small vegetable garden is maintained. Her tasks include the preparation of meals, care of the children, milking of the cows, and the feeding of the small animals. She makes butter and sews the family's clothing. She enjoys a private income from the sale of butter and eggs. Like her husband, she is expected to dispose of it for the family.

This division of labor between the sexes is upheld by means of custom, ridicule, and pity. In justifying the fact that the farmer is concerned with selling the cattle but the woman with milking them, various proofs are introduced to the effect that a woman's hands were made for milking cows. If a man does woman's work he is laughed at; if a woman attempts man's work she is pitied, for the assumption is that she has no man to do that work.

We thus observe another of the work generalizations. Work in Eire, as in Dobu, is not morally neutral. There goes with it a belief that only certain kinds of persons should perform certain tasks and, in addition, work in itself is not considered to have meaning except with reference to the family. The farm exists for the family.

The division of labor is related to age and family status as follows.

The father is the owner and director of the enterprise. In the community the farm is known as his and his sons are spoken of as "boys." The father also teaches his sons how to do farm work and how to drive a bargain at the cattle fair. The son also learns his father's dominant position. On the farm he works under his father's eye and refers necessary decisions to him. At the fair the father makes decisions: even if the son should want a drink he must ask his father for money. If the son should earn money from roadwork for the government, he will turn the money over to his father and his father may return a certain amount to him for recreational needs. This dominance is present as long as the son lives on the farm and as long as the father has not yet handed over the farm to one of his sons. Even if the son is forty-five or fifty years of age, he is still spoken of as, and is, a "boy." One said ruefully: "You can be a boy here forever as long as the old fellow is still alive" (1, p. 56).

In his relation to his mother the boy's role is that of a subordinate, but the relationship is an affectionate one. His mother assumes the the role of mediator in disputes and will protect her sons from what she feels is overly rigid discipline on the part of the father. Toward the father the son feels respect but not intimacy: they do not smoke or drink together. There is a latent antagonism which the son expresses in chafing and irritation in private to his fellows, but the controls are too strong for overt resistance.

Relations among siblings are as follows. Children are all subordinate to their parents but are considered equal. For the boys there is no primogeniture or junior right. Normally the boys do not know which of them is going to inherit the farm until the farmer makes up his mind. Boys work together; years of common effort and common dependence on their father create a strong solidarity among them. This was expressed in the old days in the form of feuds which might go on for generations. The girls are normally closer to their mother with strong affectional ties. But they are equivalent before her. They do not have to adjust to the father as the boys do, nor to the mother very much. Their big adjustment will come later—to their mother-in-law.

A boy regards his sister in much the same manner as he regards his mother, lovingly. A girl regards her brother in much the same way as she regards her father: she looks to him for protection and for assistance should she fall in need.

The complete family on the farm is the unit of life in County Clare. Incomplete families—spinsters, bachelors, widows, widowers—are unusual and are the object of pity. Arensberg and Kimball cite an illustration of a widow who tried to get a male relative to come over to her farm and to do the man's work there. A bachelor managed to get a nephew to come to his farm. He then treated him as a son and later gave him the farm. But these types of arrangements are regarded as unusual, abnormal, and unfortunate. The usual comment is: "It's a hard life she has with only the brother and no husband to help her," or else: "He's all by himself with only his son there on the land, poor fellow" (1, p. 69).

RELATIONS AMONG FAMILIES

Although the family is the work unit, there is much cooperation among families: lending tools, lending a boy's services, lending a girl to help make a tub of butter, helping a family in time of distress with gifts, and fulfilling the obligations which surround ceremonies, marriage, hay-making, and death. This process of mutual help is called "cooring" and is distinguished by the absence of any monetary payment. Cooring is restricted to those one knows and trusts and is obligatory. The expression, "I have right to go," indicating an inescapable duty, is used equally to explain why one is attending one's aunt's funeral and why one is going to assist a neighbor make a tub of butter.

The most critical inter-family relation occurs at the time of marriage —the greatest single event in the community. As in many peasant societies, marriage is arranged through the *match,* a contractual arrange-ment involving not only marriage but a dowry and the handing on to a son of the farm. At the same time, the father who is passing on his farm to his marrying son will provide amounts of money for each of his other sons and dowries to each of his unmarried daughters. Provision is also made for the father and his wife for the rest of their lives. They are accorded food, the right to "the grass of a cow," the yield of a patch of potatoes, access to the hearth, and the use of a special room—the West Room. This is a semi-sacred room in which are stored the family's treasured possessions—religious pictures, ceremonial objects brought in by the old lady when she first came as a young bride, family pictures, and heirlooms. In rural folklore, the "fairies" include the spirits of the dead who hover about the West Room to keep a watchful eye on the farm and see to it that the family's name is still on the land, that the old folks have married their children well, and the old ways have not been tam-pered with. It is into this room that the old couple moves, a gesture indicative of (1, p. 136):

. . . the sacred and semireligious nature of the attitudes surrounding the old couple and identifying them with the forces of the dead and the symbolic unity of the family, past and present.

The above is a remarkable illustration of the close ties between the organization of work and other societal elements, for in it the transfer of properties and assumption of ownership and managership of the farm are intimately knit with marriage, religion, "the fairies" (which the Catholic church has tried to banish), and the breakup of a closely knit family. But the match has still wider consequences, which manifest themselves in some peculiar statistics.

VITAL STATISTICS

Eire offers to the statistical analyst a number of very puzzling facts. First, the population between 1841 and 1926 decreased by more than one-half (from 6½ million to 3 million)—the result of migration which far exceeds that of such famous exporters of population as Norway and Italy. Of special interest is the fact that the decline was greatest in the most rural parts of the country—County Clare fell from a population of 250,000 to one of 95,000.

Second, in 1926, Eire had a larger proportion of unmarried persons of all ages than in any other country for which records are kept. Along with this went a tendency for persons to marry very late in life. For example, for men between the ages of twenty-five to thirty, the per cent unmarried in the U.S.A. is 39, in Eire's neighbor, England, the per cent is 45, and in Denmark, a country rather similar to Eire in many respects, the per cent unmarried is 49. In contrast with all these countries, the per cent unmarried in Eire is an incredible 80. By the ages of thirty-five to forty, when the per cent has dropped to 20 in the U.S.A. and to 15 in England and Denmark, it is still 50 per cent in Eire. Again, these percentages are still higher in the rural areas of small farms.

Third, there is a high sex ratio (an excess of men over women) which is especially marked in the rural areas (Dublin had an excess of women over men). And fourth, in spite of late marriage and the scarcity of women, fertility is very high. At the time of the study the fertility ratio (as measured by the number of children for every one hundred married women under forty-five years of age) was 77 in the U.S.A., 71 in England, 93 in Denmark, but 131 in Eire. In County Clare, the fertility ratio was 140.

The primary clue for explaining these statistics is to be sought in the fact that all these figures are exaggerated in the rural counties with small farms such as those in County Clare, the type of farm we have been describing.

When the old man gives up his farm and marries off his inheriting son, that is also the time when the other children must be provided for or taken care of. The farmer tries to place his children as near home as possible. He will try to marry his daughters into the towns or farms to the east and if he can, he will do so at any time before he hands over the farm. He will also try to do the same for his sons. He will try to get them government appointments or professional positions or urban occupations. This is not always possible and furthermore, the farmer needs his sons for the farm work. There is, therefore, a greater tendency for the woman to move eastward than for the man and the result is the high sex ratio in the rural western counties.

Those who cannot be provided for at home do one of two things:

1. They may go to Dublin, the metropolis, and seek a job. Dublin is not highly industrialized and this was especially true in the last century when much of the migration took place. But there was one source of employment available and that was the Irish Republican Army which was organizing for the war of independence against England. The strapping young farmers from the west counties were ideal recruits for such an army. Many of them did join it and thus the rural farm was in no small way responsible for the emergence of Eire from Ireland. This opportunity was not available to women and, therefore, if there were no jobs available, there was only one thing left and that was emigration out of the country altogether. Hence the country-wide high sex ratio.

2. They may emigrate. The Irish, through the mechanism of the farm family which required it, have dispersed all over the world. At the same time the pattern of cooring maintains itself. If one of the sons should find a good position somewhere outside of Ireland he will write home and assist his family to come out. For example, one man from the district of Cross, on the Atlantic coast, went out to Shanghai and became police chief at the International Settlement. He then sent for his brothers and friends until eventually this small district in Ireland supplied almost the whole police force of the International Settlement of Shanghai. The extent to which the Irish predominate in the New York police force is legendary.

When a person leaves Eire, his upbringing, his family ties, and the internalized pattern of cooring [12] help to maintain strong ties with the homeland. These are reflected in the provision of passage money for brothers, sisters, and friends, and gifts from parents of money, clothes, and farm delicacies. Should the emigrant return to Eire, he will usually settle at or near his place of birth.

---

[12] A unique American adaptation of cooring is the urban political machine. The machine process of informal assistance to those who are in need bears more than a superficial resemblance to cooring.

In sum, reasons for the dispersal of the Irish now become clear. When the inheriting son takes over the farm, the others must leave, for otherwise, a difficult burden of support would be placed on the son or else the farm would have to be divided up. The old family gives way to the new and the very mechanism that disperses the Irish assures the continuance of the farm and the family name on it.

The other statistics now become understandable. The population decline was due to a variety of factors—famine, periodic hard times, changes in agricultural practices—which the Irish responded to by emigration. The family, work, and inheritance patterns made it inevitable that such a course would be pursued.[13] Late marriage is explained by the reluctance of the old couple to give up control of the farm *and* the dependence of the children on their parents. Only one boy gets the farm, and since no one (including the father) knows who this will be, all the sons can do is wait. In any case, all are needed on the farm. The girls require dowries which take years to save; the boys receive either the farm, or money, or support in learning a trade or emigrating. Consequently, it is not surprising that marriage is delayed: the girl has no dowry and the boy is unable to support a wife. Finally, the high fertility figures are to be explained in terms of the need of a large family to work the farm *and* the attitudes of the old couple in the West Room. There is a new woman in the house and the old couple watch and help her all they can. They hope she will soon have a son who will carry on the family name, and they hope she will have *many* children to run the farm successfully after the old couple dies.

THE COMMUNITY

Besides cooring and marriage, families also meet in the local community. Two phases of community participation deserve mention: the old men's Cuaird and the town fairs.

When a man hands over his farm, or is about to do so, he is far from having "retired" in the American sense. For it is such old men who are the real controlling force in local community affairs. They form a small group or clique, known as the Cuaird, who meet nightly to discuss community matters.

They discuss agriculture—the time of sowing or harvesting, the merits of different seeds and of innovations in practice. They relate the community to the outside world. It is the Cuaird that may originate a petition for a new road, request relief-work for their sons, and, in fact,

---

[13] For a striking description of a people who were confronted with many of the same problems as the Irish but who did not emigrate, see (5).

conduct all political business. They review the candidates for public office and decide to whom to give their support. After the meeting, the men of the Cuaird return home and inform their wives and sons of the decision of the Cuaird. There may be argument but in the end all will usually vote as they were told to. The Cuaird concerns itself also with new members of the community—the new priest or school teacher— and with their behavior. If sanctions become necessary against anyone, the Cuaird invokes them. Finally, the Cuaird is the fountainhead of traditional lore. It reaffirms the past and acts as link with it. In sum, it is the seat of judgment in the community. It is a clearing house of information and a court in which the decisions of the community are made and the traditional knowledge of the peasantry is applied and disseminated. The young men also have their cliques. They meet at dances or to play cards, and a young man may win acclaim as a good dancer or gambler. But these activities do not seriously affect the community. As Arensberg and Kimball point out, the young men's meeting unites the young; the old men's meeting unites both the young and old.

The second phase of community participation brings the farmer into contact with the town. The farmer comes to town for the fairs and produce markets. While there he meets two persons. The first of these is the large farmer who has come to buy cattle from the small farmer. This relationship is an economic one but again we find that work is surrounded with conceptions of right and wrong and with a ritual.

Arensberg and Kimball describe the meeting as follows (1, pp. 300–302):

As dawn breaks, the buyers arrive. They are nearly always cattlemen and big farmers. Only occasionally are they local men. One can recognize them as they hurry about, business-like, wearing trench coats, bowlers, and leggings. The costume is practically a uniform with them, quite different from the drab coats and boots of the countrymen. They carry chalk or scissors and pencils and a notebook to mark the beasts of their choice and record their purchases.

In the good days of high prices, as during the world war, the buyers arrive even before and buy by lantern light. All the good beasts at the fair may be gone by the time the sun comes up. On occasions of little demand, however, the buyers have time to look about carefully and make the exhaustive tests of quality that long experience has convinced them are the secret of commercial success.

The procedure of choice, of bargaining and sale is as unchanging a ritual as any church provides. The buyer—dealer or farmer—strolls unconcernedly along the lines of farmers and their beasts. Here and there he greets an acquaintance. But he is appraising the animals all the while. Rigid customs forbid his breaking in on a bargain already begun. He must find a farmer who is free for the moment. Should he catch sight of an unoccupied owner of a likely animal, he crosses over to him and begins the business of the day. His first move is to ask the price, knowing full well he will get one larger than the farmer really hopes to receive. This first exchange is merely the occasion for the closer inspection of the cattle and a notice to the other that a bargain is in process.

Such a move is a signal. As questions and offers pass between buyer and farmer, a crowd of bystanders soon collects. They offer suggestions, shout out commentaries, encourage one party or the other, contributing animatedly to the debate, which will eventually culminate in a sale at a price which instantly becomes the knowledge of buyers and sellers alike.

One of the bystanders almost invariably adopts a well-recognized role. He becomes an intermediary between buyer and seller. He turns all his energy, backed by the plaudits of the crowd to the consummation of the sale. He may be a friend of either buyer or seller, brought in for his shrewdness or experience or skill, or he may be a wandering tinker in hopes of a commission from one or the other. He may even be only a disinterested bystander.

The intermediary is almost always a major factor in the transaction. He is the one who forges an agreement over the distrust and shyness of the farmer and the autocratic impatience of the buyer. All the parties are vociferous, the farmer in praise of his wares and the buyer in depreciation of them. The intermediary turns grandiose claims into laughter, wears down the resistance of the farmer by wit, and raises the offers of the buyer by appeal to fair dealing. Time and time again he will drag back a buyer who rushes off in well-feigned disgust at an outrageous demand or push forward the hand of a reluctant farmer to be received by the buyer in a handclasp that marks the completion of the sale. Amid the encouragement of the bystanders, he repeats the old bargaining cries. He shouts "split the difference!" when taking price and asking price approach one another, and he wrings concessions from each party until an agreement is reached. They end with a handshake between them. The sale is made.

If a buyer is ready to pay for his purchase on the spot, the older custom, all three parties step off the fairground to any convenient nearby pub. There they celebrate the transaction at the expense of the buyer, and the purchase money changes hands, and they make assurances all around. The seller turns back a "luck penny" out of the purchase price. This is a payment often as large as half a crown depending upon the transaction, repaid to the buyer in token of good faith.

The buyer is important to the farmer, but the relation between the two is, after all, limited to a business transaction, even though the transaction is ritualized. A much more intimate relation exists between the farmer and the second person he meets in town—the shopkeeper.

FARMER AND SHOPKEEPER—MUTUAL EXPECTATIONS

The shopkeeper depends on the countryman for trade and the farmer looks to him for credit. The farmer secures cash mainly only at the fairs and produce markets and this is also the time when the farmer makes his purchases. Normally the farmer will have an account with a given shopkeeper and it is this account that is the symbol of the tie between them. The farmer is always in debt to the shopkeeper and the shopkeeper wants it that way. The debt is seldom brought up to date and may even be carried over from one generation to the next. If a debt is paid off in full this usually means that the farmer is no longer going to trade at that shop and is symptomatic of an argument or of bad blood between the farmer and the shopkeeper. The debt is a bond between the two. The farmer regards the shopkeeper as a "cut above" him. The shopkeeper associates with the townfolk—the priest, the police officer, the teacher—and he associates to a greater extent with the large farmer with whom he has more in common. Both are businessmen and both deal directly with Dublin. The shopkeeper is also more concerned with the outside world. He knows the news through his contacts and participates more actively in politics.

Because of this prestige difference, the farmer will usually try to marry his daughter to the son of his shopkeeper or apprentice his son to a trade or profession in town if he can possibly arrange this. If this result is secured, then there occurs upward mobility for the children.

When a farm girl is to marry the son of a shopkeeper in the town, the marriage fits itself neatly into the pattern of family cooperation. There is a tendency for a family, including the extended kin, to carry on its trade at the same store. Therefore, if a girl marries the son of a shopkeeper she will bring with her her whole group of extended kin who will then swell the shopkeeper's trade. In this manner, a shopkeeper when looking for a wife for his son, which he will do through the match, will usually look for a country girl because she is hard-working and does not have fancy ideas. But also she will bring with her a large group of kindred. Thus, marriage literally fosters trade and the shopkeeper's prestige in the town will go up.

This brings us to the conclusion of the descriptive materials on County Clare. We turn next to the task of deriving a conceptual framework that will be applicable to the analysis of work in our own society.

CONCEPTUAL FRAMEWORK FOR ANALYSIS OF WORK RELATIONS †

Two very different societies have now been examined, with special emphasis on work relationships. Our objective—it will be recalled—was to secure clues which will tell us what to look for in our own society.

† The framework is developed as follows for pedagogical reasons. The major categories were first divided by E. C. Hughes.

The most important clues so far have been the five work generalizations, and we may conveniently begin with them.

THE MAJOR CATEGORIES

We have seen that work involves authority relations both in Dobu (the man's relation to his mother-in-law) and in County Clare (the relation of son to father, daughter to mother, and young to old). These observations suggest that it may be worth-while to examine the relation between authority and work in our society. It was also noted that authority relationships were usually also status relationships and carried implications of rights and privileges or obligations. Therefore we may consider as a valuable analytic category what we shall call *The Status and Authority System.*

The second proposition dealt with the division of labor. In Dobu, it was sexual. In County Clare, we observed both a sexual division of labor and a division of labor based on age—the old *vs.* the young with reference to work around the farm. We also saw a division of labor according to occupation—the relation of farmer to shopkeeper and of small farmer to big farmer. The function of the division of labor was that of *structuring* relationships among workers; that is, work relationships are formally arranged or *instituted* through the division of labor.

Our third proposition about work simply broadens the notion of structuring or instituting to include the whole social system. It stated, it will be recalled, that work is related to other parts of the social system. This we saw in Dobu in the intimate relation between magic, land ownership, residence, inheritance, and so on, on the one hand, and yam-growing on the other. In County Clare, we observed the close relationship between the work of the farm and the family, the fitting of work needs into the cooring pattern, the relationship of the dowry to the work of the farmer, and the relation of the West Room to the transmission of the farm and the reformation of the family. Indeed, although highly complex, what was striking about the Irish material was the manner in which it all fitted together into a functional whole. In this manner, we note that both propositions two and three deal with similar matters—the relation of different kinds of work and workers to each other, on the one hand, and the relation of work and workers to other parts of the social system, on the other. We may conveniently think of them together as suggesting an analytical category that we shall call *The Institutional System.*

The fourth proposition dealt with the moral implication of work. In both societies, such moral sentiments were upheld and enforced by a group with power—by the Owners in Dobu, and by the Cuaird in County Clare. In our society, we shall wish to pay attention to which kind of groups have such power and how they exercise it. These phenomena will be discussed under the heading of *The Work Group*.[14]

The fifth proposition dealt with the individual in the system. In Dobu it was shown how men get married in spite of their desire to remain single. The significant effect of this event is that a man's work career is determined for him by events over which he personally has little control (the alternatives, it will be recalled, were unpleasant). In County Clare, we saw the individual caught up in a vast set of expectations organized about the match in marriage, cooring, and the selection of a career. If he was a marrying son, then his career would be that of a farmer. If not, then what he would become was a function of his father's ability to apprentice him to an occupation in town, his brother's ability to send him passage money to other parts of the world, or, failing these, the need of the Irish Republican Army for recruits. These observations suggest that we should pay attention to the factors that influence the individual's entry into the world of work and his movement through it. The discussion dealing with those factors we shall call *The Career*.

In this manner, we emerge with four major categories which may be stated in the following order for reasons of increasing clarity in the subsequent presentation:

A. The Institutional System
B. The Status and Authority System
C. The Career
D. The Work Group

Beginning, then, with the five work generalizations that were observed in Dobu, we found that they were equally applicable to County Clare. But it was also true that those five generalizations alone did not, by any means, adequately describe work relations in County Clare. Therefore, using the five generalizations as clues, we were able to derive the above four categories, which have much wider scope, and which, in fact, enable us to study work relations in our own society. There remains only the task of spelling out the details within the four major categories.

---

[14] Although many of the Owners and none of the Cuaird actually *do* the work themselves, it is important not to confuse their functions with that of owners (or management) in our society. The work group members implement the folkways and mores associated with work, whether they themselves do the work or not. In our society, the work group usually does the work as well.

THE FRAMEWORK

A. The Institutional System

We are concerned here with the structuring of work relations. It is convenient to analyze these relations in terms of three subjects: the relation of work to other instituted structures in society (the Work Complex), the division of labor (The Work Structure), and the recognition of differential positions in the division of labor through economic payments (The Economic Complex).

I. *The Work Complex*

This, our most obvious category, will deal with the manner in which the world of work is related to other parts of society. We shall ask: How is work related to the family, to the church, to recreation, to politics, to migration, and to the community?

II. *The Work Structure*

We noted in Eire the relations of the farmer to the shopkeeper, the big farmer to the small farmer, and the relations among family members when they worked closely together (turf-cutting and "saving the hay"). In both Dobu and Eire, work was carried out according to a clearly understood division of labor. These observations suggest the importance of the following questions: How is work divided up and within what kind of structure? What is the nature of the division of labor and specialization? How is one type of work related to another type of work?

III. *The Economic Complex*

We noted in Eire that cooring involved no payment of money, but required a repayment in kind; that the large farmer used (much more often than the small farmer) cash to secure the things and services he needed to carry on his work; and that the large farmer had higher prestige. We noted, further, the privileges of land ownership and farm operation in both Dobu and Eire. These observations lead us to ask: How is payment for work provided for? What services are supplied free and what are not? What is the symbolic significance of the manner of payment (wages, salaries, fees, etc.)? What is the significance of the ownership or non-ownership of the tools of an occupation? What privileges and what limitations attach to such ownership?

B. The Status and Authority System

This discussion will deal with the determination of status (The Status System), controls on new entrants to the occupation (Teaching and Learning), and controls on those already in the occupation (Systems of Control).

I. *The Status System*

In Dobu, we observed the relation between magic and land ownership, and the relation between the power of women's magic and their control over the work of men. In Eire, we observed the importance of ownership and the effect of age, occupation, and membership in the old men's Cuaird on one's rights and privileges. These observations lead us to ask: What work factors place persons in authority relationships with each other? What privileges or rights and duties attach to different work positions or statuses? How is authority expressed? [15]

II. *Teaching and Learning*

In Dobu, the young man learns his magic from his mother's brother. In Eire, the boy learns work practices from his father, the girl from her mother. We are led to ask: How do persons learn the skills required in their occupations? Who does the teaching? Again, we noted that, in Eire, the father selects the person who inherits the farm and consequently it is that person's learning which would be most important, as far as the farm is concerned. This leads us to ask: Who is permitted to learn? And since all occupations require on-the-job learning, how is the learning process controlled by controlling the entry of new persons into the occupation?

III. *Systems of Control*

We observed in Dobu the close relation between magic and yam-growing. We observed in Eire the yearly round, and the ritual of the cattle sale at the fair. These observations lead us to ask: What are the attitudes of right and wrong that surround work performance? What are the folkways, mores, and codes? In Eire, a person who refuses to coor may become an object of ill-feeling and even be ostracized. This leads us to ask: What forms of deviant conduct exist and what are the sanctions that are imposed on deviants?

C. The Career

Our concern here is with the selection of the career (Social Selection), career success and movement (Mobility), crucial career decisions (Career Contingencies), and the relation between work and personality (Work and the Self).

I. *Social Selection*

In Eire, a young man might become a farmer, a shopkeeper, or, eventually, a member of the New York police force. In each case, he would need his father's or other member of the family's sponsorship and financial assistance. Whether a girl became a wife or emigrated and

---

[15] For example, may a factory foreman order a worker to shift from the work he is doing to something else? May he order him to buy flowers for his (the foreman's) wife's birthday? May he order him to "cover up" for him in time of emergency? And under what circumstances are any of these orders likely to be given or likely to be obeyed?

took a job, she would also need familial help. These considerations lead us to ask: What factors determine an individual's selection of an occupation? What is the role of family, religion, race, and other background characteristics? To what extent does the occupation itself determine the kinds of people that will enter it?

II. *Mobility*

In Eire, a girl might marry up, or a boy might, with his father's help, be apprenticed to a shopkeeper or adopt an urban occupation. We are led to ask: How does a person change his work status? How does he rise or fall? What factors may assist or retard him?

III. *Career Contingencies*

In Eire, we saw the phenomenon of delayed marriage and why this delay was related to the need to wait until the father accumulated sufficient capital to finance the children's future. In addition, the choice by the father of the inheriting son may not be made until quite late in the father's life. We are led to ask: At what point in his life does the individual make crucial decisions about his occupational future? At what point does he decide to secure the necessary occupational education? To what extent does the occupation determine these points of crucial decisions?

IV. *Work and the Self*

In Dobu, we noted the relationship between authority and the ownership of land, and the very great difference between the power a man possessed in his own village and in his wife's. In Eire, we noted the attachment of children to the parental home and locality and the importance of keeping the name of the family on the farm. We noted the obligations that surround cooring. These observations lead us to ask: Wherein lie a person's identifications—with his work, or with some outside group or cause? What sort of personality does the occupation require? To what extent is it true that the occupation selects persons of a certain personality type and to what extent is it true that the occupation itself tries to mold persons to fit a certain personality type?

D. The Work Group

Two categories seem appropriate here—the determination of membership (Inclusion and Exclusion) and informal group structure Informal Relations).

I. *Inclusion and Exclusion*

One was identified in Dobu as an owner or one of "those-resulting-from-marriage." We noted in Eire the matters of membership in the old men's Cuaird, family work, and community cooring. The latter took place only among those known and trusted. We therefore ask: Who make up the work groups or colleague groups within work situations? What kinds of persons are trusted and what kinds regarded as marginal members of the occupation? Who gets into the inner circles of work organizations and how do they maintain themselves and exclude outsiders?

II. *Informal Relations*

In Dobu, a person's magical knowledge is kept secret. The "boys" in Eire chafe under their father's discipline but do not express this irritation openly. We recall also the old men's Cuaird. These facts lead us to ask: What kinds of secret behavior go on in a work organization and why? What types of behavior are considered correct to discuss with one's colleagues only, and what kinds of information is it considered appropriate to discuss with outsiders? What kinds of informal specialization exist? What, finally, is the relation of the small group or clique to work behavior? Why do cliques appear, what are their functions, and what effects do they have on work conduct itself?

The above set of categories, with their accompanying questions, make up the conceptual framework for the analysis of work in our society. For convenience, the framework is summarized in abbreviated form in Fig. 2.

In examining the framework, one might wonder where certain traditional or expected categories are. Neither the labor union nor the subject of race relations are mentioned. Such subjects are not included because the framework is intended to provide an optic for the analysis of work *anytime* and *anywhere*. But we do not see unions everywhere. They are obvious in our own society but were missing in both Dobu and County Clare. Nor did we observe any minority groups or racial divisions in either place. However, the omission of these categories does not mean that the framework leaves them out. They will come in, as will be seen, under the appropriate headings. The union comes in for discussion in many places: a union affects the institutional system—is actually part of it—it affects status and authority relations, and may affect the career and work group. Race relations, similarly, will be relevant to the work complex, the economic complex, status, teaching and learning, systems of control, the career, and, eminently, the work group.

The discussion of the conceptual framework brings us to the conclusion of Part One. Our procedure in Parts Two and Three will be to take the framework and apply it to the two major areas in the sociology of work relations: occupational and industrial sociology. We shall first discuss the sociology of occupations. After that, we shall focus on three industries: the farm, the restaurant, and the factory.

A. THE INSTITUTIONAL SYSTEM

I. *The Work Complex*
Relation of the work to other parts of social structure

II. *The Work Structure*
Nature of the division of labor and specialization

III. *The Economic Complex*
Nature and types of payment; significance of ownership

B. THE STATUS AND AUTHORITY SYSTEM

I. *The Status System*
Factors determining status; nature of power structure

II. *Teaching and Learning*
Determination of who teaches and who is permitted to learn; nature of on-the-job learning

III. *Systems of Control*
Folkways, mores, and codes; sanctions for deviant conduct

C. THE CAREER

I. *Social Selection*
Factors in selection of given work as career; extent to which the work selects distinctive types of persons

II. *Mobility*
Rising and falling in career levels

III. *Career Contingencies*
Crucial decisions—timing and significance

IV. *Work and the Self*
Work identifications and counter-identifications; occupational personality

D. THE WORK GROUP

I. *Inclusion and Exclusion*
Make-up of work groups and colleague groups; inner circles and exclusiveness

II. *Informal Relations*
Informal specialization; types of secret behavior; cliques and informal groups

FIG. 2

CONCEPTUAL FRAMEWORK FOR ANALYSIS OF SOCIAL RELATIONS WITHIN AN OCCUPATION OR INDUSTRY

45

CHAPTER REFERENCES

1. Arensberg, C. M., *The Irish Countryman,* London: Macmillan, 1937.
2. —— and Kimball, S. T., *Family and Community in Ireland,* Cambridge: Harvard University Press, 1948.
3. Benedict, R., *Patterns of Culture,* Boston: Houghton Mifflin, 1934.
4. Fortune, R. F., *Sorcerers of Dobu,* London: Routledge, 1932.
5. Hughes, E. C., *French Canada in Transition,* Chicago: University of Chicago Press, 1943.
6. Malinowski, B., *Argonauts of the Western Pacific,* London: Routledge, 1932.

PART TWO

OCCUPATIONS:
PROFESSIONAL
WHITE-COLLAR
BLUE-COLLAR

INTRODUCTION

The Sixth International Conference of Labour Statisticians (47, p. 54) agreed upon this definition of the term "occupation":

"Occupation" is the trade, profession or type of work performed by the individual, irrespective of the branch of economic activity to which he is attached.

This definition, in its last clause, suggests that care must be taken to avoid confusing occupation with "branch of economic activity," and, in fact, most censuses make a similar distinction. Usually, the term "industry" is used to describe the appropriate "branch of economic activity." Thus occupational data will describe the number of electricians, whereas industrial data will describe the number employed in in "electrical installations, cables and apparatus." People employed in the latter will include *some* electricians, but also machinists, engineers, salesmen, clerks, and many others.

This distinction has two serious defects. First, it breaks down in practice because occupation and industry overlap, in some cases extremely. It is easy enough to decide, for the case of a nurse attached to a factory, that her occupation is "nurse, medical" and her industry is "manufacturing." But a great many occupations cannot be defined apart from the industry in which they are practiced. This is particularly true of semiskilled and unskilled occupations. What shall one do with an unskilled worker in an ammunition works who loads completed shells into boxes? The U.S. Census (24) would probably classify him under the general heading of "Operatives and kindred workers, n.e.c." or

"Laborers, Except Farm and Mine, n.e.c." [1] But such omnibus categories tell us precious little about the type of work performed by the individual. Would it help to create a genuine occupational category, say, "those who pack light objects into containers" and put our worker in it? [2] But this would put him in the same category with persons who pack canned-soup cans into cases, persons who pack cigarettes into cartons (a highly skilled operation in some places), and those who fill bags of salted peanuts (an activity which, in one firm, is performed by feebleminded girls). Important occupational differences among these people would be ignored and an expert in packing canned soups might be wholly unsuited to the requirements in the ammunition works. [3]

The second defect in the occupation-industry distinction is more serious from a sociological viewpoint. When one insists that occupation is something wholly separate from industry, there is a strong tendency to think in terms of the isolated individual apart from his fellows. Thus, one important official source (48, p. 9) makes the following statement:

> The nature of the factory, business or service in which the person is employed has no bearing upon the classification of his occupation, except to the extent that it enables the nature of his duties to be more clearly defined.
>
> It is a person's occupation, *i.e.,* the nature of his work, which determines the type and degree of the strains, physical or mental, to which he is subjected, and the conditions generally under which his working life is lived. These are in the main independent of his industrial association, *i.e.,* of the industry or service which affords him employment.

But we shall show in this book that the "type and degree of the strains" to which a man is subjected are only *slightly* determined by the type of work he does. We shall show that "type of work" means that a man is thrown into association with a peculiar group of fellows on which his work destiny largely depends. And this is just as true of doctors or lawyers in private practice as it is of factory laborers. Consequently, the definition first quoted on p. 49 *is* satisfactory provided we do not insist on any rigid separation between type of work and "branch of economic activity."

The four chapters which make up Part Two deal with occupations in our culture and are organized according to the conceptual framework which was presented in Chapter Two. Chapter Three deals with the

---

[1] "N.e.c." is short for "not elsewhere classified."

[2] The categories of "packer" and "loader" both occur as detailed occupations under both the Operative and Laborer headings.

[3] A detailed occupation, "nut packer (not factory)" does occur, but this simply adds an *industrial* feature—which illustrates the point we are making.

institutional system of occupations; Chapter Four is concerned with the status and authority system in occupations; Chapter Five deals with the career; and, finally, Chapter Six analyzes the occupational work group.

CHAPTER THREE

THE OCCUPATIONAL
INSTITUTIONAL SYSTEM

THE OCCUPATIONAL WORK COMPLEX

We are concerned here with the manner in which occupations are related to each other and to the social structure as a whole.

Work, as a societal complex, has been considered by a number of social scientists of whom the most noteworthy have been Adam Smith and Emile Durkheim. Adam Smith, in his classic work (71, Pt. I, Chs. I, III), pointed out that the larger the society, the more refined is its occupational specialization. In turn, the great increases in economic productivity of modern times have rested on the evolution of a complex division of labor. Mass production depends on a division of labor because it requires repetition of minute tasks in order to speed up production. He illustrated this process in his famous description of the effects of mass production on the manufacture of pins (71, pp. 44–45). But Smith omits the most important thing of all—the social significance of the division of labor. He treats the division of labor as if it were purely an economic phenomenon—as if the whole thing were essentially a convenient, highly efficient mechanism for getting society's work done. He has very little to say about the meaning of the specializations in which the division of labor puts people. There is no explicit attention given to the fact that where one puts people occupationally has powerful, if not decisive, consequences for their behavior in society: their prestige positions in the community, their family relations, their religious and civil affiliations, their interests and non-work activities in general.

Durkheim (33) is concerned with pointing out the effects of the division of labor on personality. He shows how the division of labor leads to a type of solidarity which he calls *solidarité organique*—a solidarity which rests on the fact that specialists, by the very act of specialization, become dependent on one another. *Solidarité organique* is contrasted with *solidarité mechanique*—a type of solidarity based not on interdependence, but on similarity or consensus, as illustrated in strongly knit primitive societies, the modern family, labor unions, and the modern state. The modern division of labor is therefore a means by which society is held together, a substitute, as it were, for the disintegrating unities of family, religion, and locality. At the same time, Durkheim goes on to show, the division of labor becomes so complex and involved that the individual becomes unable to see his place in the whole. The individual becomes lost and the total system, of which he is a small cog, becomes meaningless—a condition Durkheim called *anomie*. In one place,[4] Durkheim suggests, as a solution, the creation of occupational groups modeled, to some extent, along guild lines. But his discussion is quite general, and he gives little attention to particular occupations.

An adequate discussion of the work complex in modern culture must accomplish two objectives: first, it must be specific—we cannot be satisfied with a general discussion of "occupations and society," however insightful the discussion might be; and, second, the discussion must encompass the entire range of modern occupations. Perhaps the most efficient approach is through the examination of occupational trends.

TECHNIQUES OF CLASSIFICATION

As both Adam Smith and Emile Durkheim pointed out, one of the outstanding characteristics of our own society, as compared with preliterate and non-industrial societies, is the tremendous elaboration of the division of labor and the degree of specialization. The *Dictionary of Occupational Titles* (84) describes well over 20,000 occupational specialties in the United States. Not only are there a large number of occupations, but each occupation is broken down to a minute degree. From doctors to pretzel-benders, from professional dancers to gandy-dancers, specialization proceeds. Our first task is to reduce this great welter of occupations to manageable proportions, and to do it in a meaningful way that will bring out the relations of occupations to each other and to other parts of society.

There are many comprehensive schemes of classification in use but few of them satisfy the criterion of meaningfulness. The U.S. Census (20) recognizes such categories as professional, technical, and kindred workers,

---

[4] (33), Preface to the 2nd ed., pp. 1–31. First published in 1902.

farmers, and farm managers, managers, officials, and proprietors, except farm, private household workers, operatives and kindred workers, etc. This type of classification includes everyone, but we learn little about the people or their relation to each other.[5]

Most schemes of classification that attempt to be socially meaningful are systems of ranking occupations from high to low, using, in general, intelligence [6] or prestige [7] (as measured by a sample of the population or specially selected judges) as criteria of rank. We shall not pause to examine these scales critically [8] except to note that the lack of complete success or even agreement in the use of such scales strongly suggests that there is no single variable by which occupations may be arranged in rank order (44). Instead we shall here make use of a scale which seems to be superior to most others in terms of its comprehensiveness, meaningfulness, and the relative lack of bias. It has, further, the very great advantage that it has been applied to census data over a considerable period of time, so that comparable data on occupational trends may be derived. The scheme was developed by Alba Edwards (34) [9] and is limited to *gainful* workers: that is, it does not include rentiers (persons living off of investments), children and women doing only uncompensated housework or chores in their own home, some parts of institutional populations, and some others.

THE EDWARDS OCCUPATIONAL SCALE

Gainful workers are arranged in a hierarchy of six main categories:
1. Professional Persons
2. Proprietors, Managers, and Officials
3. Clerks and Kindred Workers
4. Skilled Workers and Foremen
5. Semi-Skilled Workers
6. Unskilled Workers

No distinction is made with reference to what people are doing. We do not know, for skilled workers, for example, whether they are working on farms, in factories, or offices.

---

[5] The first object in any census is that of comprehensiveness. One must be sure that everyone is counted, and if meaningfulness must occasionally be sacrificed to that objective, then little can be done. See, however, for excellent discussions, using the standard census categories, (1, 2).

[6] See (4, 14, 37, 38, 73, 78).

[7] See (5, 6, 21, 27, 28, 29, 41, 50, 61, 63, 70, 72, 79).

[8] For a good discussion of the assumptions underlying occupational scales, classified by the author as socioeconomic, intelligence, and prestige scales, see (16, pp. 42–57).

[9] Edwards' scheme was not completely original but a great improvement over previous classifications.

The notion of socio-economic grouping involves three major assumptions. First, the income of persons in our culture is derived, for the most part, from gainful occupation. In eliminating persons not so employed, the assumption is that we are not eliminating a significant segment of the population as far as the work of society is concerned. Second, occupation and form of income are not just matters of individual merit or distinction but are contingent on many factors such as education, training, skills, rural-urban location, and ancestry. These factors in turn affect movement up and down the occupational ladder. It is possible to move but there is competition for available positions and the competition is a sticky one. It depends on the apprenticeship opportunities, on unionism and on the state. Third, it assumes that however indifferent we may insist we are to different ways of living we do, by reward or by ascription of status, recognize a hierarchy of occupations and professions. What one does for a living has implications for where and how one lives, for opportunities that one can provide for oneself and one's children, for status, and for the interest groups that the individual will belong to.[10]

The six categories listed above are in turn subdivided into other categories. The first category of professional persons is self-explanatory. It includes only those in the recognized professions and conceives of a profession as that which requires a good deal of specialized education and experience. Examples of occupations included in this category are actors, architects, artists, chemists, clergymen, professors, veterinarians, photographers, and physicians.

Proprietors, Managers and Officials, the second category, is subdivided into three subcategories:

1. Farmers, including both owners and tenants.
2. Wholesale and retail dealers.
3. Other proprietors, managers, and officials.

Examples of occupations in this general category are: livestock buyers, hucksters and peddlers, funeral directors and embalmers, and proprietors, managers, and officials in various industries. We note that both owners

---

[10] Edwards himself, however, claims a good deal more for his categories. He writes: ". . . it is evident that each of these groups represents not only a major segment of the Nation's labor force, but, also, a large population group with a somewhat distinct standard of life, economically, and, to a considerable extent, intellectually and socially. In some measure, also, each group has characteristic interests and convictions as to numerous public questions—social, economic, and political. Each of them is thus a really distinct and highly significant social-economic group." (34, p. 179) While such assertions may be partly true of occupations, they become dubious when applied to such categories as "Proprietors, Managers, and Officials" or "Semi-Skilled Workers."

and tenants are put together in the "farmers" category although their opportunities are likely to be different.

The category of Clerks and Kindred Workers is self-explanatory. Examples include radio operators, advertising agents, baggagemen, mail carriers, office machine operators, salesmen, and other white-collar workers. In early days the occupation of clerk was a high-status category. The clerk did not perform dirty work, he was literate and could figure, and he worked close to management. Originally the scribes were churchmen (58, Vol. I, Ch. I). Their activities have gradually become secularized but they have tended to carry the early prestige with them. However they had prestige only as long as they were scarce. At the present time, when large numbers are literate and the mere ability to read and write is no longer a scarce skill, the clerical group has lost much of its prestige.

Also, over the same period labor union organization has tended to raise the wages of manual workers above that of many clerical workers. And the value of the clerical worker's broad or cultural education has been greatly lessened by the introduction of the machine into the clerical office. A visitor to the modern business office would find it difficult to distinguish the office from the factory with the office's typewriters, duplicators, bookkeeping machines, addressograph machines, and even IBM equipment. As a consequence, a great deal of the work of the clerical worker is itself manual work. To many persons the significant difference is that the office workers are segregated from the factory workers in an *office;* this in turn has certain symbolic significance to the office workers themselves. However, the lower pay check, the less sure tenure that the office worker is likely to have, and the very much poorer opportunity for advancement produces a tendency to evaluate office work more highly than it is worth. For the future, the trend seems likely to be that office work will become more and more manual, more and more like factory work.

The last three categories differ from the first three. Here for the first time the matter of skill is brought in explicitly. Distinctions between the last three categories are made in the manner of a continuum. Edwards includes among skilled workers and foremen those occupations that require mainly, "education, judgment, and manual dexterity," [11] the semiskilled workers include those that require "less" education, judgment, and manual dexterity, and, finally, the unskilled workers are simply those that require no education, judgment, or manual dexterity (34, p. 176). Let us look at each of these three skill criteria.

[11] These criteria are undoubtedly related to Adam Smith's discussion (71, p. 43) of the division of labor, where he speaks of the "skill, dexterity, and judgment with which it (labor) is anywhere directed."

Education with reference to skilled work consists of two components: acquisition of the general cultural traditions and heritages, and training in the particular skills requisite for the occupation. The most important question here is the extent to which persons can be trained on the job—apprenticeship—and the extent to which they can be trained apart from the job in formal institutions of learning. The medieval guilds provide the classic illustration of apprenticeship, but the guild involved much more than a symbiotic tie between apprentice and master. The tie was direct and personal with the apprentice even living with the master.[12] At the present time even apprenticeship is not personal. Instead it is an impersonal association which is restricted to the *work alone*. It furthermore involves an association *not* with a master but with an organization, for the teacher is likely himself to be an employee like the apprentice. Standards of craftsmanship are dictated not by the master but by engineering design. In addition, with the increase in the use of machines the sheer amount of skill needed for a given occupation is declining. Consequently the length of training necessary is declining. Therefore the importance of master or teacher tends to decline, and with that his status.

As a matter of fact the whole conception of "craft" is becoming obsolete. The type of skill being increasingly asked for is the operation of a machine. The company advertises not for a tailor but a sewing machine operator, not for a mechanic but for a riveter or punch press operator. The extent to which this is true is illustrated in the U.S. Census classification of Operatives. Some illustrations are: operatives in electric light and power plants, operatives in gas works, operatives in lime, cement and artificial stone factories, operatives in paint factories, and in many other types of industries (20, pp. 10, 14, 15).

As a consequence, the craft becomes less and less the unit of organization, and is replaced by the industry as the major unit of organization, or by the process, or by the machine. One finds the United Automobile Workers (CIO) including within their ranks persons who have nothing at all to do with the making of automobiles.[13] One finds the Teamsters including clerks, employees of Boeing Aircraft, and salesmen.[14] And

[12] See (10, pp. 65–66, 68).

[13] Included are not only persons directly involved in the manufacture of farm, automobile, automotive propelled products, aircraft and agricultural implements, but also "employees engaged in office work, sales, distribution and maintenance thereof, and such other branches of industry as the International Executive Board shall decide in accordance with the jurisdiction committee of the Congress of Industrial Organizations" (65, p. 63). See also (55, pp. 198–99; 64, Chs. 3, 4).

[14] Jurisdiction includes: "teamsters, chauffeurs and helpers, stablemen; all who are employed on horses, harnesses, carriages or automobiles in and around stables or garages (other than mechanics); warehousemen; all classes of dairy employees inside and

this trend gives an entirely new dimension to social organization. It means further that there is a greatly decreased interest in beauty or in fine workmanship—the machine takes care of these matters—but instead an interest in uniformity, in the correct operation of the machines.[15]

Because apprenticeship has declined and, therefore, persons can be trained quickly, there has been a tendency for schools to take over part of the training process and we have had the development within modern times of vocational schools (68, ch. 7). Labor unions have tended to oppose this trend because it means the bringing in of outsiders who are difficult to control and because it upsets seniority within the plant.

We get, therefore, a picture of skill being increasingly transferred to the machine and of less skill being required to operate these machines. This in turn means a decrease in the need for skilled workers and an increase in the need for semiskilled workers. However, the *designing* of these machines then becomes a highly complex activity and is lifted up into the *professional* group, and produces the engineer and the designer. The fact that the worker spends much of his time before a machine also raises the question of efficiency and of boredom and one gets the emergence of the personnel man and efficiency personnel who also are listed in the professional group. This in turn means that there is still less opportunity for the machine operator to exercise his ingenuity or originality.

Manual Dexterity does not appear to be a major factor in work any more. It may be a function of length of experience on a machine. Because skill no longer is so important, manual dexterity is not.

---

outside; workers employed in ice cream plants; all truck terminal employees." In some cases, vendors and owner-operators of a team or vehicle are eligible (65, pp. 373–74).

[15] This great change was recognized—and advocated—by one of the earliest apologists for modern factory methods, Andrew Ure, who wrote, in 1835: "Wherever a process requires peculiar dexterity and steadiness of hand, it is withdrawn as soon as possible from the *cunning* workman who is prone to irregularities of many kinds, and it is placed in charge of a peculiar mechanism, so self-regulating that a child may superintend it.

"The principle of the factory system, then, is to substitute mechanical science for hand skill, and the partition of a process into its essential constituents, for the division or graduation of labour among artisans. On the handicraft plan, labour more or less skilled, was usually the most expensive element of production-*Materiam superabat opus;* but on the automatic plan, skilled labour gets progressively superseded, and will, eventually, be replaced by mere overlookers of machines.

"By the infirmity of human nature, it happens that the more skillful the workman, the more self-willed and intractable he is apt to become, and, of course, the less fit a component of mechanical system, in which, by occasional irregularities, he may do great damage to the whole. The grand object, therefore, of the modern manufacturer is, through the union of capital and science, to reduce the task of his work-people to the exercise of vigilance and dexterity—faculties, when concentrated to one process, speedily brought to perfection in the young" (82, pp. 192–93).

Judgment implies the ability to apply one's knowledge to new situations, or problems, and also the ability to synchronize one's activities with others. Such judgment as remains tends to rest with the foremen. The foremen are recruited usually from the ranks of the skilled workers but they enjoy few of the privileges of the worker such as union membership, and very little of the authority of the managers. Consequently they find themselves in an anomalous position. They are at the mercy of the employer without the protection that the worker has. One result has been the growth of foremen's associations.

1. Professional Persons
2. Proprietors, Managers, and Officials
    a. Farmers (owners and tenants)
    b. Wholesale and Retail Dealers
    c. Other Proprietors, Managers, and Officials
3. Clerks and Kindred Workers
4. Skilled Workers and Foremen
5. Semi-Skilled Workers
    a. Semi-Skilled Workers in Manufacturing
    b. Other Semi-Skilled Workers
6. Unskilled Workers
    a. Farm Laborers
    b. Factory and Building Laborers
    c. Other Laborers
    d. Servant Class

FIG. 3
GAINFUL WORKERS OF THE UNITED STATES *
(AFTER ALBA EDWARDS)

Comparable to the foreman, is the shop union steward and he is put into the same category.

Edwards has therefore three categories according to degree of skill. The skilled workers and foremen are not subdivided. The semiskilled workers are divided into two categories, one—those in manufacturing, two—those in others. The unskilled workers are broken up into four subcategories:

1. Farm Laborers.
2. Factory and Building Laborers.
3. Other Laborers.
4. Servant Class.

It is in the unskilled category that persons who make use mainly of

---

* From *Population: Comparative Occupation Statistics for the United States, 1870 to 1940*, Table XXVII, p. 187.

their muscles occur; and as the machine is increasingly used, the jobs that depend on the use of muscles alone decline. It will be noted that in the last two categories Edwards does give some attention to the industries in which people work.

We thus have six major categories subdivided so that we end up with twelve groups. We have noted that there are certain faults in this scheme. It is not by any means a perfect description of society's evaluation of these occupations but is a coagulation into common-sense groupings based upon categories used in the past. Edwards still distinguishes white-collar workers from manual workers though that distinction is breaking down; he still distinguishes those who are in business for themselves from those who work for others, when in many cases those who work for others may enjoy greater financial rewards. But these criticisms mean only that social status involves more than occupation alone. It involves income, urban-rural location, nationality, recency of migration, race, and many other variables.

OCCUPATIONAL TRENDS

The trends in each of the major occupational categories are presented in Table 1 [15a]. Two special features of this table should be noted.

First, there is the shift from the "gainful worker" concept of 1930 and earlier to the "labor force" concept of 1940 (and later). The main difference is that a worker was counted as "gainfully employed" if he was *usually* employed at a given occupation, whether he happened to be working when the census enumerator called or not. By contrast, a worker is counted as a member of the "labor force" only if he is actually working during the week the census is taken, or is actively seeking work at the time.[16] The lack of comparability between 1940 figures and those gathered earlier was in part remedied by excluding from the 1940 figures "new workers." [17]

[15a] Data for 1950, comparable to that in the table, are not available.

[16] The census statement is as follows: " 'Gainful workers' were persons reported as having a gainful occupation, that is, an occupation in which they earned money or a money equivalent, or in which they assisted in the production of marketable goods, regardless of their activity at the time of the census. The labor force, as defined in the 1940 census, includes all persons who were employed for pay or profit, or at unpaid family work, during the week of March 24 to 30, 1940, or who were seeking work or were on public emergency work during that week" (34, p. 11). The major groups affected by the change are new workers, seasonal workers, inmates of institutions (not counted in 1940), and retired and disabled persons.

[17] In 1940, a person just out of school and actively seeking a job would qualify as a member of the labor force. But in 1930, such a person, never having worked regularly, could not report a "usual occupation."

TABLE 1
CHANGES IN PER CENT OF WORKERS, CLASSIFIED ACCORDING TO EDWARDS, UNITED STATES, 1910 TO 1940 *

	PER CENT OF GAINFUL WORKERS			LABOR FORCE	PER CENT INCREASE	PER CENT INCREASE OF OTHER WORKERS	RATIO OF CATEGORY INC. TO INC. OF OTHER WORKERS [a]
	1910	1920	1930	1940	1910–1940	1910–1940	
Professional Persons	4.4	5.0	6.1	6.5	107.2	36.5	3.0
Proprietors, Managers, and Officials	23.0	22.3	19.9	17.8	7.6	49.1	.2
Clerical and Kindred Workers	10.2	13.8	16.3	17.2	134.6	28.8	4.7
Skilled Workers and Foremen	11.7	13.5	12.9	11.7	39.9	39.5	1.0
Semi-Skilled Workers	14.7	16.1	16.4	21.0	98.9	29.3	3.4
Unskilled Workers	36.0	29.4	28.4	25.9	.4	61.6	.0

TOTAL NUMBER OF WORKERS	
1910	37,271,360
1920	41,236,185
1930	48,594,592
1940	52,020,023

* Source of data for first four columns: Edwards, A. M., Population: Comparative Occupation Statistics for the United States, 1870 to 1940, Table XXVII, p. 187. The three right-hand columns, which make comparisons, are based on calculations by the author.
[a] Figures rounded to one decimal place.

Second, the three right-hand columns in Table 1 involve a unique trend analysis which prevents spurious comparisons. In each case a particular category, say, "Professional Persons," is compared, not with all workers including "Professional Persons," but with all *other* workers.[18] The result of the comparison is the ratio of the increase of "Professional Persons" to the increase of all other workers—the figure in the right-hand column.

Table 1 reveals that, whereas the number of other workers increased by 36.5 per cent from 1910 to 1940, the number of Professional Persons increased by 107.2 per cent, or almost three times as fast. A very different situation is seen to have prevailed for Proprietors, Managers, and Officials, who increased by only 7.6 per cent, much more slowly than did the rest of the workers. Furthermore, the proportion of Proprietors, Managers, and Officials has declined steadily. Clerical and Kindred Workers show an increase of 134.6 per cent or close to five times as fast as the increase of other workers, the highest increase of any occupational category. Skilled Workers and Foremen increased by 39.9 per cent, or at almost the same rate as the rest of the workers. This figure is, however, misleading, for it suggests that Skilled Workers and Foremen are holding their own, which is not the case. If we look at the figures for each census decade, we see the following. Between 1910 and 1920, Skilled Workers and Foremen increased by 27.7 per cent whereas other workers increased by only 8.4 per cent—a real increase. But from 1920 to 1930, the situation reversed itself, with Skilled Workers and Foremen increasing by only 12.8 per cent when the rest of the workers increased by 18.6 per cent. In the decade from 1930 to 1940, Skilled Workers and Foremen actually *decreased* by 2.8 per cent when the total number of other workers increased by 8.5 per cent. Looked at in this way, we see a net downward trend in this category.

For Semi-Skilled Workers we observe a very large increase of 98.9 per cent, or almost three and one-half times as fast as did the other workers. Finally, Unskilled Workers increased by only 0.4 per cent, or very much more slowly than did other workers. As with Skilled Workers

[18] The result is achieved simply by subtracting the number of "Professional Persons" from the total number of workers, and using the *difference* as the group with which to compare "Professional Persons," instead, as is more common, of using the entire number of workers. The latter procedure introduces a spuriousness since "Professional Persons" are themselves obviously a part of the group they are being compared to. If "Professional Persons" are increasing much faster, or changing much faster in any direction than the rest, obviously this will affect the increase or change in the total group. The problem is especially serious when we are using categories which include as large a proportion of all workers as Edwards' do.

and Foremen, we get a clearer picture by breaking up the trend. From 1910 to 1920, when the other workers increased by 22.0 per cent, Unskilled Workers *declined* by 9.6 per cent; from 1920 to 1930, when the other workers increased by 19.5 per cent, Unskilled Workers increased by only 13.8 per cent; and from 1930 to 1940, when the other workers increased by 10.8 per cent, Unskilled Workers again *declined* by 2.4 per cent.

We proceed next to the interpretation and explanation of these trends.[19]

The striking increase in professional workers is to be attributed to two major factors. First, the actual number of persons in traditional professions has increased, reflecting an increasing emphasis on education, growing public awareness of the need for expertly trained persons,[20] and the greatly increased technological complexity of professional activities. Second, wholly new professions have emerged in such areas as public health, teaching, accounting, engineering, social work, and so on. The most striking increase within professional ranks has been in connection with professions related to industry (1, p. 498)—such occupations as technical engineers, chemists, designers and draftsmen—many of which hardly existed in the nineteenth century. Professionalization thus reflects the increasing complexity of man's working life.

Proprietors, Managers, and Officials have declined, and are declining for two reasons. First, this category includes farmers, both owners and tenants. The figures for this group are presented in Table 2 below.

TABLE 2
NUMBER AND PER CENT OF FARMERS (OWNERS AND TENANTS) UNITED STATES, 1910 TO 1940

	NUMBER	PER CENT OF ALL WORKERS
1910	6,132,368	16.5
1920	6,387,358	15.5
1930	6,012,012	12.4
1940	5,274,706	10.1

We observe that at each census year, the farmers (owners and tenants) made up a smaller and smaller proportion of all workers, dropping from about one-sixth in 1910, to almost one-tenth in 1940. We observe also that the trend years take in a great war and great depres-

[19] The discussion which follows is necessarily general. Perhaps the best detailed discussion is presented in (1).
[20] "When, in 1839, medical authorities were requested to assume responsibility for training dentists, the faculty of the most important medical school replied that dentistry was not important enough to be included in the curriculum" (1, p. 540).

sion. An inspection of the actual number of farmers, as presented in the table, shows that since 1920, not only have the farmers declined proportionally, but they have declined in actual numbers as well.

The second reason for the decline in Proprietors, Managers, and Officials is the over-all decline in *self-employment*. The figures reflect a decline in small business particularly, and a tendency for persons in such businesses to become skilled or semiskilled workers in some one else's employment. In Table 3 below are presented the figures for Proprietors, Managers, and Officials, with the farmers excluded. It may be observed in Table 3 that this group is increasing but that it is

TABLE 3
NUMBER AND PER CENT OF PROPRIETORS, MANAGERS, AND OFFICIALS (FARMERS EXCLUDED), UNITED STATES, 1910 TO 1940 *

	NUMBER	PER CENT OF ALL WORKERS
1910	2,447,090	6.5
1920	2,793,125	6.8
1930	3,653,447	7.5
1940	3,958,937	7.6

* Data for this table from Edwards, A. M., *Population: Comparative Occupation Statistics for the United States, 1870 to 1940*, Table XXVII, p. 187.

doing little better than holding its own. A considerable part of the increase it does show must be attributed to the increase in complexity of modern business, rather than to an increase in proprietorship.[21]

Clerical and Kindred Workers have increased faster than any other group; this is due to two main influences: first, the increase in the complexity of administrative activity—the increase in business accounting, the emphasis on promotional and sales activity; and second, the complexity and growth of governmental services. The clerical workers now become a very large part of the working force, and as their numbers have increased, their prestige has declined. Further, because the machines that clerical workers make use of are relatively small and inexpensive it is possible for this group, perhaps more than any other, to be trained in separate vocational schools. This produces a profound contrast with a great deal of factory work. Factory workers tend to be unionized to a considerable extent, and one of the functions of a union is to prevent too great an increase in the numbers of those employed. But if workers are trained in vocational schools, then there is no obvious control on their numbers. Vocational schools can turn out as many as wish that kind of training. As a consequence, large numbers of clerical workers are

[21] See (3, Ch. 7, pp. 454 ff.; 26; 46, pp. 12–18).

trained every year by the vocational schools and these then descend on businesses. With little unionization there is little to prevent the increase in their numbers.

The clerical workers make up a large group but one that is perhaps the most impotent politically. Clerical workers are, first, a poorly organized group. To a considerable extent there still remains among the white-collared group the lingering hope of upward mobility because of their traditions and because of their closeness to management. The clerical worker is still unable to avoid a feeling that, because he works next to the centers of power in business, to some extent he is also a center of power and that his opportunities for being formally vested with those powers are great (13, pp. 65–67). It is also of course among the clerical group that the middle-class values and the faith in upward mobility are likely to be strongest (56, pp. 259–65). Attempts to organize the white-collar workers have so far not been as successful as such attempts have been among the factory workers. A second reason for the lack of potency is its sex composition. Females make up a large proportion [22] and the position of the females in the work situation tends to remain an ambiguous one. Children may cut short or seriously limit the woman's earning ability, and normally the wife is expected to *supplement* the family income rather than to be its sole or main provider. Consequently she is not so likely to have as strong a feeling of job identification as her husband does (7, pp. 179–80).

But the situation is changing. The many labor-saving devices in the home, the marked decline in the birth rate, and the rise of the day-care nursery tend to change the work status of women. An increasing number of women who are married are taking jobs [23] and regarding them as full-time careers. Also, unionization is making headway among the clerical workers.[24]

The role of clerical workers in our society has not been sufficiently

[22] In 1950, of 6,865,960 "clerical and kindred workers," 4,272,930 or 62.2 per cent were women.

[23] In 1950, of 37,606,720 married women over 14 years of age, 8,634,560, or 23.0 per cent were in the labor force (83).

[24] C. W. Mills (56, p. 302) offers the following picture of white collar unionization: 1900: 2.5 per cent; 1920: 8.1 per cent; 1935: 5.0 per cent; 1948: 16.2 per cent. These figures are roughly one-third of the corresponding percentages of hourly wage workers. From figures supplied by L. Wolman (89, pp. 220–21), we have calculated the following percentages: 1910: 1.9 per cent; 1920: 5.3 per cent; 1930: 3.3 per cent. The latter figures are based on Wolman's categories of "Clerical Service," "Commercial Service," and "Professional Service," which are, of course, narrower than Mills' "white collar" group. A third source (81) estimated that "about one-eighth" of "clerical and professional" workers were unionized in 1944. See also (7, pp. 136–186; 52; 56, Ch. 14; 74) and the perceptive, though perhaps unduly pessimistic, article, "Why White Collar Workers Can't Be Organized" (88).

studied. Many persons think of the factory or of industry as being composed essentially of manual workers with, perhaps, a few clerical workers
in the head office of the company. But in 1940, clerical workers made up
close to one-fifth of the labor force. They are not a potent group but
they represent a great potential. They could control labor unions, determine price and wage policy, and even swing elections. If they are
ever organized or develop group consciousness on a large scale, they
may become the most powerful occupational group in our society (cf. 74,
pp. 550–51).

Referring again to Table 1 and observing trends in the last three
occupational categories, we note two facts: (1) both the skilled and unskilled groups have fallen; (2) the semiskilled group has risen. These
changes and the contrast are to be traced largely to the mechanization of
work over the thirty-year period. The skilled worker has tended to
become increasingly a machine operator, who is classified as semiskilled.
The unskilled worker who depends primarily on his muscles is actually
declining in sheer numbers as his work is taken over increasingly by
machines. We see here the effects of the decline in craftsmanship and
the rise of industry.

It is the change among the categories based on skill that represents
the second most revolutionary change in the thirty-year period.[25] Crafts
have been gradually disappearing and being replaced by work broken
down into minute acts which most persons can easily learn. Public
awareness of this change was dramatized in the Oregon Minimum Wage
case of 1917 (77, pp. 944–54) which established the constitutionality of
provisions for minimum wages and maximum hours for women and children, based, not on health, but on general principles. The pay of workers
was not to be determined solely by skill or marginal contribution, but
rather a minimum wage was to be guaranteed to all, irrespective of skill.
The ruling suggested also that besides skill, the successful operation of industry depended on wholly new personality requirements—regularity,
docility, absence of fatigue, and attentiveness. This change has tended to
have a leveling influence among such workers. It has become increasingly
difficult to arrange workers according to skills because the operations
they are required to perform have been made so elementary that workers
themselves have been made as interchangable as the parts they work with.
This trend has also produced important changes in the employers' attitude toward the workers. Formerly, the employer would ask a new worker:
"What experience have you had?" Now the question is likely to be, at

[25] The first being the increase in clerical workers.

least implicitly; "Are you docile? Can you be depended upon?" There is a tendency to emphasize, as much as skill and experience, the qualities of loyalty or low absenteeism. Further, while it was difficult to replace a skilled worker, it is by no means difficult to replace a semiskilled worker because his job is so simple that it can be taught to another in a relatively short time. The result has been a great increase in the power of the employer, a fact which has given labor unions one of their strongest talking points with workers.

As the crafts decline and work becomes routinized, the worker finds his job yields him little personal satisfaction or pride of workmanship. The end of the working day sees the worker turn from his vocation to an avocation that is often as unlike his work as possible. The man who spends his day reading dials in an oil refinery looks forward to spending the evening creating bows and arrows, by hand, in his "shop" in the basement, whereas the punch press operator daydreams of getting out to the country to do some sketching.[26] But the hobbies to which men turn have themselves become mechanized and routinized. Recreation itself has become commercialized and we see spectatorship developing in which the individual secures vicarious satisfactions, thrills, and shocks.[27] Leisure, the great gift of the industrial revolution, now becomes a problem (cf. 60, ch. 13; 67, ch. 1).

In addition to turning outward for personal satisfaction, the worker also tries to impose personal meanings, if not on his job, then on the situation surrounding his job. Working conditions, opportunities to work with others, and availability of status symbols are all taken into account in evaluating the job and some may even be spelled out as fringe benefits in union contracts. Public relations staffs proclaim that the company is a "good" one to work for, and personnel staffs try to make such claims true.

OCCUPATIONAL TRENDS, BY INDUSTRY

Up to this point, we have examined occupations by themselves. We shall now look at occupations according to the field or industry in which the occupation is found. Fortunately the Census provides us with comparable data from 1870 to 1930 so that long-term trends may be ascertained. In addition, we have made an attempt to bring the data up to 1950 so as to have an eighty-year trend before us. The data are presented in Tables

[26] Cf. (22, Vol. III, p. 149; 23; 31, p. 90; 66, pp. 351 ff.; 75, p. 17).
[27] See (3, pp. 243–63; 19, Pt. 1, Chs. 8, 9 and Pt. 2; 53, pp. 22–35, 46–50; 75, pp. 100–02; 85).

TABLE 4

PER CENT DISTRIBUTION OF GAINFUL WORKERS BY OCCUPATIONS, 1870 TO 1930,[a] AND LABOR FORCE BY INDUSTRIES, 1940 AND 1950.[b]

	GAINFUL WORKERS							LABOR FORCE	
	1870	1880	1890	1900	1910	1920	1930	1940	1950
AGRICULTURE	53.0	49.4	42.6	37.5	31.0	27.0	21.4	18.7	12.2
FORESTRY AND FISHING	.5	.6	.8	.7	.6	.6	.5	.2	.2
EXTRACTION OF MINERALS	1.4	1.7	1.9	2.4	2.6	2.6	2.0	2.0	1.7
MANUFACTURING	20.5	22.1	23.7	24.8	28.5	30.3	28.9	24.8 *	29.0 *
TRANSPORTATION AND COMMUNICATION	4.2	4.8	6.0	6.7	7.1	7.3	7.9	5.3 *	6.0 *
TRADE	6.8	7.9	8.8	10.6	9.7	10.0	12.5	13.5 *	21.1 *
PUBLIC SERVICE	.7	.8	.9	1.0	1.2	1.7	1.8	1.7 *	2.5 *
PROFESSIONAL SERVICE	2.6	3.2	3.8	4.1	4.6	5.1	6.7	7.3	8.3
DOMESTIC AND PERSONAL SERVICE	9.7	8.8	9.6	9.7	10.1	8.0	10.1	8.9	6.2

[a] Data on Occupations from 1870 to 1930 exclude category "Clerical Occupations."

[b] Source of Table: Data from 1870 to 1930 derived from *Populations: Comparative Occupation Statistics for the United States, 1870 to 1930*, Table XXII, p. 101. Data for 1940 and 1950 from appropriate census volumes.

* Clerical workers removed.

TABLE 5

PER CENT INCREASE OF GAINFUL WORKERS 1870 TO 1930, AND ADJUSTED GAINFUL WORKERS-LABOR FORCE CATEGORIES, 1870 TO 1950.

	PER CENT INCREASE, 1870–1930	PER CENT INC. OF OTHER WORKERS, 1870–1930	RATIO OF CATEGORY INC. TO INC. OF OTHERS, 1870–1930	PER CENT INCREASE, 1870–1950	PER CENT INC. OF OTHER WORKERS, 1870–1950	RATIO OF CATEGORY INC. TO OTHERS, 1870–1950
AGRICULTURE	52.9	531.4	.1	.5	712.4	.0
FORESTRY AND FISHING	315.8	277.6	1.1	100.0	336.2	.3
EXTRACTION OF MINERALS	427.5	275.6	1.6	497.9	334.2	1.5
MANUFACTURING	433.8	237.7	1.8	517.5	288.3	1.8
TRANSPORTATION AND COMMUNICATION	611.4	263.2	2.3	520.4	327.0	1.6
TRADE	592.2	254.9	2.3	1249.3	268.4	4.7
PUBLIC SERVICE	854.0	273.8	3.1	1462.9	327.2	4.5
PROFESSIONAL SERVICE	851.1	262.2	3.3	1266.4	309.8	4.1
DOMESTIC AND PERSONAL SERVICE	295.3	275.9	1.1	178.5	351.9	.5

4 and 5. Table 4 shows the per cent distribution for each category for each census year. Table 5 presents the trend analysis in terms of two time periods: 1870 to 1930 and 1870 to 1950.[28] In this analysis, as in

[28] This separation of periods is not made because of any special interest that attaches to either period but because the manipulation necessary to secure the 1940 and 1950

the analysis of the Edwards' occupational groups, we compare the increase of each category with all *other* categories so as to avoid a spurious overlap.

1. AGRICULTURE

With each census decade, workers in agriculture have made up a smaller and smaller proportion of the working force. In 1870, over half of all workers were classified as agricultural, but by 1950, the number so classified made up less than one-eighth of the labor force. From 1870 to 1950, the absolute numbers in all other categories had increased by 712.4 per cent; yet in 1950, the number in agriculture was *almost the same* as it had been in 1870. Furthermore, over this eighty-year period, the *total* population which had to be fed by agricultural workers increased from 39,818,449 to 150,697,361. This means that practically the same number of workers as in 1870 were able to provide for the food needs of almost four times as many people. These figures are eloquent testimony to the effects of the mechanization of agriculture and the decline of subsistence farming.[29] Another effect of this great decline in numbers should also be noted. The greatly reduced need for agricultural workers, especially since 1920, has contributed overwhelmingly to the growth of cities through migration from rural areas (40, pp. 59–62).

2. FORESTRY AND FISHING

The percentage of workers in Forestry and Fishing has fluctuated over the years, but by 1930, the number in this category had increased by 315.8 per cent, or faster than the rest of the working force. This increase largely reflected the increase in processing activities in the fishing industry. In 1940 and 1950, the proportion in Forestry and Fishing decreased with result that over the total eighty-year period this category

---

data are not entirely satisfactory and some readers may prefer to ignore the 1870–1950 data. From 1870 to 1930, the census adopted the practice of putting an occupation in a category if most persons in the occupation were likely to be found in that category. For example, if most electrical engineers worked in manufacturing, then all electrical engineers would be put in that category. In addition, the census created a special category, "Clerical Occupations," and treated it like any other industrial category. In 1940 and 1950, a shift was made to a genuine industrial classification and all persons were placed in the industry in which they worked, whatever their occupations. The category of "Clerical Occupations" was dropped. Therefore to make these data comparable to the earlier data, we omit from the earlier data "Clerical Occupations" and subtract from the 1940 and 1950 data those clerical workers found in manufacturing, trade, public service, and transportation and communication. This is tantamount to removing practically all of them. The cost, then, of comparable categories is the removal of the trend effects of clerical workers. A comparison of the ratios in Table 6 for the two time periods, however, suggests that our procedure has not done serious damage to the analysis.

[29] Of course many other societal changes helped facilitate these changes, especially the great development of distribution and marketing mechanisms.

increased more slowly than did other workers.[30] This effect is partly due to the increasing use of other building and heating materials than wood,[31] and to the maturity of the livestock industry with the growth of adequate refrigeration and transportation facilities (25).

3. EXTRACTION OF MINERALS

Workers involved in the extraction of minerals made up an increasing proportion of workers until the peak years of the 1920's, and have declined, relatively, since then. Nevertheless, in both the period from 1870 to 1930 and 1870 to 1950, they increased considerably faster than the rest of the workers. The increase was not, significantly, due to any increase in the number of miners, but appears to be due to an increase in processing and maintenance activities in connection with new minerals such as aluminum and magnesium, and the alloys.

4. MANUFACTURING

In 1870, the number of workers in manufacturing was less than half as great as those in agriculture. With each census year, as agriculture lost numbers, manufacturing registered gains until in its peak year of 1920, manufacturing finally surpassed agriculture. While continuing its gains over agriculture, manufacturing declined proportionally since then, though in 1950, it showed an upsurge which reached close to the 1920 percentage. The latter effect was unquestionably due to the war and continued prosperity of the postwar period. Over both 1870–1930 and 1870–1950 periods, manufacturing increased 1.8 times as fast as did the rest of the workers.

In spite of these increases, the numbers in manufacturing have not since 1920 risen above the proportion they formed of all workers in that year. During that thirty-year period, the total population to be supplied with manufactured goods increased by over 30 per cent and the demand for goods spiralled.[32] Yet no larger a proportion of workers than in 1920 was able to meet this need. This fact reveals the tremendous revolution that machine technology has made in our culture. At the same time, the inability of manufacturing to exceed the 1920 proportion suggests that manufacturing has only been able to maintain its position as the

[30] A factor whose significance is difficult to estimate may be partly responsible. Loggers were considered part of Forestry and Fishing up to 1930, but were removed from that category in 1940 and 1950.

[31] Cf. the trend data on lumber production vs. fuel oil demand in (15).

[32] See (35). The Federal Reserve index (unadjusted) of industrial production (1935–39 = 100) rose from 93 in 1920 to 237 in 1950. *Federal Reserve Bulletin,* 38: 69, 1952. Actually, these figures, selected because they correspond to census years, understate the expansion potential for manufacturing. A better picture is drawn by noting that the index dropped to a low of 41 for the depression year of 1932, yet only 11 years later, it had jumped to a high of 360 in the war year of 1943.

largest single work category by virtue of, not only the over-all population increase, but the increased demand of that population for manufactured goods. Its continued growth will undoubtedly depend on the magnitude of that demand.

5. TRANSPORTATION AND COMMUNICATION

Transportation and Communication has shown a steady increase as a proportion of all workers until 1940, when it dropped from its 1930 peak; it recovered somewhat by 1950. The 1930–1940 drop may represent a genuine drop due to depression conditions, or may be a reflection of the lack of complete comparability of the figures. However, the latter is probably not a major factor since in 1940, the category of "utilities" was added to transportation and communication, so that, if anything, the proportion should have gone up. However, from 1870 to 1930, when the rest of the workers increased by 263.2 per cent, transportation and communication increased by 611.4 per cent or 2.3 times as fast; from 1870 to 1950, when other workers increased by 327.0 per cent, this category increased by 520 percent or 1.6 times as fast. These remarkable increases appear to be due mainly to the increased use of mass transportation (15, pp. 112–118).

6. TRADE

With the exception of a drop in 1910, the numbers in trade have shown a steady, large increase over the period from 1870 to 1950. In 1950, they had risen to the point where they made up over one-fifth of the labor force and were exceeded only by manufacturing. Over the 1870–1930 period, the numbers in trade increased by 592 per cent, or 2.3 times as fast as the rest of the workers did; over the 1870–1950 period, trade workers increased by 1249.3 per cent, or 4.7 times as fast as all other workers—the largest of all comparative increases.

Persons in trade occupations now make up the second largest category of workers. Manufacturing and trade, in 1950, accounted for slightly over one-half of all workers, in vivid contrast to the 1870 figures, when agriculture accounted for over one-half. But manufacturing and trade have not increased at the same rate: the numbers in trade have increased over two and one-half times as fast as have the numbers in manufacturing. This suggests the tremendous new emphasis on distributional activities in connection with trade, and the great rise of marketing, sales, and promotion as major elements in modern business.

On the other hand, the fact that manufacturing did not increase at anything like the speed of trade suggests that production is no longer a serious problem in the United States. It appears that we are able to produce all that we need or are likely to need—barring possible war.

But whereas production begins to fade as a serious problem, *selling* rises to the fore as a major problem. The problem is not so much to produce the goods as to sell them.[33]

The factory worker who steps into the business office of his company is likely to be amazed at the number of persons he sees engaged in activities designed to sell the product he helps manufacture—persons concerned with credit and collection, huge staffs in accounting activities, staffs concerned with foreign export, large sales staffs, merchandising staffs, and so on. Not infrequently, he expresses dissatisfaction with the very large proportion of the company budget that goes to such persons. While recognizing that goods must be sold before he can be paid, there often lingers in his mind a notion of himself as the "primary producer" (an idea by no means confined to factory workers) and of all these others in the office as "middlemen," who glean a living "off his back," as it were. Also, whereas factory workers are usually paid an hourly wage or work on piece-work and thus their contributions can be measured with great accuracy, office workers work on salary and the decision as to their contributions rests on the subjective judgments of department heads—judgments which may be arguable. To add to the factory worker's sense of injury, it is unfortunately true that, in case of a business recession, the sales force may not actually decrease at all. While persons are being laid off in the factory, the sales force may even actually increase; in a recession there is likely to be a greater emphasis than ever on sales, promotional and advertising activities.

But there is a second implication of the great increase in trade activities. It is precisely in the trade occupations that unionization is at the weakest. The unions are likely to be forced to recognize that their continued power depends on unionizing this group, particularly if the numbers in manufacturing remain at their 1920 proportion, while the proportion in trade continues to go up.

7. PUBLIC SERVICE

With the exception of one census year, persons in public service had made up an increasing proportion of the working force in each census year. In 1940 the proportion dropped slightly, in part owing to depression conditions and in part because large numbers of public emergency workers gave as their occupations whatever type of government work they happened to be working on, such as construction (34, pp. 32–3). Although this group is small in absolute numbers, it shows the highest percentage increase of any occupation category over the 1870–1950 period —1462.9 per cent—and is second only to trade in its increase relative

---

[33] This problem has serious implications for certain kinds of discontent among factory workers. See pp. 419–420.

to other workers. These figures express the increasing areas of responsibility the state has assumed for public welfare and the growth of public corporations.[34]

8. PROFESSIONAL SERVICE

Professional groups have already been considered as an occupational category. This category is different, and includes persons in health services, educational services, legal and engineering services, charitable and religious organizations. In other words it is the *services* that are professional, rather than everyone in them. This category shows a steady, undiminished increase for each census year. As pointed out earlier, this increase is to be traced to the increase in the number of professionals and the emergence of wholly new professions. In addition, the figures represent the growth of auxiliary activities incident to the increased complexity of professional activities.

9. DOMESTIC AND PERSONAL SERVICE

This category has fluctuated up and down as a proportion of all workers. From 1870 to 1930, it little more than held its own in comparison to other workers; over the period from 1870 to 1950, it increased only half as fast as did all other workers, so that a downtrend may be in evidence. Such increase as it shows appears to be due to a general rise in the standard of living, but perhaps more important, it reflects the extent to which personal services have become institutionalized, as activities such as tailoring, laundry, barbering, and so on have moved outside the home.[35]

THE WORK COMPLEX: CONCLUSIONS

The foregoing discussion of occupational and industrial trends leads to two conclusions. First, *occupations in our culture, as in other cultures, are related to one another.* This we have seen by noting that a change in the numbers in one occupation is likely to affect the numbers in another occupation. We have seen, for example, that, as the unskilled and the skilled workers have decreased, the semiskilled workers have increased in numbers. These trends are directly related to each other. It is in fact the skilled workers who have *become* semiskilled workers. We have observed further that, as the number of semiskilled workers rises,

[34] Those interested in political implications should bear in mind that the figures represent an eighty-year trend since 1870. It is, consequently, hazardous to attempt to assign blame to given political parties.

[35] For example, for the period from 1870 to 1930, the number of "Barbers, hairdressers and manicurists" increased by 1,417.8 per cent when the rest of the workers increased by 275.6 per cent, or over five times as fast. Over the same period, persons in laundering services increased by 877.7 per cent when the rest of the workers increased by 274.8 per cent, or over three times as fast. See (34, Table 8, p. 212).

the number in the professions have risen concomitantly to a considerable extent because the sheer number of semiskilled workers and the type of their work have created the need for new professions dealing with efficiency, with controlling coordination, and with machine design.

Second, *occupations in our culture are related to other parts of our society and culture.* As the administrative aspects of our culture in business and government have grown, the number of clerical and trade workers has risen. As self-employment has declined, the number of proprietors, managers, and officials has declined. With mechanization, the numbers in farming have declined and the proportion in manufacturing has not exceeded the 1920 peak. We have also observed the manner in which changes in the occupational picture affect education, unionization, the position of women, and recreation. As we shall see later, the effects reach out into still other areas of society and culture.

In sum, the data on occupational trends suggest that work, as in Dobu and in Eire, forms a complex with other elements in our society and culture. In order to understand an occupation, one must examine its relationship to other occupations and to our society and culture as a whole.

THE OCCUPATIONAL WORK STRUCTURE

The classification schemes so far discussed, though valuable, are arbitrary. The categories into which persons are put are often not meaningful to the persons themselves. We have created the category of "Proprietors, Managers, and Officials" for our convenience; the persons so categorized probably do not think of themselves as a unit. We know that clerical workers do not do so.

We turn now to a discussion of organizational categories that are meaningful to the worker himself, categories that *he* uses to describe himself and others related to him. There are four major axes around which work structuring takes place: the industrial axis, the axis of related activities, the professionalization axis, and the axis of authority.

THE INDUSTRIAL AXIS

Although censuses create industrial categories to solve their own classification problems, some of those categories turn out to be meaningful to the worker himself. If one asks a clerk for the federal government what she does for a living, she is more likely to say: "I work for the government" than she is to say she is a clerk. The same thing is likely to be true of the factory worker, who will reply: "I'm out at the Lundee

Works"; when we ask *what* he does he is likely to tell us *where* he works. This tendency gives work a positional or local character.

Going along with this is a tendency for the worker to remain attached to one industry. Theoretically, the bookkeeping machine operator has a skill which is transferable to any industry, and the maintenance man can work for the government, a restaurant, or a labor union. But in fact there is a social psychological inertia which prevents movement unless the motives are strong. The worker in any company gets used to the routine there to the point where his work becomes somewhat easier. He develops a work reputation among his fellows which, if reasonably high, may be difficult to rebuild in another place. Often, unless he is strategically placed, he does not even hear of new job opportunities that may arise elsewhere. In addition, the worker has often bought a home, has children who are enrolled in school, friends whom he values, and so on. He is therefore not a freely mobile person no matter how transferable his skill may be.

As the worker stays on in a given industry, his identification is likely to increase. He begins to speak of the company as "a good one to work for" and feels an affiliation with other members of the same industry. Such affiliations have contributed significantly to the great growth of industrial unions.

AXIS OF RELATED ACTIVITIES

Workers engaged in occupations which interlock tend to develop a feeling of identification toward the whole complex of interlocking occupations. A doctor feels closest to other doctors, but he recognizes his relation to and may be found in pressure groups with the dentist, the nurse, the X-ray technician, and others who assist the sick.

Occupations become interlocked in two main ways: either several distinct activities are performed by one man, or several men perform closely related activities. It is important to recognize that *which* occupational activities become interlocked is determined quite as much by custom as it is by efficiency. This means that interlockings may change over time and "strange" combinations may be found.

The medieval mysteries of barbering, bloodletting, and toothdrawing were known to the same man who carried out all three (49, p. 91). The church in the same period took on a great variety of functions: not only the saving of souls but also the care of the sick, the care of the needy, the subsidy of art and of education, and the control of the guilds through insistence on a "just price" for goods. The present-day church minister is expected to preach, conduct rituals, raise money, have tea with the elderly ladies in the neighborhood, and run a Boy Scout troop. The high school teacher of science is often also the football coach.

The relation between college teaching and research is a shifting one. In theory the teacher should do research and then communicate his findings to his students.[36] But powerful forces are working against such a happy marriage. There has arisen the General Education movement which emphasizes the importance of "good" teaching as a skill and a value in its own right.[37] On the other hand, increasingly persons are being hired by industry to do research—and the findings may not even be communicated to others. Private industrial concerns may not wish to inform their competitors of a new research finding.[38] In the case of government-subsidized research, the stamp of "Classified" prevents communication of findings even to the colleagues of the researcher.

The pharmacist not only prepares medicines, he also sells them. As Thorner (80) points out, in the former capacity the pharmacist is a professional adjunct to the physician; in the latter capacity, he is a businessman. However if the pharmacist sold only medical prescriptions we would have many fewer pharmacists than we do. Consequently, the pharmacist sells other things—from quasi-medical items like beauty potions to toys and nuts—and, unquestionably, many pharmacists derive a large part of their incomes from the soda fountain or the sandwich bar in the drug store.

One may extend this analysis to occupation after occupation and discover that no occupation is isolated from other occupations. However, the relationship does not extend *in the workers' thinking* indefinitely to include all occupations. We instead tend to find clusters of them which tend to be thought of as belonging together. Sometimes they are performed by different persons, sometimes by the same person. The truck driver does more than drive a truck; he is expected normally to help to load and unload the truck. He will carry a list of pick-ups that he must make. He also is expected to have elementary knowledge of engine mechanics so as to be able to make minor repairs while on the road. The factory worker operates his machine, he helps feed it, he helps others out in the operation of their machine and helps unload trucks

---

[36] This principle is maintained to some extent in some European universities. A staff member may spend considerable time in research and give only occasional lectures when he feels he has something to say—a salutary principle.

[37] See (9, Chs. VI, VIII, *passim;* 11; 32, pp. 246–47; 51, pp. 84 ff.).

[38] One of the most famous pieces of analysis in the field of statistics is known by the anonymous designation of "Student's Distribution." "Student" was the "name" adopted by an employee of a British brewery house who did statistical research of the first magnitude. He was refused permission to use his own name in publication so that the company's competitors would be unable to trace the research to the company.

of raw material. These are normally considered to be associated with the operation of the machine.

In general we must not, in describing a given occupation, pay attention solely to the formal job description. Normally we will find that there is a central core of activities which are directly associated with the occupation, and that there are surrounding related activities. The worker in thinking of the work group includes the related activities in his identification area.

THE AXIS OF PROFESSIONALIZATION

As any occupation approaches professional status, there occur important internal structural changes and changes in the relation of the practitioners to society at large. A useful way of discussing these changes is by reference to the criteria of professionalization: the unstandardized product, degree of personality involvement of the professional, wide knowledge of a specialized technique, sense of obligation, sense of group identity, and significance of the occupational service to society (43).

1. THE UNSTANDARDIZED PRODUCT

A professional activity is one in which general knowledge is applied to solve particular problems, each of which is different from all other such problems. This notion of an unstandardized product or service is perhaps best illustrated by the artist struggling to express himself on canvas, but his experience is only an exaggeration of that of all professionals. The doctor finds each case unique, if not in symptoms, then in the attitudes and anxieties the patient brings with him, the presence or absence of concern on the part of the patient's family, the degree to which the patient will follow instructions, and the likelihood of success of treatment. In education, in spite of prescribed textbooks and syllabi, it is difficult to control what takes place in the classroom. Even the most polished lecturer finds he cannot anticipate every question; or, if he does not permit questions, then he cannot control all the devices students use to express their views: the frown, the look of amazement, the five-minute-long stare out the window, the irrelevant guffaw, the deep, sad sigh, or the look upward as if appealing for help from on high. In sum, the professional possesses *both* of the types of knowledge that William James (48a, p. 221) long ago distinguished: "knowledge-about" (generalized knowledge or knowledge of scientific laws) and "knowledge-of-acquaintance." The latter refers to intimate familiarity with the individual case based on experience and insight, a type of knowledge that is essential when each case is unique and non-repeatable.[39]

[39] The fact of uniqueness of the individual case produces a dilemma in the training of the professional. Cutting up cadavers, reading legal cases, drawing up plans for

2. DEGREE OF PERSONALITY INVOLVEMENT

A special relation of confidence between professional and client or patient is involved. A doctor or lawyer is, of course, expected to be technically competent; but also, the client must respect and like him as a person. In addition to skill, there is also reputation. In teaching, the public school teacher finds, usually to her great annoyance, that not only is her teaching observed but her private life as well. But her experience is typical of professionals in general. The lawyer is expected to act for his client. As Marshall (53a) states it:

The attitude of the client to the lawyer is roughly this. "I am asking you," he says, "to act as my brain in this matter. I want you to think and judge for me, because I haven't the technical equipment to think and judge for myself. But please do so exactly as I should if I knew the law."

Since the client reposes such confidence in a professional, he must be the epitome of virtue and entirely beyond reproach. One sees this in industry also, in the case of positions that have become professionalized, particularly executive positions. In considering a man for promotion, it is not enough that he be competent. Indeed this will simply be assumed or else that man will not be considered at all. When one reaches the higher levels of management one discovers that there is a tremendous plethora of talent and experience to the point that it is often difficult to distinguish between executives on that basis. The question of competency, therefore, may hardly be discussed. Rather, other questions which have to do with the whole personality of the individual are likely to form the major subject of discussion. Is he dependable? Is he loyal? What is his wife like?

These matters are subjective. It would be difficult to reproduce them in any questionnaire and yet they form the heart of the professional experience.

3. WIDE KNOWLEDGE OF A SPECIALIZED TECHNIQUE

The professional is the man who knows. He has power precisely by virtue of being a repository of knowledge. The client is ignorant.

---

imaginary houses, and participating in mock debates are all useful but have the defect that none of them is "real" and all are unavoidably somewhat standardized. On the other hand, the use of real cases for training purposes usually involves too high an expense or risk. The major approach to the solution of the dilemma has been the development of the internship where the professional-to-be merely assists, but where he does work with real cases. Yet sooner or later, the assistance and guidance ceases and the professional finds himself alone with his case—a patient anaesthetized on the table before him—and he must take his knife and push it into the patient's abdomen. This experience is quite unique. Professional, patient, and teacher can do no more than hope for the best.

He (the client) often hardly knows what to ask for, let alone how it can be provided. He must surrender all initiative and put himself in his lawyer's hands or under his doctor's orders . . . When the doctor says, "Take more exercise," it is a command. When the associated greengrocers plaster the boardings with the slogan, "Eat more fruit," it is an effort at mass suggestion. (53a)

4. SENSE OF OBLIGATION TO ONE'S ART

Talcott Parsons (62) refers to this as a norm of "Rationality." By that is meant that the professional is expected to use only the best or the most efficient techniques and not merely the traditional or dramatic one. Attention is concentrated on the art or the technique and on doing as good a job as he can possibly do. Such matters as personal friendship, money, the ethnicity, religion, race, or social class of the client are assumed to be irrelevant. The matter of money is particularly interesting. Marshall comments (53a):

The professional man, it has been said, does not work in order to be paid: he is paid in order that he may work.

The professional is not supposed to be interested in sordid money. The doctor may refuse money offered to him directly by the patient, but instead sends a bill. However his services are supposed to be so valuable that money is expected to roll in, virtually unsolicited. The client is expected to recognize that the services that he has received are so valuable, are so far beyond price, that the bill he is expected to pay does not begin to express the client's obligation to the professional. However, from time to time, money does not roll in unsolicited and then the professional may behave in a most businesslike manner. That is part of the reason that professionals attempt to control or even eliminate advertising on the part of their members. It is part of the reason that the dentist has difficulty in maintaining informal colleagueship with the doctor. Those who cannot behave in a businesslike manner and advertise—teachers would be a good illustration—may instead go out on strike (one might call this workman-like behavior). Yet they may fail because of the ambivalent attitudes they create: sympathy with their aims but disapproval of the means as a dereliction of duty.

5. SENSE OF IDENTITY WITH ONE'S COLLEAGUES

One mark of the professional is strong colleague consciousness. Such consciousness expresses itself in a concern as to who one's colleagues are and therefore in a set of admissions qualifications. There are always examinations, special degrees and certificates, and, often, experience requirements. Once in the group, the professional feels himself to be part of the group to the extent that the group opinion of him is a significant control on his behavior. Hughes (45) speaks of a profession as:

. . . entered by long training, ordinarily in a manner prescribed by the profession itself and sanctioned by the state . . . The training, however, carries with it as a by-product assimilation of the candidate to a set of professional attitudes and controls, a professional conscience and solidarity. The profession claims and aims to become a moral unit.

Carr-Saunders and Wilson (17, p. 478) state:

But this (professional) recognition may be hindered by dependence, which militates against group consciousness since it is only under the stimulus of the latter that the practitioners associate together and becomes a profession in the full sense of the word.

The controls of the group turn out to be necessary in order that mores and codes may be developed and sanctions invoked against deviants.

The group consciousness is usually expressed also in the development of professional associations with public relations activities in order to keep peace with society and to protect the membership. The layman discovers that it is very difficult to sue the doctor; he must deal instead with a medical association. It is very difficult for students to get a professor discharged; they must usually deal with a faculty council or association.

6. ESSENTIAL TO WELFARE OF SOCIETY

The professional's activities tend to be regarded as either vital to society or else involving a high degree of trust. The professional provides services which may be required at a moment's notice and which may be essential to the health or the welfare of the individual asking for the service. Consequently, the state is never indifferent to the professions but steps in and imposes regulations of various kinds through licensing and in other ways. The importance of the professions is expressed by Carr-Saunders and Wilson (17, p. 306) in their categories of the professions:

1. Vital to Individual Health—medicine, dentistry, veterinary, surgery, pharmacy, nursing, and midwifery.
2. Fiduciary in a Marked Degree—law, accountancy, patent work.
3. Connected with Public Safety—the armed services, public health.
4. Professional Activities of the State—civil service.
5. Building Planning—architects.
6. Education.

The criteria of professionalization that we have discussed represent ideal conditions. None of the recognized professions completely satisfies all of them, though there is perhaps such a tendency. The doctor finds that many of his cases can be treated in routine fashion. But there is a tendency for his work to be unstandardized; each case is to some extent unique, and some highly so. At the same time no occupation is completely devoid of any of these six aspects. A helpful way in which to observe the ideal character of the criteria is to think of two extremes or poles of a continuum. At the one end of the continuum we may place the Profession, at the other end what might be called the Job as follows:

THE PROFESSION . . . . THE JOB

At the professional pole of the continuum we postulate ideally the complete presence of all six of these criteria in their full development. No actual occupation achieves this extreme, but perhaps specialized surgery might come rather close. It should be noted that one could not place medicine as a whole at any given point on this continuum but the various branches of it would occur at different places according to the extent to which they exhibit the six criteria.

At the other end of the pole, the Job, we postulate the complete absence of these criteria. That is: the work is completely standardized; the relation to the client or customer is entirely segmented; the worker has no previous knowledge; the traditional technique is employed and friendship, money, etc., are of first importance; there is no group consciousness; and the work is not essential to society. Again, no actual occupation achieves this extreme though there is a tendency for some to come close. Certain kinds of factory work are highly standardized; the operator is a "worker" and little more—he is semiskilled; wages are of major importance and the object of direct action through unions (a device repugnant to professionals); there is little group consciousness (reflected partly in turnover), except as it is provided through a union; and the work may not be vital to society at all.

Actual professions and jobs may be placed on the continuum and the behavior of persons in those occupations may be intepreted with respect to how close they are to either pole. For example, during the Second World War, some factory work was regarded as vital to society— aircraft production for instance. In that case, greater emphasis was placed on precision and accuracy (knowledge), the worker was expected to give of his whole personality ("Work for Victory!"; "The boys are depending on us."). Employers were asked (or forced) to employ Negroes and other workers to work with them; an attempt was made to develop group consciousness through the use of slogans such as "We are all part of the same team." In this manner, this type of work was enabled to move somewhat towards the professional pole and was the occasion of considerably more pride than was the case previously.

As will be discussed in Chapter 14, the clique in industry also represents for its membership a movement in the direction of the Professional pole. The clique members know more of one anothers' personalities than the work itself requires and the clique involves, preeminently, group consciousness.

Ordinarily, the supervisor or employer desires that his subordinates shall regard themselves, or act as, professionals. He looks for demonstrations of unusual ability or the effective handling of emergency situations (the unstandardized activity), he desires that the worker shall give "his all" to the job in the form of loyalty, dependability, sobriety, etc., he desires knowledge and experience, he desires that money shall not be the worker's sole concern, and he desires that his workers shall feel that they are part of his "team." In other words, there are advantages to professionalization which the supervisor would like to enjoy. At the same time there are advantages to the members of the occupation, particularly in that they are given control over the professionalized endeavor and can enforce standards. But it is not easy to create professional attitudes. The time element is important—activities normally must be old. Remuneration is also significant. As Marshall (53a, p. 326) states,

> The professions . . . are respectable because they do not strive for money, but they can only remain respectable if they succeed, in spite of this pecuniary indifference, in making quite a lot of money, enough for the needs of a gentlemanly life.

This is not easily achievable in most occupations. W. R. Sharp (69a, p. 545) conceives of a profession as providing ". . . financial and social rewards adequate to attract persons endowed with distinguished intellectual and personal qualities to permanent careers. . . ." This requirement leads Sharp to some doubt as to whether teaching, which he is discussing, is a profession or not.

AXIS OF AUTHORITY

A large proportion of occupations in our society are carried on within formal work organizations. In those work organizations they tend to be organized in terms of a formal authority system such that persons performing related work find themselves under the same foreman or supervisor. There is a tendency for persons who work under the same supervisor or within the same authority unit to regard themselves as a unit and to feel a sense of belongingness to that unit.

In the professions, formal authority is not so important as informal controls. Professionals are not supposed to work under a formal authority but to be colleagues and owe no work allegiance higher than that to the profession. But if the lawyer secures one big client, then the client begins to have authority over him. The lawyer may be held by a "retainer," be on call, or even have an office in his client's building. Or a lawyer may become a boss himself in a law office with a number of junior lawyers under his direction. When these things occur, the lawyer's relation to his colleagues changes profoundly. In any profession, if a man has one client who is bigger than all the rest, then the profession becomes a little like a job. If a factory has a company doctor, nurse, or social worker, these persons are hired and fired like any other employee.

A professional in such a position finds he is the target of contradictory pressures (45). A doctor in private practice who could find nothing seriously wrong with a patient who claimed to be ill might simply tell the patient to go home and rest. But the company doctor must take into account the fact that management wants every worker on the job if possible. A similar role conflict was described by a social worker who was employed by the Salvation Army:

I have quite a lot of trouble with the Army. I'm a social worker, you know, and I am a graduate of a recognized school of social work. I have my Master of Science degree. The Salvation Army supports social work and I do real social work when I go out but sometimes the Army officials will give us some trouble. Usually they let us alone but just the other day a Major said to a group of us: "I don't want to interfere with the work of any of you girls. I know that you're well trained and that you know what you're doing, but this is a small thing to ask. Do you think that when you go out into the homes of the needy and the helpless that after you have done your social work, could you not then ask the family to kneel for a minute of prayer?" That sort of thing irritates me. It isn't that I object to prayer, I'm a good Baptist myself. Prayer is all right but only in its proper place and I don't think that prayer has anything to do with social work.

Of course the professor, who nearly always works in a formal authority structure, is continually confronted with the problem of balancing the demands of his colleagues for research or literary production against the demands of his university administration (who pay his salary) for superior teaching, attention to student problems, and community service. We get also a fundamental conflict between the role of the scholar and the administrator. If the professor takes on too many administrative tasks, he is likely to find that he has little time for scholarship. There is a growing tendency to separate these functions and one may meet administrators of universities who make no pretensions whatever to scholarship.

Although authority problems of the type we have been describing do come up in the professions, authority is found in its most elaborate form and is most likely to be a normal part of the everyday life of the worker close to the Job pole of the Profession-Job continuum. It is in the factory that we have one of the best illustrations of how authority is organized and we shall use it as a model in the following discussion.

A modern factory is organized bureaucratically, and a bureaucracy is a combination of two elements:

1. *a division of labor*—that is, a set of related specialists, and
2. *an authority system.*

The authority system has two functions: to *evaluate* the activities of the specialists, and to *coordinate* their separate activities so as to carry out the purposes of the organization. Theoretically, every supervisor should carry out both functions but there is a cleavage which is related to the level the supervisor occupies. In general, the closer the supervisor is to the bottom or production level, the more does he emphasize the evaluative function. This is due in part to his nearness to the production process and in part to the fact that supervisors near the bottom have often been lately promoted from the bottom and so are more conscious of the technical manufacturing problems the men must solve. But as one moves up in the organization, supervisors spend more and more of their time in the second function: coordinating men. A supervisor very high up in the organization may know very little about specific activities in the shop, a situation that creates grave communication problems in large-scale organizations.

Along with the authority system, there goes a major contradiction. The men at the bottom are paid for their ability to manipulate inanimate objects. But the greatest reward management has for demonstrated competence in that activity is a promotion which means the man must now exercise authority over other men. It is ironical that a man who shows ability in one activity should be rewarded by being assigned to a very different activity.[40] As the man moves up, the contradiction is repeated. The lower supervisor who has developed skill in evaluating the work of his subordinates is rewarded by being moved up—which means more emphasis on coordinative activities. Some factories try to meet the

---

[40] That this situation is certainly not confined to factories was brought out by the frank statement of a textbook salesman of a major publisher:

"I've got to show my boss I can really get adoptions for our textbooks. You want to know why? Because I hate the job of beating the bushes. If I get a few really good adoptions, old _____ will find me a cozy slot in the office back in little old New York, and assign someone else to beat the bushes."

problem by hiring persons known to be skilled in coordination from the outside but this practice usually creates strong resentments within the factory.

An important relationship is that between authority and responsibility. In a bureaucracy the supervisor exercises his authority in one of two ways: adherence to the rules, or, discretion. It is rule-adherence that involves responsibility; that is, the supervisor is expected to see to it that certain rules are obeyed, or certain standards met. However, he has a free hand to some extent because rules or standards can be enforced to the letter or they can be enforced only minimally. In governmental bureaucracies the traditional complaints are likely to center about these two ways of exercising authority. The supervisor who tends to over-emphasize rule adherence is accused of putting up a barrier of red tape, of lack of initiative, and of a desire to perpetuate his own position. The supervisor who exercises discretion, however, is accused of being arbitrary, and of having too much power (8, pp. 114–35; 57, pp. 1–18).

This phenomenon also turns up in any situation in which occupations are organized within an authority pattern. In the factory an order may come down from management: "Speed up production of leather belts." As this order passes down the line, the department head or foreman must decide what to do. If he complies with the order strictly, this may mean taking men off other jobs and putting them on leather belts. That tends to disrupt routines and to upset people. On the other hand, to ignore the order entirely is to bring on his own head the sharp criticism of his supervisors. He must somehow maintain a balance between the demands of his supervisors and the needs of his subordinates, perhaps by gradually shifting men to leather production and, in the meantime, pacifying his supervisors as best he can.

A. W. Gouldner, in his study of a gypsum plant (42, 42b), has taken an important step forward in the analysis of such bureaucratic tensions. He points out that there are several *types* of bureaucratic patterns of which two are of central significance: "representative" **bureaucracy**, in which a rule is expected to be obeyed because it is a means to an end which both supervisor and subordinate accept (e.g., safety rules), and "punishment-centered" bureaucracy in which a rule is expected to be obeyed simply because it *is* a rule (e.g., a rule in the gypsum plant which punished a worker who had been absent by requiring that he stay away from work for the same number of days that he had been absent). In the first case, a safety engineer, for example, might expect obedience because of his expert knowledge; in the second, a supervisor might expect obedience because of the authority inherent in his position. When Gouldner asked workers which rules they thought involved the most red-tape, more than twice as many workers mentioned the absenteeism rules as mentioned the safety rules—26 to 12—even though the safety rules and program surrounding them were, Gouldner tells us, far more complex (42a, pp. 410–18). On the other hand, the supervisor who, in our terms, is exercising "discretion," is behaving like an expert—using "judgment" based on his experience—rather than simply using the authority inherent in his position. Gouldner notes also that the representative bureaucratic pattern is most likely to elicit consent when the worker has some measure of *control* over the initiation and administration of rules, as workers did through safety meetings. Similarly, a supervisor exercising "discretion" is directly limiting the pressure of rules on his subordinates through *his* control over the rules.

The four axes of organization discussed above, the industrial, the axis of related activities, the professional and the authoritarian, co-exist within our society and form important means by which occupations become related to each other. A given industry will contain within it a number of interlocking nuclei of occupations, which in turn are still further interlocked or related to each other through their common devotion to the purposes of the industry. Existence of interlocking activities themselves may lead to the formation of an industry. Professionals may also interlock with each other in professional associations or else in the performance of their work, as in the hospital. Authority as a social bond is eminently present in the industry and, as pointed out above, comes in at various points in the professions.

THE OCCUPATIONAL ECONOMIC COMPLEX

In our society there are two major forms of concrete remuneration: payment in kind and payment in money.[41]

PAYMENT IN KIND

In our society, payment in kind is relatively rare and not likely to be the whole of a person's remuneration. In periods of economic depression, however, government doles or the benefits distributed by private clinics or social work agencies often take the form of goods or services. The sharing of housing among relatives and friends also becomes more important at such times. And speaking generally, the volume of payment in kind appears to be inversely related to the size of monetary income.

M. G. Reid (65a, pp. 125–79) has emphasized the importance of

[41] Scrip might be considered a third, but it is either a payment in kind or money depending on its convertibility.

taking into account the value of housewives' household activities in any discussion of income. Such activities are not classified as "gainful" and some have questioned the legitimacy of their inclusion in income calculations at all; yet a man whose wife dies will find that he must purchase outright many services which his wife performed as housekeeper and mother. Further it is important to be able to place an economic value on such services so that cross-cultural or trend studies may take account of the great variation in the economic role of the wife. An estimate for 1929 put the dollar equivalent of housewives' services at $23 billion (over a fourth of the national income) and Reid herself valued them at $15 and $34 billion in 1940 and 1945—about one-fifth of the national income (65a, p. 175). She also calls attention to the goods from public sources available without a means test, such as schools and parks.

Payment in kind is more important in some occupations than in others. Household servants receive their employers' cast-off clothes, restaurant workers receive meals, and presidents of colleges (and nations) are usually given the use of a house and the services of a staff. Professionals, especially doctors, exchange services.[42] Of all occupations, those in farming appear to have the largest proportion of their income paid out in kind. The survey, *Family Spending and Saving in Wartime* (12;65a, pp. 129–47), estimated the dollar value of nonmoney income for 1941 and found that, for every $100 of money income, the nonmoney income was $7 for urban families, $17 for rural nonfarm families, and $46 for farm families. The size of the last figure creates serious problems for those who wish to compare farm incomes with those of occupations in other areas.

Payment in kind is found fairly widely in the form of gifts which are regular parts of a payment system. Employees may be given company products or the opportunity to buy them at reduced prices. Nor should one ignore insurance, annuity, or sick leave provisions whether provided voluntarily by management or required by a union contract. The meals of salesmen on the road may differ considerably from those they eat at home. It is difficult to decide whether the fifth of whiskey used to seal business contracts is a payment or not. Bribes, whether concealed or not, often take on the form of goods also. Businesses make donations of company products to fire inspectors and buy their "quota" of tickets to the annual policemen's ball. Of course gifts of properly labelled company

---

[42] This is not the same as the mutual exchanges that occur in farming, e.g., cooring in Eire. A doctor who receives free services from another doctor may be willing to return the favor, but may never be asked to since his benefactor may seek *his* help from another doctor whose competence he values more highly.

goods for use as prizes at community carnivals can be justified in cold business terms, but as with the tickets to the policemen's ball, one is also purchasing a vague fringe benefit—"goodwill"—which may later be converted into an expectation or understanding.

Because payment in kind is rare in our society, its significance is often to be sought in terms, not of its amount or type, but of its symbolic reference. On some occasions, an offer of a payment in kind may be rejected as insulting. To some persons, such payments are associated with doles, and limit one's freedom to spend one's income; others reject them because they reject the bond created by such payments—the expectation of repayment. On the other hand, others regard the bonds created by such payments as symbolic of their membership in an exclusive group, for example, doctors' treating each other. Here the payment in kind begins to verge on the prize for valor or excellence—the cup or trophy— which would be rendered wholly meaningless if converted to its monetary value by being sold.[43]

PAYMENT IN MONEY

1. FORMS OF PAYMENT

Monetary payments take many forms: wages, fees, salaries, rents, insurance income, interest, commissions, bonuses, profit-sharing income, dividends, profits, market gambling receipts, inherited money and many others. It is difficult to look at form of income apart from occupation yet it seems reasonably clear that form of income may carry prestige in its own right. Income from salaries is usually rated more highly than is income from wages, income from interest or dividends may be rated still more highly, and inherited money may be rated the highest of all. Partly the prestige that attaches to different forms of income reflects the sentiments attached to *freedom* in our society. We respect the dignity of labor but we feel also that one's work should not tie one down: the more freedom an occupation offers, the better is it felt to be. Therefore, if one's income is directly connected to effort and varies with that effort, one is tied to the job and is to that extent unfree—a "wage slave." The typical wage worker who is late is docked a proportional amount of pay—many firms divide the day up into 10-minute intervals. By contrast, consider the statement of a highly successful business executive:

[43] Hence the monetary value of trophies is usually kept deliberately low, which leads, occasionally, to subterfuges, as in amateur athletics where players were given pocket-watches from which the works had been removed and money substituted. On the other hand, the player who was "given the works" was obviously being honored—not paid, which must have been disappointing to some or the expression would not have arisen.

How much money do I get? Oh, if you consult the salary rolls of the company you'll see my name there. I get $25 a week . . . but that money would hardly keep me in my cigars . . . I get a bonus. My job here is that of attempting to create new products . . . I get an idea and sketch it out on a piece of paper. I talk it over with one of the foremen in the factory and we make up a model. Then we show it to the president of the company and he passes judgment on it. If he decides we should go ahead why then we go ahead on quantity production and we see how it goes. Then if the article sells at all well I may get a bonus at the end of the year of a $100,000. (The writer then asked him what would happen if the article did not sell.) The company would still carry me. I could probably get along here for as long as two years. (The writer asked what would happen at that point.) Oh, that's simple, I would be fired.

In this case, the executive clearly did not depend on his salary but lived on an unpredictable bonus which might or might not come. If it did come, the actual size of the bonus was dependent on sales, a matter over which he had no control. Apart from the man's position in the firm, his form of income in itself carries high prestige. Of course the sheer size of his bonus makes a great deal of difference for his standard of living and his ability to "get along" between bonus payments. But if one holds size of income constant, one will still find that form of income and prestige are closely related. An outstanding illustration of this relationship was provided by W. L. Warner (86, pp. 11-12, *passim*) who, in contrasting the Upper Upper and Lower Upper classes in Yankee City, found that the members of these top classes had about equal amounts of money. But the Upper Uppers were the old families in the community who had inherited their money, whereas the Lower Uppers had earned theirs. The superior prestige position of the Upper Uppers was conceded by the Lower Uppers who emulated them.

2. SIZE OF INCOME

Obviously the sheer amount of wealth that a man possesses is of significance, quite apart from the question of how he got it. But hoarded money is of little social significance; we must discover how the money is spent. This raises an important question that must be asked of each culture: What are the things that money can buy? Jewels can usually be bought; the Crown Jewels, rarely so. Western culture, and the United States especially, might be called monetary cultures in the sense that a powerful attempt has been made to make as many goods and services purchasable as possible. Although some have deplored this fact, it has given to our culture a very great dynamic quality in contrast to feudal cultures where goods and services may be monopolized by privileged groups. Money has the great advantage of impersonality, and if an object is opened to free purchase, then it is made available alike to Negro and white, man and woman, Jew and Gentile. Money is also convertible to honor and power, either directly through the purchase of industry, or indirectly through contributions to political parties or causes. This possibility creates a situation in which new groups, through acquiring money, may upset existing honor and power structures and create new ones. This still leaves open the important question of the freedom of new groups in a culture to acquire money, for money may be used to consolidate old, as well as create new, power. Yet even where this power is consolidated to a high degree, the situation is still more fluid than one in which family name, religion, or race are enough to disqualify a person from even trying to acquire honor or power.

The analysis of size of income in relation to occupation is a *status* phenomenon and forms part of the discussion in the next chapter. Yet the fact that size of income is not simply a measure of "reward" for a valued service but is part of a total societal complex is nowhere better illustrated than in difficulties encountered by income researchers (39, pp. 25–47). Income itself is not easy to define but depends on what one is trying to measure. If one is interested in knowing about occupational differences in pay, one will wish to know gross earnings before deductions for taxes; but if one wishes to know about purchasing power, then earnings-in-hand (after taxes) will be more meaningful. The sheer problem of gathering reliable data about income should also be taken into account. The resistance to the inclusion of a question on income for a sample of the population in the U. S. Censuses of 1940 and 1950 is typical, for income is felt to be a highly personal matter. D. V. Glass (40a) quotes a critic of the proposal for a British Census as saying in Parliament, in 1753, that such an action would be "totally subversive of the last remains of English liberty" and further, that if any interviewer tried to get data about the

. . . number or circumstances of my family, I would refuse it; and if he persisted in the affront, I would order my servants to give him the discipline of the horse-pond.

When such resistance is overcome (and it usually is), there remain errors of response for income data are based on memory and are usually given by the wife of the family head rather than the earner himself. Since persons forget minor or irregular income sources (to take the most charitable point of view), practically all surveys produce an underestimate of income. It is difficult to assign an income figure to many persons because they hold double occupations, or shift employment at various times. The farm population, for example, derives much of its income from nonfarm occupations: in 1950, about one-third of farm families received *more* cash earnings from nonfarm work than from farming itself.

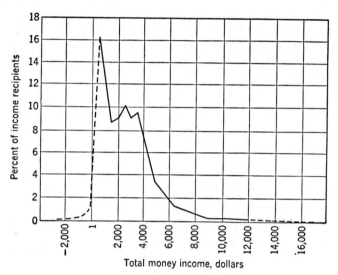

FIG. 4

INCOME RECIPIENTS BY INCOME IN 1951 *

A useful approach to the analysis of size of income is through an examination of the income curve. For this purpose, we may draw on the major work of H. P. Miller (54). As is well known, the income curve is badly skewed, with a preponderance of cases at the lower end. For the population fourteen years of age and over who were income recipients in 1951, Miller provides the chart shown in Fig. 4. Over one-quarter of all income recipients are found in the range between $1 and $1,000. To look at the matter in another way: 20 per cent of income recipients received less than $650 in 1951 but they accounted for only 3 per cent of the aggregate income; by contrast 20 per cent received more than $3,860 but they accounted for nearly one-half of the aggregate income. This lopsided distribution becomes more meaningful if we examine the component groups more closely.

* From Miller, H. P., *Income of the American People*, New York: Wiley, 1955, Fig. 2, p. 11. Curve includes only income recipients (including losses) 14 years of age and over. Dashed line at extremes indicates data for those parts of curve representing rough approximations.

First, women workers are concentrated at the lower end of the curve because of their different orientation to the labor market and because of their restriction to certain types of jobs. If we separate the women from the men, the two resulting curves are still found to be skewed, and bimodal, as is shown in Fig. 5. But then if one takes the curve for women and breaks it up into a curve for women who worked fifty weeks or more and a curve for all others, one gets two highly symmetrical curves. The skewness and peakedness for women, then, seems to be due largely to part-year work and nonworkers who will, of course, be found at the lower end of the curve.

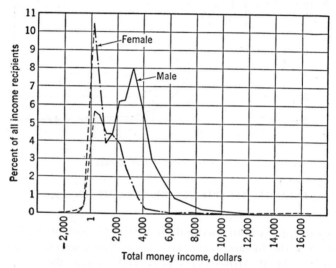

FIG. 5

INCOME IN 1951 OF PERSONS BY SEX *

If one next takes the curve for men and breaks it up into the groups of employed and not employed, the curve for employed men is fairly symmetrical but still has a definite bulge at the lower end and a long tail out to higher incomes. Miller found that much of the bulge at the lower end was due to two groups: farmers and farm managers (9 per cent) and service workers and laborers (17 per cent). The remaining three-quarters of employed men formed a highly symmetrical curve,

* From Miller, H. P., *Income of the American People,* New York: Wiley, 1955, Fig. 3, p. 19. Curve includes only income recipients (including losses) 14 years of age and over. Dashed line at extremes indicates data for those parts of curve representing rough approximations.

though it is peaked and still contains a tail running out to the high income end of the distribution. These points may be seen in Fig. 6. Service workers and laborers have a "box-like" appearance because they have a low upper limit to the amount of income they receive and because they only work for a part of the year, or part-time. The asymmetry of the farmers is due, Miller believes, to the high proportion of small low-production farms whose owners or operators are not forced out as

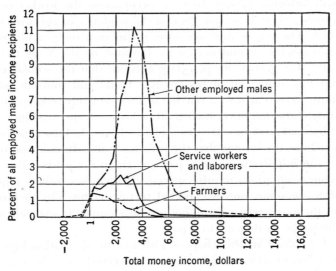

FIG. 6

INCOME IN 1951 OF EMPLOYED MEN BY CERTAIN OCCUPATION GROUPS *

abruptly as is, say, the small shopkeeper, by a low return or even a loss. Finally, Miller finds that the high income tail in the curve is due largely to the independent professional, business and managerial group who include about three-quarters of all men with incomes over $10,000.

In sum there appear to be a number of separate universes within the population of income recipients and a large part of the skewness of the overall income curve is removed when these universes are considered separately. The universes appear to be a consequence of the operation of the following factors: sex differentiation of work roles, part-time work, part-year work, ability to stay in business even when income drops

* From Miller, H. P., *Income of the American People,* New York: Wiley, 1955, Fig. 6, p. 24. Curve includes only income recipients (including losses) 14 years of age and over. Dashed line at extremes indicates data for those parts of curve representing rough approximations.

very low, and the upper limit to the income range. Consequently, it is of the first importance—in estimating size of income—not to throw together or compare groups from different universes, such as a person whose job is of such a character that he works a full year and a person who works only part of the year or part-time all the year, without taking into account these differences.

Another factor in estimating the significance of size of income has to do with hidden expenses. In some occupations the worker must buy his own tools although as time goes on the tendency in this direction has diminished. The doctor does not own all his own tools, a phenomenon which increases his dependence on the hospital, on the X-ray technician, and others. Max Weber (87, p. 131) points out that the scholar does not and never has owned all of his "tools"—books and journals, although his attempts to own at least a portion of them is likely to keep him poor. The engineer also has never owned all of his tools, the machines. Insofar as the individual must buy his own tools, we have a hidden expense which actually reduces the income that the person receives. In many occupations laundry is an important expense, particularly in the white-collar occupations. Some occupations require special work clothes; others require an automobile. In some, one is expected to take clients out to lunch and entertain them—activities involving not only monetary expenditures but time, which may be difficult to repay.

We have dealt in this chapter with instituted relationships among members of occupations. We have been concerned with the relationship of occupations to society and to each other and with the formal rewards that the occupation offers. Our discussion of the last found us referring, in passing, to honor, power, and prestige. We turn to the explicit discussion of these matters.

CHAPTER REFERENCES

1. Anderson, H. D. and Davidson, P. E., *Occupational Trends in the United States,* Stanford, California: Stanford University Press, 1940.
2. ———, *Recent Occupational Trends in American Labor,* Stanford, California: Stanford University Press, 1945.
3. Arnheim, R., "The World of the Daytime Serial," in Katz, D.; Cartwright, D.; Eldersveld, S., and Lee, A. M. (eds.), *Public Opinion and Propaganda,* New York: Dryden, 1954, pp. 243–263.
4. Barr, F. E., "A Scale for Measuring Mental Ability in Vocations and Some

of Its Implications," in Terman, L. M. *et al.*, *Genetic Studies of Genius*, Stanford, Stanford University Press, 1929, Vol. 1, pp. 69 ff.

5. Baudler, L. and Paterson, D. G., "Social Status of Women's Occupations," *Occupations*, **26**:421–424, 1948.

6. Beckman, R. O., "A New Scale for Gauging Occupational Rank," *Personnel Journal*, **13**:225–233, 1934.

7. Bell, D., "No Boom for the Unions," *Fortune*, **53**:179 ff., June, 1956.

8. Bendix, R., "Bureaucracy and the Problem of Power," in Merton, R. K. *et al.* (eds.), *Reader in Bureaucracy*, Glencoe, Ill.: Free Press, 1952, pp. 114–135.

9. Breed, F. S., *Education and the New Realism*, New York: Macmillan, 1939.

10. Brentano, L., *On the History and Development of Gilds and the Origin of Trade-unions*, London: Trubner, Ludgate Hill; (No date, Preface dated 1870).

11. Broudy, H. S., *Building A Philosophy of Education*, New York: Prentice-Hall, 1954.

12. *Bureau of Labor Statistics Bull. 822*, and Department of Agriculture *Miscellaneous Publication 520*; brought together by Reid in 65a.

13. Burns, R. K., "Unionization of the White Collar Worker," in Shister, J. (ed.), *Readings in Labor Economics and Industrial Relations*, Chicago: Lippincott, 1956, pp. 65–75.

14. Burt, C., *A Study of Vocational Guidance*, Industrial Research Board, Report No. 33, London, 1926.

15. *Business Statistics, 1955*, U.S. Dept. of Commerce, Supp. to *Survey of Current Business*, Washington, D.C.: U.S. Government Printing Office, 1955.

16. Caplow, T., *The Sociology of Work*, Minneapolis: University of Minnesota Press, 1954.

17. Carr-Saunders, A. M. and Wilson, P. A., "Professions," *Encyclopaedia of the Social Sciences*, Vol. 12, pp. 476–480.

18. ————, *The Professions*, Oxford: Clarendon Press, 1933.

19. Cauter, T. and Downham, J. S., *The Communication of Ideas*, London: Chatto and Windus, 1954.

20. *Census of Population: 1950*, U.S. Dept. of Commerce, Bureau of the Census, U.S. Government Printing Office, 1953, Vol. II: Characteristics of the Population.

21. Centers, R., *The Psychology of Social Classes*, Princeton: Princeton University Press, 1949.

22. *The Chicago Recreation Survey 1937*, Vol. III, 1938.

23. Clarke, A. C., "The Use of Leisure and Its Relation to Levels of Occupational Prestige," *American Sociological Review*, **21**:301–307, 1956.

24. *Classified Index of Occupations and Industries*, Washington: U.S. Government Printing Office, 1950.

25. *Consumption of Food in the United States*, Bureau of Agricultural Economics, Miscell. Pub. No. 691, Aug., 1949.

26. Converse, P. D., *Business Mortality of Illinois Retail Stores from 1925 to 1930*, University of Illinois Bureau of Business Research, Bull. No. 41, 1932.

27. Counts, G. S., *The Selective Character of American Secondary Education*,

University of Chicago, Supplementary Educational Monographs, No. 19, May 1922.

28. ———, "The Social Status of Occupations: A Problem in Vocational Guidance," *School Review*, 33:16–27, 1925.

29. Deeg, M. E. and Paterson, D. G., "Changes in Social Status of Occupations," *Occupations*, 25:205–208, 1947.

30. "Distribution of Nonmoney Income," in *Studies in Income and Wealth*, New York: National Bureau of Economic Research, 1951, Vol. 13, pp. 125–179.

31. Dulles, F. R., *America Learns to Play*, New York: Appleton-Century, 1940.

32. Dunkel, H. B., *General Education in the Humanities*, Washington, D.C.: American Council on Education, 1947.

33. Durkheim, E., *The Division of Labor in Society*, Geo. Simpson (trans.), Glencoe, Ill.; The Free Press, 1949. First published in 1893.

34. Edwards, A. M., *Population: Comparative Occupation Statistics for the United States, 1870 to 1940*, U. S. Bureau of the Census, Washington: U. S. Government Printing Office, 1943.

35. Fabricant, S., *Employment in Manufacturing, 1899–1939: An Analysis of Its Relation to the Volume of Production*, New York: National Bureau of Economic Research, 1942.

36. *Federal Reserve Bulletin*, "Business Indexes," 38:69, 1952.

37. Fryer, D., "Occupational-Intelligence Standards," *School and Society*, 16:273–277, 1922.

38. ——— and Sparling, E. J., "Intelligence and Occupational Adjustment," *Occupations*, 12:55–63, June, 1934.

39. Garvy, G., "Inequality of Income: Causes and Measurement," in *Studies in Income and Wealth*, New York: National Bureau of Economic Research, 1952.

40. Gist, N. P. and Halbert, L. A., *Urban Society*, New York: Crowell, 1942.

40a. Glass, D. V., "Population Controversy in Eighteenth-century England," *Population Studies*, 6:69–91, 1952.

41. Goodenough, F. L. and Anderson, J. E., *Experimental Child Study*, New York: Century, 1931.

42. Gouldner, A. W., *Patterns of Industrial Bureaucracy*, Glencoe, Ill.: Free Press, 1954.

42a. ———, "Red Tape as a Social Problem," in Merton, R. K. *et al.* (eds.), *Reader in Bureaucracy*, Glencoe, Ill.: Free Press, 1952, pp. 410–418.

42b. ———, *Wildcat Strike*, Yellow Springs, Ohio: Antioch Press, 1954.

43. Gross, E., "Some Suggestions for the Legitimation of Industrial Studies in Sociology," *Social Forces*, 33:233–239, 1955.

44. Hatt, P. K., "Occupation and Social Stratification," *American Journal of Sociology*, 55:533–543, 1950.

45. Hughes, E. C., "Dilemmas and Contradictions of Status," *American Journal of Sociology*, 50:353–359, 1945.

45a. ———, "Personality Types and the Division of Labor," *American Journal of Sociology*, 33:754–768, 1928.

46. Hutchinson, R. G. and A. R.; and Newcomber, M., "Business Life and Death

THE OCCUPATIONAL INSTITUTIONAL SYSTEM 97

in a Hudson River Town," *Dun's Review,* Dun and Bradstreet, New York, June, 1939, pp. 12–18.

47. International Labour Office Studies and Reports, New Series, No. 7 (part 4): *The Sixth International Conference of Labour Statisticians,* Resolution I, paragraph 14 (Geneva, 1948).

48. International Labour Office, *International Standard Classification of Occupations,* Studies and Reports, New Series, No. 15, Geneva, 1949.

48a. James, W., *The Principles of Psychology,* London: Macmillan, 1890, Vol. I.

49. Jones, L. W., "Dentistry," *Encyclopaedia of the Social Sciences,* Vol. V, pp. 91–93.

50. Kefauver, G. N.; Noll, V. H.; and Drake, C. E., *The Secondary School Population,* National Survey of Secondary Education, Bull. No. 17, 1932, Monograph No. 4, U.S. Government Printing Office, Washington, 1933.

51. Kelly, E. C. and Rasey, M. I., *Education and the Nature of Man,* New York: Harper, 1952.

52. Kirstein, G. G., *Stores and Unions,* New York: Fairchild, 1950.

53. Lazarsfeld, P. F. and Stanton, F. N. (eds.), *Communications Research, 1948–1949,* New York: Harper, 1949.

53a. Marshall, T. H., "The Recent History of Professionalism in Relation to Social Structure and Social Policy," *Canadian Journal of Economic and Political Science,* 5:325–340, 1939.

54. Miller, H. P., *Income of the American People,* New York: Wiley, 1955.

55. Millis, H. A. and Montgomery, R. E., *Organized Labor,* New York: McGraw-Hill, 1945.

56. Mills, C. W., *White Collar,* New York: Oxford University Press, 1951.

57. von Mises, L., *Bureaucracy,* New Haven: Yale University Press, 1944.

58. Moore, G. F., *Judaism,* Cambridge: Harvard University Press, 1927, Vol. I.

59. Mumford, L., *The Culture of Cities,* New York, Harcourt, Brace, 1938.

60. Neumeyer, M. H. and Neumeyer, E. S., *Leisure and Recreation,* New York: Barnes, 1936.

61. Nystrom, P. H., *Economic Principles of Consumption,* New York: Ronald, 1931.

62. Parsons, T., "The Professions and Social Structure," *Social Forces,* 17:457–467, 1939.

63. Paterson, D. G., Gerken, D. d'A.; and Hahn, M. E. *Revised Minnesota Occupational Rating Scales,* Minneapolis, University of Minnesota Press, 1953.

64. Peterson, F., *American Labor Unions,* New York: Harper, 1945.

65. ———, *Handbook of Labor Unions,* Washington, D.C.: American Council on Public Affairs, 1944.

65a. Reid, M. G., "Distribution of Nonmoney Income," in *Studies in Income and Wealth,* New York: National Bureau of Economic Research, 1951, Vol. 13, pp. 125–179.

66. Riesman, D.; Glazer, N.; and Denny, R., *The Lonely Crowd,* New Haven: Yale University Press, 1950.

67. Robbins, F. G., *The Sociology of Play, Recreation, and Leisure Time,* Dubuque, Iowa: Brown, 1955. Cp. I.

68. Scott, J. F., *Historical Essays on Apprenticeship and Vocational Education,* Ann Arbor, Michigan: Ann Arbor Press, 1914.

69. Seligman, E. R. A., *Two Chapters on the Mediaeval Guilds of England,* American Economic Association, 1887 (originally written as Ph.D. dissertation, 1882–3).

69a. Sharp, W. R., "Teaching Profession," *Encyclopaedia of the Social Sciences,* Vol. XIV, pp. 543–553.

70. Sims, V. M., *The Measurement of Socio-Economic Status,* Public School Publishing Co., Bloomington, Ill., 1928.

71. Smith, A., *The Wealth of Nations,* New York: Collier, 1902. First published in 1776.

72. Smith, M., "An Empirical Scale of Prestige Status of Occupations," *American Sociological Review,* 8:185–192, 1943.

73. ——, "University Student Intelligence and Occupation of Father," *American Sociological Review,* 7:764–771, 1942.

74. Solomon, B., "Dimensions of Union Growth, 1900–1950," *Industrial and Labor Relations Review,* 9:544–561, 1956.

75. Steiner, J. F., *Americans At Play,* New York: McGraw-Hill, 1933.

76. ——, *Research Memorandum on Recreation in the Depression,* Social Science Research Council, Bull. 32, 1937.

77. Stettler, V. O'Hara, *The Lawyers Reports Annotated, 1917 C,* 243 U.S. 629.

78. Super, D. E., *Appraising Vocational Fitness,* New York: Harper, 1949.

79. Taussig, F. W., *Principles of Economics,* New York: Macmillan, 1939, Vol. II.

80. Thorner, I., "Pharmacy: The Functional Significance of an Institutional Pattern," *Social Forces,* 20:321–328, 1942.

81. "Unionization of Clerical and Professional Workers, 1944," *Monthly Labor Review,* 58:1229, 1944.

82. Ure, A., *Philosophy of Manufactures,* 1835; quoted in Friedmann, G., *Industrial Society,* Glencoe, Ill. The Free Press, 1955.

83. *U.S. Census of Population: 1950, Employment and Personal Characteristics,* 1950 Population Census Report P-E No. IA, Preprint of Vol. IV, Part I, Washington, D.C.: U.S. Government Printing Office, 1953.

84. U.S. Dept. of Labor, Bureau of Employment Security, U.S. Government Printing Office, 1949, Vols. I and II.

85. Warner, W. L. and Henry, W. E., "The Radio Day Time Serial: A Symbolic Analysis," *Genetic Psychology Monographs,* 37:3–71, 1948.

86. ——, Meeker, M. and Eells, K., *Social Class in America,* Chicago: Science Research Associates, Inc., 1949.

87. Weber, M., "Science As A Vocation," in Gerth, H. H. and Mills, C. W. (trans. and eds.), *From Max Weber: Essays in Sociology,* New York: Oxford, 1946.

88. "Why White Collar Workers Can't Be Organized" (anonymous), *Harper's Magazine,* August, 1957, pp. 44–50.

89. Wolman, L., *Ebb and Flow in Trade Unionism,* New York: National Bureau of Economic Research, Inc., 1936.

CHAPTER FOUR

THE OCCUPATIONAL STATUS
AND AUTHORITY SYSTEM

In this chapter, we examine the ways in which society evaluates its occupations, how persons attain a desired occupational status, and how their occupational behavior is then controlled.

THE OCCUPATIONAL STATUS SYSTEM

When we speak of "status," we are referring to *social location* within a system of human relationships. Any society or organization may be thought of as a set of related statuses and any person may then be located by naming the status he occupies. This "naming" consists of describing the rights expected by, and duties expected of, anyone who occupies the status, though, in practice, we give names to statuses or select one outstanding feature of the status as a way of identifying it. Thus, "husband" is a status, as is "member of the landowning class." This usage is broad and defines status, simply, as "position in a group." [1]

Although there are always minimal specifications, statuses vary in terms of how precisely the rights and duties are defined, a situation that permits the incumbent some latitude. [2] When we are speaking of the

[1] This approach is that of Ralph Linton (28, pp. 113 ff.) and is very close to that of Kingsley Davis (12). Davis, in what remains one of the most lucid discussions of stratification concepts, prefers to restrict "status" to "position in the general institutional system" (e.g., "professor"), and adds the concept of "office" for "position in a deliberately created organization" ("associate professor at the State College of Washington"). Status, for us, includes both types of positions.

[2] For example, occupations—all of which are statuses—vary widely in the freedom society permits incumbents to decide what to do and how society rewards them. One

manner in which the incumbent enjoys the rights and fulfills the duties of a status, we are speaking of his "role."[3] Obviously, since an individual has many statuses, he will also have many roles.

Following Mead (33, pp. 152 ff.; 11, pp. 151–53) we think of the status a person will occupy and the way he will play his role in any organization as depending on two phenomena: the person's self-conception, and the conception that others have of him.[4] James (25, pp. 293 ff.) pointed out long ago that a divergence between these conceptions could not last very long, and our researches have shown that such divergences typically suggest a breakdown in the system of relationships. A useful indicator of such divergences is often provided by the social types[5] that a group identifies. Strong (46, 47), for example, found Negroes referring to one person as an "Uncle Tom" and another as a "high yaller,"[6] and Wirth (51), examining European Jewish migrants to the United States, found such social types as the "allrightnick," "mensch," and "schnorrer."[7] In industry, we have the "company man," "union man,"

---

architect not only builds buildings, but takes into account who lives in them, their ability to pay, and community problems of the area, while another architect does little more than conform to the legal building code. One incumbent gives payment and recognition hardly a thought, while another demands them before he will begin work.

[3] Kingsley Davis (12) suggests the use of "esteem" to refer to the invidious value attached to a role, that is, to the degree of success or failure of the incumbent in meeting the expectations of his status. For example, the expectations associated with "private" and "colonel" are different, yet each may receive a medal (sometimes the same one) for "bravery beyond the call of duty." Such a medal would reflect esteem, not status.

[4] Strictly speaking, it is not the conception of others of him, but *his* conception of the conception of others; that is, what he thinks others are thinking. For example, others may think of a man as an amusing clown and may continually call upon him to amuse them. The man may interpret this as a tribute to his sense of humor and acting skill (which it is, in part) and act in accord with this interpretation. But if he later comes to feel that others are laughing at him with a strong component of ridicule, then he may act in accord with *that* interpretation and refuse to perform any longer. In both cases, the behavior and conceptions others had were the same, but the individual's interpretation varied. In other words, the individual compares two self-conceptions: himself as he sees himself, and himself as he thinks others see himself. To avoid cumbersome language, we shall speak, simply, of "the conception of others."

[5] One of the first to explicitly identify and describe social types was Nels Anderson (1, Chs. VI, VII; 2, pp. 19–20, 33–34) who studied homeless men. He described the hobo (who works and wanders), the tramp (who wanders but does not work), the bum (who neither works nor wanders), the homeguard (a casual laborer) and many others such as mushfaker, wangy, straight crip, stew bum, etc. One of the most careful descriptions of a single social type is provided by Zorbaugh (52, pp. 98–105; 53, Ch. IV).

[6] An "Uncle Tom" bows and scrapes to get favors from whites. A "high yaller" is a light-skinned Negro woman who thinks this gives her an excuse for putting on airs.

[7] An "allrightnick" is a person who has achieved success but has forgotten his religious and social obligations to the Jewish group. The "mensch" is also a success but has remained a loyal Jew and is, therefore, a model for Jewish mothers to point to for their sons. The "schnorrer" was once simply a beggar, but then he took the view that

"slacker," "rate-buster," and others. Such types are worth careful scrutiny since the name always carries with it an attitude which provides the researcher with clues to the conception of others of the behavior. Further, since the group (and not the sociologist) has made up these names, the behavior to which they refer is probably important to the group or at least occurs often enough to be worth naming.

Status problems—divergences between self-conceptions and the conceptions of others—are usually involved in minority group relations in industry. A good example was provided by Japanese Nisei in the United States during World War II who, after having been interned, were permitted to seek jobs in the midwestern states.[8] Faced with a divergence between self-conceptions and the conceptions of others— the Nisei thought of themselves as loyal but their internment led them to believe that others thought they were disloyal—they set about trying to change the conceptions of others. They became "model" workers according to the capitalistic (management) ethic: docile, diffident, silently efficient, above all avoiding horseplay. Unfortunately this behavior created even more problems, for the average white worker was (and is) not a "model" worker and therefore was placed in the position of being "shown up" by the Nisei.

But the Nisei are not a special case. Persons in our culture are forever attempting to change their status or are being forced to change it as society changes. In examining status, then, we shall always find it important to ask whether the self-conception the individual has is affirmed or challenged by his work associates. The answer to this question usually provides important clues to structural strains.[9]

So far we have discussed status in general terms. The most important kind of statuses appear to be those that are *ranked* and we shall confine our attention in this chapter to those. We shall discuss the general criteria used to rank statuses, status symbols, and then specific factors which determine status rank.

GENERAL STATUS CRITERIA

The three major criteria used to rank statuses are economic factors, power, and prestige.[10]

---

he was doing the donor a favor in accepting his money since he was enabling the donor to perform a charitable act.

[8] The following case is based on conversations with Dave Okada who was making a study of Japanese Nisei in Chicago industry in 1948.

[9] The answer may, of course, provide clues to personality strains as well.

[10] This differentiation follows that of Max Weber and is used, substantially, as suggested by Lipset and Bendix as a fruitful approach to rank problems. See (17, pp. 180-95; 30).

1. ECONOMIC FACTORS

A person's status may depend on whether he owns his own business, is a free-floating professional, or is employed by someone else. It depends also on how the person derives his income (whether from gainful employment, investments, inheritance, or a wealthy wife), and on the size of his income. The last affects the individual's freedom to participate in honorific activities which cost a great deal of money, and, possibly, his ability to control the affairs of persons in a significant sector of the economy.

2. POWER

By "power" we understand the ability of an individual intentionally to influence [11] the behavior of others. Davis (12) points out that a status may give its incumbent power because of the importance of the activity performed (for example, a professional activity),[12] because of the scarcity of the means of performing the activity (for example, great knowledge, training, or talent), or because of the number of persons controlled [13] and the degree of control of each. When a person's power is institutionally recognized, we speak of authority.[14] That is, a person possesses authority when the legitimacy of his exercise of power is acknowledged by those the power-holder influences.[15] Thus we say a king, who has been properly anointed and crowned, has authority, as do the duly elected president of the United States or the owner of a business. In any work situation, there are persons who have authority—e.g., the foreman or department head—but there are others besides them who have power, such as informal leaders.[16]

---

[11] Goldhamer and Shils (20) suggest the following definition of "influence": "Influence is to be understood as both an alteration of behavior and a maintenance of behavior as it was, but other than what it would have been without the intervention of the power-holder."

[12] Davis also points out that "importance" is not always easy to define, as when comparing, for example, the importance to public health of doctors and scavengers.

[13] Sheer number may not be so significant as how large a segment of the society is affected; that is, whether control is purely local or extends over whole sectors of the society as in the case of major powerholders such as heads of large businesses, union leaders, armed-forces leaders, and government policy-makers.

[14] This definition is substantially that of Parsons (37).

[15] It must be emphasized that acknowledgement of legitimacy does not necessarily imply obedience. A thief, being pursued by a policeman, acknowledges the legitimacy of the policeman's act but does not, for all that, stop running.

[16] Most discussions of the sources of power legitimation refer to Max Weber's three major types: legal, traditional, and charismatic (23, Pt. 3). It is difficult to decide where to put the informal leader since he may, at times, assume traditional or quasi-charismatic qualities, but may also subvert bureaucratic authority or help initiate a wildcat strike. But, perhaps the latter may be regarded simply as a breakdown of authority.

3. PRESTIGE [17]

Statuses may be ranked according to the amount of honor or deference persons in society accord their incumbents. Prestige differs from both economic position and power in that it is primarily an attitudinal phenomenon. It must be discovered by asking a sample of the population where they place various statuses, such as occupations, where they place various persons (whose status is known), or, perhaps, where persons place themselves or their occupations.

Although these three types of rank may be distinguished, we recognize immediately that they are related to one another. Economic position may often be converted to power, or a powerful person may use his influence to increase his wealth. If persons have enough wealth, they may sometime "buy" prestige by associating themselves with worthy causes, or a person of power may try to influence advertising and public relations organizations or the public press to describe him favorably so that his prestige may rise.

At the same time, high rank in one area does not necessarily imply high rank in another.[18] Expatriate nobility who have lost all their power and money may still be accorded high prestige. Successful racketeers may have a high economic position but very low prestige, whereas a politician may have a middle economic position and prestige position, but a very high power position. Medical doctors rank near the top of all prestige scales, yet their power is low indeed.[19]

Status does not only manifest itself as an attribute of the individual. Typically, all societies organize statuses into clumps or groups of persons of similar rank. Persons of high economic position may come to know each other, form economic associations for their common benefit, join or create exclusive clubs, and encourage their children to intermarry. High powerholders discover they need large sums of money and make temporary alliances with wealthy persons, or try to secure high-prestige names on the mastheads of their letters. When persons of a similar rank begin to act together or develop feelings of "we-ness" and regard themselves as

---

[17] Translators of Max Weber have usually rendered his term "Stand," in this context, as "status." However, consistent with our broad use of "status," we do not do so but use instead the clearly understood "prestige." To use "status" here would also involve confusion with the use of this term by Linton and Kingsley Davis, as we have pointed out above. See Parsons' discussion of the translation problem (37, p. 347, footnote 28).

[18] Goldhamer and Shils (20) mention the peculiar case of "polite manners," by which a person can influence someone else by expressing deference toward him.

[19] In terms of the size of the segment of the society controlled. It is interesting to note, however, that the context in which most persons meet a doctor is one in which he is in a position to influence a great deal of the patient's behavior.

different from others, social stratification begins to take place. By "social strata" we understand categories which express such differential ranking of persons who compose a social system and their treatment as superior and inferior relative to one another in certain respects (37, p. 841). Examples of social strata are castes and classes.[20] It does not, of course, follow that persons of similar rank will necessarily either think or act alike.

STATUS SYMBOLS

The analysis of status is complicated by the existence of status symbols (45). When we judge a person we are likely to do so not on the basis of careful study but on the basis of external symbols that we can see or hear easily. Our judgments are mostly prejudices, that is, prejudgments we make before we have had time to examine the full evidence, and in life we never have the time. Therefore we make a cultural judgment that we were taught to make when we were too young to be critical. When a white in our society meets a Negro, he is apt to make a judgment of what to expect on the basis of an external, highly visible symbol—skin color—and race is one important status symbol in our society.

A second status symbol of importance is that of family descent or kinship. This has tended to be shaken with the decline of feudalism and the rise of urbanism but it is still of some importance. Nor is it simply a belief. It is illustrated with certain families in government—the Adamses and the Roosevelts—and with certain families in science and in literature. This sort of symbol is transferable by inheritance, and implies a certain degree of wealth, of office, of claims to property, of opportunity, and of a tradition. The tradition is of considerable significance. Frequently, a person is able to rise to a position because he has been brought up to believe that he can do it. It is easier for him to rise to the position with poise and grace rather than to have to fight through the opprobria of *nouveau riche* and "upstart." The son of a banker has at least the option of following in his father's footsteps; the same thing is true of the doctor. This phenomenon, the tradition of success, is of particular importance to minority groups. Through the name, one secures a transmission not only of wealth but of a position, of an estimation by others of one, and an estimation of oneself.

The symbols by which we identify status are not necessarily the

---

[20] A caste system organizes all members of a society into a series of levels and isolates these levels from each other by such devices as endogamy, fixed position, and religious sanctions. Class systems also organize persons into levels but the levels are not so rigidly isolated from one another. Individual upward mobility occurs and occasionally the members of an oppressed class may unite and overthrow their oppressors.

factors which actually confer status. But the fact that they go with status means that the symbols themselves may become objects of pursuit. One may then get a dissociation of the symbol from the thing symbolized, a situation which not only creates confusion but leads to misrepresentation. Goffman (19, p. 298) points out that attempts are made to avoid this problem by such devices as "intrinsic restrictions"; that is, the use for a symbol of the symbolized thing itself:

We symbolize our wealth by displaying it, our power by using it, and our skill by exercising it.

Sometimes one can use objects or features closely associated with an occupation: the doctor's black bag or the manual worker's calloused hands.

But in spite of these and other devices, status symbols come to be valued and pursued in their own right.[21] One sees outbursts in fraternal orders (15, 34, Ch. 3), many of which are modelled on feudal orders: practically all statuses are ranked in lengthy hierarchies, and few persons are found in the bottom ranks. There is some evidence that the lower a man's actual status is, the more likely is he to seek the symbols of high status.[22] It is not surprising therefore to find fraternal orders drawing many of their adherents from Negroes, immigrant groups, and others who have low statuses in society. During the day a man may be merely a janitor on the third floor of a large company. But come nightfall he dons the robes and sweeps majestically into the lodge-hall where all must bow before this potentate.

Not only low status but *anxiety* about status may lead to emphasis on status symbols. Such anxiety is common among white-collar workers in business offices because their status is marginal and uncertain. Nearness to centers of authority becomes symbolic of status. If the big boss is located in an office at the end of a corridor, then the clerk whose desk is closest to his is likely to feel—and be treated—as if his status were more exalted than that of the clerk whose desk is farther away. To have a desk at all means one stands higher than those who have only a table. A telephone on the desk, a wastebasket, whether one has a blotter on one's desk or not, the manner in which one is paid, whether in cash or by check, and whether the check is presented to the individual by his

---

[21] Goffman notes the peculiar problem created by "curator groups." As status symbols are accumulated, their creation and care require special personnel—interior decorators, teachers, servants—who then become expert in manipulating these symbols, without themselves occupying the statuses they symbolize.

[22] There are, of course, other motives. See (15, Ch. I).

superior or sent by mail—all of these things are ranked and assumed to reflect status.[23] Since this is true, once status symbols have been assigned, they are difficult to reassign. A worker who has had a telephone on his desk for a year is likely to assume that its removal implies that his status has been changed. Of course this interpretation is most likely where workers are not sure of their status. One is likely also to find emphasis on symbols in relatively new situations where relationships have not as yet been clearly defined (16, pp. 247–250).

Scott and Lynton (43, pp. 45–46) have shown, through an illuminating illustration, that status symbols need not be the occasion for discontent or anxiety. They describe an old established Belgian factory which had—for the first time—to add a number of engineers to its staff. A small number of foremen who had been with the company for many years were accustomed to running their shops without interference. Consequently, status conflict between foremen and engineers was anticipated. Management, however, did two things, both inadvertently, which had favorable results. Instead of hiring experienced engineers, management hired young college graduates who were hardly "dry behind the ears" and who could be counted upon to know little about getting along with the old hands. But age was a status symbol. The company had for years promoted men slowly on the basis of experience so that the older men were usually the most experienced and respected. Not only was age on the foremen's side, but the foremen were the only ones permitted to hold the keys to the factory doors. An engineer who desired admission after hours found himself having to secure a foreman's permission. Through these means the engineers were introduced with a minimum of conflict.

Symbols—whatever problems they create—serve to identify status.[24] We turn next to the factors which affect status itself.

SPECIFIC FACTORS WHICH AFFECT STATUS RANKING

Economic factors, power, and prestige were identified earlier as the major means by which the rank of a status was determined. There remains the question of what specific factors determine the economic position, power, and prestige that come to be assigned to any status. Although our main emphasis will be on occupation, we find we must consider other factors as well.

[23] See (3, pp. 50–52; 14; 16, pp. 180. 26–32; 44).

[24] This is not their only function. Goffman (19) notes that symbols also have expressive significance; that is, they express a point of view, style of life, and cultural values, or they may satisfy needs, e.g., dueling. Horse-racing, play-going and hunting may serve to identify those who can afford them, but that does not make them less enjoyable.

1. KINSHIP AND FAMILY AFFILIATION

Kinship is not only a status symbol: it may confer an increment of status as well. One inherits ancestors and with them certain advantages and opportunities. In primitive and feudal societies kinship is a major status factor and often defines a person's career. One secures a *name* which may imply differential rank; it makes a difference to have an ancestor who fought in the American revolution. One may inherit property which in turn may give the owner power.

Important also is the extent to which such transference may be made through marriage. In our society it is easier for women to marry "up" than it is for men. We applaud the poor girl who marries the millionaire but pity the poor man who marries the rich girl. This ability of a husband to confer his status on his wife is seen also in the German practice of adding the husband's title to the wife's name.

2. WEALTH

Other things being equal, the greater the wealth associated with a status, the higher the rank of the status. Often the power inherent in a status (e.g., head of an advertising agency) may be made to earn money for the incumbent. Similarly, the prestige that surrounds an army general (ret.) or sports hero may be used to help sell products or services. When such conversions from one criterion of rank to another occur, it is often difficult to decide which criterion is most important in determining the rank of a status. Sheer amount of money is often sneered at; yet the impersonality of money gives it a flexibility which the other two criteria lack. Money can be handed around without losing or even changing its value; power and prestige are much more difficult to pass on.

3. ETHNICITY AND RACE

Ethnicity and race confer status in their own right but a large part of their significance lies in the fact that they may depress other status determinants. There have been approximately 35 million immigrants to the United States and priority of immigration of one's family has come to be an important status determinant. The earliest immigrants were able to secure land and enter favored occupations. When a new wave of migrants came in, they lifted up the previous waves and this process went on repeatedly. Yet priority of immigration, as a status increment, does not apply significantly to the Negro nor to the earliest immigrants of all—the Indians. Nor is this all. A man may come of good family, have wealth, and be in an occupation of high rank; but unless he is white, his status remains limited.

4. OCCUPATIONAL FACTORS

As we stated earlier, occupations are themselves statuses and, in addition, often become involved in key ways in determining the rank of other statuses. We shall here concern ourselves with the major factors determining differential occupational rank; namely, type of industry, size of income, white-collar–manual distinction, authority, freedom permitted, amount of preparation, and manipulation of symbols.[25]

The type of industry in which one practices one's occupation affects one's status. In England, traditionally, authority, power, and prestige are derived from land ownership. In the United States, the possession of land has not been a source of power except on a local basis, owing in part to the profusion of free land. Instead, high status rank has become attached to the heavy industries: railroads, shipping, iron and steel, oil and coal, and the great producing enterprises.[26] Commerce and trade has tended to enjoy much more prestige than is the case in Europe. The new country found it needed bankers and financiers to finance its rapid growth.

Little prestige has been associated with contraband activities or to those that smack of such activities, such as brewing beer, though the leaders in those industries may be men of great wealth and power.[27] Little prestige is attached also to the tobacco industry and, strikingly, to government service. The low prestige which attaches to government service is traceable in part to the Jacksonian tradition and with it the notion that no special ability or training are required. In addition, in part owing to experience and in part to the low prestige of governmental occupations, there has grown a feeling that government is unclean. Many persons think of politicians in terms of false promises, unsupported accusations, corruption, waste, and inefficiency. The civil service, in contrast to a country like England, enjoys little respect, a fact which partly explains the low salaries paid for government work.

Intellectual and artistic pursuits are not, in general, accorded high status, at least in comparison to some European and Far Eastern countries. This situation is in part due to the Jacksonian tradition, the newness of the country, the disillusionment of many with the brain-trusters of the

[25] Our discussion is general and will attempt to make only crude distinctions. This procedure is necessary in spite of the fact that there have been several attempts to rank occupations precisely (see p. 54) for in most cases prestige has been the only measure of rank utilized. Without denying the importance of persons' evaluation of an occupation, one cannot ignore the power and economic position an occupation may give its practitioner, whether the general population is aware of these things or not. On this point, see (31). At the local level, such popular evaluations may be more reliable, assuming persons know the local occupations well, but even the prestige of an occupation may be different in a small town from what it is in a large city. In any case, one should be extremely cautious for in a democracy, power is often hidden and economic position deemphasized in open discussions.

[26] With certain exceptions, for example meat-packing.

[27] A Canadian university chose to increase student tuition fees to pay for a new stadium rather than accept the offer of a brewer to make a free gift of the stadium to the university with the single provision that the stadium should bear his name.

New Deal, and, possibly, the very great heterogeneity of the population with the lack of any great common intellectual or artistic tradition.[28] On the other hand, an *occasional* writer, musician, or artist may be idolized to an extent quite unapproached in other countries. The latter situation is related to the development of fast transportation (for "going on tour"), centralization in the mass media (networks, syndication), "saturation" distribution techniques,[29] and the association of entertainment and selling.[30]

A second factor affecting occupational status is size of income. This factor is important not only because money can often be converted into prestige and power but also because one may purchase directly the more expensive status symbols. Prestige is a delicate matter which one may lose through no fault of one's own, and one must learn how to exercise power. But the man with money may forthwith buy ("acquire," in the language of the dealer who will tell him what to do) paintings, precious jewels, and first editions.

Adequate data on the relation between occupation and size of income are not easy to gather in part because of the difficulties of measuring income (35) and in part because of the problem of classifying occupations. The U.S. Census provides income data, broken down by occupation, which are worth looking at in spite of the necessarily omnibus character of the occupational categories. We present the data for males and females separately and, in order to reduce the problem created by part-year workers, restrict our attention to the labor force who worked 50 to 52 weeks of the year. In Tables 6 and 7, the occupational categories are ranged in order of median income for males and females. To describe the range of incomes, we provide, first, the name and median income of the detailed occupations having the lowest and highest median incomes. Beside this very crude measure we provide the interquartile range. The data for "Professional, technical and kindred workers" (male) then inform us that: one-half of the men in this category received less than (or more than) $4,311 in 1949, ranging from a low median of $2,379 for "Musicians and music teachers" to a high median of $8,704 for "Physicians and surgeons"; however, one-half of the men earned between $3,190 and $6,010 for the year. The medians and interquartile ranges have been charted in Figures 7 and 8.

Looking first at the data for males, the range for each occupational

---

[28] The implications of these trends for "status politics" are discussed in (29, Ch. 7).

[29] For example, making magazines available almost everywhere.

[30] This relationship goes both ways. An artist or entertainer who has the power to hold the attention of large audiences can obviously use this power to sell products. In turn, a high volume of sales enables a manufacturer to pay out large sums of money to attract some (though not all) of the finest talent available.

TABLE 6
MEDIAN INCOME, AND RANGE OF MEDIAN INCOMES AND INTERQUARTILE RANGE IN 1949 OF THE EXPERIENCED MALE LABOR FORCE WHO WORKED 50 TO 52 WEEKS IN 1949, FOR THE UNITED STATES: 1950 *

	MEDIAN INCOME	LOWEST DETAILED OCCUPATIONAL MEDIAN INCOME	HIGHEST DETAILED OCCUPATIONAL MEDIAN INCOME	INCOME RANGE INCLUDING ONE-HALF OF PERSONS IN CATEGORY (INTERQUARTILE RANGE)	
Professional, technical, and kindred workers	4,311	2,379 (Musicians and music teachers) a	8,704 (Physicians and surgeons)	3,190	6,010
Managers, officials, and proprietors, exc. farm	4,158	2,468 (Managers & superintendents, building)	8,377 (Managers, officials, and prop'rs n.e.c.—self-employed in banking and other finance) b	2,895	6,190
Craftsmen, foremen and kindred workers	3,395	2,245 (Shoemakers and repairers except factory) c	4,896 (Photoengravers and lithographers)	2,685	4,235
Sales workers	3,364	1,878 (Hucksters and peddlers) d	4,932 (Stock and bond salesmen)	2,385	4,690
Clerical and kindred workers	3,213	1,446 (Telegraph messengers)	4,026 (Agents, n.e.c.)	2,570	3,870
Operatives and kindred workers	2,969	2,058 (Operatives and kindred workers, n.e.c. in sawmills, planing mills and mill work)	4,080 (Operative and kindred workers, n.e.c. in petroleum refining)	2,260	3,605
Service workers, except private household	2,502	1,548 (Attendants, recreation, and amusement)	3,365 (Policemen and detectives—Private)	1,840	3,250
Laborers, except farm and mine	2,392	1,294 (Laborers, n.e.c. in personal services)	3,301 (Laborers, n.e.c. in petroleum refining)	1,750	3,030
Farmers and farm managers	1,655	1,644 (Farmers-owners and tenants)	2,572 (Farm managers)	825	2,910

Private household workers	1,505	.... [e]	....	930	2,155
Farm laborers and foremen	1,129	1,248 (Farm laborers, wage workers) [f]	2,571 (Farm service laborers— self-employed)	560	1,875

* Medians copied directly and interquartile range figures calculated from 1950 Population Census Report P-E No. 1B, Preprint of Volume IV, Part I, Chapter, B, *Occupational Characteristics*, U.S. Bureau of the Census, U.S. Government Printing Office, 1956, Table 20.

[a] Includes large proportion of part-time workers. Others earning below $3,000 are clergymen, religious workers, and professional nurses (male).

[b] This category is an extreme case. The second highest (managers, officials, and proprietors, n.e.c., self-employed, in insurance and real estate) had a median income of $5,875.

[c] Ignores Armed Forces.

[d] Ignores "newsboys" with a median income of $347.

[e] Data not supplied by Census.

[f] Omits "farm laborers, unpaid family workers" with median income of $483.

category gives a picture of great overlap. Yet there is considerable consistency in the order of the categories in Table 7 whatever column one follows, including the very crude measures of the extreme occupations. In view of the considerable heterogeneity of the census categories, even moderate consistency is gratifying. Comparing the two top categories, it may be seen that professional, technical, and kindred workers have a

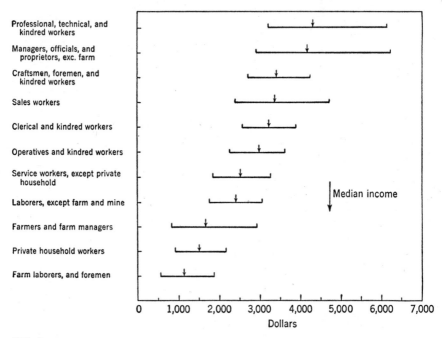

FIG. 7

MEDIAN INCOME AND INTERQUARTILE RANGE IN 1949 OF THE EXPERIENCED MALE LABOR FORCE WHO WORKED 50 TO 52 WEEKS IN 1949 FOR THE UNITED STATES: 1950 *

higher median income than do managers, officials, and proprietors, but the interquartile range of the latter category is wider than is the range of the first. This suggests that persons in the latter category have a better chance to make more money, *and* to make less. The categories which include craftsmen, sales, and clerical workers are all close to each other in median income and not much above the median for operatives. Sales workers show the widest spread—thus resembling the quasi-business category of managers, officials, and proprietors. In view of the

* Based on Table 6.

decline in prestige and the low level of political and union organization of clerical workers, it is worth emphasizing the fact that craftsmen are above the clerical workers in median income and operatives are next below them. The figures for the bottom three categories—farm operators, private household workers and farm laborers and foremen—do not mean very much because of the importance of perquisites and hidden

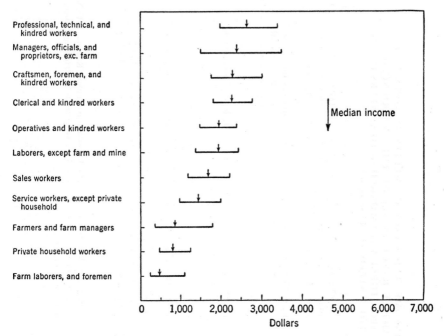

FIG. 8

MEDIAN INCOME AND INTERQUARTILE RANGE IN 1949 OF THE EXPERIENCED FEMALE LABOR FORCE WHO WORKED 50 TO 52 WEEKS IN 1949 FOR THE UNITED STATES: 1950 *

expenses and part-time work in these occupations. Worth calling attention to is the wide range exhibited by the farmers and farm managers; yet wide as it is, the 75th percentile actually is less than the *median* for operatives.

Turning next to the females (Table 7), we are struck immediately by how much lower the medians are. Even for comparable occupations which are practiced full-time, this generalization holds. For "Physicians and surgeons," the median for women is almost half what it is for men;

* Based on Table 7.

TABLE 7
MEDIAN INCOME, AND RANGE OF MEDIAN INCOMES AND INTERQUARTILE RANGE IN 1949 OF THE EXPERIENCED FEMALE LABOR FORCE WHO WORKED 50 TO 52 WEEKS IN 1949, FOR THE UNITED STATES: 1950 *

	MEDIAN INCOME	LOWEST DETAILED OCCUPATIONAL MEDIAN INCOME	HIGHEST DETAILED OCCUPATIONAL MEDIAN INCOME	INCOME RANGE INCLUDING ONE-HALF OF PERSONS IN CATEGORY (INTERQUARTILE RANGE)	
Professional, technical and kindred workers	2,615	1,217 (Clergymen) a	4,375 (Physicians and surgeons)	1,965	3,385
Managers, officials, and proprietors, exc. farm	2,382	1,288 (Managers & superintendents building)	3,638 (Managers, officials & prop'rs self-employed in manufacturing)	1,490	3,470
Craftsmen, foremen, and kindred workers	2,280	c	....	1,750	2,895
Clerical and kindred workers	2,255	1,807 (Attendants, physicians & dentists office)	2,743 (Telegraph operators)	1,795	2,765
Operatives and kindred workers	1,926	c	....	1,485	2,380
Laborers except farm and mine	1,912	c	....	1,375	2,415
Sales workers	1,658	c	....	1,180	2,210
Service workers, except private household	1,445	1,337 (Waitresses)	1,785 (Barbers, beauticians and manicurists)	985	2,003
Farmers and farm managers	845	....b	....	371	1,805
Private household workers	799	419 (Laundresses Living out)	1,199 (Private household workers, n.e.c. Living in)	451	1,260
Farm laborers and foremen	474	c	....	236	1,095

* Medians copied directly and interquartile range figures calculated from 1950 Population Census Report P-E No. 1B, Preprint of Volume IV, Part I, Chapter B., *Occupational Characteristics*, U.S. Bureau of the Census, U.S. Government Printing Office, 1956, Table 20.
a Omits Student professional nurses with median income of $413.
b Data not applied by Census.
c Insufficient number of entries in Census data.

for "Floormen and floor managers, store," the median is $3,352 for men and $1,892 for women; and for operatives in confectionery and related products factories, the median for men is $2,779 and for women is $1,880. The great differences for most occupations are, however, due to the fact that many women work part-time, and their orientation to the labor market is quite different owing to sex role differences. In Table 7 and Figure 8, we note an overlap between categories similar to that we saw for males, and that managers, officials, and proprietors have a wider spread than does the top category. The clerical category—a major one for women—moves only one step up in rank, and is sandwiched between craftsmen and operatives; but its median is slightly below that of craftsmen and only a little above that of operatives. It does, however, have the highest floor (as measured by the 25th percentile) of the three categories, and, in fact, is exceeded in that respect only by the very top category—professional, technical and kindred workers. Women in the clerical category do not, then, make a lot of money—on the average—but they are not likely to make a very small amount either.

Because of the difficulties created by the all-inclusiveness of the Census occupational categories, we are fortunate in having a special analysis by L. G. Thomas (49, Ch. 6, Appendixes A, B) which overcomes many of the usual objections to the data we have presented.[31] He makes five important changes: (1) Elimination of occupations not representing self-supporting lifetime careers (newsboys, apprentices, and unpaid family farm workers); (2) Elimination of occupations in which a considerable part of the pay takes the form of perquisites of unknown cash value (clergymen deleted from professional-technical category, and members of armed services deleted from craftsmen, foremen and kindred workers); (3) Breaking of the professional-technical conglomeration into two categories: "standard professions"[32] and "semi-professional and technical;"[33] (4) Breaking of "service workers, except private household" into "police and fire protection" (partly restoring the "protective service" category used in earlier censuses), and "other services;" (5) Inclusion of estimated value of

[31] Thomas' material was secured from the Bureau of the Census in advance of publication of the data we have presented above and does not include those from whom income was not reported nor those who reported that they had no income in 1949 from work in their 1950 occupational classification.

[32] Includes accountants and auditors, architects, chemists, college presidents, professors, and instructors, dentists, technical engineers, lawyers and judges, natural scientists, professional nurses, osteopaths, physicians and surgeons, social scientists, teachers, and veterinarians.

[33] Consists of what remains after removal of the occupations listed in previous footnote. There would be argument about some of the occupations listed here, especially airplane pilots and navigators, authors, chiropractors, clergymen, actors and actresses, funeral directors and embalmers, optometrists, and pharmacists.

perquisites where applicable. The latter were applied to farmers and farm laborers, private household workers living out, and cooks, housekeepers and stewards, and waiters and waitresses. The result of these manipulations—especially of the estimates of perquisites—is to provide a more meaningful and comparable set of categories. Thomas goes on to treat these data in terms of the theory of income distribution of Harold F. Clark (9). We have taken Thomas' raw data and computed the medians and interquartile ranges presented in Tables 8 and 9. These data are charted in Figures 9 and 10. We have, also, bracketed the categories which are so small as to present unfair comparisons with much larger categories: for example, "firemen and police" turn out to be the top category for females.

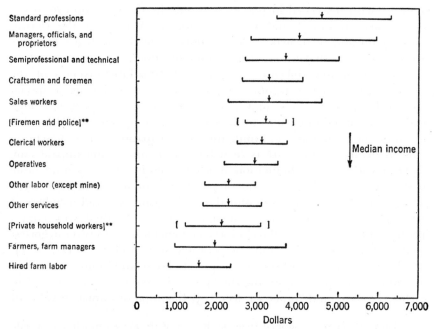

FIG. 9
MEDIAN INCOME AND INTERQUARTILE RANGE OF MALE OCCU-
PATIONAL GROUPS WHO WORKED 50 WEEKS OR MORE IN 1949,
INCLUDING ESTIMATED CASH VALUES OF PERQUISITES AND
OMITTING CERTAIN OCCUPATIONS *

* Based on Table 8.
** Number in category too small to offer adequate case for comparison with other categories.

Looking first at males, we see that the standard professions and managers, officials, and proprietors are still at the top, although the limitation of those included in the top category increases the magnitude of the difference between the medians, and makes the dispersion for the two groups about equal. The craftsmen, sales, clerical, and operatives categories preserve their relative rank, with sales workers still showing a large dispersion. And we note that, in spite of the inflation of incomes by inclusion of dollar value of perquisites, the two farm categories are at the bottom. The farm operators have a wide dispersion but the 75th percentile is below that percentile for clerical workers. The importance of part-time work is being reflected here.

For females we see a rough correspondence in rank of occupations

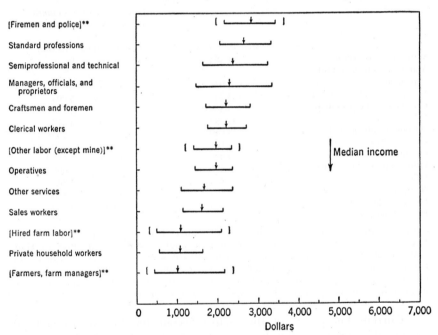

FIG. 10

MEDIAN INCOME AND INTERQUARTILE RANGE OF FEMALE OCCU-PATIONAL GROUPS WHO WORKED 50 WEEKS OR MORE IN 1949, INCLUDING ESTIMATED CASH VALUES OF PERQUISITES AND OMITTING CERTAIN OCCUPATIONS *

  * Based on Table 9.
  ** Number in category too small to offer adequate case for comparison with other categories.

to that we saw for men.[34] The most important change is that the clerical category moves up distinctly above sales workers which drop way down to a median of $1,630 compared to $2,240 for clerical workers. Private household workers, a much more important category for women than for men, is practically at the bottom—in spite of the inclusion of perquisites. Part-time work is also an important factor here. Again, as we saw with the Census categories, the overall medians for women are much lower than those for men.

TABLE 8

MEDIAN INCOME AND DISPERSION OF MALE OCCUPATIONAL GROUPS WHO WORKED 50 WEEKS OR MORE IN 1949, INCLUDING ESTIMATED CASH VALUES OF PERQUISITES AND OMITTING CERTAIN OCCUPATIONS *

| | | INCOME RANGE INCLUDING ONE-HALF OF PERSONS IN CATEGORY | |
	MEDIAN INCOME	(INTERQUARTILE RANGE)	
Standard professions	$4,585	$3,440	$6,340
Managers, officials, and proprietors	4,025	2,805	5,880
Semiprof. and technical	3,755	2,735	5,004
Craftsmen and foremen	3,350	2,645	4,160
Sales workers	3,330	2,350	4,575
[Firemen and police]	[3,240]	[2,735]	[3,755]
Clerical workers	3,140	2,510	3,770
Operatives	2,920	2,230	3,525
Other labor (exc. mine)	2,360	1,740	2,965
Other services	2,355	1,700	3,120
[Private household workers]	[2,165]	[1,280]	[3,115]
Farmers, farm managers	1,995	955	3,750
Hired farm labor	1,570	850	2,420

* Calculations of medians and interquartile ranges from data supplied in Thomas, L. G., *The Occupational Structure and Education* (Englewood Cliffs, N.J.: Prentice-Hall, 1956), Table B-1, pp. 480–483. Thomas' material was secured from the Bureau of the Census in advance of publication and does not include those from whom income was not reported nor those who reported that they received no income in 1949 from work in their 1950 occupational classification. See text discussion above.

Current knowledge of the factors accounting for the differential income of occupations is aptly summed up in the title one authority gives to his discussion: "Wages: A Parade of Theories" (26, Ch. 7). Labor economists, who have done a great deal of thinking in this area, have

[34] The leading position occupied by "Firemen and police" is an artifact resulting from the very small size of this category. The calculations of the median and interquartile range were based on only 3,180 persons. The total number in this category accounted for only .03 per cent of all females employed, but this small group happened to enjoy a high median income.

offered very broad theories (subsistence, wage fund, surplus value, marginal productivity, bargaining) and "lists" of factors [35] which overlap and vary greatly in significance. The poor state of knowledge seems to be due to research difficulties,[36] the tendency to offer subjective explanations based on the writer's own experience,[37] and the attempt to cover too much in too great a hurry.[38] We shall content ourselves with pointing out certain major sociological factors, with the caution that these should be regarded as hypotheses rather than explanations.

TABLE 9

MEDIAN INCOME AND DISPERSION OF FEMALE OCCUPATION GROUPS WHO WORKED 50 WEEKS OR MORE IN 1949, INCLUDING ESTIMATED CASH VALUES OF PERQUISITES AND OMITTING CERTAIN OCCUPATIONS *

	MEDIAN INCOME	INCOME RANGE INCLUDING ONE-HALF OF PERSONS IN CATEGORY (INTERQUARTILE RANGE)	
[Firemen and police]	[$2,870]	[$2,200]	[$3,490]
Standard professions	2,650	2,065	3,360
Semiprof. and technical	2,440	1,660	3,265
Managers, officials and proprietors	2,340	1,465	3,370
Craftsmen and foremen	2,255	1,740	2,850
Clerical workers	2,240	1,790	2,730
Operatives	1,945	1,420	2,415
[Other labor (exc. mine)]	[1,905]	[1,390]	[2,390]
Other services	1,705	1,120	2,415
Sales workers	1,630	1,175	2,145
[Hired farm labor]	[1,150]	[502]	[2,100]
Private household workers	1,090	570	1,645
[Farmers, farm managers]	[1,000]	[431]	[2,175]

* Calculations of medians and interquartile ranges from data supplied in Thomas, L. G., *The Occupational Structure and Education* (Englewood Cliffs, N.J.: Prentice-Hall, 1956), Table B-2, pp. 484–487. Thomas' material was secured from the Bureau of the Census in advance of publication and does not include those from whom income was not reported nor those who reported that they received no income in 1949 from work in their 1950 occupational classification. See text discussion above.

[35] For example, Peterson (39, pp. 284–85) lists serially: training and skill, custom, responsibility and authority, advancement opportunities, regularity, unpleasant features or hazard, perquisites, employers' financial condition, prevailing wage, cost of living, labor market, potential labor substitutes, elasticity of product demand, union organization.

[36] Caplow (7, p. 148), in his intriguing approach in terms of labor markets, mentions the difficulty of determining the incomes of the self-employed and others, the cash value of perquisites, and the extent of income concealment.

[37] For example, overconcern with "disagreeable" occupations without supporting data that their practitioners so find them.

[38] That is, trying to have all, or a large number of occupations neatly accounted for, in the face of scarcity of research.

Obviously, the "importance to society" of an occupational service will make a difference,[39] but one could spend a fruitless hour discussing the relative importance of teaching the young and burying the dead without explaining why the latter yields more income than the former. To put the matter plainly, society—like any person in it—will pay as little for an activity as possible; therefore, the reward for an activity depends, in part at least, on what society can be required to pay, a fact which makes occupational pay frequently a *power*[40] phenomenon. Such power manifests itself in various ways. A service in high demand (for whatever reason) places those who supply it in a position to demand high pay. If the service is, in addition, of an emergency character, then those who supply it (doctors, lawyers, plumbers, TV repairmen, drug smugglers) can demand more money than those who supply services that can (relatively speaking) be postponed (architects, librarians, many types of researchers, gardeners, rug-shampooers, pimps).[41] Assuming moderate to high demand, the power of the practitioner to control his income depends further on the rarity of the service and on his market position. A service can remain rare if it involves a natural scarcity (a service requiring great talent or beauty, or risk of being imprisoned, or of being killed), if it requires a long period of education and experience, or if its providers are organized to prevent too many entering the occupation (10). Professional services (and craft services, to some extent), as a group, tend to meet these requirements and they help explain the relatively high pay of professionals. But a professor of dentistry can demand more money

[39] Caplow (7, p. 145) draws a relation between importance and numbers: "The most essential activities are those which engage labor on a large scale—agriculture, manufacturing, and transportation." The assumption is that since the total wage bill will be high, a limit on what society can afford is soon reached. By contrast, the "least essential activities, the arts and sciences perhaps . . ." require fewer workers and therefore persons in those activities can push up their wage demands. But such a use of numbers, without holding constant degree of technological development, would appear to be hazardous. The numbers in agriculture in the U.S. decrease with each census without agriculture's becoming any the less essential.

[40] This should not, of course, be construed to mean that power and income are directly related. We are speaking here only of one kind of power: the power to exact money. Talcott Parsons, in a discussion incidental to a broader treatment of social stratification (38, pp. 121–22) describes three ways of earning money which differ in terms of the occupational incumbent's power to exact money. These are: (1) income derived by one's own "entrepreneurial" activity by selling services or products in a free market; e.g., independent craftsmen, professionals, and businessmen; (2) payments received from a firm on the basis of its earnings in a competitive market; e.g., salaries, wages, bonuses, commissions; (3) income from occupations which are subsidized out of taxation or philanthropic sources; e.g., income of government employees and employees of "non-profit" organizations such as hospitals and universities. Such differences create the serious problem of a possible lack of correspondence between evaluations of occupational roles and income derived from them.

[41] The demand for postponable needs is usually less also.

than a professor of English not only because the demand for dentistry is higher but also because the professor of dentistry is in a better market position: he can *withdraw* his services and go into private practice. Similarly, those who are in a position to charge per service or per person (doctors, dentists, lawyers, private investigators, plumbers) can earn more than those who cannot do so (nurses, social workers, teachers, police detectives, maintenance men). Their poor market position helps explain the low wages paid to casual laborers (who, when *seeking* work, must take what they can get), to semiskilled manual workers (who include women, high-school students, etc.), and to policemen, firemen, and soldiers (who, though rendering vital and emergency services, are forbidden the right to withhold their services). On the other hand, a good market position is enjoyed by those who are parts of large unions [42] or in industries in which a union settlement with one firm is forthwith adopted in other firms. And strong indeed is the market position of the professional in private practice whose services are in high demand: he can take whatever the traffic will bear (which includes the risk of occasionally getting nothing).

The power to exact money is important but the pay of an occupation may depend on quite different factors. Sheer prestige may mean high income but the money does not come by magic; there must be an *intervening mechanism* for converting prestige to money; for example, a connection with advertising or business (as in the case of sports heroes or movie stars) or direct association with a power organization, such as a congressional committee, which can determine the salaries to be paid to high government officials. The economic position of the occupational incumbent may be involved especially for those occupations which authorize money payments (above all, owners and managers) to others and those occupations that are concerned with the manipulation of money (stock-brokers, middlemen, bankers). To some extent, the economic position of such persons is a power position also. Still remaining are a variety of other factors such as tradition, work group controls which may enforce restriction of output (and therefore of earnings), and fringe benefits. The last includes security of tenure and other values often associated with bureaucratic positions, continuous employment, and opportunities to increase one's pay through piece-work. Many of these factors are also associated with the power of the occupational incumbent or of his organization. One should not ignore the importance of regional differences in making generalizations. For example, L. E. Lewis (27) re-

[42] A number of studies support the statement that unionized workers receive—on the average—higher wages than do nonunionized workers though there are important regional differences. See (41). Such differences will, it may be expected, affect most the categories including craftsmen and operatives.

ports that office workers' weekly salaries are nearly 25 per cent higher in San Francisco than in Boston but both cities fall considerably below New York City in the case of wages in the building construction industry.[43] Income is positively related to size of place, a phenomenon that is especially marked for females and nonwhites, which in turn suggests that occupational opportunities are an important factor. Of course, a group which is severely restricted by such a factor as race will find its power to exact wages greatly reduced. H. P. Miller (35, pp. 42–48) finds that income differences between whites and nonwhites hold even when age, sex, education, region, and size of place are held constant. Finally there are the many controls (and limitations) government[44] places on wage payments.[45]

The third factor affecting occupational status is the white-collar-manual distinction. The distinction between white-collar and manual work has tended to become obscured but it still is made and is important to people. The white-collar worker does hold his head up higher in the community and the blue-collar worker envies[46] him and often encourages his children to prepare themselves for white-collar jobs. Our attitudes toward white-collar work may in part be traced back to feudal society when manual work was frowned upon[47] and to religious attitudes toward work as a penalty for sin. Part of the reason that white-collar work has tended to lose its prestige has been precisely that it has become more manual as time has gone on. That itself is evidence that the distinction is still a real one in people's minds. The status of white-collar workers seems to be almost wholly a matter of prestige, for a high proportion of manual workers outrank them both in power and in economic position.

A fourth occupational status factor is authority. In general, status rank is related to power and therefore those occupations which, by definition, give the incumbent the legitimate right to exercise power (authority) tend to have high status. These include managerial, political, and military occupations. Although authority and rank are clearly related,

[43] H. P. Miller (35, Ch. 4) found that the major regional cleavage was between the South and the rest of the nation, a division which held when data were controlled by color, sex, residence, and size of community.
[44] Ober (36) finds that over time the percentage difference between skilled and unskilled work has narrowed and that this is due in considerable part to the *raising* of the wages of unskilled labor because of the general concern for welfare and the lifting of the wage floor.
[45] Those interested in a broad approach to the assessment of income should see (13).
[46] An attitude often mixed with that of contempt.
[47] This attitude found its major expression in the large cotton plantations of the antebellum South, the closest thing we have seen in the United States to a land-based aristocracy. It has persisted even where social conditions have changed drastically. See the discussion on p. 339.

it is difficult to measure the relationship. To some extent, the number of persons controlled is a crude measure (e.g., lieutenants *vs.* generals, in the field) but numbers do not help much in evaluating the relative status rank of a U.S. senator and a state governor. A second problem is that different authority statuses are rarely comparable. It is difficult to compare the degree of authority of a national union leader (very high power, but moderate prestige), a U.S. senator (very high power *and* very high prestige), and the head of a huge business (very high power *and* very high economic position). In these cases, one cannot ignore the relation between authority and prestige and economic position.

The fifth occupational status determinant is the freedom permitted by the occupation. The extent to which an occupation offers the incumbent the opportunity to dispose of his time as he sees fit is directly related to the degree of prestige of the occupation itself. The more the individual is tied to the job, the more he is forced to be present at a given time, and the more his work is standardized and controlled by others, then the lower is the status of the occupation likely to be.[48] This phenomenon is a variable even within a given occupation and may be found in the degree of freedom that is permitted a supervisor to influence the behavior of a subordinate. It is the source of important types of resentment and some kinds of low morale that may be found among factory workers or office workers. The following case illustrates the importance of freedom from direction to the worker in terms of self respect: [49]

Just like the Boss's son. On a nice hot day like today, he is over at Michigan Beach; he really believes in takin' it easy. He knows the business, but when the old man, his father, isn't around, he doesn't work too hard. Well, maybe I guess I'd do the same thing, too, if I was in his boots.

But the company isn't bad, though, now. If a fella don't feel like workin' today, O.K. Tomorrow is another day.

Interviewer: Do you mean that if you don't feel like working very hard today you can leave your work go until the next day?

Mr. A: Yes. You see, it's like this. The designers think up a design, and then they tell us just how it goes. The carriers bring us the material and tell us how many are wanted in what sizes. Then we go to work, cutting sometimes 150 with one operation. They have you down for so many garments for the day; but if you don't get them all done in one day, they don't run up and

---

[48] Caplow (7, pp. 120–21) warns of the danger of identifying control with coercion. Thus the independent professions and crafts often suffer little from coercion but have many *unfelt* controls because these controls have become internalized, the rules change rarely, and for other reasons.

[49] Thanks are due to Burleigh B. Gardner for permission to reproduce this case.

want to know right away why you didn't do them all, like they would in some places. But they wait for a couple of days, and then if you still are behind, they come around and want to know why.

For a while there, it wasn't like that though. They got in some of those efficiency experts from New York, and then it really was funny. Why, this one guy really got worked up in two weeks.

Interviewer: How do you mean, "worked up"?

Mr. A: Well, it was like this. We are used to going at our own rate, like I told ya. So they bring this guy in. You know, he used to go and sneak behind the posts to spy on us and try to catch us doing somethin' we weren't supposed to be doin'. Well, he was there only two weeks when he had to go to the hospital and had to have two blood transfusions. A couple of the guys from the shop went down and donated him some blood. They wanted me to go, too. Hell, I wouldn't give that guy nothin'.

You know he was one of these guys that wants you to work like nuts from the time you step inside the door in the morning 'til the time the bell rings at night. I suppose that was his job but he really was tough. First, he wanted the girls to stop chewin' gum. When they put in that order the girls started quittin' left and right. Guess they figured that for what they were gettin' paid at R—— it wasn't worth quittin' to chew gum, so they began to quit. The company couldn't get anybody else to do their work at the machines, so they could chew gum on the job after that. Then this efficiency expert decided that the fellas were takin' too much time off goin' to the washroom for a smoke about once every couple of hours, so he hollered about that. I guess you know what happened then—they started goin' out every fifteen minutes; so the company had to cut that order out.

Some people are so money hungry they work all the time. Hell, if I wanted to, I could make $100 a week like some of these defense workers, too—that's if I want to work myself to death. What good is the money if you don't have time to spend it and no time to go out and have a good time? I worked like that for a while there, but then I said, "Nothin' doin'! I'm not that greedy for the money." Why I worked day and night. For what? I was so tired when I got home that I didn't feel like goin' out anywhere, what little time I had to go out.

It is in part because of the importance that is attached to freedom in our society that the occupation of the professor tends to have high prestige. It helps explain also the prestige that attaches to self-owner-ship, which includes the idea of being independent. One reason that members of minority groups frequently encourage their children to get into one of the independent professions is precisely that they will then be in a position where they will not be working directly for anyone. For Negroes, for example, anti-Negro attitudes will not hit them so directly as they might if they were forced to work under the direction of a white person or in direct association with other white persons.

Degree of freedom is a major factor accounting for the low status of domestic work in our society. Such work usually involves personal subordination to a unique master [50] with all his whims, with little recourse for the servant except at law or by threatening to quit.[51] A part of his remuneration is likely to be in kind which further restricts his freedom to choose his food and clothing. And there is a limited life outside of work because of the uncertainty of the hours of work. Domestic work not only involves low power, but low prestige and economic position as well. As is usually the case with occupations that are thrice-cursed, the fact of low status (and attendant low pay) makes it difficult to attract persons to it with the result that those who do come are likely to be those who can find nothing better. This situation helps keep the status low.[52]

A sixth occupational status determinant is amount of preparation. Prestige tends to be related directly to amount of preparation. This is in part a matter of *numbers:* prestige is lost if spread around too much. Consequently, occupations will frequently try, whether successfully or not, to control entry by apprenticeship or other restrictions. Important exceptions are provided by business and government where the "self-made man" and scrappy underdog are still heroes in many persons' eyes. To the extent that it is true that little preparation is required, the status structure of our society becomes confused.[53] But as both business and government become increasingly bureaucratized, education, training, and preparation come to be more important in those areas as well as others, a factor contributing to the rising status of the university in the United States. Control on entry through increase in amount and kind of training not only keeps prestige high but power as well since the occupation can attempt to monopolize the service it provides. Further, when the numbers who supply a service in high demand are kept low, their economic position is likely to rise.

Seventh, and lastly, the status rank of an occupation is related to the

[50] As opposed to subordination to a foreman or department head who controls by virtue of authorization from *his* superior, and who may be replaced at any time.

[51] The force of this argument is hardly weakened by those who point out (usually with glee, for some reason) that servants also control their masters insofar as their masters are dependent on them. No human relationship is one-sided, and the question, in any case, is one of degree.

[52] The fact that typically only high status persons can afford servants creates the interesting situation that persons from opposite ends of the status scale interact intimately. This fact has probably contributed to the exaggeration of the degree of control of the servant over his master. A person of high status may find it galling to be made aware of his dependence on a person of low status, as when a servant dumps the soup in the guest-of-honor's lap.

[53] In Europe, by contrast, certification requirement for jobs are much commoner and one is not surprised to find Ph.D.'s in private businesses.

extent to which the occupation involves the organization, intermediation and management of symbols. One might classify occupations into the following three categories:

1. Those concerned with things.
2. Those concerned with people.
3. Those concerned with ideas, or the symbols of things or people.

It seems to be true that prestige tends to rise as one moves from (1) to (3) in this classification. We observe the significance of the manipulation of symbols in the rise of the advertising man to a position of importance in the business structure. To an increasing extent, the dependence of the manufacturer on sales for his very existence has tended to increase the power of the advertising agency personnel. In some cases, such personnel are taking over the companies whose advertising accounts they formerly handled. Theirs is not a manual skill, nor is it simply a matter of manipulating persons but rather of selling an idea, of showing persons how the symbol can be applied to their business or profession. After posing for a statue in Madame Tussaud's wax museum, Mickey Mouse helped rescue the Lionel Corp., manufacturer of toy trains, from receivership, sold more than 8,000,000 Ingersoll watches, and, since 1929 (50, p. 45),

. . . Mickey's name or picture has appeared on 5,000 different lines of merchandise, from milk of magnesia to a $1,200 diamond bracelet to a radiator cap, and has sold more than $250 million worth of goods . . . Mickey is likely to be remembered . . . for one decisive moment when he stood at the absolute center of human affairs. On June 6, 1944, the D-day of the Allied invasion of France, the code word for the entire Allied operation was "Mickey Mouse."

The creation and dissemination of ideas gives to some occupations high prestige (teaching), to some high power (labor relations and public relations occupations), to some high prestige and power (the clergy, government diplomats), and to a few who can use ideas to keep the attention of 30 or 40 million persons focussed on a television screen, ideas give prestige, power, and high economic position.

CONCLUSIONS ON OCCUPATIONAL STATUS

We may draw two major conclusions from our discussion of occupational status:

1. STATUS IS A COMPLEX OF MULTIPLE FACTORS

In the study of pre-literate societies, there is a tendency to deal with status in a unilinear fashion; that is, to take the most prized element and relate its distribution to status. This element may be self-abnegation, cleanliness, or the accumulation of wealth. Among the Kwakiutl, status has been related to the magnificence of the potlatches that the individual can put on (6, pp. 332–38). On the other hand, our discussion of Dobu, brief as it was, indicated at least three factors—magic, kinship, and residence—which affected status. In any society, the factors which confer status may be few but there is never only one. We have discussed kinship and family affiliation, wealth, ethnicity and race, and a number of occupational factors. Nor do these even begin to exhaust the subject. Of importance also are religion, rural-urban origin, regional origin, personal beauty, sex, education, or even speech accent.[54] Some of these factors go together, whereas others work against each other, a fact which contributes both to the richness of life and to the exasperation of researchers who are seeking a unidimensional status scale.

2. OCCUPATION IS ONE OF THE MOST IMPORTANT STATUS DETERMINANTS

All occupations are statuses in their own right and have powerful effects on the other statuses in society. But it is never enough to use occupation alone for a balanced picture of an individual's status. A fruitful way to look at status in relation to occupation is as follows. The individual brings a status to the occupation with him and the occupation in turn confers still another status on him. A person comes to the job with an already existing status, with a conception of himself formed in part from the conception that others have of him. This he may secure from his family, from his race, from his ethnicity, from his origin, from his sex. Then when he takes the job, he gains a new status. The job may in turn force him to redefine his status. He may discover for example that in spite of his abilities or his experience the fact that he does not have a college degree may prevent him from entering certain technical positions. He may then have to make a different estimation of himself and what he can ever hope to be, or provide for his family.

Occupation therefore introduces a dynamic element in status because through it the individual can, at least theoretically, change his status. Many, perhaps the major, determinants of status in our society are of such a character that they do not admit of change. Family descent, race, ethnicity, origin, or sex are none of them easily modifiable.[55] But the occupation that the individual enters is related to a *decision* which he can make and through it he can to some extent change his status. Occupation is to a degree a free variable in our society and is not determined

[54] It is hardly a difference in the languages which explains why German immigrants quickly reduce their accents to a minimum while British immigrants carry theirs to their graves.

[55] Both religion and education are modifiable, but religion does not seem to be a major status determinant in the United States, and education exerts its major effect *through* occupation.

automatically by family or by race or by region. Occupation therefore provides a major medium of status change.[56]

TEACHING AND LEARNING

Having considered the occupational status system, we consider now the manner in which the individual is assigned an occupational status.

Among some educators we find the notion that *teaching* means simply the *transmission of skills or of ideas*. This approach is illustrated in the claim that one can teach persons a great deal in school and that those persons are then able to fill a job vacancy. What is not realized is that taking a job implies a *change of status*. The individual changes his conception of himself—he is no longer a student but a machinist or social worker—and he hopes that others will too. Sometimes they do but often they do not. For example, a student who takes a summer job is often irked because he is paid a low wage. He conceives of himself as a full-fledged employee (does he not put in a full day and do his job?) but his employer conceives of him as "summer help"—a wholly marginal status. Ability is rewarded, but so are permanence and dependability.

Taking a new job, therefore, involves the assumption of a new status—new self-conceptions and new conceptions by others of one's self. The conceptions others have are not randomly determined. Rather, one's colleagues have *standards* by which they judge the new person in order to decide whether he measures up to the characteristics they think colleagues should have. One of the most important standards is *training,* which the members of the occupation will try to control for two reasons: to make sure novices secure what is considered the right training and to prevent many from entering at all. This control is exercised through three mechanisms: restricting the number permitted to learn, controlling the learning itself, and requiring an initiation.

RESTRICTING THE NUMBER PERMITTED TO LEARN

This restriction is implemented by setting up both formal and informal criteria—the former being public, the latter being simply "understood."

1. FORMAL CRITERIA

Prerequisites, before one may enter dental or law schools or schools granting advanced degrees, often prevent persons from ever pursuing the occupation. Such prerequisites may include college degrees or educational requirements which take a long time to meet or cost a great

---

[56] Wealth might be regarded as a second major variable that can change status, but unless it is inherited or married wealth, it must be secured through an occupation.

deal of money, or may involve regional and scholastic restrictions; that is, giving preference to applicants from the immediate area and/or establishing minimal grade point averages. The sheer length of the occupational education itself will stop many persons even after they have begun their course of study. Many occupations require internships which are, in fact, parts of the learning process.[57] Further, there are good and poor internships: a Negro physician may be prevented from entering practice on the same level as whites by preventing his securing an internship in a good hospital. In law, the individual may be required to serve a period in a law office, the accountant may have to serve in an accounting firm or business office before he can be articled, and many crafts preserve apprenticeship requirements even when the skill might be taught (partially, at least) in a formal school.[58]

Where much of the learning must take place on the job, still other devices are used. The factory personnel office screens persons and the union may use the device of the hiring hall or the closed shop, if legal, to exercise control on the persons who are permitted to take a job at all and therefore to secure the learning that the job requires. This becomes a circular process whereby persons are unable to learn the skills that the job requires except by taking a job and they are unable to secure the job because they do not have the skills.

2. INFORMAL CRITERIA

These are varied, but the most important of them revolve about race, religion, age, and sex. They are of necessity informal, that is not proclaimed, because of democratic ideals and because of the desire to maintain a favorable public opinion. Informal criteria may be applied in various ways. One technique is the informal quota in the school. It may be decided that no more than a certain fixed percentage of the student body shall be Jews, or Negroes, or women. If such an understanding exists it is extremely difficult for the outsider either to prove that it is used or discover how it is enforced. The individual applying to the school for entry may simply be told that his qualifications do not meet the requirements of the school, without any particular reason being given. Or he may be told that limitation of funds require that classes be held to a certain maximum size and that this size has already been reached. Another device is the use of the performance test in dentistry and in medicine. Persons who apply to a school of dentistry may be

[57] A physician stated: "If I'd started practicing as soon as I got out of medical school, I would have been a menace. Where I first really began to learn was in my internship. That's where I had my first chance to work with live patients in a real situation."

[58] The resemblance of the modern crafts to the medieval craft guilds is not a mere ritualistic imitation. See (7, pp. 166 ff.).

required to pass a performance test which is intrinsically a simple procedure. The individual may be given a set of wooden blocks of varying shapes and told to put them together, jigsaw-fashion, in order to make a sphere. He performs the test in the presence of the examiner who makes notes as he proceeds. When the test is over the person may be told that he has failed. It is difficult to discover why. The explanation may be (if one is offered at all) that the candidate made false moves, did not exercise sufficient care, or had too cavalier an attitude. The vagueness and subjectivity of such judgments makes decisions based on them impossible to combat.[59]

Informal criteria are seen in their most highly developed forms in the professions, but they are not absent from occupations lying closer to the Job pole of the professionalization continuum. The personal interview before hiring may be used to restrict persons on any desired basis. A common requirement is a photograph to accompany an application form. These facsimiles are often useless for identification purposes, but they will usually reveal one fact which state laws may forbid being asked on the questionnaire itself—race.

CONTROLLING THE LEARNING ITSELF

Besides controlling entry, an attempt is usually made to control the learning itself. Where this learning consists in part of a formal education off the job, control is exercised by having accepted members of the occupation do the teaching. When the members of the teaching staff of a medical school are also practicing doctors, they can be counted upon to convey to students not only facts and skills but the desired professional attitudes as well. For similar reasons, accountants teach accounting students and engineers teach engineering students.

But the most important control on learning is the control on the learning that occurs on the job itself, a statement that remains true however much formal education an occupation requires. Matters learned on the job may be discussed under three headings: regular technical skills, tricks of the trade, and social skills.

1. REGULAR TECHNICAL SKILLS

The individual acquires real facility in the skills of the occupation only when he begins to practice them. A stenographer described some of the skills she had to acquire on her first job as follows:

---

[59] One should not interpret the presence of such tests as *prima facie* evidence of a silent (sometimes illegal) conspiracy. Obviously the major (sometimes only) purpose of tests is to weed out the incompetent in advance, and, given the nature of many occupations, subjective tests may be the best means of discovering incompetence. But *if* it is desired to restrict on an informal basis, such tests *may* be used to do so.

In the (business) school the thing that had always been emphasized was accuracy along with speed. But in this particular company it turned out that they didn't give a hoot about speed at all. The important thing was accuracy. I was told again and again that they didn't want any whiz-kids around here and when I was typing up an order the important thing was that the figures be right, that if I type a 6 instead of a 1 let us say why that might mean the difference between producing 600 parts and producing 100 parts, that a simple mistake on my part could create wholesale chaos out in the factory. So I was to type slowly, pay particular attention to any figures and to check them again and again until I was sure they were right. I had to learn the quirks of my boss, the way he liked his letters to be made up. I had to learn how to compose a letter myself in imitation of his letters since, after awhile, he told me he would expect me to be able to answer mail myself. But worst of all was trying to type in the midst of some of the things that go on. I would get started on a letter and suddenly my boss would come over to me and tell me to stop working on that one and to start on something else. I had to learn to concentrate in the midst of the jabber of voices that was always going on all around me, and that was quite a trick. And you had to be able to do that not just with one letter or for one hour but hour after hour and day after day without getting tired.

No matter how realistic or ingeniously contrived a model used in a school may be, it remains a model deliberately brought forth to "illustrate a point." Further, the student conceives of himself as a student and is not surprised to receive criticism from his teachers. But these matters are not at all clear in on-the-job learning. Much of the time the individual is unaware he is learning something (as when, for example, an action of his does not receive expected praise or is ignored) and almost anyone may assume, momentarily, the role of "teacher" by prefacing his remarks with: "Here's the way to do it." Since the right to assume this role is not clear (as it was in school) a considerable discriminatory burden is placed on the worker. After a time, the supervisor who says to a subordinate: "You ought to know better than that by now," is criticizing the speed of the subordinate's learning, although his remarks are likely to be interpreted as a criticism of immediate work performance. In one sense this interpretation is correct: work performance at any given time is a reflection of technical skills developed or sharpened on the job. This means they will change—and are expected to change—continuously.

2. TRICKS OF THE TRADE

A trick of the trade is a device which saves a person from his own mistakes. The most important are tricks that save time, save energy, and prevent a man's being hurt. All occupations have their short-cuts and part of the efficiency of the experienced worker is attributable to them. The new teacher marks each examination paper in its entirety before moving on to the next; the old hand marks one question or one page on each person's paper at one time. Nell Giles (18, pp. 49–52), a newspaperwoman, in describing her experiences as a worker at the West Lynn, Mass., plant of General Electric, mentions the following:

My job tonight was what is called "boosting . . ." For the first hour, the job went very slowly . . . I was only "picking 'em (electric rotors whose electrical strength was to be boosted) up and puttin' 'em down!" . . . and then the girl who does the magnetizing came over and showed me the short cuts with finger motions. As the left hand picks up the next rotor, the right hand inserts the first one in the "boosting" machine and the foot presses the lever. Think what a whiz an octopus would be on this job.

In some occupations, one must learn how to lift heavy weights without strain; in others, one learns to avoid cutting oneself or hitting one's thumb with a hammer. Matthews (32, pp. 46–53) has described how a rookie fireman must learn never to look up, when scaling a ladder, lest burning material fall on his face. The fireman learns also to put on his helmet before he buttons his fire coat so that if he falls off the "rig" (fire-engine) his head will be protected, and he learns to change from his street shoes to his firemen's boots one shoe at a time so that if the alarm should go off, he will never have more than one shoe left to put on. Perhaps the most ingenious is the trick of the "smoke eater" (one who can stay in a smoke-filled room for a long time) of getting breaths of fresh air from the nozzle of the hose, before water is pumped through it. Of course professional criminals run a continuous risk of being "hurt" so it is not surprising to find them using tricks of the trade in great profusion. The professional pickpocket often stations himself right below signs reading *BEWARE OF PICK-POCKETS* (because most men carrying a lot of money feel automatically for their wallets when they read the sign, thus informing the pickpocket where the wallet is kept) and the professional motel thief rarely enters a room when the guests are away (they might return at any time) but waits until they are in bed, fast asleep (48, pp. 44–45, *passim*).

3. SOCIAL SKILLS

The worker must learn how to get along with fellow workers. To do this he must learn what their social world is and what their code is. One of the commonest ways of teaching social skills is by *horseplay*, including all the legendary devices for making the novice look foolish: tripping him as he passes, hiding his tools, sending him to nonexistent places to get nonexistent tools from nonexistent persons, and making obscene remarks about his youth. Such devices—often dismissed as "mere kidding around"—have the definite function of letting the individual know that there is a group there and that the individual cannot regard himself as a member of the occupation until he has been accepted by that group.

Acceptance in turn involves learning how to behave. The individual must learn what is considered to be a day's work and to restrict his output to that point. He must learn what to keep his mouth shut about, and what it is safe to talk about. He must learn *whom* he can talk to and whom he must avoid. He must learn how to protect other workers from criticism. It is these social skills that are the most difficult to teach *away* from the job. C. I. Barnard (3), formerly president of the New Jersey Bell Telephone Company, has suggested that in the training of executives the social skills of the executive are far and away the most important kind of skills that he should have, and it is precisely these skills that cannot be taught in the schools of business administration or in vocational schools. He states that there is little point in attempting to teach precise executive skills in schools because they change and because the appropriate skills are peculiar to each industry. Therefore, he recommends a broad course.

INITIATION

When the new individual has been permitted to learn and when he has completed his learning, then there are often certain devices for admitting the individual to the occupation. In some cases the individual may go through an initiation which is just as arduous as that in any primitive society at the time of the *rites de passage*.[60] The worker in industry may be hazed, or forced to perform a particularly unpleasant or dirty task. The final examination for the Ph.D. degree is, to *some* [61] extent, such an initiation. In many occupations the individual may be expected to give an expensive dinner or buy drinks for his fellow workers.

The ceremonial nature of these practices is no accident for they have ceremonial functions. They let the man and others know he has at last been admitted to the occupation as a full member, and they impress upon him what an *honor* this membership is. In sum, a change of status has been recognized.

It should now be clear why we discuss the subject of "Teaching and Learning" in a chapter devoted to occupational status, for the function of teaching and learning is to provide the individual with the means by which he can change his status and become an occupational member. The mere fact that one has completed a course of study does not in itself admit one. One is admitted, instead, when one has learned the regular

[60] Ceremonies accompanying important, non-unique crises in the life-cycle of the individual which involve a great change in his relations to others. See (1, Ch. 20, *passim*).

[61] Of course the fact that any act is ceremonial does not make it any the less important, nor—for the case of the Ph.D. examination—any less difficult to pass.

technical skills, the tricks of the trade, and the social skills, *and* when one has been recognized. Then one's status actually changes; then one is actually a member of the occupation.

OCCUPATIONAL SYSTEMS OF CONTROL

We turn next to the means used to control recognized occupational members. These are of two main sorts: those controls that come from within the occupation—which we shall discuss under the headings of folkways, mores, and sanctions—and those that come from outside the occupation.

FOLKWAYS AND MORES

In any new occupation there is considerable floundering around at first. Since persons do not know which situations are likely to recur, they do not know which situations should be subjected to group control and definition. But gradually persons come to know what to expect of one another. Bendix has described this process in the early industrial period in England. A great problem was the lack of an "internalized ethic of work performance" on the part of the workers owing largely to traditional beliefs and practices (5, pp. 203–4; 40, Ch. V).

In practice, the workers were managed by a reliance upon the traditions of craftsmanship and of the master-servant relationship. However important these traditions were for industrialization, they were not always compatible with the requirements of industrial production. Traditionally, skilled work was performed at a leisurely pace or in spurts of great intensity, but always at the discretion of the individual worker. In modern industry work must be performed above all with regular intensity. Traditionally, the skilled worker was trained to work accurately on individual designs; in modern industry he must adapt his sense of accuracy to the requirements of standardization. In handicraft production, each individual owned his own tools and was responsible for their care; by and large this is not true in modern industry, so that the care of tools and machinery is divorced from the pride of ownership. Traditionally, skills were handed down from generation to generation and, consequently, were subject to individual variations. In industry the effort has been to standardize the steps of work performance as much as possible . . .

. . . The problems of labor management have come to the fore, wherever the organization of production involved the concentration of all work operations within the enterprise and depended to some extent upon an *internalized* ethic of work performance on the part of unskilled as well as skilled workers. Under the conditions of factory production, such an ethic involves a number of variables. Workers must be willing to do the work assigned with a degree of steady intensity. They must have a positive interest in accuracy and exercise reasonable care in the treatment of tools and machinery. And they must be willing to comply with general rules as well as with specific orders in a manner which strikes some reasonable balance between the extremes of blind obedience and capricious unpredictability. And it is this last qualification which brings the general attributes of an ethic of work performance within the framework of an industrial organization; for under conditions of factory production the intensity of work, its accuracy, and the careful treatment of tools and machinery cannot remain the attributes of an individual's performance. Rather these qualities of work must be coordinated with the production schedule, and that coordination depends to some extent on the good judgment of each worker in his every act of complying with rules and orders.

Under such conditions, folkways and mores develop that define duties and obligations. In some occupations, usually in those with pretentions of becoming professions, one gets a code (24, Ch. IV). The code is often formal and as such may get further and further away from the actual work situation. It may then become a creed or faith, a statement of what occupational members are supposed to live up to. Such a code functions as an *apologia* which states what the occupation does for the world and justifies its contribution. However, in back of this code there is a real working code and it is this that is usually more significant.[62] Laymen sometimes feel that the creed was once lived up to and the working code is a departure from it. This view is a fallacy because in life action precedes words, and the working code is usually much tougher than the formal code. It is important, therefore, to look behind the parchment scroll for this working code. For example, during World War II, the slogan, WORK FOR VICTORY, was unquestionably accepted by most American factory workers. Yet this did not mean that all controls were removed and each worker became a rate-buster. However high the rate of production in a shop may have been lifted, it was still an *agreed* rate. To make such a control possible, means must have been present to control deviants—both rate-busters *and* slackers. We turn next to this type of control—the sanction.

SANCTIONS

Sanctions may be imposed in many ways. One of the best is to make it appear that the sanction is coming from the outside—like the old schoolboy technique of punishing a fellow pupil by getting him in bad with the teacher. The rate-buster may find rejected pieces slipping into his work pile which may lead to his being criticized by the foreman or the inspector. Or the group may work at top speed in order to cause the

[62] In terms of day-to-day control of work behavior. It is interesting that actual working codes, even when written down, are rarely called "codes." A good illustration is the "Rule Book" of the building crafts. The term "building code" usually refers to *legal* regulations (which, of course, the crafts have had a hand in creating).

rate-buster to get behind in his work. As the pieces pile up on his desk the foreman appears and wonders about him. The worker himself is puzzled. Actually he is working at a very rapid pace, but to all appearances he is a slow worker. The man will then get a reputation as being a slow worker, and may be shifted out of the work group to another one, by which means the work group will have achieved its objective. These are informal sanctions.

There are also formal sanctions. The individual may be rejected from the occupation, the priest may be excommunicated or reprimanded or unfrocked. In law the person may be disbarred, in medicine he may have his license taken away. These things happen but they are much less common than informal exclusion from an inner circle. In most professions legal sanctions are rarely applied. If they are, they are usually applied by a group outside of the professional body altogether. Normally informal sanctions are applied first and formal sanctions only if the person gets very far out of line.

In most professions the device of *referral* is a major source of clients. This is found to be true eminently in medicine and in law but it is also true in accounting, in many of the crafts, in business, and even in teaching: professors refer students to one another's courses. This means that one of the ways that one can hurt an individual the most is to stop referring clients to him.

When such sanctions are imposed, a man is hurt in two ways: he finds it more difficult to make a living; and he feels the force of group disapproval, that is, he is insulted. A forced reduction in earning power is always highly painful, but it is worth asking what the conditions are under which group disapproval is highly painful. Our answer is: only when the person *identifies* with the group; that is, when his status in the work group is his most important status. If, then, the person has an *escape* into another status, group sanctions may not hurt him so much at all. The best illustrations of those with status escapes are minority groups: Negroes, Jews, Mexicans, Japanese, women. A Negro who finds rejected pieces slipping into *his* work pile can interpret this as an attack, not on him, but on the Negro race. As such, he may simply shrug his shoulders in resignation or seek solace or help from fellow Negroes, but the insult has not hurt him personally. A woman being subjected to group disapproval may express her resentment with the words: "You're doing that to me *because I'm a woman!*" There is, of course, pain [63] here but not so much as there would be if she had no status escape.

---

[63] *Some* pain is always involved when there is group disapproval since, allowing for certain marginal otherworldly or artistic escapes, no one can escape one status—that of human being.

The question is: Who can insult you? To be an insult it must hurt. Therefore only if a person values the opinion of the group will he be very much upset if the group disapproves of his behavior.[64]

CONTROL FROM OUTSIDE THE OCCUPATION

Outside controls include those from clients, other professions and occupations, and public opinion in general. Such outside control is typically mediated through an authority structure (for example, work duties of electricians employed in a factory), the market-price mechanism (charges self-employed electricians are able to collect for their services),[65] governmental controls (the building code, licensing) and the general controls of custom (few electricians would refuse to respond to an urgent night-call from a householder whose electricity has failed for no obvious reasons).[66] But it is among the independent professions that we get the most striking illustrations of outside controls, for their very independence, coupled with the fact that they supply a vital service which the individual cannot begin to supply for himself, makes the independent professions peculiarly vulnerable to pressure from outside.

The professional is, after all, a man and member of society for the function he performs is too important to be reserved only for supermen. The very importance of this function makes us insist that its performance be unaffected by monetary or social class considerations.

[64] The concept of the *status escape* provides an important clue to understanding minority group relations in work situations where minority groups are partially or tentatively accepted. Having undergone prejudice and discrimination and having had to fight for entry, minority group members are, naturally, sensitive and quick to take offense. If a sanction is imposed by the majority group on a minority group member, it is likely to be interpreted by him as another attack on his group; that is, he escapes to minority group status. But any individual who, by his behavior, indicates that group sanctions do not hurt him is suggesting that he cannot be controlled by the work group. Groups will permit varying degrees of criticism of themselves, but one type of action no group of any permanence or self-consciousness will tolerate is action which implies that the group itself is of little importance or is not powerful enough to control a member's behavior. Status escape behavior, therefore, is likely to result in more drastic sanctions and to impede the development of harmonious intergroup relations. It becomes important for those interested in facilitating intergroup harmony to be able to distinguish sanctions from prejudice, for the attacking of sanctions with the weapons used to attack prejudice is likely to increase intergroup hostility.

[65] The market price mechanism exerts many other controls, of course, such as affecting the number of electricians a community will support and their credit rating. Since credit rating is, by definition, a way of evaluating occupations, it is possible to rank them by credit rating, an attempt made by Robert S. Hancock (22). Interesting implications for their position in the community are suggested by the fact that college professors and railroad clerks turn out to be not very far apart, but both are much better credit risks than policemen or lawyers.

[66] In some cases, the labor union may come as an outside control, for example, for crafts that may be isolated (a single linotype operator in a small town) or for occupations which may be in a minority in an industrial union (clerks in the UAW).

At the same time, when we seek out his services we want *him* and not the dubious help of a subordinate or flunkey. Therefore he soon reaches the limit of as many clients as he can see in one day. How then is he to secure a high income which, considering his training, experience and the high demand for his service, he feels is due him as a member of society? Obviously, only by "selecting" his clients, which means excluding those of low income and those whose skin color or religion are disliked by his "better" clients. So we get "society" doctors and "successful" lawyers. But the low income patient does meet the "society" doctor—at the out-patient clinic—where the patient who could not secure access to the doctor's waiting-room is now treated for no fee at all. On the other hand, those excluded only by skin color or religion may turn to their own. Therefore the same mechanism that produces the "society" doctor produces the "Jewish" doctor.[67]

The power of other occupations is seen in cases where engineers are able to set standards that members of the building crafts must follow and when members of some self-employed occupations (and therefore businessmen) are able to pressure members of other self-employed occupations to keep certain hours because of their common membership in the Chamber of Commerce. Because the training of professionals takes place increasingly in universities, interoccupational relations often take the form of interdepartmental relations. Sociologists question the right of the Home Economics department to produce Family and Home Consultants, mathematicians bemoan the limited amount of mathematics training required of the high school mathematics teacher by the Education department, psychologists dispute the right of the Sociology department to train group dynamics leaders, and all the arts and sciences shudder at the Ph.D.'s being let loose in the community by the Physical Education department.

Public opinion influences the independent professional in many ways. A famous criminal lawyer once stated that any man, whatever he had done, was entitled to a good defense. But what if the lawyer knows his client is guilty of a serious offense and that knowledge of this would affect his chances of acquittal for the crime for which he is being charged? If he conceals this knowledge is he making himself an accessory after the fact, or can he regard himself as being in a position similar to that of the priest who learns of a crime in the confessional? What also shall the accountant who discovers irregularities in his client's conduct of business

[67] A unique form of client control may be experienced by the psychotherapist who finds that a patient whom he is treating for an anxiety neurosis is becoming increasingly anxious because of the psychotherapist's mounting bill.

do? At what point, in other words, do the obligations of confidence and secrecy cease?

Although he is not an independent professional, the social science researcher is worth mentioning in the present context. A special problem has been created within recent years because of the great growth of indirect research techniques (participant observation, projective techniques, forced-choice questionnaires, hidden microphones). In many cases, persons are being studied without their being aware of the real purpose of the research or, in some cases, without their even being aware they are being studied at all. What are the rights, not of scientific inquiry, but of human subjects to be *free from* scientific inquiry? If subjects could prevent such inquiry, they would very likely do so. But then how could social science researchers study many intimate human affairs, such as what takes place in jury rooms, the confessional, and bed (21)? The problem of answering questions such as these and of building a favorable climate of opinion for occupational members have contributed overwhelmingly to the great growth of professional associations in recent years.

In sum, no occupations, even the independent professions, escape societal controls. The liquor interests advocate moderation. We allow the playwright and actor some license to satirize society and be risqué, but the censor is never far away. Society keeps a wary eye on its occupations, on some more than others.

In this chapter we first described the occupational status system. We saw that status rank was affected by many factors, such as family, wealth, ethnicity, and race but that occupation was one of the most important and dynamic of all. Occupational status itself was related to type of industry, income, the white-collar—manual distinction, degree of authority, freedom permitted, amount of preparation, and the manipulation of symbols.

Our attention then turned to the means by which persons can acquire occupational status. We described how occupations restrict those permitted to secure the requisite learning, control the learning itself, and ceremonially admit those considered worthy. Once admitted, the individual is controlled by folkways, mores, and sanctions from within, and by clients, other occupations, and public opinion from without.

We are now in a position to study the career of the individual as he moves through time in his occupation.

CHAPTER REFERENCES

1. Anderson, N., *The Hobo,* Chicago: University of Chicago Press, 1923.
2. ———, *Men On The Move,* Chicago: University of Chicago Press, 1940.
3. Barnard, C. I., "Education For Executives," *The Journal of Business of the University of Chicago,* 18:175–182, 1945.
4. ———, "Functions and Pathology of Status Systems in Formal Organizations," in Whyte, W. F. (ed.), *Industry and Society,* New York: McGraw-Hill, 1946.
5. Bendix, R., *Work and Authority in Industry: Ideologies of Management in the Course of Industrialization,* New York: Wiley; London: Chapman and Hall, 1956.
6. Boas, F., "The Potlatch of the Kwakiutl Indians," in Kroeber, A. L. and Waterman, T. T. (eds.), *Source Book in Anthropology,* New York: Harcourt, Brace, 1931.
7. Caplow, T., *The Sociology of Work,* Minneapolis: University of Minnesota Press, 1954.
8. Chapple, E. D. and Coon, C. S., *Principles of Anthropology,* New York: Henry Holt, 1942.
9. Clark, H. F., *Economic Theory and Correct Occupational Distribution,* New York: Teachers College Bureau of Publications, 1931.
10. ——— and Pancoast, O., Jr., *Occupational Mobility,* New York: Columbia University Press, 1941.
11. Cooley, C. H., *Human Nature and the Social Order,* New York: Scribners, 1902.
12. Davis, K., "A Conceptual Analysis of Stratification," *American Sociological Review,* 7:309–321, 1942.
13. Dublin, L. I.; Lotká, A. J.; and Spiegelman, M., *The Money Value of a Man,* New York: Ronald, 1946.
14. Endres, F. C., *The Social Structure and Corresponding Ideologies of the German Officers' Corps Before the World War,* in *Archiv fur Sozialwissenschaft und Sozialpolitik,* 58:282–319, 1927. Ellison, S. (trans.), New York, 1937.
15. Ferguson, C. W., *Fifty Million Brothers,* New York and Toronto: Farrar and Rinehart. 1937.
16. Gardner, B. B. and Moore, D. G., *Human Relations in Industry,* Homewood, Ill.: Irwin, 1952.
17. Gerth, H. H. and Mills, C. W. (trans. and eds.), *From Max Weber: Essays in Sociology,* New York: Oxford, 1946, pp. 180–195.
18. Giles, Nell, *Punch in Susie! A Woman's War Factory Diary,* New York: Harper, 1943.

19. Goffman, E., "Symbols of Class Status," *The British Journal of Sociology*, 2:294–304, 1951.
20. Goldhamer, H. and Shils, E. A., "Types of Power and Status," *American Journal of Sociology*, 45:171–182, 1939.
21. Gross, E., "Social Science Techniques: a Problem of Power and Responsibility," *Scientific Monthly*, 83:242–247, 1956.
22. Hancock, R. S., "Occupation and Credit Risk: The Occupational Credit Pattern," *Current Economic Comment*, 14:27–35, 1952.
23. Henderson, A. M. and Parsons, T. (trans. and ed.), *Max Weber: The Theory of Social and Economic Organization*, New York: Oxford, 1947.
24. Hughes, E. C., *A Study of a Secular Institution: The Chicago Real Estate Board*, Ph.D. thesis (unpub.), Dept. of Sociology, University of Chicago, 1928.
25. James, W., *The Principles of Psychology*, London: Macmillan, 1890, Vol. I.
26. Lester, R. A., *Economics of Labor*, New York: Macmillan, 1941.
27. Lewis, L. E., "City Comparisons of Wage Levels and Skill Differentials," *Monthly Labor Review*, 74:643–647, 1952.
28. Linton, R., *The Study of Man*, New York: Appleton-Century, 1936.
29. Lipset, S. M., "The Sources of the Radical Right," in Bell, D. (ed.), *The New American Right*, New York: Criterion, 1955, Ch. 7.
30. ———, and Bendix, R., "Social Status and Social Structure: A Re-Examination of Data and Interpretations: I," *The British Journal of Sociology*, 2:150–168, 1951.
31. ———, "Social Status and Social Structure: A Re-Examination of Data and Interpretations: II," *The British Journal of Sociology*, 2:230–254, 1951.
32. Matthews, T. J., *The Urban Fire Station: A Sociological Analysis of an Occupation*, Unpub. M. A. thesis, Department of Sociology, The State College of Washington, 1950.
33. Mead, G. H., *Mind, Self and Society*, Chicago: University of Chicago Press, 1934.
34. Merz, C., *The Great American Bandwagon*, New York: Day, 1928.
35. Miller, H. P., *Income of the American People*, New York: Wiley, 1955.
36. Ober, H., "Occupational Wage Differentials, 1907–1947," *Monthly Labor Review*, 67:127–134, 1948.
37. Parsons, T., "An Analytical Approach to the Theory of Social Stratification," *American Journal of Sociology*, 45:841–862, 1940.
38. ———, "A Revised Analytical Approach to the Theory of Social Stratification," in Bendix, R. and Lipset, S. M. (eds.), *Class, Status and Power*, Glencoe, Ill.: Free Press, 1953.
39. Peterson, F., *Survey of Labor Economics*, New York: Harper, 1951.
40. Richmond, A. H., *Colour Prejudice in Britain: A Study of West Indian Workers in Liverpool, 1941–1951*, London: Routledge and Kegan Paul, 1954.
41. Sanford, E. P., *Hourly Earnings of Employees in Large and Small Enterprises*, Temporary National Economic Committee, Monog. 14, U.S. Government Printing Office, 1940.

42. Sanford, E. P., "Wage Rates and Hours of Labor in the Building Trades," *Monthly Labor Review*, 45:281–300, 1937.

43. Scott, J. F. and Lynton, R. P., *The Community Factor in Modern Technology*, UNESCO, International Documents Service, New York: Columbia University Press, 1952.

44. Speier, H., "Honor and Social Structure," *Social Research*, 2:74–97, 1935.

45. Spencer, H., *The Principles of Sociology*, New York and London: Appleton, 1910.

46. Strong, S. M., "Negro-White Relations as Reflected in Social Types," *American Journal of Sociology*, 52:23–30, 1946.

47. ———, "Social Types in a Minority Group: Formulation of a Method," *American Journal of Sociology*, 48:563–573, 1943.

48. Sutherland, E. H. (annot. and interpret.), *The Professional Thief*, Chicago: University of Chicago Press, 1937.

49. Thomas, L. G., *The Occupational Structure and Education*, Englewood Cliffs, N.J.: Prentice-Hall, 1956.

50. *Time*, 64:45, Dec. 27, 1954.

51. Wirth, L., "Some Jewish Types of Personality," in Burgess, E. W. (ed.), *The Urban Community*, Chicago: University of Chicago Press, 1926.

52. Zorbaugh, H. W., "The Dweller in Furnished Rooms: An Urban Type," in Burgess, E. W. (ed.), *The Urban Community*, Chicago: University of Chicago Press, 1926.

53. ———, *The Gold Coast and the Slum*, Chicago: University of Chicago Press, 1929.

CHAPTER FIVE
THE CAREER

In this chapter, we turn our attention to the movement of the individual through the occupational system: how he enters it, increases, maintains, or decreases his occupational prestige, power, or economic position, and seeks some sense of personal worth in his work which has meaning in his family and in the community.

In recent years students of social stratification have done a good deal of research on social mobility. This research will be of help to us, but it must be borne in mind that it is tangential to our interest which is in *work as represented by occupations,* and not in social stratification processes themselves. Our major categories are: occupational social selection, occupational mobility, occupational career contingencies, and occupation and the self.

OCCUPATIONAL SOCIAL SELECTION

Parsons, in a capsule introduction to his general theory of social action (143, p. 93), states:

We conceive action to be oriented to the attainment of goals, and hence to involve selective processes relative to goals.

If we bear in mind that "selection" does not necessarily imply that the individual is himself conscious of the fact that he chooses, and, further, that the choice may be made by others for him, then we have the core of the idea of social selection. Theoretically, persons in our culture are free to enter any occupation, and through compulsory education and subsidies we try to equalize opportunities to secure needed training. But many other factors affect the probability of entry to an occupation. Instead, then, of speaking of persons as *choosing* an occupation (though all may try), we find it more revealing to ask how they are selected for the occupation. This approach leads us to focus on such factors as family, location, sex, age, access to education, social class, race, and national origin. This process we call *social selection* by analogy with the process of natural selection in Darwinian theory.[1] And it is no more than an analogy: humans are often aware of the choices they make or might have made. We may, therefore, examine social selection under three general headings: the relation between the individual's conscious choice and his subsequent occupation: forces that affect the individual as he grows up and which move him, inexorably, in certain directions; and, finally, the resistance that occupational groups themselves offer to the outsider who seeks entrance.

THE ROLE OF CHOICE

Although we agree with Caplow's assertion (25) that there are universal principles governing the recruitment of persons to occupations, we add that cross-cultural differences are also important. In Dobu and Eire, it will be recalled, the individual had little chance to exercise any choice of occupation. The culture largely determined what an individual would do when he grew to maturity. In our culture, there is much more choice possible, and in most discussions, the range of choices is strongly emphasized. This emphasis occurs for two reasons. First, most studies simply ask a person, usually a high school or college student, what occupation he would like to enter. And if one adds up all occupations, the total number is well over 20,000, so that it looks like the individual has a tremendous number from which to choose. But this is as fallacious as saying that since there are millions of eligible men in the world at any given time, a woman should have no trouble finding a husband to her liking. Obviously, the *actual* choice available to the individual will be within a much smaller range. A second reason why the range of choices is likely to be overemphasized is that most studies are not followed up.

[1] It will be recalled that under this theory it is assumed that if some animals are better adapted than others to survival in the environment through special characteristics which they attained through mutations, then those animals will survive and the others will die off. There are thus certain forces which operate which determine what sort of animal shall survive. Similarly in the occupational world, we maintain that there are certain forces operating which determine which persons shall enter an occupation and which shall not. This we conceive of as a process of *social* selection.

Therefore, one gets a picture only of what people would *like*, and that will be very different from what a realistic appraisal of opportunities would show. And, speaking generally, it is important to bear in mind that ours is a culture that emphasizes choice as a virtue and a duty. Parents are expected to choose wisely a neighborhood in which to live so that their children will have wholesome playmates. Children in school, often at an untimely age, are expected to choose a course of study which may affect their whole careers. Later, they must exercise intelligence in the choice of a wife or husband. When an election comes, they are told that they may vote for whom they choose, but they have a moral obligation to vote. In such a culture, when one thrusts a questionnaire at a person and asks him to *choose* an occupation, even the person who has not thought much about it or imagines vaguely that he will go into his father's business, is likely to put down his "choice" like everyone else.[2]

It is not surprising, then, that many studies show a discrepancy between expressed choice and actual occupations. Miller and Form (123, pp. 588–92) refer to an unpublished survey made in Canton, Ohio high schools in 1937, in which the choices of students in the twelfth year of school are compared with the occupations of the students who left school six years previously (1931). The comparison shows a considerable divergence. For example, over one-half of twelfth year males wanted professional positions, but only about one-seventh of the previous graduates were in professional positions. By contrast, less than one-twentieth wanted clerical jobs, whereas over one-fifth of previous graduates were in such jobs (123, p. 591). This was a depression study, and such a discrepancy might be expected from that fact alone, but later studies seem to confirm the findings. Thus, Slocum (174) compared the occupational preferences of students who were high school seniors in Washington in 1954, with the distribution of occupations in the Washington labor force and found large discrepancies. Well over one-third wanted professional positions whereas less than one-tenth of the labor force were in such positions. Clerical work was preferred by almost one-fifth whereas about one-eighth of the labor force were doing clerical work. "Crafts and trades" was chosen by only 7.6 per cent, compared with a figure of 16.0 per cent for the labor force (15).

The existence of such indeterminacy obviously makes prediction

[2] The romantic character of much choosing, especially by the young, was brought out in a recent national survey of youngsters aged thirteen to nineteen. It was reported that the huge proportion of 38 per cent chose one of the professions as their occupational goal. Survey by Gilbert Youth Research Co., reported in syndicated column in *Lewiston (Ida.) Morning Tribune*, Aug. 25, 1957, Sec. 1, p. 5.

hazardous. The indeterminacy, plus the large amount of job-shifting which persons go through, leads some analysts to introduce "accident" as an explanation for the jobs people get (34, p. 301; 123, pp. 651 ff.), or to refer to "trivial" bases for occupational choice. For example, Caplow (26, p. 218) states:

> The bases for decision are often trivial. A student decides to study law because he has gotten his highest grades in history courses, dislikes the idea of teaching, and knows that courses in history are required for entrance to law school. A grade school pupil elects the vocational high school because someone has told him that automobile mechanics get high wages. A high school sophomore transfers from the academic sequence to the clerical course to be with her best friend. The crucial decision to leave school and go to work may reflect the most casual dissatisfaction or the lure of a passing opportunity.

But such factors hardly constitute explanations. In many cases they are rationalizations after-the-fact because the person is himself not aware of the factors motivating him. In any case, the question is why these "accidental" or "trivial" occurrences affect some and not others. In the case of the student who goes to the vocational school because "someone" has told him automobile mechanics make high wages, why is it that another student who hears the same story does not transfer schools? Or it may be that the "someone" did not get a chance to tell him to begin with. Everyone is exposed to accidental occurrences and contacts and, therefore, we must ask why some are apparently in a state of readiness to respond and others are not. The problem is one of selectivity. In any case, "accident," as an explanatory factor, should only be introduced as a last resort after generations of research have failed to turn up anything better. And in this area of study, we are at the very *beginning* of research. Furthermore, such explanations are in many cases superficial. A *particular* choice may be based on a trivial factor, but here we are talking about a precipitating rather than an underlying factor. Thus, it may well have been the suggestion of a friend that led a person to seek a job at a factory rather than, say, at a warehouse. But if we look more closely, we note that the job at the factory and the job he would probably have gotten at the warehouse are both semiskilled, and manual, and if we consult a study by Lipset and Bendix, we learn that although they record much shifting of persons between different occupations, they find little permanent shifting between manual and nonmanual occupations.[3] Finally, the influence of friends is not trivial, but a very important selective force. In short, "choice" should be ex-

[3] See (103). The authors' sample was made up of 935 working heads of families in Oakland, California.

amined in the context of the realistic alternatives open to the individual, his knowledge of them, and his access to them.[4]

THE CULTURAL PERSPECTIVE

By the cultural perspective we understand the process by which a culture channels the occupational ambitions of its young by limiting the alternatives available and endowing some with higher value than others. The occupational perspective is wider in Eire than it is in Dobu, and wider by far in our society than in Eire. Indeed, the very width of this choice helps keep alive the American dream. But the range is, nevertheless, limited.

Further, although Sharp (169, p. 89) has pointed out how the *lowering* of the status of government work in France has led to recruitment problems, while Green (67), in contrast, tells us that the *high* status of government work in Ceylon has led to the neglect of other much-needed work, nevertheless we tend to find in all stable cultures a well-defined set of ambitions. Davis and Moore (40) point out that a function of any stratification system is to attract persons to statuses and then to get them to fulfill the duties associated with each status. This the culture accomplishes by a set of differential rewards.[5] The result is that, in every society, occupations have different amounts of prestige, economic rewards, and power, and this situation has the effect of holding up certain occupations as more worthy of pursuit than others.[6] Any occupational scale, then, is not only a record of differential rank, but is also a crude picture of the values of the society and the directions in which young persons are being encouraged to go. If we look at one of the most widely used scales—the North-Hatt or NORC scale (135, pp. 411–26)—in this manner, we find that the national sample that was asked why they said a job had "excellent standing," gave the following reasons.

The job pays so well	18%
It serves humanity; it is an essential job	16

[4] This is not, of course, to deny the value of studying the hopes and dreams of persons and the relation of these dreams to reality. Indeed, some cultures—ours is one of them—encourage such dreaming—a factor that helps explain the "open-class" character of our culture as we shall note below.

[5] This is not, of course, to deny that there are inconsistencies and clumps of occupations which may not even be comparable with one another. See (71, 187).

[6] This process may get out of hand and become perverted. Thus, Merton (119, pp. 125–49) has pointed out that although rewards are intended to be motivations, they may become detached from the legitimate means prescribed for their achievement. If a society emphasizes success as the major reward, but does not also distribute widely enough the means to success, then some persons will engage in deviant behavior to achieve success. In this sense, deviance has been "built into" the social structure.

Preparation requires much education, hard work and money   14
The job carries social prestige   14
It requires high moral standards, honesty, responsibility   9
It requires intelligence and ability   9
It provides security, steady work   5
The job has a good future; the field is not overcrowded   3
The job is pleasant, safe, and easy   2
It affords maximum chance for initiative and freedom   *
Miscellaneous answers; don't know; no answer   10

* Less than 0.5%.

It is interesting to note that although amount of pay heads the list, that category does not dwarf any other; indeed, no category does, a fact suggestive of lack of emphasis of our society on one particular goal, as Parsons (144, pp. 112–115) has pointed out.[7] On the other hand, Taft (182) reports that an Australian sample felt that the status of an occupation depended *most* on the required amount of education, intelligence, the interest of the work, and its importance to the community, and depended *least* on size of income, working conditions, and stability.[8]

The foregoing discussion relates to the culture as a whole. No one, however, participates wholly in all of Western culture but instead, each person participates only in a small part of it. As a consequence, his cultural perspective is considerably narrower than has been indicated thus far. We shall give special attention to the roles of the family, physical location, sex and age, education, and social class.

The family is the medium through which cultural imperatives are brought to bear on the growing child. It is not, then, surprising to learn that a considerable part of his job horizon is defined for him by his family. A major question is how many occupations the individual's family knows about or is sympathetic towards. Mangione (115, pp. 232–33) has given us an excellent illustration in his record of the attitudes of his family—Sicilian immigrants to Rochester, N.Y.—to his decision to become a writer:

My relatives were nettled to hear that instead of studying medicine, law, or pharmacy I planned to study no particular subject but a number of subjects, with the idea of equipping myself for newspaper work. My aunt Giovanna threw up her hands. *"Ma chi si stupiddu!,"* she said. "Such dirty work printing a newspaper. Why don't you take up a cleaner profession?"

[7] It should, however, be borne in mind that respondents were asked to give *only one main thing*. The results might have been quite different if several could have been listed by each respondent.

[8] On this point, see (22, 62). There is also evidence that persons in different countries tend to rate occupations in a remarkably consistent manner. We shall consider this evidence presently.

I tried to explain how clean the newspaper profession was, and that writing for a newspaper did not mean setting type. She could not understand. "If you intend to dirty your hands, why waste your hard-earned money and your parents' on a college education? Why not become a *briccoliere* like your Uncle Luigi? When there is work he makes ten dollars a day."

My mother was not sure what I was talking about when I told her I was going to write for a living. She looked worried and said she should never have permitted me to read so many books. She begged me not to waste my education on something so uncertain as the writing profession. Could I not become a teacher instead; or at least train to be a teacher, so that I would have something to fall back on if I couldn't earn a livelihood as a writer? *Maestro*. It was obviously the fourth item on her list of the most respected professions. I was the oldest, the only one in the family who was going to get a college education. It was important to her that I bring honor to the family by training myself for a profession my relatives recognized and respected. Writing was no profession. Anyone who had any education at all wrote. So she argued. I didn't want to hurt her; I promised I would train myself as a teacher as well as a writer.

Mangione's experience illustrates the significance of the cultural perspective for immigrant ethnic groups who have suffered restriction over many generations. As a consequence of such occupational restriction, a child's father knows only his own and a few related occupations, and it is these occupations the growing child is exposed to. It makes a difference to his ambition pattern whether the voices from the living-room that he listens to in bed (when he should be asleep) are those of successful lawyers or of successful pickpockets. Only in connection with the occupations that his father and his friends know about is the child likely to receive assistance or even understanding. This process, after many generations, produces the ethnic and religious concentrations in certain occupations and industries which, although often much exaggerated, do exist: Italians in the fruit and vegetable business and in the needle-trades; Eastern European Jewish persons in retail business and the professions; Japanese in fishing; and the Irish on the police force.[9] Here, then, we have a powerful restriction on the individual's career goals which operates *from within*. It is not simply a matter of an outside group's forbidding the individual entrance; rather, he is effectively prevented from entering by the fact that the group in which he grows up simply does not know [10] about the occupation, does not understand it,

[9] See (82, pp. 83–93; 85, p. 165; 90, pp. 131–46; 99, pp. 312–15; 148, pp. 184–87; 172, Chs. 12, 13; 208, pp. 60–61, 64).

[10] The phenomenon of ignorance of occupational alternatives is not, of course, exclusively a family phenomenon. Some occupations are esoteric and simply not widely known, while others are given widespread publicity. Thus American teenagers are aware of the possibility of a career in the entertainment industry, for that industry has often been the locale for movie and TV dramatic plots. By contrast, Elbridge Sibley (170)

or is unsympathetic toward it. This situation places an additional burden
on him who would enter such an occupation: he must fight his own group.

Occupational inheritance is a continuing theme in analyses of social
mobility, but it is also relevant to an understanding of the role of the
family in occupational selection. On the whole, most studies confirm

TABLE 10
OCCUPATIONAL INHERITANCE IN TWO GENERATIONS
IN MARION COUNTY, INDIANA *

	ACTUAL INHERITANCE (in percentages)		ACTUAL INHERITANCE COMPARED TO EXPECTED	
	1910	1940	1910	1940
Professional	20.95	28.27	5.53	5.10
Semi-professional	27.03	19.30	14.61	6.23
Proprietors, etc.	21.07	17.62	2.96	2.66
Clerical and sales	43.70	42.21	2.40	1.91
Skilled	48.65	32.25	1.52	1.47
Semi-skilled	31.60	43.22	1.85	1.60
Unskilled	34.24	28.61	2.87	4.14
Protective Service	2.50	8.30	2.60	3.58
Personal service	14.73	10.37	4.04	3.07
Farming	10.65	4.16	3.17	3.92

* Rogoff, N., *Recent Trends in Occupational Mobility*, Glencoe, Ill.: The Free Press,
1953. Left-hand column figures from Tables 52 and 53, pp. 118 and 119; right-hand
column figures from Table 11, p. 57.

each other in the finding that there is a strong tendency for a son to be
found in the same occupational category as his father. In Table 10
we present the findings of a major study of social mobility trends by
Natalie Rogoff (152).[11] The figures in the left-hand columns are self-
explanatory: they are the percentages of, say, sons of Professionals who
are also Professionals: 20.95 per cent in 1910, and 28.27 per cent in 1940.

---

reports that only one-twentieth of graduate students stated they had decided on graduate work in social studies before entering college, as compared to one-eighth for students in the natural sciences, a fact which he partially attributes to lack of general
knowledge of the possibility of social science careers.

Worth noting also is the finding that manual workers, as compared to nonmanual
workers, are less likely to have had any job plans while still in school and more likely
to have taken a job which was the *only* job they knew of. See (104). Nor is such ignorance always dysfunctional for the whole social system. See (131).

[11] The figures in the left-hand columns are drawn from Tables 52 and 53, pp. 118
and 119; the figures in the right-hand columns are drawn from Table 11, p. 57. We
shall discuss Rogoff's study more thoroughly presently. For the moment, it may be
noted that her study was based on information supplied in marriage application forms
in Marion County, Indiana (Indianapolis and a suburban and rural fringe) for two
periods: July, 1905 through 1912, and from 1938 through the first half of 1941. Her
study was of the entire population of applicants (males only) but she was forced, for
various reasons, to use 57 per cent of this population, which came to around 21,000
applications, divided about equally between the two periods. Although we present
only the data for large occupational groups, it should be remembered that Rogoff in
fact used a more detailed classification involving about 100 occupational categories.

The figures in the right-hand column represent an analysis based on the method of expected cases which Herbert Goldhamer and Natalie Rogoff applied to occupational trend data. Essentially it is a means of controlling the effect of changes in the number of vacant positions in an occupational category. Thus, if an occupational category makes up a large proportion of all workers, then it will not be surprising to find a large proportion of sons of men in the occupation following in their father's footsteps; the demand is high. For example, the table shows that in 1910, 20.95 per cent of the sons of professionals were themselves professionals whereas 48.65 per cent of the sons of skilled workers were themselves skilled workers. From these figures alone one would conclude that occupational inheritance was much commoner among skilled workers than among professionals. But these figures ignore the fact the demand for skilled workers (in numbers) was much higher than the demand for professionals. We get quite a different picture if we ask: what is the probability that the son of a professional will also be a professional? Clearly, if we knew nothing else, the best estimate we could make would be: the probability that the son of a professional will be a professional is the probability that *anyone* will be a professional. The probability that anyone will be a professional is, on the average, the proportion of professionals in the population; in Rogoff's case, this is 3.79 per cent. Therefore on the average, 3.79 out of every 100 sons ought to be found to be a professional. But we find that 20.95 per cent of sons of professionals are professionals. This is 5.53 times as many as we would expect on the basis of chance and this is the figure we find in the right-hand column. On the other hand, a similar analysis for skilled workers produces a surprising result. Although the proportion who followed in their father's footsteps was more than double that of professionals, skilled workers made up 31.99 per cent of the population. Therefore, it turns out that the sons who followed their father's occupations did so only 1.52 times as often as they might have done if the probability of their doing so were a chance phenomenon. Allowing then for the size of the categories, inheritance appears to be more characteristic of professionals than of skilled workers.

Looking now at the table as a whole (152, p. 59) we note the following. In terms of actual proportions: (1) All categories except protective and personal service [12] are high, and, in fact, the occupation of the

[12] We omit reference to "farming" since Miss Rogoff's population was an urban one. Inheritance, in her population, refers to a son of a farmer who is himself a farmer *and* is living in Indianapolis or its immediate environs. Since American farmers do not typically live in town but right on their farms, we can secure an estimate of the degree of inheritance from the data from a national sample which we present below. See Table 11.

father is the *single* most likely destination for any son. (2) The proportions inheriting their father's occupation have increased only for professionals, semiskilled workers, and protective service workers over the
two generations being compared. When we turn to the figures in the
right-hand column, the picture changes in one important respect. We
see that: (1) Occupational inheritance is again high, with every figure
being over one, indicating a greater tendency to enter one's father's occupation than chance requires. (2) The inheritance of sons of protective
service workers has gone up higher than expected, but that of professionals and semiskilled turns out to have *dropped.* Further, inheritance
has increased among the *unskilled* workers.

Rogoff (152, p. 56) herself notes the relatively low ratios for clerical
and semiskilled occupations and attributes them to the weakness of two
factors: "(a) the extent to which the sons consider the father's class to
be rewarding and (b) the extent to which characteristics associated
with the sons' origins (e.g., education, ambition) inhibit mobility out
of the class of origin." But she expresses puzzlement over the low ratios
for skilled workers, a category traditionally thought of as one of those
in which father passed on his skills and secret lore to his son; this
certainly is puzzling. She notes, as we have done, that actual inheritance
is very high among skilled workers; the ratios drop because skilled
workers make up a large proportion of workers. In other words, the
denominator in the ratio or fraction is *high.* We shall offer an alternative explanation presently.

Rogoff's study, in spite of its unique picture of trends and its technique of mobility analysis, is limited to one community. It is worth
while, therefore, to look at a national study for further data on the
subject. In Table 11 we present data from the National Opinion Research Center study (135, pp. 424–25).

TABLE 11

**OCCUPATIONAL INHERITANCE AS REVEALED BY A
NATIONAL SAMPLE OF THE UNITED STATES
POPULATION: 1947** *

	PER CENT OF SAMPLE IN SAME OCCUPATION AS FATHER
Professional people	23
Businessmen	31
White-collar workers	15
Skilled workers	30
Semi-skilled workers	19
Domestic and personal service workers	8
Farmers	84
Non-farm labor	19

* National Opinion Research Center, "Jobs and Occupations: A Popular Evaluation,"
pp. 424–425.

The NORC categories are not comparable to Rogoff's, and there is a period of almost a decade between the two studies (in which occurred World War II), but such rough comparisons as can be made are important. We note again the high proportions of sons who engage in their fathers' occupations and these are roughly near those found by Miss Rogoff. There is only one which is very different: In 1940, 43.22 per cent of the sons of semiskilled fathers were themselves in semiskilled occupations in Marion County, Indiana. By contrast, only 19 per cent of a national sample of semiskilled workers had fathers who were or had been semiskilled. Although it is not revealed, the explanation may lie in the fact that the NORC study included women whereas Miss Rogoff's population did not: the sons of semiskilled workers are far more likely to engage in such work than are the daughters.

We should note, finally, the enormous figure for "farmers." This category positively dwarfs all others.[13]

With these facts in mind, we may next address ourselves to the major factors associated with occupational inheritance. It is important, first, to distinguish the *transmission* of an occupation from what might be called "forced inheritance." The former refers to the situation in which a father actually teaches his son certain skills or helps him in some way to enter his own occupation; for example, the teaching of farm practices to a farmer's son by his father. But the son of a factory laborer may wish to stay *out* of his father's occupation, and may *try* to do so, but because of economic or educational limitations or because of a narrow cultural perspective, may end up, like his dad, as a factory laborer. A statistical study will, of course, record this case as one of inheritance but the mechanisms are clearly very different from the transmission situation just described. A factor of this kind may help explain Rogoff's findings. In Table 11 we note that the right-hand columns in both 1910 and 1940 exhibit U-shaped distributions. It is possible, therefore, that her high ratios among the occupations of high status (professional, semiprofessional, proprietors, etc.) represent transmission, whereas her high ratios among the low-status occupations (unskilled, protective and personal service) represent forced inheritance. At the top, persons follow their fathers because the rewards are high and because their fathers can and do help their sons in various ways; at the bottom, sons also follow their fathers because their fathers are *unable* to help them get out of

[13] Other studies worth consulting are one which also used a national sample (29) and one which, like Rogoff's, concentrated on a single community, that of San Jose, California (36, pp. 162 ff.). A unique type of inquiry has been the degree of self-recruitment into elites. See (183, p. 139; 198, p. 38). The latter found that 26 per cent of the business elite had fathers who were business executives and another 26 per cent had fathers who were business owners.

those low-status occupations. But *in the middle*—clerical and sales, skilled, and semiskilled—the pulls in and out are roughly equal: fathers *can* transmit skills and know-how of various kinds and so make it easy for their sons to follow in their footsteps, but also the forces holding them in to the occupational category are not as strong as they are further down.[14] Of course, an important aspect of any inheritance analysis must be consideration of the size of the occupational groups. One must beware of statistical artifacts.[15]

A second factor influencing occupational inheritance is the presence of a proprietarial element. Caplow (26, pp. 76–77) points out that such an element is especially likely to be present in farming, retail stores, service enterprises, small factories, sales agencies, truck companies, and commercial schools.[16] Here some relatively concrete thing is present

[14] Rogoff herself feels that a factor of this kind may operate for skilled workers when she writes that the ". . . sons of skilled workers were neither as immobile nor as mobile as other sons" (152, p. 57).

[15] One of the most important is the following. Goldhamer, in his preface to Miss Rogoff's book (p. 15) mentions that the ". . . proportion of sons, with fathers in occupation k, who will enter occupation j is a (linear) function of . . . the demand of the society for persons to enter occupation j as defined simply by the proportion of gainfully occupied persons in occupation j." In other words, in the case of the ratios in the right-hand columns of Table 6, when the denominator goes up, the numerator also tends to go up. This produces some strange results. For example, using the Goldhamer-Rogoff ratios, we find that in 1940, the category exhibiting the *highest* inheritance (over expected) was "semi-professional" (draftsmen, embalmers, chiropractors, newspaper writers, nurses [male only, of course], actors). Inheritance among actors does not surprise us but this writer, at least, is amazed to learn that inheritance is so high among male nurses. If we look next at the figures of actual inheritance in the left-hand columns, we find that semi-professionals are about *in the middle* in both 1910 and 1940 (a trifle over 27 per cent and 19 per cent respectively), but they made up only *small* proportions of all workers (2 per cent in 1910 and barely over 3 per cent in 1940). Surely, then, a great part of high inheritance ratios must be attributed to the low size of the denominator (low demand) rather than high size of the numerator (high inheritance). In other words, there appears always to be a great deal of inheritance in every occupation either because of restrictions or because sons have a clear advantage over outsiders in many occupations. But, if the demand for a particular occupation is low, then the sons of men in that occupation will loom particularly large. The net result will be the enormous figures for semi-professional that Miss Rogoff secured. This reservation does not however obviate the clear fact that Miss Rogoff's study is head-and-shoulders above any other trend study because it does take into account the size of occupational groups.

[16] Caplow also calls attention to the "strictly hereditary" occupations, in which an assortment of very special skills are passed down from generation to generation as family secrets: "bell casters, circus performers, croupiers, . . . chefs, gondola (makers), certain kinds of perfumery . . ." (pp. 76, 251). But as Caplow himself hastens to point out, a major factor here is not so much the transmissibility of these skills to children, but rather the very limited markets involved. If there were any significant rise in the demand for bells, we feel confident that those families that have kept their secrets for generations would soon be happy to sell them to a manufacturer rather than face the risk of imitation by a skilled research staff.

which can be handed on intact to the next generation, especially if the inheriting son has become known to and accepted by the steady customers. A similar set of circumstances seem to operate for services. Caplow (26, p. 77) states the essence of the matter as follows:

Occupational inheritance is much more frequent among the children of physicians, who can take over their father's practice intact, than among the children of architects, who cannot.

Of course other factors are involved here, such as differential prestige and income, and the character of the educational process.

The structure of the family is a third factor which affects the likelihood of inheritance of parental occupation. Parsons (142, p. 852) has called attention to the fact that the conjugal family with dependent children is, probably, best adapted to social mobility.

Dependent children are not involved in competition for status in the occupational system, and hence their achievements or lack of them are not likely to be of primary importance to the status of the family group as a whole.

In other words, children remain dependent and share the status of their parents until they are old enough to achieve a status for themselves. But at such a time, they leave the family and strike off on their own. Such a family system, then, would tend to work against the development of occupational inheritance. Barber (8, pp. 361–66) has described the contrasting situation where an extended family in classical China might, for example, support a member in the long education necessary for entrance to the imperial bureaucracy. If the son secured a favorable position, he would be expected to share his good fortune and so raise the position of his family. Such a process might, of course, be used to assist another son to achieve success. Our own discussion of the transmission of farming in the extended family system of Eire provides another illustration.

A fourth factor affecting inheritance has to do with the content of what is transmitted. It is one thing to teach one's son a specific craft, juggling, for example. Quite another thing is the transmission of drives and ambitions, or, simply, a set of attitudes. Faris (48) has pointed out the importance to family stability of the continuous transmission of atmospheres and traditions. But when skills and the character of the market change as rapidly as they do in modern times, it may be that the general attitudes or atmosphere the father transmits is the only thing that has meaning by the time the child reaches adulthood. Of particular importance is the transmission of a belief in the desirability of attending college because of the overwhelming significance of education in occupational advancement within modern times.

A variety of other factors affect the inheritance of occupations. In some occupations, antinepotism rules may be deliberately created to prevent transmission. On the other hand, the reverse may occur as when medical schools give special preference to the applications of sons of physicians, especially previous graduates of that school, or when the sons of craftsmen find it easy to secure admission to their fathers' craft unions. Also important is the difficulty of passing on some kinds of skills or positions in spite of the attempt to do so. The headships of family businesses do not appear to remain in the family's hands for more than two or three generations at the most. Sons are simply not competent to run the business, are not interested in it, or else conditions change so radically that methods that worked so well for a grandfather may be disastrous for the grandson. Still other factors are certain contingencies that we describe below (see pp. 196–201). If occupational requirements change, then what a father teaches may be meaningless, a situation especially likely if an occupation that formerly was learned on the job now requires a college degree, as is the case increasingly with all the professions. Another contingency is related to the period of maximum earnings of the father. If this occurs when a boy is in his teens and thinking seriously about an occupation, he is much more likely to follow his father's occupation than in the situation where his father is still struggling very hard for success, or has already passed his peak.

The occupational perspective of the growing youngster is affected by the location in which he grows up. A rapidly growing area, such as southern California, is likely to present a very different set, not only of ambitions, but of occupations themselves, as compared to a stagnant or declining area such as one sees in some parts of New England or the southern border states. Warner and Abegglen (198, pp. 69–77) report "productivity ratios" of greater than one (indicating a particular region produced more business leaders than was expected on the basis of population at the time the business leaders were born) in the middle Atlantic states, New England, the Pacific states, and the East North Central states. Productivity ratios below one were reported for the South—a broad swath from Texas east and including Kentucky, West Virginia, Maryland, and Delaware. Important also are the occupations that are traditional in a region or in a town. When a town population is dependent on a single industry for its living, the probability that a child will enter that industry is greater than it would be otherwise. Such a factor is, perhaps, especially important for extractive resource industries. On the other hand, small towns may—in a negative way—widen the job horizons of its young people by the very fact that it offers very little to them. Warner and Abegglen (198, pp. 17–18) criticize studies of mobility in small communities as follows:

. . . these community studies were concerned with the problems of the ongoing social structure as seen in a specific locale. Examination of emigration and the subsequent careers of emigrees from these communities were not included in the research designs. It is likely that much of the mobile or potentially mobile populations of these communities was not available to the researchers.

In other words, since the predominant current of migration has been from rural areas to the cities, farm areas and small towns, by forcing their young people to leave, open to them the wider choice available in larger cities. Of course training, experience, and other factors help determine whether they actually get particular jobs or not. But the choice is, nonetheless, much wider than it was in their place of origin.

An important selective factor in every society is that of sex: certain jobs are "men's jobs" and others are "women's jobs." In our society, the matter has become confused because of the entry of women into the labor force in increasing numbers. In 1890, there were about four million women workers, making up about one-sixth of all women over ten years of age and about one-sixth of the working population. By 1956, there were twenty-two million women workers, making up about one-third of all women over fourteen years of age and about one-third of the civilian labor force.[17] These figures do not take account of the volume of women who enter and leave the working population and therefore may not be counted in a census enumeration. It is worth noting, then, that at the close of the century about one-half of adult women worked outside the home *at some time in their lives,* whereas now at least 90 per cent do. Over this same span the average number of years worked increased from eleven to twenty. Of particular significance are changes associated with age and marital status. In 1890, of women who worked, 70 per cent were single and 50 per cent were under twenty-five years of age. By 1956, only 25 per cent were single and 60 per cent were married, whereas around 50 per cent were over forty

[17] It is important not to measure trends solely by census data since the particular proportion employed in a census year may be low, medium, or high. For example, in 1890, women made up 17.4 per cent of all gainful workers ten years of age or over; in 1950, they made up 29.0 per cent of the labor force fourteen years of age and over. But these figures do not measure the potential for in 1945, women made up *36.1* per cent of all workers, though the percentages were high all during World War II. There was a sharp drop of close to 7 per cent in 1946, but then the percentages quickly rose again and have not since dropped below what they were in 1941. See (5).

years of age. Clearly, then, not only are larger proportions of women working, but they are working for larger parts of their lives, and have managed to integrate working with their other important roles of wife and mother. There has also been a distinct shift in the fields in which they work. There have been profound shifts away from unskilled and semiskilled manual work and agriculture, and proportional declines in "traditional" fields like domestic and personal service, teaching, and the clothing and textile industries. On the other hand, they have loomed ever larger in the white-collar ranks which now account for about one-third of all women workers as compared to one-twentieth in 1890.[18] Their motives for working are aptly summarized by the National Manpower Council (134, pp. 19, 20) as follows:

The fifteen-year-old girl who takes a part-time job while in high school in order to earn additional spending money; the twenty-year-old wife who is willing to help her husband complete college by holding a secretarial job, but who looks forward to being a full-time housewife and becoming a mother; the woman of forty-five who took a job in an airplane factory during the war, and has since remained in the labor force; the mother who returns to the teaching profession when her children are of school age; the grandmother in her late fifties who has been practicing medicine throughout her adult life; the sixty-year-old woman who, having just lost her husband, takes a job as a housekeeper; the wife who carries on her husband's real estate business when he is ill; the wife and mother who is a migratory farm worker; the middle-aged mother who works in a department store during the holiday season in order to provide additional family income; the woman who has been a machine operator in garment factories all her adult life; the hourly domestic worker. . . .

Yet in spite of the great increase in numbers, and the strength of these motives, sex-typing appears still to be present and shows little sign of declining in significance. It is true that "traditional" men's jobs have often been invaded by women, but the net effect is usually simply to make these jobs into "women's jobs"; shifts occur, but sexual discrimination appears to have remained. The nature of this sex-typing is well brought out in Table 12.

In Table 12 it is seen that twenty occupations account for nearly three-quarters of all employed women; over one-half are in *eight* occupations. In addition, the occupations in which women are concentrated tend to be *dominated by women:* nearly one-half of all working women are in occupations in which three-quarters or more are women. Women's occupations turn out to be: professional nurses; private household workers;

---

[18] Our figures are drawn from what is perhaps the most thorough study of women workers (134).

stenographers, typists, and secretaries; waitresses; operatives in apparel and other fabricated textile products factories: cashiers; bookkeepers; and teachers.[19] Men, by contrast, are found concentrated as managers and proprietors, craftsmen and foremen, farmers and farm workers, and laborers. Sex-typing goes further than these figures indicate, however. The National Manpower Council (134, p. 60) states:

TABLE 12

OCCUPATIONS EMPLOYING 1 PER CENT OR MORE OF ALL EMPLOYED WOMEN, 1950 *

OCCUPATION	THOUSANDS	PER CENT OF ALL EMPLOYED WOMEN	PER CENT OF TOTAL IN OCCUPATION
1. *Stenographers, typists, and secretaries*	1,501	9.5	94
2. *Clerical and kindred workers, n.e.c.*	1,440	9.2	49
3. *Private household workers*	1,334	8.5	95
4. *Salesmen and sales clerks, n.e.c.*	1,260	8.0	38
5. *Teachers, n.e.c.*	835	5.3	75
6. *Operatives, apparel and other fabricated textile products manufacturing*	655	4.2	81
7. *Bookkeepers*	556	3.5	77
8. *Waiters and waitresses*	546	3.5	82
9. *Nurses, professional*	389	2.5	98
10. *Operatives, textile mill products manufacturing*	355	2.3	53
11. *Telephone operators*	342	2.2	53
12. *Farm laborers, unpaid family workers*	318	2.0	35
13. *Service workers, except private household, n.e.c.*	311	2.0	62
14. *Laundry and dry-cleaning operatives*	288	1.8	67
15. *Cooks, except private household*	242	1.5	56
16. *Retail proprietors*	242	1.5	17
17. *Barbers, beauticians, and manicurists*	190	1.2	50
18. *Operatives, food and kindred products manufacturing*	186	1.2	38
19. *Cashiers*	184	1.2	81
20. *Operatives, electrical machinery, equipment and supplies manufacturing*	180	1.1	54
TOTAL	11,354	72.2	

(n.e.c. = not elsewhere classified)
* National Manpower Council, *Womanpower*, New York: Columbia University Press, 1957, p. 58.

[19] It is worth noting that certain occupations often thought of as nearly completely female turn out to be far from it; especially telephone operators. In turn, certain other occupations have much higher proportions of women than is commonly thought; for example, bookkeepers. From other data (134, pp. 63, 64) we learn that women make up 35 per cent of "authors, editors, reporters," 29 per cent of "personnel and labor relations workers" and a whopping 43 per cent of all postmasters. These are not "clerical" who are reported separately.

Men comprise 25 per cent of the 1.1 million teachers reported in the 1950 census, but most men teach in high schools while most women teach in elementary schools. In high schools the physical sciences and some of the social sciences are usually taught by men, while languages and literature are usually taught by women. In vocational, commercial, and industrial arts classes and physical education, men generally instruct boys, while women teach girls.

Caplow (26, p. 82) has described sexual segregation in retail selling as follows:

The prevailing pattern is that salesmen serve male customers, and saleswomen serve female customers. Where the customers are mixed in gender, the sales force follows the majority. An exception is made for very heavy or very valuable commodities, which are commonly sold by men. A whole set of folkways is developed on the basis of these principles. Thus, in a normally organized department store, there will be men in the sports-goods department, women to sell curtains and dishware, men to sell hardware, women to sell books, but men to sell wedding silver and furniture.

Even more remarkable than these cases is the fact that what is regarded as a man's job in one city may be considered a woman's job in another city close by. For example, in 1950, 43 per cent of those who wait on tables in New York City were men whereas 85 per cent in Philadelphia were women (134, p. 82). But in spite of these striking differences one should certainly not conclude that sex-typing is purely arbitrary or always based on mythical foundations. The very fact that women will work for lower wages may lead management to hire them for "traditional men's jobs" whether the men so employed like it or not.[20] The National Manpower Council (134, p. 236) calls our attention to the fact that the role of women as purchasers of retail products has affected their likelihood of being employed:

The recognition of women's importance as purchasers has had a direct effect upon the employment of women in sales, demonstration, and advertising. Women are now commonly employed to sell men's shirts and other men's furnishings in department stores because it was found that women constituted a majority of the buyers of these items.

But whatever the reasons, the evidence speaks loudly for the existence of sexual segregation in the United States as in all other cultures.

We have then two sets of facts to reconcile: on the one hand is

[20] Employers themselves, however, rarely give this as an explanation for why they hire women workers (134, p. 88).

the increasing number of women, of all marital statuses and ages, who are employed; on the other hand, there is a definite conception of men's and women's jobs, so that women find entry into many jobs very difficult or impossible. Does the former trend imply that sex-typing in occupations will disappear or decline greatly in the United States?

The answer seems to be a loud NO. The National Manpower Council (134, Ch. XI) classifies the motives for women's working into five major groups: the desire to earn money; the preference for, say, office work over unpaid housework; the search for meaningful activity when the family has shrunk or the children need little care for much of the day; the desire to utilize their earlier education or training; and the plain desire to avoid wasting time. It is important to note that *not one* of these motives involves or even suggests a rejection of the roles of wife and mother.[21] Slocum and Empey (175, p. 26), in turn, confirmed the findings of many researchers, when they reported that even college girls (who might be expected to be comparatively more career-oriented than a general sample of women) definitely prefer marriage over a career, or marriage *and* a career over a career without marriage:

Seven out of ten college undergraduate girls said that they believed they could successfully combine marriage and an outside occupational career. But their responses indicated a much greater loyalty to traditional definitions of sex roles than to the idea of occupational emancipation for women.

In the first place, eight out of ten college women said they preferred marriage to a career. Only 8 per cent said they preferred the latter, and the remainder were unsure. Secondly, in reply to the question, "What, in your opinion, is the most important duty of a woman to society?," their replies were strikingly similar to those of college men . . . over two-thirds of both sexes felt that woman's most important duty was to marry and have a family; most of the remainder said it was to combine marriage and a career. Only 2 out of each 100 women listed "a productive occupational career" as woman's most important duty.

The evidence, then, tends to fill out in more detail the picture given by Parsons of the functional significance of sexual role segregation for the American family. Whereas the husband is expected to have a job and be the family breadwinner:

[21] Some might argue that the rejection of unpaid household work represents a kind of role rejection of the traditional (especially rural) housewifely role. For some women it unquestionably does, particularly in cases where the rejection of household chores is only symbolic of more deep-seated personality or adjustment problems. But for a large (and unknown) proportion this rejection is simply a realistic recognition that household chores are today, with the help of labor-saving devices, hardly even a decent challenge to the modern woman. These remarks are, it should be added, more distinctly characteristic of middle-class, rather than lower-class women.

In the case of the feminine role the situation is radically different. The majority of married women, of course, are not employed, but even of those that are a very large proportion do not have jobs which are in basic competition for status with those of their husbands . . . In . . . (the) urban situation the primary status-carrying role is in a sense that of housewife. The woman's fundamental status is that of her husband's wife, the mother of his children, and traditionally the person responsible for a complex of activities in connection with the management of the household, care of children, etc.

Parsons (142, pp. 608–09) goes on to point out that in addition to housewife, there are three other roles a wife may assume: "common humanistic" role (art, community welfare, "serious" interests), "glamor" role, and careerist. Then, since housewife and "common humanistic" roles are not satisfying to many wives, and the latter two roles threaten the stability of the family, the married woman's role is, in sum, unstable. But the data we have just presented show that a fifth role is possible and being assumed by an increasing number of women: the housewife who works but continues to regard her role as wife and mother as her major one. She is able to accomplish this by *limiting* herself to a distinct set of occupations (which may, however, change over time) rather than to try to enter full scale into direct competition with men, for the latter would force her to give her primary attention to her job rather than to her family. The increased employment of women appears to have been accomplished (134, p. 234) :

. . . more through increased employment in occupations held by women and by the emergence of new "women's" occupations than through the entrance of women into occupations formerly considered exclusively male.

The cost of such segregation has been lower wages and a reluctance of employers to promote persons who clearly regard their jobs as of secondary significance.[22]

Education, as a selective force, presents a paradox. On the one hand, it is now the major avenue of entrance to high status occupations and of upward occupational mobility. Warner and Abegglen (198, pp. 99–114), for example, report that their business leaders were highly educated men, whatever their level of origin and that this phenomenon was accentuated in their group as compared to the group studied earlier by Taussig and

---

[22] Of course we do not deny or fail to recognize the great importance of careerists among women workers. Such a group appear, however, to represent quite a different group from those we have been discussing (though they dominate the proportions in the profession). Further, they seem to enjoy distinctly higher wages and faster promotion than women who try to carry on both family and job. See (134, pp. 67 ff.).

Joslyn. But on the other hand, the educational system itself is one of the greatest of all restrictors in our society. Its restrictive efforts are manifested in three important ways. First, our junior and senior high schools are organized into curricula (general, academic, vocational) which force students to make a selection when very young. Once made, the student has, in effect, rejected a large number of possible occupations to which his chosen curriculum does not lead, and by the time he finds out, it is often too late to change. Caplow (26, p. 220) describes how this process is continued into college:

As the processes of occupational selection are moved into the educational system, they take on an academic coloration. Intellectual competence becomes a requirement for many occupations in which dexterity or mere inclination were once sufficient. The humanities and the social sciences are considered essential for the well-rounded realtor or veterinarian. This has the effect of continually lengthening the curriculum, especially that part of it which precedes professional training. The effect is to lower the age of occupational choice *within* the educational institution and to raise the age at which the working career begins. The sophomore at a university finds himself already restricted to a particular group of occupations. If preparing for a course in business, he will be fairly well debarred from specialization in science or medicine. If his studies are centered in an agricultural field, he cannot, without considerable loss of time, turn to journalism or social work. Increasingly, then, occupational choices are made at a time when the student is still remote from the world of work. They are made in terms of school requirements, which may call for quite different abilities and tastes from those which will be related to the eventual job.

Except for that tiny minority whose occupational choices are crystallized in childhood or early adolescence, choices occur at points where they are built into the educational system. They cannot be evaded. Under the emerging system of occupational determination, complete passivity on the part of the student is itself a choice. If he does not elect the appropriate subjects in his early years of high school, he rejects in effect the occupations for which college training is required. If he omits the natural sciences in favor of the social sciences, he eliminates himself as a candidate for thousands of industrial jobs, and if he ignores both of them, he will never be qualified for the beginning ranks of government service.

Second, the school is one of the major places in which social class restrictions on occupational choice make themselves apparent. As we have pointed out earlier, teachers tend to encourage middle-class children to go on to college, with the result that lower-class children will choose the vocational or general curriculum. The result is that middle-class children get a chance to enter the professions and semiprofessions which require higher education, whereas lower-class children leave high school and find themselves forced to take manual or clerical jobs requiring little education.[23] And third, the particular school attended affects one's probability of entering certain occupations, especially those of high status. Of course, upper-class schools, which deliberately prepared the sons of the great to replace their fathers, have always tried, as Mack (114) has shown, to teach not only appropriate knowledge (whether it was Greek and Latin, or music, or skills considered proper to a certain style of life, e.g., riding, fencing, etc.) but also appropriate attitudes and standards. Patricia S. West (203, pp. 465–80) has examined the selectivity of American colleges and found a considerable cleavage between students who supported themselves in college and those who did not. She found that though the former are very important as a proportion of the increase in college attendance, they tend to enter the *more poorly paying* professions (education, ministry, or the arts, rather than medicine, dentistry, or law). Further, when she restricted her attention to the self-help group alone, she found that college attended made a definite difference in subsequent earnings, with the Ivy League colleges scoring at the top. Clearly, then, the relation between education and occupational selection is not simply a matter of widening one's job horizons, for factors restricting choice are present right up to the end of even the college graduate's education (72).

A final factor which strongly affects one's job horizon is that of social class. Like education, the primary effect of social class restrictions on one's occupational perspective is to narrow one's choice to those one's class knows about, is sympathetic toward, or can help one with. In practice, however, this turns out to be primarily a mobility or aspirational matter, rather than one of social selection. That is, the social class of a person seems to affect more the prestige, power, or economic position of the occupation he tries to enter rather than the particular occupation itself. But since occupations do differ in prestige, power, and economic position, a net effect here is to shunt lower-class persons to semiskilled and personal service occupations and to open the possibility of professional positions to middle-class persons. The nature of this process will be described below.

POSITIVE RESTRICTIONS

Our discussion has been concentrated thus far on selective factors which operate from *within* the individual's orientation groups. These are especially important to examine since they are often hidden. On the other hand, there are also a set of factors within occupations which

[23] We shall discuss the role of social class itself presently. But see A. B. Hollingshead's intensive study of the role of social class in curriculum selection (78, pp. 168 ff.).

deliberately resist the attempted entry of persons to the occupation. Since these are usually more obvious and easier to detect, we need not give so much attention to them here. We have already discussed the major restriction on entry which results from preventing persons from securing the learning necessary to enter an occupation. (See pp. 128–134.) But even though persons have this learning, occupations will often attempt to be as exclusive as possible: in part because they wish to regulate the numbers who enter (and therefore control the market for the occupation's services), and in part because members of occupations are also members of society and will reflect, in their attitudes toward race, religion, ethnicity, or in their occupational stereotypes, whatever the society happens to believe. Rogoff has given us the data on the mobility of whites as compared to Negroes, presented in Table 13 below.

TABLE 13
RATIO OF AVERAGE MOBILITY OUT OF EACH CLASS TO AVERAGE MOBILITY INTO THAT CLASS, BY RACE AND OCCUPATIONAL CLASS *

OCCUPATIONAL CLASS	OUT: IN RATIO	
	NEGRO	WHITE
Professional and semi-professional	2.29	0.76
Proprietors, etc.	1.56	0.93
Clerical and sales	6.95	0.72
Skilled	4.44	0.88
Semi-skilled	1.68	1.81
Unskilled	0.13	1.56
Service	0.36	1.04
Farming	4.51	2.50

* Rogoff, N., *Recent Trends in Occupational Mobility*, Glencoe, Ill.: The Free Press, 1953, Table 19, p. 71.

As the title of the table suggests, the ratios in the table compare the average mobility out of an occupational class with the average mobility into that class. This is a measure of "reciprocity"; ratios below one indicate occupations which are more likely to be the destination than the origin of occupational movement. It is noteworthy that for the Negroes, the ratio is below one for only two occupational classes: unskilled and service. Rogoff (152, p. 71) comments:

These two classes represent the occupational destination of two-thirds of all Negro sons. Therefore, in all other classes in the Negro occupational structure, the flow of movement is preponderantly out of the class of origin and into the unskilled and service classes.

The American Negro will be made aware of such restrictive patterns, and the result will be more Negroes in occupations wherein Negroes do not compete with whites for jobs or clientele: we are likely to find proportionately more Negro preachers than we will Negro doctors. Rogoff finds only one partial exception to the engulfing movement of Negroes into unskilled and service occupations: the proprietor class. This group more nearly resembles the white pattern than does any other occupational group. Rogoff (152, p. 73) says of this group:

> For the most part, the Negro proprietors are self-employed in retail trade or contracting work. These are the only occupations in the Negro structure (apart from the few professionals) which perform services for the Negro population alone. Unlike the other Negro classes, the demand for workers in the proprietor class is determined solely by the needs of the Negro population. In all other occupations the mobility of Negroes is determined by the opportunities made available to them in the predominantly white social structure.

The Negro sharecropper may not be sensitive to these blocks; his cultural perspective may prevent his knowing or thinking seriously about careers in engineering, accounting, or public relations. But the sophisticated, educated Negro is very much aware of and perhaps belligerent about such blocks. Sometimes he may try to protect his child by not telling him of these restrictions, but the child is likely to find out later.

These restrictions—whether based on race, religion, social class or sex—turn up in school (87). Warner, Havighurst, and Loeb (199, pp. 101–05) have pointed out that the school is a bearer of our cultural values. Who are the teachers? They are likely to be Protestant, white, middle-class, native-born Americans. There is evidence that teachers tend to favor children who are like themselves, and their preference shows up in the giving of high marks, in recommendations for honors, scholarships, and so on.[24] Their middle-class values with reference to sex (91, pp. 148–51, 239–42; 92, Ch. 10), drinking, ambitiousness,[25] and so on are likely to be reflected in their attitude towards the child. To the middle-class teacher the discovery of sex-play or experimentation on the part of a lower-class pupil in her school room may be the occasion for severe reprimand and a consequent coloring of the teacher's attitude toward the child. Such a child may not be encouraged to go on to college or otherwise secure the training that may be necessary for high prestige occupations in our society.

[24] "Teachers represent middle-class attitudes and enforce middle-class values and manners. In playing this role, teachers do two things. They train or seek to train children in middle-class manners and skills. And they select children from the middle and lower classes who appear to be the best candidates for promotion in the social hierarchy" (199, p. 107). See also (117).

[25] See (2; 12, pp. 451–65; 86; Ch. 14; 179, pp. 9–101; 194, pp. 175–84; 195, pp. 72–3; 200, Ch. XV, XX–XXII).

OCCUPATIONAL MOBILITY

The study of mobility is of particular interest to students of American society for ours has been, traditionally, the model *par excellence* of the open-class society. Research in this area has tended to revolve about two major questions: how much mobility is there and what are the processes by which persons change their social positions? The answer to the first question will help us to give a partial answer to the crucial question of whether class lines in the United States are tightening or not, whereas the answer to the second will give us clues for understanding how the traditional "openness" of the United States status structure may be preserved or increased.[26] But before we can discuss the extensive literature on these questions, we must first discuss the very serious problems that are involved in studying mobility so that we will be in a position to assess the relative worth of this literature. Our discussion of mobility will, then, be divided into three sections: the nature of mobility, the amount of mobility, and the process of mobility.[27]

THE NATURE OF MOBILITY

Our concern here is with occupational mobility, which is one type of social mobility.[28] By "social mobility" we mean the *rate of movement* of humans from one social position to another. There are clearly many possible kinds of social mobility: religious mobility (for example, the rate at which Protestants are converted to Catholicism), marital mobility, income mobility,[29] and changes in community prestige and power.[30] Our interest is limited to occupational mobility, though we are, of course,

[26] Assuming, of course, that it is desired to keep open the lines of mobility.

[27] One of the best summaries of the literature on these subjects (written from the point of view of social stratification) is provided by Barber (8). Useful bibliographies are (89; 111; 145; 198, pp. 301–11).

[28] It is important, at the outset, to distinguish social from physical mobility. The latter is that involved in migration or in the movement of a population in or out of the central business district of a city. Although it might seem that there is no danger of confusion, the fact that physical movement is often associated with social movement (as when the employee of a company is sent out to manage one of the company's outlying branches) has led, sometimes, to physical mobility being discussed as if it were another type of mobility, side by side with social mobility. See (26, pp. 88–98). The two belong to totally different orders of analysis.

[29] For example, Mason and Gross (116) found salary to be the best single predictor of prestige among school superintendents. On the other hand, the lack of correspondence between income and prestige leads to confusion and the problem of the four-flusher. See (66).

[30] See (124, pp. 144–54). Lipset and H. L. Zetterberg (107, pp. 155–177) have identified the following dimensions of social mobility: occupational rankings, consumption rankings, social class (interaction), and power rankings.

concerned with the relation between occupational and other kinds of mobility. In a strict sense "occupational mobility" refers to *any* changes in occupation [31] of which the following appear to be the main types.[32] First, we may distinguish between studies of changes between a man's occupation and that of his father (intergenerational mobility) and changes that may befall a man within his own work lifetime (career mobility). For example, a man whose father was an unskilled laborer may himself start his work career as a semi-skilled machine operator and end his career as a factory foreman. But whether one reckons the point of change from what one's father did or what a man did at some previous time in his life, the types of occupational change appear to be of the following main types.

1. A man's *position in his occupation* with relation to his colleagues may change. For example, a businessman may increase or lose customers or trade, a dentist may suffer a change in the kind of clientele he serves, a lawyer may specialize in real-estate work, a man may go to work for a new employer, or a man may move up, or down, or may change departments in a bureaucracy (26, pp. 68–73). In each of these cases, the basis of comparison may be what a man's father did before him, or what the man himself did at some previous time. For example, a businessman may have more trade than his father had before him, or more trade than he himself had last year. Similarly, a man may be higher up in a bureaucracy that his father was, or than he himself was ten years ago. In this type of case, the occupation is the same and is comparable.

2. There may be a *change of occupation* to either an occupation of the same status as the previous occupation, or an occupation of different status from the previous occupation. Again, the son of a carpenter may become a mortician, or a factory operative may go into business for himself. When such a change of occupation occurs, there may occur a change of position *in the occupation* as well. Here there is a problem of com-

---

[31] Such a usage is close to what economists frequently call "labor mobility," though discussions in sociology of occupational mobility rarely include changes in employment status (employed to unemployed, for example). See (140, Ch. 1).

[32] We are deliberately avoiding use of the space analogy first given wide currency by Sorokin (177); namely, "vertical" and "horizontal" mobility. Talcott Parsons (143, pp. 841–42) stated the reasons very well: "This usage is dangerous. It states the analytical problem in terms of a two-dimensional spatial analogy. On the one hand, because stratification constitutes one important range of differentiation, it does not follow that all others can be satisfactorily treated as a single residual category. Thus sex differentiation, occupational differences apart from their relation to stratification, and differences of religious affiliation should not on a priori grounds be treated as if they all involved only values of a single variable with a common unit of variation, 'horizontal distance.' On the other hand, it is equally dangerous to assume a priori that stratification itself can be adequately described as variation on a single quantitative continuum, as the analogy of a dimension of rectilinear space suggests."

parability, but it is perfectly clear that men quite often start their careers not only in a different occupation from their parents' but at the bottom of the new occupation as well. And, in general, within a career, when a man shifts occupations radically, he may have to start anew at the bottom. Such positional changes are, however, generally discussed without reference to the fact of occupational change as such.

3. A man may retain the same occupation and even the same position in it (compared to his father or himself at an earlier time) but the *occupation itself may change* in relation to other occupations. For example, Strauss (181) describes a case in which a loss of status by a group of master mechanics led to a loss of status by the set-up men who typically worked with the mechanics. A man may still own and operate the automobile filling-station he did twenty years ago, but if his business is now a unit in a petroleum company chain and he must buy all his supplies from the company, then his position with reference to other businessmen has changed.

Although it is quite clear that a man who takes over his father's small lunch-counter cafe and converts the business into a national chain of high-prestige restaurants has experienced a very great deal of movement upward in the occupational structure, it is customary to restrict the use of the term "occupational mobility" only to those cases where there has been a change of occupation on the part of a man. In addition, the case of occupational change attributable to changes in the occupational structure is generally treated residually, or as a facet of "occupational trends." (See pp. 67–73.) The net result is that "occupational mobility" comes, in most studies,[33] to refer only to our type (2): the case of a man's changing from the occupation of his father to a different occupation, or of a man's changing from one occupation to another in his own lifetime. We shall follow this practice in the present section, but will also consider our type (3). We shall give attention to intraoccupational changes in the following section.[34]

Before turning to the data, let us note, in passing, some of the major technical problems in the study of occupational mobility. The findings of any mobility study depend, in part, on the *number* of occupational categories the researcher uses: the more detailed the occupational breakdown, the greater the amount of mobility likely to be revealed. The problem is most serious at the lower levels of the occupational scale where such vague designations as "laborer" are closer to invidious prestige judgments than to accurate occupational descriptions. Men doing very different kinds of work in very different industries are all thrown

---

[33] With one very important exception which we shall discuss in detail.
[34] See *Career Contingencies*, pp. 196–201.

together, so that a change within this category does not show up as an
occupational change (141, Ch. 2). Subjects themselves, however, are
likely to make very fine distinctions, especially where *they* are concerned.
A man who has quit his job as lineman for one city and taken the same
job with a private utility company in another city may feel he has improved his occupational future and therefore has moved "up," but the
researcher will remain unimpressed.[35] The fineness of division made by
the subjects of research, in contrast to the broad categories usually preferred by the researcher, may go far toward explaining the frequent
finding of continued faith in the ideology of upward mobility when research studies show relatively little change in mobility over time.[36] The
seriousness of this problem lead A. J. Jaffe and R. O. Carleton (83) to
suspect that all occupational mobility studies are studies of *relative*
rather than absolute mobility.[37] A related problem is brought to our
attention by MacRae's finding (110b) that Massachusetts legislators
often have another occupation to supplement their income. This raises
the question of how persons with two occupations ("moonlighters")
should be classified. More serious is the question of whether to classify
a person by his "present" job or not. Most studies do, yet a finding (to
which we will refer presently) suggests that there is a tremendous amount
of occupational shifting so that one's present occupation may be temporary. The labor force concept of the U.S. Census classifies persons by
present job (job during the Census week). On the other hand, if one
uses "usual job" one gets into the problem of respondents' hopes and
dreams. Perhaps if one were to use the job on which a person has spent

---

[35] A striking illustration of the fineness of division of function in a low-status occupation is provided by J. J. Hecht's study of the domestic servant in 18th century England
(74, Ch. 2). "Upper" domestics were divided into land steward, house steward (if there
was little land), clerk of the kitchen, man-cook, confectioner, baker, valet, butler, and
gardener; and "lower" domestics into coachman, footman, underbutler, undercoachman,
park keeper, gamekeeper, porter, and various "boys." The above groups leave out entirely the various types of female domestics.

[36] This raises the general question of what "success" means in a society; that is, what
change is considered sufficient for an individual to regard himself as a "success." Palmer
(139) reports that a sample of Norristown, Pa. residents studied in 1952 had quite diffuse conceptions of success: "Owning a home, money in the bank, and a 'good' job with
'decent' pay or steady income appear again and again as the visible signs of a successful
life" (p. 19). Job or work career achievement appeared secondary to other values. Obviously, if occupation is of secondary importance, it is hazardous in the extreme to make
judgments about whether class lines are tightening in America on the basis solely of
occupational changes, especially over large categories. See (188, pp. 35–43) for an examination of the effects of increasing emphasis on education.

[37] They write: ". . . since there is no uniquely correct number or classification of
occupations, there can be no uniquely correct levels of occupational mobility. In short
only relative levels of mobility can be measured. If the same measuring procedures are
used for several time periods or several populations, then we compare the relative
amounts of mobility among them" (83, p. 36).

the highest proportion of his working life, one would avoid many problems but this procedure could only be used with mature workers, and
many persons have a number of jobs for considerable periods.[38]

Another problem is presented by the fact that different parts of the
occupational range in any scale are rarely comparable. There are data
which suggest that movement from manual work to owning one's own
business is a much easier move than is moving to semiprofessional status.
Yet most studies would count each such move equally. The sheer number
that move is important; but so is the occupational distance over which
they move, and so is their starting point.[39] Various lesser problems in
the study of mobility may be listed more briefly. When persons have
held many jobs, the usual problem of errors of memory may arise. Most
studies confine themselves to men, or deal with men and women as a
conglomerate group; yet we know the occupational roles of the two
sexes are usually quite different. All occupations are often dealt with
as equivalent (for mobility purposes); yet certainly temporary jobs or
those "between jobs" (say, for seasonal workers) are clearly of different significance than "usual" jobs. Many job changes are of little
significance; for example, a man may be shifted from one to another job
in a factory because of a reshuffling of work schedules. Most students of
this area are concerned about whether mobility is "up" or "down" and
this is certainly an important question; yet often the judgment is made
by the researcher on whatever grounds he thinks proper. Nor is the
subject's judgment any better. Perhaps this should be regarded as a
problem for research, rather than an assumption.

Finally, there is the problem of studying occupational changes over
time. The results from a national study may vary from those of a small
community for, as we pointed out earlier, the more highly mobile persons
may have left the small community. The time at which a study is carried
out may be important: a good deal of our knowledge of occupational
trends is based on studies done during the great depression of the thirties,
and these studies often showed that class lines were tightening. On the
other hand, studies carried on in the post World War II period of prosperity have been notably more optimistic. It is sometimes forgotten that

[38] Form and Miller (55) are among the very few who have moved in this direction in
their use of a three-year period as a minimum for a "stable" job period.

[39] For example, Warner and Abegglen (198) found that one's chances of becoming a
business leader varied depending on the industry one entered. For example, sons of
laborers had the best chances in highway transportation, railroads, electrical machinery,
and personal services, whereas sons of the business elite themselves and professional
men loomed large in brokers and dealers, and a variety of other industries (Table 79,
p. 146). The size of firm also made a difference, with most inheritance occurring in the
smaller firms. In studying those who became proprietors, then, it would be important
to stratify by size of firm, or even type of firm.

in order to study a trend one needs more than one point in time. A considerable number of studies simply ask a sample of men their present occupation and that of their father's. It is then difficult to do more than guess what the trends are, for such a study tells us only how far men have moved relative to their fathers. It does not tell us whether they have moved, on the average, farther than did some previous generation. Nor will comparison of younger men with older men solve the problem. A study of the business elite by *Fortune* magazine which used this procedure was criticized by W. Lloyd Warner and James C. Abegglen (198, p. 18) as follows:

Inevitably, larger proportions of the younger men were found to be from higher status occupations. While *Fortune* concluded that this reflects increased occupational inheritance, the more accurate conclusion is of course that men from higher status backgrounds, advantaged in both tangible and intangible ways by education, money, friends, and way of life, attain these positions at an earlier age.

Equally dangerous are studies which ask men to recall not only their father's occupation but their grandfather's as well. Not only are there memory problems, but as Rogoff (152, p. 108) points out, this procedure means comparing men in different towns or countries with each other. Finally, one should not lose sight of the fact that the relative rank of occupations changes over time [40] as well as of the fact that changes in the relative proportions of the working population found in each occupational category clearly affects the opportunity structure. It is plainly easier to become a professional when the demand of a society for professionals is increasing.[41]

THE AMOUNT OF OCCUPATIONAL MOBILITY

Although J. A. Schumpeter's (162, p. 165) comparison of a social class to an ". . . hotel or an omnibus, always full, but always of different people" gives the impression that there is a great deal of mobility, we wish to know with some precision what the rate of movement is and whether the rate has changed over time or not. Chinoy (31), in what is perhaps the best short statement of the literature on trends, ends up on a note of indecision. Clearly, all the facts are not in yet,[42] and such studies

[40] A good example is the finding by Janowitz and Wright (84), that the prestige of public employment—traditionally low in the United States in belief if not in fact—has risen in recent times.

[41] It is, in part, the fact that this seemingly obvious factor was taken into direct account that makes the Rogoff study so much better than most others.

[42] A situation which makes it possible for such a major figure in social stratification as W. Lloyd Warner to shift his ground from that stated in a book published in 1952 (196), where a rather pessimistic position is stated, to practically the opposite position in a book published in 1955 (198).

as we have are often difficult to assess because of the technical problems we have just discussed. Yet, however serious the problems, the need for knowledge about occupational mobility requires us to see how far these data will lead us. Lewis Corey (33) has pointed out, for example, the significance of the rise of a new middle class for Marxian theory. The industrial proletariat, which under Marxian theory was soon to rebel against its masters, is now challenged by an entirely new middle class— salaried white-collar workers and professionals, rather than the small owners of old. And the rise of this new class provides entirely new avenues of upward mobility and may be helping to prevent the development of the sort of class consciousness Marx foresaw.

Our discussion will divide the studies into two groups: those dealing with local communities, and those with American (and other) societies as a whole. As we pointed out above, local community studies suffer from the grave defect of a shifting population and therefore may understate the actual mobility. In any case, the two types of studies are not comparable, no matter how "typical" the community may be.

The studies by the Lynds (109, 110) of Middletown, though dated, produced findings that do not vary much from studies conducted more recently. They report that the class structure of this relatively small town had expanded greatly from one that could, roughly, be described as a two-class town—working class and business class—to one in which there was a considerably wider gap between top and bottom. The changes were attributable to changes in population, in social organization, and especially in technology. Warner in his equally famous study of Yankee City (199a, pp. 79 ff.) explains a strike in this "stable" community by reference to the breakdown of a traditional age-graded skill hierarchy and the shifting of control out of local hands. Davidson and Anderson (36) in a study of San Jose, California, found that about two-thirds of the men studied were in or near their father's occupational level, and that such movement as had taken place was of relatively small degree (79). These studies give one an impression of relatively little occupational movement and, perhaps, a tendency for career movement to be getting more difficult. Yet on the other hand, Lipset and Bendix (103), using data derived from a study of a sample in Oakland, California, report that whereas only 32 per cent of the sons of fathers in nonmanual occupations had "dropped" to manual occupations, 47 per cent of the sons of fathers in manual occupations had "risen" to nonmanual occupations.[43]

In view of the fact that these studies leave us quite uncertain conclusions, it is a real relief to be able to turn to a study which, in its

---

[43] Our quotation marks are due to the fact that decisions on whether movement is up or down are subjective, and because Lipset and Bendix found that most of the movement out of manual occupations was to small business or sales.

technique, fairly dwarfs all other studies of occupational mobility in local communities: Rogoff's study of Marion County, Indiana.

She derived her information from marriage license applications in Marion County, Indiana (Indianapolis and a suburban and rural fringe) which were made over a period from 1905 to 1912 (usually labelled "1910" in her tables), and from 1938 through the first half of 1941, (usually labelled "1940"). Her sample is a total population, though she was able to use only 57 per cent of the applications,[44] or a total of 20,145 persons. As we explained above, she made use of a measure which is called "social distance mobility." This has the effect of measuring the rate of movement from one group into another in terms of the relation of this rate to chance expectations. For example, in 1910, about one-fourth of the sons of unskilled fathers were skilled workers compared to less than one-fifth of unskilled fathers who were semiskilled workers. From this alone, one might get the impression that it was actually easier for the son of an unskilled worker to become a skilled worker than to become a semi-skilled worker. But in 1910, the proportion of skilled sons in Rogoff's population was nearly twice as high as the proportion of semiskilled sons. Therefore, a higher proportion of *any* category of sons ought to be found in skilled work for the demand for them was higher. When we divide the proportion of sons in each category by the proportion of that category in the whole population, we find the situation reversed, with sons of unskilled workers entering semiskilled work at a faster rate than chance would require (1.11), whereas they entered skilled work at a lower rate than chance would require (.84). Miss Rogoff's findings are presented in Tables 14 and 15. In them, we present the actual proportions of sons of each fathers' occupational class who entered the corresponding sons' occupational class. For example, the figure in parentheses in the upper left hand corner of Table 16 tells us that 20.95 per cent of the sons of professional fathers were themselves professionals in 1910. The figures not in parentheses tells us that this proportion was over five times as high as chance distribution would have produced.

When Rogoff summarized her measures to get an over-all impression of trends, she obtained the results presented in Table 16. The mean (unweighted) mobility rate for 1910 is found to be almost identical with that in 1940, indicating *neither less nor more* mobility in 1940 than in 1910. The fact that the standard deviations (a measure of spread or dispersion) are high for each mean indicates that restrictions on occupational movement *varied* as between occupational classes; nevertheless, it

[44] The shrinkage was due to her having to reject application from nonresidents of the county, and those on which the information was inadequate. There were other sampling problems. See her Ch. III.

TABLE 14
SOCIAL DISTANCE MOBILITY (AND ACTUAL PERCENTAGES) OF ALL SONS, 1910*

SONS' OCCUPATIONAL CLASS

FATHERS' OCCUPATIONAL CLASS	PROFESSIONAL	SEMI-PROFESSIONAL	PROPRIETORS, MANAGERS AND OFFICIALS	CLERICAL AND SALES	SKILLED	SEMISKILLED	UNSKILLED	PROTECTIVE SERVICE	PERSONAL SERVICE	FARMING
Professional	5.53 (20.95)	2.01 (3.71)	1.71 (12.20)	1.32 (24.14)	0.68 (21.75)	0.64 (10.88)	0.27 (3.18)	0.55 (0.53)	0.58 (2.12)	0.16 (0.53)
Semi-professional	1.07 (4.05)	14.61 (27.03)	1.33 (9.46)	1.19 (21.62)	0.42 (13.51)	0.79 (13.51)	0.45 (5.41)	2.81 (2.70)	0.74 (2.70)	— (0.00)
Proprietors, managers and officials	11.92 (7.26)	1.51 (2.79)	2.96 (21.07)	1.51 (27.53)	0.63 (20.19)	0.61 (10.45)	0.41 (4.95)	1.00 (0.96)	1.05 (3.83)	0.29 (0.96)
Clerical and sales	1.48 (7.69)	1.56 (5.22)	1.04 (7.61)	2.40 (42.21)	0.69 (15.11)	0.62 (16.39)	0.30 (2.38)	0.48 (1.28)	0.67 (1.92)	0.36 (0.18)
Skilled	0.49 (3.26)	0.85 (2.86)	0.57 (4.29)	0.83 (19.05)	1.52 (32.25)	0.99 (26.90)	0.58 (5.64)	0.84 (2.13)	0.88 (3.04)	0.21 (0.59)
Semi-skilled	0.64 (2.50)	0.81 (2.11)	0.51 (4.14)	0.75 (17.25)	0.99 (18.36)	1.85 (43.22)	0.86 (5.33)	0.77 (2.24)	0.90 (4.28)	0.29 (0.59)
Unskilled	0.21 (2.36)	0.39 (1.53)	0.39 (2.78)	0.60 (13.06)	0.84 (15.42)	1.11 (30.00)	2.87 (28.61)	0.92 (2.36)	0.92 (3.61)	0.19 (0.28)
Protective service	0.33 (2.49)	0.34 (0.83)	1.49 (6.64)	1.17 (22.82)	1.02 (17.01)	1.13 (31.54)	0.73 (8.71)	2.60 (8.30)	0.86 (1.24)	— (0.41)
Personal service	0.21 (4.88)	1.68 (4.27)	0.54 (5.49)	0.98 (17.07)	0.82 (22.56)	1.22 (29.88)	0.97 (3.66)	0.81 (1.83)	4.04 (10.37)	— (0.00)
Farming	0.91 (3.79)	0.62 (1.65)	0.85 (5.87)	0.80 (15.17)	0.87 (23.12)	0.98 (28.75)	1.17 (8.87)	1.32 (3.55)	1.18 (5.08)	3.17 (4.16)

* Rogoff, Natalie, *Recent Trends in Occupational Mobility*, Glencoe, Ill.: The Free Press, 1953, pp. 47 and 118.

TABLE 15
SOCIAL DISTANCE MOBILITY (AND ACTUAL PERCENTAGES) OF ALL SONS, 1940*

SONS' OCCUPATIONAL CLASS

FATHERS' OCCUPATIONAL CLASS	PROFESSIONAL	SEMI-PROFESSIONAL	PROPRIETORS, MANAGERS AND OFFICIALS	CLERICAL AND SALES	SKILLED	SEMISKILLED	UNSKILLED	PROTECTIVE SERVICE	PERSONAL SERVICE	FARMING
Professional	5.10 (28.27)	2.04 (6.33)	1.14 (7.59)	1.26 (27.85)	0.70 (15.40)	0.35 (9.49)	0.37 (2.53)	0.36 (0.84)	0.44 (1.48)	0.20 (0.21)
Semi-professional	2.85 (15.79)	6.23 (19.30)	0.53 (3.51)	0.79 (17.54)	1.08 (23.68)	0.45 (12.28)	0.38 (2.63)	0.75 (1.75)	1.04 (3.51)	— (0.00)
Proprietors, managers and officials	1.38 (7.65)	1.10 (3.41)	2.66 (17.62)	1.38 (30.59)	0.65 (14.30)	0.73 (19.78)	0.36 (2.49)	0.68 (1.58)	0.62 (2.08)	0.47 (0.50)
Clerical and sales	1.39 (7.69)	1.68 (5.22)	1.15 (7.61)	1.91 (42.21)	0.69 (15.11)	0.61 (16.39)	0.34 (2.38)	0.55 (1.28)	0.57 (1.92)	0.17 (0.18)
Skilled	0.59 (3.26)	0.92 (2.86)	0.65 (4.29)	0.86 (19.05)	1.47 (32.25)	0.99 (26.90)	0.82 (5.64)	0.92 (2.13)	0.90 (3.04)	0.56 (0.59)
Semi-skilled	0.45 (2.50)	0.68 (2.11)	0.62 (4.14)	0.78 (17.25)	0.84 (18.36)	1.60 (43.22)	0.77 (5.33)	0.97 (2.24)	1.27 (4.28)	0.56 (0.59)
Unskilled	0.43 (2.36)	0.49 (1.53)	0.42 (2.78)	0.59 (13.06)	0.71 (15.42)	1.11 (30.00)	4.14 (28.61)	1.02 (2.36)	1.07 (3.61)	0.26 (0.28)
Protective service	0.45 (2.49)	0.27 (0.83)	1.00 (6.64)	1.03 (22.82)	0.78 (17.01)	1.17 (31.54)	1.26 (8.71)	3.58 (8.30)	0.37 (1.24)	0.39 (0.41)
Personal service	0.88 (4.88)	1.38 (4.27)	0.83 (5.49)	0.77 (17.07)	1.03 (22.56)	1.10 (29.88)	0.53 (3.66)	0.79 (1.83)	3.07 (10.37)	0.00 —
Farming	0.68 (3.79)	0.53 (1.65)	0.89 (5.87)	0.69 (15.17)	1.06 (23.12)	1.06 (28.75)	1.28 (8.87)	1.53 (3.55)	1.50 (5.08)	3.92 (4.16)

* Rogoff, Natalie, Recent Trends in Occupational Mobility, Glencoe, Ill.: The Free Press, pp. 48 and 119.

is noteworthy that this variation is about the same in 1940 as in 1910. The use of "minimum mobility" as another measure of rate of movement seems less defensible. Here she simply took the lowest social distance mobility ratios in her table (ignoring zeros), but both of these were those of farmers: in one case, the sons of professionals who were farmers and in the second the sons of "clerical and sales" who were farmers. Any of Rogoff's findings on farmers must be considered highly atypical, for these are farmers living in urbanized Marion County. If instead we take the next to the lowest figures, we find them to range from .21 to .33 in 1910 (involving movement of sons of unskilled or service occupations to the professions, and movement of the sons of professionals to unskilled work); in 1940,

TABLE 16

SUMMARY MOBILITY MEASURES, 1910 AND 1940 *

MEASURE	1910	1940
Mean Mobility Rate	.82	.81
Standard Deviation	.47	.43
Minimum Mobility	.16	.17
Mean Minimum Mobility	.30	.37

* Rogoff, N., *Recent Trends in Occupational Mobility*, Glencoe, Ill.: The Free Press, 1953, Table 5, p. 49.

the lowest figures ranged from .34 to .37 (involving various kinds of "downward" mobility and one interesting one: sons of protective service workers who became personal service workers). The fact that there was a slight rise in these figures indicates somewhat easier mobility, albeit in a "downward" direction. Her final measure is the average size of the smallest entries in each row. In sum, then, Rogoff (152, p. 49) found that:

. . . *no significant changes took place in over-all mobility rates between 1910 and 1940.* [Italics, Rogoff's.]

It is essential to recognize that this conclusion refers to *all kinds* of movement: contributing *equally* to this conclusion would be the case of the son of a porter who became the owner of a factory, and the case of the son of a physician who became a household servant. It is worthwhile, then, to look at her attempt to measure the *direction* of movements. For this purpose she makes use of the collapsed categories of white-collar,[45] blue-collar,[46] and farming. Her results are presented in Table 17.[47]

[45] Includes professionals, semiprofessionals, proprietors, managers, and officials, and clerical and sales.

[46] Includes skilled, semiskilled, unskilled, and service workers.

[47] The diagonal categories here do not, of course, indicate inheritance. Rather they refer to, say, the son of a white-collar worker who became a white-collar worker, but in

From Table 17 we see that the easiest move in both 1910 and 1940 was from one white-collar occupation to another. Insofar as movement from a blue-collar to a white-collar occupation represents upward mobility, the ratios are found to be almost identical in the two time periods. Insofar as movement from a white-collar occupation to a blue-collar occupation represents downward movement, the ratio is somewhat lower in 1940 than in 1910, indicating the move was a little harder to make. Then, if we divide the ratio for upward mobility by that for downward mobility, we find that the quotient is .96 for 1910, and 1.20 for 1940. The latter indicates a possible "net" in favor of upward rather than downward mobility, though this seems to be due to a lowering of the amount of downward mobility.[48]

TABLE 17

AVERAGE INTER-CLASS MOBILITY, 1910 AND 1940 *

	CLASS OF DESTINATION		
	WHITE-	BLUE-	
CLASS OF ORIGIN	COLLAR	COLLAR	FARMING
1910:			
White-collar	1.47	0.72	0.20
Blue-collar	0.69	0.91	0.14
Farming	0.80	1.10	—
1940:			
White-collar	1.39	0.59	0.21
Blue-collar	0.71	0.92	0.35
Farming	0.70	1.29	—

* Rogoff, N., *Recent Trends in Occupational Mobility*, Glencoe, Ill.: The Free Press, 1953, Table 13, p. 60.

Certain other of Miss Rogoff's major conclusions deserve mention. We shall list them.

1. The most likely occupational destination of any son at each time period was the occupation of his parent. If his father was in a white-collar occupation, then the next most likely destination was another white-collar occupation. If his father was not, then the most likely destination was a manual or service occupation.

2. About 70 per cent of sons are in occupations different from their fathers.[49] But she did not find, as have others, that occupational inherit-

---

a different occupation, for example, the son of a travelling salesman who became a labor union official.

[48] Owing to smallness of numbers, Miss Rogoff was forced to exclude Negroes from the above groups, and presents data for this group only for the later period. If it is true that mobility chances for Negroes in the United States have improved over the 30-odd years under consideration, then we might guess that, had Negroes been included, the results would probably not have tipped the scales in the direction of more downward mobility.

[49] A finding which, Rogoff notes, is similar to that found in other studies.

ance was highest for skilled workers: on the contrary, it was in last place.

3. About two-thirds of the Negroes in her later group are in un-skilled and service classes, as compared only to one-eighth of the whites —a very great difference in occupational structure. The likelihood of a Negro's becoming a laborer was unrelated to occupational origin. In sum, then, we may say that Miss Rogoff agrees with many studies that there is a great deal of occupational movement between generations but that the rate of such movement does not appear to have changed over the period studied. She throws cold water, then, on *both* the pes-simists and the optimists.

If we turn, next, to career mobility we find we do not have studies as definitive as Rogoff's. Davidson and Anderson (36) report that around one-half of their San Jose, California group were in a different occupa-tion from the one they started in, whereas Form and Miller (55) found that they could fit only about one-half of their Ohio group into the career patterns they found to be modal.[50] Perhaps the best single com-munity study we have is Lipset and Bendix' report (103) on Oakland, California. Without trying to reproduce the tremendous mass of materials they present, certain major findings may be noted. They found a great deal of job movement within the career. The 935 working heads of families studied reported 4,530 jobs; or an average of 4.8 jobs each for an average of 25.3 years in the labor force. Those who owned or managed a business were found to be the most heterogeneous in past experience: almost 40 per cent of the shifts into self-employment were from manual jobs, slightly under 30 per cent were from various nonmanual jobs, and only 21.6 per cent were from one form of business ownership to another. Shifts *within* the occupation were found to be most characteristic of professional, semiprofessional and upper-white-collar groups, though skilled workers also were high on this dimension. In spite, however, of this great volume of shifting, they found that most of the shifting between groups was with *adjacent* groups, and there was very little permanent shifting between manual and nonmanual occupations. The latter lead Bendix and Lipset to say (103, p. 371):

This is perhaps the most fundamental cleavage in American society.

A final important finding is that "upward mobility" has come to mean quite different things for the working class as compared to the middle class. Based on their data, they write (103a, p. 507):

[50] Rogoff (152, p. 27) comments that career mobility seems to involve a smaller por-tion of the population than does intergenerational mobility.

It is our guess that the creed of "individual enterpriser" has become by and large a working-class preoccupation. Though it may have animated both work-ing class and middle class in the past, it is no longer a middle-class ideal today. Instead, people in the middle class aspire to become professionals and, as a second choice, upper-white-collar workers.

It is unfortunate that we do not have trend data to check the relative significance of those goals at different points in time.

We turn next to studies of the United States as a whole. Unfortu-nately, we do not have trend studies here on the model of Rogoff's; there-fore, we shall content ourselves with presenting the results from two na-tional surveys of the actual mobility at the time of the studies. In Table 18,

TABLE 18
MOBILITY (AND INHERITANCE) IN A NATIONAL U.S. SAMPLE. I *

FATHER'S OCCUPATION

	PROFESSIONAL	BUSINESS	WHITE-COLLAR	SKILLED	SEMISKILLED	SERVICE	FARM	NON-FARM LABOR	DON'T KNOW
All those interviewed (per cent)	7	16	8	17	11	3	31	5	2
RESPONDENT'S OCCUPATION:									
Professional people	23	24	10	13	5	5	17	2	1
Business men	4	31	9	18	8	3	25	2	**
White-collar workers	9	23	15	21	10	3	16	3	**
Skilled workers	3	7	4	30	14	5	29	7	1
Semi-skilled workers	2	11	6	19	19	3	32	7	1
Domestic and personal service workers	4	6	3	20	12	8	28	12	7
Farmers	2	2	2	3	4	*	84	3	—
Non-farm labor	3	12	—	9	17	1	32	19	7

   * "Jobs and Occupations: A Popular Evaluation," *Opinion News,* 9:3–13, Sept. 1, 1947, pp. 424–425.
   ** Less than 0.5%.

there are the findings from the National Opinion Research Center study to which we have referred previously. (See pp. 147–148.) In Table 19 are the findings from the study by Richard Centers, which has the advantage of breaking up the usual omnibus owners-and-managers category into two groups of different size. Both studies roughly confirm Rogoff's findings. There are exceptions, but in general the father's occupation is the most likely or a highly likely destination for the son. However, the majority have occupations different from their father, though the occupation is not likely to be very much higher or lower than the father's occupation.[51]

   [51] An intriguing type of study, to which space limitations permit no more than this passing reference, is that of mobility into elites, such as business or professional elites. Although some studies (127, 183) suggest that movement into the elite may be more

We may conclude our survey of the data on amount of mobility by examining attempts to estimate changes in the opportunity structure. We have earlier (pp. 67–73) presented the data on occupational trends. Here we shall consider the general question of whether class lines have grown tighter or looser in recent decades.

TABLE 19
MOBILITY (AND INHERITANCE) IN A NATIONAL U.S. SAMPLE. II [*]

PER CENT WHOSE SONS ARE OF VARIOUS OCCUPATIONAL STRATA

OCCUPATIONAL STRATUM OF FATHER	N	LARGE BUSINESS	PROFESSIONAL	SMALL BUSINESS	WHITE-COLLAR	FARM OWNERS OR MANAGERS	SKILLED MANUAL	SEMI-SKILLED MANUAL	FARM TENANT OR LABORER	UNSKILLED MANUAL
Large Business Owners & Managers	16	50	19	6	25	—	—	—	—	—
Professional	41	15	32	17	10	5	12	5	2	2
Small Business Owners & Managers	145	10	11	32	24	3	8	10	1	1
White Collar	77	8	9	10	45	6	9	7	1	5
Skilled Manual	190	6	6	8	17	4	31	20	1	7
Semi-Skilled	127	1	2	6	11	4	22	43	1	10
Unskilled	41	—	6	5	10	4	17	20	1	37

[*] Centers, R., "Occupational Mobility of Urban Occupational Strata," *American Sociological Review*, 13:198, 1948.

One difficulty in drawing any conclusions about trends is the real possibility of overemphasis on the amount of social mobility in past generations. We have indicated above (p. 180, fn. 51) that the studies of William Miller and his associates suggest that business and industrial elites in the nineteenth century were drawn for the most part from middle and upper classes, and that therefore the picture of the free-swinging entrepreneur who rose from poverty to the top represents a great exaggeration. Overestimates of present "rigidities" may then be due to overestimates of *past* mobility. One of the most important of beliefs coloring discussion of mobility trends is the labor-safety-valve theory. This theory, generally attributed to the historian, Frederick Jackson Turner (though it was

difficult than it has been, other studies (137, 198), and goodly number of studies of professionals suggest that movements into elite positions are no *more* difficult to make than they have been in the past. Of particular importance are the studies by Miller and his associates. A good deal of current belief that upward mobility is more difficult is due to an apparent overemphasis on the supposed amount of mobility in the 19th century because of the stereotype of the free-swinging entrepreneur. Miller (125, 126) found that only about five percent of the business elite at the turn of the century had been recruited from the lower class. Gregory and Neu (68, pp. 193–211) checked Miller's work for the period of the 1870's and found that approximately 90 per cent of business leaders in textiles, steel, and railroads had been reared in middle- or upper-class milieus.

not originated by him), explains the traditional openness of the American class system by reference to the open frontier: any man who could not "make a go of it" in the Eastern labor market could always pack up, and go out West. Goodrich and Davison (65, 65a) have examined this theory with such evidence as they could accumulate. If the theory is true, they reason, then we should find Eastern laborers making up significant proportions of the migrants to the western states. They first report that the various supporters of the theory do not offer evidence that such groups did make up large proportions of the migrants. Their own evidence, gathered from Eastern and Western newspapers, state and county histories and other available data (between 1830 and 1890) leads them to conclude (65a, p. 114):

. . . the movement of eastern wage-earners to the western lands was surprisingly small.

Further, those who did leave apparently did not push up the wages of those they left behind, and very often those who left failed as homesteaders and returned home. Their evidence suggests that the western movement did draw *farmers,* and in the sense that the latter might otherwise have migrated to Eastern cities and competed with other wage earners, then there is some substance to the theory. Shannon (167) casts still further doubt on the theory. He points out that the Homestead Act was only facilitating and provided little or nothing to help the prospective settler get to the West; nor did the Act provide for credit or guidance in the settler's early years of occupancy. He writes (167, p. 645):

It was hard enough for an experienced farmer to make a success of the venture. To the industrial laborer of the second generation it was virtually an impossibility.

There may, then, have been less occupational movement in the past than is often thought (77, 168).

The data on changes in the opportunity structure in the United States are inconclusive. Sibley (171) points out that a number of factors stimulated upward mobility in the past: technological progress, with the opening up of new opportunities in new industries (but often with attendant "temporary" unemployment [52]), immigration (in which new immigrants typically took the bottom jobs in the industrial hierarchy

---

[52] Haber and Stanchfield (68a, pp. 32–33) refer to the Henderson report on technological changes in the automobile industry:

"One-piece stamping of the under-body has saved 50 hours in the manufacture and assembly of parts. In one plant a one-piece top brought a saving of 43 hours of labor. The labor cost of a door in one plant has been reduced from $4.00 to 15 cents, in the brief space of five years, by the use of fewer parts and the installation of a weld-

and thus lifted their predecessors up), and differential fertility (with the white-collar and upper groups failing to reproduce themselves and therefore providing openings for lower-class persons). But immigration has now been reduced to a trickle, there is evidence that differential fertility may be declining,[53] and industry has only a limited number of promotions to offer.[54] In another article, Hertzler (76), summarizing a number of studies, repeats Sibley's points and refers in addition to race and ethnicity, and to restrictive elements in the educational system, and in labor unions (190). The process by which class lines may be forming is suggested by Hollingshead (78, pp. 387–88):

The association between education, job levels, and prestige in the social structure is so high that the person with more education moves into the high-ranking job and the person with little education into the low-ranking job. Furthermore, and this is the crucial fact from the viewpoint of the person's relation to the social structure, each tends to remain in the job channel in which he starts as a young worker. This is especially true if he has less than a high school education; then he starts as an unskilled menial and has few opportunities in later years to change to skilled labor, business, or the professions. Therefore, his chances to be promoted up through the several levels of the job channel in which he functions are severely limited. As the years pass, his position in the economic system becomes fixed, and another generation has become stable in the class structure. These young people come from families near the bottom or on the bottom. They start where their parents are, and they are likely to remain about where they started. As a young class V (lowest class) mother of two babies put it, "Mother said, 'Toil and trouble is our lot.' She had her share, and it looks like I got mine comin'." Her husband had been arrested that morning for driving a car he did not own across a state line. This pressure of everyday events is likely to keep these young people where they are in the social structure for the rest of their lives.

---

ing machine. Welding of back and quarter panels, once requiring 6 welders and 12 finishers, now is completed with two men with a welding machine and one helper for finishing. The installation of conveyors in handling stock has long been recognized as a potent and efficient means of eliminating man power. The use of a quick change holding jig in the rough boring of connecting rods has enabled one man to turn out more work than the combination of four men and four machines before the new method was put into operation."
Haber and Stanchfield are well aware of the fact that such developments often produce only temporary unemployment. But nevertheless, they do "compel the individual worker to change from his accustomed occupation to some new type of work. The intervening period may be long enough to exhaust his savings and other resources. Technological unemployment has a special bearing on the status of the skilled worker in industry. Jobs once highly specialized can now be filled from the larger supply of semi-skilled and unskilled workers. American industrial history contains many examples of skilled crafts which have been wiped out by mechanical innovations."

[53] The evidence on this subject is shaky. One of the best statements is in (204). See also (93).

[54] We discuss this phenomenon in greater detail on pp. 476–478.

On the other hand, some writers have suggested that there are equally strong forces working toward the prevention of class rigidity. Sjoberg (173) refers to the emergence of new power groups, such as bureaucrats and labor leaders, to the wider dispersion of achievements and personal possessions, and to the decline in inter-class distinctions such as dress and language. He also points out that the very fact of changes in mobility and class alignments tends to produce a greater *awareness* of social class and this awareness may be mistaken for greater rigidity. Our discussion of the great increase in professional and clerical workers, and in semiskilled workers, with a concomitant deline in un- skilled workers may also be recalled. Foote and Hatt (54) tried to measure the over-all trend and concluded that the *net* occupational movement in recent times has been toward occupations of higher prestige.[55] Finally, it is worth noting that Kuznets (97) reports that changes in income distribution show an increase in the proportions of the population in the *middle* income categories and a decline at both ends.[56]

What, then, shall we say these data indicate? When the opportunity structure is taken into account, as it was by Rogoff, the data do not indicate an increase in intergenerational mobility over time. On the whole, the other studies that we have discussed offer no evidence to contra- dict this statement. Most studies agree that there is a great deal of inter- generation movement but that sons are most likely to follow their fathers' occupation rather than any other particular occupation. Career mobility seems to be somewhat lower than intergenerational mobility, but there are too few studies to make any reliable conclusion here. Again, the data do support the statement that there is a great deal of interjob movement within a man's career, though much of this movement is that of manual workers moving into private business, if only tem- porarily.

The data on the opportunity structure that we have just discussed leave us unsure of any conclusion except one: the opportunity structure has apparently not made it *more* difficult for persons to change jobs from that of their fathers' or from their own previous jobs. In sum, the picture is neither dark nor rosy. Class lines have not tightened,[57] but they have not, apparently, loosened either. On the whole, the data seem to support

[55] Kolko (95) however, quarrels with their conclusion. His data (based mainly on income) show no predominant trend either up or down, but rather a steady level.

[56] Worth consulting also is the attempt by Kahl (88) to measure various types of mobility which affect the opportunity structure, especially technological mobility, re- productive mobility, and immigration mobility. See Ch. IX.

[57] Even the authors who called the manual-nonmanual distinction a "fundamental cleavage" have, in a later article, insisted that the distinction holds as a *tendency* rather than a hard and fast rule. See (19).

the picture Parsons (143) drew in his now classic article wherein he saw the American class structure as a relatively loose one characterized by a certain vagueness. As he pointed out, this very indefiniteness makes possible a reduction of strain in cases where there is a discrepancy between income and occupational status (so that a leading scientist of low salary does not compete directly with a corporation lawyer of much higher pay) and where a son begins to make more money or is in an occupation of higher prestige than his father is. The vagueness, then, is functional, and our class system need not be regarded as transitional to something else, but a genuine type in its own right which is capable of persisting.[58]

THE PROCESS OF MOBILITY

We turn our attention, finally, to the means and conditions that facilitate or retard movement from one occupational position to another. Although this process is perfectly general, our discussion will, inevitably, reflect the fact that most research has been concerned with situations in which there is a change of occupation, and, particularly, the case where this change involves a change in economic position, power, or prestige. However, the latter kinds of changes are perhaps the most significant to a society.

Lipset and Zetterberg (107, pp. 155-77) suggest four relatively distinct kinds of phenomena that should be taken into account in any study of the process of social mobility: the supply of vacant statuses (e.g., an increase in demand for professional persons, or demographic changes), the interchange of ranks (that is, when the supply of vacant statuses is held constant, a movement on the part of one person is only possible if someone else moves to make room for him), motivation, and ego-needs to increase one's self-evaluation through increasing one's rank. We will follow this general division of subject matter, but will combine the latter two because of their close relation and because of the scarcity of sociological research on the last factor.

We have pointed out the need to take into account the supply of vacant statuses in measuring amount of occupational mobility and have presented the data on this subject. Here we need only note that one of

[58] Recently, attention has also been given to the question of the amount of social mobility in other countries in comparison, especially, to the United States. Although the technical problems are very great, the data suggest that there is less difference in social mobility between the United States and other countries, than is often thought. See (106), and the set of charts adapted from certain unpublished materials in Barber (8, pp. 472-76). These are presented in highly compressed form in (107, p. 165) a volume which contains papers valuable to the student interested in comparative analysis.

the most important ways in which social mobility is made possible is through a change in the number of available occupations. If a society increases in population and must supply its economic needs from somewhere else, then the number of jobs available in the supply area will probably go up, if a reservoir population is available. In any society, a sudden increase in the number of babies (without concurrent rise in the death rate) may produce new jobs, and, indeed, any change in size may affect the supply of vacant job statuses. Of course a major determinant is the swing of the business cycle.

Changes and differences in fertility are also important. In the case of the Roman Catholic church in the Western world, the development of a celibate priesthood has also meant the prevention of the development of an hereditary priesthood.[59] And speaking more generally, Carr-Saunders (28, pp. 316–19) has called attention to the low birth rate of persons in the high-status professions, a situation which seems to be a special case of a more general phenomenon: the higher the status, the fewer the children.[60] Although this phenomenon has caused concern to the Eugenicists, the differential fertility has a salutary effect on upward mobility: the professions and other high-status occupations must continually recruit new members from the children of lower-status occupations.[61] Another factor that may affect the supply of vacant statuses is immigration. However, the manner in which immigration affects mobility is by no means always the same. If immigrants enter at the bottom, and if, in addition, a generation of time intervenes so that children of earlier migrants have a chance to learn the language and secure education, then those who entered earlier will be enabled to rise. It is the latter combination of circumstances that occurred in the United States and that has led to the frequent assumption that immigration increases upward mobility. On the other hand, if immigrants enter at the *same* level as certain groups in the society, then the immigrants will compete for available jobs and may depress wages or make upward mobility *more* difficult for those already in the society; the latter situation may be particularly likely when an immigrant group is a highly educated elite uprooted from their lands by political changes. Hence the not infrequent concern of labor unions about the volume of immigration.

[59] This development took many centuries and its history is directly relevant to the understanding of occupational mobility process. See (98).

[60] See (32, pp. 234–43; 132, pp. 139 ff.; 176, pp. 218–21; 184, Ch. IX, X). As we noted previously, divergences between social or socioeconomic classes appear to have declined somewhat in recent years, but still seem to be present. See (138, pp. 167–78).

[61] Thrupp (186, pp. 199–200) has called our attention to the fact that the merchant class in this early period had difficulty replacing itself because of low fertility and high mortality of offspring, and this made possible mobility into this class from lower-class groups.

Political self-government in the United States has tended to open up new statuses. Frequently it is better not to be too rich if one wants to go into politics. Also politics has often been depreciated as a profession by the rich. As a consequence, the poor are provided with a new avenue of advancement, one which has been especially noteworthy since the advent of Jacksonian democracy and the belief that no special qualifications are needed to govern.[62] Patronage itself tends to increase the interest of lower classes in politics and political advancement. Also the development of competition for civil service positions on the basis of objective examinations has opened up new positions for those who might previously not have attained them.

Finally, technological change has been a major provider of new jobs in the United States. The automobile industry, for example, created with it a whole new group of positions—mechanics, designers, engineers, salesmen. The radio and television industries have created new positions for designers, manufacturers, repairmen, and private businessmen. Related to this phenomen has been the rise of new professions, such as those in the area of social work, accounting, nursery school teaching, and public opinion polling.

The second type of mobility process is through the interchange of ranks. For this to take place, a major prerequisite is the existence of some *hope of success*. That is, ability must count for something. The paths must be open so that a person who has the required training and experience has a chance to try for an available position. Hence the importance of the vagueness of the United States class system so that persons are not automatically limited to a set of occupations solely by virtue of parental position, as they might be in countries which have more rigid class, or caste systems.[63]

But in addition to the general characteristics of the society as a whole, we may ask what factors in particular facilitate and retard the interchange of ranks. We may divide them, roughly, into group mobilities and individual mobilities.

Obviously, in the United States, the individual may rise above his fellows under certain circumstances. But just as important are situations

[62] The fact that political campaigns have become very costly in recent years, and the fact that top governmental positions (such as ambassadorships) often pay less than may be considered proper for fulfilling the expectation of the office, has created a dilemma. On the one hand, the rich tend to avoid politics, and, at the same time, no one wants politics to become a special prerogative of wealth. This fact has tended to increase the strategic significance of the political party, for few can afford to go it alone, even if they could win or secure political office in that way.

[63] An important area of research has been on the question of whether the U.S. class system is better described as a set of discrete classes, or as a continuum of statuses. See (100).

in which the *group* that the individual belongs to changes its relation to other groups in the society. This type of mobility is seen in the rise of social classes, as, for example, in the replacing of the French feudal lords by the bourgeoisie, but it is also present when an important technological change takes place. When a new industry begins, not only are new statuses provided, but also if the significance of the industry increases, then those who got in "on the ground floor" will rise with it. One of the most remarkable instances of a profound change in the position of an occupational group—from one of illegality in some places—has been the rise to national eminence of some labor union leaders (128). On the other hand, other occupations—particularly some of the traditional crafts— have lost prestige and dropped in economic position.[64] One of the commonest ways by which occupations try to raise their relative position is, Hughes (81) has pointed out,[65] to try to make themselves into professions. At the same time, the high status and rewards that attach to the professions may lead some occupations to strive for this status before they may be technically ready for it, or at a sacrifice of the values of a "general" rather than specialized approach (80, 101, 151). Finally, a type of group mobility is certainly involved in the rise of an entire occupational structure of the sort suggested in Foote and Hatt's conclusion (54) that the net occupational movement in recent times in the United States has been toward higher prestige occupations.

When we examine factors facilitating the interchange of ranks through individual mobility, we find a considerable variety. One of the most frequently expressed goals of mature workers has been that of owning their own business, a fact supported by many studies. When *Fortune* magazine (57) asked the 54.7 per cent of their sample who worked for others and the 9.8 per cent who were unemployed whether they would like to go into business for themselves, they found that just over one-half answered "yes." The desire is not, however, a completely general one: it is strongest among the young, the single, and the lower income groups.[66] Parsons (144) calls attention to another type of individual

[64] An excellent illustration of a group change in societal position is provided by the case of the Pasi subcaste in India who changed their occupation from the low-status one of hunting to the higher-status one of fruitselling. See (39, pp. 378 ff.).

[65] An interesting point of view, in this context, is that of N. Foote (53) who points out that labor as a whole is tending to become professionalized. The indices he notes are: technology has been the preoccupation increasingly of engineers or else it has become automatic, trade unionism is, in one sense, a movement to assure each worker of a career, and there is a growing emphasis on "rules" and general knowledge.

[66] The last finding is consistent with that of Lipset and Bendix (103) who found that the greatest social mobility of manual workers in their sample was into their own business. They also report, however, that the rate of failure is high, and there is much moving back and forth.

mobility when he notes that the "status of a clergyman is roughly a
function of the prestige of his parishioners." By implication, if the status
of one's parishioners rises, then the status of the clergyman does. This
situation is also found in other situations and accounts for a good deal
of movement, especially, of private businessmen who hope that a "new
location" may help business and therefore move into a district of higher
status. This factor is important in restaurant location (see p. 390).

Without subscribing to the labor-safety-valve theory, we can still
recognize that, in many cases, migration is a technique of effecting occupational change. Although the data are difficult to gather because of
sampling problems, the studies of Freedman and Hawley (59), Scudder
and Anderson (164), and Pihlblad and Gregory (147) tend to agree that
migrants are likely to be more mobile than those they left at home and
to attain higher positions than comparable groups. In a sense, of course,
the skimming off of those who would otherwise have occupied high
positions at home may make it *easier* for those who remain as well. In
this context, it is worth noting that some occupations *require* that the
person move around, for example, in large concerns that have many
branches. For some groups, moving up often means moving away, as is
often the case for farmers, professors, or city managers (51). On the other
hand, the requirement that one be on the move may, as in the case of
migratory workers, lead to lower yearly wages and a depressed existence
in other respects. Yet Caplow (26, p. 97; 27) suggests that for some occupations such as dance-band musicians, journeyman potters, and railroad
men, the fact of transiency may itself create the need for in-group solidarity and a highly-elaborated status system. These may in turn be utilized, as
they often are, to increase wages and control deviants.

The fact that occupations are related to other parts of society has
meant that persons can achieve occupational mobility by increasing
their economic position, power, or prestige in a nonoccupational area of
life. As we have pointed out previously, wealth, power, and prestige,
however achieved, may be converted into rights to property which may
include the ownership of factories or other private businesses. Access to
other occupations may also be secured. Ross (154, 155, 156) has recorded
the important shift from the traditional need of successful businessmen
to engage in church-related activities to their current tendency to engage
in philanthropic activities. On the other hand, they must necessarily
engage in such activities toward the *ends* of their careers, when they have
already accumulated the money and leisure to do so.

Many societies accord prestige to the scholar. But in our society,
education has come to be of significance, not so much as a value in its
own right, but with reference to its relation to the professions. As the

professions become the major goal of middle-class persons, and as more and more occupations become professionalized, the role of education in the process of upward mobility becomes increasingly important. And in this sense education can assist a person to rise in both group and individual-mobility situations. Our experience is quite different from that associated with the European tradition. In the Middle Ages, education operated in connection with patronage: if an unusual person was found, a feudal lord might take him as a ward and put him through. Or else the philanthropic system operated in the form of the poor boys' school. A college professor of German origin contrasted his European experience as follows:

One thing that surprised me at first in this country was the period of time between degrees. When I looked in our catalog which states the time at which the man gets his degree I was very surprised. I would find things like: B.A. 1921, M.S. 1924, Ph.D. 1935. What puzzled me was why there was such a long interval between these degrees. It could not be that American students were so stupid that it took them so long to get the higher degree. If we did a corresponding thing in our European catalogs it would look very different. It would be B.A. 1921, M.A. 1922, Ph.D. 1924. I later learned what was the reason for the long delay in this country. It is because the individual seeks some employment because he is not being subsidized and so he leaves his education for a time and then later comes back. In Europe this would not be done. The individual would not pursue a higher degree to begin with unless his family had the money with which to carry it through from the beginning to the end.

In spite of our earlier reservations about the role of education as a restrictor of opportunities, and in spite of the fact that many worthy students get eliminated because of race, ethnicity, or a lack of money, there is no doubt that education has had powerful consequences for our society. The more a society emphasizes education, without at the same time permitting the right to an education to become the prerogative of any special group, then the more likely it is that the interchange of ranks can go on. For education cannot be inherited.

The mobility processes that we have discussed thus far—the supply of vacant statuses and the interchange of ranks—are, after all, only permissive or facilitating. The fact that a position is available does not guarantee that someone will turn up to fill it: *motivation* is also required. Lipset and Zetterberg (107, p. 164) call attention to the strange paradox presented by the United States: the same society that insists that all are equal also continually reassures its young that upward mobility is the right of all. Yet if all are equal, then there are no superior and inferior positions and there is nothing to strive for. The paradox is resolved by

Lipset and Zetterberg by their pointing out that the very emphasis on equalitarianism makes it necessary to stimulate persons to try to move up; in more rigid societies which freely concede the existence of large class differences, those very differences provide obvious reasons for striving to rise to a higher class. In the United States, then, motivation to strive is a *problem,* and special means must be provided for assuring that persons will strive for upward mobility.

Merton (120, Ch. 7) has described the mechanism of the "self-fulfilling prophecy" by which belief that a goal will be achieved generates the action that actually achieves it. Such a mechanism appears to be at work in the elaboration of the American success ideology, for there is a very strong and persistent belief that upward mobility is possible to those who will try.[67] *Fortune's* (57) self-portrait of America included the finding that 56.3 per cent of the national sample felt that "the years ahead hold for (them) personally a good chance for advancement." [68] The latter belief is all the more remarkable in view of the fact that the same survey found that the wants of the sample were exceedingly modest; 49.9 per cent named a figure lower than $2,500 per year, and 72.2 per cent named a figure lower than $5,000 a year. In a later survey in 1947, *Fortune* found that their income wants had not even kept pace with the rise in the cost of living. Lipset and Bendix (103) report two findings that are relevant: they found that manual workers interpreted "upward mobility" to mean owning their own business and this was highly characteristic of manual workers; in turn, nonmanual workers very often had spent some part of their work life in manual work. Therefore, manual workers could point to their own experience as proprietors (however brief) and nonmanual workers to their earlier experiences as manual workers—both experiences which would result in estimates that mobility chances were good.

Another important kind of evidence on the vitality of beliefs in upward-mobility chances is involved in perceptions of social class. *Fortune's* self-survey (57, p. 133) found that 56.2 per cent of the sample thought that "the interests of employers and employees are, by the very nature . . . basically the same." But more famous is the finding of the same survey (57, p. 14) that a huge 47 per cent of the population sample used "middle class" or a term like it to describe their own class position.[69]

[67] Two leading students of social mobility have suggested that it may be this belief in equalitarianism, rather than actual differences in mobility chances, that distinguishes the United States from the more status-oriented European countries (102, pp. 34–5).

[68] It is worth noting, however, that when a question like this one was asked again in a later self-portrait (35:6, Jan., 1947) there was a definite drop in the percentage.

[69] This was the percent that *volunteered* the term or something like it. But there was also a huge 27.5 per cent who answered "don't know" and many others who gave

Here is clearly a "middle-class society" in which the goals of upward mobility are believed in by a very large proportion of the population.[70]

This belief in the chances of success could hardly persist if it were founded on nothing and there is evidence that there *is* as great deal of upward movement, as we pointed out earlier.[71] But even more remarkable is the persistence of this belief in the face of evidence to the contrary. For example, a special *Fortune* survey of factory workers (58) showed that while a high proportion of workers believed personal qualities (ability and effort) are, in general, the basis of promotion, yet almost one-half did not believe that such qualities would yield such results in their *own* jobs. We pointed out above that the income wants of the population were very modest, even for the time of the survey. Yet modest as they are, even the editors of *Fortune* (57, p. 134), with every desire to paint as bright a picture as possible, are forced to say:

Based upon 40,000,000 families and self-supporting unmarried adults, it would require $132,000,000,000, or more than twice as much as the national income estimated for 1938 to pay everyone who knows what he wants (not to mention providing for 5,000,000 who don't) the income he would regard as satisfactory.

Katherine Archibald (4, pp. 151–84), describing the class consciousness of workers in a shipyard in Oakland, California during World War II, provides a major insight into this phenomenon. She found very little of the traditional spirit of individual enterprise. On the contrary, her fellow-workers resented authority, especially of the front office (whose

---

other answers. Therefore *Fortune* took the 56.5 per cent who had not used the actual words "upper," "middle," or "lower" to describe their class position, and asked them which *of those three* they would use if they "had to describe the class to which (they) belong." Then they added what they got on the earlier question and came out with these percentages: upper class—7.6; middle class—79.2; lower class—7.9; don't know—5.3. This 79.2 per cent figure is often quoted, but although it does make the point more dramatically, it must be recalled that the sample was *forced* to use these categories. Other studies have suggested that the categories one forces persons to use affects the findings. Meanwhile, it is worth noting that Montague (130) in a comparative study found that although American boys more generally accepted mobility as a goal than did British boys, American boys were *more* conscious of social class than were English boys.

[70] It is partly for this reason that Faris (49) challenges the existence of a class system in the United States. He claims we need another way of describing the variation in the population in terms of money, power, prestige, and occupational way of life.

[71] Lipset and Bendix (102) mention the following factors as sustaining the belief in success possibilities: the lack of a feudal tradition, the actually high rate of mobility, the increase in educational opportunities, the possibility of business careers (at the top and bottom of the ladder), the effects of immigration and of ethnic and racial minorities (on the shoulders of which others could climb), and the relative wealth and distribution of goods through mass production.

power, they felt, was *not* due to merit), and they felt that education would not get a man very far. BUT THEY DID NOT REJECT THE SYSTEM for they recognized that a man *could* move up, though the means for doing so were either beneath their dignity (bootlicking) or beyond their control (luck). Even more revealing is Wohl's finding that, contrary to common belief, the typical Horatio Alger story is *not* that of a slum boy who rises to the top by practicing middle-class virtues (207, pp. 388–95).[72] Rather, the "Horatio Alger hero" has become a success *symbol* and is adjusted to fit whatever the mobility pattern is at the time; no one reads the novels anymore.

In addition to the motivating influences that originate in the society as a whole, the more intimate experiences of the growing youngster— especially in his home—are of significance in motivation to seek success. It is of the greatest importance that the child grow up among adults who talk with pride of their latest accomplishments and look forward optimistically to tomorrow rather than with adults who lament their status and look fearfully into the future.

The individual must have *precedents* for upward mobility. Others just like him must have succeeded so that he can secure a conception of himself in that role. Such a tradition of success is of particular importance for minority groups. Negroes have relatively few precedents of success and are forced to fight, not only a hostile white world, but the expectation of their own group that they will not succeed. Hence the importance of "race heroes" who are not simply "successes" but models and symbols which become all the more precious because they are scarce.[73]

Such a model may generate an ambition, but as Hall (70) has shown, a mere "itch" is not enough. Besides that, he writes (70, p. 328), one needs help from family and friends for:

[72] Based on his reading of 55 of the 125 novels written by Alger, Wohl finds the typical Alger hero to be a country boy who has come to the city and who takes a low-status job. He *does* practice middle-class virtues, but these get him nowhere. Instead, *luck* intervenes (he stops a pair of runaway horses and is rewarded by their owner). And the story ends not with him at the top, but with his foot on the first rung of the ladder only.

[73] The hero, however, is quite distinct, sociologically, from the success. All societies seem to contain the heroic role, whether such a person is found in the military, sports, entertainment, gambling, exploring, invention, or occasionally, in work ("hero of socialist labor"). But by definition, no one can make an occupation of being a hero, which involves a unique noncomparable accomplishment (Listen to the eternal question: Was Joe Louis as good as Jack Dempsey? *etc.*). However, the fact that a hero depends so much for his role on talent has meant that skyrocket mobility can happen here —from the slum to a position of national prominence in just a few years. Hence his role as a success model (94, 201).

. . . encouragement, helping establish the appropriate routes, arranging the necessary privacy, discouraging anomalous behavior, and defining the day-to-day rewards.

He provides a striking comparison between a moderately successful doctor of Armenian extraction and a highly successful Yankee doctor. The former came of a poor family, though he did get some financial help from his aunt. He had difficulty getting a good internship, and had, at first, to take only patients other doctors were reluctant to see (for example, late night cases). By contrast, the Yankee doctor came of a medical family in which medical literature was literally lying around the house when he was a child. His biology instructor in college urged him to go on to Harvard Medical School and one of his college instructors was also the superintendent at the best hospital in the city and welcomed his application for an internship. His father bought him his instruments and paid his office rent for two years. Finally, he was invited to join the specialty board as a charter member (which meant he did not have to pass the examinations that others had to). Hall notes that both these men had ambition but the Yankee doctor was continuously assisted by groups who had inside knowledge of the profession and its requirements.[74] On the other hand, Warner and Abegglen (198, pp. 201–03) in their study of recruitment into the business elite found that the possession of influential friends did not have much effect upon the time necessary to achieve success though having relatives in the firm did. They found also that marrying the boss's daughter did *not* seem to shorten the time it took to enter the business elite, though such a marriage does have other social effects.

We may examine, finally, the significance of reference groups and of social class. How high up a man tries to go on the social ladder depends in part on the platform from which he surveys the possibilities. Reissman (149) found that rookie policemen regarded themselves as successful, though their aspirations were low, because they were comparing themselves to their own brothers. Similarly, Stouffer (180, p. 250) found that the better educated in the army, even though their own chances of promotion were superior to most others, were the most critical of promotion chances, a fact attributable to the high expectations their education had given them. But it is Merton and Kitt (121, pp. 40–105) who have given us one of the most meaningful analyses of the role of reference groups in upward mobility. They interpret "brown-nosing" and "sucking up" in

[74] It is this factor that helps explain why the "outsider" often seems uncouth. The medical family can transmit not only knowledge and help, but also the little nuances associated with professional behavior.

the army as a type of anticipatory socialization; that is, a man in one group takes as his reference group the group above him and adopts their mores. This action serves the double function of helping get the man into the superior group and of helping him adjust when he joins the group.[75]

Oswald Hall (69, pp. 327–28) has stated:

One function of ambition is to discipline present conduct in the interest of a future goal.

On the basis of this supposition, one would expect that the person who wishes to move to a high-status occupation in society must learn to give up the possibility of current lesser rewards in the interest of the larger occupational reward later. This phenomenon—often called the deferred gratification pattern—has been related to social class by Schneider and Lysgaard (161). They find a tendency in the middle class toward "impulse-renunciation" as illustrated in restrictions on fighting and physical sex expression, the pursuit of a long education, obedience to parents, restrictions on spending money, and high aspirations. By contrast, the lower class tends to be characterized by "impulse-following" behavior, or the reverse of the above.[76] The work of Hollingshead (78, pp. 176–78) provides one of the most intensive analyses of the class patterning of occupational aspirations, as revealed by high school students in Elmtown. He describes how children in his top two classes are urged by parents and teachers to stay in school and go on to college: it is almost taken for granted. Class III children may come from relatively secure families or from "climbers." If from the former, then *some* education is expected, say, high school at least; if from the latter, then their parents usually expect their children to achieve more than they did. This group will identify with the top-class students. Class IV children tend to enroll in the secretarial, agriculture, shop, and homemaking courses, but most parents are dubious that school has any but a limited vocational value. Class V students do not expect to finish high school but to quit when they can, escape both school and parental authority, and get a job. Although these limitations occur in the school, since high status positions in our society, especially the professions, so often require a college educa-

---

[75] It is necessary to bear in mind, however, that when the system is closed so that a man who engages in such behavior cannot move up, then the man will be rejected by those above him and by those below him to whom he is a renegade. In any case, such behavior may shake the solidarity of the group he is trying to leave.

[76] In another place, Lysgaard presents evidence that these differences are not due simply to differential opportunities but to different motivational patterns in the two social classes (110a, pp. 364–77).

tion, a very powerful restrictive force is in operation here. Another type of study has examined class differences in techniques of child rearing: there is evidence to support the belief that the middle class tends to be more restricting and controlling, and the lower class more permissive. Then, insofar as the former pattern helps to discipline a child toward rewards in the future, this pattern may help account for a difference in levels of aspiration of the two classes.[77] The findings are not, however, as reliable as once thought.[78] Nevertheless, although group differences may not be in the direction once thought, and though future research may yield many refinements, there seems little doubt that group experience affects not only the range of occupations but how high one will strive.[79]

This brings us to the conclusion of our discussion of social mobility. We turn next to an examination of career contingencies.

CAREER CONTINGENCIES

The word "career" is derived from a French word meaning "race-course" and connotes a relatively orderly sequence in a man's life: one starts at some definite point and ends at a predictable place. The fact that such orderliness is more characteristic of the high-status professions had led, sometimes, to the word "career's" being applied only to those in such professions: others simply have "jobs." Yet there is little reason for such restriction of usage. We can speak of a career irrespective of the status of an occupation, and even in situations where the person changes occupation. All that is necessary is that there be some type of recognizable *pattern* with at least roughly known probability. This means that we have some knowledge of the major kinds of events or phenomena which can produce these patterns and determine their probability of occurrence. These are career contingencies.

All studies of career mobility agree that a tremendous amount of job-changing is almost a characteristic of American workers.[80] It is

[77] These conclusions are associated with the so-called "Chicago school" and may be found in (38, 47, 112).

[78] See esp. the Boston study (113) in which class differences were found to be the reverse of the above studies on some variables. These researchers suggest that Ericson, Davis and Havighurst may have been describing the *upper* middle class, for Maccoby and Gibbs found the lower middle class to be quite permissive with their children. See also (73) where the serious sampling problems involved are discussed.

[79] Important also are studies of the actual interpersonal process by which ambition may be generated or striving may be encouraged. See the masterly description of how early parental patterning began in middle class homes in (1). See also the descriptions of the effects of childhood rejection on the striving patterns of children in (44, 46).

[80] See our discussion of mobility above, pp. 185 ff. See also (83, pp. 56–7), where the estimate is made that only about one man in five remains in the same major occupation group for his entire working life.

important therefore to examine the *sequence* of jobs. The data that we have on *first jobs* strongly suggest that these often serve the function of a "jockeying for position" while the individual surveys the course before him. Form and Miller's study (55, 56) of a sample of the Ohio labor force revealed two important kinds of unstable work patterns: the initial work period (jobs held before the individual completed his formal education) and the trial work period (jobs held less than three years). Although the initial work period was limited to the school period by definition, the authors found that the trial work period might occur many times in the life of a worker. His first job might, then, lead to quite a different job, though usually at the same level. Even for the case of business leaders, Warner and Abegglen (198, p. 118) found a considerable variety of first jobs: 34 per cent started as clerks or retail salesmen, 14 per cent as laborers, and 24 per cent in the professions (with engineering and law dominating). Lipset and Malm (105) remind us that the first job is, for many, taken for the experience it may provide for a later job, or it may be a low rung on a ladder the person is sure to climb.

While persons assess the opportunities before them (as they see them), occupations themselves may engage in deliberate recruiting. One of the best ways to secure a surplus of recruits (so that one can then start being choosy about who shall be let in) is to try to raise the prestige of the occupation. Since prestige cannot be simply manufactured, it is not surprising to find the quasi-magical practice of name-changing. Everett C. Hughes (81, pp. 313–14) writes:

The names (of occupations) are tags, a combination of price tag and calling card. One has only to hear casual conversation to sense how important these tags are. Hear a salesman, who has just been asked what he does, reply, "I am in sales work," or "I am in promotional work," not "I sell skillets." Schoolteachers sometimes turn school-teaching into educational work, and the disciplining of youngsters and chaperoning into personnel work. Teaching Sunday School becomes religious education, and the Y.M.C.A. Secretary is "in group work."

Yet sheer change of name and attempts to influence public opinion [81] will avail little unless there is a genuine change of function and an increase in the economic position of the practitioners. Hence, the occasional sense of outrage on the part of men who feel that the recruiting programs of the armed services have misled them. There is no "self-fulfilling prophecy" here.

[81] See Theodore Caplow's description (26, pp. 139–40). See also R. C. Myers description (133) of the tenacity of the myth of the boy apprentice in the old-line trades, such as carpentry and bricklaying. Such beliefs are strong enough to force the inclusion of minimum-age clauses in union contracts.

In what is perhaps the best theoretical statement of the categories of the career, viewed in sequential terms, Becker and Strauss (14) note that some occupations may take care of the recruiting problem by having established "feeding occupations" which provide a continuing stream of persons,[82] although sometimes the desire for "new blood" can mean that a person of divergent background can secure entry easily. A further problem is that of notifying persons. For example, the possibility of a career in art is known to high school students, but that of a physiologist may not be; yet one who would be a physiologist should begin taking biology in high school. Becker and Strauss refer also to the problem of recruiting into low-status occupations. These, they point out, may be recruited from failures in other areas,[83] from those who reject traditional values (such as jazz musicians who may play in dives because only there do they have the freedom to play as they want), and from transients who regard their present job as temporary.[84]

It is important to recognize that once a person is recruited into an occupation, he does not necessarily want to move up. Personal attachments and pride of competence may make a person wish to remain at his job or level, or a person (for example, a schoolteacher in a slum school) may prefer a snug berth rather than face the problem of adjusting to a new situation even though it is a promotion (to a school in a "good" neighborhood). Therefore, Becker and Strauss (14, p. 259) write:

. . . the institution has devices to make him forget, to plunge him into the new office, to woo and win him with new gratifications, and, at the same time, to force him to abandon the old.

At the other end of the career, it may be necessary to force persons out. Sometimes this is needed to keep alive the upward mobile hopes of others further down, or the person may himself refuse to recognize that he is no longer capable of carrying on as usual because of aging—as in the case of persons in sports, airline pilots, prostitutes, and many types of criminals. The experience of continued failure may make it plain to some that they must leave, but where the lives and futures of others are involved, one cannot wait that long. So one gets honorific promotions,

[82] A phenomenon often incident to downward movement from other occupations, as illustrated by the often-stated (and untested) belief that there is a sequence as follows: medical student, dental student, pharmacy student, salesmen of medical and dental supplies.

[83] A remarkable contingency is presented here by the fact that one man's failure may be another man's success. For example, a white person whose own business has recently failed is forced to take a clerical job next to a Negro who has fought to get up that high.

[84] A frequent source of workers for taxi companies and mail-order houses.

demotions, bribing persons to leave, downgrading persons, or sending them "out to the sticks." [85]

A major occupational career contingency revolves about *age grading*. There are "young men's jobs" and "old men's jobs." A rough measure of the likelihood of mobility into various occupations is presented by Natalie Rogoff and is reproduced in Table 20. Since our interest here is not in trends, we present only the data for 1940.

TABLE 20

AVERAGE MOBILITY INTO EACH CLASS OF DESTINATION BY SON'S AGE, 1940 *

CLASS OF DESTINATION	SON'S AGE		
	UNDER 24	24–30	OVER 30
Professional	0.41	1.39	1.53
Semi-professional	0.96	1.10	0.70
Proprietors, etc.	0.56	0.79	1.21
Clerical and sales	0.93	0.91	0.96
Skilled	0.84	0.75	1.01
Semi-skilled	1.01	0.83	0.58
Unskilled	0.94	0.49	0.62
Protective service	0.82	1.14	0.56
Other service	0.98	0.82	0.74
Farming	0.25	0.27	0.39
All classes	0.77	0.85	0.83

* Rogoff, N., *Recent Trends in Occupational Mobility*, Glencoe, Ill.: The Free Press, 1953, Table 46, p. 101.

The table refers only to those who moved out of their father's occupational group. The following rough conclusions can be drawn: (1) Men twenty-four or older found it easier to enter any occupational group than did men under twenty-four. (2) "Young men's occupations" seem to be: semiskilled, other service, semiprofessional, and unskilled. (3) "Older men's occupations" appear to be: professional, proprietors, etc., and clerical and sales.[86] There is a definite relation to degree of preparation, need for capital, and status here.

The increased emphasis being placed on education has tended to keep young persons off the labor market to an older age, particularly those men who are upward-mobile. One should not, however, ignore the effect of what Parsons (142, p. 606) has called the "youth culture" in examining the selective effects of age. He writes:

[85] See (64). Especially interesting has been the recruitment of retired army generals into manufacturing, finance, education, and government. See (150).

[86] Strictly speaking these are not young or old men's occupations, but rather those young or old men are likely to have moved into from other occupations their fathers held.

Perhaps the best single point of reference for characterizing the youth culture lies in its contrast with the dominant pattern of the adult male role. By contrast with the emphasis on responsibility in this role, the orientation of the youth culture is more or less specifically irresponsible.

This irreponsibility Parsons illustrates by reference to the emphasis on "having a good time," athletics, attractiveness to the opposite sex, and rebelliousness. The very fact that these activities contrast with the "bitter reality" of maturity may, suggests Parsons, help explain them. There is something here of the "have fun while you may" pattern. Young persons, then, should not be thought of primarily as occupation-holders. Though many, of course, do work at an early age, in 1950, there were less than three-quarters of a million workers between the ages of ten and fifteen in the United States.

Within an occupation, there is often a conception of a proper rate of movement which is also related to age: one is expected to have passed certain points by a given age. During the great depression of the thirties, many persons over forty years of age who had held academic positions were unable to secure jobs in spite of their willingness to accept bottom-rank instructorships: an instructorship is a young man's job. Ambitions and hopes are themselves related to age: we have the paradox that, especially in middle-class occupations, hopes for success are highest and drives strongest when persons are young, but one may not achieve that success until one is too old to share it with one's children or even to enjoy it oneself. What was exciting at twenty-five may be boring at fifty.

Age-grading is frequently upset by technological change or by rapid expansion. During World War II, we had to train many officers, who, because of need, were advanced very rapidly. Then the colonel who was a career officer and had spent twenty-five years reaching that rank might suddenly find a mere baby at a nearby desk who was also a colonel (and worse, had "stars in his eyes"). One gets a similar occurrence in industry in a period of expansion. At such time, many persons of the same age enter at once, and reach the appropriate age of advancement at about the same time. Yet they obviously cannot all be promoted. Then there are failures of expectations due to changing technical processes (193) or the plant itself may be moved, leaving many workers other than those who depended on their earnings, in a state of disorganization (157). Quite another kind of upset of expectations occurs when a neighborhood population changes radically in ethnicity or social class. In one kind of change, the "foreign" restaurant finds it must leave or face bankruptcy; whereas in the opposite kind of a change, a schoolteacher, Becker (11) tells us, who has settled down in a school in a "nice" neighborhood finds that it is not "nice" any more.

These things provide occupational career hazards. In the academic profession there has developed the notion that one should not be an instructor or an assistant professor too long. Some schools formalize the requirements and insist that after a given period the person shall either be promoted or discharged.

Furthermore, we expect that a person will go through each of the steps or stages and will not skip any on the way. One of the greatest causes of resentment in the work situation is provided by the individual who skips from one stage to a considerably higher one. This makes meaningless the career plans of others. One cannot very easily count upon being promoted to that position oneself if one's competitors include not only those at the same level as oneself but also those at lower levels as well.

Coupled with the notion of age-grading is also the principle of the point-of-crucial-decision in the career. When does one decide to enter on occupation? In physics, the student may decide in high school that he will make physics his lifelong career. He may then proceed in a fairly well-defined pattern through high school, college, graduate work, to employment in teaching or as a research physicist, or on the staff of a factory. We have here a straight career line. The point of crucial decision has been pushed down.

In sociology as recently as a generation ago we had just the opposite situation. The decision might be made when the individual was a graduate student or when he already had left school and had been working for a number of years. The ranks of sociology were made up to a considerable extent of former preachers, school teachers, politicians, newspaper men, and others who had come upon sociology at relatively late points in their lives. This phenomenon has by no means vanished but the attempt is being made to push the point of decision down. The same thing is true in the field of social work.

This phenomenon comes to the attention of the individual in a particularly bitter form. The individual may wish to make what would otherwise be a crucial decision but he finds it is too late to do so, that he has already reached an age or a degree of responsibility where he is unable to turn back in his tracks. To many such persons the area becomes a hobby or else they seek friends among the members of the group that they might otherwise have joined.

THE OCCUPATION AND THE SELF

C. Wright Mills divides all philosophies of work into two great categories: the various forms of Protestantism (and their secular derivatives) which saw work as a means to salvation (or to some external reward), and the Renaissance view which saw work as intrinsically meaningful, creative, and satisfying in its own right. But, he says (129, p. 219), work is neither of those to the modern worker:

If there is little Calvinist compulsion to work among propertyless factory workers and file clerks, there is also little Renaissance exuberance in the work of the insurance clerk, freight handler, or department-store saleslady. If the shoe sales-man or the textile executive gives little thought to the religious meaning of his labor, certainly few telephone operators or receptionists or schoolteachers ex-perience from their work any Ruskinesque inner calm. Such joy as creative work may carry is more and more limited to a small minority.

Although Mills is referring to white-collar workers, his picture could be generalized to other groups as well. However, instead of settling, it raises the question: what meaning *does* work have to modern workers? And certainly the twofold division is overly broad, for we will wish to know how whatever meaning work does have is articulated with other areas of life.

THE OCCUPATION AS A VOCATION

The term "vocation" means literally a "calling" and as such refers to occupational situations in which the person's work is felt to be his whole life. He identifies with his work as a burden and feels an obligation to try to be especially good or proficient. As such the term is used most commonly among the clergy and among professionals in general.[87]

Sometimes, however, the enthusiasm hoped for may get out of hand and the group may be forced to use repressive measures. Barrett, an ex-Jesuit, in describing his experiences in the Order complains of what he feels was unjustified chastisement. He had done considerable research on the dubious (to the Jesuits) field of psychoanalysis and was getting ready to publish a book on the subject. Flush with excitement, he describes his shock at the reaction of the Order (9, p. 327):

When my two years of special study in biology and psychology at London Uni-versity were finished, my Provincial showed his appreciation of these sciences by sending me to teach spelling, reading and recitation to little country boys in an out of the way village in Ireland.

One commonly finds the conception of the occupation as a "calling" in new instructors or teaching fellows. Often they are very enthusiastic,

---

[87] (13) gives a picture of the identifications of graduate students in physiology, mechanical engineering, and philosophy. (185) points out that the internalization of the desired role personality may best be carried out when students live in a separate professional community. The latter situation is found for physicians and nurses, but not for pharmacists and optometrists. Hence some of the professional problems of the latter.

and worry intensely about their lectures. When a student asks a question which they are unable to answer immediately they feel embarrassed and may scurry out and search the literature to present a thorough, definitive statement. Each student they are forced to fail is like the stab of a dagger. "It is not the student that has failed; it is *I* who have."

At the other extreme is the casual attitude. The individual looks upon the occupation for its money and prestige alone and would change readily to a different job if a higher wage or other inducement were offered. His work does not enter much into his personality.

Most workers are likely to fall somewhere in between. Bakke has described (6, p. 96; 7, pp. 68–70, 256–61) the situation with reference to skilled workers. He found that they did tend to feel some identification with the job. When these men became unemployed they did not immediately rush out to seek another job at the same level in a different occupation. Instead they were likely to wait awhile. In order to change occupations one must change one's self-conception. One must alter the feeling that one expresses when one says, "This is the sort of man I am." Everett Hughes [88] has described the situation in industry in which a recession occurred and a man who was accustomed to receiving over two dollars an hour was offered a position at $1.90 an hour. He refused the job and in explanation said, "You don't understand. I am a two-dollar man."

All occupations have a little of the vocation in them. The extent to which this element is present is likely to be significant in predicting the behavior of the worker.

IDENTIFICATIONS

Occupation is not the only thing the person has. He has also sex, family, church, race, hobbies, politics, and each of these involves identifications which are also part of the self. Morse and Weiss (132) reported that 80 per cent of a random sample of employed men said they would keep on working even though they did not have to in order to earn a living. But when asked for their major reasons, about two-thirds referred to such factors as "to keep occupied," "feel lost, go crazy," "not know what to do with my time, can't be idle," or "keeps individual healthy, good for person," and only 9 per cent referred specifically to the kind of work they did or its satisfactions. Morse and Weiss are led to conclude (132, p. 192) that work serves to: ". . . anchor the individual into the society." That is, work has diffuse functions outside the job itself.[89]

[88] In private conversations.
[89] See (43 and 60, especially the article by the editors), and (108). On the other hand, note the emphasis on the satisfactions that *some* workers get from conveyor belt or repetitive work in (61).

At the same time, the other roles the individual has may conflict with the demands of his occupation. The major kinds of alternative loyalties may be classified as loyalties to a cause, to an outside group, to the organization within which one works, and to one's clients.

Identification with a cause is probably illustrated better nowhere else than in Pearl Buck's description (23, pp. 68–69) of her father's behavior as a missionary: he identified with God only:

> He never obeyed any rules at all, because they always seemed to conflict with what was his duty, and he always knew his duty. The others might vote and decide, for the Work was supposed to be carried on by a sort of democratic decision of all the missionaries, subject to their financial boards in America. But Andrew [her father] listened only to God. Lack of money never stopped him. If he had no money, and he never had it, he wrote to anybody he knew who had any, asking for it shamelessly. If he got it, and he often did, he was supposed by mission rule to report it and put it into the common budget. But though he would report it if he thought of it, he never gave it up and he used it as he liked—always to push on into the interior (of China), to open up new little centers for his preaching. I have seen other lesser and more bureaucratic missionaries grow almost demented trying to control Andrew. They shouted bitter words at him, they threatened him with expulsion if he did not cease disobeying rules, over and over they called him a heretic, once even called him insane because he seemed to hear nothing they said. He was a rock in the midst of all the frothing—unmoved, unresentful, serene, but so determined, so stubborn in his own way, that I know there have been those who, seeing that high, obstinate, angelic tranquillity, have felt like going out and groaning and beating their heads against a wall in sheer excess of helpless rage. But Andrew did not know even that they were angry with him. Had he not told them God's will? He must obey God's will.

The leadership of an occupation wish members to obey *its* rules. But occasionally someone like Andrew comes along and insists that he has a higher allegiance: he gets his instructions straight from God himself. How can one control such a man?

When the late Nurse Sister Kenny met opposition to her method of treating poliomyelitis from the medical profession, she made her method into a cause by taking her case to the public. The result was that some fairly worshipped her, but others regarded her as a quack.

The matter comes to this. If one identifies with one's colleagues, one has to learn to keep certain silences, and one of the most important kinds of silences are about new developments in the occupation. The accepted procedure is to let one's colleagues pass judgment on new things. If one takes the new idea or technique to the people, one is rejecting one's colleagues and their opinions. The resulting criticism may be harsh, but it should not be surprising.

Another kind of identification is with a group outside one's occupation. Among the most important kinds of groups are ethnic or racial groups, women, and labor unions. Ethnic or racial identifications often turn up with the entry of ethnic or racial groups into an occupation previously preempted by another ethnic or racial group. For example, the first Negro physician in an area has often engaged in a fight to secure the right to practice. The question then arises: which identification is uppermost in his mind, that with his medical colleagues or that with his race? His medical colleagues will expect him to behave like a trusted member of the profession; the members of his race will hold him up as a model for their children and as a symbol of hope and will expect him to be mindful of the needs of his group. But suppose that the Negro doctor learns that a hospital has a racial policy, for example a quota system on Negro nurses. Shall he then notify Negro leaders in the community? If he does not and it is found out anyway (as it is likely to be), then the Negroes will accuse him of deserting them. On the other hand, if he does inform the group then it is likely that other doctors will reject him as a man who cannot be trusted to keep his mouth shut. It may be perfectly well-understood why he would feel the pressure that he does feel. Nevertheless it may be felt that if he is unable to maintain silence in that subject then he cannot be trusted to maintain silence on other delicate matters.

Oswald Hall (69, pp. 97–98) has described the dilemma of the doctor of Italian descent. Often he has risen from the slums and wishes to be successful. In order to earn the respect of his colleagues, he will desire a widespread clientele which will include others besides Italians. He may find that in order to secure this clientele he has to refuse to treat some of his poorer Italian patients. This may lead to his being rejected by his own friends, and accused of being a renegade, or else they may say "Success has gone to his head."

The Negro personnel man in industry is not likely to be considered a full member of the colleague group of personnel men. He is usually expected and hired to deal with the peculiar *Negro* problems in the plant. That is he is expected to deal with problems which arise because a part of the working force are Negroes. As Hughes (82, pp. 77 ff.) has pointed out, his position is really that of a straw boss: his job is to interpret management to the Negro and vice versa. The question then arises in his mind: what is he, a Negro or a personnel man?

A similar problem is faced by the woman in personnel work. She is usually hired because there are many women working in the plant and she is to provide the "women's point of view." Shall she be a feminist and fight for the rights of women, or shall she identify with her personnel colleagues? [90]

Some persons become active in union affairs at the local level until they begin to think of themselves primarily as members of the union. Occasionally this identification takes on the elements of a cause, but since labor unions are so widely accepted, it is more often a role alternative to that of employee of the company, which has its own rewards. O. W. Phelps (146) has pointed out that union leaders typically have low community prestige, a fact related in part to their own background, but in part also to the occupation itself. But this prestige may not compare at all with their power, and, occasionally, with their income. A man may rise high in the union and yet still never be invited to his boss's home for dinner.[91]

Where do these people belong—to their race, sex, labor union, or occupation? If the number of Negroes in the plant be reduced, will management keep the Negro personnel man on as a general personnel man? Probably not. This may push him to identify with Negroes, for what chance does he have anyhow? [92] The situation is similar for the woman, while the union man may find there are greater personal rewards and satisfactions in his union role than in that of worker.[93]

Besides other groups, there may be identification dilemmas with reference to the relation of one's occupation to the organization in which one's occupation is carried out. In a factory, for example, the foreman is expected to interpret management to the workers and also carry the complaints of the workers up to management. If he insists on the workers' problems too much then he is likely to be felt to be an agitator. But in order to get a hearing he frequently *has* to insist. If he listens to the workers too much, management may feel that he is encouraging questions and that therefore he is encouraging discontent.

In teaching, one finds a conflict between the claims of the college administration and of professional ethics. How many failures shall the instructor give in a class? Usually this is clearly specified in the catalogue

[90] Josephine J. Williams (206) has described the marriage-career dilemma of the woman doctor. If she marries, she will practice medicine less, especially at night. Worth noting is Miss Williams' caution about regarding women as minority groups for they are quite different in three respects: they marry, they compete for the best clientele, and they expect special consideration (at least men often think they do).

[91] See the discussion below of this phenomenon, pp.

[92] A similar situation confronts the Negro union official. See (96). Even holiness and sacredness may be racially defined. See (52).

[93] It has often been noted that the phenomenon we describe may give persons like the Negro or female personnel official, or anyone who lives "off the backs" of such groups, a stake in the continued existence of segregation. For if segregation ceased, they might lose their jobs or positions. See (42, pp. 430 ff.) on the doctrine of the "double-duty dollar."

or else there exists a set of expectations. The administration will not wish an instructor to give too many F's and yet by the instructor's own standards or the standard of excellence that he has been taught he may feel that half the class should receive F's.

Burchard (24) has studied the problem of the military chaplain who must reconcile his role as one who helps the men adjust to the task of killing others with the Biblical injunction against the taking of life. Some, he found, had not thought about it, some saw no conflict, and some claimed the injunction has been mistranslated and should read "You shall not murder" rather than "You shall not kill."

In a broad sense, the whole society is an organization within which all occupations are practiced, and that has meant, especially in recent years, meeting the demands that may be made by the state. Ralph S. Brown, Jr. (21) estimates that about one-fifth of jobs now require some type of security or loyalty test. In Soviet Russia, the physician occupies a unique role. A medical excuse is needed to explain tardiness at work. If a physician gives too many, he may be exposed to state pressure; if he gives too few, he will be exposed to pressure from his patients (50).

A final type of orientation one may adopt is identification with one's clients. Hall's distinction (70) between what he calls the "colleague type" of doctor and the "individualistic type" is essentially a distinction between one who is oriented to his colleagues and one who is oriented to his patients (often because he has no alternative). As Hall points out, the former does not have to be aggressive about getting patients for the referral system keeps him occupied; the other, however, must depend on attracting patients directly, a much more difficult job. Among college professors one gets, occasionally, the "student man"—one who spends much time counselling students, helping them put on dances, and so forth, to the possible neglect of his teaching or research.

The accepted colleague personality is a balance between the various identifications, but the nature of this balance is usually not clearly defined within the occupation. The man whose identification on the job is to *break* all of management's rules is likely to be pitied but the man who obeys all of the rules is apt to be disliked. Neither is tolerated.

In the professions a similar balance is expected. Within medicine, the man who never tries anything new until it has been demonstrated beyond all possible doubt is considered to be a conservative and fuddy-duddy. On the other hand, the man who snatches up any new technique or any new drug as soon as he hears of it is felt to be attempting to curry public favor and is also rejected. One is expected to take up the new advances in the profession but before doing so to talk them over with one's colleagues. In the case of the Negro it is expected that he will behave like one. He is not fooling anyone by attempting completely to identify with the white doctors. It is expected and considered normal that he should be interested in Negro problems but it is expected also that he should not let them obscure his professional allegiances. Again, the proper procedure is to discuss matters with one's colleagues first.

Incentive systems must tie themselves to these identifications. Most of them tend to appeal to the lone individual and to take little account of his identification with his colleagues or with other groups that may be important to him. There is frequently an assumption that the worker identifies only with management, is interested only in getting ahead by individual mobility. Consequently a reward is held out which appeals to the individual. The worker is told *"You* work hard and *you* will get more."* There are at least two considerations here in attempting to predict the effect of such an incentive system on the worker. The first is the matter, already referred to, of where the worker's identification may in fact lie. But for those who may be tempted, a second matter must be considered and that is the likehood of success. Hughes (82, pp. 80 ff.) has referred to the ambivalence of management with reference to pro- motion and upward mobility. It is desired that persons will orient them- selves toward management's goals. At the same time it is not desired that *too* many people will do so, particularly those of ethnic membership dif- ferent from that of management. Management may not actually promote the Negro or promote the Japanese. Consequently the worker will raise in his mind the question of whether there is any point at all in striv- ing for those goals. The higher rungs of management, after all, are trodden by very few and are not likely to be trodden at all by persons of an ethnic group being discriminated against.

OCCUPATIONAL PERSONALITY

Although both Veblen and Bogardus (192, 20) called our attention long ago to the problem of the relation between occupation and personality, it is a subject about which we know surprisingly little. We have many impressionistic descriptions (129, pp. 183–84) but few empirical studies. One that has received considerable theoretical and some research atten- tion has been the bureacratic personality. Merton, in a famous article (118), described how Veblen's concept of "trained incapacity" or Wundt's "heterogony of ends" (both implying a displacement of goals wherein what is a means to an end becomes an end in itself) apply especially to the bureaucrat. In order to achieve the bureaucratic goals of precision, reliability, and efficiency, emphasis is placed on rule-adherence, duty- specification in the office, and motivation not through competition, but through tenure, seniority, pensions, and so on. But, Merton points out, these very devices which increase the likelihood of conformity to expectations may also lead to too much concern with strict adherence to regulations with the results of timidity, conservatism, and technicism. The latter qualities are then characteristic of the personality of the bureaucrat. Davis (37) provides us with a striking case of overconcern with rule-compliance in a description of bombers out on submarine patrol whose crews avoided the possibility of being criticized by their superiors for errors by sticking to their patrols exactly as charted beforehand. This meant ignoring unknown objects which happened to lie a few miles abeam.[94] But on the other hand, Turner (189) reports that the Navy disbursing officer, who was also diverted from ideal-typical bureaucratic behavior by various pressures, moved not in the direction of ultra-formalism but toward *personal* functioning. He found the commonest type was not the Regulation type but what he calls the Realist ("Rules specify chiefly the papers which must be filed . . ."). Such a person responded to pressure from friends, and from simulated friends ("earbanging") and participated in the exchange system of favors. He might also use his position to enhance his status. The bureaucratic personality, then, seems to be a *possibility*, rather than a certainty.

Another type that has been examined empirically has been the successful business executive. Henry (75), using the Thematic Apperception Test, a short undirected interview and a projective analysis of a number of traditional personality tests, found the following characteristics to be common to over one hundred business executives (the majority in distributive industries): high drive and achievement desire; strong mobility drive; a view of authority as controlling but helpful; strong ability to impose order on unstructured situations (though often this order is a forced one); ability to make decisions; strong self-structured (they know what they are and what they want); need to keep active; fear of failure; strong reality orientation (the immediate, the practical, and the direct; a concern may prevent their being men of vision): interested in their superiors (treating subordinates in a detached, though not cold, manner); attitude to parents one of having cut ties with home; and a need to operate within an established framework [that is, they are not empire-builders (197, Chs. 4, 5)]. A variety of other occupations have been studied with varying degrees of intensity and reliability, including dentists, ministers, industrial rate-busters, taxi-dancers, prison guards and wardens, nurses, lawyers, boxers, and others.[95]

In addition to the actual personality type or patterns that may be

---

[94] For a thorough discussion of the diffusion of conformist tendencies into almost all areas of life, see (205).

[95] See (10; 26, pp. 130–37; 30; 35; 41; 158; 159; 160; 163; 201).

associated with particular occupations, there is also the question of the kinds of pictures we carry around in our heads of occupational members. We think of the bank clerk as a cold, cautious, suspicious, meticulous individual. We like to think of the doctor as a person of middle age, gray at the temples, slow spoken but self-confident. The lawyer is a glib talker and the professor is someone who is never able to come to a conclusion.

While these are unquestionably exaggerations or stereotypes, an interesting consequence is that because of them we tend to expect that kind of behavior from these persons and may judge them in terms of whether they fit what is *considered* to be the appropriate personality. If they do not our confidence may be shaken. We expect the bank clerk to be suspicious and even though we are upset when he questions our checks, it is behavior that we have come to expect. The bank clerk who makes only a desultory attempt to verify the customer's identification may please the customer for the moment but at the same time may make him worried about the safety of the money he has on deposit in the bank. Although we may recognize, intellectually, that a young doctor might be just as capable as a middle-aged one, we are likely to feel safer in the hands of the latter.

As a consequence, the member of the occupation who does not have the expected occupational personality may not enjoy as much success as the member who does. There operates a type of personality selection here.

Actual occupational personality may be related to temperament or intelligence. The ability to learn certain manual skills is, as we know, a variable. The Vocational Guidance Movement at one time attempted to convince persons of the philosophy that there was a definite person for each job. It was maintained that individuals must be selected in such a manner they they would then fit into the required job on the basis of skills. But there is a growing feeling that these skills are not so crucial as they used to be. This has been true particularly as machine industry has grown and as the need for semiskilled persons rather than skilled persons has increased. However, other personality traits may then be important; docility, the ability to resist fatigue, or satisfaction in performing simple tasks may increase in significance.

An important question in this connection is whether the occupation produces the personality or whether persons of a certain personality tend to be *selected* by the occupation. In the case of the bank clerk, for example (assuming he *is* a cautious, suspicious person), does the occupation itself tend to make the individual cautious and suspicious, or does the occupation *attract* persons who are suspicious and cautious to begin with? A study of particular significance because it deals with bureaucratic personality is that by Sperling (178). He raises the question, implied by Turner (189), as to why *some* persons develop the personality extreme described by Merton and others do not (178, p. 90):

Pedantry is not the logical result of precision. The sense of limitation of one's authority does not by itself degenerate into avoidance of responsibility. Specialization does not necessarily turn into "trained incapacity," and it is naively benevolent to assume that chicanery stems from the "sanctification of routine."

Using as subjects twenty bureaucrats whom he psychoanalyzed, Sperling reports that the majority were compulsive, with the rest being fanatics and psychopaths, and these patterns had developed when the subjects were children. He found that the most important motivation among the compulsives was unconscious sadism;

Direct gratification of sadism being excluded in our culture, officialism in government provided for my patients an opportunity to vent their sadism in occupations which provide rational motives, and to change socially acceptable action, by a small variation, into chicanery.

For example, he cites the case of an army officer in a displaced persons' camp who issued an order forbidding keeping pets under the pretence of cleanliness but actually to secure an inmate's dog which the officer's mistress wanted.[96]

There is not, however, any necessary contradiction between Sperling's findings and those of the other studies we have discussed. Merton pointed out that, given the role expectation of the bureaucrat, the so-called "bureaucratic personality" (over-emphasis on conformance) was possible, and Davis provided a concrete instance from the Navy. Turner showed that this kind of behavior did not necessarily happen, and Sperling, finally, suggests that such behavior may be more characteristic of persons who have a compulsive personality to begin with. In sum, there is probably both a process of personality selection and one of molding for occupations. A certain type of personality may be attracted to an occupation with higher probability than another type. But whatever the original personality, the occupation takes the person and further molds his personality until it becomes one felt to be appropriate to the occupation. If the individual is unable to adjust to this process or unable to redefine the status so that it conforms more with his own talents and conceptions, then the hypothesis would be that he would move on to some other occupations.[97]

---

[96] Roughly confirming Sperling's findings is (45). See also (3).

[97] An important kind of research on which no more than a beginning has been made is the association of mental disorders with occupations. See (31a, 97a).

A further question for research has to do with the extent to which the occupational personality is emphasized. Certainly our conception of what constitutes the ideal physician is a much clearer one than is our conception of what constitutes the ideal sewing machine operator. Our images with reference to many occupations are not at all clear. It is probably true that it is among the recognized professions that we find the most highly developed conceptions of occupational personality. In part this is due to the fact that the professions are considered vital to society. It is, therefore, these that we watch and picture more clearly, though not necessarily more accurately, than others.

CHAPTER REFERENCES

1. Aberle, D. F. and Naegele, K. D., "Middle-Class Fathers' Occupational Role and Attitudes Toward Children," *American Journal of Orthopsychiatry*, 22:366–378, 1952.

2. Abrahamson, S., "Our Status System and Scholastic Rewards," *Journal of Educational Sociology*, 25:441–450, 1952.

3. Allen, P. J., "Childhood Backgrounds of Success in a Profession," *American Sociological Review*, 20:186–190, 1955.

4. Archibald, K., *Wartime Shipyard*, Berkeley and Los Angeles: University of California Press, 1947.

5. Baetjer, A. N., *Women in Industry: Their Health and Efficiency*, Philadelphia, 1946.

6. Bakke, E. W., *Citizens Without Work*, New Haven: Yale University Press, 1940.

7. ———, *The Unemployed Man*, New York: Dutton, 1934.

8. Barber, B., *Social Stratification*, New York: Harcourt, Brace, 1957.

9. Barrett, E. B., *The Jesuit Enigma*, New York: Boni and Liveright, 1927.

10. Barthuli, E. F., "Occupational Attitudes of Dentists," *Sociology and Social Research*, 20:548–551, 1936.

11. Becker, H. S., "The Career of the Chicago Public Schoolteacher," *American Journal of Sociology*, 57:470–477, 1952.

12. ———, "Social-Class Variations in the Teacher-Pupil Relationship," *Journal of Educational Sociology*, 25:451–465, 1952.

13. ——— and Carper, J. W., "The Development of Identification with an Occupation," *American Journal of Sociology*, 61:289–298, 1956.

14. ——— and Strauss, A. L., "Careers, Personality, and Adult Socialization," *American Journal of Sociology*, 62:253–263, 1956.

15. Bell, H., *Youth Tell Their Story*, Washington, D.C.: American Council on Education, 1938.

16. Bendix, R. and Lipset, S. M. (eds.), *Class, Status and Power*, Glencoe, Ill.: Free Press, 1953.

17. ———, "Social Mobility and Occupational Career Plans: I. Stability of Jobholding," *American Journal of Sociology*, 57:336–374, 1952.

18. ———, "Social Mobility and Occupational Career Plans: II. Social Mobility," *American Journal of Sociology*, 57:494–504, 1952.

19. ——— and Malm, F. T., "Social Origins and Occupational Career Patterns," *Industrial and Labor Relations Review*, 7:246–261, 1954.

20. Bogardus, E., "The Occupational Attitude," *Journal of Applied Sociology*, 8:171–177, 1924.

21. Brown, R. S., Jr., "Loyalty-Security Measures and Employment Opportunities," *Bulletin of the Atomic Scientists*, 11:113–117, 1955.

22. Brown, M., "The Status of Jobs and Occupations as Evaluated by an Urban Negro Sample," *American Sociological Review*, 20:561–566, 1955.

23. Buck, P. S., *Fighting Angel*, New York: Reynal and Hitchcock, 1936.

24. Burchard, W. W., "Role Conflicts of Military Chaplains," *American Sociological Review*, 19:528–535, 1954.

25. Caplow, T., "Los Principios de la Distribución Ocupacional," *Revista Mexicana de Sociologia*, 15:363–374, 1953.

26. ———, *The Sociology of Work*, Minneapolis: University of Minnesota Press, 1954.

27. ———, "Transiency as a Cultural Pattern," *American Sociological Review*, 5:731–739, 1940.

28. Carr-Saunders, A. M., *The Population Problem*, Oxford: Clarendon, 1922.

29. Centers, R., "Occupational Mobility of Urban Occupational Strata," *American Sociological Review*, 13:197–203, 1948.

30. Chapman, S. H., "The Minister: Professional Man of the Church," *Social Forces*, 23:202–206, 1944.

31. Chinoy, E., "Social Mobility Trends in the United States," *American Sociological Review*, 20:180–186, 1955.

31a. Clark, R. E., "Psychoses, Income, and Occupational Prestige," *American Journal of Sociology*, 54:433–440, 1949.

32. Cook, R. C., *Human Fertility*, New York: William Sloane Association, 1951.

33. Corey, L., "Problems of the Peace: IV. The Middle Class," *The Antioch Review*, 5:68–87, 1945.

34. Cuber, J. F. and Kenkel, W. F., *Social Stratification in the United States*, New York: Appleton-Century-Crofts, 1954.

35. Dalton, M., "The Industrial 'Rate-Buster.' A Characterization," *Applied Anthropology*, 7:5–18, 1948.

36. Davidson, P. E. and Anderson, H. D., *Occupational Mobility in an American Community*, Stanford: Stanford University Press, 1937.

37. Davis, A. K., "Bureaucratic Patterns in the Navy Officer Corps," *Social Forces*, 27:143–153, 1948.

38. Davis, A. and Havighurst, R. J., *Father of the Man*, Boston: Houghton, Mifflin, 1947.

39. Davis, Kingsley, *Human Society*, New York: Macmillan, 1949, pp. 378 ff.

40. Davis, K. and Moore, W. E., "Some Principles of Stratification," *American Sociological Review*, 10:242–249, 1945.
41. Desenberg, B. N., "Occupational Attitudes of Taxi-Dancers," *Sociology and Social Research*, 25:258–263, 1941.
42. Drake, St. C. and Cayton, H. R., *Black Metropolis*, New York: Harcourt, Brace, 1945.
43. Dubin, R., "Industrial Workers' Worlds: A Study of the 'Central Life Interests' of Industrial Workers," *Social Problems*, 3:131–142, 1956.
44. Dynes, R. R.; Clarke, A. C.; and Dinitz, S., "Levels of Occupational Aspiration: Some Aspects of Family Experiences as a Variable," *American Sociological Review*, 21:212–215, 1956.
45. Eliasberg, W. G., "Psychodynamics of the Industrial Executive," Committee on Public Information of American Psychiatric Association, *Proceedings of Meetings May 13–17, 1957*, Paper No. 118.
46. Ellis, E., "Social Psychological Correlates of Upward Social Mobility Among Unmarried Career Women," *American Sociological Review*, 17:558–563, 1952.
47. Ericson, M., "Child-Rearing and Social Status," *American Journal of Sociology*, 52:190–192, 1946.
48. Faris, R. E. L., "Interaction of Generations and Family Stability," *American Sociological Review*, 12:159–164, 1947.
49. ———, "The Alleged Class System in the United States," *Research Studies, State College of Washington*, 22:77–83, 1954.
50. Field, M. G., "Structured Strain in the Role of the Soviet Physician," *American Journal of Sociology*, 58:493–502, 1953.
51. Floro, G. K., "Continuity in City-Manager Careers," *American Journal of Sociology*, 61:240–246, 1955.
52. Foley, A. S., "The Status and Role of the Negro Priest in the American Catholic Clergy," *American Catholic Sociological Review*, 16:83–93, 1955.
53. Foote, N. N., "The Professionalization of Labor in Detroit," *American Journal of Sociology*, 58:371–380, 1953.
54. ——— and Hatt, P. K., "Social Mobility and Economic Advancement," *American Economic Review*, Papers and Proceedings, 43:364–378, May, 1953.
55. Form, W. H. and Miller, D. C., "Measuring Patterns of Occupational Security," *Sociometry*, 10:362–375, 1947.
56. ———, "Occupational Career Pattern as a Sociological Instrument," *American Journal of Sociology*, 54:317–329, 1949.
57. "The Fortune Survey; XXVII The People of the U.S.A.—A Self-Portrait," *Fortune*, 21:14 ff., Feb., 1940.
58. "The Fortune Survey: The American Factory Worker," *Fortune*, 35:5 ff., May, 1947.
59. Freedman, R. and Hawley, A. H., "Migration and Occupational Mobility in the Depression," *American Journal of Sociology*, 55:171–177, 1949.

60. Friedmann, E. A. and Havighurst, R. J. (eds.), *The Meaning of Work and Retirement*, Chicago: University of Chicago Press, 1954.
61. Friedmann, G., "Outline for a Psycho-Sociology of Assembly Line Work," *Human Organization*, 12:15–20, 1954.
62. Froomkin, J. and Jaffe, A. J., "Occupational Skill and Socioeconomic Structure," *American Journal of Sociology*, 59:42–48, 1953.
63. Gilbert Youth Research Co., *Lewiston (Ida.) Morning Tribune*, Aug. 25, 1957, Sec. 1, p. 5.
64. Goffman, E., "On Cooling the Mark Out: Some Aspects of Adaptation to Failure," *Psychiatry*, 15:451–463, 1952.
65. Goodrich, C. and Davison, S., "The Wage Earner in the Westward Movement I," *Political Science Quarterly*, 50:161–185, 1935.
65a. ———, "The Wage Earner in the Westward Movement II," *Political Science Quarterly*, 51:61–116, 1936.
66. Gold, R., "Janitor Versus Tenants: A Status-Income Dilemma," *American Journal of Sociology*, 57:486–493, 1952.
67. Green, T. L., "Vocational Problems in Education in S. E. Asia," *Journal of Educational Sociology*, 26:380–391, 1953.
68. Gregory, F. W., and Neu, I. D., "The American Industrial Elite in the 1870's: Their Social Origin," in Miller, W., *Men in Business*, Cambridge: Harvard University Press, 1952.
68a. Haber, W. and Stanchfield, P. L., *The Problem of Economic Insecurity in Michigan*, Lansing, Michigan, A Report to the State Emergency Welfare Relief Commission, August, 1936.
69. Hall, O., "The Stages of a Medical Career," *American Journal of Sociology*, 53:327–336, 1948.
70. ———, "Types of Medical Careers," *American Journal of Sociology*, 55:243–253, 1949.
71. Hatt, P. K., "Occupation and Social Stratification," *American Journal of Sociology*, 55:533–543, 1950.
72. Havemann, E. and West, P. S., *They Went to College*, New York: Harcourt, Brace, 1952.
73. Havighurst, R. J. and Davis, A., "A Comparison of the Chicago and Harvard Studies of Social Class Differences in Child Rearing," *American Sociological Review*, 20:438–442, 1955.
74. Hecht, J. J., *The Domestic Servant Class in Eighteenth-Century England*, London: Routledge and Kegan Paul, 1956.
75. Henry, W. E., "The Business Executive: The Psychodynamics of a Social Role," *American Journal of Sociology*, 54:286–291, 1949.
76. Hertzler, J. O., "Some Tendencies Toward a Closed Class System in the United States," *Social Forces*, 30:313–323, 1952.
77. Hibbard, B. H., "Homestead," *Encyclopaedia of the Social Sciences*, Vol. VII, pp. 436–441.
78. Hollingshead, A. B., *Elmtown's Youth*, New York: Wiley, 1949.
79. ———, "Trends in Social Stratification: A Case Study," *American Sociological Review*, 17:679–686, 1952.

80. Hughes, E. C., "Professional and Career Problems in Sociology," in *International Sociological Association, Transactions of the Second World Congress of Sociology*, London: International Sociological Association, 1954, Vol. I.

81. ———, "Work and the Self," in Rohrer, J. H. and Sherif, M., *Social Psychology at the Crossroads*, New York: Harper, 1951.

82. Hughes, E. C. and H. M., *Where Peoples Meet: Racial and Ethnic Frontiers*, Glencoe, Ill.: The Free Press, 1952.

83. Jaffe, A. J. and Carleton, R. O., *Occupational Mobility in the United States, 1930–1960*, New York: King's Crown Press, 1954.

84. Janowitz, M. and Wright, D., "The Prestige of Public Employment: 1929 and 1954," *Public Administration Review*, 16:15–21, 1956.

85. Janowsky, O. (ed.), *The American Jew: A Composite Portrait*, New York: Harper, 1942.

86. Jones, A. W., *Life, Liberty, and Property*, Philadelphia: Lippincott, 1941.

87. Junker, B. H. and Loeb, M. B., "The School and Social Structure in a Midwestern Community," *School Review*, 50:686–696, 1942.

88. Kahl, Joseph A., *The American Class Structure*, New York: Rinehart, 1957.

89. Kaufman, H. F.; Duncan, O. D.; Gross, N.; and Sewell, W. H., "Problems of Theory and Method in the Study of Social Stratification in Rural Society," *Rural Sociology*, 18:12–24, 1953.

90. Kephart, W. M., "What Is Known About the Occupation of the Jews," in Rose, A. M. (ed.), *Race Prejudice and Discrimination*, New York: Knopf, 1951.

91. Kinsey, A. C. *et al.*, *Sexual Behavior in the Human Female*, Philadelphia: Saunders, 1953.

92. ———, *Sexual Behavior in the Human Male*, Philadelphia: Saunders, 1948.

93. Kiser, C. V., "Fertility Trends and Differentials in the United States," *Journal of the American Statistical Association*, 47:25–48, 1952.

94. Klapp, O. E., "The Creation of Popular Heroes," *American Journal of Sociology*, 54:135–141, 1948.

95. Kolko, G., "Economic Mobility and Social Stratification," *American Journal of Sociology*, 63:30–38, 1957.

96. Kornhauser, W., "The Negro Union Official: A Study of Sponsorship and Control," *American Journal of Sociology*, 57:443–452, 1952.

97. Kuznets, S., *Shares of Upper Income Groups in Income and Savings*, New York: National Bureau of Economic Research, 1953.

97a. Lantz, H. R., "Occupational Differences in Mental Disorders," *Social Problems*, 2:100–104, 1954.

98. Lea, H. C., *History of Sacerdotal Celibacy in the Christian Church*, New York: Macmillan, 1907, Vol. 1.

99. Lee, R. H., "Chinese Americans," in Brown, F. J. and Roucek, J. S. (eds.), *One America*, New York: Prentice-Hall, 1952, pp. 312–315.

100. Lenski, G. E., "American Social Classes: Statistical Strata or Social Groups," *American Journal of Sociology*, 58:139–145, 1952.

101. Levine, D. L., "Teacher-Counselor: Role and Qualifications," *Marriage and Family Living*, 15:313–315, 1953.
102. Lipset, S. M. and Bendix, R., "Ideological Equalitarianism and Social Mobility in the United States," in *Transactions of the Second World Congress of Sociology*, London: International Sociological Association, 1954, Vol. II.
103. ———, "Social Mobility and Occupational Career Plans: I. Stability of Job-holding," *American Journal of Sociology*, 57:366–374, 1952.
103a. ———, "Social Mobility and Occupational Career Plans: II. Social Mobility," *American Journal of Sociology*, 57:494–504, 1952.
104. ——— and Malm, T. F., "Job Plans and Entry into the Labor Market," *Social Forces*, 33:224–232, 1955.
105. Lipset, S. M. and Malm, T. F., "First Jobs and Career Patterns," *American Journal of Economics and Sociology*, 14:247–261, 1955.
106. ——— and Rogoff, N., "Class and Opportunity in Europe and the U.S.: Some Myths and What the Statistics Show," *Commentary*, 18:562–568, 1954.
107. ——— and Zetterberg, H. L., "A Theory of Social Mobility," in *Transactions of the Third World Congress of Sociology*, London: International Sociological Association, 1956, Vol. III.
108. Lyman, E., "Occupational Differences and the Value Attached to Work," *American Journal of Sociology*, 61:138–144, 1955.
109. Lynd, R. S. and Lynd, H. M., *Middletown*, New York: Harcourt, Brace, 1929.
110. ———, *Middletown in Transition*, New York: Harcourt, Brace, 1937.
110a. Lysgaard, S., "Social Stratification and the Deferred Gratification Pattern," in *Transactions of the Second World Congress of Sociology*, London: International Sociological Association, 1954, Vol. II.
110b. MacRae, D., Jr., "The Role of the State Legislator in Massachusetts," *American Sociological Review*, 19:185–194, 1954.
111. MacRae, D. G., "Social Stratification: A Trend Report and Bibliography," *Current Sociology*, 2:3–74, 1953–1954.
112. McGuire, C., "Family Life in Lower and Middle Class Homes," *Marriage and Family Living*, 14:1–6, 1952.
113. Maccoby, E. E. and Gibbs, P. K., "Methods of Child Rearing in Two Social Classes," in Martin, W. E. and Stendler, C. B. (eds.), *Readings in Child Development*, New York: Harcourt, Brace, 1954.
114. Mack, E. C., *Public Schools and British Opinion, 1780–1860*, London: Methuen, 1938.
115. Mangione, J., *Mount Allegro*, Boston: Houghton Mifflin, 1942.
116. Mason, W. S. and Gross, N., "Intra-Occupational Prestige Differentiation: The School Superintendency," *American Sociological Review*, 20:326–331, 1955.
117. May, M. A., "The Teacher as a Transmitter of Culture," *Educational Administration and Supervision*, 26:161–175, 1940.

118. Merton, R. K., "Bureaucratic Structure and Personality," *Social Forces,* 18:560–568, 1940.

119. ———, "Social Structure and Anomie," *Social Theory and Social Structure,* Glencoe, Ill.: Free Press, 1949.

120. ———, *Social Theory and Social Structure,* Glencoe, Ill.: Free Press, 1949.

121. ——— and Kitt, A. S., "Contributions to the Theory of Reference Group Behavior," in Merton, R. K. and Lazarsfeld, P. K., *Continuities in Social Research,* Glencoe, Ill.: Free Press, 1950.

123. Miller, D. C. and Form, W. H., *Industrial Sociology,* New York: Harper, 1951.

124. Miller, S. M., "The Concept and Measurement of Mobility," *Transactions of the Third World Congress of Sociology,* London: International Sociological Association, 1956, Vol. III.

125. Miller, W., "American Historians and the Business Elite," *Journal of Economic History,* 9:184–208, 1949.

126. ———, "The Recruitment of the American Business Elite," *Quarterly Journal of Economics,* 64:242–253, 1950.

127. Mills, C. W., "The American Business Elite: A Collective Portrait," *Journal of Economic History* (Supplement), 5:20–44, 1945.

128. ———, *The New Men of Power,* New York: Harcourt, Brace, 1948.

129. ———, *White Collar,* New York: Oxford, 1951.

130. Montague, J. B., "Conceptions of the Class Structure as Revealed by Samples of English and American Boys," *Research Studies, State College of Washington,* 22:84–93, 1954.

131. Moore, W. E. and Tumin, M. M., "Some Social Functions of Ignorance," *American Sociological Review,* 14:787–795, 1949.

132. Morse, N. C. and Weiss, R. S., "The Function and Meaning of Work and the Job," *American Sociological Review,* 20:191–198, 1955.

133. Myers, R. C., "Myth and Status Systems in Industry," *Social Forces,* 26:331–337, 1948.

134. National Manpower Council, *Womanpower,* New York: Columbia University Press, 1957.

135. National Opinion Research Center, "Jobs and Occupations: A Popular Evaluation," *Opinion News,* 9:3–13, Sept. 1, 1947.

136. National Resources Committee, *The Problems of a Changing Population,* Washington: U.S. Government Printing Office, 1938.

137. Newcomer, M., *The Big Business Executive: The Factors That Made Him, 1900–1950,* New York: Columbia University Press, 1955.

138. Osborn, F., *Preface to Eugenics,* New York: Harper, 1951.

139. Palmer, G. L., "Attitudes Toward Work in an Industrial Community," *American Journal of Sociology,* 63:17–26, 1957.

140. Palmer, G. L., *Labor Mobility in Six Cities,* New York: Social Science Research Council, 1954.

141. Parnes, H. S., "Research on Labor Mobility: An Appraisal of Research Findings in the United States," Social Science Res. Council *Bulletin 65,* 1954.

142. Parsons, T., "Age and Sex in the Social Structure of the United States," *American Sociological Review*, 7:604–616, 1942.

143. ——, "An Analytical Approach to the Theory of Social Stratification," *American Journal of Sociology*, 45:841–862, 1940.

144. ——, "A Revised Analytical Approach to the Theory of Social Stratification," in Bendix, R. and Lipset, S. M. (eds.), *Class, Status and Power*, Glencoe, Ill.: The Free Press, 1953.

145. Pfautz, H. W., "The Current Literature on Social Stratification: Critique and Bibliography," *American Journal of Sociology*, 58:391–418, 1953.

146. Phelps, O. W., "Community Recognition of Union Leaders," *Industrial and Labor Relations Review*, 7:419–433, 1954.

147. Pihlblad, C. T. and Gregory, C. L., "Selective Aspects of Migration Among Missouri High School Graduates," *American Sociological Review*, 19:314–324, 1954.

148. Rademaker, J. A., "The Japanese of the Region," in Reuter, E. B. (ed.), *Race and Culture Contacts*, New York: McGraw-Hill, 1934.

149. Reissman, L., "Levels of Aspiration and Social Class," *American Sociological Review*, 18:233–242, 1953.

150. Reissman, L., "Life Careers, Power and the Professions: The Retired Army General," *American Sociological Review*, 21:215–221, 1956.

151. Riesman, D., "Recreation and the Recreationist," *Marriage and Family Living*, 16:21–26, 1954.

152. Rogoff, N., *Recent Trends in Occupational Mobility*, Glencoe, Ill.: The Free Press, 1953.

153. Rohrer, J. H. and Sherif, M., *Social Psychology at the Crossroads*, New York: Harper, 1951.

154. Ross, A. D., "Organized Philanthropy in an Urban Community," *Canadian Journal of Economics and Political Science*, 18:474–486, 1952.

155. ——, "Philanthropic Activity and the Business Career," *Social Forces*, 32:274–280, 1954.

156. ——, "The Social Control of Philanthropy," *American Journal of Sociology*, 58:451–460, 1953.

157. Rothstein, E., "Plant Relocation and Discarded Workers," *Social Problems*, 1:28–31, 1953.

158. Roucek, J. S., "Social Attitudes of the Prison Warden," *Sociology and Social Research*, 21:170–174, 1936.

159. ——, "The Sociology of the Nurse," *Sociology and Social Research*, 24:526–533, 1940.

160. ——, "Sociology of the Prison Guard," *Sociology and Social Research*, 20:145–151, 1935.

161. Schneider, L. and Lysgaard, S., "The Deferred Gratification Pattern: A Preliminary Study," *American Sociological Review*, 18:142–149, 1953.

162. Schumpeter, J. A., *Imperialism and Social Classes*, New York: Kelley, 1951.

163. Schwab, J. B., "Occupational Attitudes of Lawyers," *Sociology and Social Research*, 24:53–62, 1939.

164. Scudder, R. and Anderson, C. A., "Migration and Vertical Occupational Mobility," *American Sociological Review*, **19**:329–334, 1954.

165. Seymour, H. C. and Tremer, C. E., *We Left School a Year Ago*, Rochester Public Schools, 1941.

166. *No entry.*

167. Shannon, F. A., "The Homestead Act and the Labor Surplus," *The American Historical Review*, 41:637–651, 1936.

168. ——, "A Post-Mortem on the Labor-Safety-Valve Theory," *Agricultural History*, 19:31–37, 1945.

169. Sharp, W. R., *The French Civil Service: Bureaucracy in Transition*, New York: Macmillan, 1931.

170. Sibley, E., *The Recruitment, Selection, and Training of Social Scientists*, *Bull. 58*, Social Science Research Council, 1948.

171. ——, "Some Demographic Clues to Stratification," *American Sociological Review*, 7:322–330, 1942.

172. Simpson, G. E. and Yinger, J. M., *Racial and Cultural Minorities*, New York: Harper, 1953.

173. Sjoberg, G., "Are Social Classes in America Becoming More Rigid?" *American Sociological Review*, 16:775–783, 1951.

174. Slocum, W. L., "Occupational and Educational Plans of High School Seniors from Farm and Non-Farm Homes," Pullman, Washington: *Washington Ag. Exp. Sta. Bull. 564*, 1956.

175. —— and Empey, L. T., "Occupational Planning by Young Women," Wash. Ag. Exp. Sta. *Bull. 568*, Pullman, Wash., 1956.

176. Smith, T. L., *Population Analysis*, New York: McGraw-Hill, 1948.

177. Sorokin, P. A., *Social Mobility*, New York: Harper, 1927.

178. Sperling, O., "Psychoanalytic Aspects of Bureaucracy," *The Psychoanalytic Quarterly*, **19**:88–100, 1950.

179. Stendler, C., *Children of Brasstown*, Urbana: University of Illinois Press, 1949.

180. Stouffer, S. A. *et al.*, *The American Soldier*, Princeton: Princeton University Press, 1949, Vol. I.

181. Strauss, G., "The Set-Up Man: A Case Study of Organizational Change," *Human Organization*, 2:17–25, 1954.

182. Taft, R., "The Social Grading of Occupations in Australia," *British Journal of Sociology*, 4:181–187, 1953.

183. Taussig, F. W. and Joslyn, C. S., *American Business Leaders*, New York: Macmillan, 1932.

184. Thompson, W. S. and Minnis, E. D., *Population Problems*, New York: McGraw-Hill, 1953.

185. Thorner, I., "Nursing: The Functional Significance of an Institutional Pattern," *American Sociological Review*, 20:531–538, 1955.

186. Thrupp, S. L., *The Merchant Class of Medieval London, 1300–1500*, Chicago: University of Chicago Press, 1948.

187. Tumin, M. M., "Some Principles of Stratification: A Critical Analysis," *American Sociological Review*, 18:387–394, 1953.

188. Turner, R. H., "The Changing Ideology of Success: A Study of the Aspiration of High School Men in Los Angeles," in *Transactions of the Third World Congress of Sociology,* London: International Sociological Association, 1956, Vol. V.

189. ———, "The Navy Disbursing Officer as a Bureaucrat," *American Sociological Review,* 12:342–348, 1947.

190. ———, "Occupational Patterns of Inequality," *American Journal of Sociology,* 59:437–447, 1954.

191. Veblen, T., *The Instinct of Workmanship,* New York: Macmillan, 1914.

192. ———, *The Theory of Business Enterprise,* New York: Scribners, 1904.

193. Wance, W. and Butler, R., "The Effect of Industrial Changes on Occupational 'Inheritance' in Four Pennsylvania Communities," *Social Forces,* 27:158–162, 1948.

194. Warner, W. L., *American Life: Dream and Reality,* Chicago: University of Chicago Press, 1953.

195. ——— et al., *Democracy in Jonesville,* New York: Harpers, 1949.

196. ———, *Structure of American Life,* Edinburgh: The University Press, 1952.

197. ——— and Abegglen, J. C., *Big Business Leaders in America,* New York: Harper, 1955.

198. ———, *Occupational Mobility in American Business and Industry, 1928–1952,* Minneapolis: University of Minnesota Press, 1955.

199. ———, Havighurst, R. J. and Loeb, M. B., *Who Shall Be Educated?* New York: Harper, 1944.

199a. ——— and Low, J. O., *The Social System of the Modern Factory,* New Haven: Yale University Press, 1947.

200. ——— and Lunt, P. S., *The Social Life of a Modern Community,* New Haven: Yale University Press, 1941.

201. Weinberg, S. K. and Arond, H., "The Occupational Culture of the Boxer," *American Journal of Sociology,* 57:460–469, 1952.

203. West, P. S., "Social Mobility Among College Graduates," in Bendix, R. and Lipset, S. M. (eds.), *Class, Status and Power,* Glencoe, Ill.: The Free Press, 1953, pp. 465–480.

204. Westoff, C. F., "Differential Fertility in the United States," *American Sociological Review,* 19:549–561, 1954.

205. Whyte, W. H., Jr., *The Organization Man,* New York: Simon and Schuster, 1956.

206. Williams, J. J., "The Woman Physician's Dilemma," *Journal of Social Issues,* 6, No. 3:38–44, 1950.

207. Wohl, Richard R., "The Rags to Riches Story: An Episode of Secular Idealism, in Bendix, R. and Lipset, S. M. (eds.), *Class, Status and Power,* Glencoe, Ill.: Free Press, 1953.

208. Zeleny, C., "Irish Americans," in Brown, F. J. and Roucek, J. S., *One America,* New York: Prentice-Hall, 1952.

CHAPTER SIX

THE OCCUPATIONAL COLLEAGUE GROUP AND THE WORK GROUP

In preceding chapters we dealt with the institutional and status orders of occupations, and with the individual career. Now we turn to the intimate work ties that an occupational member has with co-members of his occupation (his colleague group) and with co-workers (his work group). A colleague group is illustrated by two school teachers who argue whether school teaching has become more, or less, difficult over the years. A work group is illustrated by any set of persons who work together on a particular job or problem, for example, a work crew in a factory. Relations among colleagues are, by definition, relations between members of the same occupation. A work crew *may* be made up of members of the same occupation,[1] but the significant characteristic remains that of coming together to do a job cooperatively.[2]

OCCUPATIONAL INCLUSION AND EXCLUSION

We examine first the general question of who are regarded as members of an occupation, and then consider the obligations and rewards of membership-status.

[1] For example, two assembly-men who cooperate in putting together a piece of equipment. Or, the two schoolteachers referred to above would *become* a work group if, for example, they were appointed by their principal to a committee which supervised the school-lunch program.
[2] Obviously, since colleague relations are confined to members of the same occupation, we can discuss them in *this* chapter only. In subsequent chapters—which deal with relations among coworkers (formal and informal) in specific work organizations—our discussion of intimate work relations becomes one of the work group only. Hence the double-barrelled title of this chapter and the dropping of "colleague group" in subsequent chapters.

COLLEAGUESHIP

When a chairman at a public meeting introduces a speaker as "my col-league," he usually means no more than that they are both engaged in a similar kind of work. But often he means also that he *recognizes* the other man's right to membership in their occupation. Many occupations admit persons provisionally or to a marginal satus which falls short of such recognition. There are persons who are in the occupation for only a short time, such as students taking summer employment. And there are some whose minds are not there. Kenneth Burke (11, pp. 303–16) has distinguished the occupation from the preoccupation—the latter il-lustrated, for example, by many women who work but whose primary identification is with their families. Such workers are "preoccupied." Another important kind of marginal person is the man who is trying to gain entrance, but meets opposition because of his race or religion. Such a person may have to content himself (perhaps for his lifetime) with doing the dirty work for his colleagues as when an upper-class lawyer is able to maintain his reputation by handing over shady cases to lawyers who have no choice but to accept.[3]

Occupational marginality may be found not only with individuals but also with whole occupations. The X-ray technique developed out-side the field of medicine, but its enormous utility in medical diagnosis and treatment soon required the establishment of control over its use. Two procedures were possible and both occurred: the development of a new specialty (radiology) and the inclusion of the X-ray technician as a regular member of the hospital staff but subordinate to the physicians. Similarly, midwifery, nursing, pharmacy, surgery, and eye-measuring were all historic trades or mysteries which once existed alone outside the field of medicine.[4] All have now become either medical specialties or their practitioners have become subordinate or auxiliary to physicians.

[3] See (41, p. 358). A similar mechanism seems to operate in medicine, occasionally, for patients who desire illegal operations or who wish to keep some "unmentionable" disease secret from their usual doctors.

[4] On midwifery, S. P. Breckinridge (8, p. 221) writes: ". . . in classic times midwives commonly attended women during confinement and . . . physicians were summoned in abnormal cases." On nursing, the following statement is revealing: ". . . Radegonde in the sixth century and Hildegarde in the twelfth, might study all the medical knowledge available to their day; but the rank and file of nursing nuns at-tended to the laundry and other menial tasks, prepared the meals and prayed beside the dying without benefit of even a modicum of scientific training. Nursing became a disagreeable drudgery performed for an ultimate reward in heaven." (36, p. 405) Pharmacy had a varied position being first inside medicine, then moving out to a more or less independent existence in eighth century Europe, and then later coming under the control of, though not coming into medicine. See (24, p. 279; 77, pp. 283–89).

The situation is however a dynamic one. Technicians originally brought in in a subordinate position may later develop self-consciousness and break away from the group or even attempt to control their masters. The accountant was a creation of capitalistic industry and existed to serve it. But the certified public accountant—articled by the state and responsible only to his colleagues—is a man whose prestige and power are at the point where the businessman who employs him regards him with respect and not a little fear. Still in process of definition is the position of key-punch operator. The increased use of punch cards in business and manufacturing operations has created an increasing need for this operator whose skill is somewhat like that of a typist, and who is often required to be able to type as well. These similarities to typing have resulted in its assignment as a "woman's job" but its relative status remains unclear. On the one hand, key-punch operators work with the professionals and semiprofessionals who know how to run the giant automatic calculators; on the other hand, those persons are rarely the heads of offices or executives with whom the typists are often associated.[5]

Such considerations touch only formal colleagueship—those who have the right to call themselves occupational members at all. *Within* an occupation, colleagueship implies a deeper relation: members of colleague groups are bound together by a strong sense of *esprit de corps* which Blumer (7, pp. 205–06) has described in these terms: [6]

In itself, it is the sense which people have of belonging together and of being identified with one another in a common undertaking. Its basis is constituted by a condition of rapport. In developing a feeling of intimacy and closeness, people have a sense of sharing a common experience and of forming a select group. In one another's presence they feel at ease and as comrades. Personal reserves break down and feelings of strangeness, difference, and alienation disappear. Under such conditions, relations tend to be of cooperation instead of personal competition. The behavior tends to facilitate the release of behavior on the part of others, instead of tending to inhibit or check that behavior; in

[5] W. I. Wardwell (81) has given us an excellent picture of occupational marginality in his study of chiropractors. They suffer from what Talcott Parsons has called "socially structure strain" because their freedom to practice is limited in most states (illegal in some), they must compete with physicians, and they have low prestige and income. To reduce the strain they engage in the following types of behavior: realistic patterns (uniting for mutual aid, practicing massage, civic activity), aggression (toward the American Medical Association, one another, or patients), withdrawal (from the occupation, or from difficult patients), deviant practices (fee-splitting, advertising), and, the claim that their work is *not* a type of medicine and therefore should not be so judged.

[6] Blumer's description is presented in the context of social movements, but has more general applicability.

this sense each person tends to inspire others. Such conditions of mutual sympathy and responsiveness obviously make for concerted behavior.

In sum, members of a colleague group feel that what happens to any one of their number is of importance to the others, that all are "in the same boat" and that what one of them does affects the interests of the others.

Certain elements appear to be important in building such a sense of colleagueship. First is some control on the entry of new members: with such control, other, more intimate controls become possible; without it, other controls—whatever their character—are largely ineffective. Among occupations requiring relatively little skill or training, the most serious threat (apart from elimination of the occupation itself through mechanization) is the existence of a reservoir population willing to compete with regular occupation members. Most important are groups who leave as easily as they enter the occupation because they have an alternative identification, and groups who will take work at low wages because they can find little else to do—women, youngsters still in school, minority group members. Labor unions waver between trying to keep these persons out of the union and insisting that they join. The former is possible only where union membership is a prerequisite to hiring—a situation more difficult to arrange since the Taft-Hartley law was passed—while the latter meets strong resistance from those to whom union benefits (tenure, pensions, minimum wages) are of little significance since they are willing to accept low wages or do not intend to work long. White-collar workers—especially those whose work involves a moderate skill such as those in the business office—present a special problem since they are trained outside in business schools or colleges. In addition, they resist unionization for other reasons.

Controls on entry to occupations which require a considerable skill or amount of learning are both more complex and more effective. These occupations include the professionals and semi-professionals, and the skilled crafts. The controls on entry have been discussed above in connection with occupational teaching and learning but may be restated briefly. An occupation may restrict the numbers permitted to learn either through formal criteria (formal education, restrictions on hiring for the case where most of the learning is acquired on the job) or informal criteria (restriction on the basis of race, religion, sex, or age). For those permitted to learn, the learning process is itself controlled by having members of the occupation teach (especially the tricks of the trade and social skills) and pass on prospective candidates, and entry is itself controlled through licensing, articling, or entrance rituals. Obviously, control on entrants is easiest when occupations require much learning or training.[7] Those who are disturbed at the increase in vocational emphasis in the universities should remember that the term *universitas* was originally applied to the early *guilds* and that the great universities at Bologna, Paris, Cambridge and Salamanca were each formed of the *professional* schools of law, medicine, and theology. The emphasis on a broad, liberal education was an element added much later by the Renaissance.

A second means of building a sense of colleagueship is the development of occupational consciousness. The attempt will be made to develop an image of the practitioners as the unique purveyors of a service to a world that would be much the worse without them. Such an image cannot, of course, be maintained unless it is believed in by the occupational members themselves. In order to achieve it, it is obvious that obligations to the occupation must stand high, in priority, over obligations to other occupations or to clients.

First, then, the members of an occupation must regard the services they provide very highly, higher than do members of society in general and certainly higher than members of occupations providing related services. Caplow (12, p. 131) comments that—at least for the major professions—even some exaggeration is functional:

. . . the degree of disproportion (between relative prestige and relative earnings) is invariably exaggerated. This mild paranoia serves as a constant support for the militancy of professional organizations in promoting their economic interests.

But the phenomenon is more general and, indeed, more likely (because more necessary) among occupations at the bottom of the status hierarchy. Hughes (43, p. 316), referring to research among Negro industrial workers who had jobs of the lowest status, notes:

It was from these people that we learned that the common dignifying rationalization of people in all positions of a work hierarchy except the very top one is, "We in this position save the people in the next higher position above from their own mistakes." The notion that one saves a person of more acknowledged skill, and certainly of more acknowledged prestige and power, than one's self from his mistakes appears to be peculiarly satisfying.

The general character of this tendency is suggested by the finding of a National Opinion Research Center (65, p. 415) study of occupations that

---

[7] A factor which helps explain the tenacity of such beliefs as the myth of the boy apprentice in the old-line trades (64).

persons rated their own jobs almost always considerably higher than the average evaluation of the job.[8]

The fact of high evaluation of one's own occupation appears to develop occupational consciousness more easily when there goes with it a sense of rejection of other occupations and of superiority over clients. In what is one of the most intensive studies of a single labor union (and certainly one of the best studies of a craft union)—the study of the International Typographical Union by Lipset, Trow, and Coleman (55)—the authors advance what they call the "marginal status hypothesis." Printers regard themselves (as they always have) as the elite group among the manual workers. They are literate (their occupation required they be), better educated, and tend to have a stronger middle-class orientation than do other manual workers. Consequently, they would be expected to prefer to associate with middle class persons, but if that is not possible, then they would associate with other printers. Such was the finding (55).[9]

Occupational consciousness is also related to the development of attitudes toward the client or society in general. Becker (5) reports that jazz-band musicians must somehow come to terms with the "squares" (the audience) who do not appreciate good jazz but, unfortunately, are the ones who pay to hear them play. A technique may be simple avoidance which the elevated stage helps provide; if there is no stage, then a few chairs in front of the bandstand will, it is hoped, have a symbolic effect.[10] Sometimes an occupation will cultivate among its members a feeling that society is attacking it. Actors, artists, and writers find that supersensitivity increases attendance at national conferences, while the

---

[8] Relevant also is R. K. Kerckhoff's finding (49) that clergymen, physicians, attorneys, and social workers were highly reluctant to accord marriage counseling professional status in its own right because each of these professions chose itself as the *best* equipped to give such services. In a later article (48) Kerckhoff reports that though all four of the professions resisted a special profession of marriage counseling, the attorneys objected most strongly.

[9] Lipset, Trow, and Coleman also report a very high proportion of printers who "like printing as an occupation" and use this datum as a further reason why printers associate with one another. But such a conclusion is hazardous in view of the fact that job satisfaction seems always to be quite high (though not, certainly, as high as in the case of the printers). Thus Nancy C. Morse and R. S. Weiss (62) found that 80 per cent of a random sample of employed men in the U.S. were either "very satisfied" or "satisfied" with their jobs. But the reasons for such satisfaction were quite diffuse, with only service workers mentioning the kind of people they were likely to meet as a factor. Nevertheless, the factor of job satisfaction, along with other factors, may well contribute to occupational consciousness. Further, job satisfaction definitely varies among occupations, being, for example, relatively low for railroad workers, as Lipset, Trow, and Coleman themselves report.

[10] Becker (5, p. 137) illustrates the extremes to which high and unique self-evaluation may go when he tells us that there is a belief that ". . . only musicians are sensitive and unconventional enough to be able to give real sexual satisfaction to a woman."

attack on the "eggheads" may have increased membership in the American Association of University Professors. In the case of the professional
criminal, it is not necessary to offer proofs that society is out to destroy
the profession.

But the sense of being attacked is, perhaps, found most commonly
among members of occupations that do society's dirty work (43, pp. 319
ff.). The work may be physically dirty (janitors, plumbers, garbage col-
lectors), may involve the incidental learning of offensive or shameful
facts (doctors, lawyers, journalists, barbers, and bartenders), may involve
the care of persons that we do not like to think about too much (prison
guards, mental hospital attendants, orderlies in homes for "our senior
citizens"), or those rendering services which remind us of our frailties
and which, we wish, did not have to be performed at all (money lenders,
at times—bootleggers and smugglers, and prostitutes). And when one is
attacked (perhaps by being assigned a low prestige position) one fights
back as well as one can. Hughes (43, p. 320) says of janitors:

By a *contre coup*, it is by the garbage that the janitor judges, and, as it were,
gets power over the tenants who high-hat him. Janitors know about hidden
lover-affairs by bits of torn-up letter paper; of impending financial disaster or
of financial four-flushing by the presence of many unopened letters in the waste.
Or they may stall off demands for immediate service by an unreasonable woman
of whom they know from the garbage that she, as the janitors put it, "has
the rag on." The garbage gives the janitor the makings of a kind of magical
power over that pretentious villain, the tenant. I say a kind of magical power,
for there appears to be no thought of betraying any individual and thus turning
this knowledge into overt power. He protects the tenant, but, at least among
Chicago janitors, it is certainly not a loving protection.

So, too, the plumber may take his own sweet time (in the opinion of the
householder who is paying for it) about repairing the very necessary
toilet drainpipe, a situation all the more exasperating when the householder *could* do the job himself but does not want to, for then the
plumber is being paid *only* for doing a dirty job. The lawyer is the object of mixed feelings: most persons rarely if ever need his services but
when they do, they may need them very badly indeed. He becomes, to
many, a necessary evil [who, Riesman (69) tells us, does the dirty work of
the client, including some that the client would not approve of, if he
knew]. The lawyer has to content himself with trying to develop a
favorable stereotype of the profession, as does the money lender who
would prefer that persons think of him as "helpful," rather than as a
"loan shark." Prison and hospital personnel know (and it should be more
widely known) that because of overcrowding and scarcity of professional

help, it is they, and they alone, who know the inmates best, and have as much to do, sometimes, with changing the likelihood of a man's release as the professionals do. Perhaps this knowledge is itself enough to offset the sense of outrage from maltreatment by the professional gods. The bootlegger, however, who often deals with the pillars of the community, gets back something of his own by "soaking them good," while the prostitute does the same, if she may, and hates her clients as well. Among such varied groups as these the sense of a common threat or of actual pain helps bind the occupational group together.

A third procedure that helps develop colleagueship is the presence of mechanisms for facilitating informal interaction among colleagues. Among craft unions, the *local* is not merely a convenient organizational unit: it forces occupational members into one another's society at regular times, and is often the springboard for picnics, parties, and contests directly related to the occupation, as in the case of the corn-husking and log-rolling contests of several decades ago. Lipset, Trow and Coleman (55, Chs. 5, 6) provide us with one of the best descriptions of the significance of informal interaction among members of an occupation. They found that printers have an extensive "occupational community," which takes the form of voluntary associations and of informal visiting with one another. Those most active in this community were found to be also most interested in and informed about union political affairs. The occupational community also had important functions for those interested in political action or careers in the typographers union. The clubs helped men to learn the skills of politics by providing for them the chance to become club officials and helped men to build up their reputations and win recognition throughout the union. Another factor that helped bind the printers together as an occupation was the substitute system. Substitutes, who are taken on irregularly (in accord with demand), are hired daily by a lottery system; this forces men looking for work to show up every day in case their name is drawn from the lottery. In the case when a regular printer is ill or has a day off, then he has the privilege of naming his substitute; thus, friendship can mean that a substitute is named by a printer. In both cases, then, printers are forced into one another's company more often than might otherwise be the case.

A final condition that seems to have more general applicability is described (55, p. 138) as follows:

As one printer put it in an interview, "Night workers don't have to punch the family time clock." Day workers, finishing work in the late afternoon, are under pressure to rush home to dinner and to conform to a time schedule set by their children or by plans for evening activities of the family. For the day worker, the end of the day's work often means the end of relations with fellow workers unless special arrangements are made to return or to stay over for a meeting later in the evening. Thus it requires an added effort and inconvenience to see other printers after work—either missing a meal at home or leaving again after supper.

Night workers, on the other hand, finish work after their wives and families are asleep. Their schedule is so completely in conflict with that of the children that they are not expected to conform as are day workers. If a fellow worker suggests that a group go down to a local bar or go bowling or talk for a while over coffee in a cafe, no one at home will object. Many night workers, in fact, have reported such a pattern of afterwork activity. Similarly, the night worker can take his time going to work. Unlike the day worker, who is usually rushed in rising, breakfasting, and reaching work on time, the night worker customarily does not go to work for many hours after he has risen. He may and often does arrange to meet his friends downtown before work. One worker who had spent most of his time on night work reported having had a regular pattern through the summertime of meeting two printer friends in the early afternoon, going to the baseball game together, and then coming to work together afterwards.

Night work, then, seems to break up the normal pattern of family and recreational life. Neighborhood organization and mass entertainment does not fit night-workers' needs, and as a consequence they will be motivated to associate with one another. While it is easy to exaggerate the matter, there seems little question that occupations that, for various reasons, pull the worker away from his family and normal recreational activities often exhibit very great solidarity. It is difficult to abstract the occupational element, for many occupations which involve such a break, especially those of migratory laborers and hoboes, also involve many other elements, such as racial and ethnic factors, and community rejection. On the other hand, railroad men, travelling musicians, actors, and professional soldiers (and, to some extent, salesmen) have formed what amounts to separate sub-cultures.[11]

A fourth factor that contributes to colleagueship derives from the fact that every occupation supplies a limited market. One type of action that can easily create antagonism, cleavages, and even a loss of the market to charlatans is *uncontrolled competition.* Consequently every occupation (even that of private business) tries to regulate competition by securing consensus on the "rules of the game." The most celebrated form that such controls take are professional "ethics," of which Oswald Hall (37, p. 248) gives us a good illustration in the following quotation from one of the physicians in his sample:

[11] See (4; 12, pp. 95–8; 18).

One young woman came to me when her obstetrician was out of the city. I took care of her and delivered her child. When she became pregnant again she came back to me. I told her that she could have any obstetrician in town whom she preferred over her original one—anyone, that is, but me.

Where professional identification is weaker, then competition may be controlled through a labor union, especially a craft union. For example, a plumber may refuse to re-lay the floor and linoleum he was forced to tear out in order to get to the pipe he repaired; the latter activities involve other craftsmen with whom there is a mutual agreement, mediated through the respective unions. Among the most dramatic controls are those enforced, not by a colleague group, but by a work group on rate-busters. These persons, who threaten the welfare of the work group, are the object of powerful pressures. The controls on entry that we discussed above have an effect, also, in ensuring that only persons who possess the "proper" attitudes will get into the occupation. This is one reason why many occupations prefer that their membership shall be a *homogeneous* one, for persons of diverse background and affiliation are difficult to weld into a body with high consensus. This factor is of first significance in understanding the work problems of migratory laborers.

A fifth method of developing colleagueship is the deliberate formation of formal occupational organizations—professional associations, craft unions, and, sometimes,[12] industrial unions. The functions of these organizations are varied: they regularize and help facilitate controls on the entry of supplicants by establishing standards, provide a formal expression of group consciousness, help punish violators of occupational folkways and mores, especially those relating to internal competition and prices and wages, and help the occupation maintain a monopoly on the services it provides. Relevant to these functions—and a function in its own right—is that of relating the occupation to the outside world through propaganda. The attempt is made to create a set of attitudes favorable to the occupation so that its claim to be the uniquely qualified suppliers of the service may be legitimized.[13]

Although there are many types of formal organizations associated with the work situation, it is important to distinguish the *occupational* organization from all others for it is that type that is most important for

---

[12] This limitation (with reference to industrial unions) refers to the fact that industrial unions usually do *not* consist of the members of *one* occupation, though some come fairly close to doing so.

[13] It is important not to confuse this phenomenon with advertising, which is directed at the individual. However, propaganda may, of course, provide an attitudinal atmosphere within which advertising of a particular product may be facilitated.

colleagueship. For example, an organization may include only one major occupational group (American Association of University Professors, International Typographers Union), or several occupations (perhaps the Teamsters are the best illustration, though they come close to being an industrial union) but each of these is still occupational in the sense that it is concerned with the welfare of its component occupation(s). This situation is quite different from that of the white-collar union which is so broad that it represents a class or prestige level rather than an occupation.[14]

The outstanding illustration of a formal occupational organization —one that is important not simply historically but because of the light it sheds on colleagueship—is the medieval guild.[15] Of course there is no question that membership in a craft or merchant guild carried with it direct economic benefits as Charles Gross (29, pp. 46–47) shows us in the following quotation from the ordinances of Southampton (presumably in the fourteenth century):

And no one shall buy anything in the town of Southampton to sell again in the same town, unless he be of the Gild Merchant or of the franchise; and if anyone does it and is found guilty, all that he has thus bought shall be forfeited to the king . . . And no one, except a gildsman, shall buy honey, suet, salt herring, nor any kind of oil, nor millstones, nor fresh leather, nor any kind of fresh skins; nor keep a wine tavern, nor sell cloth by retail, except on market and fair day; nor keep more than five quarters of corn in his granery to sell by retail, if he is not a gildsman; and if anyone shall do it and be found guilty, all shall be forfeited to the king.

But the purely economic or occupational function of the guilds was only *one of many* functions, as Lewis Mumford (63, pp. 29–30) has emphasized:

When one first encounters the guild in England in Anglo-Saxon times, it is primarily a religious fraternity under the patronage of a saint, meeting for brotherly comfort and cheer, insuring its members against the dire accidents of life and providing a decent burial. It had features not unlike those of the later English friendly society, or the Society of Freemasons, Elks, or Odd Fellows. The guild never lost this religious color: it was a brotherhood adapted to specific economic tasks but not wholly engrossed in them: the brothers ate and drank

[14] Another important factor is that persons in a white-collar union tend to identify with the office at which they are employed much more than they do with the union or occupation *per se*.

[15] Although there were many types of guilds, the most important were the religious fraternities (with mainly benevolent and protective functions), the craft guilds (including professional organizations), and the merchant guilds. The craft guilds were concerned with manufacturing goods or dispensing services, while the merchant guilds regulated conditions of sale and the economic life of the town as a whole.

together on regular occasions: they formulated regulations for the conduct of their craft: they planned and paid for and enacted their parts in their mystery plays, for the edification of their fellow-townsmen: and they built chapels, endowed chantries, and founded schools.

For a specific instance, E. R. A. Seligman (72, pp. 87–88) provides an excellent description of the closeness of the tie between apprentice and master: [16]

The apprentice formed a member of the master's family. For the principles of the law of parent and child were made applicable to a certain extent, and all responsibility for the purchases of the apprentices as well as for their behavior were imposed on the masters by city ordinance. From one of the indentures that have been preserved we can obtain a clear view of his position. The apprentice is to keep his master's secrets, do him no injury nor commit excessive waste on his goods. He is not to frequent taverns, commit fornication or adultery with the housemaids or in town, nor betroth himself without his master's permission. He is not to wear certain garments, play at dice, chequers, or any other unlawful game, but is to conduct himself soberly and piously as a good and faithful servant, or in default to serve double time. The master, on the other hand, agrees to find him in all necessaries, food, clothing, bed, and so on, for four years. In the fifth year he finds himself, but receives twenty shillings and the tools of the trade; and in the sixth year he gets forty shillings but finds his own tools. The master agrees on his side to teach him the craft without any concealment.

Another area of life that the guilds were associated with was that of town administration, particularly town finances. Gross (29, p. 54) points out that the obligation of the merchant guild members "to be in scot and lot" with other burgesses meant that: [17]

". . . the gildsman was expected to render the authorities of the borough assistance, according to his means, whenever they needed money,

In sum, then, the guild was related not only to the economic needs of the town but also to its religious, educational, recreational, familial, and political needs as well. A man might join a guild because he had to in order to earn a living at all, but, having done so, he would find he was also a member of a health and old-age insurance society, a burial association, a group of intimates, and a dramatic society. When an organization touches so many areas of a man's life, his sense of identification with it is

---

[16] See (1, 9, 80).
[17] See also the description of the important role that the Spanish guild merchants played in juridical procedures related to international trade in (74).

likely to be high, and, in turn, the cohesiveness among the members is likely to be strong.[18]

In the United States, craft guilds did not develop fully on anything like the scale of the European medieval guilds. Instead, from a rather early period, labor came to conceive of itself as separate from capital and became interested in improving its economic position: the broader functions of the guilds were not emphasized. By and large, the growth of labor unions in the United States exhibited two phases. On the one hand, there was a fluctuating involvement of laborers in a labor movement with distinctly political objectives, as reflected in the National Labor Union, the Knights of Labor, the various farmers' movements, and the International Workers of the World. On the other hand, there was the formation of craft unions, beginning in the latter part of the nineteenth century in the skilled trades—printing, the building trades, and railroad engineers. This distinction is still a tenable one, but Caplow (12, pp. 195–98) comes closer to the mark in conceiving of the AFL as "restrictive" and the CIO as "expansive." The former type of union tries to maintain a monopoly or near-monopoly of a service by controlling entry into the occupation, and is, therefore, exclusive. The latter, however, being composed of semiskilled and unskilled workers, recognizes that it cannot control entry and therefore tries to control the market for labor by encouraging minority groups, women, and others who would otherwise form a reservoir labor supply to join the union. In turn, the inability of the expansive union to control its policies from within (in the manner the "restrictive" union can) has led it into active involvement in state and national politics to secure favorable legislation. Of course, when whole industries, which affect the national welfare, are involved, it is difficult to keep state and federal governments from entering into labor relations. The white-collar unions seem to represent a tendency closer to the model of the CIO than to that of the AFL. C. Wright Mills (58, pp. 195–98) has characterized their unionism as "expedient and instrumental, rather than principled or ideological." That is, when white-collar workers go union, they seem to do so mainly from a desire for the economic benefits that a union can supply rather than from an

---

[18] The guild form of organization is still important in several parts of the world, especially in Latin America and (probably) China. See (17, 61). A later work by John Stewart Burgess (10) estimates that there were 128 guilds in Peking at the time of his study. Particularly interesting is Burgess' reprinting (from an earlier work) of a description of a meeting of the Gild of the Blind (singers, storytellers, and entertainers)—pp. 103–106. When a sample of guild representatives were asked to decide what factors held the guild together, the ordering of replies (of those that replied at all) was, from most to least frequently mentioned: cooperation in making a living, tradition, religious belief, the sense of solidarity or unity, and the inspiration of the leaders.

identification with the labor movement or with a political swing. The CIO is, perhaps, better set up to handle such narrow interests, and, in any case, the white-collar group is a highly heterogeneous one to which entry is very difficult to control.[19] These are, however, considerations which involve labor unions *per se,* rather than occupational associations.

Sixth, and lastly, reference should be made to the general tendency of occupational associations to develop distinctive ceremonial behavior and objects. Songs, cheers, secret handshakes, uniforms, and the like will be invented to identify the member. Parades, large meetings and ceremonies that commemorate the founder (or patron saint) will be held. John Stewart Burgess (10, p. 164) describes the ceremony signifying admission of apprentices to the Cooks Guild of Peking:

After three or five years, when the term of apprenticeship has been completed, several of the masters gather together with their respective apprentices and formally sign a document which signifies that the apprentice has graduated or finished his term of training. The apprentice kowtows to his master and also to the guarantors, while his father or brother provides a feast of several tables for the party. The document that has been written must be in the handwriting of the master. Among the forms of thanking the master are: (1) the presenting of four hair pins to the master's wife; (2) the presenting of two bolts of cloth, a hat and a pair of shoes to the master, together with providing a feast for him; (3) the presenting of a hair pin called *Chiu-Lien-Luan* to the master's mother.

Distinctive paraphernalia are often displayed such as the engineer's ring, or the fireman's vest. The annual convention of the professional or business association, or the labor union has many functions, but the ceremonial one is certainly not unimportant. Such ceremonial behavior or objects have two functions: they are intended to *remind* the member of his membership and the obligations that this membership entails, and they are intended to provide him with a strong sense of group support. When large numbers are involved—as when the conventioneer finds himself in the midst of a tightly packed mass, all gasping for air—the individual may feel uncomfortable but he cannot help but secure a sense of ego-expansion: "Look at us all!"

THE OBLIGATIONS AND REWARDS OF COLLEAGUESHIP

Through the means we have described, the attempt is made to increase occupational unity and, with this unity, to create the feeling that what

[19] Our use of "AFL" and "CIO" does not suggest that the recent merger of the two organizations is unimportant or temporary. It is too early yet to see what shape this union will give to American occupational association, and the two groups have, in any case, been of great importance historically and still preserve their identity.

happens to any one member is of importance to all the others. Yet, obviously, even in the case of the guilds—which reached deep into the lives of their members—there remain areas of privacy. This raises the question: *which* actions have a man's colleagues the right to be concerned about? The answer seems to be clear: One's colleagues have a right to be concerned about any actions which affect the welfare of the occupational group. With reference to such actions, then, the members of a colleague group will have expectations of or obligations toward one another, and since these expectations or obligations are important to group welfare they are occupational *mores*.

Mores are most likely to be found among groups in which the *conscience collective* [20] is strong. At the same time because they are considered essential to group welfare—and often to group survival—they come to be taken for granted to the point where the member who even raises a question about them is immediately suspect as a possible threat to the group. The major professions rest on public confidence and any member who shakes such confidence—say by criticizing another professional to a client—is felt to be threatening the occupation. A dentist described another type of violation of *mores* as follows:

People don't get thrown out of the (local) dental Society very often but it happens, occasionally, and for the flimsiest reasons. For instance there were the two Simpson brothers who set themselves up in a fleet of offices which they named the "Simpson Clinic." The term "clinic," you know, has a precise meaning in medicine—it refers to an association of specialists in which the patient may be referred from one man to another for a complete treatment. But this wasn't true of these men: they were just two brothers practicing dentistry together.

At a meeting of the Society they were told it wasn't a good idea to confuse the public with this term. They were ordered to drop it from their letterhead and scratch it off their windows. The Simpsons refused and were kicked out of the Society.

That's not necessarily disastrous: a man can still get along. But there's an understanding between the Society and the property owners in the business district that office space will be leased only to members of the Society. This means an outsider may have to practice in a third or fourth rate building off on the byways of the city. That can hurt a man. The Simpsons went ahead and built their own building, although it is out of the way somewhat. I don't know how well they're doing.

The seriousness of the misuse of the term "clinic" is not a subject on which we can pass judgment. But another matter is clear from the interview statement: The Simpsons defied the Society. Many groups will per-

[20] A phrase of Emile Durkheim (19, Bk. 1, Ch. 2; Bk. 2, Ch. 3) which refers, roughly, to the degree of consensual and moral unity of a society.

mit criticism of themselves and some may encourage it; but no group
with any degree of self-consciousness or permanence can permit behavior
which suggests that the group itself is of little significance and may be
defied with impunity.

Another important work situation in which *mores* are usually found
is in the work group—whether composed of colleagues or not. The "rate-
buster"—who produces at a much faster rate than that agreed upon by
the work group as "proper"—is a threat to group welfare for his productivity is a demonstration to management that the other members of
the work group are slackers.

One of the most important obligations of colleagueship is the
obligation of secrecy. Of course one keeps one's clients' affairs secret if for
no other reason than that any other course would bring eventual economic
ruin. But at a deeper level secrecy includes the obligation to doubletalk [21]—to talk in one frame of reference to one's clients or society at
large and in a different frame of reference to one's colleagues. Nor is this
simply a matter of "fooling the client." If a doctor were to tell the patient
the truth in scientific language, he might tell him nothing or simply
alarm him. Consequently he must learn to tell the patient in language
that he will understand. It is the professional and skilled craftsmen who
experience the most difficulty here for they are forced to deal, as cases,
with events that may be of the utmost significance to the client. David
Riesman (69, p. 128) may overstate the matter when he tells us that
lawyers "learn not to take law seriously," but Hughes (43, p. 323) drives
the point home eloquently:

It would be interesting to know what the parish priest thinks to himself when
he is called for the tenth time to give extreme unction to the sainted Mrs.
O'Flaherty who hasn't committed a sin in years except that of, in her anxiety
over dying in a state of sin, being a nuisance to the priest. On Mrs. O'Flaherty's
side there is the danger that she might die unshriven, and she has some occasion
to fear that the people who shrive may not take her physical danger seriously
and hence may not come quickly enough when at last her hour has come. There
may indeed be in the minds of the receivers of emergency services a resentment
that something so crucial to them can be a matter for a cooler and more objective
attitude, even though they know perfectly well that such an attitude is necessary
to competence, and though they could not stand it if the expert to whom they
take their troubles were to show any signs of excitement.

Westley (82) tells us that almost all the policemen whom he studied
stated they would perjure themselves rather than testify against a fellow
policeman they felt sure had stolen money from the wallet of a drunk

[21] This phenomenon was pointed out first, to my knowledge, by E. C. Hughes.

whom they had brought in together. The manifest functions of secrecy he found to be: a shield against possible attacks of a usually hostile public and newspapers, a protection from criminals who would profit from knowledge of internal police affairs, and a protection of themselves on those occasions when their use of violence exceeded that legally permissible (83) or when political corruption was involved.[22] But the most important latent function of secrecy was that it (82, p. 256):

. . . makes the individual policeman identify with other policemen and distinguish himself from non-policemen. Thus it functions as a social bond among the police by giving them something in common (if only a sense of mutual incrimination).

The members of any occupational group will have a set of peculiar interests and needs which, if more generally known, might seriously affect their ability to carry on their occupation. Sometimes these require the ability to discuss clients (from the doctor's patient to the janitor's tenant) in an objective manner (which would be disturbing to patient or tenant, if they heard it), and sometimes these involve behavior of which the worker himself is unsure or occasionally even illegal behavior.

This means that one wants colleagues who are more than merely technically competent: one wants persons whom one feels one can communicate with and who can be counted upon to understand. And this knowledge—being esoteric—often is expressed in a distinct argot or occupational language. Cottrell (18, p. 101) reports the following statement of an engineman:

We were called for a three-thousand-ton drag, and the master maniac gave us a wet hog. We had a flock of slow orders and they were relaying curves. It was a nigger local, and we had to set out and pick up at almost every whistling post. We had to go into the hole twice for highliners and once for a red ball that was on our tail. Then we had to double over the hill and cut and run for water. After we got rolling down the grade the brains gave me a washout. We had a cut journal; we brassed it and tried to freeze the hub with a keeley, but it was no go. We had to cut it out and drop it on a blind siding. We got so far behind our orders that we were on the other fellow's time, so we had to

[22] Violence is legally permissible only when persons such as drunks, criminals or rioters resist arrest. He found, however, that violence beyond such cases was most likely in cases where a "good pinch" (of a felon or much sought criminal) was possible and would earn the policeman greater prestige, and in cases of suspected sexual deviants (where public pressure for arrest is high but victims are usually loathe to cooperate). Westley found the most important justification for the use of illegal violence to be "disrespect for the police"; that is, violence was legitimized when it would (perhaps) increase public respect for the occupation.

go in the hole and ring up the detainer. The shack brought me the flimsies, the skipper gave me a highball, and we were on our way. Then a dumb hoghead on a work train reached into his pocket and got five minutes of my time. He didn't clear the block and when I hit it I had to big-hold her or run a red board. We had a dynamiter about thirty cars back and when it let loose we pulled out a lung. By the time we got it chained up the monkey had us and they had to send a caboose hop with a dog chaser to bring us in.

The layman would express the statement quite differently.[23] The sheer length of the "translation" suggests one major function of an argot: communication. It is shorter and more precise, and therefore, there is less chance of misunderstanding. But in this respect, it does not differ in function from a technical vocabulary. When we note that argots are most common and most elaborately developed among occupations which are highly integrated, and especially among soldiers and criminals, who are besides, isolated from the general population, this suggests that the argot has colleague functions as well. Elkin (20) notes that the soldier's language is related to his image of solidarity ("GI" or "Mac"), to his freedom from

[23] "We were told to prepare to move a slow freight train with cars and lading totaling three thousand tons in weight. The master mechanic assigned for our use on this train a locomotive on which the superheating elements which convert the wet steam to dry were not functioning properly. This made for inefficiency, since a great deal more water has to be heated and the wet steam responds less slowly to the throttle. We were unable to maintain speed once we had gained it, since the track was being repaired and we were required to proceed slowly over those sections. We had to take cars out of the train and add others to it at almost every stop. As the weight of the train was too great for the engine to pull it over a steep grade, we divided the train, pulling it over the hill in sections. But this used up so much water that we were required to leave the train and go to the nearest water tank to get water. When the train was once more moving, the conductor signaled violently to stop. A bearing on one of the cars had become overheated and had scored the axle. We put in a new bearing and tried to cool it by attaching a small tank of water to the side of the car with a hose leading to the bearing box. As this was unsuccessful, we were forced to take the car out of the train; and since the car was to be placed on a track with only switch connecting it to a through track, we put both car and engine in motion, uncoupled the car from the engine, ran past the switch with the engine, closed the switch and allowed the car to roll into this side track.
"The delays thus occasioned were such that the special orders we had concerning the movement of other trains and their orders concerning us were no longer adequate. Putting the train on a side track we notified the dispatcher, who issued new orders concerning our operation. The brakeman brought me these orders and the conductor signaled to go ahead. But the engineer of a work train tried to get to a passing track beyond that which he could reach in time to leave the automatic block signals showing a clear track. I was required to make an emergency stop or pass this signal. When I made this stop, a car with defective brake mechanism, which allows too much pressure to be built up before it releases, caused such a shock to the draft gear that a coupler was pulled from its fastenings. We had to improvise a substitute out of a heavy chain; but by this time sixteen hours had elapsed since we had left the terminal and we could not legally move our train. Another crew with an engine and caboose came and brought it to the terminal" (18, pp. 101–103).

customary social restraints (the omnipresent obscene word prefix), belief in his strength ("sweat out"), and his attitude to authority ("sad sack" or "chicken shit").[24] It is among criminals that one of the most important of the argots appears. Chic Conwell told Edwin H. Sutherland (78, pp. 16–17):

> Because the underworld is an exclusive society, it is necessary that the stranger be identified before he is admitted. The language of the underworld is both an evidence of this isolation of the underworld and also a means of identification . . . A professional thief can tell in two minutes' conversation with a stranger whether he is acquainted with the criminal underworld and in two minutes more what particular rackets he knows intimately. If a thief were in the can and another person were brought in, the first might ask, "Where were you nailed?" The second might say, "In the shed." It is possible that an amateur might know that "nailed" in that connection meant "arrested," but no amateur would use the word "shed" for railroad station.

At the same time, Conwell goes on the point out, no professional would be so stupid as to use the argot within earshot of outsiders for some might be policemen.[25]

When such an argot is fully-developed, it serves to identify colleagues, to make possible free-and-easy communication, and to symbolize the strength of the ties between them. These considerations direct our attention to the major function of the colleague group. In medicine, no matter how skilled the doctor is, some of his patients are going to die. In religion, no matter how hard the priest tries, some of his charges are undoubtedly going straight to hell. In teaching, no matter how skilled the instructor is, some of his students are going to fail. In industry, no matter how skilled the mechanic is, he may occasionally ruin an expensive piece of equipment. It is the colleague group that comes in at such times to give the individual a sense of assurance so that he does not crack up in the face of failure. Here is the group to which the individual can turn, can "let his hair down," and recount his mistakes (41). The members of the group can then tell him of their mistakes or in other ways reassure him and give him back his faith in himself. A criminal lawyer spoke as follows:

[24] Although glossaries are of dubious value because the words or expression they report are defined out of context, the reader may find it useful to examine (56, Ch. IX; 68, pp. 308–25). Some students of argots have claimed that obscenity ought more properly to be treated as a class or social psychological phenomenon, than an occupational one. While there seems to be little question that such factors are involved, it remains true that when obscene phrases or prefixes become a part of the argot, they are *then* argot and may be treated as such. See (57, pp. 291–292).

[25] See (27, 59, 67).

The first important case I lost really upset me. The poor fellow got 20 years. I went back to my office and sat there staring through my window. He wasn't going to get to stare through a nice open window like that for a long, long time. Finally I couldn't stand it anymore and I called up a friend of mine who'd been in this business a lot longer than I had. He was really a good egg. He went over the case with me from start to finish. Finally he leaned back and said: "Put the whole thing out of your mind. You did as fine a job as anyone could have possibly done. That fellow got a better defense than he deserved. In anybody else's hands he would have gotten the electric chair." That certainly bucked me up, I can tell you that. Of course I knew he was probably exaggerating but hearing that was just what I needed.

The presence of a colleague group is an intimate part of the whole phenomenon of self-confidence. A major reason why the new teacher, the new lawyer, the new social worker, the new carpenter, or the new worker in general feels anxiety and self-doubt is not simply that he lacks experience: it is also because new workers are not admitted to colleague groups until others feel they can trust them. When he has earned this trust, he may then experience the powerful group support the occupation has to offer to its members.

INFORMAL RELATIONS

The motives which lead a man to enter an occupation or remain within it are extremely varied. The majority, certainly, are working in order to achieve or maintain a standard of living which they consider appropriate to themselves. This standard of living may involve a need for money with which to buy possessions and to make easier their (or their children's) entry into certain status groups. To some their occupation means access to power—the means of influencing others—and some enter an occupation because of their desire for the prestige or public honor that the occupation will confer on them. Family or tribal custom influences many, and some have an intense interest in the occupation because of the challenges it offers and the high degree of skill and knowledge required.

But whatever the original motives may be, when an individual enters an occupation and secures a job he finds himself thrown into forced association with other persons, who, in a highly mobile society like ours, are likely to be strangers. These co-workers need have no more to do with each other than the job itself requires. But we find that, since workers bring the *whole* of their personalities with them to the work situation, they interact with co-workers at more intimate levels than the job alone requires. They make informal arrangements with each other for dividing up the job—informal specialization—and what is more important, they form informal groups or work cliques.

INFORMAL SPECIALIZATION

The sheer complexity of the work in the recognized professions leads to informal specialization. The law itself does not distinguish between corporation lawyers and divorce lawyers, but lawyers themselves usually do. All doctors are doctors, but this fact does not prevent the formation of a college of surgeons or an association of pediatricians, which are important, even though they do not have the force of law. Then there are more informal distinctions. In the ministry or priesthood, one will find "church builders," "clean-up men" (clergymen skilled in arranging the settling of church debts), "peace men" (who know how to patch up splits and cleavages), "example setters" (for those clergymen who have not quite lived up to moral expectations) and "funeral preachers."

These divisions are not formal and may be called "functional specialties." Hughes (42, Chs. XII, XIII) calls our attention to the distinction in the real estate business between the "bird-dog," who spots the customer, and the "closer" who gets his name on the dotted line (14). In any well-established factory, there will be persons in a shop who are repositories of technical knowledge: when one wishes to know something, one will be told: "Ask Joe. He knows." There are persons who handle the factory lottery, and persons who, because their job enables them to move freely in and out of several departments, are "relay stations" in the factory grapevine and are looked to for news of forthcoming changes.

Such informal specialties appear to be important in two contexts. First, for those occupations practiced primarily within large-scale bureaucratic organizations, informal specialties are of major importance in the distribution of power. Informal specialties lead to the emergence of a set of informal leaders who are looked to for guidance by other workers and may, therefore, partly determine the probability that an order that comes down the line will be obeyed. Second, for those occupations in which the member himself deals with the client, informal specialties are part of the secret behavior about which silence is an obligation of colleagueship. If the client himself were aware of the specialization, he would probably try to choose his specialist himself. The secrecy that surrounds specialization is therefore designed to retain the locus of decision in the hands of members of the occupation, rather than of their clients. For example, the members of a college department, say sociology, will have such informal specialization. We do not refer to the "fields" in sociology such as criminology, social theory, or the family: there is no secrecy here. (The Catalogue may itself provide the names of the instructors.) There is yet another division of labor: one man is known to his colleagues as a scholar, another as an outstanding teacher, another as a good administrator, another as one skilled in securing grants of research funds. *These* specialties will not be publicly announced.

INFORMAL GROUPS

The study of the *small group,* dating at least back to the theoretical speculations of Charles H. Cooley and Georg Simmel, has become a major subject of sociological interest. It is important to understand the place of the study of the informal group in this larger area. Three major subjects of interest may be distinguished. There is, first, what has come to be called "group dynamics," in which the attempt is made to understand and change individual behavior by the use of group resources.[26] That approach is oriented to action or therapy. The second subject deals with the formal group—the meeting, the seminar, the classroom —which has the great advantage that it can often be studied under relatively controlled conditions, with recording devices, one-way glass, and other instruments.[27] The third subject—and the one we are concerned with here—is that of the study of the small group which is not contrived or set up deliberately but which occurs spontaneously or "naturally," such as cliques, friendships, and colleague circles. There is also the limitation that we are not interested, primarily, in *using* the group to change individual behavior, though we are certainly interested in observing the effect that group membership has on individual behavior. There is, of course, the further limitation that, in the present context, we are interested mainly in groups which appear in *work* situations.[28]

On the one hand, informal work groups are sometimes regarded as innocuous associations which are of little significance. What, after all, is more natural than a few friends meeting for coffee or chatting informally around the water-cooler? Surely this is merely a recreational activity (is it not called a "break"?) which bears little relation to the important activity of the participants: their work. But on the other hand, informal groups are often not so regarded. For example, Hall (37) reported that the final or crowning stage in a medical career was acceptance into an "inner core" of specialists who had access to and dominated the main hospital posts in the community. This group integrated the various specialties, organized the market, and constituted a "fraternity." By the latter is meant that they were an informal group or clique who knew one

[26] See (13, 35, 52, 60).

[27] Perhaps the outstanding figure in this field is Robert F. Bales (2). See also (79).

[28] Those interested in the broad area of the small group will find the following bibliography useful (13; 21, pp. 155–84; 39; 68a, pp. 786–832; 76).

another well. The existence of such cliques—with their frequent association with power, prestige, and economic position—has often created bitter feelings and resentment (especially on the part of those who seek to join them) and, when they occur in formal work organizations, attempts are often made to stamp them out as "ugly centers of gossip" or worse. But the persistence and universality of informal work groups suggests that they must perform important functions for their members. We wish, in this discussion, to attain a balanced view of the nature of the groups and their place in the work life of occupational members.

1. THE NATURE OF INFORMAL GROUPS

Informal groups take different forms in different work situations. Although we partially anticipate the discussion in later chapters (for work groups in factories, restaurants, and farms are often involved), certain general points may be made here. In formal organizations which bring together a variety of occupations, informal groups are often work groups; that is, the members of an informal group are persons who customarily cooperate in the performance of a given task. These persons may be members of different occupations. For example, the cliques described in the classic Western Electric studies (70) were composed of wiremen, soldermen, and an inspector who cooperated in producing a piece of equipment, as may be seen in Fig. 11 below.

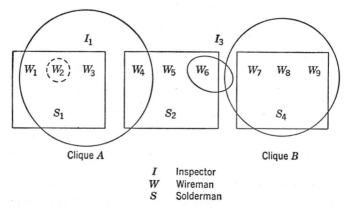

Clique A   Clique B

I Inspector
W Wireman
S Solderman

FIG. 11

INFORMAL ORGANIZATION OF WORK GROUPS IN
THE BANK WIRING OBSERVATION ROOM IN
THE WESTERN ELECTRIC STUDIES *

* Roethlisberger, F. J., and Dickson, W. J., *Management and the Worker*, Cambridge, Mass.: Harvard University Press, 1940, Fig. 45, p. 509.

From the figure it is clear that, in spite of overlapping, and in spite of the way in which the central soldering unit was broken up, there was a distinct tendency for the cliques to mirror the formal organization itself; that is, both cliques A and B were largely restricted to soldering units (the unit composed of one solderman and three wiremen). The formal organizaton itself, then, breaks up the factory (or other work organization) into crews or division-of-labor units and the informal groups that manifest themselves are affected by the formal division. Homans (40, Ch. 6) has emphasized the importance of the relation between frequency of interaction and sentiments (especially friendship),[29] though one must be careful not to assume a direct and invariant relationship under any conditions.[30]

In offices, the work group may not be so important. One may get an informal group composed of private secretaries each of whom works for a different person: they do not form a work crew at all. However, they are formal equals and perform similar work. As such, each member can count on the other to understand his problems and to offer, if not direct help, then the collective support of colleagueship. The fact of status equality seems to be important. If one confesses a serious blunder to one's boss, he may be sympathetic but he can hardly fail to take it into account in evaluating one as a worker. The members of one's informal group, on the other hand, do understand, but are not placed in a position where they must act on such knowledge. Homans (40, p. 243) notes the limitation that status difference or leadership places on informal interaction when he states, in summary, that:

. . . The more frequently persons interact with one another, when no one of them originates interaction with much greater frequency than the others, the greater is their liking for one another and their feeling of ease in one another's presence.

[29] The hypothesis stated by Homans [". . . the more frequently persons interact with one another, the stronger their sentiments of friendship for one another are apt to be." (30, p. 133)] should not be accepted or criticized without taking into account Homans' cautions that the hypothesis is "hedged in" by others, and that it does not settle, but raises, the question of why persons interact with one another or find one another's company pleasant. A large part of the difficulty stems, perhaps, from the fact that Homans takes a functionalist or systematic approach, which forces one to pay attention to one thing at a time, even though the approach insists that *any* thing must be seen in relation to other parts of the system.
[30] An especially imporant situation in which formal organization and informal group may be related is provided by cases of men who form work teams in isolation, as for example, radar or communications site crews, ship crews, and the crews on a bomber. Whether such men are compatible or not may be related to their efficiency as work teams. See (45, 70a, 89).

The qualification, it is later suggested, introduces the possibilities of respect or hostility, and a limitation of the frequency of interaction. For example,[31]

A sea captain may prefer not to meet one of his crew in a beer hall, but if they do meet he is apt to be the one to take the initiative in ordering beers for both.

Informal work groups tend to form spontaneously. If one asks a member when the group began, one rarely gets a specific date although the occasion of first assemblage may be recalled: "I guess we first got together that time when we found out we all like the blueberry pie at the Bluetile Restaurant." Yet not all co-workers who liked this pie were included then, and no outsider could secure entry now if that were his only qualification. The beginnings of these groups are not important. Propinquity itself may be enough to account for the *origins:* persons are thrown together by the accident of nearness in space to one another, a factor which seems to be significant in many situations. The factory cliques described above are a case in point, for not only did the men form work crews, but they worked in physical proximity to one another as well. It is difficult to separate the factor of physical proximity from that of working together, but the former cannot be ignored, especially since other studies show it to be of significance in other than work situations.[32] But sheer physical nearness is important only insofar as it *forces* persons into contact with one another in situations where freedom of physical movement is restricted. It is almost tautological to point out that persons who cannot interact with others do interact with each other more frequently than with others.[33] Nevertheless, the work situation *does* often force men into association with those near them in space and restricts their freedom to move elsewhere. Therefore we should expect a relation between location of work and of on-the-job friends. The rate of inter-

[31] See (40, p. 246). The illustration is attributed to S. A. Richardson.

[32] Residential proximity has been examined in (23a; 56d, pp. 163–217; 88). The last named work, for example, describes a housing project at the Massachusetts Institute of Technology which involved U-shaped courts built for occupancy by married veteran students. Occupants were assigned housing according to the order of name in a waiting list. Friendships developed more frequently between next-door neighbors than between those farther apart; and between those whose houses faced one another, rather than those that did not. In another case, which involved apartment buildings, friendships tended to develop among residents of the same building, same floor, and nearby apartments. In more general terms, sociometric choice has been found to be related to propinquity in (56a). Intriguing also is the finding (74c) that persons in discussion groups tended to interact more frequently with those *opposite* to them than those next to them.

[33] We say "almost tautological" for there is the possibility of little interaction of any kind, or of psychotic developments, as when small groups of men become completely isolated.

action and its degree of friendliness would depend, in addition, on degree of previous acquaintance and common values. Where a group is homogeneous (as has often been the case in housing studies, and in the many studies which utilize college students as subjects), then it may be a matter of indifference to the individual whom he interacts with when working. The situation is obviously different when there is an important cleavage or when persons bring with them a set of attitudes which are likely to result in antagonism toward those they are forced to be near. An outstanding illustration of the latter is provided by Leon Festinger and Harold H. Kelley (23a, 22) in their study of a housing project which was occupied by persons who had formerly worked in wartime shipyards and persons forced to move in (later) by the housing shortage. Both groups regarded themselves as "victims" of a set of circumstances beyond their control (the wartime emergency and the housing shortage) and regarded their neighborhood as a "government housing project," which was occupied, "obviously," by undesirable persons. Interaction and friendship was very low in this neighborhood. This situation has important implications for work situations where persons of different cultural backgrounds are forced to work in close proximity. It is hazardous to predict that such persons will become friends or that antagonisms decline. Also important is the extent to which the friendships that develop on the job among those near one another are generalized to off-the-job situations. Lipset, Trow, and Coleman (55, Ch. 8) report the finding that men who work in small print shops do not develop as close friendship ties with co-workers as do those in larger shops. Yet, they say, surely in the small print shops propinquity and forced interaction are more likely to be in operation. The significant point, they find, is that interaction or friendships which develop mainly from propinquity (that is, because a man has no alternative) tends to be confined to on-the-job matters. When persons *do* have a choice—as in the larger print shops—they are more likely to select as friends persons with similar values to their own, especially in regard to union politics.

Whatever brings men together, a crucial element in the development of informal groups is that of *time*. There must be a sufficient amount of time for men to get to know one another intimately. It is only when this point is reached that they can begin to share confidences and trust one another.

The work of Kurt Lewin and his followers (28, 53) and the major experiment of Muzafer Sherif (72a) on the autokinetic effect [34] have

[34] The autokinetic effect is the illusion of movement of a stationary point of light which is flashed on in a darkened room. Sherif had subjects estimate the amount they thought the point had moved, alone, and then in small groups. He found that indi-

served to emphasize the effect of group values on personal behavior and values. One mark of informal groups—in work situations and many other situations—is that they tend to develop a common way of looking at the world—what Katz and Lazarsfeld (47, pp. 53–56), drawing upon the Lewinians, call the "social reality" function of the small group. In the case of informal work groups, the "world" is that of the work situation. Members of informal work groups are likely to be agreed on such matters as efficiency, salary, the union, and what one has a right to expect from one's formal superior. There is consensus on these matters, and indeed this is one of the bonds that holds the group together; the individual feels at home in such a group.

However, it is important to emphasize that although informal groups often *do* exhibit a high degree of consensus, this is not always true, nor always important. For a work group may offer its members other reasons for making membership worth while. Some groups, certainly, are those in which the individual is "happy"—in which he likes his fellow-members, or enjoys the benefits of good fellowship. But many groups—especially task-oriented groups such as work groups—are those which have a specific reward (other than "fellowship") to offer their members, one which they cannot achieve alone. Such is the case of a work crew assembling a piece of equipment. The reward is the wages each receives, or, in some cases, the completed piece of equipment (say a house) itself. In the latter case, the individual may only mildly like his co-workers or actually dislike them; but he needs them *now*. Therefore he remains a member of the work group at least for a time.[35] Such a situation is one of constraint but, after all, most work situations are. It remains, of course, problematic how long a group which is held together *only* by the ability of the group to give the person a desired reward can persist. It is likely that if the reward is chronically needed—and money is such a reward—such groups can persist indefinitely. In addition, consensus often begins to develop as interaction continues over time.[36]

-----

viduals varied their private estimates to conform more closely with the norm of the group.

[35] On this point in general, read (1; 13, pp. 73–91; 34).

[36] In spite of the unquestioned significance of the matter, it is surprising how little research has been done on the relation between cohesiveness and productivity, especially since the original Western Electric Studies were very much concerned with this problem. R. L. French (24a) was unable to find a direct relationship; Babchuk, and Goode (1b) found that when a change in incentive plan among salesmen produced increased discontent, bickering and conflict, production (sales), nevertheless, continued to rise; Marquis, Guetzkow, and Heyns (56c, pp. 55–67) found that the productivity of participants in conference groups was not correlated significantly with the cohesiveness of the groups; but Van Zelst (80b) found that when he regrouped carpenters and bricklayers according to sociometric choice, labor turnover greatly decreased, as did

Often the members of an informal work group will have some objective characteristics in common. These may be religion, education, age, sex, language (which is often a matter of national or regional origin), income, or other things. Such factors probably contribute to heightened consensus. Other mechanisms as well are likely involved in the considerable tendency for membership in informal work groups to stay within ethnic lines. In one industry a very well-knit informal group was composed of unmarried stenographers who were over forty years of age (46).

A number of relatively distinct types of members can usually be found. One finds the protected member, who operates as an appendage of another member. Another type is the marginal member. He shares in group activities but is not regarded as a full member, or he may be a "hanger-on," a person who would like to get in. He acts as a suppliant and does services for the other members. Another marginal member is the former member. This is a person who was once a member but now does not take full part in the group activities, because of marriage or perhaps because he has now been promoted to a higher position. Another type that is found is the ejected member. This person is likely to be recognizable by the fact that he feels blasé about informal groups or else is indifferent to them. Occasionally he may be found to be in opposition to them; such persons occasionally are found to be management spies.

An informal work group is likely to experience two major kinds of changes over time. First there is segmentation. Generally when an informal group grows as large as, say, ten, it tends to split. It is difficult to preserve intimacy when the group grows very large; factions are likely to emerge (86). The second change is dissolution. However, the informal group does not easily dissolve; it tends to persist.[37] It dissolves only when most of its members have left the company. The presence of a dissolved informal group is often discovered by finding a person who is forever talking about the "good old days" when so and so, and so and so were here.

The members of an informal group feel close to each other. Yet leadership seems always to be present and may even be necessary to help preserve the unity of feeling or task-orientation that may be the occasion for group assemblage. A great deal of research was done in the past searching for the "traits" that would mark off "the leader" from his

---

labor and material costs, and several other factors often correlated with productivity. A part of the difficulty in coming to any conclusion in this area is the difficulty in measuring cohesiveness when it is defined differently by different researchers, as we have commented above.

[37] Cf. (87a, 90); see (68a, pp. 816–29).

followers. By and large, such trait studies have declined in favor of a recognition that leadership is not simply a characteristic like blue eyes, but involves a relationship between persons in a group. As such, it is recognized that there may be not only many leaders in *a* group but many types of leadership as well. There is the formal leader (the person oc-cupying a status in which inheres certain rights with reference to sub-ordinates—the foreman, sergeant, etc.), the person whom subjects choose most frequently,[38] and the person who exercises "influence" on individual behavior, group performance, and structure (25, pp. 877–920). Since we are concerned only with informal groups, the formal leader is not found (though persons who are formal leaders in other situations may easily be members and perhaps leaders in informal groups). Of course, the fact of being chosen is related to influence, though certainly not in any simple manner. It is helpful to think of leadership as present in a relation-ship in which one person *initiates* action for others: he suggests topics of conversation, makes suggestions as to what to do, and so forth. Whyte (84, p. 502) has described a means for observing such leadership behavior in the small group by observing changes in group activity:

> Some of the fellows are sitting around a table in a cafeteria having their evening coffee-ands. *A* leaves the group to sit down for a few minutes with people at a near-by table. *X* remains at the original table, and the conversation con-tinues much as it did when *A* was present. On another occasion, the same people are present in the same spatial arrangement in the cafeteria, but this time it is *X* who gets up and goes over to another table. The conversation at *X's* former table noticeably slows down and perhaps breaks up into twos and threes. The men talk about what *X* would be doing over at the other table, and their attention is frequently directed to that table. If *X* stays away beyond a given point in time, we may observe his friends picking up their chairs and moving over to the table with him.
>
> Observations along these lines establish that *X* characteristically initiates action for this group, that he is the leader of this group.

It is a mistake to think that there is likely to be only one informal group within a work department or shop. Frequently there are very many and they may even form a rough sort of hierarchy. Some of the groups regard themselves as superior to others. One may find informal groups among executives, among department heads, among foremen and among workers, although the hierarchy does not by any means necessarily follow formal lines. One may observe the hierarch operating at union meetings or see them together at picnics, company dinners, and so on. The groups often tend to sit together and to vote as a block.

---

[38] This is the approach of "sociometry," narrowly conceived. See (54, pp. 405–48).

2. THE FUNCTIONS OF INFORMAL GROUPS

Informal groups have a variety of functions but there are four that are particularly significant in the work situation.

a. PROTECTION AND ASSISTANCE

The members of an informal group typically stand together when one of its members is in difficulty. They will take over one another's work in emergencies, will make excuses for one another, will put in a good word with the foremen for one of their fellows, and in general support one of their members if he is attacked, maligned, or accused. Roethlisberger and Dickson (70) found that one of the major activities of the informal groups in the Bank Wiring Observation Room was mutual help. They offer the following record (70, pp. 505–06) of remarks to the observer (Int) made by one of the wiremen (W$_4$):

Int: You do move around quite a bit, do you? Then you don't always work on your own equipment?

W$_4$: Oh no, not always, but most of the time. That is, once in a while if a fellow gets behind someone will go over and help him out.

Int: Do they do that for anyone who is behind?

W$_4$: No. You know, it's a funny thing about that gang. It seems like if a fellow is loafing and gets behind, nobody will help him out, but if he is making an honest effort he will be helped. I've seen that happen time and again. Somebody who has been working along hard all day and has had a lot of tough luck will be helped out.

Int: Do you find that certain people help certain other people all the time, or do they change around quite a bit?

W$_4$: Well, some people are friendlier than others, you know, and where that's the case you will find them helping each other out. Once in a while a fellow will get behind who ordinarily is a good worker. That sometimes happens to anyone. I know one fellow down there who did that and two other fellows went over and started helping him out. That was around a quarter to four. They had their job done and thought they would give him a hand. He didn't say anything, he let them go ahead and help him out, but you know he never helps anyone else out. Since then he has never given a hand to anybody. Do you think they would help him out again? No sir! They're off of him. They don't like a guy that does that. I think it's a good idea to help a fellow out once in a while. I know I appreciate it. It makes all the difference in the world. It's a funny thing, I'll be working along and be behind, and I'll feel all fagged out. Then somebody comes over and starts in wiring on my equipment with me, and you know I perk up to beat the band. I don't know; it just seems to put new life in you, no matter if he only helps you for a couple of levels. I can pick up and work like the deuce then, up till quitting time.

Int: I wonder why.

W$_4$: I don't know why it is. You have a feeling when you're behind that you've got so much work behind it's going to be impossible to get it done, any-way. Then when somebody helps you out it gives you a fresh start, sort of.

This procedure (as well as job trading) was especially interesting in view of the fact that it was in practice forbidden by management.

b. COMMUNICATION

Sometimes—particularly in office situations or smaller industries —informal groups are made up of persons from different parts of the organization. An informal group may be composed of clerks from the sales department, accounting department, complaints department, and the filing department. In such groups a function is that of making it possible for persons in different parts of the organization to learn what is going on in other parts of the organization. The individual is also enabled, to some extent, to see where his work fits into the whole and thus his work is rendered more meaningful than it would be otherwise. This arrangement may also be used in order to discover forthcoming decisions and to prepare for them. The worker is thus protected from un-foreseen actions which may affect his welfare. A worker who is not a member of an informal group is without this protection. The following incident, from an industrial office, is illustrative (30).

At one time the company had a large inventory of expensive rain-coats which it was having difficulty selling to its dealers. It was felt to be unwise simply to reduce the wholesale price since many had already been sold at the higher price. Therefore, to get rid of them, the practice had been adopted of mixing in these more expensive coats with a less expensive line. Most dealers were pleased at what they felt was an error and simply said nothing. When one did object, he was told by the sales department that there had been a shipper's error, and the dealer was to keep the coats. But one dealer not only objected but sent the coats back where they were received, as usual, in the Receiving Room of the Shipping Office. On such occasions, a memo is sent by the Receiving Room to the Department of Complaints and Adjustments, whose function it is to decide on the legitimacy of the claim being made.

An informal group existed which included among others a secretary in the sales department and a clerk in Complaints and Adjustments. The secretary knew of the practice of mixing in expensive coats and she informed the clerk who took it into account in his work. But on the occasion being discussed the Receiving Room memo came to the *head* of the Department of Complaints and Adjustments, Henry Kennedy,[39] who belonged to no informal group. The memo simply said, "Shipment defective. Reason not given." Henry handled it routinely and issued

[39] A pseudonym.

an order to replace the goods. Therefore another mixed shipment went out. The Office Manager described what happened:

The dealer was really boiling when he received this a second time, so he wrote a hot letter to the president asking him what kind of an organization he was running anyhow. Dave (the president) became very upset when he read it and went tearing out of his office and jumped on poor Henry. Well it was just like lightning out of the sky to Henry. He didn't know what was going on. He had never heard of the change in shipping procedure. Dave insisted that he ought to have known about it and that somebody ought to have told him. Henry was so upset about the incident that he developed ulcers and was home for a week.

c. CONTROL

The small group, in part by virtue of its size and in part because of the intimacy of relationships involved, is one of the most important agencies of social control in society. It can operate directly on one of its members who, it may be felt, is deviating from a standard or goal the group considers important. This phenomenon is certainly not peculiar to work organizations (23) but it is of particular importance in work organizations because the content of the standard or goal is crucial to the work organization's ability to carry out its objectives. For example, if informal group members are being pressured by fellow group members to hold down production to an agreed level, then such groups are clearly reducing efficiency of production. On the other hand, the power of group resources may be used, equally, to step up production, or achieve any other goal that may be considered important. The group itself, then, is a center of power, but how this power is used or in what direction remains a central problem in each work organization.

d. THE PROVISION OF SATISFACTIONS

Katz and Lazarsfeld (47, pp. 50–53), in summing up a large amount of evidence on the relation between norms and small groups, speak of the "instrumental function" of small groups, by which they mean the benefits that a group has to offer those who will identify with it. And certainly one of the most important is that of personal satisfaction. Within the informal group, the member secures a haven from the impersonal, rationalized relationships within which he must move in the work situation. Here he gets intimate response, understanding, and recognition. It is here that he finds persons who understand him, are interested in his problems, and want to hear him talk about them.

Types of satisfaction that may be offered are highly varied but two major kinds are those that may be called "symbiotic" and "consensual" (33). By the former we mean that the individual finds himself in an informal group with others who can act as a complementary resource to him. One may, for example, find an informal group composed of a newcomer to the company and the "old hand." The old hand answers questions and shows the newcomer "the ropes." In exchange, he receives a sense of reassurance and a feeling that he is needed. The censensual type of satisfaction is that which the individual secures from associating with those who hold beliefs and attitudes similar to his own. A member of an informal group in a U.S. Air Force organization stated the matter as follows (31):

There's nothing that's more important to me than the mission (of the squadron) . . . The man that calls me "buddy" has got to see that.

The intimacy of the informal group—whether in the colleague group or work group—has led some persons to class them as "primary groups," but this usage may be confusing. When Cooley (16) described the primary group, he saw it as lying at the other end of a continuum from the "institution": both were conceived of as ideal types.[40] In the case of the former, persons tend to meet as "total" personalities, as, for example, the case of an intimate couple who know each other in many roles. By contrast, in the latter situation—the institution—persons meet as segmented personalities, or in terms of only one role, as in the cases of the relationships between customer and clerk, lieutenant and private, foreman and worker.

Now . . . it is the point of an ideal-type that it is an exaggeration. In no situation do persons meet as total personalities or as completely segmented personalities. This means there are no pure primary groups or no pure institutions. However intimate a husband and wife are, there remain segments of their personalities unknown to the other. The Air Force recruit salutes the uniform, and not the man, as he has been taught, but he salutes some more smartly than others and, occasionally—as in battle —this symbolic control may break down altogether under an incompetent officer. Any group, then, is a blend of primary and institutional components.

If we think of the continuum from primary group to institution, then it is possible to place particular groups along it. Rather close to the primary group pole we might place *certain* families in which there is great intimacy between husband and wife. Other families which are close to divorce or in which the couple have grown apart to the extent that they are largely performing their roles mechanically might lie

---

[40] A term referring to analytically exaggerated behavior. A famous illustration is the "economic man." See (66, pp. 601–10; 71; 71a).

considerably to the right of the primary group pole. Similarly, some churches might lie close to the institution pole of the continuum, whereas still others, such as the small store-front church, might lie quite close to the primary group pole.

The informal group in industry lies towards the middle of the continuum, perhaps slightly closer to the primary group pole than to the institutional pole. It is by no means a meeting of total personalities, although the members know considerably more about one another than the formal work requires. Nevertheless the group does not usually continue after working hours.

It is important to note that the primary and institutional components within any group have functions related to the social control of behavior. A good deal of literature within sociology has dealt with the effects of the breakdown of neighborhood (primary) control (3, Ch. XVI; 50, Chs. 1, 4, 5). It has been pointed out that when this occurs there is a tendency for institutionalized, especially legal, controls to replace primary controls. But the reverse can also occur: instituted controls may break down and be replaced by primary controls. Such is the case in crowd behavior and in situations were normal legal controls are absent as in frontier conditions (85).

Our discussion of informal work groups suggests that they also may be functional in the organizations in which they are found. The functions they perform—protection and assistance, communication, control, and the satisfaction of personal needs—may be essential for the harmonious operation of the industry itself (32). The significance of the informal group for the successful achievement of the goals of the larger organization of which it is often a part is, perhaps, nowhere better illustrated than in the finding that American combat soldiers depended heavily on their immediate buddies to support and sustain them in meeting stresses they might not have been able to face otherwise. In *The American Soldier* it is stated (75, p. 149) that: [41]

The sense of power and security which the combat soldier derived from being among buddies on whom he could depend and from being part of a strong and winning team should . . . be regarded . . . as one way in which the resources of the individual were maintained at a level at which he remained capable of coping with the stresses of combat. . . .

Informal work groups perform functions quite as important (and perhaps much the same functions) as those performed by colleague groups for their members.

[41] See also the excellent discussion by Shils (73, pp. 16–39).

CHAPTER REFERENCES

1. Albert, R. S., "Comments on the Scientific Function of the Concept of Cohesiveness," *American Journal of Sociology*, 59:231–234, 1953.

1a. Ashley, W. J., *An Introduction to English Economic History and Theory*, London: Longmans, Green, 1892, Vol. II.

1b. Babchuk, N. N., and Goode, W. J., "Work Incentives in a Self-Determined Group," *American Sociological Review*, 16:679–687, 1951.

2. Bales, R. F., *Interaction Process Analysis*, Cambridge, Mass.: Addison-Wesley, 1950.

3. Barnes, H. E., *Social Institutions*, New York: Prentice-Hall, 1942.

4. Becker, H. S., "Some Contingencies of the Professional Dance Musician's Career," *Human Organization*, 12:22–26, 1953.

5. ———, "The Professional Dance Musician and His Audience," *American Journal of Sociology*, 57:136–144, 1951.

6. Blumenstock, D. I. and Thornthwaite, C. W., "Climate and the World Pattern," in *Climate and Man: Yearbook of Agriculture, 1941*, Washington: U.S. Government Printing Office, 1941.

7. Blumer, H. in Lee, A. M. (ed.), *New Outline of the Principles of Sociology*, New York: Barnes and Noble, 1946, Part Four.

8. Breckinridge, S. P., "Maternity Welfare," *Encyclopaedia of the Social Sciences*, Vol. X, pp. 221–227.

9. Brentano, L., *On the History and Development of Gilds and the Origin of Trade-Unions*, London: Trubner (no date; Preface dated 1870).

10. Burgess, J. S., *The Guilds of Peking*, New York: Columbia University Press, 1928.

11. Burke, K., *Permanence and Change*, New York: New Republic, 1935.

12. Caplow, T., *The Sociology of Work*, Minneapolis, Minn.: University of Minnesota Press, 1954.

13. Cartwright, D. and Zander, A. (eds.), *Group Dynamics*, Evanston, Ill.: Row, Peterson, 1953.

14. Clark, J. M., *Social Control of Business*, New York, London: Whittlesey House, McGraw-Hill, 1939.

15. Clark, R. E., "Psychoses, Income, and Occupational Prestige," *American Journal of Sociology*, 54:433–440, 1949.

16. Cooley, C. H., *Social Organization*, New York: Scribners Sons, 1909.

17. Coornaert, E., *Las Corporaciones en la Edad Media y en los Tiempos Modernos*, Buenos Aires: Ministerio de Educación de la Nación, Subsecretaria de Cultura, 1950.

18. Cottrell, W. F., *The Railroader*, Stanford University, California: Stanford University Press, 1940.

19. Durkheim, E., *The Division of Labor in Society*, Glencoe, Ill.: Free Press, 1949.

20. Elkin, F., "The Soldier's Language," *American Journal of Sociology*, 51:414–422, 1946.
21. Faris, R. E. L., "Development of the Small-Group Research Movement," in Sherif, M. and Wilson, M. O. (eds.), *Group Relations at the Crossroads*, New York: Harper, 1953.
21a. Fenneman, N. M., *Physiography of Western United States*, New York: McGraw-Hill, 1931.
22. Festinger, L., "Architecture and Group Membership," *Journal of Social Issues*, 7, Nos. 1 and 2:152–163, 1951.
23. ———; Back, K.; Schachter, S.; Kelley, H.; and Thibaut, J., *Theory and Experiment in Social Communication*, Ann Arbor: Research Center for Group Dynamics, University of Michigan, 1950.
23a. ——— and Kelley, H. H., *Changing Attitudes Through Social Contact*, Ann Arbor, Michigan: Research Center for Group Dynamics, 1951.
23b. ———, Schachter, S.; and Back, K., *Social Pressures in Informal Groups*, New York: Harper, 1950.
24. Fischelis, R. P., "Medical Materials Industry," *Encyclopaedia of the Social Sciences*, Vol. X, pp. 279–282.
24a. French, R. L., "Sociometric Measures in Relation to Individual Adjustment and Group Performance Among Naval Recruits," *American Psychologist*, 4:262, 1949.
25. Gibb, C. A., "Leadership," in Lindzey, G. (ed.), *Handbook of Social Psychology*, Cambridge: Addison Wesley, 1954, Vol. II, pp. 877–920.
26. Gold, R., "Janitors Versus Tenants: A Status-Income Dilemma," *American Journal of Sociology*, 57:486–493, 1952.
27. Goldin, H. E.; O'Leary, F.; and Lipsius, M. (eds.), *Dictionary of American Underworld Lingo*, New York: Twayne, 1950.
28. Grabbe, P. and Lewin, K., "Conduct, Knowledge, and Acceptance of New Values," *Journal of Social Issues*, 1, No. 3:53–64, 1945.
29. Gross, C., *The Gild Merchant*, Oxford: Clarendon, 1890, Vol. I.
30. Gross, E., "Characteristics of Cliques in Office Organizations," *Research Studies*, State College of Washington, 19:131–136, 1951.
31. ———, "Primary Functions of the Small Group," *American Journal of Sociology*, 60:24–29, 1954.
32. ———, "Some Functional Consequences of Primary Controls in Formal Work Organizations," *American Sociological Review*, 18:368–373, 1953.
33. ———, "Symbiosis and Consensus as Integrative Factors in Small Groups," *American Sociological Review*, 21:174–179, 1956.
33a. Gross, E., "Informal Relations and the Social Organization of Work in an Industrial Office." Unpublished Ph.D. dissertation, University of Chicago, 1949.
34. Gross, N. and Martin, W. E., "On Group Cohesiveness," *American Journal of Sociology*, 57:546–554, 1952.
35. Gurvitch, G. (ed.), *Sociometry in France and the United States*, Beacon, N.Y.: Beacon House, 1950.
36. Haines, A. J., "Nursing," *Encyclopaedia of the Social Sciences*, Vol. XI, pp. 405–412.

37. Hall, O., "The Stages of a Medical Career," *American Journal of Sociology,* 53:327–336, 1948.

38. ———, "Types of Medical Careers," *American Journal of Sociology,* 55:243–253, 1949.

39. Hare, A. P.; Borgatta, E. F.; and Bales, R. F. (eds.), *Small Groups: Studies in Social Interaction,* New York: Knopf, 1955.

40. Homans, G. C., *The Human Group,* New York: Harcourt, Brace, 1950.

41. Hughes, E. C., "Dilemmas and Contradictions of Status," *American Journal of Sociology,* 50:353–359, 1945.

42. ———, A Study of a Secular Institution: The Chicago Real Estate Board, unpublished Ph.D. Dissertation, University of Chicago, 1928.

43. ———, "Work and the Self," in Rohrer, J. H. and Sherif, M. (eds.), *Social Psychology at the Crossroads,* New York: Harper, 1951.

44. ——— and H. M., *Where Peoples Meet,* Glencoe, Ill.: Free Press, 1952.

45. Jacobs, J. H., "The Application of Sociometry to Industry," *Sociometry,* 8:181–198, 1945.

46. James, J., "Clique Organization in a Small Industrial Plant," *Research Studies, State College of Washington,* 19:125–130, 1951.

47. Katz, E. and Lazarsfeld, P. F., *Personal Influence,* Glencoe, Ill.: Free Press, 1955.

48. Kerckhoff, R. K., "Interest Group Reactions to the Profession of Marriage Counseling," *Sociology and Social Research,* 39:179–183, 1955.

49. ———, "The Profession of Marriage Counseling as Viewed by Members of Four Allied Professions: A Study in the Sociology of Occupations," *Marriage and Family Living,* 15:340–344, 1953.

50. Landis, P. H., *Social Policies in the Making,* Boston: Heath, 1947.

51. Lantz, H. R., "Occupational Differences in Mental Disorders," *Social Problems,* 2:100–104, 1954.

52. Lewin, K., "Dynamics of Group Action," *Educational Leadership,* 1:195–200, 1944.

53. Lewin, G. W. (ed.), *Resolving Social Conflicts,* New York: Harper, 1948.

54. Lindzey, G. and Borgatta, E. F., "Sociometric Measurement," in Lindzey, G. (ed.), *Handbook of Social Psychology,* Cambridge, Mass.: Addison-Wesley, 1954, Vol. I.

55. Lipset, S. M.; Trow, M. A.; and Coleman, James S., *Union Democracy: The Internal Politics of the International Typographical Union,* Glencoe, Ill.: Free Press, 1956.

56. Lovette, L. P., *Naval Customs: Traditions and Usage,* Annapolis, Md.: U.S. Naval Institute, 1939.

56a. Maisonneuve, J.; Palmade, G.; and Fourment, C., "Selective Choices and Propinquity," *Sociometry,* 15:135–140, 1952.

56b. Mangus, A. R., *Rural Regions in the United States,* Washington: U.S. Government Printing Office, 1940.

56c. Marquis, D. G.; Guetzkow, H.; and Heyns, R. W., "A Social Psychological Study of the Decision-Making Conference," in Guetzkow, H. (ed.), *Groups, Leadership and Men,* Pittsburgh: Carnegie Press, 1951.

56d. Merton, R. K., "The Social Psychology of Housing," in Dennis, W. *et al.* (eds.), *Current Trends in Social Psychology*, Pittsburgh: University of Pittsburgh Press, 1948.

57. Miller, D. C. and Form, W. H., *Industrial Sociology*, New York: Harper, 1951.

58. Mills, C. W., *White Collar*, New York: Oxford University Press, 1951.

59. Monteleone, V. J., *Criminal Slang*, Boston: Christopher, 1949.

60. Moreno, J. L., "Origins and Foundations of Interpersonal Theory, Sociometry, and Microsociology," in Gurvitch, G., *Sociometry in France and the United States*, Beacon, N.Y.: Beacon House, 1950.

61. Morse, H. B., *The Gilds of China*, London: Longmans, Green, 1909.

62. Morse, N. C. and Weiss, R. S., "The Function and Meaning of Work and the Job," *American Sociological Review*, 20:191–198, 1955.

63. Mumford, L., *The Culture of Cities*, New York: Harcourt, Brace, 1938.

64. Myers, R. C., "Myth and Status Systems in Industry," *Social Forces*, 26:331–337, 1948.

65. National Opinion Research Center, "Jobs and Occupations: A Popular Evaluation," *Opinion News*, 9:3–13, Sept., 1947.

66. Parsons, T., *The Structure of Social Action*, New York: McGraw-Hill, 1937.

67. Partridge, E., *A Dictionary of the Underworld: British and American*, New York: Macmillan, 1950.

68. Pye, A. B. and Shea, N., *The Navy Wife*, New York: Harper, 1942.

68a. Riecken, H. W. and Homans, G. C., "Psychological Aspects of Social Structure," in Lindzey, G. (ed.), *Handbook of Social Psychology*, Cambridge, Mass.: Addison-Wesley, 1954, Vol. II, pp. 786–832.

69. Riesman, D., "Toward an Anthropological Science of Law and the Legal Profession," *American Journal of Sociology*, 57:121–135, 1951.

70. Roethlisberger, F. J. and Dickson, W. J., *Management and the Worker*, Cambridge, Mass.: Harvard University Press, 1940.

70a. Rogers, M., "Problems of Human Relations in Industry," *Sociometry*, 9:350–371, 1946.

71. Salomon, A., "Max Weber's Methodology," *Social Research*, 1:146–168, 1934.

71a. ———, "Max Weber's Sociology," *Social Research*, 2:60–73, 1935.

72. Seligman, E. R. A., *Two Chapters on the Mediaeval Gilds of England*, Baltimore: American Economic Association, 1887.

72a. Sherif, M., "Social Factors in Perception," in Swanson, G. E.; Newcomb, T. M.; and Hartley, E. L., eds., *Readings in Social Psychology*, New York: Henry Holt, 1952.

73. Shils, E. A., "Primary Groups in the American Army," in Merton, R. K. and Lazarsfeld, P. F. (eds.), *Continuities in Social Research*, Glencoe, Ill.: Free Press, 1950, pp. 16–39.

74. Smith, R. S., *The Spanish Guild Merchant: A History of the Consulado, 1250–1700*, Durham, N.C.: Duke University Press, 1940.

74a. Smith, T. L., *Brazil: People and Institutions*, Baton Rouge: Louisiana State University Press, 1946.

74b. Stark, M. C. and Whittlesey, D. S., *Major Geographic Regions of North America*, Bloomington: McKnight and McKnight, 1923.

74c. Steinzor, B., "The Spatial Factor in Face-to-Face Discussion Groups," *Journal of Abnormal and Social Psychology*, 45:552–55, 1950.

75. Stouffer, S. A. *et al.*, *The American Soldier, Vol. II: Combat and Its Aftermath*, Princeton, N.J.: Princeton University Press, 1949.

76. Strodtbeck, F. L. and Hare, A. P., "Bibliography of Small Group Research," *Sociometry*, 17:107–178, 1954.

77. Sudhoff, K., "Medicine—History," *Encyclopaedia of the Social Sciences*, Vol. X, pp. 283–289.

78. Sutherland, E. H. (annot. and interpret.), *The Professional Thief*, Chicago: University of Chicago Press, 1937.

79. Thelen, H. A. and Whithall, J., "Three Frames of Reference: The Description of Climate," *Human Relations*, 2:159–176, 1949.

80. Unwin, G., *The Gilds and Companies of London*, London: Methuen, 1908.

80a. U.S. Department of Agriculture, *Soils and Man: Yearbook of Agriculture, 1938*, Washington: U.S. Government Printing Office, 1938.

80b. Van Zelst, R. H., "Validation of a Sociometric Regrouping Procedure," *Journal of Abnormal and Social Psychology*, 47:299–301, 1952.

81. Wardwell, W. I., "The Reduction of Strain in a Marginal Social Role," *American Journal of Sociology*, 61:16–25, 1955.

82. Westley, William A., "Secrecy and the Police," *Social Forces*, 34:254–257, 1956.

83. ———, "Violence and the Police," *American Journal of Sociology*, 59:34–41, 1953.

83a. Whittlesey, D. S., "Major Agricultural Regions of the Earth," *Annals of the Association of American Geographers*, 26:199–240, 1936.

84. Whyte, W. F., "Observational Field-Work Methods," in Jahoda, M.; Deutsch, M.; and Cook, S. W. (eds.), *Research Methods in Social Relations*, New York: Dryden, 1951, Part Two, Chapter Fourteen.

85. ———, "Social Organization in the Slum," *American Sociological Review*, 8:34–39, 1943.

86. ———, *Street Corner Society*, Chicago: University of Chicago Press, 1955.

87. Williams, W., *What's on the Worker's Mind*, New York: Scribners, 1920.

87a. Williams, S. B., and Leavitt, H. J., "Group Opinion as a Predictor of Military Leadership," *Journal of Consulting Psychology*, 11:283–291, 1947.

87b. Willis, J. C., *Agriculture in the Tropics*, Cambridge: The University Press, 1909.

88. Wilner, D. M.; Walkley, R. P.; and Cook, S. W., "Residential Proximity and Intergroup Relations in Public Housing Projects," *Journal of Social Issues*, 8, No. 1:45–69, 1952.

89. Zeleny, L. D., "Selection of Compatible Flying Partners," *American Journal of Sociology*, 52:424–431, 1947.

90. ———, "Sociometry of Morale," *American Sociological Review*, 4:799–808, 1939.

PART THREE

WORK ORGANIZATIONS

INTRODUCTION

By a "work organization" we mean an organization of work specialties which are related to each other for the purpose of achieving a definite objective. For example, an aircraft factory has within it a large number of persons engaged in different specialties—designers, riveters, tool-and-die makers, mechanics, inventory storesmen, clerks, engineers, and stenographers. These activities are all related to one another in such a way that the objective of the organization—the production of airplanes—is achieved. The same general analysis could be made of an army, a broker's office, or a farm.

The main characteristic is the *definite objective*. In a sense, of course, all organizations have objectives. The objective may have changed over time and the original objective (perhaps unstated or unrecognized) may be lost in antiquity, or the organization may have only a vague purpose, such as "fellowship." In work organizations, *the objective is clear* and formally recognized by the participants at start of their involvement in the organization.[1] When objectives are clearly enunciated, then the

[1] In speaking of "the objective" we do not, of course, ignore situations where there are many objectives (as when a factory makes several products) or where a major objective—in addition to whatever else the organization does—is that of making money. Structurally the presence of several objectives presents no special problems unless the achievement of one conflicts with the achievement of another. We are, however, deliberately postponing discussion of the problem raised by Alvin W. Gouldner (16) of the fact that different parts of the same organization may have conflicting goals. We look on the organization as a whole. Therefore, the objective is determined primarily by those in high authority positions in the organization, and for ease of classification, we consider the objective to be the major product or service the organization provides to consumers or clients.

organization necessarily requires that relationships within it shall be *defined* so as to achieve those objectives. A work organization is, therefore, a control body for its members.

The degree of this control will vary depending on the type of organization and on the culture. In nontotalitarian countries, the control is only of a segment of the worker's personality—his role as a work specialist. The boss's control is minimal: he expects of the worker only enough to make his appropriate contribution to the achievement of the objectives of the organization. The boss does not expect, in addition, to be loved by the worker (though he is usually pleased if he is), and he does not expect the worker to abandon all loyalties—to his family, his church, his friends, and the state and give completely of himself to his work. In totalitarian countries (including Western industry when it leaves home and goes to the East Indies or Africa), by contrast, a much larger portion of the worker's personality is controlled. In Communist countries, for example, the worker is told that he is not working for this or that manager in this or that industry. Rather, he is working for the community at large which needs his contribution. Managers, no less than workers, are servants of the community which is the ultimate authority. The community or workers' interest is represented by the Communist party which, it is maintained, is simply the "vanguard" who understand more clearly the "dialectic of the historical process." Consequently, the worker must give his "all," not just his role as a worker, to the work organization. If other loyalties—family, friends, church—interfere, then they must be given up, for a loyalty which interferes with his obligation to the community is, by definition, subversive or treasonable. The worker who slows down on the job is therefore not simply "lazy" but is guilty of sabotage. By contrast, the worker who gives his "all" and produces beyond expected minima (the "activist"), is rewarded not simply with money and other emoluments, but by being made a "Hero of Labor" —a political rather than economic reward (2, Ch. 6; 55). Owing in large part to a paucity of data, the discussion in the subsequent chapters will be largely confined to Western work organizations. Thus we shall say that only a segment of the worker's personality is controlled.

Part Two dealt with occupations. When we turn to work organizations, we are focusing special attention on the *relationships among* occupations, for a work organization is essentially a set of related occupations which are coordinated for the achievement of a specific goal. At the same time, there is a tendency for occupations to vary in terms of the type of work organization in which they may be found or indeed in whether they tend to be found in a work organization at all. The nature of the relationship between occupations and work organization is a function of the extent to which the occupation is professionalized. In general, the closer an occupation approaches professionalization, the greater is the tendency for the occupation to become to some extent independent of a *particular* work organization. It is here that private practice is likely to make its appearance. The members of the recognized professions resist being included in any work organization. The doctor uses and is part of the hospital, but doctors attempt to control the hospital. The "company doctor" is felt to be atypical and his loyalties are confused. The association of lawyers in a law office is felt to be, and is, different from the association of workers in a factory.

Nevertheless, even among the most individualistic of professional practitioners there is normally some type of continuing relationship with a work organization. The doctor is associated with the hospital, the lawyer with a court system. Artists, perhaps, come closest to avoiding a regular relation with a work organization, but this is true of only a small portion of their numbers. The vast majority are likely to be included within art schools or within commercial organizations. On the other hand, certain professions are inalienably associated with work organizations, as, for example, teaching [2] and social work.

It is true, however, that the greater the extent to which an occupation is professionalized then the more it is likely to retain a distinct identity and a special group consciousness even though it is practiced within a work organization. As we move over to a consideration of occupations that are less and less professionalized, those occupations tend increasingly to be practiced within a work organization and to be practiced only there. They become specialties within the work organization and may almost lose their separate identity. In this case, the industry, as contrasted with the colleague organization, begins to demand the workers' identification and loyalty, and the industrial union increases, *pari passu* in power and significance.[3] The difference between group consciousness as developed by a professionalized occupation ("we doctors"), and group consciousness as maintained through a work organization ("the boys out at the mill"), becomes evident (18, p. 239).

---

[2] The private tutor or music teacher who gives lessons in her home is a rare exception.

[3] A case in point (and one that poses serious problems) is the difficulty large scale date-gatherers (e.g., censuses) have in classifying such categories as "operatives" or "craftsmen, foremen and kindred workers" except *by the industry* in which they are practiced (e.g., transportation, manufacturing, etc.). See (53).

TYPES OF WORK ORGANIZATIONS

Work organizations in our society include governmental staffs, schools, universities, restaurants, farms, business offices, armies, churches, and factories. They do not ordinarily include families, children's gangs, cliques, communities, or racial and ethnic groups.[4] The latter may, however, *become* work organizations on certain occasions as in the case of household-manufacturing, or when a group of friends constitute themselves as a committee. Any organization has an element of work in it to the extent that its activities are directed or controlled in the service of a stated or recognized objective.

There are in every work organization two major sets of relationships. The first of these is a division of labor, which functions to relate specialisms to one another. Here, the separate occupations which we have discussed in Part Two *become* specialisms.

The second set of relationships is an authority structure by which the activities of persons are coordinated and directed toward the achievement of objectives of the organization. These two sets of relationships may be conceived of as substructures within the larger structure.

Each worker occupies two positions, one in each substructure. This occurs as a consequence of the fact that the two substructures interlock. An illustration may be drawn from the business office of a factory (17).

Mr. A is head of the Accounting Department. Under him are two supervisors, Mr. B and Mr. C who are in charge of Accounts Receivable and Accounts Payable respectively. The relation between Mr. A and Mr. B, and the relation between Mr. A and Mr. C are both authority relations. Mr. A, in turn is related to the Treasurer and the Treasurer to the President of the company. This is the "line." In turn, both Mr. B and Mr. C have clerks under them in an authority relation. However, the authority structure does not relate the two supervisors to one another. Nevertheless the two are, in fact, closely related and are in continuing

---

[4] This distinction is related to the threefold division of "major collectivities" which Talcott Parsons (42, p. 115) marks off: (1) organizations such as business firms, schools, and hospitals in which roles (other, of course, than those of client and consumer) take the "full-time" occupational form; (2) diffuse-function "associations" such as political units and churches (and specific function associations such as labor unions, professional and trade associations) which "represent their constituencies"; and (3) "diffuse solidarities" in which individuals are embedded such as local communities, kinship, and ethnic groups. He notes immediately, however, that type (2) associations ". . . in proportion to their size and extensiveness of interests also tend to become organized in occupational-type roles for the more responsible and specialized functions, but with many limitations on how far this mode of organization, i.e., their bureaucratization, can be carried."

conference with one another. The tie between them is one of a division of labor.

These relationships may be diagrammed as follows:

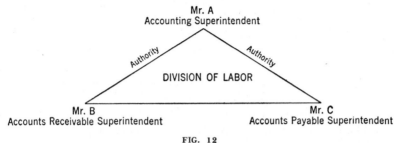

FIG. 12

In this manner it may be seen that authority and division-of-labor substructures interlock. The authority substructure creates various status levels. At each such level, work is divided among specialists.

In addition to interlocking, the two substructures also overlap. In his capacity as head of the Accounting Department, Mr. A is authorized to supervise the work of Mr. B and Mr. C. However, Mr. A does more than supervise. He makes decisions on whether salesmen should be allowed large advances on their salaries or not; he acts as a liaison between the company and its lawyers in case of litigation; he handles matters such as conflicts between the company and its customers with respect to the balance owed, claims of customers with regard to payment, unexplained deductions made by customers, questionable adjustments with regard to shipping costs, and other matters. All of these activities are of an unusual character; yet in his performance of them, Mr. A is placed in the division of labor. Mr. B or Mr. C refer such matters to him, just as Mr. B would refer an accounts payable item to Mr. C. In this manner one can see that the three persons in fact make up a division-of-labor organization. Thus, the relationship between Mr. B (or Mr. C) and Mr. A is both an authority and division-of-labor relationship.

It might be claimed that the two substructures are not only overlapping but are in fact identical. If one chose to regard the exercise of authority as a type of labor, the division of labor would emerge as the major or only structure: managing would be merely one type of work among others. Such a point of view would do violence to an adequate description of the social relationships involved. The work of managing is different from other types of work in that managing requires that the person shall coordinate the work of various specialists placed under him. The division of labor serves to divide up the work among persons who

then confine their attention to a given area. The manager is expected
to see to it that these specialisms mesh and that unity results. The manager does this by evaluating the work of his subordinates both by itself
(as an occupation) and in relation to the work of others. Only he is placed
in such a position that he can see his work organization *as a whole*. The
very nature of evaluation requires that a set of supervisor-subordinate
relationships shall exist. It is for this reason that an authority structure
is formally necessary.

When such an organization is set up, each person in it will have a
status composed of his positions in the two substructures. All statuses
will then be related to each other so that the total organization exhibits
unity. The kind of unity will vary depending on the type of work organization. We may classify work organizations on the basis of type of unity
by thinking of two extremes—unity based on *consensus* and unity based
on *symbiosis*.[5] To speak generally, a consensual tie is one in which people
subscribe to the same set of values, or are united by agreement, illustrated, for example, by the citizens of a state, the members of a church,
or the members of, say, the Society of Mozart Lovers. A symbolic tie is
one in which people are united because each has something to give which
the other needs; that is, a tie of interdependence, illustrated, for example,
by the family in the U.S. of 100 years ago, the tie between storekeepers
and customers, or the tie between nations or regions which trade with one
another. Consensual relations tend to be governed by emotions and sentiments, by mores, and implicit understandings. Symbiotic relations tend
to be governed by reason, by self interest, by laws, and formally agreed-
upon rules.

A self-sufficient farm in the hill country of Tennessee will fall close
to the consensual extreme. There is a division of labor and an authority
structure that come into play in the running of the farm, but it is highly
dominated by traditional, consensual elements. An army, on the other
hand, will fall close to the symbiotic extreme. It is a highly rationalized
organization in which rules and other symbiotic elements loom large. Yet
neither the farm nor the army are purely consensual or purely symbiotic.

In Fig. 13 the continuum is pictured, with various types of work
organization located on the continuum. The actual location of particular
work organizations is only intended to be suggestive. We have the farm at
the extreme left, yet some farms probably belong further right. Some
armies, perhaps the Papal army, or that of Monaco, belong further left.

As one moves from left to right on the continuum, work organizations tend to increase in size and complexity, and to become more heavily

[5] These concepts were first given wide currency by Robert E. Park who utilized
them in the study of the community. See (38; 39, pp. 165–166, 505–511; 41).

bureaucratized. As the size of an organization increases, it becomes increasingly difficult to maintain unity on a primarily consensual basis and symbiotic elements become of increasing importance. Since there seems to be an historical trend toward increase of size, complexity, and bureaucratization, we may speak of a trend from consensus to symbiosis. But it should more properly be spoken of as a shift of emphasis, for neither element ever entirely vanishes.

		Old,		Schools and		Govt.			
	Some	Small,	Restau-	Univer-	Some	Civil	Large		
Farm	Churches	Factory	rant	sities	Churches	Serv.	Factory	Armies	

CONSENSUS .... SYMBIOSIS

FIG. 13
CONTINUUM OF WORK ORGANIZATIONS

There are other distinctions between consensually based and symbiotically based work organizations. In the former type, specialists will be distinguished from one another by informal agreement, and are likely to be taken for granted and hardly even discussed. This situation is common in the small, long-established work organization which undergoes little change. At the same time, authority relations tend almost to vanish or rather to overlap with the division of labor to the extent that the two substructures become almost coincident, for there is little need for formal coordination at all. At the other pole, we have the work organization in which the specialties are rigidly defined by stated rules. Yet the rules are being forever changed in the light of varying conditions. This situation is common in the new, large work organization, which undergoes change as the demands for its products or services change, or for other reasons. Here authority becomes more rigid and much more in evidence as the tasks of coordination and evaluation become more complex. This type of organization is characterized by continuing meetings among personnel, by conflict among specialists, and the like.

In the first type of organization status is hardly discussed; persons know where they stand. In the second type, status becomes an object of major concern to the worker, precisely because the division of labor and authority substructures are products of discussion and therefore may vary substantially depending on individual decisions. In the search for a clearer definition of status and rights, status symbols are emphasized and labor unions make their appearance. Such categories as race, religion, ethnicity, and social class may be major status symbols.

Informal groups make their appearance in both types of work organization, but there is less need for them in the first type. The worker feels an identification with the organization and a high degree of security. In the second type there is a greater need for informal fellowship which is not directly related to the work because work relations themselves do not supply such fellowship. The very impersonality of work relations drives the worker to other identifications which command his interest and loyalty. One important identification is with fellow workers *vis-à-vis* management, which may be reflected, in say, restriction of output.

The continuum provides the basis for the selection of work organizations to be analyzed in Part Three. It would be desirable if we could select organizations at random, but unfortunately research in work relations does not yet permit us this freedom. Instead, we shall confine ourselves to work organizations about which we have sufficient reliable data. We have chosen the farm, which lies fairly close to the consensual pole of the continuum, the restaurant, which lies toward the middle, and the large factory which lies fairly close to the symbiotic pole. Since we will be discussing quite different kinds of work organizations, it will be useful to begin each discussion by pointing out the special features of each kind that mark it off from other kinds.

CHAPTER SEVEN

THE FARM: THE WORK COMPLEX

Most studies of work outside of Western society are studies of the farm for it comes closer to being a universal work activity than does any other activity.[1] Industrialization, trade, and urbanization have greatly affected the character and form of Western farming without, however, decreasing its significance. In the United States—where these trends have gone on rapidly—farmers comprise most of those classified as "rural farm" who, in 1950, still accounted for over one-sixth of our population.

DISTINCTIVE CHARACTERISTICS OF THE FARM

The farm exhibits the following characteristics which mark it off from other types of work organization: closeness to other areas of life, peak activities, low degree of predictability, and small scale of operations.

CLOSENESS OF FARMING TO OTHER AREAS OF LIFE

We have pointed out repeatedly that work is related to other segments of the total life of a community. But farming tends to be characterized by a remarkable degree of closeness to the family, to religion, to education, to politics, and to recreation. It is this closeness of relationship that is a primary factor in the making of the farmers' world into a distinct social world. Three major aspects of farming are relevant:

[1] In addition to the works of Fortune and Arensberg and Kimball, already discussed in detail, see (7, 8, 9, 11, 33, 34, 43, 44, 45, 46).

1. NEED FOR SPACE

Farming, by its very nature, requires a great deal of space, and the desire of the worker to be near his place of work has tended to produce a close relation between farm and residence. The factory worker will desire to live near his place of work, but for him to be only one mile away usually means living in a neighborhood where he may be surrounded by persons of divergent occupations, marital status, age, religion, and income. The farmer, by contrast, lives right on his farm, surrounded by the farms of others, or else he lives in farm villages with other farmers or persons with interests similar to his.[2]

One result, then, is the creation of a special or reserved set of institutions or facilities to cater to the farmer's total needs. This isolation tends to give the farmer some independence of action and helps to create peculiar characteristics. The ecological base, further, favors the development of consensual unity and gives rise to the farm community. The factory community does exist, but is relatively rare; one could, if one wished, call Washington, D.C. a "government community" or a resort town a "restaurant community." But these are both uncommon and do not, in any case, adequately describe the work make-up of such communities. On the other hand, to speak of an area as a "farm community" is both an adequate description and a characterization of a dominant type.

2. ABSENCE OF URBANIZATION

By definition, and owing to special space needs, a farming area is not urbanized. The farmer may produce for sale in an urban market but his place of dwelling is not an urbanized area. To some extent, therefore, he escapes one major effect of urbanization. Urbanization is one of the forces which help separate work from other areas of life. In Western society where urbanization is well developed, with consequent formalization and the growth of impersonal relations and secondary contacts, work becomes compartmentalized along with other areas of life. Formal mechanisms embodied in government, law, and institutionalized churches and clubs arise to maintain integration. These trends do not operate so strongly on the farmer in the United States; they operate hardly at all in many other areas of the world. Work is not so much separated from other areas of life as it is in cities.

3. THE FAMILY BUSINESS

Farming is usually a family affair. The family business is found in many types of work but it tends to be declining; in farming, however, the family farm is still the dominant form. Even on the huge wheat farms of the Palouse country of Washington, the very fact of extreme

---

[2] The migratory laborer is a partial exception. He often moves without his family, but many of them take their families with them.

mechanization makes it possible for a *single family* to run a farm of five hundred acres with occasional help.

These three factors—the need for space, absence of urbanization, and the family business—make of farming a complex which is particularly closely articulated and well-integrated with other cultural elements.

PEAK ACTIVITIES

Many work activities exhibit a seasonal or even daily variation, but few industries approach farming in the overwhelming concentration of work at the time of harvest.

At the time of harvest there is not only an enormous concentration of work, but also a concentration of attention. Where a whole year's income is involved, then all of the family's and the whole community's attention become focussed on the harvest and on prices if the crop is commercial. The periods of non-peak activities are usually neatly integrated into the pattern of total community activities. In Ireland, for example, as we have pointed out, the time of the Christmas ceremonies comes conveniently when the farmer has little else to do. This tends to be true of other rural peoples that celebrate Christmas. Vance (54, pp. 164–66) refers to the peak of crime, fighting, and campground meetings in the cotton areas in the time of the "lay-by," when workers are waiting for the cotton to bloom.

DEGREE OF PREDICTABILITY

Except for crops with a very short growing period there is ordinarily a considerable time lapse between planting or calving and harvesting or marketing. This makes it necessary for the farmer to take long range chances. He doesn't know what the weather will be like, what the prices will be, or whether he will be able to get labor in the week or on the *day* when he needs it. He is unable to control his inventory in a manner comparable to that of a shopkeeper.

This means the farmer must try to reduce the severity of these risks. He will make use of insurance, will try to spread the risk through loans, and most significantly, will seek government support.

HUMAN SCALE OF OPERATIONS

Farms attain great sizes in some areas, but they are exceptional and the typical farm varies from one or two acres in size to two or three hundred. Further, the need for labor on any *given* farm is small compared to a factory or a department store. There is typically only a small resident population of farmers on a farm at a given time. Usually there is only the family, and a few hired workers (rarely more than nine).

There is almost a complete absence of a "line" in the factory sense. There may be a foreman on a large ranch, or an overseer on a cotton plantation, and below them miscellaneous laborers. But, except for the giant enterprise, there is normally no formal hierarchy of any consequence. The result is that mobility takes fundamentally different forms in agriculture than it does in the factory, involving moving from laborer status to tenant status, or from tenant status to owner status. In this process migration becomes one of the most significant of mobility techniques.

THE INSTITUTIONAL SYSTEM OF FARMING: THE WORK COMPLEX

Our first concern is with the manner in which farming is related to other activities in the local community or to society at large. These relations are manifold but two of them are of particular significance: the *degree of isolation* and the *degree of commercialization*.

The more isolated the farm community is, then the closer is farming likely to be related to the community and to local culture. Tradition is strong then and farming is likely to dominate the community. Commercialization is related to the degree of isolation, for, in general, the more isolated the farming area is then the less commercialized agriculture is there likely to be. Broadly speaking the farmers of the world may be divided into two great groups—subsistence farmers and cash farmers. The subsistence farmer grows his crops for his own needs and sells little or nothing. He tries to satisfy all of his immediate needs in the community. Under these conditions, the nexus between work and the rest of the local society is very close. In cash farming the farm is a business. This farmer is linked intimately with the urban world and therefore with the world at large.

The nature of the relation of the farm to other parts of society may be examined first with reference to the ecological basis of settlement.

RESIDENCE PATTERNS

Three major types of residence patterns are observable.

1. THE FARM VILLAGE

In the farm village the farmer and his family live in a village with other farmers and the farmer goes out daily from the village to his farm. The farm village should not be confused with the rural or small town in the United States which the farmer *uses* for marketing and for the purchasing of supplies; the farmer does not himself live there, as he does in the farm village.

The farm village is extremely common, especially outside the United

States.[3] In general, the community consists of a nucleus of homes and common facilities—church, school, shops and an administrative center or meeting place. These make up the village proper. Near the homes are garden plots and perhaps sheds for livestock. Further out are the fields and interspersed among the fields or outside them is a pasture or woodland if the area permits them.[4]

The farm village requires considerable travel to and from work but the distance is not likely to be very much greater than that which the average city worker travels. It does mean that tools and other heavy equipment have to be carried back and forth or else stored in sheds on the farm. Livestock and other matters requiring continual attention must usually be kept fairly close to the home. T. Lynn Smith (49, pp. 216–18) mentions the problem of establishing boundaries, especially if there has been much fragmentation of farm land. In this pattern we often have very small parcels of land in different locations in order to allot the favorable pieces of land equitably. Under those conditions there may be severe boundary disputes and the problem of using heavy equipment may be serious. Further, it may be necessary for the farmers all to plant the same crop at the same time, if they are located on adjoining pieces of land.

But the pattern has certain definite economic advantages. When people live in a village they need not make as great expenditures for roads. They can support a good school, churches, and civic activities. Visiting is easier and more frequent and group integration is facilitated. In isolated areas, the most valuable property and storage places are centrally located and can be more easily defended.

But it is perhaps the level of group consensus that is the most significant factor in explaining the emergence of this form of settlement throughout the greater part of the world. When a group exhibits a high degree of consensus there is likely to be a desire to live near one another, particularly if this consensus is expressed in the form of common education, common folkways and mores, and ceremonies. For then the people can more easily assemble and exercise group control, providing the numbers are not great, and they usually are not. The importance of the relation between physical closeness and group control is well illustrated in the case of the Russian *mir* (23, pp. 19 ff.; 56, pp. 9–21).

We tend to find the village pattern then among groups where there

[3] The outstanding illustrations in the United States were the New England "plantations" with their central green, the Spanish-settled areas built about a plaza, and in the Mormon community. See (3, pp. 164–83; 28, pp. 231–34; 31; 38).
[4] See (47; 48, Ch. 2; 49, pp. 201–09).

is a high level of consensus, where primary ties are strong, and where neighborhood controls work. Farm villages are likely to exhibit great uniformity of composition and to be little subject to social change. O. Leonard and C. P. Loomis (26, p. 273)[5] tell us that though the residents of El Cerrito, New Mexico have sold their grazing land on the mesa, the villagers recognize that to sell the irrigated plots in the village would be to sell their birthright.

2. THE LINE SETTLEMENT

This form of settlement is usually related to a natural phenomenon which threads its way through the countryside, such as a river or the levees of a marsh country. In this case the pattern is for each farm to front on the river and to extend a considerable distance back in the form of a wedge. The home is usually located on the farm and other facilities are found stretched along the river.

The line settlement appears to have originated with the French line villages in the early Middle Ages, but it was used also by the Dutch and Germans (49, pp. 235–37). As far as we can determine it seems to have been brought to the United States by the French where it is still seen in Quebec and Louisiana as well as in other places.

The line pattern preserves most of the social and economic advantages of the farm village but the fact that the farmer lives on his land makes agricultural operation economically more efficient. It tends also to make for a more equitable distribution of wealth since all have access to the river if that is the basis of settlement. But under an inheritance system in which land is divided among all the sons, one may get progressively narrower strips stretching back for miles whose boundaries are often difficult to maintain.[6]

3. THE SCATTERED SETTLEMENT

In the case of the scattered settlement, the farmer's house, his barns, his livesetock, and all his possessions are on the farm and usually located near its geographical center. Such farms often are laid out in a rectangular pattern as well. The result is a maximum of physical isolation of farmers from each other. In actual practice one may get the farm houses themselves built along the road so that isolation is somewhat reduced.

This type, characteristic of the United States, is found in various

---

[5] It is important, however, not to underestimate the potentialities for change especially under the impact of the importation of Western technology (and Western social scientists). See (22, Ch. 14; 29; 30).

[6] E. C. Hughes (24, p. 7) discussing the need to pass on the French-Canadian farm to one, and only one, child, speaks of this as the ". . . great vulnerable spot of the system. For, if a man has enough children to work his farm without outside help, he has more children than he can provide with land. If, however, the farm were split up among them, none would be provided for. It is a question, not of all or none, but of one only or none."

other places, especially in the countries that border the Baltic Sea. Its development in the United States was largely a result of rapid westward expansion and the profusion of land. The basic factor seems to have been the existence of large amounts of land and the increased heterogeneity of the immigrants. A village requires homogeneity and relatively small parcels of land for easy accessibility. When we shift from the twenty to twenty-five acre farm to the 200- to 300-acre farm and when there are not just English and Scotch settlers, but Irish, German, Scandinavian, and Polish settlers, then the village form is not likely to be found appropriate. Also the laying out of land in squares by the Ordinance of 1785 and the requirement of the Homestead Act that a person live on his land in order to establish residence there helped to contribute to the growth of scattered settlements.

This type has many important economic advantages. It facilitates care of livestock and it makes possible a careful attention to crops. Most important, it provided the basis for the large-scale mechanized farming that was to come later.

The isolation produced by the scattered settlement pattern in the United States produced many of the traditional characteristics of our rural life. Physical isolation tended to produce provincialism and the isolationist sentiment that has been associated with the midwest farm region. It has also meant high costs for water, sewage, and for electricity and the prevalence of some of the features that are dear in our tradition such as the use of the well and the kerosene lamp, and some that are not so dear, such as the outdoor privy. It produced the open-country church and the one-room school. At the same time, the higher incomes from these larger farms made possible the later consolidated school and the use of buses and other facilities to enable farmers to get to town. Further, through the use of radio and telephone a great deal of the former isolation has gone.

Above all it laid the basis for the great transformation—the shift from subsistence to cash farming—which has profoundly altered the relation of the farmer to the city and to the rest of the world.

The scattered farm settlement meant a shift from emphasis on the community to emphasis on the family. Where farms were isolated, the farmer maintained contact with his neighbors and locality groups were of importance. But under isolated conditions, the neighborhood did not ever attain quite the same dominance as it did in the case of the village. There was an emphasis instead on the family and the family virtues of loyalty, of selfhelp, and love of home which have left their marks on the farm-derived population up to the present day. The scattered settlement also helped lay the basis for the later conflict between the generations, when the effects of mechanization produced the great rural-urban trend and the invasion of the countryside by the city.

THE FAMILY AS A WORK UNIT

Family work is a universal phenomenon. Chapple and Coon (7, pp. 144, 181, 252) note that there is a tendency for men to be concerned with the seasonal cycle of activity on the farm and for women to be concerned with the daily cycle of activities. Such a division of labor does not separate the sexes, but instead binds them together through inter-dependence.

The family division of labor is seen in many forms. It was significant in manufacturing in the "putting-out" system (13, pp. 7–11; 25, pp. 255–60) where the whole family might cooperate in a small manufacturing process. This very system was used in Japan as recently as World War II; it was part of a highly efficient war machine. The family business exists in small urban American enterprise such as the grocery store, the restaurant, the meat market, etc., but its most important expression (and where it may be found even in large enterprises) is on the farm. Where we find subsistence farms, the farm is almost invariably run by the family. Even when the farm shifts to a cash activity it tends to be a family enterprise—for with machinery, a farmer and his sons can handle three or four hundred acres; only at harvesting are extra hands likely to be necessary.

The family on the farm is not a work unit everywhere. In some cases it may only so function at periods of critical labor demands. M. J. Hagood (quoted in 51, pp. 42–43) makes the following statement:

In a study of 117 white tenant farm women in the Piedmont area of North Carolina, where tobacco was the dominant crop and cotton was second, over three-fourths of the wives did a considerable amount of fieldwork. In fact the usual practice was for the wives to do as nearly full time work as their housekeeping and cooking permitted during chopping, hoeing and picking times on the cotton farms, or on the tobacco farms during the summer and also during the fall, which is largely spent in grading and preparing the tobacco for market. The urgent need for extra labor on the tobacco farms at harvest time, when the tobacco must be "saved" or "housed" usually meant obtaining work from every member of the family—from the youngest child able to handle leaves to the oldest grandparent, who may be relieved from fieldwork at other times of the year because of age. And of these tenant farm women, seven-eighths reported that they liked field and tobacco-barn work better than housework.

On highly prosperous farms the farm wife is of course not likely to participate as much as on less successful farms. Types of tenure may also make a difference. The owner or tenant is more likely to draw upon the services of his family than is the regularly hired or migratory worker. But where the family farm exists, and it exists almost everywhere, the work unit operates with a clearly defined division of labor and this division of labor in turn is translated into status.

The father as the director and performer of the major tasks assumes a leading role. This is one reason why the farm family is usually considered "patriarchal." His dominant position is usually reinforced by the association of his name with the farm, and by his assuming the role of relating his family to the community. If the farm produces anything for sale, then he is the one who takes it to market and meets the trader or buyer. He is the one who is likely to be active in politics and in the implementation of community controls on members. The mother maintains a close association with the raising of children and the feeding of the family. She assumes a superior position because of age and because she also may have some things to sell. She acts as a unifying influence and usually takes the lead in the religious participation of the family in the community. She is usually not dominated by her husband. C. E. Lively quotes (27, pp. 29–30) a description of the relationship on a North Dakota farm as provided by a farmer's son:

The father was boss in the family with reference to finances. He did all the business and money transactions. The chief items, such as furniture and clothing, were purchased. The remainder were made at home and did not necessitate a great deal of expenditure. Mother is the boss of household affairs though father asserts his "say so." With reference to children both parents were boss, with greater responsibility to the father. His was the final word. Mother would handle the cases that needed attention when in her presence. Father controlled the activities of children in his presence. Cases that could not be handled by the mother were referred to the father.

My Father's attitude toward my Mother was that of the German family head. The father had the greater say so. He did not consider Mother his inferior. She belonged in the house and he took over the place in general. He didn't consider her equal in some cases for the reason that he did transact most of the business and was acquainted with it. Furthermore, mother wasn't interested in detail. Mutually, they both decided to make things go, and they did go. Mother did not feel inferior to Father and she never felt that he expected her to feel so. She knew that he knew what he wanted and both were interested in making things go. They worked together. Even with all the drudgery they enjoyed working together and going places together.

Children's roles vary in different societies. Usually the sons operate under the father's direction and the girls under the mother's. In some societies, a son may come under the influence of someone other than the biological father. But probably always he is supervised by a man. The sons may vary in their rights and obligations according to age, especially under a primogeniture system. The daughters are more likely to have equivalent status before the mother.

When the family operates as a work unit on the farm, the family is the major medium of learning, often completely over-balancing the school. In closed societies where occupational choice is limited, what the boy and girl learn on the farm is likely to make up almost the whole of their education. The boy learns planting and harvesting techniques, and how to buy and sell for farm needs. The girl learns the care of the barnyard, preserving and canning, the making of butter, and how to cook. If they go on to their own farm later in life, they are likely to be well prepared.

The son may receive not only his training but his capital as well, that is, the farm. This procedure is of course not peculiar to the farm but it has important implications for the maintenance of neighborhood control and the preserving of local traditions. The fact that the farm occupies a large area and tends to be conducted by the family, produces an association of the family name with the land. A worker may occupy a bench in a factory for years and may assume some proprietary interest in it, but his son will not likely move into his place. But where 500 acres are involved, the situation is very different. The fact that the whole family is on it and works it produces a fundamental sense of ownership. As a father in *The Grapes of Wrath* says, "It's working a farm that makes it yours."

The association of the family with the land is also related to the practice of the arranged marriage, with appropriate dowries or the bride price. Marriage means a shift of roles and is the concern of the entire family, for a new economic unit is being formed. It will be recalled that in County Clare if the man marries into a farm then he must pay a large dowry because the name on the land changes.

One of the most remarkable features of the family as a work unit is that it grows its own labor force. A large family is needed for the performance of the work on the farm. In turn, a large family is a source of pride and of support in old age. Therefore the attitudes toward and the custom of the large family is economically useful. However, with mechanized farming this becomes less true. The customs and attitudes persist, however, and the large farm family is the source of one of the most striking features of the farm family in the United States, namely, its role as a reservoir for migrants to our cities.

THE FARM AND THE COMMUNITY

Farming is always associated with a distinctive culture or set of inter-personal relations. The major characteristic of this culture everywhere is the intimacy and closeness of articulation of the various segments of life. The nature of farming itself, which requires a large space, forces association based on physical isolation. The emphasis on the land gives a *locality* basis to all social relationships. A person tends to become identi-fied with an area, religion comes to be characteristic of a given area, education is adapted to the needs of the area, and politics is land-centered, and because our legislature is land-centered also we can often predict a congressman's stand if he is elected from an agricultural district.

In a farming area a high proportion of the residents have the *same* occupation. There is no comparable phenomenon in urban areas. We may get white-collar areas, areas of homeless men, and factory-worker areas; but each of these areas in fact represents a great occupational diversity and in any case the total area occupied by any one of them would account for little more than a moderate-sized farm. The nature of the soil and the growing process means a considerable similarity of agri-cultural practice over a wide area. Thus, there is produced a remarkable uniformity of attitudes and needs and a consequent fitting together of life elements into an integrated whole.[7]

1. RELIGION

The closeness of the relation of other areas of life to farm work is well-illustrated in the case of religion. Almost all of the world's religions have produced groups who have tried to flee the world and live away from its temptations and evils, such as the Jesuit "Reducciones" of Paraguay, the Jewish Essenians, the Buddhist Mahayanas, and the Mohammedan Sufis. We also find groups splitting off from the church altogether and founding colonies in sparsely settled areas, such as the Doukhaboors, the Rappists, the Shakers, and the Amana and Oneida groups. Groups like this, having decided to live apart, found that they had to concentrate on agriculture and therefore these have tended to be

---

[7] Horace Miner (35, p. 70) reports that even the farmers of a relatively mechanized corn-growing community—Hardin County, Iowa—had few clubs based on different interests because their interests were largely the same. This is not, of course, to deny the significance or possibility of very deep cleavages in an agricultural community as illustrated, for example, by the division between unskilled laborers and others in the factory agriculture of the California central valley. See (15). In that situation, there is a strong occupational split, as well as important ethnic divisions. Nevertheless, even this case is poles apart from the consensual diversity presented by even a medium sized city.

communities of farmers (21, pp. 832–37). But such groups are relatively rare; and religion has not usually created a community but instead grows up *with* a community.

Usually a farming community is characterized by relative uniformity of religion. This is not to deny that there may not be very real religious differences between farmers and competition among them. But at least in contrast to the industrialized traders of the city there is very much more uniformity. This uniformity may be a function of the fact that the farmers' church, to be successful, must orient itself to the special problems of farmers. And the significant point is that the uniformity of occupation makes this possible and distinguishes the farmers' church from the urban church which must make a broader appeal.

Of particular concern to the farmer are problems that arise out of unpredictable aspects of farming, or those which are only subject to limited control. The combination of unpredictability and peak activity creates a situation of great potential tension. The farmer does all he can in the choice of crops and equipment, in the method of plowing and seeding, and thinning or "chopping," but then he must wait and hope. The weather, prices, boll weevils, a scarcity of labor at the needed time— any one of these may create disaster. The lack of control and the uncertainty, if it becomes chronic because of the area's being a poor one for farming, or for other reasons, produces a social environment conducive to the rise of holiness and fundamentalist sects, which emphasize highly emotional behavior. Both McCormick (32, p. 14) and Holt (20) point out that the greatest expansion of the holiness sects has occurred among the marginal farm groups most subject to uprooting and economic shocks.

But apart from such extremes, the peak character of agriculture has produced, all over the world, what Chapple and Coon (7, pp. 398 ff.) call *rites of intensification.* They distinguish between these rites and Gennep's concept of the *rites de passage,* which involve the restoration of equilibrium after a crisis, or a change of status involving an individual, as in the case of birth, age grading, marriage, and death. By contrast, the rites of intensification involve a disturbance of the equilibrium of the whole group. The most important of these among agricultural peoples are those associated with the oscillating waxing and waning of effort as the seasons progress. They tend, therefore, to exhibit a periodicity as at planting and harvest. The rites of intensification act as a proclamation and dramatization of the need for increased interaction. The priest or shaman will then initiate a ritual involving intensified interaction.

James G. Frazer pointed out long ago that the timing of Christian ceremonies is associated with annual changes in agriculture in the Mediterranean countries. Thus, Christmas occurs at a time when there is little work, when there is an abundance of food, but when there is also no technological system to order interaction. A function of these ceremonies is to increase family and community interaction and to symbolize unity. They also reorder social relations in accordance with technical needs, reinforce the farmer's faith in those techniques and provide him with group support to face the attendant risks and uncertainty. Horace Miner (36, p. 97) in describing St. Denis, a French Canadian parish, says as follows:

> As has already been indicated, the duality of sacred and secular is a logical one used for its value in presenting a philosophy of existence. To the *habitant* of St. Denis there is no such division in life. He could understand such a separation, but it has no part in his daily life. Nature is both sacred and secular. A crop which could grow without sacred influence is merely an idea, not a fact. To the farmer, the plowing of the land, the singing of masses for its productivity, the harrowing of the soil, the planting of blessed seed of each sort, the spreading of fertilizer, and the processions to secure the fruits of the soil are the ways to get a good crop. Some or any of them might be omitted, but with definite detrimental effect to the crop.

Chapple and Coon (7, pp. 398 ff.) conceive of the function of a ritual as involving the restoration of equilibrium after or during a crisis. The ritual prescribes a certain kind of rate of interaction which is appropriate to the crisis. For example, the practice of sexual intercourse in the garden in Melanesia symbolizes the intense and close interaction that gardening will require. In the case of potentially disastrous phenomena such as drought, then there is likely to be worship *in common* and rituals to manipulate environmental forces. These have the function of reaffirming the group's faith in itself and the need of the individual for a group.

Rituals of this kind are of particular significance in agriculture practiced without benefit of modern science, and they are therefore found among preliterate and peasant peoples to a high degree. They are found in any society, but when science intervenes, fundamental changes may take place. The Irish countryman needs the fairies to explain why butter will not churn, but the dairy farmer of Wisconsin who uses an electric churn has no need of them. When butter does not churn, he does not have to turn to his group and ask "What ritual did I not perform correctly so that the fairies are angry at me?" He calls the maintenance man or writes a strong letter to the manufacturer.

But agriculture even under the most highly mechanized conditions presents uncontrollable elements and is subject to serious risks. Many of its processes are still not mechanized. Also the isolation of the farmer is still a factor in most of the world and therefore helps to preserve his unique religious beliefs and practices. Yet, as time goes on science increasingly invades even these areas and one gets complaints of "the passing of the church."

In the United States, one of the most important changes has been the gradual disappearance of the open-country church and the growth of the trade center or urban church (4, Ch. VIII; 5, Ch. XII). The open-country church finds it difficult to get services of a full-time minister or pastor. The fact that these persons can only come occasionally means that they must confine their attention largely to preaching. The trend has been toward larger but fewer churches. The movement of the church to the trade center or the village means changes in the nature of church activities themselves. When the church is larger and has a more scattered congregation then it must broaden its basis of appeal. It must include youth groups, offer opportunities for the young people to play basketball, offer vocational services, meeting facilities, and so on. That is it must bid for a congregation since over a wide area there is a choice available to the population among several churches and there are, furthermore, alternatives and distractions from church attendance itself. As such the church becomes less distinctly a farmers' church and the farmer moves into the main stream of American religious trends.

2. EDUCATION

Education is ordinarily the concern of four major structures: family, state, church, and work organization. These four structures both supplement and compete with each other.

In a simple or peasant society, the family and church reinforce each other. Training in Sunday school or in church rituals is related to the work life. The church may bless the first fruits or the seed. But where science enters, one gets the formal school with its rational and rapidly changing techniques. The extension agent begins to overlap the priest, and the agricultural extension bulletin begins to appear beside the Sears, Roebuck catalog and the Bible. The farm itself develops an authority line (however short), employees, marketing co-op, and lobbyists in Washington. As such it desires to train its own people and brings the college expert in on a consultant or staff basis only.

But besides these media of education, informal education goes on through the press, the radio, and through associations. Through these means the farmer hears of new techniques and ideas and also learns attitudes. A farm radio commentator for example was discussing the agricultural program of agricultural colleges and said, "A young farm expert is one who has had no experience, an old one is one who has tried and failed."

The latter influences are often spoken of as informal media. It is implied that the objective is not to educate, except incidentally, but to sell or entertain. Such distinctions are arbitrary or invidious. In the simple, relatively static society, all education is likely to be "informal." The nature of the association between the family and the farm means that a significant part of a boy's training in farming takes place at home. The boy does not have to be trained in punctuality or in getting to work on time. The whole family is up at five o'clock. The smell of breakfast, the mooing of the cows, the clucking of the chickens, the ringing of church bells, are all going on. It seems as though the whole society conspires to get the boy up on time. The father's control on farm work is but *one* of many areas of control. There is no need for him to dock the pay of the boy if he is late and there is no need for incentive. Most important, the work training is functional. Where there is little change, the man with 30-years' experience is a better farmer than the man with only five. It is then that farm lore grows and becomes encrusted in folk saying and rural philosophy.

But when change begins to occur, when alfalfa is introduced, when new equipment comes in, when prices enter as a control on type and quantity of crop, and where prices are determined in Chicago or in Winnipeg or by government policy in Argentina, then the father's 30-years' experience may be a source of rigidity and of little help to the son. Then we may get important changes in the total educational pattern, with increased need for special education for farm children.

The role of the teacher in the farm community varies. Where there is isolation and the one-room schoolhouse, the teacher is usually a native of the area, a woman, and is poorly paid. Being a woman she is likely to marry and, consequently, turnover among teachers is high. In any case a person with ability is likely to be promoted which usually means moving to a city school. Yet such persons often enjoy a high prestige in the rural community. This is likely to be so particularly if the teacher is a man. He may be turned to for discussion of the affairs of the day, politics, and for questions about matters requiring a knowledge of the outside world.

A teacher in a village is likely to be regarded as a specialist along with the priest, the doctor, the policeman, and the shopkeeper. As such he enjoys considerable prestige and turnover may not be so high for the male. But his interaction in that society is circumscribed. For there he meets the ideology of success in American society. Yet he is not supposed to participate in that struggle. If he buys real estate or makes investments, that is, behaves in the way his neighbors are behaving, then his behavior is likely to be frowned upon. At the same time he is likely to be judged by his neighbors' criteria of success which includes such things as home, car, clothes, and so forth, and his lack of those things makes him a considerable object of pity.

This problem of course is by no means peculiar to the rural teacher. Education in our society has a high value but a low price.

3. POLITICS

Utopian social movements have usually had to separate themselves from the rest of society in order to try out economic experiments. Usually small, and not based on factories, they had to grow their own food and this meant that they tended to be agricultural collectivities.

What distinguished these agricultural communities was the presence of an economic or social ideal which required close political control for its realization. Therefore, agricultural practices, especially buying and selling, were or are directly prescribed by a formal body or government. Consequently, one gets under such circumstances a very close relation between farming and government. In fact the farm becomes the medium through which the government tries to test its ideas on desirable human arrangements.

A close relation between government and farming is by no means confined to experimental settlements. Because small numbers of persons are present in rural villages, rural local politics emphasizes personal ties: the farmer is likely to know the local politicians personally and the smallness of numbers makes each vote highly significant.

This situation is changing. As the farmer faces problems of prices and the swings of the business cycle, he finds the local country or town government to be increasingly non-functional. The increased control of the state means increased professionalization and bureaucratization of local government through the county manager and other plans and focuses the attention of the farmer on Washington. But the remarkable uniformity of farmers as an occupational group has tended to produce powerful agricultural lobbies and to create the will-of-the-wisp that is called the "farm vote."

4. THE FARM AS AN ETHNIC MEETING PLACE

In a separate chapter on ethnic relations the role of the farm is to be discussed. Here should be noted two important facets of ethnic relations on the farm.

First, movement of Western Europeans to the "underdeveloped" areas of the world has been prompted in part by the search for raw materials. That has meant that one of the most important stages of ethnic contact and conflict has been on the farm which was set up on the native's land to harvest the raw material. In general, native labor has been encouraged or forced to work and that has meant violent changes in the native economy, family, and community life. It has produced the rise of nationalisms and the revolt of colonial peoples.

Second, in the United States the farm has played a strategic role in ethnic and race relations. The American Negro entered the American economy and labor system as a slave on the rice farms and cotton plantations. With the cutting off of immigration in the early twenties, the most important groups to enter the country have been Mexicans, Puerto Ricans, and Filipinos—and these have to a considerable extent come in as migratory laborers for the fruit and vegetable harvests.

Although much of the literature on the American Negro deals with the rural South, ethnic and race relations are often thought of and treated as urban phenomena. The melting pot concept is generally thought of in terms of the giant steel mill, the road gang, or the petty shopkeeper. Yet the Negro, the Mexican, the Puerto Rican, and the Filipino have all met the native white American on the farm. Before him the Norwegian, the Swede, and the German were (and still are) a significant part of the farming group in the United States. The farm is therefore one of the major places where peoples meet and where ethnic attitudes may take shape.

THE BALANCE OF BIRTHS AND DEATHS

Agricultural people typically exhibit a high fertility, and with the exception of Western Europe and America, a high mortality as well. The result is to produce a relatively stationary population subject to the controls of the Malthusian population principles. The high death rate is unquestionably due to the lack of knowledge of the control of disease, to malnutrition among the children, and to the uncertainties of agricultural life as practiced under primitive conditions. The causes of the high fertility are however by no means as clear. Here, most of the explanations we have are *post facto* lists of plausible factors. Sorokin, Zimmerman, and Galpin (50, p. 141) mention the Biblical injunction to "multiply and replenish the earth" which is beside the point in cultures operating without benefit of the Western Bible. Loomis (29, pp. 73 ff.) emphasizes the *Gemeinschaft* character of rural life with the emphasis on family values which would include children. In the United States, the high cost of raising children in the city and the emphasis on individual values and success in the city has been employed to help explain the differential birth rate. The lack of knowledge of or ability to afford contraceptives has been mentioned, although there is evidence that peasant and primitive peoples practice birth control (1; 19; 52, pp. 10–14).

While all these explanations make some sense, they remain speculative in part because of their use of a causal or meaningful approach. It is useful to seek a functional explanation: we ask how the large family is related to other parts of the society. Is it needed? The answer to that question is, in most agricultural places, yes. The size of family bears a close functional relation to farming as a work activity. On the subsistence farm it is the family that makes up the labor force. Where agricultural laborers are absent or cannot be afforded, then the family produces its own laborers. They are needed and even from an early age children can be of some help in the field or in the barnyard. As they grow older they become still more useful.

If the death rate is as high as the birth rate, then there may remain only one son to take over the farm. But if the death rate is low, as in Western Europe and America, then on reaching maturity, the children form an excess population which must be drained off to make possible the continuation of the family on the farm. Some peoples have tried subdividing their lands among their children but farms then have become increasingly small. Therefore the typical procedure has been for those who do not inherit the farm to migrate. Migration may be to foreign lands, as in the case of the Irish, Italians, and Norwegians. Or it may be to cities within the same country as in the case of the United States within recent years. These are not the only alternatives; for example, industry may come into the agricultural area as it has done in the United States and in other parts of the world.[8]

It is remarkable that in the United States, though mechanization has decreased the need for a large family on the farm, farmers continue to have large families. This is due in part to the fact that because the large family was once functional it tends to persist as a cultural trait. There is also some evidence that highly mechanized farmers do have smaller families. Also the low fertility of the population in the cotton plantation (49, pp. 137 ff.) area of the United States may be due to the factory nature of that agriculture.

The pouring of rural migrants into cities had profound effects on entire societies. The migration has been selective with reference to sex and age. In general with the exception of migrants over long distances and migrants to young, industrial cities, women have outnumbered the men. The reasons for this selectivity are not known. The usual explanations are the greater opportunity for women's employment in the city as compared to the farming area, the shift from subsistence to cash farming with the decline in need for family labor, and the search for freedom from the

[8] A recent invasion of importance has been the coming of industry into the upper south of the U.S., a movement which may eventually check the great rural-urban migration streams out of the south.

narrow controls of the farm community (14, pp. 267–69). Whatever the reasons the result has been to produce basic and quite large differences in the sex ratio between cities and farming areas. In 1950, using the "new urban" definition,[9] sex ratios were as follows: Urban—94.6, rural non-farm—103.6, and rural farm—111.1 (52a, p. 1–88). This means then a considerable excess of women in cities and an excess of men in farm areas.

The fact that the women who migrate are in the marriageable and working years has serious effect on both marriage rates and employment patterns. T. Lynn Smith (49, p. 410) comments that cities bring together two groups: (1) foreign born males who are in the marrying years, and (2) native born females from the farms who are also in the marrying years. He hypothesizes that the social barriers between these two groups may depress the marriage rate since the two groups make up a considerable proportion of the eligible persons in cities.

The farm requires a large labor force normally but it also requires that most of this labor force shall leave shortly after reaching maturity. This combination of high fertility and the migration in the youthful years produces striking differences in age structure between farm areas and cities. The population pyramids of cities tend to bulge in the middle, whereas those of farm areas bulge at the bottom and are concave in the middle (52a, p. 37). This means also that cities have a high proportion of persons in the active, wage-earning years, whereas farm areas suffer a corresponding scarcity. Urban persons are thus better able to support public projects and community developments. This difference is especially marked in the distribution of educational facilities. Cities have a large population in the working years to pay taxes to support the education of only a small proportion of children. By contrast farms have a small proportion in the working years to support a large proportion of children. The result has been a claim, particularly from the rural states of the deep South, that they educate the children who then leave and confer the benefit of that training on the city. This has been one of the bases for their requests for federal aid to ease the burden and as no more than a just recompense for their contribution to the prosperity of cities.

Except since 1940 cities have not reproduced themselves through births. They have instead been overwhelmingly dependent on migration for their growth.

The symbiotic tie between town and country in the United States therefore operates at two key levels: in the provision of food, and in the provision of population. But in mechanized cash farming, there is a still

[9] Which classifies many part-time farmers as "urban."

further intimate tie. In subsistence farming, the farm is a world unto itself. By contrast, one of the most important factors leading to rural-urban interdependence is the shift to cash farming. The farm becomes a factory where finished products are produced from raw materials for sale in the urban market. The major effect is to put money into the hands of the farmer. This is a tremendous change and is perhaps the first time in world history that the farmer on a large scale has had money. That in turn has made it possible for him to buy not just his food but the other peculiarly urban things the city has to sell. The Far Eastern farmer may know about radios, books, fashionable clothes and the like, and he may want them, but he has little money with which to buy them. The American farmer *can* buy them and this process provides a major medium for the influence of urban folkways on farm behavior.

But once the farmer begins to sell his crops, then he must pay attention to prices. This leads to efforts to reduce price uncertainties through the influencing of Federal government policy, and leads to the linking of farming to the swings of the business cycle. As such, the farmer moves into the center of the flow of world economic and social trends.

CHAPTER REFERENCES

1. Apteker, H., *Infanticide, Abortion and Contraception in Savage Society*, New York: Goodwin, 1951.
2. Bendix, R., *Work and Authority in Industry*, New York: Wiley, 1956.
3. Blackmar, F. W., *Spanish Institutions of the Southwest*, Baltimore: Johns Hopkins University Press, 1891, pp. 164–183.
4. Brunner, E. deS. and Kolb, J. H., *Rural Social Trends*, New York: McGraw-Hill, 1933.
5. ——— and Lorge, I., *Rural Trends in Depression Years*, New York: Columbia University Press, 1937.
6. *No entry.*
7. Chapple, E. D. and Coon, C. S., *Principles of Anthropology*, New York: Holt, 1942.
8. Fei, H. T. and Chang, C-I, *Earthbound China* (rev. English ed. prepared in collaboration with Cooper, Paul and Redfield, Margaret P.), Chicago: University of Chicago Press, 1945.
9. Firth, R. W., *Malay Fishermen: Their Peasant Economy*, London: Paul, Trench, Trubner, 1946.
10. ———, *Primitive Economics of the New Zealand Maori*, New York: Dutton, 1929.
11. ———, *Primitive Polynesian Economy*, New York: Humanities Press, 1950.

12. Forde, C. D., *Habitat, Economy, and Society,* London: Methuen, 1937.
13. Gay, E. F., "Putting Out System," *Encyclopaedia of the Social Sciences,* Vol. XIII, pp. 7–11.
14. Gist, N. P. and Halbert, L. A., *Urban Society,* New York: Crowell, 1956.
15. Goldschmidt, W., *As You Sow,* New York: Harcourt, Brace, 1947.
16. Gouldner, Alvin W., "Discussion of Industrial Sociology," *American Sociological Review,* 13:396–400, 1948.
17. Gross, E., "*Informal Relations and the Social Organization of Work in an Industrial Office.*" Unpublished Ph.D. Dissertation, University of Chicago, 1949.
18. ———, "Some Suggestions for the Legitimation of Industrial Studies in Sociology," *Social Forces,* 33:233–239, 1955.
19. Himes, N. E., *Medical History of Contraception,* Baltimore: Williams and Wilkins, 1936.
20. Holt, J. B., "Holiness Religion: Cultural Shock and Social Reorganization," *American Sociological Review,* 5:740–747, 1940.
21. Honigsheim, P., "Rural Collectivities," in Loomis, C. P. and Beegle, J. A., *Rural Social Systems,* New York: Prentice-Hall, 1950, Appendix B.
22. Hoselitz, B. F. (ed.), *The Progress of Underdeveloped Areas,* Chicago: University of Chicago Press, 1952.
23. Hourvich, J. A., *The Economy of the Russian Village,* New York: Columbia University Press, 1892.
24. Hughes, E. C., *French Canada in Transition.* Chicago: University of Chicago Press, 1943.
25. Knight, M. M., "Handicraft," *Encyclopaedia of the Social Sciences,* Vol. VII, pp. 255–260.
26. Leonard, O. and Loomis, C. P., "Culture of a Contemporary Rural Community, El Cerrito, New Mexico," as reprinted in Loomis, C. P., *Studies of Rural Social Organization in the United States, Latin America, and Germany,* East Lansing: State College Book Store, 1945.
27. Lively, C. E., *Readings in Rural Sociology,* Columbus, O.: Hedrick, 1932–33, Bk. I.
28. Loomis, C. P. and Beegle, J. A., *Rural Social Systems,* New York: Prentice-Hall, 1950.
29. ———, *Rural Sociology: The Strategy of Change,* Englewood Cliffs, N. J.: Prentice-Hall, 1957.
30. Loomis, C. P., et al., *Turrialba, Social Systems and the Introduction of Change,* Glencoe, Ill.: Free Press, 1953.
31. MacLear, A. B., *Early New England Towns,* New York: Columbia University Press, 1908.
32. McCormick, T. C., "Rural Social Organization in South Central Arkansas," *Ag. Exp. Sta. Bull. 313,* University of Arkansas, 1935.
33. Malinowski, B., *Argonauts of the Western Pacific,* London: G. Routledge: New York, Dutton, 1932.
34. ———, *Coral Gardens and Their Magic,* New York: American Book Co., 1935.
35. Miner, H., *Culture and Agriculture: An Anthropological Study of a Corn*

Belt County, Occasional Contributions from the Museum of Anthropology of the University of Michigan, No. 14, Ann Arbor: University of
Michigan Press, 1949.

36. ———, *St. Denis: A French-Canadian Parish,* Chicago: University of Chicago
Press, 1939.

37. Nelson, L., *The Mormon Village,* Provo, Utah: Brigham Young University
Studies, 3, 1930.

38. Park, R. E., "Human Ecology," *American Journal of Sociology,* 42:1–15, 1936.

39. ———, "Reflections on Communication and Culture," *American Journal of
Sociology,* 44:187–205, 1938.

40. ———, "The Urban Community as a Spacial Pattern and a Moral Order,"
in Burgess, E. W. (ed.), *The Urban Community,* Chicago, Ill.: University of Chicago Press, 1926, pp. 3–18.

41. ——— and Burgess, E. W., *Introduction to the Science of Sociology,* Chicago
University Press, 1921.

42. Parsons, T., "A Revised Analytical Approach to the Theory of Social Stratification," in Bendix, R. and Lipset, S. M. (eds.), *Class, Status and Power,*
Glencoe, Ill.: The Free Press, 1953.

43. Redfield, R., *A Village that Chose Progress: Chan Kom Revisited,* Chicago:
University of Chicago Press, 1950.

44. ———, *The Folk Culture of Yucatan,* Chicago: University of Chicago Press,
1941.

45. Richards, A. I., *Hunger and Work in a Savage Tribe,* Glencoe, Ill.: Free
Press, 1948.

46. ———, *Land, Labour, and Diet in Northern Rhodesia,* London: Oxford
University Press, 1939.

47. Seebohm, F., *The English Village Community,* New York: Longmans, Green,
1926.

48. Sims, N. L., *Elements of Rural Sociology,* New York: Crowell, 1940.

49. Smith, T. L., *The Sociology of Rural Life,* New York: Harper, 1953.

50. Sorokin, P. A.; Zimmerman, C. C.; and Galpin, C. J. (eds.), *A Systematic
Source Book in Rural Sociology,* Minneapolis: University of Minnesota
Press, 1932, Vol. III.

51. Taylor, C. C., *Rural Life in the United States,* New York: Knopf, 1949.

52. Thompson, W. S. and Minnis, E. D., *Population Problems,* New York,
McGraw-Hill, 1953.

52a. U.S. Bureau of the Census, *Characteristics of the Population,* Washington:
U.S. Government Printing Office, 1953, Vol. II, Pt. 1, U.S. Summary,
Table 36, pp. 1–88.

53. U.S. Bureau of the Census, *Classified Index of Occupations and Industries,*
Washington: U.S. Government Printing Office, 1950.

54. Vance, R. B., *Human Factors in Cotton Culture,* Chapel Hill: University
of North Carolina Press, 1929.

55. Vucinich, A., "The Structure of Factory Control in the Soviet Union," *American Sociological Review,* 15:179–186, 1950.

56. Yermoloff, A., *La Russie Agricole,* Paris: Hachette, 1907.

CHAPTER EIGHT

THE FARM: THE WORK STRUCTURE AND THE ECONOMIC COMPLEX

THE WORK STRUCTURE OF FARMING

In farming, the social organization of work is a direct function of the relation of man to the land. The fact that land takes up a large amount of space tends to permeate all aspects of human relations in agriculture. Agriculture varies in many ways, but the one constant is the presence of land of some kind. We can never discuss farming without asking the fundamental question: Where?

The close relation to the land and soil has given rise to an environmental deterministic position among some students of agriculture. Several classifications of farmers are based largely on the type of soil.[1] Different soil types do give rise to different human requirements, but it is better to begin the other way around and ask: What is involved in agriculture as a work activity so far as human organization is concerned? Then the various soil types, crops, and techniques may be seen as *human* creations, which in fact they are. Man adjusts to the soil but he imposes himself on it. It is necessary to conceive of man as the actor and the land as the raw material. The level and type of his social organization and culture will then help to explain agriculture as a human work structure.

THE RAW MATERIALS—TYPES OF AGRICULTURAL PRODUCTS

Although many thousands of species of vegetation have been domesticated by man, almost all of them belong to the broad leaf-family. Of these it is the annuals that provide humans with most of their food. Chap-

[1] See (1, 6a, 6b, 13, 17a).

293

ple and Coon (4, pp. 171–74) have classified them into major types according to the part of the plant that is eaten.

a. SEEDS

Here are included the cereals (wheat, barley, rye, oats, millet, sorghum, rice and maize), the legumes (beans, peas, chick-peas, lentils, vetches, and peanuts), and oil seeds (sesame and flax). These are the most widely used of all plants for food by human beings, and the stems of many of them provide fodder for animals. Many of them may be sown broadcast, making them well adapted to mechanical contrivances. They may be reaped with sickles or scythes, or thrashed with flails, or by the trampling of animals. They are easily stored because of their small size.

b. SEED PODS AND POD FIBRES

The most important of these are not used for food but for the fibres that protect the seed: cotton, tree cotton and kapok.

c. FRUITS

Included are the annuals such as the gourds, melons, squashes and tomatoes, and the perennials that grow on trees or bushes. In Western cash-farming, fruit may be the principal or sole crop. They need relatively little attention, but they require large numbers of persons for picking in the short harvest period. Among subsistence farmers they are not usually the sole crop. They are valuable because they will grow where other crops will not, for example, on steep slopes or in moist land.

d. NUTS

Most nuts are grown for food, including the almond, the walnut, the chestnut, the kola nut, and the cocoanut.

e. ROOTS AND TUBERS

These include turnips, beets, cassava, yams, potato and taro. Turnips are used mainly for fodder and beets for sugar. These require much labor to cultivate but they will grow where many seeds will not, especially in damp soils.

f. LEAVES

Here are included cabbage, lettuce and spinach, which are used mostly as relishes. But important non-food uses are possible in the case of flax, hemp and sisal for rope and textiles. Also there are the products of tobacco and tea.

g. STEMS

These are not much eaten except for rhubarb and asparagus. We do not include the use of trees for lumber and pulp here.

The remaining three categories mentioned by Chapple and Coon are not very important. These are piths (sago in New Guinea), saps (sugar cane and maple), and poppies for opium and barks (the paper mulberry).

Many of these products are gathered in their wild state by hunting-

and gathering-people. But in their cultivated or domesticated state they may go through profound changes. Chapple and Coon (4, p. 174) comment:

> After a crop has been harvested, the farmer must set aside some of it to be used for the next year's seed. Sometimes he selects this at random, but more frequently he will choose it on some particular basis of discrimination.
>
> As a result of this selective process, farmers have profoundly altered many of the species of plants grown for food; a great example is the turnip, which has been altered by selection into such diverse vegetables as cabbage, Brussels sprouts, broccoli, and cauliflower. According to the botanists the most changed of all is maize, which has acquired a husk to keep off birds during the ripening season, but which at the same time prevents the plant from reproducing without human aid.

The animals domesticated by man are much fewer in number of types than is the case of the plants. Domestication in the case of animals involves not only selection but also training. Animals differ also in that their introduction usually involves profound changes in agricultural practices and greatly increases the productivity of the land.

Relatively few animals are bred for food alone. The animal in most widespread use is the pig, for reasons aptly summarized (4, p. 176) by Chapple and Coon: "The pig grows rapidly, matures quickly, produces many young in one litter, will eat almost anything, and can be fattened rapidly to a great size."

Certain animals are bred for both food and secondary products, such as the sheep, the reindeer, and the cow. But the most significant uses for animals are for the provision of secondary products, for assistance in agriculture, and for transportation. The secondary products include food, clothing, and materials for implements and ornaments. The food may be milk (cows, goats, sheep, camels, and reindeer), eggs (mainly hens, but also ducks and geese), and honey. The clothing secured includes wool (sheep, llama, alpaca, and others), and silk which involves the mulberry bush also. The implements and ornaments include the use of skins for leather (the cow, reindeer, and others), and feathers (the turkey among the United States Indians, and geese in medieval Europe, and the ostrich in modern Western culture). Animals, especially the horse and the dog, are also much used for assistance in herding and for hunting. Other uses for assistance in agriculture we will say more about later.

THE ORGANIZATION OF FARMING

Perhaps the central characteristic of farming as a work structure is its *cyclical* nature. This is of two main types—daily and seasonal. The daily cycle includes household tasks and chores and those centering about the barnyard and the feeding and care of small animals. These are usually performed by women. The seasonal cycle revolves about the yearly rounds of clearing, plowing, weeding, harvesting, and perhaps marketing. These are usually the prerogatives of the men. In connection with the seasonal cycle and the usual situation is for the labor demand to fluctuate, sometimes violently, between periods when a farmer and a son may spend their time inspecting or mending fences, to a period when the whole family and neighbors, and for some crops, hundreds of temporary workers, work at a fever pitch at the harvest.

The organization is further related to the type of implements used and the type of crop. We shall present, first, a general survey of the typical organization of agricultural activities and then turn to the special crops in the modern United States because of the complexities which they exhibit.

The first work activity in the yearly round is the clearing of the land if this is necessary. In tropical areas one of the commonest procedures is the use of fire agriculture or the slash-and-burn technique.[1a] Here the trees are cut down and burned to let in the sun and simultaneously to provide a good soil from the resulting ashes. This procedure requires the use of axes or machetes. It is a common occasion for interfarmer cooperation.

Where domestic animals are present, the work is easier. The ox is used to haul large stones, as it was in early New England. With tractors and dynamite, stumps and large logs are easily removed. The latter activities involve usually just one man, though a son may assist in leading the animal or in guiding the stones or stumps as they are pulled along.

Where there is little cover, as in the prairies and steppes, not much labor is involved in clearing. The great problem in such areas is selection of the land. However it is really only a severe problem where the land is arid, for then the location of streams is a determining factor. Since only a small amount of land is usable near the stream, it is usually necessary to *irrigate*. For example, the Hopi in Northern Arizona make use of a system of natural gullies and arroyos. They also build stone walls to catch silt and gullies to spread the water to the fields in flood periods (8).

Irrigation has several effects. It increases the land available for cultivation, makes possible a longer growing season since the people are then less dependent on rain, and the stream usually brings in minerals to replenish the soil. The latter is especially significant in its effects on residence. The exhaustion of the soil would mean that the whole tribe would

[1a] See (16a, Ch. 3; 17, pp. 334–38; 22).

have to move periodically. But if irrigation is used, then the people can remain permanently in the same location.[2]

The fact that irrigation is usually an elaborate process involving the work of many means that it is only useful if spread over a wide area. It normally requires large-scale cooperation.

In the absence of mechanical power, irrigation means leading the water from a stream to follow a more gradual slope over the field. Usually animals are used if they are available, though the Papago, Pima, and Hopi do not employ them (4, p. 184). Animals are not used just for pulling rocks to build walls; they provide the fertilizer which is usually necessary to supplement the river's minerals, since the people must stay relatively close to the stream and use the same land over and over again. The major use of animals is to haul water. For example the Yemenites train camels to walk down slopes to pull up buckets of water (4, p. 191). Great irrigation areas are seen in the Mediterranean areas, in the Middle East, in Java, and in the Orient, especially in the valleys of the Nile, the Hwang-Ho, and the Tigris-Euphrates. These may involve building large retaining walls to keep the flood waters in, or dikes to prevent too great a flood. These also involve the cooperative work of all the residents of the area. In addition there is cooperation necessary in repairing the ditches (10, p. 322).

Where irrigation is used, there is likely to be a system of allotting water if it is scarce. With the use of mechanical power, windmills and water wheels are used to pump the water. In the Columbia Basin in the United States irrigation becomes entirely a commercially organized matter and the farmer simply pays a fee for his water.

A last operation before sowing is preparing the soil to receive the seed. In the case of fire agriculture or irrigated land the land is usually ready right then. Otherwise it is necessary to break up the soil so as to hold the moisture and to make room for the plants to spread their roots. Ground-breaking activity does not involve much social interaction. Plowing is usually a one-man operation, though a man's son may guide the horse or the ox if they are used. If animals are scarce, as in the Mediterranean, two men may combine their animals and plow together.

The next step is planting. The seeds may be simply scattered broadcast, as in the case of the small grains, or it may be necessary to dig a hole, or to build a mound, as with potatoes. Planting is usually a family activity, except where mechanical planters are used. The mechanical planter can

[2] Ralph Linton has related the growth of confederacies among the Mayas and southeast Indians to the desire to slash and burn far out from the village without danger of attack from hostile groups. See (11).

be operated by one man. It digs the hole, drops the seed at desired intervals, and covers the seed.

With most crops, after planting there occurs a period of waiting. This is the period for the performance of small chores, visiting, and perhaps religious ceremonies. Soon, however, weeding and thinning are necessary with many crops. These may be done by hand; if so, they are usually left to the women. The use of mechanical weeders ordinarily involves the work of solitary men. In cotton the work of "chopping" (thinning) involves the whole family.

Then comes the climax of the agricultural year, the harvest. Here we witness one of the most remarkable transformations in work activities in any work structure. The whole countryside seems to come alive with people. Grains usually must be harvested just when they are ripe, which means a fight against rain or frost. Entire families, townspeople, and all available help is mobilized. Harvesting may involve cutting, binding, perhaps shocking to permit drying and then the movement of the grain to a barn or storage place. The grain may be cut with a sickle or scythe and then dropped into a basket. Mechanical equipment may perform almost all of these operations in one step. Other crops, especially roots, do not have such precise harvest periods and they are usually taken out of the ground when there is time.

We have not given special attention to livestock in the above discussion. These also involve a yearly cycle which reaches its peak in the round-up when calves are branded, animals castrated, or calves are sold. This is contrasted with the lonely, long periods of sheepherding when the herder goes with his sheep over vast areas.

There is a close relation between domestic animals and agriculture. The animals assist in clearing land, in plowing, and in harvesting. They may also be used to haul crops away for sale and to bring back fish or other fertilizer. Their excrement is itself a valuable fertilizer. In turn, the use of animals means that fodder must be provided. The farmer may use stalks of the grains that he grows. Indeed, the great shift in the United States from animal to mechanical power has meant a decline in the growth of hay and oats. In one remarkable case, the corn belt in the United States, corn may actually not be a cash crop at all, but be used instead to feed pigs. This area might more properly be called the pig belt.

We now turn to detailed consideration of the major crops grown in the United States.

United States farming exhibits great variation. Farms vary in size from two or three acres to thousands of acres. They differ in types of crop and in degree of mechanization. There are subsistence-diversified farms and there are farms which produce a single crop for sale. There are family

farms and farms which make use of thousands of migratory laborers annually. There are even farms which do not exhibit to a marked degree a
seasonal cycle, as is the case in dairying.

But this great variation is not a chaotic one; definite and far-reaching
patterns are observable. One of the most efficient ways to discover these
patterns is to look at farm work in terms of the type of crop or animal that
is raised. We shall use the categories devised by Raper and Taylor (19,
Ch. 19): general and self-sufficing, range-livestock, Western specialty crops,
cotton, dairying, corn and wheat.[3]

1. GENERAL AND SELF-SUFFICING AREAS

The general and self-sufficing areas lie in the East Central area of the
United States and include the uplands east of the Rockies.[4] There are two
main sections within the region according to type of crop: the northern
areas in Pennsylvania and New England (which are gradually shifting to
general crops and animals for sale with emphasis on dairying), and the
Appalachian-Ozark section (which includes the major proportion of self-
sufficing farms).

These areas are rugged country, ill-adapted to large farms or to the use
of machinery, rather isolated from urban centers, and covered with relatively poor roads. The fact of desirability of land near the rivers still places
a premium on the bottom lands: houses and even roads may be built on
hills in order to save land.

At first, farms were large and located in the bottom lands. Then
began the process of subdividing the land for the benefit of offspring, and
soon it was necessary to push up into the highlands. The hillside farms
suffered badly from erosion and the whole area tended to become one of
small, relatively poor farms.

The crops grown represent a considerable diversity. Corn is used for
fodder and meal, and hay is grown for animals. Most farms have some
cows, chickens, and hogs. Potatoes, vegetables, and fruit are raised for
home consumption. A large proportion of the produce is for the family's
own consumption but if there is any left over it will be sold. The products
sold usually include eggs, chickens, milk, butter, and cured meats.

Allowing for variations particularly in New England and Pennsylvania, the farm work-group is the family itself with the assistance of
neighbors in peak periods. The yearly round is essentially as described
above for agriculture generally. There is a busy period in the spring when

[3] Loomis and Beegle note the correspondence of the Raper-Taylor classification to
A. R. Mangus's regional system and to Loomis's own social systems scheme based on
Tonnies' concepts of *Gemeinschaft* and *Gesellschaft*. See (12, p. 258 and Fig. 83, p. 259
and pp. 281 ff.).
[4] Included are most of Kentucky, Tennessee, West Virginia, Pennsylvania, Virginia,
and much of Missouri and Ohio, parts of the New England states and Oklahoma.

all members of the family participate in plowing, planting, weeding, and thinning. There then occurs the cutting of hay and home preserving. This is succeeded by a quiet period. In the fall comes the corn harvest, potato digging, the making of syrup, and the sowing of winter wheat. Then comes a time when there is some hunting and trapping.

Since the farm is a family enterprise with some neighborhood co-operation, money is scarce. This of course tends to produce low income figures for this area, but such figures, as is usual in a self-sufficing area, do not paint the full picture. As Raper points out (19, p. 453) though this area shows the lowest gross farm income of any major farming area, in 1945, its level-of-living index was 74, whereas that of the cotton belt was only 53 (national average equals 100).

The need for self-sufficiency, geographical isolation, and the relative absence of extremes in levels of living, produce an emphasis on informality of social contacts outside the family. Indeed, an outstanding character-istic is the absence of any kind of formal organizations.

The role of the family as a work group coupled with physical isola-tion, places a great value on familism and family loyalty. Because of limited transportation facilities the family must usually travel as a group. The father will usually try to provide a farm for his son when he marries.

Informal contacts and visiting are neatly articulated with the seasonal round. The most intense period occurs in the summer slack between cul-tivation and harvesting. This is when revivals are likely to be held and when bazaars and socials are attended. Also, the children may go to school then so they will be available for the fall harvest. Therefore this is the period when the children meet as a peer group. In the winter there is also a slack period but the cold and the condition of the roads prevent intensive interaction. The winter is the period when the family interacts informally to an intense degree, though there is some hunting as we have said for rabbits and squirrels and other animals.

But the entire area is in process of transition. We mentioned earlier the turning to dairying in New England and Pennsylvania. The low level of living is a source of dissatisfaction to young people influenced by the movies and by the tourists who frequent the area. Adding cash to family income by off-farm work is becoming increasingly prevalent. Persons seek employment at saw mills as laborers and in the nearby cotton belt. Also, many families run tourist camps and motels.

While their wants multiply, the pattern of the large family con-tinues. The absence of land to accommodate the population has lead to an increasing urbanward migration. With the increase in cash farming, the farmers have been lead increasingly to look to the state and federal gov-ernment for aid instead of to their family and neighbors. With this trend there goes the growth of farm organizations, particularly the Grange in the northern portion.

But even with these changes, family work still remains the dominant pattern, though hired men may assist in milking and other tasks associated with dairying. Perhaps the most significant effect of the changes will be a breakdown in isolation and a decline of the neighborhood, trends which are already far gone in other areas. With these trends may go the traditional values of independence and security associated with the subsistence farm.

2. RANGE-LIVESTOCK FARMING

Of all forms of farming in the United States, range-livestock farming comes the closest to having produced a distinctive way of life or a unique sub-culture. It has produced a folklore, songs and a literature, and still represents the frontier in the United States.

Its vast area includes two-fifths of the land area of the United States. It begins in southwest Texas in a broad belt along the Rio Grande, and stretches north to include most of Arizona and New Mexico, all of Nevada, a large part of Utah, and most of western Colorado, a large chunk of Oregon to the southeast, practically all of Wyoming, and great slices of Montana and South Dakota.

The land is even more rugged and varied than is the case in the General and Self-sufficing areas, and it is perhaps this ruggedness more than any other single factor, that helps to explain the presence of the range lands. Range land is simply land that will not grow anything else more profitably.

There are four major ethnic groups in the range lands: native-born white ranchers, whose ranches are scattered throughout the entire area; Mormons, who practice mixed farming along with ranching and do so in or near Utah; Spanish Americans who are found in the Southwest and who grow subsistence crops of beans and other products with the help of irrigation, but who also carry on some sheep ranching; and Indians, who also try to grow crops on arid lands and keep some livestock. Large numbers of Mexicans come in to work as hired hands on the ranches of non-Spanish Americans.

In examining ranching as a work organization we note first the Indians' and Spanish Americans' practice of subsistence farming. They usually experience a low standard of living because of their small ranches and because of the poor grazing land to which they are limited. The work is ordinarily carried on as a family enterprise. For the most part, the rest of the ranchers are commercial farmers who sell calves, meat, land, and wool.

The most remarkable feature of the ranch is its enormous size in comparison to other farms. It often extends over many thousands of acres. The owner is himself usually the manager though he may live in town and do his managing from there.

Ranching is not normally a family work activity. Riding the range, herding, and branding are not jobs in which women and children can help very much. They are usually run by the owner with the help of a few hired hands, plus some men who may be hired temporarily for brief periods such as the round-up. If winter fodder is grown, then the farm family may function there, as it does in crop raising generally.

The daily round consists of caring for wells in arid areas, checking windmills, riding fences to look for holes or broken posts, and moving cattle herds to new pasture areas if necessary. These are for the most part solitary activities and may even be carried out in an automobile.

For the seasonal round, in the Southwest there may be year-round grazing for sheep. But usually herds shift north with the coming of warm weather and on these occasions a solitary herdsman and his dogs will go with them, often traveling hundreds of miles. Many cattle are sent into the winter wheat areas for grazing.

In the North, sheep must be corraled and fed fodder. The activities of shearing and dipping are crucial and involve the labor of several co-operating men. Usually one man brings the sheep up and turns it while another sits on a stool and shears the sheep with a pair of electric clippers. Another man or perhaps the first one will then carry the wool away.

For the cattle, the high point of the year is the round-up in which usually all hired men cooperate. Cattle are brought in, calves are castrated and branded, or shipped to fattening areas. Castration usually involves two or three men—one or two to hold the bull who will wiggle around a good deal even though he is tied up, and a third to perform the castrating itself. In the case of branding, usually one man will rope the calf and a second will perform the branding. They may use a runway and lead the calf up to it for the branding operation.

Mechanization is observable in the use of electric clippers, automobiles, and the use of railroad cars to transport sheep and cattle to market. Of the various specialists associated with ranching, the cowboy has been the most celebrated. However, Eric Thane (20, pp. 294–95) tells us about the cowboy in the following terms:

Cowboy. The word spells romance. As a matter of fact, his job was never romantic—it was too dirty, too dangerous, too low paid. Old timers of the country say that a cowboy's usefulness was ended after ten years in the saddle, a decade of badly cooked food, of rotgut liquor, of wind, blizzard, frost, and searing heat. There were other dangers, such as rattlesnake and the semi-wild cayuses of the prairie. Doctors were scarce in the earlier days and medical attention was almost non-existent. Primitive self-help meant, for all internal disturbances, the slapping of a hot stove-lid against the abdomen, and for any other injuries, crude splints and copious doses of whiskey.

They were a heroic tribe, those early day cowboys. At least to hear the old timers tell it . . . their stories are of a vanished race of horsemen that has been glorified out of all proportion by Western pulp magazines and moving pictures; they are campfire sagas of the centaurs of the plain. They are tales of old, for the golden age of the cowboy, begun in the 70's, ended when the reign of the beef baron was over, around 1893. When the panic of that year swept across the land at the same time that drylanders, flooding in, began to break the feudal supremacy of the mighty owners of mighty herds—of men like Pierre Wibaux, whose bronze statue stands today in the town named after him on the Montana-Dakota border. Wibaux's herds, it is said, ran into the hundreds of thousands. And he was not the mightiest of the barons—others surpassed him. Their riders were centaurs of the golden age of the cowboy; when they began to pass, their men went with them.

The "skim-milk" and "mail-order" cowboy then began to come into ascendancy, though Easterners doubt this. He still rides the ranges, but he carries his horse in a trailer behind his car until he reaches the country beyond roads. He no longer packs a gun. He listens to the radio and reads movie magazines.

The vast grazing spaces required for range land have produced far-reaching effects. The livestock area is one of a few scattered towns which function as social and recreational centers for large areas. Here the people meet as neighbors and gossip over beer or else in the department store. People are accustomed to travel long distances and to know their neighbors for many miles around. The sparseness of settlement produces few local formal organizations, though there are livestock producer associations which function as pressure groups. Also because of the scarcity of persons in a given area they find it difficult to support local schools or churches. Persons must then travel many miles to the town for these services. The vast spaces have also had important effects on attitudes and values in the area as will be pointed out below.

3. THE WESTERN SPECIALTY CROPS

The area characterized as Western Specialty Crops produces most of the nation's almonds, apricots, alfalfa, asparagus, carrots, cantaloupes, cherries, lettuce, prunes, walnuts, lemons, and grapes. This area includes the greater part of California (except for the northernmost portions), a considerable chunk of Arizona, the Mormon areas of Utah, a broad strip of southern Idaho, and the Columbia basin of central Washington. Most of it has been reclaimed from arid grazing land by the use of irrigation. It is also an area containing a great mixture of ethnic groups and persons of diverse origins and orientation to the land.

The individual farm (or "ranch" as the owners prefer to call it) tends to be devoted to one crop only. If the farmer must rotate his crops, he is likely to shift to a farm in a different area where he can grow the same crops. This in turn means an almost complete commercialization of farming, and has earned for this area the name "seed catalog agriculture." There is less home consumption of food grown by the farm than in any other farming area in the United States.

In spite of the dominance of cash farming, mechanization has not gone far. There is spraying from airplanes, and irrigation is highly mechanized, but the major task—as in all farming—the harvest, has been hardly touched by the machine. Most of the leading fruits, except for nuts (which may be shaken out of the tree) or plums (which are to be dehydrated to form prunes), require gentle handling to prevent bruising and squashing. The result is that the area has need at the harvest period for thousands of temporary laborers, of which Mexicans, Filipinos, American Negroes, Puerto Ricans, and large numbers of whites from the southwest and others seeking temporary work make up the greater proportion.

Through the use of piece work and the fact of a short harvest, and the further fact that a large part of the laborers are barred from jobs elsewhere, the laborers lead a depressed, migratory existence. They are poorly housed and mostly disfranchised, with their children denied education through the need to follow the harvest north. We shall have more to say about migratory laborers in the chapter on Ethnic Relations.

There is one important exception to the emphasis on commercialization in the area: the Mormons. Because of tradition, the pattern of village living, and the controls of the church, they have greater attachment to farming as a way of life and more use of the farm family on the land. But they too are becoming increasingly commercialized.

It is difficult to describe the work on a "typical" farm owing to the great variety of farms. But most of them involve a yearly round of remarkable regularity. We shall illustrate this round by reference to apple-growing in the Yakima Valley of Washington.[5]

The modal farm is a small one of ten or eleven acres, run by the owner himself, who normally has no year-round hired help. He does his own irrigation. From January to the end of March, he hires a pruner, who assists him to cut off suckers, and branches that may be hidden from the sun. April is apple blossom time and the apple rancher can occupy himself with helping to elect an apple queen. For two weeks in June he will hire a thinner, who removes small and scrawny apples. The owner will then do his own spraying. In September and October, at har-

---

[5] The following description is based on personal observation and consultation with specialists in the Dept. of Agricultural Economics, State College of Washington.

vest time, he will hire three apple-knockers (pickers) for from fifteen to twenty days. Apple picking is an individual activity. A man props a ladder up against a tree, climbs the ladder with a basket or sack, and picks the apples individually. Then he pours the apples into a box which he leaves at the foot of the tree.

The owner decides who works where and tries to apportion the lean pickings. At the end of the day he drives about the orchard with a truck, picks up boxes, weighs each one, and records the weight opposite the picker's name in a notebook. The men are usually paid at the end of the harvest and then move on. The owner hauls the apples to a depot, or to the wholesaler. It may be noted that the farm family is absent from work, though a son may drive the truck.

On a medium-large ranch of thirty acres, the only significant change, outside of the increase in numbers needed, is the hiring of one full-time man. He is a foreman and not a manager, however, for the owner still lives on and operates the farm. The owner and foreman work side by side in spraying and irrigation. Irrigation involves turning on the water at appropriate times, repairing canals, and watching the water level. This time five or six pruners will be hired and perhaps eight or nine thinners. The foreman assigns and supervises their work. His busiest time comes in the harvest when he must allot work, collect and weigh boxes, and deliver them.

In the relatively rare big operation, which may include as much as one hundred acres, the owner may not be present at all. He lives in Wenatchee or Yakima, pursues an urban way of life, and concentrates on marketing his apples. He hires a resident manager who acts for him. Under the manager is a foreman as before. This time they will hire two full-time irrigators, who are also likely to do spraying. On this farm there will be nine or ten pruners, and twenty thinners, hired for appropriate periods. There are likely to be ninety or a hundred pickers hired in the harvest who will be divided into three crews each with a picking-sub-foreman in charge. The foreman supervises the sub-foreman or straw-bosses, who spend much of their time in weighing boxes. The latter also watch that one picker does not take another man's box and put it on his own pile.

Ordinarily, two truck drivers are hired and three swampers, the latter to put boxes onto the truck. The truck drivers and swampers normally work a little later in the day since they must complete work that others make available to them. All of these are temporary workers.

The apples are driven to storehouses or to a depot or to a wholesaler as before. The men are paid and the apple year is at an end.

Even on the very large apple ranch, only about a hundred and twenty men are at work; and at any given time the number rarely goes over a hundred, even in the harvest period. Thus the numbers are very small by factory standards. Yet an orchard of this size may mean an income for the owner comparable to that of a factory owner who has as many as one thousand workers. Note also the paucity of skilled or professional full-time personnel. Irrigation requires some skill, and the manager and foreman of course must have supervisory ability. But as for the rest, skill is primarily a matter of experience. Furthermore, because of the method of piece-rate payment, skill need not be sought out or rewarded.

The owners of specialty crops tend to be a highly urbanized group. They look to the city for their market and in many cases actually live there. As such they join formal organizations and are active in farm organizations. In California they are active in politics. The result is a striking absence of the pattern of informal visiting and country life so characteristic of agriculture elsewhere.

The average income of owners and tenants is the highest in the nation. But that serves only to exaggerate further the enormous gulf between the operators (owners and tenants) and laborers. It is quite unmatched in any other major farming area in the United States.

4. COTTON

The cotton belt stretches in a broad curve from eastern North Carolina, into and including much of South Carolina, then across the Deep South, and into Oklahoma and west Texas.

Through this vast area, cotton is by no means the only crop. Corn, sorghum, tobacco, and rice are also grown and there is considerable dairying. There has been some movement of industry into the area, especially in northern Alabama, but most of it is related to cotton. The most notable exception is in the western part of the belt where oil and natural gas vie with cotton; and if the reserves are substantial, then cotton gives way.[6]

But in spite of these variations, the pattern over the cotton belt is a remarkably persistent one. A single crop, cotton, dominates the area in a manner comparable to no other farming region in the United States. This domination is related to weather and soil. Cotton requires a long growing season of two hundred or more days between killing frosts, moderate autumnal rains and an annual rainfall of more than twenty inches. It is helped in the growing season by hot dry days and damp nights. These conditions are found in the cotton belt.

The soils of such areas as the Piedmont, the Upper Coastal Plains of the Deep South, and the Black Waxy Prairie of Texas, while adapted

---

[6] Raper (20, p. 352) quotes an Oklahoma farmer: "It's hard to keep your mind on the plough, when oil is coming up from down under."

to cotton, have also been much subject to erosion. This helps to produce recurrent droughts and floods in the river areas, and makes the cotton belt into the greatest consumer of fertilizer of any major farming area in the United States.

The rural residents (and it is an overwhelmingly rural area) are practically all native born. The notable exceptions are the Mexicans, most of whom are employed on large plantations and farms as migratory laborers in the picking season. Most white residents can trace their ancestry back to early American settlers. The Negroes also, at least after the middle 1800's, are an overwhelmingly native American group. Negroes, in spite of migration, still make up over one-third of the rural farm population of the South; and the vast majority of U.S. Negro farmers are found in the cotton belt.

Hand labor is traditional through most of the cotton belt, at least in connection with the two most time-consuming phases of cotton growth—chopping (thinning) and picking. The use of hand labor is related to the plantation system which involves managing rather than working the farm, with the use of a large number of slaves, or later, tenants and hired laborers. The existence of large families and the presence of sufficient cheap labor help it to persist. In west Texas and Oklahoma, the newest area of cotton growth, there has been considerable use made of machinery, but this development is recent and confined to a relatively limited area. Cotton production is still to a considerable extent a hand process.

There are two major forms of work organization in cotton—the family-owned farm and the plantation. In the former, the owner is independent and makes use of his own family for labor with temporarily hired laborers, especially Mexicans in the Western part of the belt.

Essentially the term "plantation" refers to land, owned by a person or corporation, which is worked by tenants. The average plantation of two hundred acres before the Civil War employed around six field hands and two hands in the house. Operating the plantation for the owner was the overseer. Since he has been painted as a vicious brute in so much of our literature, it is worth noting that his function as intermediary between master and slave created for him a difficult, marginal position (22, pp. 48–9). In this respect he resembles the factory foreman.

Slaves were quartered on the land. If a plantation were large enough for several crews, then there were straw-bosses put in charge of each crew who supervised the crews under the eye of the overseer.

U. B. Phillips has described the daily round in connection with hoeing on such a plantation as follows:

The first horn was blown an hour before daylight as a summons for workhands to rise and do their cooking and other preparations for the day. Then at the summons of the plow driver at the first break of day, the plowmen went to the stables whose doors the overseer opened. At the second horn, just at good daylight, the hoe gang set off for the fields. At half-past eleven the plow men carried their mules to a shelter house in the fields, and at noon the hoe hands laid off for dinner, to resume work at one o'clock, except that in hot weather the intermission was extended to a maximum of three and a half hours. The plowmen lead the way home by a quarter of an hour in the evening, and the hoe hands followed at sunset.

The planter usually sold his cotton through the factor. His role was well described by Vance (22, pp. 50–51) as follows:

The cotton factor was likely to be a man of money and brains. Since the prevailing prejudice against trade did not operate against him, he was always from a good family. His relations with the planter were personal and intimate as well as economical. Since factorage reflected the hazards of cotton planting, a large profit was allowed him without complaint on the part of the planters. The confidential nature of their relationship attached a high value to the moral hazards. If the planter consigned his cotton to the factor and accepted his accounting usually without quibble, the factor lent the planter money with nothing more definite than a personal pledge. In southern cities such as Charleston, South Carolina, the factors either paid the proceeds of the Sea Island cotton over to the growers or acted in the capacity of a bank for them, honoring their checks when presented. As a matter of fact, the factor was wholesale merchant, banker, and cotton agent. He supplied the necessities for the slaves and the comforts and conveniences for the home in jobber's lots. He handled the planters' money and thus concentrated it in the larger cities. If in some instances he built up a system of rebates on weighing, storing, and drayage, no one blamed him particularly. He was a busy and hard working man but cotton was the only agriculture commodity that could have stood the delays and exposure at export ports without serious deterioration. If the factors sometimes retired rich men, the hazards of their business were just as likely to wipe out their fortunes over one or two bad seasons. The factors retarded the growth of fair-sized cities in the inland, because they kept out small merchants and country banks. They developed a high standard of business honor, occupied a high social position, and if often angered at seeing their loans for cotton production spent at northern watering places or on European tours, they remained on intimate terms with the planter, directing and advising his undertakings.

After the Civil War, some attempt was made to retain the plantation system through the use of hired laborers with wage contracts. Because of the scarcity of money, the need to wait a year for wages which might not be payable, because of crop failure, and because of the mobility of workers resulting in a rise in wages especially in the west cotton states, this system did not work. Eventually the share system was introduced, and it is still the dominant form on the plantation.

Under this system the owner leases part of his land to tenants who work it in return for a share of the income. The sharecropper owns no stock or tools. The owner provides these together with a house (of some kind) and also provides credit at the plantation store or elsewhere for the cropper's needs. The sharecropper pays half of the cost of the fertilizer and of ginning. The cropper and owner then split the crop fifty-fifty, with the cropper repaying his debts.

T. Lynn Smith (17, pp. 279 ff.) and others, including the Georgia Supreme Court (7, pp. 584–85), have argued that the term "tenant" is hardly applicable to the sharecropper. Usually he is under the direct supervision of the manager or owner and has no choice of tools, stock, or even what type of farming he shall engage in. In their view, he is essentially an annual wage laborer, without any guaranteed wage. He thus shares in the risks.

A second type of tenant, though not differing greatly from the cropper, is the share tenant. He owns his own mules and implements. For rent he usually pays the owner one-third of the corn and one-quarter of his cotton. Thus the fortunes of the owner are still tied to the tenant. At the top of the tenant scale are cash or standing renters. These persons pay a fixed amount of money, which may, however, be related to the crop. In this case the owner takes a minimum risk, though he usually reduces the risk even further by taking a lien on the crop.

In the following discussion of the yearly round we shall deal with renters, and shall focus on the small or medium-sized holding.[7]

After the tenant has chosen a farm and made an appropriate agreement with a landlord (usually in December), the first process is securing equipment. If he is a share tenant, he owns stock and tools; if he is a cropper, the landlord supplies them. In addition, on a plantation, the landlord will open a charge account for the tenant at the plantation store; small owners will do likewise at the village store. Credit prices are likely to be considerably higher than cash prices.

---

[7] We do so for purposes of simplification, but it should be borne in mind that this restriction has the effect of passing over the increasing use of the mechanical cotton picker. Although the problems were great (e.g., the various bolls on one plant matured at different times, and the leaf might get into the cotton and lower the grade), most of these have now been solved and efficient pickers may be purchased. But their high cost and their adaptability mainly to flat ground has restricted their use to large holdings, especially in the Mississippi delta area and in Arizona and Southern California. The picking of cotton is, then, still overwhelmingly a hand-operation, but this is changing.

In the extreme South, there is an initial period of slack, except for chores and the necessary tending to animals, unless there are other crops, such as vegetables. The farmer may seek outside work, such as road work, levee repair work, or else work in town.

The first task of the farm year is clearing the land, which is carried out in January or February. The withered stocks from last year's crop lie about in confusion unless the farmer has burnt them to destroy the boll weevils. Stocks are cut and may be burnt or plowed under. This is not a laborious job, and it may be done by the tenant or the owner and his son.

On most cropper and plantation farms, the next operation is the plowing of the soil. Cotton is planted in long furrows built up to form beds. It is common to plant in the same bed as the previous year in order to take advantage of any leftover fertilizer. The following (22, pp. 158–59) gives a description of plowing in the eastern part of the belt:

> A one-horse plow is run along the side of the old row and the dirt is thrown toward the middle by running one or two furrows on each side of the row. This leaves the old cotton stubs standing on a balk or small ridge, which is broken out with a one-horse shovel plow leaving a furrow in which the fertilizer is distributed with a one-horse fertilizer distributor. The land is bedded back on the fertilizer with a plow taking from two to four trips per row. This leaves another "balk" between the two old rows, which may be left until the cotton is cultivated. The top of the bed is leveled off with a harrow or a board and the cotton planted on top of the bed, the new row being in the same place as the old one.

Elsewhere, four-horse "middle-busters," or tractors, are used. This is an operation requiring only one man.

Next comes the planting itself which may be combined with the distribution of fertilizer. Cotton seed may be dropped or drilled into the ground. The planter machine then covers it over. Planting is usually over by the middle of May and takes about one month. It is usually hurried to try to beat the weevil.

After the plants are up a short distance, comes the first laborious task, that of chopping the cotton, which involves thinning it and removing weeds. This is carried out with a hoe; it is usually repeated two or three times, especially the weeding. Chopping is engaged in by the whole family and lasts four or five weeks. There then may be further ploughing around the plants if there have been heavy rains or the ground has caked and hardened.

For renters, ploughing, planting, and chopping are all performed under some supervision from the owner. If a farmer is a cropper on a plantation, then agricultural practices are standardized and supervision by the owner or manager is close. He may have to return his stock to the barns daily and will be advised and criticized with reference to his farm procedures. Share tenants and cash renters have less supervision, though the owner will be concerned about the crop, weevils, weather, and will visit him frequently. The tenant in turn sees his landlord for advice or for credit to buy fertilizer or spray for insects.

About the first of August begins the lay-by. The cotton plants are now well established and weeds no longer a concern. No other crops require attention. It is a period of leisure and waiting. The schools will open in some districts since the children will be picking cotton later. This is the period of religious revival and camp meetings, and a period of visiting and the expression of confidence in the high yield to come. It is not, however, a time of visits to taverns or of gambling, as the farmer has no money. Indeed, at this time he is severely in debt.

In south Texas, picking has already begun and by early September the whole of the belt is picking cotton. This is the most labor-consuming task, and the entire rural South is mobilized for it. In the western portions, large numbers of migratory laborers are hired.

Cotton pickers are paid on a piece-work basis. A good cotton picker gets his hand on a ripe boll quickly, snaps it off with a deft movement and, without getting bits of leaf or other trash in it, transfers it to his bag. The bag is a long sack held by a strap over the shoulder. The bottom of the bag drags on the ground so that its whole weight is not carried. The individual must stoop over to pick, and this position must be maintained hour after hour. Women and children make up a large proportion of cotton pickers, though all are likely to participate in this operation.

When the sack is full—fifty to seventy-five pounds—it is taken to the weigher, who records the weight in a book. The cotton is then poured into a wagon and tramped down. If it is damp it will be permitted to dry first. It is then taken to a cotton house for storage, or in the case of the small owner-operated farm, it is dumped on the front porch.

The next operation is hauling the cotton to the gin. There is a gin in every small town and even at a crossroads one is likely to be found. The farmers line up and spend their time gossiping with each other while waiting their turn. When his turn comes, the farmer drives his wagon under a shed and helps to move the flexible vacuum pipe over his cotton until it is all sucked up. He will usually sell his seed to the ginner. The finished bale is delivered to him.

Next, the baled cotton is sold. In every town there are cotton buyers, who include specialized buyers, supply merchants, street buyers, and buyers for cotton firms. The tenant may sell to his landlord or let the landlord sell for him; the small owner may sell to the merchants who lent him supplies on credit. In the small towns, selling is an occasion for excited activity. The street buyers go from wagon to wagon and place a foot on the wagon axle as a signal that a bargain is in process. Tufts of cotton are torn from the bale for examination, which may leave the bale looking very ragged.

The price depends on the buyer's estimate of quality, and this is a rather subjective matter of which the farmer may be ignorant. Standards are necessary for predictability at textile mills, and for cotton-future trading. Attempts have been made to standardize cotton classing with varying degrees of success (1a, pp. 419–23).

In the intervals between picking, corn and fodder will be pulled, usually in early November. These jobs are usually looked upon as a nuisance to be hurried through. When the weather turns cold, there is likely to be a hog-killing. Schools soon open, though attendance is random until all of the cotton is picked.

The last phase of the cotton year is the settling of debts. The cotton grower settles his note at the bank or supply store. The landlord and tenant settle with each other, paying cash for rent, or the value of a portion of the crop and the costs of supplies and fertilizer. If the yield has been good and prices are high, then tenant and owner are in a good mood and repair to the town to celebrate. If not, then the tenant begins to look for a new farm or landlord, where he feels the land is better or from whom he can get what he regards as a better deal.

The towns come to life, for this is the time of the year when the farmer, if he has money, will spend it. But he does not always have money, for raising cotton is a highly speculative enterprise. Both yield and price are subject to wide fluctuations. These fluctuations hurt, especially owing to the lack of diversification and the dependence on a single money crop. At the same time, the farmer is caught up in a nexus of debts which make it very difficult for him to diversify or shift to general farming. To grow cotton, he needs money, and to get money he must grow cotton. The price is largely beyond his control, although producers cooperatives are spreading. The yield is subject to the weather and the various pests and diseases. As Vance says, "the world's largest consumer of raw cotton is the boll weevil."

In the cotton belt, as in all of the South, all formal and informal relations are of course cut across by race, which we shall discuss in Chapter 16. Here we note that the economic and occupational inequities of ethnic relations hit the Negro hardest, and that it is he who looms largest among cotton-belt laborers and tenant groups of all kinds.

Yet the pattern of race relations in the South is changing and these changes are directly related to the changing role of cotton-growing. We have seen the tremendous importance of cotton to the economy of this area, but it should also be noted that this importance is steadily lessening because of competition from other cotton-producing areas (e.g., Egyptian long-staple cotton), from the synthetic fibres (nylon, orlon, dacron, etc.), and for other reasons. In the period 1925–1929, the average annual acreage devoted to cotton was 42,600,000; by 1954, the cotton-growing area had shrunk to 19,187,000 acres (15, p. 57). The resultant decrease in demand for southern rural labor, especially since World War II, has speeded up the urbanization of southern Negroes. And they have migrated not only to northern cities but to many southern ones as well—where they are beginning to make themselves felt as a political force because, for one thing, it is harder in the cities to limit their right to vote. Changes in the position of the Negro may, in the long run, be found to depend not only on legal changes but also on one simple economic fact: in the South, cotton is no longer king.

5. DAIRYING

Dairying in the United States, like truck farming, is intimately tied up with urban populations who provide the sales market for raw as well as processed dairy products. Consequently it is found in the neighborhood of all medium and large cities. But the areas in which dairying is dominant form a broad belt skirting Lake Superior, enveloping Lake Michigan, and hugging southern Lake Huron, then extending in horseshoe fashion along Lake Erie and Lake Ontario and into New England, down through New Hampshire and Vermont, and somewhat inland back into New York, eastern Pennsylvania, and north Virginia. Patches of importance are also present in central and southern California and in western Washington.

The dairying area, though dominated by native-born persons, exhibits a great variety of ethnic strains. This variety is in part a reflection of the fact that dairying came late to the United States. It had to await the growth of cities and the development of good roads and efficient transportation because of the perishability of dairy products.

While western fruit and vegetable growers themselves often live in cities and are oriented to urban life, dairy farmers exhibit perhaps the greatest day-by-day intensity of interaction with the urban population insofar as interaction is related to agriculture itself. The relation to the urban population is most obviously apparent in the production of raw milk. After the milking, cooling, pasteurization, and bottling have been done, milk must move to the consumer quickly. This means that distances to cities must be as short as roads and railroads will permit. This need is not so great with cream which is to be canned or with cheese, but butter too must be hurried to the grocer's refrigerators daily.

The emphasis on the immediate relation to the urban population has produced a network of all-weather roads which are the envy of farmers elsewhere. It means the use also of the latest and fastest trucks. The presence of good roads and the nearness to cities has also made the dairying area into one having the largest rural nonfarm (small town) and urban population of any major farming area. Suburban areas stretch into the dairy lands and the homes and estates of the city wealthy are found side by side with the dairy farms. It is also a favorite tourist region, particularly near its many lakes. The total picture is one of a farm-urban mosaic, in which relations are both symbiotic and accommodative, though not, as we shall see, consensual, as in the case of the western specialty area.

The most important distinctive characteristic of work is the emphasis on a *daily* rather than a seasonal round. Milk and its by-products, cream and butter, are not seasonal phenomena and are part of the daily menus of the consumers. Nor does their production involve directly a planting-harvest cycle. This fact tends to make dairying unique in agriculture and most nearly comparable to urban factory work. There is no summer lay-by or winter quiet period; work revolves about a daily pattern which repeats itself week after week and month after month.

The major object of attention is the dairy herd. The cows must be milked twice daily usually in the morning and in the afternoon. The work unit is the farm family, though on a large farm there will also be hired men. Milking, if done by hand, is often shared by the whole family and particularly by the women among the Polish and the Germans.

On a larger enterprise, milking machines will be used. These involve a crew of two men usually. The cows are all chained to individual stalls and the milkers operate on a wide catwalk located between the stalls. The barn is equipped with compressed air pumps. The milking equipment itself is located on a wheeled truck which also includes a scale and a tank of hot water. The first operation is to wash the udder with warm water to remove excrement and bits of straw. The four-teat-cups on the milking unit are attached to the cow's nipples and the other end is attached to a pipe leading to the pump. Then the loud sounds of what seems like a giant's deep, jerky breathing are heard as the pump sucks out the milk into the can. Meanwhile a milking unit is being attached to another cow.

In such an arrangement there are likely to be four milking units so that three or four cows are being milked at once. From the sound of the sucking noise, the milker can tell when no more milk is coming out.

The unit is removed and dipped in hot water to clean it. Then the milker must usually finish by "stripping"—using a gentle hand massage to draw out the last of the milk.

The relation between milkers is one of sharing work, with little specialization evident. If the herd is large enough, there may be a third man who carries the milk away to the cooler and shortly after feeds the cows. Of course on large farms there will be two or three milking assemblies. This routine takes place twice daily. The cows may then be let out to graze, though on many farms this is not done.

Milk pails and machines must be cleaned, often by the women, when the milking is finished. If the farmer operates a cream separator, as in southern Wisconsin and Minnesota, that will be the next operation. Then the milk or cream may be hauled to a processing plant or put out on the roadside to be picked up by the dealer's truck. This operation is repeated daily. Anything else must be done between milking.

A seasonal rhythm is not entirely absent. Usually once a year, the cows are given the opportunity to be bred. When the cow is close to having her calf, she is usually put into an enclosed stall. The calf when born stays there with the mother, or is permitted to stay near her while she grazes.

The most important other seasonal activities are centered around the other crops, if raised, and the sale of livestock. The farmer usually sells some of his calves; this means attending auctions or sales in town, held usually in the spring. If he grows his own feed, then he is exposed to the same yearly round as on general farms—clearing, planting, and harvesting. The farmer who does that is likely to have a smaller farm and to make use of his family. However, if it is a large farm this will mean more hired hands and the use of casual laborers. The latter possibility is not likely in the eastern sections where fields are small and grain yields are low, and near metropolitan areas where land prices are too high. Other products such as potatoes, hogs, and fruits and vegetables may also supplement dairying.

The family farm is still extremely common. The work is, unlike ranching or western specialty farming, something that women and children can assist in. The children early learn to drive the cattle in from pasture and may be assigned certain animals as their own responsibility. Very soon too, sons and daughters can do milking and can help in cleaning the equipment.

The importance of sanitation and the dependence on commercial agriculture has made the dairy farmer profoundly interested in mechanization or any procedures which will save time or money. Animal refuse is put back into the soil of grazing lands or fodder crops; tractors, manure spreaders, milking-machines more complex than those we have described, and other machines are widely used; and cattle breeding and selection are also objects of such attention. Nevertheless the mechanization of dairying hardly approaches the levels reached in corn and wheat.

6. CORN

Corn is a widely distributed crop. Florida grows more corn than it does tangerines, and the United States actually grows about three times as many bushels of corn as it does of wheat. The states which produce the most corn are those associated with the Midwest. Their distribution resembles a giant frying pan. The handle of the pan begins in northwestern Ohio and continues through all but the southern parts of Indiana and Illinois. Then the area broadens for the frying pan itself, taking in south Minnesota, all of Iowa, and northern Missouri, southeastern South Dakota, eastern Nebraska, and the northeast corner of Kansas. It is surrounded by other major agriculture areas. This produces along its borders fringe areas which represent a compromise between corn and the neighboring area.

Mechanization is beginning in cotton and has made great strides in dairying, but it is with corn that we reach for the first time a farm crop in which mechanization is taken for granted. In the time it takes a good corn husker to produce 75 to 100 bushels by hand, the mechanical corn picker produces a thousand. In addition, plowing, planting, and cultivation, and the preparation of feed for animals are all done with the aid of tractors, multiple-row planters, cultivators, elevator pick-up balers, and manure spreaders.

As mechanization increases, the farmer has been unable to keep up with its complexities; an elementary knowledge of "fixing things" is no longer enough, as Croy (5, p. 295) points out:

> But machinery has its toll. It is always getting out of whack and this has brought in the "Fix It" man who travels around repairing parts and equipment that have begun to act up. He carries everything—seemingly—in his truck; it's a rolling storehouse of parts and replacements. And it's a job many mechanically trained men took up at the end of the war. Here's a list of the things the "Fix It" man does: Wires houses and barns, installs water softeners, puts in bathtubs and sewerage systems, fixes the spring on the screen door, clears out the kitchen drain, overhauls the tractor, puts new shoes on the spring-tooth harrow, finds out what is wrong with the refrigerator, welds a new a point on the plow share, repairs the radio, and dispenses the neighborhood news. On rainy days the farmer used to try to do these things himself, but now he telephones the "Fix It" man who takes care of the matter. It was vastly different when Pa and I did it. I mean Pa.

The important general consequences of mechanization have been a decreased need for a large family and consequent rural-urban migration, the use of some hired help, a greater separation between husband and wife in terms of the division of labor, and the focusing of attention from the farm and its traditional values to the city where prices are determined.

But corn farms were and still are, for the most part, family farms. The typical farm is diversified and produces much of the food needs of the family. As a consequence, all of the family can and do share in some aspect of farm work. The men are concerned with the field crops and the women with poultry, dairy products, and gardening. The children perform chores and help with the milking. Because of mechanization and diversification, corn farming does not exhibit violent seasonal swings. Also, the family itself can do more of the work than otherwise they might.

The yearly round is now that typical of mechanized agriculture. In March, April, and early May, the fields are prepared, the crops are seeded, and the newly born livestock are taken care of. In June, the corn is cultivated for weeds. In July, there is haying and the harvesting of oats and other small grains. August is a period of waiting. It is the time of fairs, camp meetings, and visiting. In September begins harvesting. Formerly this was carried out by hand, and it still is in some places. This activity was once celebrated in the corn-husking contests.[8]

However, the contest has vanished since the mechanical corn picker has removed the need for this skill. Corn is husked and stored, or else cut for fodder, or shelled, all by machinery, and is the concern of the farmer himself and his sons. Another procedure that is used in season is "hogging down," that is, turning the hogs into the corn fields to eat the corn as it stands on the stocks. In the winter there is the matter of the care of livestock—feeding them and protecting them against the weather.

Like dairying (which many corn farmers also engage in), the yearly round is accompanied by a daily round. Taylor (19, pp. 367–68) describes them and also comments on recent changes:

During rush seasons the schedule was: Out of bed at 4:30 or 5 o'clock to do the chores, eat breakfast, and be in the fields by six or seven; an hour off at noon for "dinner" and rest; back to the fields until 6:30 or 7, when there were more chores and supper before going to bed by 8:30 or 9. During the winter months the getting up was an hour later, and more time was taken at noon, but since the burden of chores was increased at this season, work was generally not completed much before dark.

[8] Croy (5, p. 224) describes corn husking as follows:
"1. The left hand flashes out and seizes the butt.
2. The right hand shoots out and, as it passes, rips open the husk. The left hand gives the ear a squeeze, forcing it out of the shuck.
3. The right hand returns, seizes the ear, and hurls it at the wagon.
That's all there is to it—just those three simple movements. Anyone can master them. I wish you luck."

Basically these old time rhythms are still followed. With the advent of tractors and electricity, however, the daily rhythms have become more irregular on most of the family sized, commercial farms of the corn belt. Even on the subsistence farms, which are on the fringes, the working day now more nearly conforms to urban patterns. Most corn belt farmers and their families, living on all-weather roads, are now relatively free, except at the peak seasons, to run into town, visit auctions and markets, and attend Farm Bureau, home economics, 4-H, or other meetings. This change in rural life is due to the fact that the arduousness and urgency of farm work are not as great today as they used to be. Although seasonal peaks still have to be met in planting, cultivating, and harvesting, many more acres can be handled with heavy modern equipment in fewer days and with much less physical exertion on the part of the operators. In fact, the production of corn, now grown from hybrid seed and with the use of powerful tractors and heavy planting, cultivating, and harvesting machines, is so fully mechanized that the corn is seldom touched by human hands.

Mechanization, together with the use of the family-sized farm which grows its own food but is geared to the urban market for the sale of its livestock, have produced a high level of living in the corn belt. It is characterized, however, by a relative absence of income extremes. The feeding and growing of livestock is not conducive to huge incomes nor does it lend itself to speculation to a marked extent. However, corn-belt farmers exhibit a profound tendency to sell their farms on retirement and to move into town. This has led to over-capitalization of farm values and periodic swings of farm prices. Taylor (19, pp. 372–73) describes this process as follows:

. . . between 1890 and 1920 those who had homesteaded their land, or had purchased it cheaply in pioneer days, were dying or retiring in steadily increasing numbers. Their profits from current production had for twenty to fifty years gone into houses, barns, fences, and orchards; and the value of their land had multiplied by many times over. They could therefore sell their farms and live comfortably during the declining years of their lives. Many corn belt towns became filled with retired farmers. Furthermore, a large percentage of the pioneer farmers who retired or died left no son or daughter on the farm, because the children had entered some profession or town business; and when the estates were divided among the children, many transferred their equities out of farming. In fact, in probably no other area of the country has so large a volume of farm-created wealth been transferred out of rural life, for in no other area has the out-migration been so largely composed of persons who had wealth to carry with them.

On the other hand, during the period of development commercialization automatically capitalized high annual incomes into higher land values, and these increases tended to be calculated a half generation to a generation in advance. As a result, the corn belt has been subject to booms and busts, with

THE FARM: WORK STRUCTURE AND ECONOMIC COMPLEX

many farmers losing the ownership of their farms during the bust periods. Thus the risks in corn belt farming have not been due to periodic crop failures, such as occur frequently in the wheat belt, and they have not been as great as in pure cash-crop farming. But in the troughs of relatively long time price cycles, men with heavily mortgaged farms, and with large investments in operating equipment, have found themselves unable to carry the financial burden. The first of these busts came in the early 1870's, before the western sections of the belt had been fully developed; the second came in the 1880's, when most farms were still in the hands of original settlers, and before land valleys had risen to dangerous levels. The third and most devastating came at the end of World War I, after the fine farms of the corn belt, so profitable during the war, had risen to three and four times their 1900 value; and after the average farm had been sold three or four times since it was homesteaded or originally purchased, and had been bought by the final owner with little prospect of gaining any unearned increment by reselling it. The census report of 1920 showed that farms in Iowa with their full complement of buildings, livestock, and machinery were appraised at $40,000, because both loaning agencies and farmers had developed the utopian faith that farms, which have moved up in value per acre from $10 in 1870 to $50 in 1890 to $100 in 1910 and to $200 in 1920, would continue to rise in value. This fake was a direct outgrowth of the fact that corn belt farming had developed into highly commercial agriculture, the dizzy heights of which had been attained by such a constant and long time trend that few corn belt farmers thought of the climb as inflationary, or of the attitudes and practices of the participants as speculative.

The orientation to sales and to urban markets has long made formal special interest organizations powerful in the corn belt. The Grange in the 1870's, and the Farmers' Alliance in the 1880's and 90's, were important organizations. Today the Farm Bureau is very active. These operated as co-ops and exerted and continued to exert a considerable political influence.

7. WHEAT

Wheat is the major crop in three western regions: the spring-wheat area of North Dakota and the fringes of the surrounding states of Montana (plus a chunk of north central Montana), South Dakota and Minnesota; the winter-wheat area of central and western Kansas, plus contiguous fringes of southwestern Nebraska, eastern Colorado, Oklahoma, and the Texas Panhandle; the spring *and* winter wheat region of the Columbia Basin and the Palouse area of eastern Washington, the Panhandle of Idaho and northeastern Oregon.

Wheat areas are semi-arid and wheat is not profitably grown unless extensive farming is practiced with full mechanization. In 1945, the average size of farm was 621 acres, and in the Grand Coulee area of Washington, the average was 3,000 acres. This leads to as great a sparseness of settlement as is found in the range area. Towns are few, widely scattered, and small. Neighbors may be many miles distant.

Wheat farming carries with it some of the greatest risks to which farmers anywhere in the world are subject.[9] Insects, pests, and prices (before parity) are all serious problems, but the one that hangs like a spectre over the wheat farmer is *weather*. When there is no rain and the winds sweep the dry earth, great dust bowls may be and have been created. Besides there is the fear of an early winter or of a too late spring. One result is "dry farming," that is, techniques to preserve soil moisture. These involve summer fallow, strip cropping, and repeated harrowing. In addition new varieties of wheat requiring less moisture have been developed. Sometimes the problem is one of rain at the wrong time.

The large farm (the only profitable kind of farm for the wheat belt) goes hand in hand with a degree of mechanization which exceeds even that of corn. It is with wheat that the mechanization of agriculture reaches its apex and man becomes a machine-tender. The tractor and combine represent one of the most remarkable of man's accomplishments. These behemoths cut the grain, thrash it, clean it, bundle it and deposit the bundle neatly on the ground. The sight of one of them at work makes the cotton-farm owner look on skeptically and mutter "That's not farming."

But large-scale mechanization, while essential, adds one more risk—debt—to wheat farming. The wheat area experiences disastrous booms and busts and a fluctuating population—especially in Kansas—as a string of bad years follow one or two good ones. The risks and occasional "killings" involved have led to the appellation of "slot-machine agriculture."

Wheat farming exhibits a more violent yearly cyclical variation in work than does any other major type of farming. Approximately five-sixths of the year's work is concentrated in the two seasons of seeding and harvesting. Since the big wheat farmer does not diversify to any great extent, the result is a profound swing between periods of continuous labor every minute of the day and periods of complete leisure. Mechanization is a significant causal factor, so that *total work* is probably less than any other major type of farming also.

Farms are overwhelmingly run by the farm family, though extra help is hired at harvest. In addition, custom harvesting is done: a crew comes through and does a man's harvest for him for a fee, or a resident farmer may do such work for his neighbors. A picture of the make-up of such a crew in the Big Bend country of Oregon is provided by Dubbé (6, pp.

---

[9] The situation is succinctly summarized in the motto of the Board of Trade of Hanna, a town in the dry-belt wheat area in Alberta, which states (referring to their wheat): "The Best in the West When We Get It" (2, p. 4).

170–79). It is now somewhat out of date since the threshing and bagging operations described are now done by the combine. A modern combine is likely to have only a crew of five. The one described by Dubbé required twenty-six men. It is worth describing, however, for the excellent picture provided of the division of labor.

A full crew listed the following workers:

The "Boss"	Three hoe-down men
Engineer	Sack jig
Fireman	Sack sewer
Separator tender	Two header punchers (drivers)
Derrick boy	Two loaders
Roustabout	Eight header-box wagon drivers
Two cooks	

In addition to these workers, horses and mules were required as follows:

Two header teams, eight on each	16
Eight header-box wagons, four on each	32
Water wagon	8
Derrick	2
Saddle horses and extras	5
Total	63

And wagons, machines, and tools made a long list, too:

One steam traction engine	Watering troughs
One separator	Feed racks
One derrick table	Saddles
Two headers	Bedding
Eight header-box wagons	Forks
Two water wagons (500 gallon capacity)	Sacks
Cook wagon and trailer for cooks to sleep in	Needles
A hack or Ford for the roustabout,	Sack twine
	Etc., etc., etc.

So a harvest crew and outfit is quite an affair. It moves to central positions, and makes camp until a region of great field has been cut and brought in to the machine to be threshed and sacked. The whole crew sleeps out in the field where the work is done, sometimes several miles from the ranch house. Men sleep on blankets which they throw down in the straw pile, or put in a wagon bed, or spread on the ground. First come, first served! The women, of course, have beds in the cook-house trailer. The only clothes the men remove at night before going to sleep are their boots—or possibly trousers with lumpy pockets.

Everyone is up before the sun—about 3:30 or 4:00 a.m. Each man of the field crew has four horses or mules to care for before breakfast. He waters them,

feeds them, cleans them, and puts harnesses on them. It is a beautiful sight to
see the teams moving around the camp early in the morning, especially when
the boys take pride in their teams and when they vie with each other in their
currying and trimming.

In the meantime, the cooks who have had to get up earliest of all are frying
eggs and salt pork—and potatoes by the bushel. . . .

Sometime between 5:30 and 6:00 the wheels began to turn, whips to snap,
and mules to be called unmentionable names. The header-puncher drove his
team at a half-run. The box drivers crowded their teams to keep the wagons
under the spouts, and a river of gold poured out of the spout into the wagon.
The loader reached high with his fork and pushed great sliding heaps to the
corners until the wagon was filled. Then he leaped out and into another wagon,
already waiting behind—and so he went on loading wagon after wagon, day
after day. Each header-box driver rushed his load of grain heads in to the derrick
table, hooked the cable to the ring on the net and jumped clear. The derrick
boy called to his team and marched off with the cable. When it tightened, the
load on the wagon shifted and rolled and then slid down over the derrick
table.

"Back! Back!" the derrick boy cried.

He loosened the cable from his team, and drove it around to be ready for
the next load. Another load was standing ready to pull up alongside the table,
and another was probably trotting in, while empties were going out and following the headers.

On the derrick table, two *hoe-down* men forked the headed grain on to a
travelling belt—a relentless lapping tongue which must be evenly and constantly
fed. The headed grain was heavy. The two men stroked down the grain and
pushed it to the belt. These strokes had to be powerful and reserved. The
hoe-down job was the man-killer of the outfit.

Up the belt and into the mouth of the separator, the grain was soon beating
against the metal walls of the hopper, the straw flying from the blower to the
stack, the grain streaming into sacks in the "dug-out." The jig was the man
who hung up the sacks, turned on the wheat spouts, jigged the bags full, and
handed them over to the *sack-sewer*. The sewer hooked a thread in his needle,
whipped a loop over the ear of the bag, and topped the first ringer with a second.
Then he drove his needle like a snake through the edges of the sack which he
had already furled together with his left hand. A jerk brought three or four
stitches tight. Once more, and a loop and another loop, a snap to cut the twine
—and there it was. He carried it out to the pile. Each grain bag held about
one hundred twenty to one hundred forty pounds when tightly packed.

Such a crew harvested Dubbé's peanut-sized farm (one hundred acres)
in two days.

The great peaks in wheat farming have led to the creation of a class
of farmers who are known as "suitcase farmers" and "sidewalk farmers."
The former live outside the area and only come in for seeding and har-

vesting, and the latter live in town and run other businesses or professions in addition to their wheat farms.

This concludes our discussion of the work structure of farming.

THE ECONOMIC COMPLEX OF FARMING

We turn next to an examination of resources, to land, tools, and effort as scarce goods and values whose aid must be enlisted in the work process. There are many to whom a discussion of the "business" aspect of farming is a travesty and "prices" a bad word. The attachment of man to the soil, to "mother earth," is felt to be discussable only in poetic or romantic terms. Interestingly enough, this point of view affects the cold-blooded researcher as well as others. A large proportion of that subsidized breed known as "rural sociologists" betray a nostalgia traceable in many cases to their own childhood for the good old days when men loved the soil for itself. Indeed, Loomis and Beegle (12, p. 327) elaborate the following statement: "It is the thesis of the authors that the more land is used as a means of making money, rather than as a value in and of itself, the more it will be misused." Indices of "misuse" are stated to be degree of tenancy and the farm operator's equity in the land. We are not denying that there will be correlated differences according to degree of ownership; the question is whether such is "misuse." "The plow that broke the plains" created the rolling fields of golden wheat, but produced also the dust bowls of the thirties. The uprooted farmers of the latter in turn helped to reclaim the arid deserts of California and to create the pied orchards that are so dear to the inhabitants of that latter-day Eden.

When farmers settle, their motives are complex, but a large proportion of them are those who are uprooted from other areas and they come seeking greater economic opportunity, as Miner (14, p. 8) points out in the case of the corn farmers of Hardin County, Iowa. Attachment to the land is likely to come later and may be just as characteristic of tenants and migratory laborers as owners.

There is at least this substance to the nostalgias and emotings of students of farm life—the high frequency of ownership. There is probably no other work organization on earth in which ownership is so common. In the United States, over 60 per cent of persons directly involved in agriculture are owners or tenants in spite of the high cost of land and agricultural implements (cf. 21). In many areas the tenant owns everything except the land itself and has a status about as high as the owner, who may be an absentee landlord. In such a case the tenant is no different from the factory owner who rents his property from someone else—a common procedure.

The importance of ownership in the economic complex means that we must first give attention to the matter of land tenure.

LAND TENURE

In primitive village society, though there is usually private property in movable possessions, land is usually felt to be the property of the whole village and often a contribution is made to the over-all needs of the village for ritualistic occasions and for the headman, if there is such. In feudal society, the situation is complicated by the need for a large labor force. The latter might be slaves, who could be sold, or serfs, who are bound to the soil. The latter had the right to protection from theft and marauding.

With the break-up of feudalism, two parallel tendencies were set in motion: the emergence of a free but poor peasantry who owned tiny patches of land, and the emergence of huge estates, latifundia, which made use of hired labor or established a tenant system.

In the modern period, when westerners went out to conquer the world, various systems of land assignment were employed. T. Smith (17, pp. 246–52), following P. J. Treat, refers to a "principal type" of land division as "indiscriminate location." However, it is doubtful that land is ever divided in an indiscriminate manner. What is significant is the fact that in New England, Pennsylvania, and Virginia, it was customary for persons to select the best land they could find and make use for boundary definition of whatever "metes and bounds" were handiest at the time. The latter might be large rocks, ridges, or trees, which might be marked by temporary notch or the owner's initial carved into the bark of the tree. This system, however, may be quite satisfactory in a society living in villages as was the case in New England, and where people knew each other and the population was relatively constant. As new waves of migrants entered and as settlement pushed into the Appalachian valleys, the system of squatters proved inadequate, and led to much confusion.

Quite apart from such confusion was the fact that squatters usually choose only the very best land, which might mean cutting others off from access to needed resources. For example, a man could lay out his farm to lie lengthwise along an important river.

The first successful attempt to cope with the problem was made in the United States, in 1785, under the aegis of Thomas Jefferson. It was required that land be surveyed before it could be sold; a rectangular or square system of surveying by reference to fixed astronomical points was instituted. This gave birth to what is often regarded as the "typical" American farm, laid out in quarter, half, or full sections. The system did not, however, do away with squatting and problems of multiple ownership claims.

The rectangular system, with the farm house on the land, gave rise to serious problems of long distances between families and raised the costs of roads, education, electricity, and other group facilities. But these problems are probably inherent in the *size* of the farms rather than their layout as such. If farms are small, then it makes no difference whether they are laid out in squares, rectangles, circles, or parabolas; no one will be far from anyone else.

One other type of land division, which we have noted earlier, is the river-front system associated with the French, Spanish, and Portuguese (though it was also used by the English). The characteristic form is that of a number of thin strips laid out in wedge-shaped fashion. The result is to give all farmers access to a common base such as a river, both for water and for transportation. However, streams may meander a good deal or change their course in time. Nevertheless, where it was adopted it has usually been retained up to the present. Since houses were customarily located on the river bank, neighbors were close and interaction easy.

OWNERS, TENANTS, AND LABORERS

In new areas, land is bought and sold as a commodity and may change hands with fluctuation in price, weather, or consumer preference. But in old areas, such as French Canada, the name of the family is on the land and the land is passed on in the male line. In the self-sufficing farm regions of America, ownership is likely to persist at least for the lifetime of the resident.

The American owner enjoys the privilege of disposing of his land if he can, but the tenant enjoys the freedom of moving when he wishes, providing he can pay his debts. In the corn belt, tenancy is frequent and indeed is positively correlated with the value of the farm; owner farms tend to be of lower value than rented farms.

Smith (17, pp. 283–85) has suggested a useful classification of owners and tenants, applicable wherever private property in land is the custom. Farm operators are distinguished from farm laborers. Farm operators include owners, those who manage the farms of others, and renters. It is in connection with the latter that Smith proposes a change from the United States Census procedure. The Census places share tenants and share croppers in the category of farm operators. The latter, sometimes called "half hands," are given half of the crop. They are supplied with mules and implements. A man who has his own mule and implements is given a larger share and is known as a "share tenant." The main point is that neither of these two enjoy rights on the land comparable to tenants elsewhere. Their work is usually supervised very closely and they ordinarily do not have the right to grow what they please.

However, the problem is not solved by calling these persons laborers, for they share the risks of production to a major degree. A poor crop means poverty and debt for owner *and* cropper. This is not true of a hired laborer or of a migratory laborer who receives a fixed wage whatever the crop. It is perhaps best to create a special category called, "Share Tenants and Croppers." With this change we would then have the following classification:

I. Farm Operators
   A. Owners
   B. Managers
   C. Renters
      1. Cash—pay owner a fixed amount of money.
      2. Standing—pay owner a fixed amount of produce (bushels, bales, pounds). This means rent varies with price of such produce.
      3. Share—pay owner a fixed share of the crop—½, ¼, etc., but retain full tenant rights with reference to anything not forbidden in the lease.

II. Share Tenants and Croppers
   A. Share Tenants—pay owner a fixed share of crop. Have own farm implements and stock but operate under close supervision without right to initiate action unless permitted by the owner.
   B. Sharecroppers—like share tenant, but does not have own implements and stock.

III. Farm Laborers
   A. Wage Hands
   B. Unpaid Family Laborers

Broadly speaking, agriculturalists fall into two groups—those who have a direct interest in the harvest, and those who do not. In the former category are owner-operators, all classes of tenants, and unpaid family laborers. To these persons, the size of the harvest and the price of the crop are the major objects of attention. With the exception of the cropper, they also own the tools of production, provided no custom work is employed. These tools must be bought, paid for, and looked after. The average farmer must be a better than average mechanic. Learning to operate and repair at least some farm implements is a considerable part of the farmer's sons' education.

Those who do not have the same direct interest include managers and wage hands; they are paid a fixed sum whatever prices or weather conditions may be. The manager is comparable to the manager of a business anywhere; if poor profits are attributable to poor management, he may lose his job. The only important difference is that the number of persons under his control is small and thus he usually takes a share in many of the tasks on the farm.

Wage hands will be discussed below. Here we note that they fall into two major subcategories—temporary and permanent. Permanent hands include the "hired hand," found on many corn and dairy farms, and in ranching. He is paid a salary and is usually expected to perform any task that may be required. If he has a family, they often have a house on the farm.

Temporary workers include those hired as extra hands at peak periods and migratory laborers in agriculture which requires large numbers for the harvest period. The latter are usually paid on a piecework basis.

One person who is marginal to the wage hands is the labor contractor who is particularly important in the specialty crops of the far western states and in the cotton crops of Oklahoma and Texas. Usually he is of the same nationality, ethnicity, or class as the migratory laborer and acts as an agent for them through the grower. He arranges work schedules, provides for transportation and often housing, supervises work, and often pays the workers. He is paid a fixed sum by the grower but may also work in the harvest himself. His marginal position as a straw boss gives him bargaining power which he may use to enhance his position. We shall have more to say about him in Chapter Sixteen where we deal with Ethnic Relations.

SHARING WORK

The farm is customarily a family enterprise; the division of labor is based primarily on sex and age. Adult men usually concern themselves with the field crops and with activities requiring long-range planning; women are concerned with barnyard activities, small gardens, milking, and the making—and often sale as well—of butter. Boys usually assist the father and girls the mother. This pattern is found even on the largest and most highly mechanized farms in the United States. Indeed, it is mechanization itself that makes it possible for a single family to run a five hundred acre wheat farm.

In farms that are not highly mechanized—and that includes most farms—the large family is a labor necessity. At peak periods even they may not be equal to the task. Consequently, throughout the world there is usually a patterned relation among neighbors for mutual aid and the sharing of work. We have described in Chapter Two the practice of cooring among farmers of County Clare in Eire. In the United States, especially in the early days, the quilting bee and the husking bee were characteristic of New England.

Two factors of significance about neighbor-sharing work should be noted.

1. PATTERNED RELATIONS

One does not help just anyone. In Ireland, the cooring relation is restricted to "friends," that is, extended kin and those one feels close to. Elsewhere matters of nationality, origin, ethnicity, race, religion and recency of settlement may enter in.[10]

Basically, the selection of sharing-partners rests on stability. One finds it only where farmers have been on their farms for long periods, perhaps generations, and where they have come to trust each other. Farmers must feel a sense of colleagueship with each other before they establish work-sharing ties.

The relation also implies mutual confidence. Before a farmer will accept help and let others onto his farm, he must feel that the others will do a good job, give their full cooperation, and not abuse or steal some of the produce.

There are more important matters in which trust is involved. When you let a man on your farm, into your barns, into your house (for share partners are almost always fed) and let him use your animals and machinery, he gains knowledge of intimate matters about which he must be trusted to maintain silence. The state of repair of the machines may suggest that the farmer is skimping on them. Then when they all sit down to dinner, the share partner may notice that the farmer's wife has been indulging herself in fripperies, such as city-bought window drapes or "modern" furniture. That helps explain the poor state of the machines. Helping in herding cattle permits a close scrutiny of the cattle and estimates can then be made of the owner's knowledge of feed and his competence as a cattle raiser. Through sharing work farmers are thus enabled to size each other up as farmers and farm operators. That in turn builds confidence and helps knit the group more closely together.

2. ABSENCE OF MONEY

In sharing work, no money is paid out for help, although any children involved may get a few pennies with which to buy candy. The payment of money signifies a totally different relation. Money is paid to hired hands and casual laborers, who do what they are paid to do and no more. Their relation is entirely segmented and contractual. In the harvest labor

---

[10] Gladys H. Carroll, in her realistic novel of dairy farmers, *As the Earth Turns*, has described the reluctance of neighbors to help out a new Polish settler family in securing ice. See also (2, pp. 41 ff.).

of California, the grower may not even meet any of his laborers except the labor contractor.

In Eire, it will be recalled, cooring is a duty. A person setting out to help a "friend" will say: "I have right to go." That is the same expression that is used when setting out to attend a wedding, a funeral, or to assist in any crisis. But the relation is by no means uneconomic; it is to the farmer's interest to help others since he can then count on their helping him.

But such considerations miss the symbolic significance of work sharing. Money does not pass and a farmer would feel insulted if some were offered to him. He would interpret that as meaning that the farmer offering him money does not plan to help out in *his* farm work when his turn comes. It would mean the end of the share-work relation. As such, the lack of money payment serves as a means of recognizing those who have share-work understandings with each other. It acts to proclaim the strength and permanence of the symbiotic tie that unites them.

The ties established in sharing work provide the basis for more generalized visiting and friendship. Indeed, researchers have learned to ask the farmer whom he helps or shares work with (12, Ch. 5, pp. 150–51). These turn out also to be his friends and their wives and his wife's friends. These are also the persons who customarily visit each other; and visiting is a major recreation among farmers, owing largely to the physical isolation that farming often involves. A recent development that represents a compromise between work sharing and wage labor is custom work.

WAGE LABOR

Agriculture is the world's largest consumer of labor. In spite of mechanization and the profound rural-to-urban trend, this holds true also for the United States. About one-ninth of the U.S. labor force is involved primarily in agriculture—almost 7 million of the population fourteen years old and over (18). In the peak periods of the year the number may be almost double. Of this vast number, those working for salary or wages make up only about one-fifth. Farm operators and their families constitute the other four-fifths. But the latter do not account for the largest proportion of farm products produced: in 1944, one-tenth of the farms provided nearly one-half of all agricultural produce; and it is on these farms that hired labor is most used.[11]

[11] Our discussion focusses on those who work for wages. The Census and most discussions of farm labor include the category of "unpaid family labor" when there is little point in doing so. The ability of the farmer to use his own wife and children varies according to type of crop and location. But in any case, to include the family in the same category as the migratory and the casual laborer does not make much sense. The relation to the "employer" is fundamentally different.

The thread that runs through the entire agricultural labor fabric is that of peak demands. Granted that all work organizations exhibit diurnal, seasonal, or longer-term swings of labor demands, and that some types of diversified agriculture do not show profound swings; it remains true that no other industry even resembles most agriculture in the violence of the seasonal swings. In the Yakima Valley of Washington, before World War II, the number needed during the peak demand in the hop, apple, and other crops was seventy times that needed at the trough of low demand (9, p. 448).

With the exception of California, Texas, and Florida, where winter fruits and vegetables are grown, this labor need is concentrated in the non-winter seasons, especially in the summer. The needs of farms for hired labor are, however, highly variable. Only about 9 per cent of farms in the United States employ as much as one man year of labor, only 3⅓ per cent employ the equivalent of two laborers a year, and 1 per cent require as much as five man-years of hired labor (16; 19, p. 285). Most farmers do not employ any labor, and some that do, employ laborers only for brief periods. The vast proportion of wage laborers work for a very few farmers. In September, 1945, seven-tenths of all hired workers worked on farms employing four or more hired workers, and about one-half of them worked in crews (17, p. 291). This is far from the picture often presented of each farmer with his good, faithful hired hand.

Wage laborers may be classified in four categories as follows:

1. THE HIRED MAN

Though romanticized, he does in fact exist and is found on the large farm particularly if the farm is diversified, as for example in dairying, corn, and also in fruit. He is rare in the South where the share cropper is likely to take his place. He may live in the farmer's house or be given a house on the farmer's land. His scarcity, the lack of nearness to other hired men, and social distance from the owner make him isolated. He is therefore likely to seek associates in nearby towns.

2. RESIDENT LABOR FORCE

This includes persons who live in town, do odd jobs, or have part-time work, and get their major income in times of cultivation or harvest. In the South many persons work as maids and cooks and then go out to chop or pick cotton. This group includes farmers who may seek work in nearby areas when there is little for them to do on their own farm. A large number of these are found in the great "sugar bowl" area whose farmers depend on persons recruited from the cotton belt and nearby towns and who are able to offer continuous employment from October to January.

3. CASUAL LABORERS

This category includes a very large number who work for extra money, e.g., students and housewives. It also includes persons who are temporarily unemployed in urban factories, and hoboes.

4. MIGRATORY LABORERS

These include single men, men away from their families, and whole families. The migratory laborer follows the crops as much as possible, and agricultural labor then becomes a way of life. The most significant groups are the Negroes, Mexicans, Spanish Americans, and Puerto Ricans who are unable to get other work, but a large number of native white Americans are included. These include many who were dispossessed from their farms and who continued in farming because it is the only work they know. Owing to the importance of ethnicity in this category it will be discussed in more detail in the chapter on ethnic relations.

Taylor (19, pp. 289–90) has described the major American labor migration currents. There is the great wheat belt migration which moves from Texas to Canada and which was important between the years 1900 and 1920, when mechanization removed the need for 250 thousand men. Second, there are the cotton migrations from Mexico to Oklahoma and from Mississippi to North Carolina. Third are the berry crop migrants from the Gulf of Mexico to the strawberries of north Florida to the grapes and peaches of northern Michigan. Another important migration includes the eastern coastal migrants from Florida to New Jersey to pick peaches, vegetables, and truck products. Finally there is the California fruit and truck migration which is perhaps the largest of all, involving migration to California, north to the Willamette and Yakima Valleys, and into the beet fields of Montana, for which 188 thousand persons were recruited in 1935.

Most farms require such labor for very short periods, ranging from two or three days to two or three weeks. Then the workers must move on.

The remuneration of hired labor is very low. It runs to about 50 per cent of what unskilled industrial workers get. Migratory laborers in general get more per hour than others and the hired man is likely to get more per year. The lowness of the income is due primarily to the following four factors: (1) The lack of steady work. (2) The piece-rate system. This system forces the maintenance of a furious pace and means that any number of workers can be employed, making it difficult for any one person to make much money. (3) The lack of organization. Migratory laborers include such a heterogeneous and mobile group that there is little chance for interaction and for the development of *esprit de corps*. (4) The inclusion of disadvantaged groups. A large proportion are Negroes and Mexicans who are discriminated against in other work and therefore are forced to work at low wages. This operates to keep everyone else's earnings down.

Hourly or yearly cash earnings do not present the full picture. Laborers often get "perquisites" such as housing, the yield of a potato patch, or fuel. On the other hand, there are serious hidden expenses: the cost of travel; cost of an automobile; the fact that the workers are forced to take whatever is available and therefore to pay higher prices; and most important, the lack of any employment while the individual or family is traveling, which is tantamount to expense.

Expenses and perquisites roughly balance off, and farm laborers remain among the poorest paid workers in the nation. They are continually on the move which means that they are unable to get unemployment compensation, are deprived of legislative protection, have poor and unsanitary housing, lack adequate medical care, lack an opportunity to send their children to school, and are continually forced to battle the antagonism and prejudice of the community in which they are transients. As the President's Commission on Migratory Labor said of them: "As crops ripen, farmers anxiously await their coming; as the harvest closes, the community, with equal anxiety, awaits their going."

The number of agricultural laborers fluctuates, and is related to opportunities for alternative employment, mechanization, type of crop and harvest practices, and to changes in those practices. Commercialization and the use of one crop increases the seasonal swing of agriculture and therefore the need for more workers for shorter periods of time. When mechanization enters (and it often goes with commercialization), fewer workers are needed. Fruit farming represents a maximum commercialization and specialization without mechanization; that is why that industry exhibits such a hunger for workers. Mechanization or commercialization in one crop may dispossess farmers, who then become migratory or casual laborers in another farm area. This is true, for example, in the invasion of the self-sufficing areas by dairying.

Mechanization is usually applied first to cultivation and related tasks; the harvest is likely to be mechanized last of all, as we see in the case of cotton in Oklahoma and Texas. The result is to create the need for a large number of workers for that short harvest period. But if the mechanical cotton picker becomes generally used, then cotton will go the way of wheat, and with it, probably, will go the share cropper.

Mechanization and commercialization, however, are not all-engulfing trends. The self-sufficient farm is still common in certain areas; e.g., mechanization has made almost no progress in the fruit harvest, and there we may expect to see the farm laborer for a long time to come.

MONEY AND THE RURAL-URBAN COMPLEX

Farming includes unpredictable or poorly controlled elements which make planning of any kind difficult. The farmer plants so many acres and then hopes for the best. Weather, insects, and moisture may make the difference between a poor and a bumper crop. These risks, combined with the use of hand labor and destructive soil practices, account for the fact that farmers are rarely wealthy (except in the rich river valleys); and the vast majority live at the subsistence level.

But when the soil is fertile and agriculture comes more under human control through the use of machinery, fertilizer, insecticides, and the growth of specialized and specially bred crops, then the farmer begins to produce a surplus. With this surplus comes cash.

At first the cash may be used to improve the farmer's standard of living and to buy luxuries. But as the farmer shifts increasingly to the cash crop, he needs money for the farm itself. Machines must be repaired or replaced with new ones, fertilizer and insecticides cost money, and the growth of a paying crop requires large acreages. He thus becomes more dependent on his cash crop and becomes more specialized.

At the same time he comes to recognize that the difference between poverty and wealth is determined by the bidding of men in the stock markets of Chicago, New York, Portland, and New Orleans, who know nothing about farming and care little about it. In the 1870's, he discovered that the wheat for which he got fifteen cents a bushel sold for seventy-five cents in New York. An attempt was made then to control this process. One consequence was the "green rising" that swept Europe after the First World War. In the United States, farmers have fought the railroads to try to get lower rates and have organized cooperative buying and selling companies, factories, banks, and insurance companies. Organizations such as The Grange, The Farmers' Alliance, The American Society of Equity, The Farmers' Union, The Non Partisan League, and The American Farm Bureau Federation have fought for those objectives and have tried to influence legislation. The Greenback and Populist movements were largely agrarian. With all of these developments, the picture of the independent farmer hoeing his patch of potatoes and "beholden unto no man" becomes caricature and fantasy. The farmers become a pressure group ("the farm bloc") with enormous influence in Washington. Louis Wirth [12] once stated that the farmers in the United States were the closest to being a social class on the model of the European classes. The farmer is caught up in the total society.

At the same time, cash binds the farmer to urban producers and markets. The refrigerator, the electric stove, and the automobile are not considered luxuries but part of normal expectations. He looks to the city for money and with that money buys what the city has to sell. And the city has not only agricultural implements and fertilizer but also movies, fashions, and ideas. If the farmer can resist, his children often cannot. And

[12] Lectures, University of Chicago, ca. 1945.

with the inability to absorb its own population, the country pours out its daughters first (to whom the farm offers least) and then its sons.

The city takes the farmer's money and his children. In exchange it gives him automobiles, movies, and "modern" furniture. To many farmers this seems like a bad bargain. Yet the farmer is caught in a cash nexus which holds him rigidly. Within it he finds it difficult to retain the love of the soil or to cherish the first green shoots. The corn farmer feeds his crop to his pigs and the Baptist teetotaler sells his grain to produce whiskey.

The urbanite may laugh at the "rube" and the farmer may smile tolerantly at the "city slicker." But they are intimately bound together; and though it is an uneasy marriage, the prospect of divorce is nil. The trend seems to be manifest all over the world, at least wherever Westerners go.

CHAPTER REFERENCES

1. Blumenstock, D. I. and Thornthwaite, C. W., "Climate and the World Pattern," in *Climate and Man*, U.S. Government Printing Office, 1941.

1a. Brown, H. B., *Cotton*, New York: McGraw-Hill, 1938.

2. Burnet, J., *Next-Year Country*, Toronto: University of Toronto Press, 1951.

3. Carroll, G. H., *As The Earth Turns*, New York, Macmillan, 1933.

4. Chapple, E. D., and Coon, C. S., *Principles of Anthropology*, New York: Holt, 1942.

5. Croy, H., *Corn Country*, New York: Duell, Sloan and Pearce, 1947.

6. Dubbé, M. C., *Grains of Wheat*, Caldwell, Ida.: Caxton, 1934.

6a. Fenneman, N. M., *Physiography of Eastern United States*, New York: McGraw-Hill, 1938.

6b. ———, *Physiography of Western United States*, New York: McGraw-Hill, 1931.

7. Georgia Supreme Court, *Appling vs. Odum*, 46 Georgia Reports, 1872.

8. Hack, J., "The Changing Environment of the Hopi Indians of Arizona," *Peabody Museum Papers*, Cambridge, Massachusetts: 35, No. 1, 1942.

9. Landis, P. H., *Rural Life in Process*, New York: McGraw-Hill, 1948.

10. Leonard, O., and Loomis, C. P., *Culture of a Contemporary Rural Community, El Cerrito, New Mexico*, in Loomis, C. P., *Studies of Rural Social Organization in the United States, Latin America and Germany*, East Lansing, Mich., State College Book Store, 1945.

11. Linton, R., "Crops, Soils, and Culture in America," in *The Maya and Their Neighbors*, New York: D. Appleton-Century, 1940.

12. Loomis, C. P. and Beegle, J. A., *Rural Social Systems*, New York, Prentice-Hall, 1950.

13. Mangus, A. R., *Rural Regions of the United States,* Washington: U.S. Government Printing Office, 1940.

14. Miner, H., *Culture and Agriculture: An Anthropological Study of a Corn Belt County,* Occasional Contributions from the Museum of Anthropology of the University of Michigan, No. 14, Ann Arbor: University of Michigan Press, 1949.

15. National Industrial Conference Board, *The Economic Almanac, 1956,* New York, Crowell.

16. Smith, T. L., "The Agricultural Population: Realism vs. Nominalism in the the Census of Agriculture," *Journal of Farm Economics,* **20**:679–687, 1938.

16a. ———, *Brazil, People and Institutions,* Baton Rouge: Louisiana State University Press, 1946.

17. ———, *The Sociology of Rural Life,* New York: Harper, 1953.

17a. Stark, M. C. and Whittelsey, D. S., *Major Geographic Regions of North America,* Bloomington: McNight and McNight, 1923.

18. *Statistical Abstract of the United States, 1955,* Washington: U.S. Government Printing Office, 1955, Table No. 218.

19. Taylor, C. C., *et al., Rural Life in the United States,* New York: Knopf, 1949.

20. Thane, E. (pseud. for Henry, R. C.), *High Border Country,* New York: Duell, Sloan and Pearce, 1942.

21. 1950 U.S. Census of Population, "Occupational Characteristics," Special Report P-E No. 1B, Table 1.

22. Vance, R. B., *Human Factors in Cotton Culture,* Chapel Hill: University of North Carolina Press, 1929.

22a. Willis, J. C., *Agriculture in the Tropics,* Cambridge: The University Press, 1909.

23. Wirth, L., *Lectures,* University of Chicago, 1945.

CHAPTER NINE

THE FARM: STATUS, CAREER, AND THE WORK GROUP

THE STATUS AND AUTHORITY SYSTEM OF FARMING

STATUS IN FARMING

In studies of the United States rural population, there is a tendency to see farmers as a group without major distinctions of power, prestige, and economic class. The home of democracy is nostalgically found in the New England town; the Midwest is felt to be the backbone of the nation. The farmer is looked upon as a plain fellow who works hard and has little use for urban status symbols and luxuries.

This attitude seems to be based on two main factors. First, agriculture historically in some parts of the world has shown the most highly and rigidly stratified systems ever known to man. European feudalism was based on rights in the land and aristocracies generally have maintained themselves by land ownership. The distinction between the feudal lord and the serf was so great that the near-absence in the case of American agriculture of any distinction that even comes close to it [1] has led researchers to consider that such distinctions as are found are unimportant. This is true by *comparison,* but real status distinctions are still made, and at least in the case of cotton were and still are of major significance.[2] Second, the United States is almost unique in having had a great expanse of land which the settler could have almost for the asking. This helped prevent the development of rigid strata.[3]

---

[1] With one major exception to be noted presently.

[2] Cf. (10, 32, 38).

[3] In so saying, we are not espousing the labor safety-valve theory which, as we document elsewhere (pp. 181–182), has been largely discredited. We are referring here only to farmers and not to workers in general.

To some extent, of course, it is true that status distinctions are not pronounced among United States farmers. In the early period of settlement, isolation was important in preventing severe barriers from developing. The farmer needed his neighbors and his neighbors needed him for mutual help. There was a need for a participation of *all* members of the community in organizations such as schools and churches, in order to make them possible at all. The forced self-sufficiency and lack of commercialization in the early period produced an emphasis on independence and individual effort. Later, when the farmer did begin to sell his crops in the cities, the long distances made the railways a common enemy and helped foster a sense of solidarity among farmers. Other factors were the lack of a feudal tradition in the United States (outside of the South) and the speed with which the country was settled. Also, the fact that agriculture in the United States required manual labor and the existence of a sparse population threw the onus on the owner himself to perform this labor. Dispersed settlement helped to prevent the development of villages and towns, particularly in the West; this was of significance since towns are often the locus for the development of status distinctions. In the town, with occupational differences and great heterogeneity, different styles of life can emerge. In agriculture areas where almost all residents are farmers, then, there is likely to be greater equality. Also the hardness of the life and the existence of self-sufficiency meant that there were not great income differences found in the average farm area. There was little money left over for goods and practices that could differentiate one group from another.

But all that we have said merely means that there is not great *rigidity* in status relations among U.S. farmers and true status groups are difficult to find. But distinctions exist and are important. And the study of stratification among farmers is valuable because in most stratification studies occupation is a variable, while among farmers, occupation is close to being a constant.

As in other work organizations, status is attached to all aspects of agriculture. Every action is tinged with a conception of right and wrong, with a conception of who ought to perform the act, and with conceptions of obligations and duties. But perhaps more than in other work organizations, status in agriculture tends to revolve about the twin factors of *permanence* and *stability*.

Sheer age of the work structure as such contributes little to prestige among urban industries. The man who has run a grocery store for thirty-five years enjoys respect and can tell many tales to youngsters of the changes he has seen, but he bows to the industrialist whose plant may be only fifteen years old. Though a family in the same business for two or three generations may have high prestige, it is likely to be inherent in the *family* rather than in the business as such. But the man who has been farming for ten years has higher prestige than one who has been farming for only five years, and the man who has farmed the *same* farm for five years is likely to have higher prestige than the man who has changed farms in the last five years. These factors run through prestige and ranking like a river, here broad and almost engulfing the rank system, there narrowing but never quite disappearing.

The importance of permanence and stability is related to the fact that farming as a work activity involves waiting. It is difficult to jump in and out of agriculture. Further, the farm involves management skills; only persons who feel that they have these skills are likely to enter agriculture, and they are likely to have acquired these skills from their own fathers. Important also, as pointed out above, is the fact that the isolation of the farmers forces a close integration of agriculture with church, school, politics, friendship, and other areas of life. These total relations take time to build. The farmer needs time to appraise the newcomer. The farmers who come and go are not known and are moral isolates in the agricultural community. One cannot size up a farmer by his clothes, by his automobile, or by his house, as is often done in urban areas. It is usually necessary to wait a year, to see what kind of crop he produces, to see how he works or how he manages his farm, how he sells his produce.

Permanence and stability are not unidimensional determinants of rank. Rather, they underlie and color a wide variety of other factors of which the more important are the following:

1. TENURE

In general, the hierarchy among farmers is: owners, tenants, laborers. And this is a stability hierarchy too. Owners are likely to remain on the land the longest, tenants next, and laborers are likely to move the most of all.

In our society, the owner tends to have higher status than does the tenant, because of the capitalistic value placed on private property and also because the owner possesses power to rent or not to rent and to select his tenant. The tenant exercises some freedom in the selection of an owner but he has no choice in whether he shall rent or not. He is there at the owner's sufferance.

The relationship between owner and tenant is not an invariant one. Schuler (37) found that while differences between owners and tenants were very great in the cotton belt, they were much less so in the corn belt. The tenant there often had as high prestige as did the owner; sometimes the "owner" is a corporation.

Of significance is how much actual day-to-day control the owner has over the tenant. In the case of the southern sharecropper this control is close and involves the use of tools, techniques of planting, and even expenditures on personal pleasure. In the corn belt, the tenant is more likely to pay a straight cash rent and the relation to the owner is more likely to be a segmented one. As such it approximates that present in many large factories and shops that rent their grounds or store space.

The highest point of status and the closest thing to a genuine aristocracy that the United States has ever seen was provided by the planter-owners in the antebellum South. They owned large amounts of land and slaves as well; they spent much time away from the plantation at resorts or in travel; their children did not work and were usually well educated; leisure was a value and manual labor was regarded as degrading. The southern planters were the originators of "southern hospitality," though it was likely to be extended only to members of their own class. As Smith (41, p. 399) says, *elegance* most fully describes their way of life.

Gray (12, pp. 481–507) distinguishes between this group and the owner group who were commercial farmers in the lowlands and who practiced general farming there. They usually owned only a small number of slaves. Next down were the "hillbillies" or "red necks" of the highlands. They practiced self-sufficiency farming and are still an important group in Kentucky and Tennessee and throughout the general and self-sufficing farm area. This group owned no slaves and worked their own fields with the aid of their families. At the bottom of the white hierarchy were the "poor whites." These tended to live on the fringes of the plantations and practiced general, self-sufficient farming. They also depended heavily on hunting and fishing for their food. This group is the only one which is in serious competition with the Negroes in the South.

Tenants are also divided in ranks. As stated above, status reflects the degree of owner-control of the tenant. At the top are the cash renters. Except for the payment of rent, they are independent and operate the farm completely on their own initiative. Next are the standing and share renters who pay the owner a fixed or proportional amount of produce. They do not turn out to be greatly different from cash renters since in practice the produce is simply converted to money. It is, however, a variable depending on the price of the produce. As such, the owner is somewhat more interested in the agricultural practices of the tenant. The share tenant and cropper work under close control and have much lower prestige as renters. They also exhibit much movement in a search for better farms or landlords.

Among the wage laboring group we observe again the importance of permanence and stability. At the top stand the small group of steadily employed hired hands. Next in line are the part-time laborers who live in town and work at other jobs, doing farm work in season. They are in the neighborhood but are not attached to a given farm. At the bottom are the migratory laborers, who are the least permanent of all. They are not members of the community at all, are the objects of strong prejudice, and their position is often made worse by racial factors.

2. SIZE OF FARM

The importance of size of farm varies in different places. At an extreme point there is an aristocracy, characterized by huge holdings, overseers, and a large number of slaves, serfs, or workers; this leads to an almost complete rigidity with status determined at birth. Though this extreme does not exist in the United States at present, it is still true that the very large plantations in the South, the large wheat farms, and the large fruit ranches of the West mean high prestige for the owners—but it is a money-based rather than a family-based prestige. High prestige is achieved by participation in urban associational life, and it is the high income and the resulting leisure that make that association possible. This leads us to a third factor:

3. RELATION TO URBAN POPULATION

In general, the commercialized farm producing for sale in the urban market has higher status than does the self-sufficient farm. Here the farmer competes with the urban population for available values that are the symbols of success, and takes his place as a small entrepreneur with a stock of machinery and capital. Also, an increasing number of farmers are becoming part-time farmers and take industrial or other employment or else operate businesses in the city.[4] As such they assume a marginal status position in the city as laborers or small businessmen.

4. RACE AND ETHNICITY

In farming, as elsewhere, race cuts across all other status determinants. Whatever else a farmer may be, if he is also a Negro his position is severely limited though he may achieve high status in the Negro community. Race and ethnic origin are especially important in two major U.S. crop areas—cotton and the western specialty crops. In the former, the Negro is still a major disadvantaged group, and in the latter Negroes, Mexicans, and Filipinos form the bulk of the laboring group.

In corn and dairying, priority of immigration was and is important. The early migrants secured the best land and learned the customs earlier. They could then look down on late comers as "greenhorns" and "bohunks." Language differences helped crystallize such distinctions.

The presence of these groups in agriculture serves to bring out the fact that the farm is one of the major places where peoples meet. In the cotton fields of the United States South, the cantaloupe orchards of

---

[4] See (6, Ch. 1, IV; 22, pp. 246–52; 33; 50).

California, the rubber plantations of Indonesia and the sugar plantations of Hawaii, Negroes, whites, and mongoloids meet and compete for scarce values. With this meeting has gone the breakup of cultures and the awakening of nationalism, as native peoples suddenly find themselves despised aliens in their own land. When native-born Ma Joad in *The Grapes of Wrath* fearfully tells her family: "They call us Okies," she is repeating what agricultural peoples the world over have said about their latter-day conquerors.

In sum, then, tenure, size of farm, relation to the urban population, and race and ethnicity appear definitely to produce status distinctions in agriculture. But what is the *degree* to which stratification has gone in American agriculture? Do farmers form a social class, or are they approaching such a position? If we think of a social class as a group with objective distinctions in level of living and with a sense of identity and self-consciousness, then we can make the following statements about farmers. In societies where agriculture is the major occupation it is difficult to think of farmers as a separate group at all. There usually is a small middle class of traders, craftsmen, and priests, and perhaps an overlord group of land-owners or nobility, as in Hawaii (24, pp. 31–6). These distinctions may express themselves in a caste form. But the farmers as such do not form a caste or a class there. Rather, caste or class distinctions are inherent in differential rights on the land.

In Western and especially American society, the flowering of specialization and urbanization has meant that farmers have become distinguished as a specialized group. They have also come to be tied up with and dependent on the urban population. This raises the question of their position vis-à-vis the urban population.

Bell (3) in his study of Shellstone, Iowa, an agricultural community, found that the town banker and his business associates were accorded the top position in the entire community. The banker was looked to for advice and help in business affairs by farmers and for aid in emergencies. Next in line were the town businessmen and professionals who had been in the town for some time. Next down were farm landowners, then farm renters, and last occasional laborers. The most remarkable feature of this system is that in it we see quite distinct urban-rural strata, although Bell says that the landowners and businessmen tended to merge.

Duncan and Artis (8, 37) in their study of a rural community in Pennsylvania found that farmers had community prestige scores close to the over-all average. They were below the village businessmen, the white-collar workers and the professionals, but were above the blue-collar factory employees. But this was only true of the farm owners. Farm tenants scored lower than any other group except laborers, with whom they were tied for bottom score. Similarly, Kaufman, in a study of a dairy and poultry township in central New York, found the "mean prestige" of farm operators to be below that of the professions, operators of "large" businesses, clerical workers and stenographers, and operators of "small" businesses, but above that of "store" clerks, skilled and semiskilled workers and laborers in general. Farm laborers had the lowest "mean prestige" of any occupational group (20, p. 10).

The farmer cannot everywhere be assigned such a position. The sidewalk wheat farmer or the large-scale grape grower in California may occupy a position of considerable importance in the town. However, such farmers achieve these positions by *moving out* of the rural structure and by joining associations and interacting in the urban world. They must learn the urban values and how to achieve them.

Farmers, then, in general occupy lower economic, prestige, and power positions than do urbanites; and because of the smallness of their numbers, the similarity of their occupation, and their common dependence on the urban market, there has tended to grow up a profound solidarity among them. Common cause is made by men who grow plums, wheat, hogs, cotton, and tobacco which cut across political party traditions and even racial attitudes.

The commercial farmers are one of the best organized groups in the United States, far exceeding in solidarity the wildest dreams of industrial labor leaders. Their influences are exerted on political and economic organizations, and through the fact that they are the only occupational group in the United States to have its own cabinet minister. This group is not a social class—on the model of European social classes—yet many of the elements necessary are present. It would be a paradox indeed if the U.S. farmer—prototype of the small, independent entrepreneur—should become a self-conscious social class.

TEACHING AND LEARNING IN FARMING

In peasant societies, the status of farmer is, for males, ascribed. There may, of course, be some specialization. In County Clare, for example, there is the storekeeper, the policeman, the priest, the teacher, and a few part-time specialists. Most men, however, are farmers and even though the question of who inherits the farm is uncertain, the sons stay on the farm until maturity and often many years later. There is thus no question, while they are young, of an immediate career choice. The boy must learn to be a farmer; there is only one place where he can learn this, and that is on the farm itself under tutelage of the father.

The latter is true to a great extent of farming everywhere. There are few other work activities which can be separated from the real situation less than is the case in farming. When agriculture as a separate specialty turns up in our culture, specialized education functions in a consultative manner. The agricultural college *assists* farmers, it does not produce them. Almost to a man, the students in agriculture at such colleges are the sons of farmers, or else they grew up on a farm and have come to acquire knowledge that will make them better farmers than they already are. There are exceptions, such as the agricultural engineer, the agricultural chemist, or the irrigation engineer. These are likely to be found as state employees or on very large farms, and are more properly regarded as agricultural specialists rather than as farmers.

The power relation between father and son is clear and is determined by family position and age. The father possesses the ability to reward and punish by utilizing off-the-job values. A job well done means a treat: the son is permitted to drive the horses to market or to drive the tractor or to own a colt of his own.

More significant than mere manual skills are other things the son must learn:

1. ENTREPRENEURIAL SKILLS

The son learns to buy and sell. This is especially important in commercialized agriculture (though no farm is ever *completely* self-sufficient). He must learn to appraise a calf at market, learn how to bargain, know what price is reasonable. The farm includes machinery, stock, buildings on large farms, laborers, and the land itself. The son must learn the care of these things, how they are bought and paid for, and how to apportion expenses wisely among them.

2. ADJUSTMENT TO ROUTINES

Farming is cyclical, as we have pointed out. The son must not simply learn what to do daily and seasonally, but he must develop an adjustment to a rhythmic way of life. He may want to go into town with his girlfriend, but when the harvest is on, he may have to work until midnight if weather forecasts are discouraging. He must learn to give up other wants without regrets or complaints. The son must learn to accept the idea of peak periods when everything but work is forgotten, and slack periods when he can visit or go fishing. And this is not simply a matter of *postponing* immediate pleasures. Rather it is a matter of *thinking* of work and pleasure seasonally. Christmas is visiting time; the harvest period is the harvest period.

3. RELATION BETWEEN FAMILY AND FARM

There is normally a division of labor. There is man's work and women's work. The son must learn the difference, learn to regard certain work as his and to take pride in it. More, he must, on the family farm, learn to balance the needs of the family and of the farm. He must learn to decide questions such as whether to buy a new set of draperies for the living room or get the tractor motor overhauled, whether to buy new seat covers for the family car or to try out the latest fertilizer. Most often these questions are decided in the favor of the farm. Then the son must learn, by listening quietly from his bed at night, how to handle the violent complaints that the farm wife may make about the decision. It is unfortunate that the great lovers of fiction are almost always urbanites who spend their time on balconies or in apartments. It takes a skillful lover indeed to convince a woman that fertilizer is more important than permanent hairwaves, and that the perfect expression of love is a new set of piston rings on the tractor.

4. THE SOIL AND SENTIMENT

Part of the process of becoming a farmer is the development of a love for growing things. In two respects farming is distinctive although not unique: It deals with living things and not with dead metal parts, and the farmer produces a relatively complete product. Work is meaningful in the extreme; there is no question of the value of the farmer's work to society. And though the farmer on the large-scale, commercialized farm may develop a segmented attitude to crops as representing profits, yet there is a feeling of gladness when the first green shoots come up out of the ground and when the wheat turns golden.

And there is more to this than the fact that they may mean a good profit. They represent a confirmation of the farmer's ability as a manager and mean the good opinion of his neighbors. Unquestionably space is important in this context. It is one thing for the tailor to stand back and look at a well-finished pair of trousers. But it is qualitatively different for the farmer to stand on a hill and look at the acre after acre of corn receding into the horizon. To that must be added the beauty of the natural setting, the clear air, the blue sky, and the pied crops themselves—the yellow and green corn, pink apples, crimson cherries, golden wheat, white cotton, purple plums. Indeed, one infallible sign that one has moved from one farm region to another is that the color of the entire landscape changes. Of course, the farmer spends very little of his time lolling about on grassy hills. But the beauty is there and only the obtuse farmer could miss it.

The emotional attachment to farming is created through informal means. One of the most important means is through ceremonies and occasions when families must come together because of the cyclical character of farming. In former times these included husking bees, the Mardi Gras, and other ceremonies associated with the fruitfulness of the earth.

Before mechanization, the need to share work was important and still is on most farms. This means a coming together of all men and often of women as well. It is an occasion for hilarity, competition, joking, praise and good-natured joshing. These are highly significant occasions for the boy. Everyone is cooperative and happy, and the spirit of friendliness and fellowship infects him as well. Often something exciting or semi-tragic happens—a wagon overturns and injures someone or two men get into a fight—and these become events by which to fix time: "Your aunt died the same year that Silas broke his arm when the wagon fell into the river."

These are also occasions when the son develops social skills. The son learns how to get along with fellow-workers, and what to laugh at and what to be silent about, what to say to boys and what to say to girls. He also secures a sense of importance and a pride, for here are all these people "Just to help us harvest our corn."

5. LEARNING TO BEHAVE LIKE A FARMER

To grow up on a farm and to work the yearly round means also acquiring a set of habits and attitudes. The son develops the interests peculiar to farming—concern about the weather, hatred toward insects, anxiety about prices, resentment toward urbanites. He becomes integrated into the visiting pattern. He learns whom it is proper to call on and when, how to behave in someone else's house or on someone else's farm. He goes to church (and that is both a religious and a recreational occasion). He may join the 4-H club and later the Grange or the Bureau and learn of the common interests of farmers the country over. He develops attitudes in politics. He learns who the farmer can trust, the value of parity, the importance of controlling prices of farm implements, and the importance of the tariff on Argentine beef.

The growing farm boy must learn finally the view of farming as an occupation that is characteristic of his crop. In wheat this means learning to "take the good with the bad," in cotton the value of ownership, in corn, the importance of good management, in dairying, the importance of steadiness. It is just these behavior traits and attitudes that the urbanite finds hard to understand and which he does not feel even when he spends time on a farm. To learn them requires growing up on a farm and coming to look on farming not simply as a living but as a way of life.

Mechanization and other developments on the farm have *simplified* rather than complicated farm work. They have tended to reduce labor needs and to reduce time. They may act therefore to reduce the actual learning that the farm son needs. It probably takes less skill to run a tractor than it does to hitch and drive a team of mules.

Such developments make farming more specialized and commercialized and therefore to emphasize the entrepreneurial aspects and to make of the farm less of a family business. The training is still on the job and from the father but it is likely to be more concerned with buying and selling and with farm administration.

A farm hired hand is likely to be a son of a farmer and to have learned his job at home. For the migratory worker, the worker is kept unskilled and therefore requires relatively little training. But he must learn which crops to follow and where, how to find out about good pickings, and how to make a remunerative deal with a labor contractor. These are social skills and unfortunately have not been studied. Fisher (9, pp. 28–9), however, tells us how the Japanese in California drove the Chinese out of the fruit and vegetable market. They bound themselves into units, systematically underbid the Chinese, and even adopted the labor union tactics of the quickie strike and a refusal to scab on each other.

Migratory workers often travel as whole families and pick crops where the whole family can work. As such there is a transmission of skills from father to son as is the case in agriculture generally.

WORK CONTROLS IN FARMING

The control of farm work and the folkways and mores of farmers as farmers exhibits two distinctive features:

1. CLOSE RELATION OF FAMILY TO WORK

The farmer usually does not "go to work." He is always nearby (except when he is in town) and normally eats his meals at home. The work group is the family usually, and therefore family controls are present at all times. There is nothing corresponding to the "office romance" in farming. It is not easy for the father to dissemble or to give his son moral instructions at night which may be different from his own behavior. He must practice what he preaches. At the end of the day, the father does not have stories to tell about what happened at the shop or what the foreman said. Supper is not a time when father comes home, but rather is a time when the two sexes come together. These things are, of course, less true of commercialized farming and of the migratory laborer.

This situation resembles family businesses everywhere, but in farming we have an extreme. In the small grocery store, the son and daughter and the wife help out, but there is not likely to be a rigid division of labor; rather, there is usually a sharing of *overtime* work. That is, the wife looks after the store in the evening, or else the son does after school. On the farm there is full participation and a genuine division of tasks—and during the harvest, the son may not even go to school.

2. CONTINUING RELATION TO THE COMMUNITY

The farmer is in an intimate and continuing work complex which includes his neighbors, the church, politics and the town. The farm is not a moral island in the midst of others as are factories or other work organizations. The shop in a given factory has its own routines, folkways, understandings, and these are likely to be very different from that of the shop next door. Further, the members of the shop are not likely even to *know* what these are next door.

But the farm, by its nature, is forever open to *public scrutiny*. There is inside work especially in dairying and the preparation of silage. But a great deal of the work is performed outside and the crop itself is for all to see. The work practices of the farmer can therefore be evaluated by anyone who cares to do so. As the farmer works in his fields, a neighbor may wave to him and stop and chat about work. Someone comes to borrow a tool. The town farm-implement dealer drops by to see how a new cultivator is working. There is also the coming together in connection with cooperative activities where neighbors may help each other, which gives farmers a chance to size each other up and to develop confidence in each other. Added to the fact that these opportunities are available is the fact that these people are his friends and intimate associates, and therefore facilitate a close neighborhood control over work.

These two factors give to the control of work certain peculiar characteristics. Besides them are various controls following from the nature of farm work itself. We shall discuss these two sets of controls in that order.

1. CONTROLS FROM THE WORK COMPLEX

a. PRIMARY CONTROLS

The importance and significance of primary controls in rural areas has been much discussed in the literature.[5] Although the control of the family and the neighborhood in rural areas is breaking down because of the influence of the automobile, radio, etc., it is still much stronger than is likely to be the case in urban areas generally. The nature of the work throws boys and girls into close and continuing contact with their parents. Cooley (5) long ago described the growth of sentiments, such as love, hate, envy, respect, jealousy, self-sacrifice, vanity, cruelty, and pity in the family. Those sentiments are all based on the fundamental trait of sympathy: the ability to take the role of the other. The development of sympathy provides a fundamental means of social control. The child obeys not because there is a rule that he should obey, but because "Pop wouldn't like it."

Isolation is still important in farm areas in the maintenance of primary controls. In wheat and range lands it may be fifty or more miles to the nearest town of any size. Therefore it is not so easy for the in-

[5] Cf. 21, pp. 228–37; 22, pp. 293–303; 31, pp. 80–81 ff.; 36, Ch. 11).

dividual to escape primary controls, and since farmers have a wide range of acquaintances, the boy is not likely to be anonymous.

The net effect is to preserve the primary control of the neighborhood. Farm areas are likely to be homogeneous and beliefs and morals similar. Therefore the child finds that precepts that he receives from his parents are reinforced by the parents of his playmates as well.

A result is to facilitate the transmission of farming skills and the way of life to children. When the father says, "It is time to go to church," the child obeys. And the same authority lies back of his saying, "It's time to spray the fruit trees." The child notes that this is not simply an arbitrary decision of his father's: His neighbors are likely already to be at work spraying.

b. TRADITION

Social and cultural changes take place more slowly on the farm than in the city. Mechanization has reduced effort and manpower needs, and stimulated rural-urban migration. But customs, beliefs, and faiths have changed more slowly. There remains a body of attitudes toward nature, farming as a way of life, the value of neighborhood help, and stability that still are dominant. Agricultural practices are transmitted from one generation to another and thus have the force of primary approval. The sponsorship by the father that is necessary for a son to become a farmer reinforces the dependence on parents. There tends also to be a scarcity of innovators in the agricultural community. Those with new ideas are likely to meet resistance and therefore to take their ideas to the city. There is in addition a stability of personnel; over many years the same families remain in the area, and this fact helps to conserve the wisdom as well as the force of the past.

c. STATUS ASCRIPTION

Because of stability of personnel, lack of sudden changes in agriculture practices and a reluctance to try anything until the neighbors have, there tends to grow up a reputation or ascribed status for each farmer. One farmer is known as a hard worker but a poor manager, another as a shrewd manager but a poor father, while another is known as well educated but as liking his bottle a little too much. These reputations stay with people and the persons in turn are likely to fit the role assigned to them.

This fact makes social adjustment easier. The farmer does not have to strive to prove himself; his self is known. At the same time it prevents his varying his status very much by individual effort. The farmer is accepted not for what he is but for what people think he is. His status is then reaffirmed by informal association at visiting, church, or in meetings. The strongly upward mobile (or downward mobile) person finds little opportunity and is in fact relatively rare in agriculture.

2. WORK CONTROLS

a. CONTINUOUS CHARACTER OF AGRICULTURE

Agriculture involves continuing work in the form of the yearly round. By the time one crop is seeded it is time for another to be harvested; when one crop is harvested the field must often be readied for the next seeding. And, once the seed is in, the farmer has a great deal invested in machinery and labor of himself and his family. Therefore he is less likely to be able or to want to "chuck it" if adverse conditions arise. He has too much at stake from a cold economic point of view. Further, whatever conditions are, the farm continues to demand his attention. As Landis (22, p. 297) says:

Even in times of agricultural depression when crops do not bring profitable returns, even in times of drought when there is no crop, there is work for the farmer. For this reason rural people face less personal frustration as an outgrowth of economic adversity than urban people. When the urban man loses his business or his job, he loses all opportunity to express himself through work channels.

The farm operator is not out of a job, however poor the yield. And he does not suffer loss of status normally (as the urban industrial worker who is laid off might); if his crop is poor, then very likely his neighbor's is too.

b. LIMITATIONS IMPOSED BY NATURE

The factory takes pig iron and molds it into any shape or form that is desired. When the completed product has been in use for, say, twenty years, it may then be scrapped and remelted to form new iron. But farming, in spite of the great changes in the use of machinery, types of crops, and the treatment of the soil, remains subject to biological rather than to mechanical principles. A seed of corn, whether sweet, flint, or hybrid, is a living thing. The farmer may put a super-seed into ground prepared by elaborate equipment and saturate it with fertilizer. But he must then wait for nature to perform the actual manufacturing process. One result is a continuing consciousness of nature and of being forced to adjust to it.

c. ROLE OF THE OWNER

The typical farm is a family farm, and even on a very large farm, the owner is likely to operate it directly. Therefore the operator has a direct, personal involvement in the farm and everything that goes on in it. The factory manager will try to do as good a job of administration as he can. But he cannot exercise control over everything and it is perhaps better that he does not. Control is delegated and the manager's function becomes that of hiring good subordinates. Further the factory is not his; if there is a fire, the insurance will pay for damages.

But when there is a fire in the barn, it is the farmer's private property that is being destroyed. Even though it is insured, the farmer feels much like the urban home owner whose house is destroyed. Insurance never gives back what one puts into it, and fire destroys memories and reminders of past crises too.

The smaller labor force on the farm also means that the farm operator knows his workers (except for migratory laborers), and in any case they are usually his own family. Since he does much of the work himself and is familiar with what others are doing from moment to moment, he has an intimate acquaintance with every part of the work activity, from how far down in the ground a given fence hole goes (he dug it himself) to how much milk Bossie gave this morning (his older daughter told him at lunch). Even in highly mechanized and multi-product farms, the owner can and does exercise close, pervasive supervision.

d. ATTITUDES ENGENDERED BY THE PARTICULAR CROP

The American farmer is becoming increasingly specialized. His dependence on one cash crop has tended to produce a set of attitudes peculiar to each crop.

On general and self-sufficing farms, values center about farm ownership: security, independence, and leisure (which is considered a necessity rather than a luxury). There is likely to be a general distrust of the "new fangled" and of outsiders; primary attachments are to the family and to the neighborhood.

The western specialty crop growers exhibit a profound solidarity as an occupational group. They are zealous of their interests and exhibit an ethnocentrism and smugness that is probably unparalleled in agriculture anywhere. Individual ownership and the emphasis on marketing makes these growers place a high value on the individual and on success. They have been little touched by the agrarian movement and on the whole are a highly conservative group.

The values of the cotton farmer are intimately related to the land. Ownership is highly prized by both whites and Negroes and is the object of hopes and planning. Toward cotton there is a speculative attitude because of its attendant anxieties and uncertainties (34, Ch. 2).

The cotton farmer enjoys the rhythm of the cotton year and prefers to work at his own pace, with sufficient time to rest or to visit. The lightning harvest of cherry picking, say, holds no glamour for him. But most pervasive is the tradition and cultural homogeneity of the areas with its roots in national history. In a sense, the Civil War was fought over cotton, and throughout the belt, in spite of recent technological changes and urbanization, the relation of cotton to all other areas of life makes it difficult to think of it as a mere commodity.

In dairy farming, stemming directly from the daily round character of dairying and the farmer's intimate relation to the urban market, is an emphasis on stability. There is no such thing as a "killing" in dairying (as in wheat or in the Western specialty crops); the result is a preminum on routine and attention to repetitive tasks. But the fact that he cannot hold or store his product has made the dairy man into one of the most profound joiners among American farmers. The organizations that he has created include cooperative dairy manufacturing plants, milk marketing associations, dairy herd improvement associations, purebred cattle associations, artificial breeding associations, agricultural fair societies, pasture and feed crop groups, and 4-H clubs for youngsters. The Farm Bureau and Grange are vital organizations. Besides these, there is a close relation to university extension programs, conservation programs, credit agencies, and milk control boards. In addition there is much participation in town-centered service clubs, fraternal orders and church organizations. The latter reflect the nearness of the dairy farmer to the town and his relative lack of a pattern of informal visiting.

The fact that he must live on a farm (in contrast to the wheat farmer) leads to a great emphasis on the farm home and buildings and their appearance. A very high proportion of dairy farm houses have electricity, refrigeration, running water, central heat, and telephones. The admired farmer is the one who exemplifies stability. He is solvent, owns his farm, and takes pride in his herd.

The corn belt farmer values what are considered "good" farming practices: the latest in mechanized devices, rotation, and the use of the results of scientific investigations. In the early days of isolation and hand labor, neighborhood cooperation was important. With the breakdown of this isolation and with mechanization, the neighborhood is not as important as formerly. The decline of neighborhood cooperation, together with the early tradition of resourcefulness, have helped to produce the feeling of independence (some call it isolationism) that is often attributed to the corn belt.

This independence and resourcefulness has made the farmer skeptical of politicians' promises, and has led him to take more direct steps to insure his own interest. These have taken the form at various times of the Greenback Movement, the Populist Party, the Equity and formal organizations of many kinds.

For the wheat farmer, the great imponderable of the weather leads to a great emphasis being placed on moisture and soil conservation practices. The weather itself is a frequent subject of conversation, perhaps more so than elsewhere because of the comparative lack of diversification.

The speculative attitude of the suitcase wheat farmer is condemned, and it has probably contributed to wheat land's being over priced. The sidewalk farmer is not regarded much more highly. But Taylor (47, pp. 390–91) tells us:

"Sidewalk" farmers argue that they have made the best or the correct, adjustment to extensive wheat farming. They reason that an enterprise demanding careful attention only during two short seasons of the year is not a full time occupation or profession, and that by having other sources of stable income, they are less speculative than are full time farmers, whose whole financial destiny rests on the precarious basis of extensive wheat farming. They argue further that since a wheat farm does not require year round attention, it is sensible to live in towns where they and their families can have the conveniences of schools and churches and the benefits of organized community life.

The resident farmer develops an attitude of "taking the good with the bad," and hopes to "make out" in the long run. All are united in respect for and use of the big machine.

The orientation of the wheat farmer to the sale of his cash crop and the sparseness of settlement leads to independence and steps to take care of his own needs. The Farmers' Alliance, Equity, and other farmers' organizations have had strong representations in the wheat areas and today the Farmers' Union is powerful in most areas. At the same time, the great distances between farms, the family size of the farm, and therefore joint family work contribute to an emphasis on the family as the major unit of organization. Further, the fact that wheat farms are expensive means that few sons can enter it without help. The son enters farming by taking over his father's farm, or else the father buys the son a farm. In the Palouse area of Washington, there has been a tendency for land gradually to pass into the hands of a relatively small number of families who then become potent political figures in the area.

The most important locality unit is the trade-center community. It is here that the wheat farmer buys and sells, and on his success in those activities rests the entire farm enterprise. The wheat farmer's eyes are therefore turned as much to Washington, where price levels may be determined, as they are to the skies.

THE FARM CAREER

Turning now to another part of our conceptual framework—the career— we examine the questions of social selection, mobility, career contingencies, and farming and the self.

1. SOCIAL SELECTION IN FARMING

Who enters agriculture? Murray A. Straus (44) calls attention to a major selective factor when he writes:

Farming is a hereditary occupation to an extent almost unknown for other occupations in modern American society. By and large, only farmers' sons become farmers.

Most persons in farming grew up on farms themselves—[6] and this experience resulted in the internalization of a set of values involving love of farming which makes it difficult for those who have not had that experience to enter farming.[7] Persons found in farming fall into two groups: those continuously in farming from boyhood on, and those who left the farm as youths and later returned.

a. THOSE WHO STAY IN FARMING

The per cent of farmers' sons who express an intent to go into farming is very high compared to the per cent of sons of men in other occupations.[8] Straus (45) found it to be around 50 per cent in Wisconsin, and others are in essential agreement. W. A. Anderson, who studied not preferences but actual entry into farming, found, for three different samples, 50 per cent, 77 per cent and 53 per cent of sons of farmers (grandfathers' generation) became farmers, compared to 19, 18, and 14 per cent of sons of non-farmers who entered their fathers' occupations. For the father's generation, the percentages for farmers were 31 per cent, 43 per cent, and 47 per cent, and for non-farmers, 15 per cent and 14 per cent (one sample had no non-farm fathers). See (15, 23, 40). This picture may understate the case because of the high birth rate on farms.[9]

And on the farm the son is inducted not just into an occupation but into a total way of life involving—as we have seen—visiting, religion, politics, and values. The father does not have to sell the lad on the farm or explain it. The son knows all about it.

The significance of the cultural perspective is brought out by Straus (44, p. 264) who reports that only 44 per cent of a sample of youths choosing farming as a career had *ever considered* any other occupation seriously. The mean number of occupations considered were 1.6 for the boys choosing farming and 2.1 for those choosing non-farm occupations.[10] Those who choose farming differ from those not choosing

[6] Relevant also is N. T. Theodorou's finding (49) that, of boys who took vocational agriculture, 93 per cent have an opportunity on their home farms.

[7] Chief exceptions are found among those who invest in farm land for speculation.

[8] Expressing a preference for an occupation is, of course, not equivalent to entering it and working in it. But for farming, the discrepancy between expressed preference and actual entry seems to be smaller than for most other occupations. Thus Straus (44) found that 42.6 per cent of boys choosing farming were certain they would enter that occupation, whereas only 18.7 per cent of boys choosing non-farm occupations felt certain they would enter them. This difference was found significant at the .005 level.

[9] See also our discussion of occupational inheritance, pp. 148–157.

[10] Significant at the .005 level.

farming significantly on the following variables: mothers less likely to be employed outside the home; fathers more likely to be full-time farm owners; spend more time working at home; prefer to work with things rather than with people or ideas; more often certain they would enter their chosen occupation; and median annual family income higher. Straus (44, pp. 260–61) relates these findings to the ability of the father to help his son and to the strong likelihood that the findings reflect the success with which the farm value system has been transmitted to the son. The value system includes the belief that work is considered a good in itself and the feeling that the family is a productive as well as a consumption unit.

The father can further stimulate the son to enter farming by sponsoring him on a nearby farm. First, the father sponsors the son financially by helping him to buy equipment and land. But also he gives his son a name. In the farm neighborhood people will tell visitors: "Fred Johnson's boy's farm lies over yonder." And the boy has a reputation already ascribed to him. If it is a good one, it is easier for him to rise to a position of respect in the community; if the reputation is a poor one, the son will have to do particularly well to overcome it.

b. THOSE WHO GO AND RETURN

There is no denying the volume of the rural-urban trend. But with it there goes on a smaller counter-movement of persons from cities to farms. This movement rises to high proportions in depression periods. In 1932, the number who moved from cities to farms actually exceeded those who moved in the reverse direction. That suggests that one of the major groups who return to farming are those who have failed in the city. They may enter farming or simply become dependent on their families.

During the depression many were motivated by the search for security. The back-to-the-land movement painted in glowing terms the security that farming offered especially in terms of food (22, pp. 245–46). In part as a residuum of this movement or at least stimulated by it, was the growth of part-time farming. Part-time farmers include persons who own or work small farms and also take other employment which constitutes a substantial portion of their income. Landis (22, p. 249), in summarizing the research, states that the chief motives for entering part-time farming are: increased income, bettering environment for children, and the attempt to escape from disadvantages of city life.

Persons enter part-time farming from both ends: Farmers take jobs in the city, and urbanites buy farms in the country. Part-time farms tend to be found near industrial areas in large cities. The movement in the direction of part-time farming appears to be growing.

There remains one large group of farmers who enter it with little or no previous experience: migratory laborers. They have often had agriculture experience of some kind though not that involved in following a particular crop. It is dubious in the extreme to speak of them as *choosing* agriculture as an occupation. In a very real sense they are selected because they are excluded from other occupations. For some, however, it is a means of entry to higher status positions in agriculture, as was the case for the Japanese and Chinese in California.

2. MOBILITY IN FARMING

Students of rural life conclude in general that there is less "upward" mobility in rural areas than there is in urban areas (41, pp. 580–93; 47, pp. 528–29. Perhaps there is an overestimate of the amount of actual mobility that there is in urban areas because there is *potentially* more mobility there. The vista open to the man at the bottom is wider although his chances of moving may *not* be much greater. A man *can* rise from assembly line to president, but he is more likely not even to rise to the position of foreman.

Yet there is less vertical movement in farm areas than in urban areas for the following reasons: (1) there is less occupational and industrial differentiation in rural areas. The latter is particularly important in cities. The rise of new industries in the manufacture of automobiles, radio and so on have offered new avenues of upward mobility. By contrast, every farm area is a one-industry area by definition, though there may be other industries close by. (2) Also limiting mobility is family reputation. The urban boy may come of parents who are failures. But that is not known to his employer and often the employer does not care. The farm boy carries a name that is known and that makes it more difficult for him to rise (or to fall). (3) The very chance of one farmer's becoming significantly more successful than his neighbors is difficult. One grocery store across the street from another in the city may move ahead through better management, pricing, or service. But farms next to one another are not likely to exhibit very much difference. The farmer is little able to manipulate his customers; and the price of grain is determined not by him. There are constants that all farmers face such as the weather, insects, and natural changes. This makes it difficult for one farmer to get the jump on another.

Mobility in agriculture has traditionally been described by W. J. Spillman (43) and Henry C. Taylor (48, pp. 380–81, Ch. XXII) by reference to the "Agricultural Ladder." The ladder seems to apply best to the Midwest and to the period before and after the turn of the twentieth century. The boy started as an unpaid laborer on his father's farm; then went to work as a hired hand for a neighbor; saved money, bought implements and stock, rented land and became a tenant; saved enough to buy land and became an owner. This picture, although less true now, still seems close to the facts. Various studies have shown the close correlation between age and position on the ladder (48, p. 267; 41, p. 583).

But movement down also occurs, especially in two types of situations: (1) During depressions many tenants are unable to pay their debts and revert to laboring status, and owners lose their farms because of a shortage of money. (2) The pattern of large farms seems to be increasing (41, p. 320; 47, p. 274), and few persons are ever able to accumulate enough money to buy one of these.

In agriculture there tends to be a fairly close relation between vertical mobility and migration. In general, moving up or down means moving to a different farm. This is seen notably in the case of the croppers who forever move to try to better themselves, and in the case of the agricultural immigrants to the United States who settled the West. The latter produced the great rural migrations in U.S. history: into the hill country of Tennessee and Kentucky, the Midwest, and the wheat lands of Kansas and North Dakota.

One important group that does *not* improve its chances by moving, does not move up when it moves out, is the group of migratory laborers, as we have seen. And since they tend to be found in crops where there are large labor demands, they work on large farms, which makes even less likely their chance of becoming owners or even tenants.

3. CAREER CONTINGENCIES

The contingencies attendant on farming as a career have already been mentioned or implied. The first contingency is whether the youth is eligible to take over a farm or not, which depends on whether his father is an owner or not. And if the son has the chance to become an owner, whether he does or not is likely to depend in turn on the ambitions of his brothers. If none of them wish to enter farming then the son may have his way clear. Even then he must demonstrate competence to his father because his father still has the alternative of selling the farm to an outsider.

If several brothers desire the farm, age is significant. Usually the eldest will have preference. The father may then sponsor the younger one on a nearby farm. As already pointed out, success or failure is in part dependent on the father's reputation in the community.

Sponsorship is possible whether the father is an owner or a tenant. He may have saved enough money to set his son up as a tenant on another farm. But if the father is a laborer, the son's chances of being a tenant or an owner are much poorer. In that case the son may try to get work as a full-time hired hand in the dairying or corn areas. But this is difficult, in part because if the family migrates he usually goes with it; and he usually must contribute part of his income to the family. Therefore he does not get a chance to save very much.

Movement up the ladder is related to the business cycle. In inflationary periods, it is easier for tenants to pay off their debts and become owners. The reverse is true during depressions when owners may become tenants or even laborers.

Race is a significant variable also. Many Negroes, Japanese, and Chinese have become owners, but it is not easy for them to do so. Most of them are found working, because of historical circumstances, in crops characterized by large investments. Theoretically they could enter other crops but training and cultural perspective limit their ability to move. The Mexicans are precluded by lack of citizenship from freedom of action.

The type of crop imposes severe rigidities on one's career chances. In crops such as the Western specialty crops, wheat and cotton, success usually requires a large investment. In dairying and truck farming, there may be fewer obstacles but also the chances of a great success are much less.

The availability of alternative employment affects the individual's decision to stay in agriculture. The dairy farmer, close to the city, may become a part-time farmer. It is not so easy for a self-sufficient farmer of Tennessee. Children are particularly affected by the rewards which urban employment can offer, and the large urbanward migration is partial testimony to this. On the other hand, the introduction of urban comforts to the farm, mechanization, and government price supports have made farming increasingly attractive.

But one thing the farmer's son is conscious of is the relative prestige of farming. In the consolidated school, he is thrown into contact with urban children with different and exciting career ambitions. When he visits them in their homes, he discovers that their fathers do not wear bib-overalls to supper. But conflicting with these troubling experiences, he also values family visiting when his family calls on neighbors. He feels more at home and comfortable in their warm society. The degree of isolation from urban influences may then be highly significant in decision-making.

4. FARMING AND THE SELF

On this subject we find in the literature in rural sociology a great rash of lists, usually under the heading of "Rural Personality" by which is meant usually American rural personality. Landis, in a *tour de force* (22, p. 120), presents such a list:

Farmers are supposed to be conservative, individualistic, superstitious, fatalistic, to possess stability, to lack cooperative qualities, to be of a magical turn of mind, mystical in outlook, to be religious, dogmatic, prejudiced, strait-laced in morals, stern and just, patient, stolid, introspective, versatile, impressionistic, suspicious, to possess much common sense, to be of sound and adequate judgment, to be independent in forming judgments, to possess deep convictions, to be meditative, to have fixed purposes, to have endurance, to be immune to radicalism, to have peace of mind, to practice simplicity, to feel aversion for fads and show, to practice thrift and frugality, to assume responsibility readily, to have initiative, to be resourceful, frank, hospitable, sympathetic, to lack socialization, to be characterized by hardiness, to be pessimistic, to brood over injuries. They are supposed to be emotionally intensive, highly suggestible, shy, sentimental, to lean toward the emotional in religious expression, to be conformists, to lack idealism, to love nature, to have a developed artistic sense, to like gossip, to be moody, to be given to resignation, to have a tendency to be discouraged, to be orthodox in religion, to be introverted, silent, to think and speak directly, to be democratic, to lean toward "fogyism," to be unprogressive, realistic, intolerant, naive, skeptical, serious, clannish, economical, complaining, honest, stubborn, easygoing, reticent, gullible, trustworthy, conventional, tenacious, nonmercenary, unselfish, neighborly, friendly, wholesome, and narrow-minded.

Such lists are based on three sources mainly: personal recollections from boyhood (most rural sociologists are of farm origin, and their lists reflect their own farming background); a small amount of research; and pure fantasy. Unfortunately, there is little else to draw upon because of the paucity of research. Such research as we have is couched in the census-defined rural-urban dichotomy, which means comparing one occupational group with a host of others. Usually the studies are biased by the fact that they make use of tests and questionnaires which are made up by urbanites. The outstanding illustration is provided by the intelligence tests which show in general that farmers are less intelligent than urbanites (11, pp. 260–64; 42, pp. 266–82). As O. E. Baker long ago pointed out "To the city child milk is associated with a bottle (perhaps a carton, now) not with a cow; an apple comes from a box, not from a tree. . . ." Myra Shimberg (42, pp. 282–86), by the use of a special intelligence test, was able to secure higher scores from rural than from urban children. To this must be added the experience of the anthropologist in studying the intelligence of Indian children (28, pp. 186–87).

Most studies other than of intelligence involve giving a sample (usually of college or high school students) a questionnaire. The sample typically is not random with respect to important differences among farmers by type of crop, region, nearness to urban facilities, and other factors, as Landis (22, p. 123) comments:

The cotton farmer on the southern plantation has a background of long tradition, as also has the share cropper on his small tract of land; psychological traits of southern farmers are in certain respects unique. The densely settled, irrigated districts of the far west, with small farms and intensive crops, are characterized by another pattern of life. The wheat farmer who operates a large ranch entirely by machines, hiring for a short season sufficient labor to harvest his crop, no doubt possesses behavior traits distinctly his own; the truck farmer in the hinterland of the large metropolis who deals in perishable produce and contacts the urban market daily is likely to be urbane in characteristics, life philosophy, and habit patterns; the backwoods farmer of the Appalachian or Ozark regions or of isolated areas of the Rocky Mountains are also a rural social type. There is probably as much difference between the psychological traits of an Ozark mountaineer and those of a California orange grower as between the traits of a resident of the slums of Chicago and Gold Coast millionaire, for the social roles of the two rural types are as different as those of the two urban types.

More important than such variations is the fact that few studies operate with a personality theory. It is almost useless to administer a personality scale to a sample and then to conclude that rural persons are, say, more introverted than some other group. Such a conclusion leads directly to *ad hoc* "explanations" after the fact. It is discovered that farmers are introverted. This is then "attributed" to the fact that farmers are isolated. Then a search is made for studies which show that isolation (perhaps in city schools) is associated with introversion. Then the study is complete.

We must start, rather, with the *process* of socialization and look at the farm from the point of view of personality *development*. We must ask what sort of culture a farm baby grows up in. This approach involves reference to the situation. On one occasion in a graduate class at the University of Chicago, a Southern white who was known to have strong anti-Negro attitudes entered a class late and discovered that all of the chairs were taken, some of them by Negroes. The white stood there for a moment, looked around and then left the room. He came back dragging a chair after him. This he pushed up against the table and sat down and began taking notes like anyone else in the class. From a knowledge of his attitudes it would have been difficult to predict how he would have behaved under the situation that he was faced with. But after all, he had paid his money and the only way he would hear the lecture was for him to get a chair himself, and this he did. A similar conclusion may be drawn with reference to studies which show that the farmer is, for example, "conservative." He is conservative, yes, but the question is in what kind of situation? And the situations that should be explained would include those that led night-riders to burn down tobacco warehouses in 1907, and that required that half of Wisconsin's national guard be mobilized in May, 1933, against milk strike pickets.

Here we may draw on the field of culture and personality. The work of such persons as Kardiner, Linton, Hallowell, Du Bois and Honigmann seems to show that where a culture is simple and relatively static, and where there is consensus, then the individual grows up to mirror the culture.[11] It becomes possible to describe a basic personality which all share. Personalities are there very much alike. The child in the modern western city grows up under quite contrary conditions: the culture is highly diverse and complex, is rapidly changing, and there is absence of consensus. The population is heterogeneous and the child is continually exposed to a host of alternative subcultures. As such, he is presented continually with a variety of modes of behavior and the effect is that personality in the city is likely to be characterized by diversity.

Now to the extent that the farm child grows up in an isolated farm area, where the culture is simple in the sense of being organized about farming and well integrated with other segments of life, to the extent that the child learns all he learns from his father, and to the extent that there is consensus, then we may say that the personalities of farmers are likely to be characterized by *similarity*. But these are ideal conditions. There is variation from one farm area to another. Some farm areas, such as dairying and fruit, exhibit considerable complexity. Some, like cotton, are undergoing great change, and the influx of immigrants and urban folkways has created considerable decline in consensus among farmers everywhere. As these things occur personality diversity is to be expected, though perhaps not to as great an extent as is found in large cities.

A second important hypothesis on the relation between farming and the self may be put forth. Rising to a dominant position, especially in America (though perhaps it is nowhere wholly absent), is a cleavage in attitude towards farming. There are those to whom farming is a business and those to whom it is a way of life.[12] The point is whether farming is looked upon as a means to other goals (wealth, security) or as a value in itself. It would seem that only in the latter case would farming come close to the self. The highly speculative sidewalk or "slot machine" wheat farmer would appear to be fundamentally different in world-view than the self-sufficing farmer of Kentucky, and any investigations of rural personality which throw them together for the sake of an "adequate" sample would seem to be doomed to insignificance.

The two types are at ideal-typical poles, and a concrete case undoubtedly combines some of both. No matter how speculative the farmer

---

[11] See (7; 13, Chs. 1, 4; 16, Chs. 11, 12; 18, Ch. II; 25, Ch. 5).
[12] This distinction is essentially equivalent to Max Weber's distinction between *Zweckrational* and *Wertrational* social action.

may be, he probably always must pay some attention to soil conservation practices even for the purpose of making money. There is
probably no crop, not even wheat, in which one can make a fortune
in just one year and then get out. This means care and planning for
the next year. Similarly, no farmer today can be completely self-sufficient
and grow whatever he pleases. Some attention must be given to what his
family, if no one else, wants to eat and what his children's ambitions are.

A third generalization or hypothesis about farm personality seems to
be supported by existing research. We have pointed out the closeness of
articulation of work, family, church, politics, and informal fellowship.
It would seem likely, then, that an individual growing up in such a
situation would develop a personality which would exhibit considerable
integration.[13] What the child learns in the family is not contradicted
but confirmed by his friends, the village priest, the school teacher, and
others which he has contact with. This should help to build a sense of
security and an integrated self. To the extent that farm society is segmented, then we would expect this to be less true: the truck farmer is
continually exposed to urban influences, the fruit and cotton farmer
to race differences; and there are likely to be ethnic and religious differences in any farm area.

A further distinctive feature of agriculture was stated to be its
peak character. The existence of a yearly round would have significance
in areas where it has not been subjected to much human control as for
example in self-sufficing farming, or cotton, or where human control has
accentuated the peaks as it has in fruit farming and wheat farming.

The effect of growing up in a culture in which all eyes are on a
yearly peak must be considerable. The farmer is forced to be purposeful,
practical, and forever conscious of the reality of farming.

Finally the fact of ownership, the small size of the enterprise, and
the fact that he runs it himself, knows every part of it, and has had a
hand in every operation would be expected to produce the farmer's
oft-proclaimed independence. The owner *is* dependent on many—family,
neighbors, and priest. But he is not dependent on a foreman or a boss.
The share cropper, the agricultural laborer, and the tenant may be
expected to feel less independent. And most farmer-owners certainly

[13] The evidence, such as it is, supports the statement that mental disorders are more
common in urban than in rural areas. See, for example (22, p. 110; 29; 30; 41, p. 120).
Landis, though, feels that farm experiences lead somewhat to introversion (22, p. 126).
However, comparative studies are extremely difficult to interpret because of a considerable tendency for rural persons to go to cities to get treatment, a tendency for rural
persons with incipient disorders to drift to cities, the fact that persons with disorders
can often be kept at home more easily in the country than in the city, and the age
distribution in rural areas, with some concentration of older people.

feel dependent on the urban market. But the tradition of independence is there, and the farmer will try to make it a reality even if it means adding still another dependence on his representatives in Washington.

THE WORK GROUP

1. INCLUSION AND EXCLUSION

The concept of colleagueship is limited by owners and tenants to refer to each other. It does not seem to apply among migratory laborers though racial and ethnic sub-groups do so regard themselves. Among owners and tenants there is a feeling of unity or of belonging which is usually restricted to the local community where it is supported by church, local politics, visiting patterns and so on. Occasionally this feeling of unity goes further to include the farmers in a crop region. The wheat farmers come to think of themselves as a group apart, as do the dairy men. Such feelings are likely to flourish in times of economic distress when distinctions of class, ethnicity and other divisive influences may decline.

But the most important manifestation of a sense of unity among all United States farmers as an occupational group may be seen in the case of the farmers' movements. These are quite old and, as Taylor (48, p. 511) comments, have been associated with commercialized agriculture where the farmer pits himself, not just against nature, but against a market composed of human beings. As early as 1620, the Virginia tobacco growers protested so vehemently against the monopoly granted by King James I that the monopoly was withdrawn. The major groups in the farmers' movements have been the following.[14]

The Grange, begun by O. H. Kelley in 1867, was originally planned as a social and educational organization but soon moved into economic and political activities. It ran cooperative stores, factories, a bank, and life and fire insurance companies. In the 1870's in the Midwest, it took part in the agitation against the railroads whose freight rates were felt to be discriminatory against farmers. The Grange played a role in creating the office of the Secretary of Agriculture. It ran into stiff competition from the Farmers' Alliance around 1890, but since then has recovered and remains an important farmers' organization. Its activities are now mainly recreational and social (as was originally planned), but it keeps the farmer's eye on legislation and uses its influence on such legislation.

[14] On farmers' social movements, see (14; 35; 46; 47, Ch. 29). An especially valuable case study is provided by Lipset's intensive analysis of the relation between wheat farming and the growth of the Cooperative Commonwealth Federation party in Saskatchewan, Canada (26).

The Farmers' Alliance, a loosely organized group of farmers made up of several sub-groups, arose on the 1880's. It entered into economic and political questions, as had the Grange earlier. The Alliance took a broader approach and tried to battle the low prices paid for farm products and to counteract the crop-lien system. Macune, a leader in the Southern Alliance, put forth the sub-treasury scheme, which provided for the storage of agricultural products in government-built warehouses where they could be held and released as prices warranted. The Alliance moved directly into politics by uniting itself with the Populist Party; and with the decline of the latter, the Alliance also declined.

The American Society of Equity, organized by J. A. Everitt in 1902, had its greatest strength in certain tobacco areas of Kentucky and in the spring-wheat areas of the northwest. The price of burley tobacco had fallen and this was attributed to a combination among tobacco buyers. Equity decided to cut the burley crop for 1908. Those who refused were visited by night-riders and their crops were often destroyed. The price then did rise, but the rest of the state rose in indignation at the tactics used, and the Equity leaders returned to their home in Indianapolis. In wheat, Equity proposed the holding of wheat off of the market for a few months. They also built a small elevator in St. Paul in 1914, to try to compete against the big terminals in Minneapolis. They carried on a fight against the grain dealers of Minneapolis. After World War I, they developed cooperative livestock shipping companies and sales agencies, and through the same means, got the farmer ground feeds and seeds at low prices.

The Farmers' Union, started in Texas in 1902 by Newt Gresham, later spread in the West; it is still active in the West Central states. Its program centers about the control of prices, acreage limitation, credit, and land tenure. It has developed functioning economic organizations: the Central Exchange, which manufactures tractors, milking machines, timber and soybean meal, and petroleum; a Grain Terminal Association; and livestock buying co-ops.

The first local Bureau of the American Farm Bureau Federation started in Broome County, New York, in 1911. It was early associated with a nationwide plan for the marketing of grain. It also supported strongly the McNary-Haugen Bill which proposed the retention of the tariff. The Bureau fought proposed increases in freight rates and helped to defeat the Pittsburgh-plus system for charging for steel. The Bureau also operated as an axis of organization of local neighborhood clubs and township organizations and was closely allied with the county agent system.

There have been many organizations like these, and some, such as the Nonpartisan League and the Farmers' Holiday Association, approached violence in the militance of their appeals. Basically, all of the farmers' movements have been concerned with price, credit, and marketing problems that affect the commercialized farmer.

For the most part, the business undertakings that were designed to eliminate middleman profits have not been as successful as hoped. The farmers' organizations have usually underestimated the managerial skills required, or else have sold too cheaply. The middleman is there for a purpose; only better management will raise the price that the farmer receives, not the elimination of the middleman as such.

Politically the farmers' movements have had important effects. They have helped to force the recognition of themselves as a distinct occupational and industrial group and have gained many discriminatory benefits for farmers. They have helped also to build a sense of unity among commercialized farmers throughout the country. The resultant *esprit de corps* may be of great significance for the future, especially as more and more farmers become commercialized.

2. INFORMAL RELATIONS

There have been almost no studies of informal work relations on the individual farm. What we do have can hardly be called studies: they consist mainly of remarks made in passing. For example, the "hired man" is often referred to as being close to the farm owner and treated as one of the family, but we have no study of the nature of this relationship and how it works out in detail. The pattern of neighborhood help is often referred to, and bees are discussed as occasions for the coming together of large numbers, but these have not been studied in any systematic manner.

The reasons for this lack seem to be twofold. First there is the normally small size of the work force on the farm (usually just the family). The work group *is* an informal or primary group, and therefore any consideration of informal relations is merged into studies of the farm family. The larger farm, employing many, is regarded as atypical and the rural sociologist, with his desire to be useful, has felt that he should more profitably study the "typical" farm. A second factor is the lack of attention to migratory laborers as a *work* group. For the most part, migratory laborers are treated not as a work group but as a problem. Because Negroes, Mexicans, and Puerto Ricans loom large in their numbers, they are usually treated from the point of view of race relations and regarded as depressed minorities. We do not deny the importance of the problem, but preoccupation with it has served to obscure or delay objective studies of work relationships. Persons interested in such studies are accused, as Dylan Thomas puts it, of fiddling while home is burning.

The only important studies are of friendships and cliques *among* the farmers. These consist usually of sociometric studies of visiting, or borrowing, and mutual aid. Loomis (27, ch. 5), one of the major figures in this work, points out that these three activities are closely related and usually overlap. They appear to be of particular importance in farming because of isolation. Under that condition farmers have to help each other and can only look to each other for informal fellowship. The peak character of agriculture has also contributed to the rise of informal groups because of the need to have extra help at peak points and therefore the need for a group on whom one can depend at such times.

It seems clear that cliques are not identical with the neighborhoods or locality groups so dear to the rural sociologist. We find many different cliques within neighborhoods and we find others that cross neighborhood boundaries. They are therefore a reality in their own right.

The functions of the clique are suggested by their content. There is first the need for mutual assistance. In addition they help the isolated farmer to secure a sense of belonging and personal worth and enable farmers to size each other up and develop mutual confidence. The exigencies and uncertainties of agriculture give cliques the further function of providing a sense of reassurance in time of failure. The farmer who sees his crop ruined by some insect secures some satisfaction and preservation of self-confidence when his friend tells him that he had the same experience, although he used the new much-advertised insecticide.

In order to function in this manner it is necessary that the clique become composed of persons who feel at ease in one another's presence or who feel they are "in the same boat." Research suggests that clique members are often united by blood ties and usually are of the same or a close social class [15] [though not necessarily the same tenure class, as Schuler (39, pp. 192–206) found in the corn and cotton belts].

An important function of informal groups is the communication of the news. This function is especially significant in isolated areas where news of a death, illness, birth, or trouble may move with great speed through an informal network.

Arensberg and Kimball [16] provide us with a picture of the informal

[15] See (27, pp. 149–150 and 152–153).
[16] See the discussion, pp. 28–38 above. Original source (2, Ch. X).

group as a medium of social control in the form of the old men's *cuaird,* which operates to unite the whole agricultural community. Unquestionably informal groups serve also as a means for mobilizing neighbors in case of danger of attack from without, whether in the form of hostile enemies on horseback, as in former days, or in the form of the anti-parity senator in the present era.

CHAPTER REFERENCES

 1. Anderson, W. A., "The Transmission of Farming as an Occupation," Cornell University Ag. Exp. Sta. Bull. 768, 1941.
 2. Arensberg, C. M. and Kimball, S. T., *Family and Community in Ireland,* Cambridge: Harvard University Press, 1948.
 3. Bell, E. H., "Social Stratification in a Small Community," *The Scientific Monthly,* 38:157–164, 1934.
 4. Bureau of Agricultural Economics, *Farm Tenancy in the United States, 1919–36,* Washington: U.S. Department of Agriculture, Agricultural Economics Bibliography No. 70, 1937.
 5. Cooley, C. H., *Human Nature and the Social Order,* New York: Scribners, 1902.
 6. Donohue, G. A., "A Statistical Analysis of Socio-Economic Factors Related to Part-time Farming in the States of Washington, Oregon, and Idaho." Unpublished Ph.D. Dissertation, State College of Washington, 1954.
 7. Du Bois, C., *The People of Alor,* Minneapolis: University of Minnesota Press, 1944.
 8. Duncan, O. D. and Artis, J. W., "Social Stratification in a Pennsylvania Rural Community," *Pennsylvania Ag. Exp. Bull. 543,* State College, Pa., 1951.
 9. Fisher, L. H., *The Harvest Labor Market in California,* Cambridge, Harvard University Press, 1953.
10. Gee, W., "A Qualitative Study of Rural Depopulation in a Single Township; 1900–1930," *American Journal of Sociology,* 39:210–221, 1933.
11. Gist, N. P. and Halbert, L. A., *Urban Society,* New York: Crowell, 1956.
12. Gray, L. C., *History of Agriculture in the Southern United States to 1860,* Washington: The Carnegie Institution of Washington, 1933, Vol. I.
13. Hallowell, A. I., *Culture and Experience,* Philadelphia: University of Pennsylvania Press, 1955.
14. Hibbard, B. H., *Agricultural Economics,* New York: McGraw-Hill, 1948.
15. Hill, G. W., and Christensen, H. T., "Cultural Factors and Occupational Mobility," *Rural Sociology,* 7:192–200, 1942.
16. Honigmann, J. J., *Culture and Personality,* New York: Harper, 1954.

17. John, M. E., "Part-time Farming in Six Industrial Areas in Pennsylvania," *Pennsylvania State College Bulletin 361,* State College, Penna., 1938.
18. Kardiner, A., *The Individual and His Society,* New York: Columbia University Press, 1939.
19. ———, *The Psychological Frontiers of Society,* New York: Columbia University Press, 1945.
20. Kaufman, H. F., "Prestige Classes in a New York Rural Community," *Cornell University Ag. Exp. Sta. Memoir 260,* 1944.
21. Kolb, J. H. and Brunner, E. de S., *A Study of Rural Society,* Boston: Houghton Mifflin, 1946.
22. Landis, P. H., *Rural Life in Process,* New York: McGraw-Hill, 1948.
23. ———, "The Territorial and Occupational Mobility of Washington Youth," Pullman, Wash.: *Washington Ag. Exp. Sta. Bull. 449,* 1944.
24. Lind, A. W., *An Island Community,* Chicago: University of Chicago Press, 1938.
25. Linton, R., *The Cultural Background of Personality,* New York: Appleton-Century-Crofts, 1945.
26. Lipset, S. M., *Agrarian Socialism,* Berkeley: University of California Press, 1950.
27. Loomis, C. P., and Beegle, J. A., *Rural Social Systems,* New York: Prentice-Hall, 1950.
28. Macgregor, G. with Hassrick, R. B. and Henry, W. E., *Warriors Without Weapons,* Chicago: University of Chicago Press, 1946.
29. Malzberg, B., *Social and Biological Aspects of Mental Disease,* Utica, N.Y.: State Hospitals Press, 1941.
30. Mangus, A. R., "Personality Adjustment of Rural and Urban Children," *American Sociological Review,* 13:566–575, 1948.
31. Nelson, L., *Rural Sociology,* New York: American Book Co., 1948.
32. Reuss, C. F., "A Qualitative Study of Depopulation in a Remote Rural District: 1900–1930," *Rural Sociology,* 2:66–75, 1937.
33. ———, "Social Characteristics of Part-time Farmers in Washington," *Washington Agriculture Experiment Station Bulletin 380,* Pullman, Wash., 1939.
34. Rubin, M., *Plantation County,* Chapel Hill: University of North Carolina Press, 1951.
35. Saloutos, T. and Hicks, J. D., *Agricultural Discontent in the Middle West, 1900–1939,* Madison: University of Wisconsin Press, 1951.
36. Sanderson, D., *Rural Sociology and Rural Social Organization,* New York: Wiley, 1942.
37. Schuler, E. A., "The Present Social Status of American Farm Tenants," *Rural Sociology,* 3:20–33, 1938.
38. ———, "Social and Economic Status in a Louisiana Hills Community," *Rural Sociology,* 5:69–87, 1940.
39. ———, *Social Status and Farm Tenure: Attitudes and Social Conditions of Corn Belt and Cotton Belt Farmers,* U.S. Dept. of Agriculture, Social Research Report IV, Washington, 1938.

40. Slocum, W. L., "Migrants from Rural South Dakota Families, Their Geographical and Occupational Distribution," Brookings, S.D.: *Ag. Exp. Sta. Bull. 359,* 1942.

41. Smith, T. L., *The Sociology of Rural Life,* New York: Harper, 1953.

42. Sorokin, P. A.; Zimmerman, C. C.; and Galpin, C. J. (eds.), *A Systematic Source Book in Rural Sociology,* Minneapolis: University of Minnesota Press, 1932.

43. Spillman, W. J., "The Agricultural Ladder," *American Economic Review Supplement,* 9:170–179, March 1919.

44. Straus, M. A., "Personal Characteristics and Functional Needs in the Choice of Farming as an Occupation," *Rural Sociology,* 21:257–266, 1956.

45. ———, "Selected Factors in the Occupational Choice of Wisconsin High School Seniors," M.S. Thesis (unpub.), Dept. of Sociology, University of Wisconsin, 1949.

46. Taylor, C. C., *The Farmers' Movement, 1620–1920,* New York: American Book Co., 1953.

47. ———, et al., *Rural Life in the United States,* New York: Knopf, 1949.

48. Taylor, H. C., *Agricultural Economics,* New York: Macmillan, 1919.

49. Theodorou, N. T., "A Study of Former Students of Vocational Agriculture in the Watkins Glen Area," Ithaca, N.Y.: *Cornell Univ. Ag. Exp. Sta. Bull. 848,* 1948.

50. Wakeley, R. E., "Part-time and Garden Farming in Iowa," *Iowa Agriculture Experiment Station Bulletin 340,* Ames, Iowa, 1935.

CHAPTER TEN

THE RESTAURANT

We shall first describe the characteristics of the restaurant that mark it off from other industries. These features, although distinctive, are not unique, and our analysis will be generalizable to bakeries, drug stores, and some manufacturing plants that operate sales rooms on the premises. We shall proceed, second, to analyze work relations in the restaurant by applying the conceptual framework presented in Chapter Two.

DISTINCTIVE CHARACTERISTICS OF THE RESTAURANT

COMBINATION OF PRODUCTION AND SERVICE

A factory begins with certain raw materials and ends up by producing a finished product. The product is then sold, usually in large lots or else goes into inventory. Once this is achieved the factory is through with it. On the other hand, a barber has the equipment but only a minimum of raw materials. His essential task is the performance of a service only. The restaurant begins with raw materials such as fruit, vegetables, meat, or fish and it then produces a finished product—a meal—*and* produces it *as ordered*—one only, or a very few at a time.

Some standardization is present,[1] but most restaurants serve a wide variety of meals and, in many cases, in a week there may be hundreds of different kinds of meals prepared.

The tie between production and service is normally a close one.

---

[1] For example, an exclusive restaurant in a western city has a variety of appetizers and drinks but only one main dish: prime ribs of beef.

If the factory product does not sell well, eventually production will be cut back or shifted. But when a cheese omelet smells bad, the chef is likely to hear about it within minutes after he has made it. The whole production process is highly sensitive to any changes in the service function in the restaurant. It is difficult for the production process or indeed for anyone to manipulate the customer very much. If the customer does not like what he secures he is able to affect the production process immediately.

HIGHLY VARIABLE PRODUCTION AND SERVICE

The menu is varied from meal to meal. There are peaks in the normal restaurant day which may occur three or four times daily: breakfast, lunch, dinner, and midnight. In addition there may be smaller peaks at points in between.

George Orwell (11, pp. 61–65), who worked in a Paris hotel restaurant during the Depression of the 1930's, describes these peaks in the restaurant day with great vividness:

The work in the cafeteria was spasmodic. We were never idle, but the real work only came in bursts of two hours at a time—we called each burst *"un coup de feu."* The first *coup de feu* came at eight, when the guests upstairs began to wake up and demand breakfast. At eight a sudden banging and yelling would break out all through the basement; bells rang on all sides, blue-aproned men rushed through the passages, our service lifts came down with a simultaneous crash, and the waiters on all five floors began shouting Italian oaths down the shafts. I don't remember all our duties, but they included making tea, coffee, and chocolate, fetching meals from the kitchen, wines from the cellar and fruit and so forth from the dining-room, slicking bread, making toast, rolling pats of butter, measuring jam, opening milk-cans, counting lumps of sugar, boiling eggs, cooking porridge, pounding ice, grinding coffee—all this for from a hundred to two hundred customers. The kitchen was thirty yards away, and the dining-room sixty or seventy yards. Everything we sent up in the service lifts had to be covered by a voucher, and the vouchers had to be carefully filed, and there was trouble if even a lump of sugar was lost. Besides this, we had to supply the staff with bread and coffee, and fetch the meals for the waiters upstairs. All in all, it was a complicated job.

I calculated that one had to walk and run about fifteen miles during the day, and yet the strain of the work was more mental than physical. Nothing could be easier, on the face of it, than this stupid scullion work, but it is as astonishingly hard when one is in a hurry. One has to leap to and fro between a multitude of jobs—it is like sorting a pack of cards against the clock. You are, for example, making toast, when bang! down comes another demanding scrambled eggs, coffee and grapefruit; you run to the kitchen for the eggs and to the dining-room for the fruit, going like lightning so as to be back before

your toast burns, and having to remember about the tea and coffee, besides
half a dozen other orders that are still pending; and at the same time some
waiter is following you and making trouble about a lost bottle of soda-water,
and you are arguing with him. It needs more brains than one might think. Mario
said, no doubt truly, that it took a year to make a reliable cafetier.

The time between eight and half-past ten was a sort of delirium. Sometimes we were going as though we had only five minutes to live; sometimes there
were sudden lulls when the orders stopped and everything seemed quiet for a
moment. Then we swept up the litter from the floor, threw down fresh sawdust,
and swallowed gallipots of wine or coffee or water—anything, so long as it
was wet. Very often we used to break off chunks of ice and suck them while
we worked. The heat among the gasfires was nauseating; we swallowed quarts of
drink during the day, and after a few hours even our aprons were drenched
with sweat. At times we were hopelessly behind with the work, and some of
the customers would have gone without their breakfast, but Mario always pulled
us through. He had worked fourteen years in the cafeteria, and he had the
skill that never wastes a second between jobs. The Magyar was very stupid and
I was inexperienced, and Boris was inclined to shirk, partly because of his lame
leg, partly he was ashamed of working in the cafeteria after being a waiter;
but Mario was wonderful. The way he would stretch his great arms right across
the cafeteria to fill a coffee-pot with one hand and boil an egg with the other,
at the same time watching toast and shouting directions to the Magyar, and
between wiles singing snatches from *Rigoletto,* was beyond all praise. The patron
knew his value and he was paid a thousand francs a month instead of five hundred like the rest of us.

The breakfast pandemonium stopped at half-past ten. Then we scrubbed
the cafeteria tables, swept the floor and polished the brasswork, and on good
mornings, went one at a time to the lavatory for a smoke. This was our slack
time—only relatively slack, however, for we had only ten minutes for lunch
and we never got through it uninterrupted. The customers' luncheon hour,
between twelve and two, was another period of turmoil like the breakfast hour.
Most of our work was fetching meals from the kitchen, which meant constant
engueulades from the cooks. By this time the cooks had sweated in front of
their furnaces for four or five hours, and their tempers were all warmed up.

At two we were suddenly free men. We threw off our aprons and put on
our coats, hurried out of doors, and, when we had money, dived into the
nearest bistro. It was strange, coming up into the street from those firelit cellars.
The air seemed blindingly clear and cold, like arctic summer; and how sweet
the petrol did smell, after the stenches of sweat and food! Sometimes we met
some of our cooks and waiters in the bistros, and they were friendly and stood
us drinks. Indoors we were their slaves, but it is an etiquette in hotel life that
between hours everyone is equal, and the *engueulades* do not count.

At a quarter to five we went back to the hotel. Till half-past six there
were no orders, and we used this time to polish silver, clean out the coffee
urns, and do other odd jobs. Then the grand turmoil of the day started—
the dinner hour. I wish I could be Zola for a little while, just to describe that

dinner hour. The essence of the situation was that a hundred or two hundred people were demanding individually different meals of five or six courses, and that fifty or sixty people had to cook and serve them and clean up the mess afterwards; anyone with experience of catering will know what that means. And at this time when the work was doubled, the whole staff was tired out, and a number of them were drunk. I could write pages about the scenes without giving a true idea of it. The chargings to and fro in the narrow passages, the collisions, the yells, the struggling with crates and trays and blocks of ice, the heat, the darkness, the furious festering quarrels which there was no time to fight out—they pass description. Anyone coming into the basement for the first time would have thought himself in a den of maniacs. It was only later, when I understood the working of a hotel, that I saw order in all this chaos.

At half-past eight the work stopped very suddenly. We were not free till nine, but we used to throw ourselves full length on the floor, and lie there resting our legs, too lazy even to go to the ice cupboard for a drink. Sometimes the *Chef du personnel* would come with bottles of beer, for the hotel stood us an extra beer when we had had a hard day. The food we were given was no more than eatable, but the *patron* was not mean about drink; he allowed us two litres of wine a day each, knowing that if a *plongeur* is not given two litres he will steal three. We had the heeltaps of bottles as well, so that we often drank too much—a good thing, for one seemed to work faster when partially drunk.

Production admits only of partial mechanization. Coffee, for example, may be made in gallons by percolator, potatoes may be sliced by machines, but roast duck must go into an oven and be watched. Almost every product is different and must be made to order.

PERISHABLE COMMODITIES

Food, especially cooked food, is highly perishable. Therefore, production cannot get very far ahead of demand. The highly standardized restaurant can reduce this problem, but usually, food must be prepared as ordered.

Consequently, there is a great emphasis on timing. It is necessary that there be a careful balancing of cooking and preparing times. Also there must be careful stockpiling in the pantries and refrigerators. This means a relationship of close dependence between appropriate personnel.

SMALLNESS

The giant restaurant, with three or four floors and perhaps as many as two or three hundred workers, is rare. The average restaurant is a small establishment. As a consequence the line from top to bottom is short. It is not far from the waitress or the cook to the owner. This means in turn a scarcity of possible promotions. Therefore ways must be provided for rewarding the workers in other ways: through pay increases, through security provisions, or through informal friendship. It means also that workers can get to know each other quite well on the job—and that has possibilities both for harmony and for conflict.

The fact that a restaurant can be very small indeed, as in the case of a man and his wife selling hot dogs across a six-foot counter on a street corner, means that *entry* is fairly easy as an owner, and little capital is required. But the uncertainties of the business, lack of experience, and other factors produce a high mortality.

PREDOMINANCE OF WOMEN

In the old country, food service was a man's job from chef to waiter. We still find this in many foreign-food restaurants in this country, but by and large our restaurant industry has been invaded by women. This factor gives it many of the characteristics of white-collar and other occupations in which women predominate: wages tend to be low; unionization is weak; a large proportion of workers do not view the work as a "career" but tend to be working only until marriage; and many work for only a short time in order to *supplement* the family income. These factors taken together produce high turnover.

At the same time the restaurant provides one of the few industries that can offer women a full-time career and can offer them supervisory positions. This in turn creates certain problems involving men who work under female supervisors or in which women are placed in a position where they give orders to men.

THE IMMEDIATE PRESENCE OF THE CUSTOMER

The customer, who can directly influence all the restaurant workers, is only there for a brief time; he is not likely to come back later as is the buyer of dresses or industrial machinery. Consequently, the customer must be introduced into the service, served quickly and efficiently at the time that he wants service. Those who meet the customer are forced to maintain a cheerful air and in some respects are forced to function lake a continuous chorus line in a vaudeville show. The waitress must be able to shift her mood as she moves from kitchen or pantry into the dining room. Orwell (11, pp. 67–69) has described his own experience as follows:

It is an instructive sight to see a waiter going into a hotel dining-room. As he passes the door a sudden change comes over him. The set of his shoulders alters; all the dirt and hurry and irritation have dropped off in an instant. He glides over the carpet, with a solemn priest-like air. I remember our assistant *maître d'hôtel,* a fiery Italian, pausing at the dining-room door to address an apprentice who had broken a bottle of wine. Shaking his fist above his head he yelled (luckily the door was more or less soundproof):

"Tu me fais—Do you call yourself a waiter, you young bastard? You a waiter! You are not fit to scrub the floors in the brothel your mother came from. *Maquereau!"*

Words failing him he turned to the door; and as he opened it he delivered a final insult in the same manner as Squire Weston in *Tom Jones.*

Then he entered the dining-room and sailed across it dish in hand, graceful as a swan. Ten seconds later he was bowing reverently to a customer. And you could not help thinking as you saw him bow and smile, with the benign smile of the trained waiter, that the customer was put to shame by having such an aristocrat to serve him.

The personal contact with the customer also means attention must be paid to personal appearance and to manners. If all goes well, then all are likely to take credit. If, however, matters go poorly, then the waitress is likely to bear the direct force of the criticism of the customer.

The customer also influences service and the manufacturing process by his social status. It may make a considerable difference whether the customers tend to be primarily factory workers or to be business executives. The customer has, further, a concrete way of expressing his feeling—tipping—which is still important in the restaurant industry.

ANALYSIS

THE INSTITUTIONAL SYSTEM

1. THE WORK COMPLEX

Like yam-growing in Dobu or raising milch cows in Eire, we find that the restaurant tends to relate itself to other structural components of society. Among other things, it relates itself to the community in the form of the labor union and in the manner in which it reflects racial and ethnic attitudes.

The restaurant, in one form or other, is very old in history. The tavern, the inn, the coffee house and tea house are universal. They exist as integral parts of cultures or have grown up to serve traders or transients or to express hospitality. When migrants have moved to another area in large numbers, there has usually sprung up a middle class of persons to supply the cultural food tastes of the people. The Negro might still want his grits, the Britisher his ale, the German his strüdel, the Hungarian his mammalege, the Japanese his fish and rice, the Italian his pizza, the Russian his borscht, and the Jew his gefüllte fish. These might be provided by the family in the home, but usually the whole family did not come or it was too difficult to import the ingredients. As a consequence, the "foreign" restaurant sprang up in the United States and is, even today, an almost infallible way to locate a distinctive nationality area in a large city. Food tastes are cultural and the restaurant symbolizes this fact.

In the United States, the rise of the restaurant as a distinct function is tied up with the decline of the traditional family functions and the rise of the city. Ogburn (10, pp. 125–30) has described these functions and has pointed out that among those that have left the family is included what he calls the "economic" function. The latter includes the provision of food to family members. Burgess and Locke (1, p. 463) have further documented this trend with figures of the increase in purchases from bakeries, the greater consumption of canned fruits and vegetables, and the increased tendency to *eat out*.

The modern restaurant assumes the function of feeding those who are not at home or who have no home. The rise of the city, with rural-urban migration, and with the great migrations out of the Deep South has greatly increased the need for the impersonal eating place. This was especially true during World War II when large numbers of persons migrated to war-industry areas. Whyte states that it is estimated that approximately 25 per cent of the food consumed in the United States is eaten in restaurants.

The restaurant is closely articulated with business in our society. It is a place where businessmen like to meet and talk over business affairs or make contracts. One business executive put it as follows:

> I like to talk business at lunch, especially if I'm not sure of myself or of the client. In the office, you have to give your full attention to the matter at hand. There is no chance for kidding or banter and it's hard to size up a man. At lunch, you get a chance to think. He can't talk when his mouth is full of veal cutlets, and I can pause while I take a drink of coffee to prepare for some question he has asked me. It's the pauses that a lunch naturally provides that makes the difference.

The restaurant provides space, privacy if needed, and an obvious excuse for meeting at all. Fraternal organizations such as Rotary or Kiwanis customarily meet in hotel dining rooms, as do many political organizations.

The restaurant is closely tied up with the dating complex in our society and a young couple normally consider an evening incomplete until they have had coffee or a milkshake. It has become a stage in the courtship pattern with symbolic significance. The young man takes his girl to a restaurant at first. When he begins to take her home to family meals, that signifies an engagement or a much closer relationship.

The restaurant is the place where friends of either sex may meet informally. This function of the restaurant seems to be universal and is illustrated in the German coffee house, the French café, or the British pub.

Union Relations. Restaurant workers were among the first to be unionized by the AFL but they suffered a decline in the post World War I period, largely because of a combination of high wages and prohibition. The union organization revived in the depression years, particularly in the speakeasies. It has since expanded, but the restaurant industry is still only about 10 per cent unionized. The low state of unionization is due in large part to the multiplicity of units, to the small size of the restaurant, and to the large number of women and transient employees. The presence of women is an especially important influence. W. F. Whyte (12, p. 191) provides us with statements from women in a restaurant union: [2]

> Why don't you look into the damn union while you are at it? As if we didn't have enough trouble making money, we have to shell out to them too!
> Another woman said, "All they do is collect money and give you nothing in return."

This is a fairly general situation in industry. Those who do not plan permanent careers are likely to feel that a union is useless.

Within the restaurant itself the major figure, so far as union relations are concerned, is the *steward* or *delegate*. This person is usually appointed or elected by union members. His is the function of collecting dues and acting as a first step in the grievance procedure.

The most significant point about his role is that it is a marginal one and is so on two levels. In the first place, the steward is a worker, often on the lowest level in the restaurant. He may be only a bus boy. As such he is used to taking orders from others. However, when he represents the union he must be able to make a radical shift of roles and carry a grievance to any supervisor even though that person might be in a totally different department. He might have to carry a grievance to his own supervisor in certain cases. This ability to shift roles means that the steward must be an expert in human relations able to exercise diplomatic skills. As might be expected, such persons are rare in any case and the hope that these talents will be found in the lowly bus boy are often not realized.

On a second level the problem is stated by Whyte (12, p. 197) as follows:

---

[2] There is little question that Whyte's study of the restaurant industry is the most thorough and meaningful research on the restaurant available. Of particular value are the interview excerpts he provides.

Is the steward a representative of the workers or is he just another person in authority over them? This question arises because the steward has authority to carry grievances upward and has the strength of the union in back of him. He is there to help the worker but he can also refuse help if he feels that the case does not warrant special attention. He may prefer to reserve his grievance visits to management for the important or big gripes. Consequently the worker must "sell" the steward on his gripe in much the same way he would have to "sell" his own supervisor if he were to carry the gripe upward himself.

The union is one means by which the worker tries to control his destiny. The union may offer him security or tenure, a chance to secure a hearing for complaints or to take care of special needs. But the union is not as yet a major factor in relations within the restaurant industry. Unionization is low and the union steward normally speaks for only a small proportion of workers.

Ethnic Relations. Race relations exhibit a special feature in the restaurant industry. The association with food preparation and serving and the Negro is very old in the United States. The restaurant is a place in which customers are not at all surprised to find Negro workers. It fits their stereotype of the kind of job in which a Negro will be found. For this reason, it has been possible for Negroes to secure jobs in restaurants with some degree of ease.

To the extent that the restaurant involves subservience and that such work has low status, the restaurant is one of the frontiers of Negro-white contact. In the factory, a white worker may refuse to work next to a Negro, yet this same man has no objection to a Negro working in the kitchen of the company cafeteria. The Negro kitchen-worker is in a subservient role, and as such the white man is willing to accept him. The entry of Negroes (and women) into the restaurant is part of a general tendency for them to enter the industrial system in service occupations and at the bottom.

Whyte notes that the attitude toward the Negro is a function of the community in which the restaurant is located. For example, the owner of a white restaurant located in an area where there was fear of residential "invasion" from a neighboring Negro area, was against hiring Negroes because this, for him, would be symbolic of the entry of Negroes into the neighborhood as residents (12, p. 173).

Strong anti-Negro feelings are especially likely with persons who have had a previous background in the South in the United States or persons who are experiencing status problems in their work. Sometimes both of these occur together, because a person may have left the South because of insecurities.

It will be recalled from the discussion in Chapter Four that a status problem may be interpreted as a divergence between the individual's self-conceptions and the conceptions that others have of him. Consequently, status problems are especially likely to occur and to be acute among downwardly mobile persons. Such persons at one time occupied positions of greater importance and now feel that they have fallen beneath their dignity. They are likely to regard themselves in the light of their former positions and feel that others do not give sufficient recognition to their competence.

The downwardly mobile person finds in the Negro a convenient target for his aggressions (12, p. 181), partly because working with Negroes affects his conception of how others will think of him. He is *forced* to work at a job that he considers beneath him and with people whom he considers beneath him (especially Negroes). Hence he may fear that his friends will decide that he has fallen indeed if he is reduced to *that,* whether he personally has anti-Negro feelings or not.

There are also cleavages among the Negro workers. The Negro, like the white, tends to behave in the way he is expected to: if he is considered lazy he will act lazy; if he is considered conscientious he is likely to be conscientious. Now, the role imposed on a Negro worker by management may cause that worker to have a split in his identity.[3] Whyte (12, p. 177) points out that "If the Negro worker was humble, hard working and willing to inform on his fellows, he was highly valued. . . ." That is, the Negro who identifies with management and accepts a humble role in that identification is likely to be valued by management. However, if he does so, he is rejected by his fellow-Negroes (1) as a fellow-worker who rejects his own work group, and (2) as a Negro who is rejecting his own race. Whyte does not comment on what happens to such people except to say that they are the objects of dislike from other Negroes. But other evidence from industry suggests that more drastic procedures may be employed. For example, such persons may be refused help in emergencies or else an attempt will be made to make things difficult for them in any activity requiring cooperation. The division of labor requires cooperation and one of the ways to hurt a man is to refuse to coordinate one's activities with his. Such a man may get a reputation for doing a poor job. For example, if the runner to the kitchen refuses to get food to the pantry worker or else gives him unreliable information, then the pantry worker does a poor job. Since management customarily tends to regard each job and individual separately, if the job is poorly done the incumbent is the one who is blamed. The person who violates group understandings is also likely

---

[3] See the heading "Identifications" in Chapter 5. For an extraordinarily perceptive fictional account of the Negro's identity problems, see (4, p. 177).

to be cut off from informal communication and informal news which may affect his welfare does not reach him.

Because of high visibility and the already existing attitudes, the Negro in industry generally is likely to be blamed for any problem that turns up. For example, if any stealing or pilfering takes place, he is the logical suspect. This means that the Negro must be particularly careful. This is also true about oppressed minorities generally. When he behaves like his fellow workers he is considered to be lazy, inefficient, or else "just like a nigger." The Negro who shows interest in shorter working hours is called lazy, the Negro who seeks a better job is called shiftless, the Negro who shows interest in sex is likely to be referred to as being "just out of the jungle." The Negro who shows interest in politics is likely to be dubbed a radical. The result is a situation of great tension in which almost all relations become colored by race.

2. THE WORK STRUCTURE

We next consider the nature of the division of labor and how specialties are related to each other. The division of labor will necessarily vary depending on the size of the restaurant. Clearly, the division of labor present in the small diner operated by a man and his wife will be different from that in a large restaurant with several kitchens and pantries. The discussion is necessarily general but it is the medium-sized restaurant that we are analyzing.

Types of Specialties. The three main specialties present in a restaurant are: food preparation, customer service, and staff activities. The last is auxiliary and includes preparatory, mediating and control activities. *Food preparation* includes all of the persons who are involved in the production of prepared food from raw materials. These are the cooks, the salad-makers, the fish preparers, and the bartenders. *Customer service* includes persons who serve the customer directly. The main group here are waiters and waitresses. But it may also include entertainers and, in some restaurants, girls who drink with the customers and girls who gamble with them. There may also be hat-check girls. These persons are often employed on a contract basis and have little to do with the others in the organization. The core of the customer-service specialists are the waiters and waitresses. Food preparation and customer service are aided by three types of auxiliary *staff activities: Preparatory* activities involve persons who prepare materials or tools for others to use—for example, the dishwashers, the clean-up men, and bus boys. In a large restaurant a maintenance man may be employed. *Mediating* activities involve persons who serve as links between the specialized departments. The most important group are the pantry workers who link food preparation and customer service. And, there are runners who link the pantry to the kitchen. Because these persons have liaison functions it is often not clear who has supervisory responsibility over them, and therefore these persons, or rather their jobs, are likely to form centers of conflict. *Control* activities involve persons who serve as a continuing check on others. They include checkers, cost control personnel, and cashiers.

These are the major formal specialties found in the normal restaurant. In a large restaurant one may have a different person performing each one. As one moves to smaller and smaller restaurants the specialties are still there but they are combined in one person. In the smallest of restaurants, a single man may both prepare the food and serve it.

Specialty Variability. The restaurant exhibits a great range in skills. The chef is a highly skilled professional. In large restaurants he receives a salary comparable to that of a top executive in a factory. In some respects he is the kingpin of the whole organization and sets the tone of the restaurant. He is often regarded and regards himself as a *prima donna.*

As we move along the scale of skillfulness we meet specialty cooks, salad workers, and bartenders. These still represent a high degree of training and skill. The waiters and waitresses occupy a middle place, though there is a great deal of difference between an experienced and an inexperienced waitress. Then we see persons of very slight skills such as dish washers and bus boys. This skill hierarchy has significance for status.

Shortness of Line. In most restaurants there are at most only three or four steps from bottom to top. This means that the worker is close to the top and this reduces the likelihood of information moving up the line and being stopped on the way or being amended very much before it reaches the top. Gripes and complaints can move up fast. Indeed it is hard to keep them from going up. We have here a factor which may help to explain why unionization is weak in the restaurant industry.

At the other end of the supervisory structure, the manager or supervisor is enabled to maintain close control of the organization. Because he is so close to the bottom he can see to it that his orders are obeyed precisely as he gives them. This situation provides a great contrast from that prevailing in a factory, where one may find an order being issued by production control in the office, then passing through several clerks, then going to the factory superintendent, then to the department head, then to the foreman, thence to the worker.

However, the possibility of closeness of supervision may itself create serious problems and prevent the development of initiative or the delegation of authority and responsibility.

Intimate Contact. Due to the small size of the restaurant, all specialists are likely to be in close contact with each other and usually work on the same floor. Horizontal communication can take place very quickly and misunderstandings may be less frequent than in the case where they have a long distance (official) to cover. But this very closeness can also lead to irritability, snappy replies, and personal conflict.

Closeness of Articulation. One remarkable feature, though not peculiar to the restaurant as such, is the extent to which the specialties are related to each other. The whole thing is like a delicate clock, which may be thrown off by a speck of dust. If the dishes are not clean on time, then food preparation is held up. If food preparation is held up then runners become agitated and pantries become empty. Waitresses become irritated and customers begin to complain. The whole thing points to the need of careful timing, planning, and skillful supervision.

The closeness of articulation of specialties also means that the restaurant worker is not likely to be seized with the *malaise* of the factory worker who may feel at times that his work is meaningless and may not be able to see his place in it. In the restaurant, even the dishwasher is not likely to experience a feeling of meaninglessness of work.

3. THE ECONOMIC COMPLEX

Most restaurant employees receive a fixed salary (though it may be computed on an hourly basis) but the situation is complicated by several factors. Some meals are usually provided and considered a part of the salary. The employer may calculate what he could get for such a meal from the customer and subtract the amount from what is considered an acceptable salary. The inclusion of meals is one reason why restaurant workers' salaries are likely to be lower than those of others doing comparable work.

As discussed in Chapter Three, any payment in kind reduces the freedom of the worker to spend his money as he wishes. It also reduces his ability to assume the symbols of middle-class status. For example, among white-collar women in offices, a great emphasis is placed upon chic clothes and a "modern" apartment. These things are gained by cutting down on food: coffee and toast is breakfast, a watercress salad and milkshake is lunch, and for dinner she may splurge and have a lamb chop with potato salad. The restaurant worker is not free to manipulate his salary in that manner. It means also, that like the servant who gets cast-off clothes from her mistress, she is often forced to take what she gets. As a consequence, meals or the food at a restaurant may be a focus of complaint. for example, Whyte (12, p. 148) reports that one waitress said:

At Blank's they specialized in steaks. But for the ones that worked there they only had a fish dish at noon and a meat dish at night. It isn't like here where you can get anything that is served to the guests.

A second factor which introduces variability in income is the tipping system. Whyte (12, p. 98) states: "In the restaurants we studied, at least half of the service employees' earnings came in the form of tips, and with some of them it was nearly as high as three-quarters." Frequently, tips are the means of producing high take-home pay. A tip is a combination of two types of payment that are widespread in our culture, *piece work* and *symbolic gifts.*

Viewed as piece work, a tip is roughly related to output. The better or the more efficient the service is, the larger the tip is likely to be. But there are rigidities: some customers tip automatically; others never tip. The waitress actually has little control over the amount of the tip. The tip tends to become standardized; books on courtship and etiquette will state that a tip *should* be 10 or 15 per cent. This makes it into a more or less straight service charge.

The tip is not only an economic reward but a symbolic gift. It may symbolize several things. First, it is an expression of feeling toward the waitress and the restaurant as a whole. A large tip means "I like this restaurant and the way I'm treated,' whereas "stiffing" (leaving no tip at all) may mean the opposite. The tip also symbolizes the customer's superior position: he can tip or not as he pleases; the waitress is dependent on him. The tip therefore binds her symbiotically to the customer in a way that the department store clerk, for example, is not bound. The uncertainty of the amount of tips makes budget planning difficult for a waitress. She does not know from week to week how much she will have, and there are seasonal variations as well.

Hidden expenses may also be important. Those whom the customers see must present a satisfactory appearance. Uniforms are usually provided by management though there may be a deduction from salary for laundry. However, the cost of make-up and hair dressing must be borne by the waitress herself. Persons such as the cashier are unable to wear a uniform and themselves bear the cost of being neatly attired.

THE STATUS AND AUTHORITY SYSTEM IN THE RESTAURANT

1. STATUS

In peasant societies, the tavern or innkeeper occupies a middle position in the prestige hierarchy: he is one of the townsfolk and is a "cut above" the rural customers. In our society, restaurant workers share the prestige usually assigned to persons whose occupations are associated with the growing or sale of food. This position is relatively low, though not at the bottom.[4] Yet there is certainly a considerable

[4] The National Opinion Research Center study (8) reported that "bartender," "soda fountain clerk" and "restaurant worker" were all rated very near the bottom of 90

range—from bus boys (who have very low prestige or marginal colleague position altogether) to chefs (who, in some restaurants, have the prestige and economic position of full professionals).

One factor of importance is size of the enterprise: prestige tends to go with bigness. The worker for United States Steel tends, other things being equal, to occupy a superior position in people's eyes than does the worker for a small steel company. Restaurants tend to be small; consequently the restaurant is not likely to be known widely in the country and the worker is unable to say, in the manner of a steelworker, "I am out at U.S. Steel." The expression "I am out at Joe's Diner" would be ludicrous.

The statuses of restaurant employee and customer may be related. In a restaurant that serves working-class people, waitress and customer may be of equal status or else the waitress may occupy a higher position. Under these conditions she may talk back to the customer and kid him. But in restaurants which serve upper- or middle-class persons, the waitress must be obsequious and deferential (12, pp. 370–71).

At the same time, the waiter or waitress attempts to control the customer, in part to offset what she may feel is her subordinate position; and a skilled waitress is precisely one who is able to manipulate the customer to some extent.

In addition to the status relation of the restaurant to the outside world, the restaurant exhibits a complex internal status structure. It tends to revolve about the division of labor and is related to the following elements: relation to the cooking range, type of food, type of activity (preparing as opposed to actually cooking), skill, background factors (experience, seniority, sex, etc.), and position in the authority structure.

The prestige of an activity was found to be related to how close the activity involved the kitchen range. The nature of this relationship is described by Whyte (12, pp. 34–5) as follows:

We found, first, that the stations themselves were socially ranked. At the top, of course, stood the range where all the cooking took place. Here were the positions that were most highly paid and were considered most skilled. Nearly everything in the kitchen revolved around the range. Next came the salad station, which also dealt in finished products with high prestige value. The work here was considered skilled, and the women vegetable cooks on the range spoke respectfully of the salad station, saying that they would be glad to work

---

occupations; "restaurant cook" was rated somewhat higher, and "owner-operator of lunch stand" was rated toward the middle but still below it. (The "ratings" are composites, obtained through summation, and involving a large number of ties.) The income of restaurant employees appears also to be definitely below the median, even for females. See (9).

there if they hadn't positions on the range. Next in this scheme came the chicken preparation and meat preparation stations, the latter being a subsidiary of the range. Toward the bottom were the chicken cooking and vegetable preparation stations. Vegetable preparation was under the supervision of the vegetable cooks, who worked at the range.

The kind of food worked on is also used in giving a prestige estimate of the individual. Whyte discovered that the vegetables were socially ranked (at the top were the decorative items such as parsley, and at the bottom were potatoes and onions); that personnel generally had a low estimate of working on fish; and that a distinction was made between persons who worked on the light and dark meat of chickens, which corresponds roughly to the preference for white meat expressed by urban persons at large (12, pp. 36, 42-3).

In general, those who prepare food *for* cooking have lower prestige than those who actually cook, in part because the former in a sense assist the latter.

Prestige tends to increase with degree of skill. But this fact may produce an attempt to rationalize in terms of an assumed skill difference when one is not actually present. For example, there is very little difference in skill between peeling potatoes and slicing them, yet slicing is accorded higher prestige. Speaking broadly, we can say that skill is a crude determinant of prestige. The waitress definitely has higher prestige than the bus boy; the chef has higher prestige than the waitress.

In addition to the *place* of the worker in the division of labor, there is also what the worker brings to the job. Experience and seniority are important. One of the most important background factors is sex. Whyte feels that a major source of conflict in the restaurant results from situations in which women originate action for men. Although authority relations between the sexes are more loosely defined in our culture than elsewhere, it is still true that men are accustomed to originate action for women. In the restaurant, because of the position of waitresses and pantry girls, the reverse often is the case; and the female supervisor is quite common. The result is that men often feel irritation and resentment (12, pp. 69, 76-8).

Generally, the higher the formal authority that the individual enjoys, the higher is his prestige. The supervisor has higher prestige than does the non-supervisor. This tends to be reflected in salary, although the waiter or waitress can increase his take-home pay through tips.

A special situation prevails for the checkers: they do not have a supervisory position, and yet possess the authority to control the work behavior of others. The work that the checker does is illustrated in the following quotation (12, p. 82):

I'm the last person who checks the food as it leaves the kitchen. So I watch to see that the waiters are giving the guests the right portions of food, not too much, not too little, and I check to see that he charges them right. I'm responsible to see that the guests are treated the way they should be.

She smiled, "Sometimes it is quite a job. With the old boys, it's easy. You just let them work along and trust them to do right. But with new men you have to be careful. . . .

Since the checker is often a woman, that is likely to create difficulties when she is checking men. Most important, she can hold things up when there is a rush on, and thus anger the waiters. The checker has a semi-supervisory function for a large number of persons, not just a restricted few as is the case for most supervisors. This further increases the difficulty which she experiences when exercising control.

Through the means that have been described, prestige and authority definitions come to be made. The object of such definitions is to provide ways by which workers shall know how they should behave toward one another. When the status system works well, workers know who should originate action, who should take the lead, and who should accept responsibility. The status system then defines a set of consistent relationships in which behavior is predictable. When the system works poorly, relationships are unpredictable, and workers become upset and anxious in ways that we have described.

2. TEACHING AND LEARNING

Who is permitted to learn and who does the teaching? We do not have much evidence, but certain matters appear to be clear. In the restaurant industry, special instruction in formal institutions of learning (e.g., college courses in institutional management) are likely to be taken only by higher supervisors and some professionals. For most persons, learning takes place on the job itself.

Two important bars to learning are race and sex. Negroes tend to be relegated to low status jobs. They are found as bus boys, runners, and dish washers. Consequently they are unable to get experiences as waiters or as cooks to any great extent. There is one notable exception: Negroes who are employed in railroad dining cars. However, it is only an apparent exception because there is usually an all-Negro crew (although the steward is very rarely a Negro). In mixed situations, then, the Negro is prevented from getting the needed learning.

Women in the restaurant are permitted considerable freedom of choice of job, but there tend also to be restrictions. Cooks and food supervisors are usually men. In a mixed situation, the woman is likely to discover that she must *prove* that she is better, a whole lot better, than the men before she is considered to be doing an acceptable job. Whyte, in addition, hints that social class may constitute a bar to becoming a hostess. To the extent that this is so, then the waitress is unable to secure the learning necessary to perform that job.

Teaching is usually done informally by the older, experienced workers. Whyte (12, pp. 212–13) provides us with an illuminating illustration of the introduction of a new worker to the organization:

Take the case of Helen, an 18-year-old girl without previous waitress experience, who went to work at Chandler's Restaurant. . . .

Helen was then introduced to Mary, a skilled waitress a little older than herself, who was highly popular among the younger waitresses. Mary was expected to carry on with the training, in an informal way, and to take Helen into her group.

For the first day and a half, Helen "trailed" Mary. She watched her taking her orders, she followed her into the service pantry, and observed how she organized her work. As they went along, Mary explained what she was doing. As Helen began to see the pattern, Mary let her begin to help in the service.

The second evening, Helen took over a table for two. She was on her own but working right next to Mary's station where she could get help if she needed it—and the hostess followed her, too, with a friendly interest. The next day she took on two tables, and, in a very short time, she was carrying a full station with the skill and assurance of a more experienced girl.

At the lunch hour the first day, Helen made sure Mary had met all her friends, and they all ate together. After lunch, in the two hour period before dinner service began, the girls sat around a table playing cards. Helen was included in the game. The second day the same friendly atmosphere prevailed.

At the end of two days, we found Helen enthusiastic about the restaurant and feeling completely at home. She had become an integral part of the organization in a remarkably short time.

It may be noted in the above quotation that a significant part of the learning included learning how to *fit in* to the work group. While the latter is always important in any work learning situation, it is particularly important in the restaurant because of the normal intimacy of contact and the close articulation of the division of labor.

All occupations and work structures are likely to have means to recognize the experienced worker and to distinguish the tyro. In the restaurant it is not easy for the worker to dissimulate. The closeness of contact and the social character of most activities is likely to show up a lack of experience very quickly.

One of the commonest techniques for recognizing the experienced worker is through the use of an argot—an occupational language which is likely to be remarkably uniform even in different regions. In the restaurant it is found in the means that are used to call out or to write orders to the food production personnel. For example, when the waitress wants two soft boiled eggs she will call out "two in the water"; when she wishes a stack of toast that is buttered, she will call out "stack of butters"; when she wishes a small order of pancakes she will call out, "short stack" and when she wishes a cup of coffee she will call out, "draw one."

The argot has several functions. First and most obviously it functions as a standardized way of giving an order quickly without possible misinterpretation. But once such a system develops it has the secondary function of identifying the inexperienced. The waitress who calls out, "I have an order for two eggs and some toast" is likely to stop the process of production. She has not said what kind of eggs—boiled, fried, poached, etc.—nor whether the toast is to be buttered or served with jam, or what. The cook must then ask her these questions.

3. SYSTEMS OF CONTROL

The institutional organization of the restaurant creates a system of closely linked specialties. Often there is the assumption by supervisors that if each person will do *his own* job, then the whole will take care of itself. But in the restaurant, as well as almost everywhere else, this philosophy is not likely to work out satisfactorily. Work is cooperative and being able to *do* one's job includes an awareness and a taking account of the jobs of others.

Approved work behavior becomes a matter of maintaining a balance between the expectations of one's own immediate job and the expectations of those whose jobs touch one's own. The significance of this balance is seen in cases where it may be upset. One of the commonest is where the individual feels he is prevented from doing an adequate job by the fact that others do not give him cooperation.

There is a specific means of controlling persons who violate understandings, namely, the withholding of supplies. The waitress who demands fast service gets slow service, the pantry worker who marks orders "rush" gets them late. In a situation of closely articulated activities, this tactic of withholding supplies can be disastrous.

A second special characteristic of work relationships is due to the fact that in the restaurant the people who give orders are often in a *subordinate* position. This reverses the usual pattern which leads to the necessity of diplomatic skills on the part of persons who may give such orders. For example, the waitress gives an order to the chef. The latter may even be the owner of the restaurant. The runner gives orders to the cooks. In order to avoid problems, one of the folkways has to do with giving orders in such a way as not to indicate that one is overstepping one's prerogatives. The person who violates the folkways is likely to meet with deliberate attempts on the part of the others chasten him. This is brought out in the following quotation (12, pp. 68–9):

Counterman Ralph's technique was particularly exasperating to the girls. One night a waitress had an order for oysters which had to be opened by Ralph. When she reached the counter, he was nowhere to be found. When he reappeared, she said abruptly, that she had been looking for him for five minutes. He nodded casually and then leaned back against the wall, ignoring her anguished expression. He did not pick up her order slip and start opening the oysters until she had moved away from the counter—that is until she had taken the pressure off him.

4. THE RESTAURANT CAREER
a. SOCIAL SELECTION

Entry is fairly easy into the industry, at the owner or other levels. Relatively little capital is needed for a small restaurant or sandwich shop. Many persons open restaurants; many fail. The running of a restaurant requires as much knowledge of business and administrative ability, as does any other business. The successful owner may be the person who has built up a core-following who spread the word about the restaurant. This following may be a consequence of the owner's personality, of the type of food, of the location of the restaurant, or of "atmosphere." When the restaurant grows, administrative skills become more and more important.

The cultural perspective may be of importance in some cases. In Europe, the family of waiters is not uncommon. That is much rarer in this country, though we still find the family restaurant. The sons of a successful restaurant owner are, of course, likely to go into their father's business.

Four kinds of persons boom large in the makeup of restaurant personnel: (1) Persons who are on the way up, such as country girls who are new to the city. The existence of a need for semi-skilled and unskilled labor in the restaurant means that these persons may find jobs there. (2) Persons who used to be something else, such as former restaurant owners who did not succeed and many European immigrants. They are able to secure such jobs because their experience is considered valuable. (3) Persons to whom other occupations are closed, especially Negroes, and some women who may not wish to fight the restrictions that they meet elsewhere. (4) Part-time persons, including here many housewives, students, and unmarried women to whom the restaurant job is not a career. Entry is easy, and the fact that the hours usually include a portion of the night makes it easier for these persons to fit their working times into their own time schedule.

It may be seen that the restaurant industry is a remarkably open one, but that marginal and transitional persons make up a significant proportion of the working force. The most important category of careerists seem to be women, who find advancement more likely here, and the male cook or waiter. We have little knowledge of the male waiter although foreign birth may be of some importance.

Of some significance are the armed services. Many poor boys become cooks in the army. The occupations surrounding the mess in the army provide one of the very few occupations involving skill in the army that the individual finds transferable to civilian life. In an air force study (3), it was found that while most personnel were not at all sure what they would do after leaving the service, the mess personnel had a very high proportion of persons who had decided that they were going to open restaurants.

b. MOBILITY

It will be recalled that in Chapter Five, the idea of group mobility was discussed—a situation in which a whole group or category moved up or down at the same time. While the restaurant industry is old, it has changed considerably within the last 50 years because of technological developments and because of changes in our culture. As mentioned previously, the restaurant is being increasingly used by the general population with the decrease in family functions, the increase in movement of persons, and the increase in urbanization.

The increased demands being placed on restaurant service have in turn lead to considerable mechanization. We have seen the evolution of prepackaged foods, automatic ovens, ice cream makers, and so on. These in turn have lead to new occupations in engineering and machine design. More closely related to the restaurant has been the development of nutrition ideas and dietetics. These have led to new careers as dieticians and in other home economics fields.

What is most significant about the latter occupations is that there is very little prejudice against women. Women have been the most important category among those given mobile opportunities, and they seem to be monopolizing the field.

For the individual, promotional opportunities are slight. The waitress can advance to hostess, and then to dining room supervisor. The man in food preparation may advance to a cook's position and then perhaps to chef. The line is usually short, and available opportunities are few. Furthermore, there are not many alternative lines.

Whyte points out that in another respect the restaurant is a significant elevator for mobile persons. It assists persons of lower-class or lower-middle backgrounds, or rural migrants, to move up into middle-class urban society. This is particularly likely to happen to the person who works in a "refined" restaurant. Such a girl learns the value of cleanliness, food standards, how to set a table "attractively" (according to upper-middle-class standards) and how to manipulate customers. Also through making friends among waitresses, she may make contacts with men and then may move up through marriage.

We do not know whether the restaurant provides similar avenues for men or for Negroes, many of whom are also rural migrants. But it is probable that it does for some.

C. CAREER CONTINGENCIES

The individual seeking a career in the restaurant meets relatively few contingencies. The owner is faced with problems in the selection of a location and in the changing makeup of his customers. What may be a good location at one time may later become a poor one when the population shifts. Or a small diner may suddenly have its facilities overworked when a new housing unit is built nearby.

The foreign restaurants are usually located where members of a given ethnic group live. As its own group moves up (and therefore away) the restaurant may have to follow the group unless the group scatters. The alternative may be to seek a broader clientele—to try to develop a taste in the general population for smorgasbord or for Chinese food. The latter step usually means employing English-speaking waiters and perhaps a "downtown" location.

Special problems are presented by restaurant personnel who are downwardly mobile, that is, persons of formerly higher prestige, or who owned their own restaurants or tearooms, or who were in "better class" restaurants. As pointed out above, these people can find a place in the restaurant. However, they usually exhibit status anxiety which may be manifested in the rejection of their fellow workers as "trash." The wide variety of types of restaurants and their permeability to many persons who have difficulty getting jobs elsewhere means that we are likely to find more downwardly mobile persons here than elsewhere.

d. WORK AND THE SELF

The person who decides to make a career as a worker in the restaurant meets certain resistances. A woman may have the pull of marriage, and must meet the questions, perhaps unstated, of friends who may wonder why she is not married. She must also work out an adjustment with actual or imagined attitudes of customers or society at large with reference to the status of restaurant work. Many persons regard it as low status work and see a close relation between "service" and "servant." The worker can overcome these attitudes to some extent by kidding or talking back to the customer, which is possible in a restaurant catering to factory workers or persons of similar status. Or she can partially overcome these attitudes by orienting herself to upward mobility and a "better class" restaurant and trying to become a supervisor. She can also attempt to develop a crust of immunity to criticism or low tips.

In order to do the latter she must normally have a group of fellows with whom she feels a close identification and who provide her with social support. This however is not often consistent with upward mobility, which may involve ignoring fellow-workers and orienting herself as an individual to management rewards.

It is among the non-careerists that the problem of identification becomes critical. A large proportion of the women employees are persons whose mind is not there. They are working to help support a family and will cease as soon as this is no longer necessary. The downwardly mobile person and the Negro also have alternate identifications. The downwardly mobile person may look back at what he once was and reject his present position. This means rejecting his fellow-workers because he feels no ties with them. Therefore, such persons may not be hesitant about becoming informers to management. The Negro exhibits a similar problem. If he responds to the management incentive for humility and informing on fellow-workers then he is rejecting his own group. Such persons become isolated; and since management cannot promote more than a few, that tends to reinforce the isolation.

This, in a circular manner, may prevent the acquisition of career attitudes and lead to still further isolation. The worker may then try to rejoin his fellow-workers and seek satisfaction there. He may be pushed into this position by the fact that he observes that his chances for promotion are actually very poor.

Perhaps because of the wide variety of temporary persons found in the restaurant, there does not seem to be any uniform relation between work and personality. Whyte comments that many are attracted to a restaurant career because they "like people" and do not enjoy working alone. It may be then that the outgoing sociable person finds restaurant work more satisfying.

Orwell (11, pp. 75–9) has given us some light into the self-conceptions of certain restaurant employees in the following passage. He is describing a leading Parisian restaurant employing male cooks and waiters.

What keeps a hotel going is the fact that the employees take a genuine pride in their work, beastly and silly though it is. If a man idles, the others soon find him out, and conspire against him to get him sacked. Cooks, waiters and *plongeurs* differ greatly in outlook, but they are all alike in being proud of their efficiency.

Undoubtedly the most workmanlike class, and the least servile, are the cooks. They do not earn quite so much as waiters, but their prestige is higher and their employment steadier. The cook does not look upon himself as a servant, but as a skilled workman; he is generally called "un ouvrier," which a waiter never is. He knows his power—knows that he alone makes or mars a restaurant, and that if he is five minutes late everything is out of gear. He despises the whole non-cooking staff, and makes it a point of honor to insult everyone below the head waiter. And he takes a genuine artistic pride in his work, which demands very great skill. It is not the cooking that is so difficult, but the doing of everything to time. Between breakfast and luncheon the head cook at the Hotel X. would receive orders for several hundred dishes, all to be served at different times; he cooked few of them himself, but he gave instructions about all of them and inspected them before they were sent up. His memory was wonderful. The vouchers were pinned on a board, but the head cook seldom looked at them; everything was stored in his mind, and exactly to the minute, as each dish fell due, he would call out, *"Faites marcher une cotellette de veau"* (or whatever it was) unfailingly. He was an insufferable bully, but he was also an artist. It is for their punctuality, and not for any superiority of technique, that men cooks are preferred to women.

The waiter's outlook is quite different. He too is proud in a way of his skill, but his skill is chiefly in being servile. His work gives him the mentality, not of a workman, but of a snob. He lives perpetually in sight of rich people, stands at their tables, listens to their conversations, sucks up to them with smiles and discreet little jokes. He has the pleasure of spending money by proxy. Moreover, there is always the chance that he may become rich himself, for, though most waiters die poor, they have long runs of luck occasionally. At some cafes on the Grand Boulevard there is so much money to be made that the waiters actually pay the patron for their employment. The result is that between constantly seeing money, and hoping to get it, the waiter comes to identify himself to some extent with his employers. He will take pains to serve the meal in style, because he feels that he is participating in the meal himself.

I remember Valenti telling me of some banquet at Nice at which he had once served, and of how it cost two hundred thousand francs and was talked of for months afterwards. "It was splendid, *mon p'tit, mais magnifique!* Jesus Christ! The champagne, the silver, the orchids—I have never seen anything like them, and I have seen some things. Ah, it was glorious!"

"But," I said, "you were only there to wait?"

"Oh, of course. But still, it was splendid."

The moral is, never be sorry for a waiter. Sometimes when you sit in a restaurant, still stuffing yourself half an hour after closing time, you feel that the tired waiter at your side must surely be despising you. But he is not. He is not thinking as he looks at you, "What an overfed lout"; he is thinking "One day, when I have saved enough money, I shall be able to imitate that man."

He is ministering to a kind of pleasure he thoroughly understands and admires. And that is why waiters are seldom Socialists, have no effective trade union, and will work twelve hours a day—they work fifteen hours, seven days a week in many cafes. They are snobs, and they find the servile nature of their work rather congenial.

The *plongeurs*, again, have a different outlook. Theirs is a job which offers no prospects, is intensely exhausting, and at the same time has not a trace of skill or interest; the sort of job that would always be done by women if women were strong enough. All that is required of them is to be constantly on the run, and to put up with long hours and a stuffy atmosphere. They have no way of escaping from this life, for they cannot save a penny from their wages, and working from sixty to a hundred hours a week leaves them no time to train for anything else. The best they can hope for is to find a slightly softer job as night-watchman or lavatory attendant.

And yet the *plongeurs*, low as they are, also have a kind of pride. It is the pride of the drudge—the man who is equal to no matter what quantity of work. At that level, the mere power to go on working like an ox is about the only virtue obtainable. *Debrouillard* is what every plongeur wants to be called. A *debrouillard* is a man who, even when he is told to do the impossible, will *se debrouiller*—get it done somehow. One of the kitchen *plongeurs* at the Hotel X, a German, was well known as a *debrouillard*. One night an English lord came to the hotel, and the waiters were in despair, for the lord had asked for peaches, and there was none in stock; it was late at night, and the shops would be shut. "Leave it to me," said the German. He went out, and in ten minutes he was back with four peaches. He had gone into a neighboring restaurant and stolen them. That is what is meant by a *debrouillard*. The English lord paid for the peaches at twenty francs each.

Mario, who was in charge of the cafeteria, had the typical drudge mentality. All he thought of was getting through the *boulot,* and he defied you to give him too much of it. Fourteen years underground had left him with about as much natural laziness as a piston rod. *"Faut etre dur,"* he used to say when anyone complained. You will often hear *plongeurs* boast, *"Je suis dur"*— as though they were soldiers, not male charwomen.

Thus everyone in the hotel had his sense of honour, and when the press of work came we were all ready for a grand concerted effort to get through it. The constant war between the different departments also made for efficiency, for everyone clung to his own privileges and tried to stop the others idling and pilfering.

5. THE RESTAURANT WORK GROUP
a. INCLUSION AND EXCLUSION

The degree of exclusiveness and sense of colleagueship among restaurant workers is not great, due in part to the large numbers of small restaurants, the presence of women, and of many who are only temporary workers. Some degree of professionalization and sense of membership is presented by the chef and the Old World waiters.

An important type of secret behavior revolves about recipes. The chef has certain recipes in which he takes pride and which the customers ask for. When the restaurant expands or new cooks are hired, the chef is frequently asked to set down his recipe in writing for others and in case he gets sick or leaves. However to do so is to de-professionalize (because it standardizes) his occupation to some extent.

b. INFORMAL RELATIONS

As we have seen, informal groups have several functions, such as fellowship and understanding, communication, and the giving of workers a sense of belonging in the impersonal work structure. Whyte (12, p. 131) points out that the presence of such groups in the restaurant helps bind the employees to the restaurant itself:

> . . . if a restaurant is not a good place for employees to make friends with each other, then it will not be considered a good place in which to work.

This may be more important to newcomers to the city or to others seeking friends than it is for persons who do not require such resources. However, the restaurant does provide such an opportunity for those who need it. Once such groups are formed, they tend to develop informal leaders and exhibit great tenacity.

The factors which clique members have in common are usually given attention. Whyte mentions age, length of service, marital status, relations with men, amount of education, social background, kinship, previous association, and location of the work station. While factors such as these help to explain how workers *come* together and why they find one another's company congenial, they do not explain the *selectivity* of clique membership. Not all persons of a given age are included, and a given clique may exhibit quite wide age differences.

Other research suggests that there is a type of clique which is made up of persons of *contrasting* characteristics who can then act as a resource for each other in a symbiotic sense. For example, the older waitress may clique with a brand new younger one; one may find a highly educated girl associating with one with little education. Such an organization may be important in giving understanding and the waitress may get more comfort from an old hand than one who may be just as upset as she is (6, 7).

Cliques tend to be made up of noncompetitors (5). This may be a major factor in explaining why members feel at ease in one another's presence and can therefore expect understanding and sympathy. To be noncompetitors, workers need not be in different work sections. An important factor may be a lack of career orientation. For example, if two waitresses work for the same supervisor then each might regard the other as a competitor for that job if it becomes vacant. Consequently, these two women would perhaps not feel at ease in each other's presence, but this is only true if both of the girls were upwardly mobile and career oriented. If they are not, then they are in fact not competitors with each other and can form a clique together.

The informal group serves essentially the same function as the colleague group among professionals. It is a resource to turn to in which understanding can be secured, especially in the face of criticism or failure. It may provide the individual with reassurance and self-confidence. All workers will feel personal inadequacies at times. A person without such a group to turn to may turn inward and increase his isolation or may turn outward and increase his aggressiveness. When this happens such persons may become marginal to the work group.

CHAPTER REFERENCES

1. Burgess, E. W. and Locke, H. J., *The Family,* New York: American Book Co., 1950.
2. Croy, H., *Corn Country,* New York: Duell, Sloan & Pearce, 1947.
3. Davis, F. J.; Gross, E.; and Miller, D. C., *Survey Report on Military Management Problems in Aircraft Control and Warning Stations in the Air Defense Command,* Human Resources Research Institute, Air University, Maxwell Air Force Base, Alabama.
4. Ellison, Ralph, *The Invisible Man,* New York: Random House, 1952.
5. Gross, E., "Characteristics of Cliques in Office Organization," *Research Studies, State College of Washington,* 19:131–136, 1951.
6. ———, "Primary Functions of the Small Group," *American Journal of Sociology,* 60:24–29, 1954.
7. ———, "Some Functional Consequences of Primary Controls in Formal Work Organizations," *American Sociological Review,* 18:368–373, 1953.
8. The National Opinion Research Center, "Jobs and Occupations: A Popular Evaluation," *Opinion News,* 9:3–13, Sept. 1, 1947.
9. *Occupational Characteristics,* Special Reports, 1950 Population Census Report P-E No. 1B, U.S. Government Printing Office, 1956, Table 20.
10. Ogburn, W. F. and Nimkoff, M. F., *Technology and the Changing Family,* Boston: Houghton, Mifflin, 1955.
11. Orwell, G., *Down and Out in Paris and London,* New York: Harcourt, Brace, 1933.
12. Whyte, W. F., *Human Relations in the Restaurant Industry,* New York: McGraw-Hill, 1948.

CHAPTER ELEVEN

THE FACTORY: THE WORK
COMPLEX AND WORK STRUCTURE

DISTINCTIVE CHARACTERISTICS OF THE FACTORY

The modern factory is the latest development in a long line of technological changes that stretches back in time to the first stone axeheads and bone anvils of prehistoric man, technological changes that mark off man, the culture-creater and tool-maker, from all the other animals. The factory is not only a technological invention, but a social invention of the most ingenious complexity. For in it, not only do men meet to make things, but they make things together as a group, and to a considerable extent, their success in making things depends on how this group interaction is organized.

Some of the distinctive characteristics of the factory are present in other work organizations. This should not be surprising. For the great achievements of the factory have led to its being imitated, both in technical and social organization, by many other work organizations.

The major characteristics distinctive of the factory are the following.

1. MANUFACTURING

The most obvious feature of the factory is that it is concerned with making things out of lifeless raw materials. But this was equally true of the hand manufacturing that was carried out under the putting-out system before the industrial revolution. We must add that manufacturing is carried out with the aid of steam, gasoline, oil, and electricity, and with large machinery. That last fact has profound implications for those employed in the factory. The very size of the machines means that the workers cannot own them—and in the large firm they are not owned by the managers either, or by any one person, but by thousands of stock-holders. But the machines are not just big; they are also complex to the point that the worker who runs one may know very little about how it is constructed or how to repair it. In this situation, he is very much like the average automobile owner. The worker, therefore, enjoys neither pride of ownership nor, usually, pride of workmanship. He tends machines which actually do the work. The fact that the work itself, unlike farming, or many of the professions, deals with lifeless things, means further that the workman has little sense of attachment to the product. He produces things (and usually not completed things) because he is told to, and not because he wants to or feels that society particularly needs the things he makes. He is paid, so he does his job. He separates himself from his product. He is simply giving the public what it wants, as those wants are interpreted by sales personnel. Nor is he likely to be rewarded for his personal opinion of the company's products. With these attitudes, and the remarkable similarity of machines from one factory to another, the worker finds it relatively easy to shift, if he should want to, from one factory to another.

2. SIZE

Not all factories are large, but the factory, unlike the restaurant and farm, is of such a nature that it can be expanded almost indefinitely at no loss of efficiency. Indeed, the very large factory may be more economical than the small one. It is with the factory that we encounter the huge organization, which may in some cases reach such size that it becomes a key element in the economy and its affairs become public business. The individual in this colossus becomes a tiny figure who is utterly incapable of affecting it by himself. He turns to help from government and from unions who grow in size to rival the big factory itself. Sheer size also creates grave problems of coordination. Top management in such organizations becomes a power elite (cf. 29),[1] major public figures whose pronouncements are listened to with respect, even when they move outside of their area of competence and speak of politics and international relations.

3. PERSONALITY SEGMENTATION

All work organizations require some segmentation of the personality of the worker, but the factory carries this almost to the limit. The worker is paid because he has some skill or is willing to contribute his time toward the manufacture of the company products. And that, ideally, is all that is asked of him. The factory asks nothing of and cares little about the other segments of his personality—his role as a family member,

[1] Mills sees the leaders of large corporations, along with military and government leaders, as together dominating the life of the society.

his role as a citizen, his role as a club member, his role as a church member, and so on. Of course, in practice, a humanitarian management will make allowances for these other roles and try not to make demands which will run counter to any of these roles [2] but strictly speaking, they are irrelevant to the efficient functioning of the factory.

The factory is a business organization and is there solely to make money. In public relations, and perhaps in the actual feeling of some members of management, it may be maintained that the factory is dedicated to public service. But the factory can continue to exist and pay its stockholders only as long as it makes a profit. Consequently, it does not ask devotion and unswerving loyalty of all of its workers (though it is happy if it gets them) but instead only enough effort to enable the company to make a profit.

This approach gives the factory an impersonality which has both negative and positive effects. On the one hand, it contributes to loneliness and depression of the sense of personal worth. Even though management does not ask for his whole personality, the worker brings that whole personality with him to the work situation, and it is continually on his mind. He then interprets how he is treated in terms of that whole personality. Thus if his wage is lowered, management may have meant that solely as a judgment of the value of his contribution to the factory. But to the worker the move is interpreted in terms of its effects on the new house he was buying. And in protesting, it is the latter consideration that he is likely to bring up to his foreman.

On the other hand, impersonality is a powerful force in the destruction of racial, religious, and social-class prejudices. For the impersonal personnel manager asks not, Who are you?, but What can you do? And when the question is asked, the Jew turns out to be as competent as the Christian, the immigrant Italian as competent as the native-born American, the Negro as competent as the white, the woman as competent as the man. In practice the factory is not actually as impersonal as this, and tends to reflect community sentiments. Yet there is a powerful tendency towards such impersonality; to the extent that it is present, the modern factory has provided one of the major frontiers where different peoples meet. It is difficult to run a factory efficiently if one must stop to ask each person what his religion is, or whether the color of his skin matches that of the person sitting on the other side of the work bench. The factory has, therefore, often broken down such barriers wherever it has been introduced.

[2] Such as, say, requiring a Jew to work on a religious holiday, or a man to work overtime when his wife is in the hospital having a baby.

4. EXTREME ELABORATION OF THE DIVISION OF LABOR

The factory is the prototype of specialization. In the interests of efficiency and speed, tasks are broken down as minutely as production planners are able to do. Partly, also, this process is a concession to and a consequence of impersonality. The factory attempts to organize its tasks so simply that it will have no difficulty in hiring workers at random from the population. The more skilled and complex the tasks are, then the more difficult will it be to find the proper persons to do them, and the more will they have to be rewarded. So tasks are divided and subdivided and simplified to the point where most persons in reasonably good health can do them.

This practice, of course, greatly increases the power of management. For the worker is highly replaceable by someone else. As a consequence, his dependence on management is very great. The elaboration of the division of labor also has contributed, as writers from Veblen on have lamented, to the making of factory work into a meaningless activity. When one spends one's whole day twisting a nut on a bolt, or doing some task that might, without too much difficulty, be taught to a chimpanzee, one's work does not command one's interest; it offers no challenge. We therefore have created the "morale problem" which the modern factory tries to solve as best it can. When work offers little to satisfy the worker's needs, management provides pleasant lunch rooms, music, recreational facilities, air conditioning, and personnel staffs to talk to. But these rarely work and in any case are not enough. Besides, management finds it must be continually doing something to *motivate* workers to keep working at all. The usual practices involve wage incentive systems of one kind or another. The worker himself is likely to turn for the satisfaction of personal needs to other workers and informal fellowship. The informal groups so formed may or may not be consonant with the objectives of the factory.

5. EXTENSION OF THE AUTHORITY LINE

In part as a consequence of size, and in part of bureaucratization, the line of authority from top to bottom is likely to be long. One finds employees, subforemen, foremen, department heads, shift superintendents, factory superintendents, plant managers, divisional managers, and vice-presidents in charge of production. The average worker interacts only with those very near him and sees those high up, if at all, only on ceremonial occasions. The great length of this line creates a tremendous problem of communication up and down the line. The simple message that begins at the bottom, may be amended beyond recognition before it reaches to top; the simple, direct order from the top may be interpreted and reinterpreted on its way down to the point where it is carried out in a manner highly different from that intended by the sender. Side by side with the line, there grows up a set of staffs to help the line do its work better. But although these staffs are theoretically auxiliary, yet the fact that they, in contrast to the line, are peopled by professionals and experts, such as engineers, chemists, accountants, and psychologists, means that staffs come to partially control line activities, and serious line-staff conflicts result. On the other hand, the length of the line means that the factory has, potentially, very great rewards to offer the ambitious worker.

These five characteristics—machine manufacturing, large size, personality segmentation, elaboration of the division of labor, and length of the line of authority—help mark off the factory from other work organizations.

We proceed next to examine the factory in terms of the conceptual framework that has been used with occupations, the farm, and the restaurant.

THE FACTORY WORK COMPLEX

The relation of the factory to other segments of society is highly complex but, unfortunately, we do not know very much about it. Partly the difficulty is that we live out our lives in the midst of this relation and therefore take it for granted. Partly the difficulty is that research on the factory has largely restricted itself to the factory in isolation. Such is the case for studies under the heading of "human relations in industry"—where the most important word in the heading is "in." [3] The worker himself has not been treated in isolation, but the factory as a total work organization has. The major reason for this restriction of research has usually been that a particular factory was subsidizing the research and that forced the researcher to stay within the factory walls. Another reason, possibly, is simple expediency. It is easier to do research when one's population is arbitrarily defined in advance. Still a third reason may be the influence of the systematic approach in theory. By this approach, the researcher is concerned with studying a self-contained social system and the equilibrium within it. If a single factory is conceived of as such a social system (and it is), then one has theoretical justification for restricting one's attention to it.

Yet, although the factory is a social system, it is not a closed system. Like all work organizations, it relates itself to other social systems in

[3] The prototype and, in many respects, still most useful and widely used book is (14). Works by Elton Mayo and those he influenced—F. J. Roethlisberger, W. J. Dickson, C. M. Arensberg, W. F. Whyte and others—are also representative in the main.

society, influencing them and being influenced in turn by them. Two major related social systems are organized about trade unions and ethnic relations. These, however, we have reserved for special discussion in Chapters Fifteen and Sixteen, in part because of their importance and in part because the special problems they present are not peculiar to the factory.

The modern family in the United States has been considerably affected by the rise of the factory to a position of dominance in the manufacturing process. When manufacturing was carried out in the home, the family was a work group. The proportion of working wives was undoubtedly very much higher then than now, and the phrase "child labor" would have been considered, if not meaningless, then certainly not an issue. Indeed, part of the opposition to the attempts to legislate against child labor in England during the early factory period came from *parents* to whom the idea of child labor was natural and traditional, and who, underpaid as they were, needed the added income their children could bring (4).

But after the industrial revolution, with the shift in source of power from human hands, wind, and water to coal and steam, and with the shift in tools from wood and small instruments to giant steel machines, manufacturing required a large and separate location. The worker then had to leave his home to go to work. There had, of course, always been a division of labor and separation of roles between male and female, but the factory served to exaggerate the differences. The man became, in the strict sense, the breadwinner and his wife became limited to the role of housewife. As time went on and appropriate legislation was passed, and cultural points of view changed, children became incompetent minors to be cared for until they were old enough to work. But by that time, they were usually also old enough to leave the family, and set up their own households. The separation in roles—father as breadwinner, mother as housewife, and children as dependents—became almost complete.

The modern family is (relatively) completely dependent on the economic efforts of the father. It is he alone who boards the bus in the morning to go to the smoking factory where he enters a world that his wife probably knows little about and may not even be interested in.[4] His job is not likely to satisfy his creative impulses and is not likely to form an interesting topic of conversation when he returns home in the evening. Unless a crisis has occurred (a fight, a layoff, a promotion, a salary increase), he may have little more to say than that he cut 100

[4] We are speaking in relative terms. The statement becomes less true as one moves up in the industrial hierarchy. On the role of the executive's wife in her husband's work success, see (44, Ch. 8).

parts that day, or put together 33 assemblies. A story or two, a joke someone at the shop told, and the work discussion is exhausted. The one
meaningful thing he does bring home is the paycheck, and the hopes and
plans of the entire family revolve about it. What happens to the members
of the family, the clothes they wear, the food they eat, the house they
live in, the kind of neighbors they have, the kind of recreation they
have, the education the children get, and even, perhaps, the church they
attend, all ultimately relate to the paycheck. The success with which
he can play the role of husband and father (and friend and member of
the community as well), therefore, is related to his success as a worker in
the factory. This places a tremendous responsibility on him which he
must carry out largely alone. Failure, or lack of expected success, is likely
to be reflected in bickering and feelings of deprivation. Family stability,
therefore, is in part dependent on the ability of the factory to reward
its employees.[5]

Family stability rests also on many other factors. A family held together by mutual understanding and love can withstand any paycheck
pressure. Yet the fact that *he,* the breadwinner earns it, and the fact that
it can be increased ("Why did Jack get a raise, and you didn't? You can't
blame that on your old 'market conditions.' "), may place a severe strain
on intra-family relations.

The modern wife in the companionship-based, individualistic
family may not be satisfied with the restricted role of housewife. The
increase in labor-saving devices and the growth of day-care nursery
facilities make it possible for many to work at gainful employment if
they wish. And many do. When such a wife goes to work, this does not
act as a binding force between husband and wife in a direct sense; unlike
the wife who, say, helps her husband in their grocery store, she engages
in employment which does not help the husband to be a success at his.
Insofar as she is personally happier because she is working, she may be
a more congenial wife. But many wives work to supplement the family
income and stop working when that is no longer necessary.[6] Her taking
a job may therefore be a direct reflection of the fact that her husband
is not successful enough in his factory job to provide her and the family
with the creature comforts they want.[7] And the inconveniences of ar-

[5] This matter has not been specifically studied to any great extent by family researchers. Burgess and Locke (8, pp. 468–69) state that ". . . regularity and continuity
of employment," through implications for personality, make for adjustment in marriage. Studies on the effects of the depression are relevant. See, for example, (2; 9, pp. 12–
28; 11, pp. 336–41; 23).

[6] Cf. (11, pp. 235 ff.; 16; 24, pp. 58 ff.; 31, pp. 268–71).

[7] "In American society the husband may still consider his wife's working as a reflection
upon his failure to maintain his role as the financial supporter of the family" (8, pp.
613–14).

ranging for the care of the children, hurried meal preparations, hurried breakfasts, perfunctory bedtime stories from an exhausted mother—only serve to drive the point home.

Work always takes time, but the special character of the factory requires that work time shall be spent away from wife and family by the breadwinner. The factory, with its elaborate division of labor, requires careful timing of the production process in order to insure that parts being made in one part of the organization will arrive at another part of the organization where they are needed at just the right moment. Time is measured to the hour (and paid for by the hour) so that the worker must be at work on time and remain in close attendance until closing time. For those hours, then, the worker must leave his family and usually has no contact at all with it throughout the working day. This emphasizes the role-separation between husband and wife and forces the wife to make many minute-to-minute decisions on her own, which perhaps might better be made in consultation with her husband. The care and discipline of the children are particularly important in this context. The average wife will do the best she can, which may include appeals to the authority of the absent father ("Just you wait till your father gets home! He'll teach you some manners!") and reserve important decisions till the husband is home. But he is often as tired and irritated as she is at the end of the day, and decisions of importance must be made hurriedly and in whispers while dishes are being wiped or late at night, when both are half-asleep, in the only place in which the couple are at last alone.

Of importance to many factories are the traditional family work arrangements of people in the vicinity of the factory. Thus, industries whose labor needs fluctuate may require a family system in which members of the family are willing and accustomed to shift rapidly from one type of work to another. Arensberg (1) has pointed out how the stability of plastics manufacturing plants in New England depends on a readiness of the working population to shift to farming when the demand for factory labor falls. The growth of part-time farming in the vicinity of large industrial centers represents a similar type of adjustment.

The emphasis on machine technology in the modern factory has led to the great growth of technical schools in the United States and to the general emphasis in the school system on "practical" pursuits. Engineering and Business and Secretarial studies are among the largest and fastest-growing departments in most American universities. With specialization, growing complexity, and, above all, rapid technological change, the value of specialized education begins to outweigh that of experience. The man who has worked steadily in the factory for thirty years may actually, because of new technological developments, be no more skilled than a man freshly out of school with only two years of work experience. At the same time, the specialized character of the work removes it almost completely from the family, so that the father can offer little except general orientation to his son. Except for professional activities, the factory is forced to do much of its training itself, and the factory becomes an educational institution in its own right.

The relation of the factory to business is of course intimate. The factory's high productivity is dependent on sales, advertising, and promotional activities. At the same time, shifts in consumer preferences and style place a premium on flexibility in production planning. When the workman reluctantly accompanies his wife on a window-shopping tour, he may not realize it, but what she sees and what she decides indirectly determine what he may be producing next year on the job, or perhaps, even whether he will have a job at all. But the balance between the factory and business is an uneasy one. Business personnel are likely to regard themselves as overlords of the whole production process ("Where would you guys be without us—hawking your wares on street corners?"). Production personnel on the other hand are likely to regard themselves as the "primary" producers, those who create the implements of war and peace.[8] Differences in remuneration, work clothes, attitudes toward unionization, and dozens of other differences become converted into status realities and foci of conflict.

There are a number of rigidities which mediate the relation between the factory and the local community. The factory's most crucial needs are an adequate source of power and cheap raw materials. If these two resources happen to be located near each other, the factory can be located there with minimum cost. Such was the case for Slocum's Hollow, which was a quiet Pennsylvania village until extensive coal deposits were discovered in 1840. Mine derricks were erected, it was subsequently honeycombed with tunnels, and its name was changed to Scranton. Whether such towns based on extractive industries will survive depends largely on the value and extent of the resources. Some become ghost towns, whereas others, such as Kimberley, South Africa, with its extensive diamond deposits, and Sudbury, Canada, with its enormous nickel resources, continue to maintain themselves.

Pittsburgh was peculiarly well located from the point of view of power and raw materials. It is near the Pennsylvania iron deposits

[8] An amusing statement of this antagonism, from the point of view of production, is provided in the *Union Oil Bulletin:* "An engineer is a man who knows a great deal about a very little, and who goes along knowing more and more about less, until finally he knows practically everything about nothing. A salesman, on the other hand, is a man who knows a very little about a great deal, and keeps knowing less and less about more, until finally he knows practically nothing about everything" (39).

(now exhausted) and near the Pennsylvania coal fields, which were and are a major source of power. In addition, it had access to the great supply of immigrant labor from the Atlantic seaboard. The city of Gary, Indiana is a perfect illustration of a city which was selected because of its appropriateness to manufacturing. In 1906, there was nothing there except scrub-grown sand. It was chosen as a site for steel mills by U.S. Steel, although there is no coal or iron ore in the immediate vicinity. But there were great bituminous coal fields to the south in Illinois, Indiana and Ohio, and there was iron ore in Michigan and Minnesota to the north which could be brought down by barge. Gary was in the middle. It was also close to a labor supply in Chicago.

Certain factories, such as those manufacturing aluminum, require access to large amounts of electric power. On the other hand, their raw material, bauxite, is found extensively in countries outside the United States. This has forced decisions to be made, in cost terms, as to whether to locate near rivers from which power may be generated, or near the bauxite supplies.

Once the decision has been made with reference to regional location, then the particular location must be chosen. J. D. Black [9] points out (5, pp. 254–56) that beside raw materials and power, it will usually be desired to locate near a good supply of labor, a market, and source of capital. The latter three usually mean locating in or near a city. And most factories are so located. Industries which have tried to move to rural areas, often in pursuit of cheap power (and often, cheap, non-union labor), have usually experienced difficulty in attracting a sufficient labor force. The inducements, in the form of housing, specially-built community facilities, and higher wages than the workers are accustomed to, often outweigh the saving achieved by the move. Yet such movement is taking place, notably into the upper South (28; cf. 10, pp. 253–55).

Within the city, factories tend to be found in two locations—near the center of the city in the Zone in Transition, and on the outskirts of the city in industrial suburbs. The division is likely to be one between light manufacturing near the center and heavy manufacturing in the outskirts. Light manufacturing, such as, say, millinery, finds it desirable to be near the retail outlets; more important, the fact that machines are small means it can build up to several stories, thus saving the cost of land. Heavy manufacturing requires solid ground on which to locate its giant machines, and cannot expand upward. Therefore, the high cost of land within the city drives it to the wasteland outside the city. Usually, taxes are lower as well. There they can expand without encountering

---

[9] On the location of industry with special reference to social factors, see (6; 12; 13; 26, Ch. 4; 42). For an industrial engineering point of view, see (20, 46).

streets, alleys, and networks of telephone and pipe lines. Usually, one finds a considerable number of factories grouped closely together. There are both internal and external cohesive forces accounting for such clustering. On the one hand, it is advantageous to be near each other. Parking space for automobiles can be planned more intelligently, and bought more cheaply, power lines can be shared, and common arrangements made for the disposal of industrial waste products. Externally, they can present a united front against the protests of residents of the area against noise, smoke and other unhappy accompaniments of factory production. The resistance of residential dwellers may lead zoning ordinances to be passed so that new factories discover they must locate near each other, even if they do not wish to do so. Also, with such a group of factories, it becomes worthwhile for railroads to build spur lines into the factory district, so that the disadvantage of being far from the freight depots downtown is eliminated.[10]

In the large city, the factory takes its place as one place of employment among many others. Management is careful to cultivate a favorable public opinion and makes a point of participating on socially acceptable committees (cf. 43). In the small town, however, the factory may come to occupy a dominant position (26, 37, 38). Such is particularly the case in the factory town or one-industry town. Here the fortunes of the entire community become one with that of the factory. If large-scale layoffs become necessary, all businesses suffer. If the factory expands, the town experiences a burst of prosperity. If, as happened in many New England towns, the factory moves out altogether, the whole town declines and may even vanish. These dangers [11] have led many one-industry towns to try to diversify as much as they can, and try to attract other factories.

As is often the case in one-industry towns (whether the one industry is a college, the movie industry, the national government, *or* a factory), there is likely to be antagonism and resentment between industry and town (35). Members of the community resent the very real hold the factory has on the fortunes of the town, and members of management resent the apparent lack of gratitude for the great boon that the factory represents. Occasionally, management will try to make its point by paying all workers in silver dollars. As these flood the community, it is hoped that merchants and businessmen will realize how much they owe to the

[10] A second distinguishing factor between factories near the downtown area and those in the fringe is that of nuisance features. If a factory is particularly noisy, gives off a lot of smoke or has waste products which are particularly fetid, it is likely to be forced to move to the outside of the city by zoning pressures. Thus on the outskirts one may find some light as well as heavy industry.

[11] On problems of closeness of relation between industry and the local community, see (17, 22, 25, 40, 41).

factory's presence. But such symbolic devices are likely only to produce a sense of outrage. Forced awareness of dependence is rarely a prelude to love.

The modern factory arose with the modern state, and the two have grown in power together. Some, indeed, have insisted that each has helped the other grow.[12] The growth in power of modern industry, with interlocking directorates and monopolization, has forced the state to take a greater and greater role in the regulation of factories. These have taken a wide variety of forms, such as legislation against trusts, price and wage regulation, legislation on hours, and employment of women and children, indirect controls through taxation, controls on unionization activities, and such controls as represented by the Taft-Hartley law. In turn, factory owners and managers are turning increasingly to lobbying activities in order to secure favors and benefits to themselves. The government, through its huge defense budgets, has become a major prop of manufacturing.

The factory in the United States, in spite of the massive changes it has introduced in all areas of social life, and even in spite of the dislocations it has occasionally produced, is now an integrated, and accepted part of our culture. It has effectively sold Americans on the usefulness and desirability of manufactured products to the point where products produced in any other way are likely to be regarded as curiosities. America has become a gadget-loving nation which looks to its manufacturers to solve many of its problems by producing a new mechanical gimmick. We look to new inventions not only to save us time, but ultimately, in the international struggle, to save our lives.

In this situation, the ideological position of the manufacturer has changed. The high-riding, individualistic entrepreneur of the nineteenth century has given way to the other-directed (36, pp. 17–24) manager, who emphasizes cooperation and getting along with people as desirable virtues (4, Ch. 5). American industry has made the great contribution of giving its workers a legitimate place in the social order by making the ideologies of management applicable to them. It is maintained that the man at the top is there by virtue not of who he is but rather of what he has done. Since his accomplishments are a reflection of teachable skills, then anyone may hope to rise by doing likewise. Such a statement cannot always be made about industry in other countries. While it is not in fact true that anyone may rise to the top, the fact that the hope is held out, and the fact that some *do* make it, acts to keep alive the American dream and creates a determination to make it true.

[12] Cf. (3, 7, 18, 30, 32).

THE WORK STRUCTURE

Among the most useful approaches to understanding the work structure of the factory is that of looking at the factory as a total *social system* of interacting parts. This means seeing all the parts as interconnected so that a change in any part produces changes in other parts. A social system is, further, conceived of as attempting to maintain itself in a state of equilibrium. To take a simple illustration.[13] A department head in a factory manufacturing airplanes had established the procedure of maintaining close, face-to-face ties with the five foremen who reported to him. The foremen felt at ease in his presence and did not hesitate to drop in on him in his office any time they wished to discuss their problems with him. When a foreman had a report to make, he dictated it to the department head's secretary who typed it for her boss. But whenever a foreman made such a report, he took advantage of his being in the department head's office to call on the department head and discuss the report with him, explaining any irregularities or unusual features of the report. The department head was suddenly transferred to another plant and replaced by a man of quite different personality. The new department head did not initiate personal contact with his foremen and discouraged it when a foreman sought him out. Instead, he insisted on written reports prepared by the foremen without consultation. For this purpose, he arranged for a stenographer to be assigned part-time to the foremen. This stenographer was located in the administrative offices of the factory in a nearby building.

The foremen resented these changes very much. The accustomed personal interview with the department head at the time of report-making, was not simply a chance to "chew the fat." Reports are necessarily general statements, ignoring details which may be sources of later trouble. Also, persons are often reluctant to put in writing some problem which reflects discredit on themselves. It was such matters that were discussed in the interview with the department head, so that he was informed and could anticipate future problems and make necessary explanations to his superior in turn.

The necessity to dictate reports to the new stenographer was a source of personal exasperation. Foremen, and workers in general, rarely went into the office. With their dirty clothes, and often begrimed hands and faces, they felt self-conscious there and, in any case, as usual, they just did not like office people, who were inclined to be "snippy" and "stuck-up."

[13] From the writer's observation.

It may be seen, then, that the accustomed equilibrium had been upset. The foremen then initiated the following changes to try to restore the equilibrium or create a new one. After a number of unhappy report-dictating experiences, one of their number was chosen to dictate all reports. He was a fancy dan and quite a lady's man, as it happened, and was a natural choice. He took to wearing neatly pressed trousers and a broadcloth shirt, over which he put on coveralls. When a foreman had a report to make, he wrote it out in longhand and gave it to the chosen man who removed his coveralls, put on a tie and then went to the stenographer to dictate it. This technique worked out very well, the man soon became known and accepted in the office, and he enjoyed the role himself, taking advantage of the opportunity to flirt with any pretty girls who looked his way. The success of this approach led the men to try it to restore the report-making interview with the department head. A second man was chosen who had considerable social skills—he spoke easily and got along with people very well. This man was given the task of taking all reports in to the department head. He waited till he had several reports in hand and then made an appointment to see the department head, with whom he discussed all the reports. When a question came up about a report other than his own, the foreman would suggest that the department head speak to the appropriate foreman, which the department head actually did on a number of occasions. In this manner, the foremen had managed to create a set of social relationships which were relatively stable again.

The concept of the social system does not necessarily imply that disturbances will always be corrected. Some social systems are highly stable and will resist strong disturbances; others are weakly integrated and upset by small changes. A strong disturbance in the latter case may produce a total breakdown, which will be reflected in work stoppages, slowdowns, absenteeism, and turnover.

The major elements in the social system of the modern factory appear to be the same everywhere. The system involves a division of labor and an authority system in which the individual is assigned a particular status which is felt to inhere in the position itself. Individuals come and go; the position remains. Thus, when we say that Joe Brown is superintendent, we mean that he occupies, for now, the position of superintendent. Before he took the position, the nature of the duties of superintendent had been worked out and were generally understood. Joe will be found to carry out these duties. Joe, of course, is different from anyone else who ever occupied the position, and he may introduce variations in how he carries out his duties, but there will remain a certain minimum of duties which inhere in the superintendency. For this, he is paid a fixed salary which again inheres in the position rather than in Joe. That is, his recompense is not a variable which depends on how much he can get out of it, as was the case with royal appointments during the Middle Ages. In the latter case, a noble might be given an appointment as director of some enterprise, or the right to collect taxes might be farmed out to him, for which he received no formal payment. He would receive as much as he could get by the imposition of special charges, cagey calculations, or economics.[14] By contrast, if the superintendent does his job particularly well and perhaps saves the company $10,000, he will be congratulated, he may be promoted, or he may get a raise in pay. But in no sense does he recognize the $10,000 saving as his own. Nor can Joe ever feel any sense of proprietorship with respect to the position of superintendent. This is not a position which was created for Joe, as was often the case, again, with royal appointments in former days (15, pp. 214 ff.). A man might be made chamberlain of the royal household and his heirs given the right to this distinction in perpetuity. By contrast, Joe occupies his position not because his father occupied it before him but because it is felt that Joe can perform the duties of superintendent better than anyone else the company knows of.[15]

This system of bureaucratic positions is organized about two major sets of relationships in the factory—technical and social relationships.[16]

THE STRUCTURE OF RELATIONSHIPS—TECHNICAL AND SOCIAL

Technical relations are concerned with activities in which the individual relates himself to lifeless objects. These typically include the use of tools, operation of machines, assembling of parts, handling of materials,

[14] Cf. (15, pp. 205 ff.). A good illustration, also, was the purchase of army commissions, a practice which persisted into the late 19th century in Germany.

[15] The man at the very top of the organization may, however, not occupy a bureaucratic office, as Weber pointed out. It is at the very top that traditionalistic elements may be present, in the case, for example, where headship passes from father to son. Where this occurs, however, if the son does not have the ability his father had, control is likely to pass increasingly into the hands of top executives, and the headship to become an honorary position. At the very top, also, charismatic elements may be present, in the sense that a particular man, often the founder, occupies the position by virtue of his remarkable past achievements. . . . While he was alive and still active, anyone else but Henry Ford at the head of his company would have been simply unthinkable. These special considerations, however, are most likely to come up in the case of the company owned by a single man, or family. With the increasing trend toward multiple ownership by thousands of stockholders, especially in large corporations, the man at the top becomes an appointed, bureaucratic official like anyone else. See (19, pp. 341–63). For a remarkable instance of traditionalism in the iron smelting industry in recent times, see (33).

[16] The discussion which follows is based on Burleigh Gardner's meaningful approach. See (14, Chs. 2, 3).

and so on. The ultimate, and often immediate, object of technical activities is to convert raw materials into finished products.

Technical activities are organized into two main organizations—a shop and an engineering organization. Shops are of two main types—product and functional.

The *shop* organization is the heart of the factory. If it ceases to operate, the whole factory stops. It is concerned with the direct conversion of raw materials [17] into finished or semi-finished products. In order to carry out this activity, persons in the shop organization use tools, machines, and blueprints, among other things.

The *engineering* organization is concerned with two activities: planning the shop's technical procedures, and planning the tools and machinery that the shop uses. In theory, the engineering organization is clearly conceived of as having an auxiliary function with reference to the shop. In practice, the engineering organization has, and conceives of itself as properly having, certain *control* functions over the shop. These conceptions are often the occasion for conflict and misunderstanding.

There is some overlapping between shop and engineering organizations. One may find chemists or engineers who directly assist at the job level with shop technical problems. Also, the engineering organization may be so large that it includes some persons who perform shop activities *for* the engineering department, such as making blueprints, special planning, and so on.

A product shop is one which performs all or a large number of the activities that are necessary to produce a piece of apparatus. The rivet shop, for example, will receive certain kinds of metal, treat it in various ways, and eventually produce the completed rivet. The shop performs all of the operations that are necessary to produce the rivets. This is the typical assembly-line type of operation in the factory in which a number of parts are put together to form a whole. This whole may not necessarily be the completed product that the factory turns out. It is a whole, however, from the point of view of the shop itself; the shop does all of the drilling, cutting, bolting, etc., necessary to produce all of the parts for its assembly.

The functional shop tends to perform only one activity, but it performs this one activity for a large number of different pieces of apparatus. An illustration is provided by the welding shop. Any parts

---

[17] By "raw materials" we understand whatever materials the factory takes as given. In many cases they are likely to consist of materials that have already gone through some processing before they reach the factory, or else they may consist of already tooled parts which are to be assembled.

that require welding will be sent to the welding shop and the welders will perform this one activity. Once they have completed it, the welded part then moves on elsewhere. They do whatever welding is done in the factory at all. Another illustration is the paint shop. Owing to the use of spray guns and the like it is usually segregated in a separate room with air conditioning and blowers to carry off the fumes of the paint. It is to this shop that all parts that require painting will come. They will then move on elsewhere. Still a third illustration would be provided by a packaging or mailing shop. All letters or packages pass through this shop.

The formal *social* organization of the factory, which has the function of relating people to each other, consists of three principal elements, which may be regarded as three interlocking organizations: the supervisory organization, the line organization, and the staff organization.

The supervisory organization is the formal authority structure. It may be described very simply: each individual reports *directly* to a superior and is directly responsible to him; each superior usually has a number of subordinates who report to him.

The result is a number of lines of authority which extend downward and branch at each level until they terminate at the level of the individual operator. This may be illustrated as in the figure below:

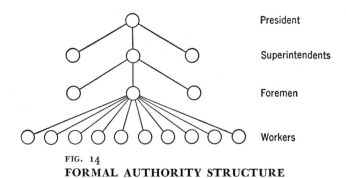

FIG. 14
FORMAL AUTHORITY STRUCTURE

It is along these lines that orders and information flow.

It should be noted that the lines from the top to the bottom do not form a simple direct relation between the top and the bottom. Rather they are *chains* of relations involving a series of superior and subordinate relations. This fact produces special problems.

Out of this series of chains there emerges the supervisory organization. Each person is directly subordinate to persons in a direct line above him but there is a tendency for the relationship of subordinates to be generalized to the whole level. For example, an employee is directly subordinate only to one assistant foreman. However, he is assigned a *formal status* below all assistant foremen. The concept of a supervisory organization refers to this idea of levels and is usually presented in the form of a pyramid.

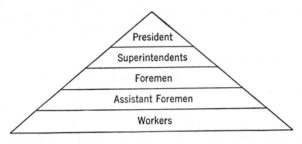

FIG. 15
SUPERVISORY HIERARCHY IN THE FACTORY

There may be gaps in the organization or special cases. Someone may have the *rank* of foreman but may have no subordinates. Occasionally a foreman may report directly to a plant manager, skipping the level in between. This again introduces special problems.

The fact that the lines of authority branch out as they go down establishes *vertical segments*. The president of a company is at the top of the major pyramid which includes the whole organization, but each supervisor is at the top of a smaller pyramid. Each of these pyramids may be regarded as supervisory units. They may in turn be divided into two types—the line and staff organizations—and it is these two types that provide the other two parts of the formal social organization.

The line organization is made up of those pyramids which are directly concerned with the process of manufacturing. It is commonly known as "the shop."

The staff organizations supply technical knowledge and assistance to the line organizations. They will include the engineering activities, research activities, chemical activities and others. A special kind of staff organization includes control or informational activities. These include accounting, cost control, production control, personnel, sales, and other activities. It is their function to gather knowledge from the line organizations and to interpret it for management in order to provide information on how the line may be operating.

These three elements—supervisory, line, and staff organizations—

make up what is usually referred to as the *formal organization*. It is called formal because it is established by administrative decree and can theoretically be changed that way.

In some factories an additional element in the formal organization is provided by a *labor union*. It is quite different from the three organizations that we have described. First, it excludes all supervisors, and it is not cut across by the formal lines of a supervisory hierarchy. For example, a man who is a machine operator in one of the shop organizations may be the president of the union local. And second, the purpose of a union organization is not, as is true of the other organizations, to facilitate the manufacturing processes. This does not mean that it necessarily hinders those processes: it is simply concerned with other things, although under certain conditions it may prevent or resist certain action on the part of supervisors or initiate changes.

INTEGRATION OF THE SOCIAL SYSTEM—COMMUNICATION

An integrated social system must provide ways for relating component parts in a predictable manner. Thus, if a manager wishes to initiate some change, he has to have some means of knowing at what point in the system this change may be introduced and how to introduce it with little strain to the system. The means consist of a complex *communication system*. A large part of this communication system is formal; that is, it is known by all persons and depended upon. There is also an informal communication system, sometimes called the "grapevine"; it is not deliberately set up, not very well known, and it may change from day to day. For the present, we shall confine our attention to the formal communication system.

There are three different media of communication each of which presents special features and problems: in *face-to-face communication,* two people communicate with each other in one another's direct presence, making use of words and gestures as symbols; in *non-face-to-face oral communication,* persons talk to each other but are unable to see each other. The most common examples are telephone communication and the use of the interoffice communication system. What is distinctive of this form of communication is that gestures are reduced to the tone of the voice; *written communication* does not permit the give and take that oral communication does. The individual writes a memo which may reach the addressee on the following day. That person may wait some while to reply. Sometimes there is no reply at all, a situation which rarely occurs in oral communication.

Whatever the medium, the communication system may be described by reference to whether it moves in a vertical or horizontal direction.

1. VERTICAL COMMUNICATION

Vertical communication ordinarily deals with two subjects: information and orders. Usually orders go down the line of formal authority. Information *may* go up the line but occasionally it will pass through other channels. The particular *path* that orders or information follow varies, but the direction is uniform: orders go down and information comes up.

The flow ordinarily involves several steps. For example, an assistant foreman may collect information about the work and give that to the foreman, who will transmit it to his supervisor, and so on. Similarly, the superintendent will give an order to a department head, the department head to the foreman who transmits it down to the next step. In both cases, at each step changes are likely to be made. The information is interpreted at each level, and the orders are restated in more detail as they move down.

Variations from the normal flow will affect the content. For example, if a foreman reports directly to the plant manager then there is likely to be less modification of information. If the plant manager himself gives an order to a foreman then there will be less restatement. Normally, persons in supervisory positions do not desire that such skipping shall occur.

Information tends to vary between two extremes: (1) generalized information in which certain details are summed up for a large number of persons, e.g., shop reports, which can summarize whole aspects of shop activities in a single set of compact figures; (2) detailed data covering a specific situation. Information of both types may move up.

Two kinds of information are of particular importance because they normally circumvent the step by step movement of information up the line: cost control information and union information.

By means of a *cost control* system information of a detailed sort is drawn from the work level, converted into monetary or numerical values, combined and summarized, and then submitted to persons high up in the supervisory hierarchy without passing through intermediate levels. It is usually transmitted simultaneously, through mimeographing, to different levels.

Cost control information is usually highly general. The figures may show only that the cost has gone up or down on certain items. The explanation of *why* this is the case must come from a particular foreman or assistant foreman or even from a given worker. This situation creates two serious problems for the effective functioning of the authority structure. First, the information leaves out the explanation as to why costs have gone up or down. Consequently, the foreman may suddenly be faced with a demand from his supervisor for an explanation of something that he may not even be aware of. Second, since the information can reach two or more supervisory levels at the same time, a given superintendent who has received a cost control report which has questionable or puzzling items in it knows that at the same moment that he is looking at the report *his* supervisor in turn, perhaps the plant manager himself, may be looking at the same set of figures. He cannot therefore amend the figures or present them in a manner that he thinks would be satisfactory to the plant manager while he scurries about in an attempt to find the reason for the puzzling figures. A foreman in a plastic manufacturing firm that also manufactured leather belts described a typical situation as follows:

It happened at the time we were making the shift from brass buckles for our belts to a chromium plated buckle. That was supposed to cut our costs quite a bit. In fact that was why we did it. I really concentrated on that one. There wasn't a man in the shop who could call his soul his own while we were making that change. I was on everybody's neck and probably made a lot of people sore, but by God I was going to bring costs on those buckles down. I even threatened one of the cost control boys. I told him that I didn't care how confidential his report was supposed to be. I wanted to see a preliminary draft that he was going to make to the superintendents and I saw it and sure enough costs were quite a bit lower.

We had just completed the changeover when I got a phone call from the superintendent. He opened his conversation by saying "I've just gotten some cost data here on your leather belts." So I was sitting there, my little heart just bursting with pride at the lowered costs which I had achieved, and so what does the old boy say? "What I want to know," he says, "is why it is that the cost of the leather belts has gone up two cents a belt. From what I am able to gather, you spent so much time worrying about the changeover from the brass to the chromium buckle that you've ignored the leather production end of it completely."

That really rocked me. He was right. I had been worrying about the buckles because that was what we were told to worry about. The last thing in the world I ever expected was that costs on the leather component would go up. I tell you, you just can't beat this game.

Union information may frequently move in the same manner as cost control information. The union steward can carry information right to the top without going through normal channels. The union *will* often move up step by step with a complaint, but it need not.

As with cost control information, the foreman or other intermediate supervisor may find pressure being put on him from above in order to explain something of which he may not be aware or for which he may not be prepared.

Even if union information does not skip levels, it forces a supervisor to give strict attention to such matters and *forces* him to carry information up the line that he might otherwise have censored or changed.

We turn now to the examination of orders. As orders flow down the line of authority there is likely to occur at each level, as in the case of information, a modification. The order as it originates at the top is likely to be very general and take little account of special problems at each level. The order may say simply "Increase production of billfolds of X-234 type." Or else "Stop production of dies on enpannade assemblies." The order is then likely to be restated at each level so as to take account of the specific situation.

Not all orders are modified to the same extent. A supervisor is likely to vary between two extremes: On the one hand he may give attention to modifying the order as much as is necessary in order to cause the least disturbance in his shop and at the same time comply at least with the general intent of the order. On the other hand he may transmit the order exactly as received and insist on its being carried out. The foreman may say, in the face of worker objections to a new order: "Those are the orders. It's no skin off my teeth if it's a crazy order. I don't make the orders here, I just carry them out. Now let's get busy." However, if the attempt to obey the order precisely causes disturbance or some mixup or complaints to the union, the foreman himself is likely to be blamed. It will not help him very much if he says, "I was only carrying out orders." He is likely to be told, "You should have known better." Also he will get a reputation for being a person who does not know how to exercise discretion. A supervisor, paradoxically, is expected by his subordinates *and* his superiors to modify an order. Indeed, the ability to exercise such discretion constitutes one of the characteristics of executive talent.

2. HORIZONTAL COMMUNICATION

Horizontal communication deals with lateral communication between persons who are on the same or closely related levels of authority, e.g., communication between foremen. How this takes place is by no means a simple matter. Usually the request by one foreman for assistance or information from another foreman must be of such a nature as not to harm the relations of either foreman with his superintendent. From a purely formal point of view, the interaction should go through a common supervisor.

If foreman A desires to consult with foreman B he should contact his department manager, A, who would in turn contact the superintendent who would contact the other department manager, B, who would finally convey the information to foreman B. Then a reverse process would take place. If this were in fact done a great deal of time would be consumed and misunderstandings would occur; normally, short cuts take place.

These short cuts save time and trouble for the person who is by-passed, but at the the same time keep information from him. This is all right as long as everything is going smoothly, but if something goes wrong then the manager may expect to be criticized for not keeping the superintendent informed. In order to meet this problem, it is common for the supervisor to handle horizontal problems through lateral inter-action and then to inform his superior afterwards of the problem and the action that was taken. Even this, however, is often not sufficient pro-tection. In an industrial office the president of a company was upbraiding one of his executives for not keeping him informed of just such a lateral interaction as we have discussed. The executive replied that he had in-formed the president in a memo. The president then replied:

Yes, you sent me a memo, I know that. Let me tell you a story that will illustrate my point. This happened during the period just before the depression. The company was riding high on paper profits and then the bottom fell out. The company went on the rocks and a funeral meeting of the officers was called. There was one man who spoke up and said, "If you men remember I warned you that all of this would happen. I told you we were riding too high and that sooner or later a break was due to come. I told you we ought to protect our investments." The president of the company said to him, "You did not tell us." The other man replied, "Oh yes I did tell you. I remember it very clearly. It was in a meeting and it was just before the July 4 picnic, don't you remember?" The president shook his head and said, "Well, it wasn't enough just to have told us. You should have pounded the table."

The extent to which horizontal interaction will take place and how harmonious this interaction is likely to be depends on a number of factors of which informal relations, the product-shop-functional shop distinction, and line-staff relations are the most important.

If the two persons who belong to different shops are part of the same informal group, are neighbors, or belong to the same club, horizontal interaction is likely to be free and easy. If two men are in competition with each other, lateral interaction may be completely blocked off.

In general, the foreman of a product shop is able to engage in horizontal communication with the foremen of other product shops with little difficulty. The product shop has relatively little interaction with other shops. It receives its material at one end and passes it out in a semi-completed form at the other end. It then has nothing further to do with it. The situation is diagrammed in Figure 16.

By contrast, a functional shop may have relations with almost every department, as indicated in the Figure. Further, whereas in the product shop the materials go only one way, in the functional shop they go both ways: a part comes in from shop A to be welded; it is then returned to shop A. The functional shop is in the position of continually working with parts which other departments regard as theirs, and for which they are usually waiting impatiently. The functional shop is therefore the place where foremen continually drop in to see how things are going and to put pressure on the functional-shop foreman. Problems are likely to arise because each job has its own problems or needs special attention.

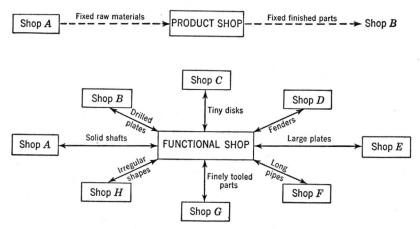

FIG. 16

INTERACTION BETWEEN SHOPS: PRODUCT SHOP VS. FUNCTIONAL SHOP

For example, if the functional shop is a paint shop, then one shop will complain because the paint has clogged up holes which must be clear for screws or rivets; another will complain because the part has been tooled to fine tolerances which are upset because paint has been applied unevenly; still another complains because paint chips off a part which must be hammered into place in an assembly. In the case of a mailing department, it is common for different shops to wish special handling for their products. Frequently these conflicts reach the point where they cannot be handled by simple lateral discussion but require the intervention of a common supervisor.

Relations between line and staff are among the most troublesome in any factory situation. They are very touchy relations in part because they are so status-colored. Generally, a member of a staff organization may go to anyone in the line organization. For example, a rate-setter who is a mere flunky in the office may go to the plant manager. An engineer may go directly to the superintendent. This means that the formal status categories break down in such relationships because the persons are not comparable. An engineering or maintenance foreman is not on the same level as a line foreman and cannot be easily compared to him. A maintenance foreman, further, can go to a line foreman and can demand action.

It is among staff and control persons that one finds most frequently elevated self-conceptions. They usually think of themselves as "professionals" (as some of them are) and therefore as persons whose orders are of the character of the doctor's, who expects to be obeyed.

Because of the peculiar role of staff organization it is customary for them to be put off to one side in a typical formal organization as illustrated below:

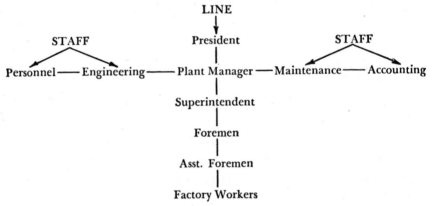

FIG. 17

SEPARATION OF LINE AND STAFF IN FACTORY STRUCTURE

The special problems created by line-staff relations mean that many line-staff conflicts can be resolved only by proceeding through a common supervisor.

CHAPTER REFERENCES

1. Arensberg, C. M., "Industry and the Community," *American Journal of Sociology*, 48:1–12, 1942.
2. Bakke, E. W., *Citizens Without Work*, London: H. Milford, Oxford University Press, 1940.

3. Bendix, R., "Bureaucracy and the Problem of Power," *Public Administration Review,* 5:194–209, 1945.

4. ———, *Work and Authority in Industry,* New York: Wiley, 1956.

5. Black, J. D., *Introduction to Production Economics,* New York: Henry Holt, 1926.

6. ——— and Brinser, A., *Planning One Town: Petersham, A Hill Town in Massachusetts,* Cambridge: Harvard University Press, 1952.

7. Brady, R. A., *Business as a System of Power,* New York: Columbia University Press, 1943.

8. Burgess, E. W. and Locke, H. J., *The Family,* New York: American Book Co., 1953.

9. Burnes, E. M., "Economic Factors in Family Life," *The Family in a Democratic Society,* New York: Columbia University Press, 1949.

9a. Cottrell, W. F., "Death by Dieselization: A Case Study in the Reaction to Technological Change," *American Sociological Review,* 16:358–365, 1951.

10. Creamer, D. B., *Is Industry Decentralizing?* Philadelphia: University of Pennsylvania Press, 1935.

11. Elmer, M. C., *The Sociology of the Family,* Boston: Ginn, 1945.

12. Floyd, J. S., Jr., *Effects of Taxation on Industrial Location,* Chapel Hill: University of North Carolina Press, 1952.

13. Fogarty, M. P., *Plan Your Own Industries: A Study of Local and Regional Development Organizations,* Oxford: Blackwell, 1947.

14. Gardner, B. B. and Moore, D. G., *Human Relations in Industry,* Homewood, Ill.: R. D. Irwin, 1955.

15. Gerth, H. H. and Mills, C. W. (trans. and eds.), *From Max Weber: Essays in Sociology,* New York: Oxford University Press, 1946.

16. Groves, E. R., "The Psychology of the Woman Who Works," *Family,* 8:92–97, 1927.

17. Havighurst, R. J. and Morgan, H. G., *The Social History of a War-Boom Community,* New York: Longmans, Green, 1951.

18. von Hayek, F., *The Road to Serfdom,* Chicago: University of Chicago Press, 1944.

19. Henderson, A. M. and Parsons, T., *Max Weber: The Theory of Social and Economic Organization,* New York: Oxford University Press, 1947.

20. Homes, W. G., *Plant Location,* New York: McGraw-Hill, 1930.

21. Hoover, E. M., *The Location of Economic Activity,* New York: McGraw-Hill, 1948.

22. Knox, J. B., *The Sociology of Industrial Relations,* New York: Random House, 1955.

23. Komarovsky, M., *The Unemployed Man and His Family,* New York: Dryden, 1940.

24. Kyrk, H., *The Family in the American Economy,* Chicago: University of Chicago Press, 1953.

25. Lamb, R. K., "Productivity and Social Structure," in Tripp, L. R. (ed.), *Industrial Productivity,* Industrial Relations Research Association, 1951.

26. Landis, P. H., *Three Iron Mining Towns,* Ann Arbor, Michigan: Edwards, 1938.
27. Lösch, A. (Wolglom, W. H. and Stolper, W. F., trans.), *The Economics of Location,* New Haven: Yale University Press, 1954.
28. McLaughlin, G. E. and Robock, S., *Why Industry Moves South,* Kingsport, Tennessee: National Planning Association, Committee of the South, 1949.
29. Mills, C. W., *The Power Elite,* New York: Oxford University Press, 1956.
30. von Mises, L., *Bureaucracy,* New Haven: Yale University Press, 1944.
31. Mowrer, E. R., *Family Disorganization,* Chicago: University of Chicago Press, 1927.
32. Neumann, F. L., *Behemoth,* New York: Oxford University Press, 1944.
33. Odaka, K., "An Iron Workers' Community in Japan: A Study in the Sociology of Industrial Groups," *American Sociological Review,* 15:186–195, 1950.
34. Pope, L., *Millhands and Preachers,* New Haven: Yale University Press, 1942.
35. *Report on the Location of Industry,* London: Political and Economic Planning, 1939.
36. Riesman, D.; Glazer, N.; and Denney, R., *The Lonely Crowd,* New Haven, Yale University Press, 1950.
37. Robinson, G. O., *The Oak Ridge Story,* Kingsport, Tennessee: Southern, 1951.
38. Smith, E. D. and Nyman, R. C., *Technology and Labor,* New Haven: Yale University Press, 1939.
39. *Union Oil Bulletin* (reprinted in *Scientific Monthly,* 83:150, 1956).
40. Walker, C. R., *Steeltown,* New York: Harper, 1950.
41. Warner, W. L. and Low, J. O., *The Social System of the Modern Factory,* New Haven: Yale University Press, 1947.
42. Weber, A. (Friedrich, C. J., trans.), *Alfred Weber's Theory of the Location of Industries,* Chicago: University of Chicago Press, 1929.
43. Welcker, J. W., "The Community Relations Problems of Industrial Companies," *Harvard Business Review,* 27:771–780, 1949.
44. Whyte, W. H., Jr., *Is Anybody Listening?* New York: Simon and Schuster, 1950.
45. Woodbury, C. (ed.), *The Future of Cities and Urban Redevelopment,* Chicago: University of Chicago Press, 1953.
46. Yaseen, L. C., *Plant Location,* Roslyn, New York: Business Reports, 1952.

CHAPTER TWELVE

THE ECONOMIC COMPLEX AND STATUS AND AUTHORITY SYSTEM IN THE FACTORY

THE FACTORY ECONOMIC COMPLEX

When the factory worker shows his identification card to the company guard and is waved on through the gates, he enters as a stranger on someone else's property using someone else's tools, machines, and materials. The worker is permitted to be there because he has a *service* to offer, for which he receives a fixed money payment. But unlike others who provide services—bootblacks, barbers, and doctors—the worker does not determine what he gets for his service. Of course, in practice, bootblacks, barbers and doctors do not completely determine what they get. They will charge the going rate, perhaps more if their customers will stand for it. But however the actual rate is determined, it is the individual who provides the service who also fixes the rate, and if the customer or patient does not like it, he can go somewhere else. In the factory, the situation is reversed. It is the person asking for the service (management) who determines the rate, and if the worker does not like it, *he* can go somewhere else.[1] In practice, the government and unions have introduced rigidities into this bargaining process so as to establish guarantees of various kinds. But these provide general conditions and averages rather than what a

---

[1] It will be recognized that in reality, neither the doctor's patient nor the worker is in fact free to go somewhere else in any sense but formally. The patient *could* go elsewhere but he does not know where things would be any better, and he is tied by feelings of loyalty, trust, and faith. The worker, similarly, may not know where better jobs can be had, may not have the money to keep his family while he looks, or may be tied to a particular locality by the fact that he is paying for a house, has his children in school, and so on. On this point, see (51).

particular individual will receive. The individual, then, must still bargain for as high a wage as he can get. For workers already employed, union contracts may provide for automatic cost-of-living increases at specified periods, but the worker will usually want more than that if he can get it. A great many factories, particularly those that are nonunionized, operate on the principle of the merit increase, which is an individual matter, based on the foreman's subjective judgment, on the estimates of higher supervisors, and on the individual worker's ability to convince his superiors that he deserves it. On the other hand, the worker who argues that his work deserves an increase will not agree that, should his work be falling down, he should get a decrease or cut. Here traditions are so strong that management will rarely dare to act in what, it could be claimed, was a rational manner.

Another important difference between others who provide services and the factory worker revolves about the question of time. The boot-black does his job, finishes, and receives a sum of money. His work is a series of disconnected jobs. It is of no concern to the user of his services that the bootblack is idle between jobs. By contrast, the factory worker is paid not only for doing a specific job but for *being there* and *staying there.* Wages therefore are pegged to *time,* and even piece work systems assume that the worker will put in a full working day.

Theoretically, wages are simply a cost of production for services rendered. They must be paid out of company receipts in the same manner than any other bill must be paid. In practice, however, wages turn out to be the most emotion-laden phenomenon in the factory. In large part this occurs because everyone, including owners and top management, are there to *make money.* This is not their only motive, but it is always a major one. Except for the very few who have independent means, this means they are dependent for a living on what money the factory can pay them. This dependence, although in theory a contractual or seg-mented one, becomes surrounded with conceptions of "rights" and "duties" and moral questions, and therefore is easily converted into an emotional reality.

Management and workers approach wages from two quite different points of view, and by looking at these points of view we gain some in-sight into the factory economic complex.

MANAGEMENT'S APPROACH TO WAGES

Management in the modern factory tends to approach the matter of wages with certain conceptions of reward and appropriateness, these con-ceptions revolve about money costs. We may state these conceptions in the form of three propositions (20a). It must be borne in mind, however, that these propositions are exaggerations, and particular managers will vary from them depending on their own personalities and the local situation.

1. ALL ACTIVITIES SHOULD BE EVALUATED IN TERMS OF MONEY

The attempt is made to assign a monetary value to every operation possible: machine operations, materials, people, objects, waste materials, and so on. These actions provide the basis for accounting and cost control and for production planning.

2. MONEY IS THE MAJOR WORK INCENTIVE

The individual is assumed to be working to make money. Therefore, if one wishes him to work harder, one should pay him more money. A promotion without appropriate wage increase is an empty act, and throughout the authority hierarchy wages should reflect work position. The top man in the company gets the most pay, the next man the second most, etc. Of two jobs, the better one is the one that pays more. The best way to recognize service or to indicate a change of status is by a change of pay. It is also felt that high wages produce satisfied, happy workers. Above all, management feels, the initiative in paying workers rests with management through its favorite technique, the merit increase.

3. ALL EFFORTS SHOULD BE DIRECTED TOWARD MAKING A PROFIT AND DECREASING COSTS

Sales should be greater than costs. To produce a profit, the worker should make a monetary contribution, through his labor, greater than what he is being paid. Every effort should be made to prevent a waste of materials or time. The attempt is made to keep wages as low as possible. It is true that occasionally management may raise wages, may assist sick employees and do other things which increase costs. Such moves may be based on what is considered "right" or "fair" in the community; but they are *ultimately* justified on the grounds of good employee morale which in turn, it is hoped, will increase efficiency and decrease costs.

On the basis of these ideas, there emerges management's conception that workers should be paid more if they are faster or more efficient, or if their jobs are more vital or require more skill, etc. But these ideas run up against a contrary conception: "the fair wage."

THE WORKER'S APPROACH—THE FAIR WAGE

What is regarded as a fair wage by the worker may differ from management's conception of what the worker should receive. The fair wage depends on two factors: community expectations and comparative work factors.

1. COMMUNITY EXPECTATIONS
H. M. Douty (18) points out:

The lower limit for labor—the wage below which labor will not work—is, in a practical sense, the prevailing wage, or perhaps slightly below this wage, for the work in question in the community or in the industry at any particular time.

The determination of "the prevailing wage" is, however, never a simple matter for there may be considerable variation even within a region or city. Federal and state legislation may fix minima but these are most important for minority groups, women, and others who often do not have labor unions to bargain for them or are forced to accept the wage offered to them because they have no alternative employment. For regularly employed men, the "prevailing wage" is a social psychological phenomenon—a conception of the standard of living that a man's family and friends consider appropriate to persons of their station. In addition, the worker brings with him a self-conception derived from his family of orientation, his sex, his place of origin, his education and any other status criteria that he feels should be reflected in the wages he receives.

2. COMPARATIVE WORK FACTORS
Within the factory (or any work situation), there is a tendency for workers to evaluate themselves by comparing themselves with other workers. The most common criteria are those of seniority, loyalty, and value to the company. While seniority admits of relatively precise measurements, loyalty and value to the company do not. These latter are likely to be matters of subjective judgment.

From the point of view of the worker's conception of a fair wage, it makes no difference if he is a fast worker, a slow worker, an efficient worker or whatever management might consider desirable. A fair wage is a fair wage. It is coming to him.

The actual wage that a worker receives, and what comes to be regarded as fair both by management and the worker, is likely to be a compromise between management conceptions, community expectations and comparative work factors. The ideal wage will be one that will place him fairly in reference to other employees, will enable him to hold up his head among his friends, and at the same time will permit management or stockholders to make a profit.[2] This ideal may never be reached and the wage must be understood as a dynamic phenomenon arrived at

---

[2] There are, of course, other factors: labor-market competition, product-market competition, centralized bargaining, common ownership of establishments, and government participation. See (57, 58).

strategically and usually representing at a given time only a temporary balance.

TYPES OF PAYMENT

As pointed out in Chapter Three, there are many types of payment found within our own society. Within the factory, the four commonest types are: hourly wage, weekly salary, monthly salary, and piece-work (individual or group).[3]

1. HOURLY-RATED VERSUS SALARIED WORKERS

The distinction between hourly-rated workers and salary workers is a reflection of the shop-office distinction that was discussed previously. Shop workers generally are paid an hourly rate and office workers are paid a salary. This distinction is in part a reflection of the differences in activities. The shop workers are concerned with the manufacture process and the office workers with the communication process and the manipulation of informational and control activities.

Among office workers, the executive group are often paid a monthly salary and the clerical group are usually paid a weekly salary. This distinction is also in part a matter of differential activities. The executive in a company supervises, controls and directs the organization. The clerical group, less skilled, assist the executives in the processes of communication and control. They include the weekly-rated clerks, stenographers, lower supervisors, and others.

The distinction, however, reflects not merely differences in activities, but also the way in which their work is *evaluated* by the company. The work of hourly-rated persons is thought of by the company as a commodity; it is felt that it can be *measured* in terms of time or units of work. But in the case of the salaried worker, work is thought of as a rather intangible thing which is difficult to measure. It is felt that the salaried worker deals with new problems, he anticipates future events, and is concerned with making complex decisions. Therefore, one cannot say that two hours of his time is worth exactly twice what one hour is worth. He may do nothing for seven hours and in the last hour may make a decision which saves the company a great deal of money. Or else the benefits of his work may not show up for a long time. Great trust and confidence is, therefore, vested in the executive. This in turn raises the question as to how long an executive may be "carried" by a company before it is considered that the results of his efforts should have made themselves evident. With the weekly salary employees, this is not as true, their work is immediately measurable.

[3] There are many variations, including profit-sharing plans which have other values as well. See (66, 77, 85).

2. STATUS DIFFERENCES BETWEEN HOURLY-, WEEKLY-, AND MONTHLY-PAID WORKERS

Status increases as one moves from hourly work to weekly-paid work to monthy-paid work. There is also a hierarchy in *numbers:* the hourly workers tend to be most frequent, the weekly workers are next, and there tend to be very few monthly-paid workers.

The hierarchy is a direct reflection of freedom from control. The hourly workers punch the time clock, it is to them that the NO SMOKING signs apply, etc. The salaried worker may be late, take an occasional afternoon off, he may leave his work without having it pile up in his absence providing he is not gone for too long a time. For the monthly workers, there may be very little formal control except from the top officers of the company itself. My own experience with top business executives leads me to think that they perhaps come the closest of any group in our society to complete freedom in their activities so far as their work is concerned. This is likely to be particularly true of the executive who is highly regarded by the officers of the company. They are among the highest paid persons in our society. The hours that they put in are likely to be a matter of their own estimate of how best to apportion their time. This does not mean that they do not work hard. Indeed, the tense executive with his stomach ulcers has become a stereotype. To a considerable extent, however, the discipline is a self-imposed one. He may not come into the office until noon or he may leave the office at three o'clock to go to his club but he may be up that night until very late making plans or attempting to sell a client. Not infrequently, an executive is a repository of experience who is retained by the company because he is able to make decisions perhaps once a month or once in six months which have long-range effects on the company. Of course all this is a source of exasperation to the clerks or other salaried workers in the office who may feel that his high salary is being paid for extremely little work. One office worker said to me:

I don't understand why they pay Mr. Lindstrom so much money. I got a look at the salary record the other day and you wouldn't believe it if I were to tell you what he is getting. It's just out of this world. Why do you know I actually do most of his work? He doesn't even see half of the letters that come in here which I answer in his name. He can't find a thing in the files and I have to go and get it for him. Then he's absent minded too. I have to remind him about his wife's birthday and about his anniversary. Can you imagine that!

3. PIECE-WORK

Piece-work tends to be found only with hourly-rated workers. If the worker is paid on a straight hourly basis then no *direct* attention is given to his output. The only formal way under such a system of recognizing efficiency or individual differences is through an increase in the hourly rate at certain specified review periods. The reduction of labor costs through the increase of output is then left entirely in the hands of the lower supervisors.

To overcome some of these problems one often finds a piece-work system—a method of payment by which the output of the worker directly determines his earnings.

In the case of individual piece-work, the worker is paid a fixed amount for every operation completed.[4] Therefore, his earnings depend on his output, although there is often a guaranteed minimum, particularly if he is a member of a labor union.

Many benefits are claimed for this system: it simplifies accounting and cost procedures; it fulfills the ideal that the faster worker should get paid more; it provides an *incentive* system to keep the person working at maximum efficiency; and, it relieves the supervisor from the responsibility of reducing labor costs.

But along with these advantages there develop serious problems of which there are four main ones.

1. Piece-work creates special problems of rate-setting. Management will desire that the rate shall be neither too high nor too low. Also rates have to be changed whenever factory procedures are changed. Therefore, there will be required skilled and trained persons in order to set rates: a fairly large staff of rate setters who add considerably to the costs of the company.

2. Piece-work increases the amount of inspection that is necessary. Because workers are paid for output, the system is liable to abuse since it would be possible to maintain a very high rate of speed but to produce many parts that would be unsatisfactory. Hence, a piece-work system is accompanied by many inspectors.

3. It is true that piece-work increases competition among workers and appeals to economic incentives. At the same time it tends to lead to individualistic attitudes on the part of the worker who takes the piece work system seriously. The worker is little interested in others under such a system and consequently it is difficult to get him to cooperate with others so as to keep the whole department running smoothly. The worker may refuse to help others, or to assist in the training of new workers.

4. It seems to be true that no matter how rates are set, some jobs turn out to have better rates than others do. A job that has a "fat" rate

---

[4] Various piece-work systems are described (6, 30, 32, 38, 39).

is one in which it is fairly easy to earn the minimum and to make extra money. A job with a lean rate is one that is just the opposite. Usually a supervisor will try to distribute the fat jobs as evenly as possible. This, however, is often very difficult and leads to charges of favoritism, to conflicts between workers, and to other disturbances.[5] In order to avoid some of these problems a system of group piece-work may be adopted.

In the case of group piece-work, the piece-work production of a work group is grouped together. Each worker is assigned an hourly rate. The earnings of the group are then expressed as a percentage earned above the total hourly rate of the group. As an illustration, let us imagine a group of four workers. Two of them have hourly rates of $1.50 an hour, one of them $1.25 an hour and the fourth $.75 an hour. The total hourly earnings of the group are then $5.00. Let us imagine that they are to receive their minimum of $5.00, if they produce one hundred assemblies of a certain kind. Let us imagine that by working at top speed they succeed in producing one hundred and fifty assemblies. Then each person will secure for that hour 50 per cent more than he would have gotten otherwise. The two men who were making $1.50 an hour secure an extra $.75 each. The man who was making $1.25 an hour secures an extra $.62½ and the man getting seventy-five cents an hour secures an extra $.37½. This is not the only way in which group piece-work may be administered. In some arrangements the increase is apportioned equally so that each member of the work group receives the same increment although his hourly rate is still different.

Through such a system the individual's earnings are partly related to his own speed and efficiency. But also his hourly rate directly affects his earnings. Group piece-work greatly reduces the amount of inspection necessary, and places more responsibility for maintaining proper quality on the work group itself and its supervisors (55, pp. 13–14, 34–36, 409–12). Group piece-work also simplifies accounting work. There are fewer records necessary since one can take the total group output rather than individual output. It has as a virtue that it recognizes the cooperative nature of work. However, it does not provide a direct monetary reward for efficient workers because they all receive the same percentage. Therefore differences in ability or efficiency are not reflected in differences in earning, and it becomes the duty of the supervisor to give such recognition in other ways.

Piece-work is essentially a device for cost control. But group piece-

---

[5] Cf. discussion in (30, Chs. VI, VII; 32, Chs. III–V; 68, pp. 235–38; 85, Chs. 5, 6). But piece-work may have other unintended values, especially, as a challenge, a game, and a means of avoiding fatigue. See (60).
Piece-work creates many other problems in the work group which are discussed in Chap. 13.

work in particular is likely to turn out to function as an important mechanism for communication and control. The earnings of the group are likely to be used by the supervisor as an index of the manner in which the organization is working. There is an assumption that if the piece-work percentage is high or is increasing, then the job is running smoothly and morale must be good, but that if the piece-work percentage is low or decreasing, then the job is being done poorly. This interpretation is related to the idea that when the worker's earnings increase he must be satisfied and when they decrease he must be unhappy. When used in this way, the earning report becomes a basis for the evaluation of the work situation and of the supervisor.

This situation causes the lowest supervisor to *focus* attention on piece-work earnings and try to keep them up. In fact piece-work earnings probably receive more attention from the supervisor than do earnings of any other kind.

Piece-work earnings are the kind of information that can skip levels in the supervisory hierarchy. When the work is completed, inspected, and counted, the work tickets will then go to the accounting department. A report may then be prepared at the end of the month which would cover the entire month. This means that the pressure or criticism or a demand for explanations from above, when they come, will be unexpected and will also be unexplainable unless something quite striking has occurred that the supervisor knows about. All that he can respond is that he will try to do better next month. Consequently the supervisor in a piece-work system is likely to be in a state of considerable tension. Perhaps this tension offsets many of the purported advantages of piece work.

MEANINGS OF MONEY

It is quite obvious from our previous discussion that payment has far more than purely monetary or economic significance. It is practically never true that money refers only to so much pay for a given amount of work done. It is used by management as a means of recognition or of reward, and may therefore be a weapon or a means of punishment. It is interpreted by the worker as a prestige symbol and enables him to maintain certain expectations among fellow workers and in the community in which he lives.

The great significance of money in our culture leads wages to become a focus about which problems converge. There is a frequent tendency in industry to express or interpret all disturbances in economic terms. Any person who is disturbed in his work may believe that the difficulty is due to a low rate of pay.

Conversely, complaints about earning or the wage system often are indicative of disturbances and maladjustments which may be due to other factors. A masterful case study of this phenomenon is provided by A. W. Gouldner's analysis of the factors responsible for a strike in a gypsum plant (24, Chs. 1–3). Workers had built up a set of expectations toward management which Gouldner calls the "indulgency pattern" and which consisted of the following: not supervising men very closely but judging them by the work they turned out; being flexible about the enforcement of plant rules; permitting workers to "bid" for a vacancy in another department; allowing an injured worker to work in the "sample room" (where the work was light) until he had recovered sufficiently to return to his old job; and allowing workers to do "government work" (use of company equipment or supplies for personal use). A new plant administration proceeded to violate every one of these expectations: closeness of supervision was greatly increased; men who violated a plant rule had to sign a formal "warning notice" indicating they would have no claim for clemency if a further violation occurred; the bidding system was curtailed; injured or absent workers had to stay away from work for as many days as they had been absent; and a worker was fired for using some company dynamite for a personal matter (a procedure common to the "government work" expectation). Yet the immediate response of the workers was to have their union leaders institute a demand for a *thirty-cent-an-hour wage increase*. New machines had been installed and workers expressed fear that these might reduce their overtime pay; the pay demand was explained as a way of preparing for a later drop in pay. While there is no question that such fears were important, it is also remarkable that expectations about wages did *not* find a place in the indulgency pattern. The explanation, Gouldner says, is that the indulgency pattern consisted of a set of expectations which were non-legitimate in that they were not contractually enforceable. Management was entirely within its contractual rights in firing a worker for using company properties for private purposes or in strictly enforcing plant rules; but if it had tried to lower costs by reducing wages, that would constitute a clear violation of the union contract. Gouldner (24, p. 29) writes:

At this time, and in accordance with the contract, the union gave management notice that it wished to re-open negotiations. The contract stipulated, however, that the only conditions permitting renegotiation were "a major change in the area rates of the industry or in the cost of living." Constrained as they were by these provisions, the union negotiating committee stuck grimly to the question of wages. They set aside all other grievances and advanced as their sole demand a request for a thirty cents an hour increase. The Company replied that, since there had been no changes in the area rates, only a two and one-half cents "cost of living" increase was warranted. Immediately, indignation at the

Company's "insulting offer" ran high. While strike threats had been heard even before this, they now became more audible. The surface workers were somewhat less intransigent than the miners. "It's thirty cents or strike," growled the miners, "None of this haggling."

Also important was the fact that outsiders (including wives, members of the community, and even the leadership of the union at the national level) could more easily understand a wage grievance and be more likely to support it. Even management—though it did argue about the *size* of the increase demanded—did not question the legitimacy of the demand. In short, says Gouldner (24, p. 34), the wage clause in the contract "served as a lightning rod attracting diffuse aggressions which stemmed from various grievances."

The significance of this "lightning rod" effect should not, however, lead the student of work to the conclusion that wage complaints are minor or merely symptomatic of other problems. Unfortunately such a position has sometimes been taken and had led to the belief that measures which increase the psychological satisfactions of the worker should result in a decrease in wage complaints.[6] This point of view has been extended to the belief that nearly all complaints and dissatisfactions can be overcome by a skillful, understanding management.[7] In argument, E. V. Schneider (65) writes of a:

. . . very real clash of interest between management and labor in several spheres. On the one hand is a cost-conscious management seeking to purchase labor and to use it most economically; on the other hand is labor seeking to maximize wages and other benefits and seeking relief from the discipline of factory life and machine. No amount of talk of "misunderstanding" between capital and labor, or "blocked channels of communication" can serve to gloss over this real area of conflict.

Schneider's statement remains true even when we recognize that it may sometimes be to management's economic interest to raise wages (both to heighten productivity and purchasing power) and when we recognize that an expanding economy may permit both rising wages and lower prices. Yet we do not have to adopt the dialectic of the pendulum in analyzing the significance of wages; it is possible to avoid an "either-or" position. We should ask of each case: what is the significance of this grievance? To what *extent* does it reflect an economic conflict and to what extent

[6] This belief is associated with Elton Mayo and his followers. See (41, Ch. 1; 55, Pt. III).

[7] Those so believing have been called "managerial sociologists." See (7, 20, 44, 47, 67).

other conflicts? The answers that research provides to such questions should be more revealing than disputation.

THE STATUS AND AUTHORITY SYSTEM IN THE FACTORY

STATUS IN THE FACTORY

We have seen that occupation is one factor among others which confers status. The status of a factory worker will be a blend of his status in the community and his status in the factory. The man brings a certain status *with him* to the job—a self-conception based in part on his interpretation of the conceptions others have of him. In turn, he will also take with him a factory status when he leaves the factory at the end of the working day. Here we shall consider first the status determinants that the worker brings with him *to the factory* and then shall consider the factory status determinants that he takes with him *back into the community.*

1. STATUS DETERMINANTS THAT THE WORKER BRINGS TO THE FACTORY

There are a large number of such status determinants but the most significant to the factory worker are the following: age, wealth, kinship, education, experience, and ethnic status. All of these have powerful effects on an individual's self-conceptions. Each of these tends to produce in the worker's mind a definite sentiment of rights and of what he feels is coming to him. He thinks and says: "Because I am sixty years old and because I have had thirty years' experience, therefore I deserve special treatment in terms of the kind of job I get, raises, promotions, *and* in terms of respect." Every one of these factors are things about which the person is willing to fight.

a. AGE

The aged in American industry are not often admired or respected: feelings toward them tend to be a mixture of pity and resentment.[8] The pity may take the form of regret that "that old geezer *has* to work," while the resentment may occur because he is holding down a job which a younger person could fill. This resentment is particularly likely to occur if the older person occupies a supervisory position. Indeed, these two sentiments of pity and resentment are related to each other. It may be precisely because resentment is felt that pity is expressed. Resentment tends not to be approved in our culture, but pity is.

Because of the speed with which industrial progress is made the aged worker tends not to be regarded as a repository of wisdom or of skill.

[8] For a good discussion of the aged in relation to industry, see (33, 46, 69, 83).

They are however repositories of memories. The aged person is often the "old timer," who will talk to anyone willing to listen. For that reason he may be looked upon with good humor and called "dad" or "pop." But the oldster is likely to feel that he *ought* to be regarded as a repository of wisdom and will resent these condescending attitudes.

At the other end of the age scale the youth is likely to feel a conflict between his self-conceptions and the conceptions that others have of him. It seems to be true that no matter how much education a person has had, no matter how much special training, how much wealth or what kind of a family he comes from, *if he is young,* then he is likely to be treated with condescension or with grudging respect. Youth in fact tends to be a status depressant. A man is expected to move along at a certain rate; and no matter what his qualities may be in general, the young person in a position of authority is resented. He is often the object of epithets such as "ball of fire" and "whiz kid."

b. WEALTH AND KINSHIP

Both of these factors provide what we have called status escapes: The worker can avoid adverse opinion and treatment by escaping to the status that may attach to his wealth or to his kinship. For example, if a person who is privately wealthy finds that his salary is lower than others like himself in ability, he is likely to express resentment and say that it is not fair. However it does not mean very much to him. The wealthy worker finds that he just cannot get too excited about a five-dollar difference in salary, when the person who is getting five dollars more than he is may have to ask him at the end of the day for a lift home in his car.

Kinship is likely to be significant in U.S. industry only if the worker is a relation of the boss. Then, it may provide a status escape. The person who is in such a position is not likely to receive adverse criticism; and if he should, he can safely ignore it because he enjoys the security of ascribed status.

Both wealth and kinship may incur resentment from other workers but they are likely to become resigned to it. In general neither wealth nor kinship tends to cause severe disturbance in industry, though they cannot be ignored. The matter of kinship *is* significant in the family business wherein all or most of the top white-collar positions are preempted by the members of one family. The effect is that of a ceiling for upward mobile persons, and the result may be high turnover among the top executives who find themselves approaching that ceiling. For example, in one plastics manufacturing concern, the top positions were filled as follows (25, p. 173):

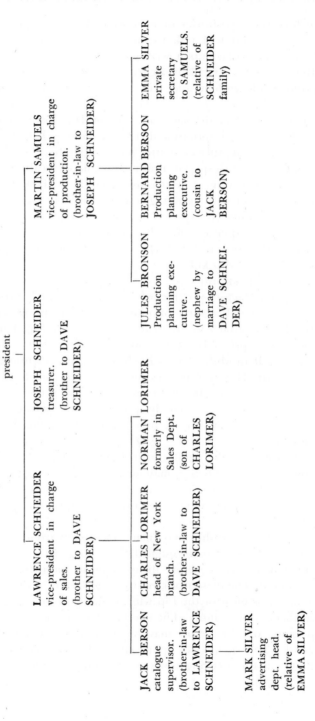

DAVE SCHNEIDER
president

LAWRENCE SCHNEIDER vice-president in charge of sales. (brother to DAVE SCHNEIDER)

JOSEPH SCHNEIDER treasurer. (brother to DAVE SCHNEIDER)

MARTIN SAMUELS vice-president in charge of production. (brother-in-law to JOSEPH SCHNEIDER)

JACK BERSON catalogue supervisor. (brother-in-law to LAWRENCE SCHNEIDER)

CHARLES LORIMER head of New York branch. (brother-in-law DAVE SCHNEIDER)

NORMAN LORIMER formerly in Sales Dept. (son of CHARLES LORIMER)

JULES BRONSON Production planning executive. (nephew by marriage to DAVE SCHNEIDER)

BERNARD BERSON Production planning executive. (cousin to JACK BERSON)

EMMA SILVER private secretary to SAMUELS. (relative of SCHNEIDER family)

MARK SILVER advertising dept. head. (relative of EMMA SILVER)

436

An executive, in charge of Credit and Collections, looked over a chart showing these positions and, commenting on his own promotion chances in the company, said: "You can see where that leaves me."

C. EDUCATION AND EXPERIENCE

On the whole, experience is accorded greater prestige than is education *per se*. It is through education that the individual may be enabled to secure a position in the first place. However, if the individual secures the position because of his experience then he is likely to be accorded higher status by his fellow-workers.[9]

One of the first questions asked of the new worker is: "Where did you work before?" It is by that means that workers are able to place people. It is through that means that one can decide how much respect or attention the person deserves.

In spite of the respect accorded experience, increasingly the worker is led to recognize the value of a formal education, especially a college education. There is considerable resentment on the part of those who do not have that education if this lack in any way acts as a ceiling for them. It leads some workers to attend night school and make other attempts to make up for their lack of formal education. It points therefore to a profound respect which the worker has if not for education then for the *power* of education. One will find the same worker who himself belittles white-collar work urging his own children to secure a college education so that they may be provided with at least the formal prerequisites for moving into those positions.

d. ETHNIC AND MINORITY GROUP STATUS

Sex, ethnicity, race, and religion tend to act on status in two ways: as status depressants and as status escapes. It is often not recognized that

---

[9] An executive emphasized the significance of experience as follows: "How do you know these things? How do you know what will sell? Experience. Take someone like Jules Bronson. He's not a good salesman . . . He's learning, but he isn't a good salesman. He doesn't have the experience . . . I was out on a trip a while ago, breaking in a new salesman. Naturally I wanted to put on a good show. We went into a women's clothing shop. A woman was the owner. She was bawling somebody out. I could see she was in a bad mood. So we go up to her and I tell her I've got some raincoats to sell. 'How much are they?' she asks. So I tell her: '$9.95.' 'What?' she says. 'They won't sell here. There isn't a coat in the store that sells for less than $25.' So I says to her, 'You're feeling pretty snappy today, aren't you? Well, I've got something here that's really wonderful. It's out of this world.' So she becomes interested. I'm so enthusiastic. She wants to see this something that's out of this world. So I pulled out one of the metallic elasti-glass coats in green. I ask her to let one of her salesgirls model it. So she calls over one of the girls. She put it on and she really looked good. The other girls saw what was going on and they came running over. 'How much is the coat?' I told them: '$9.95.' So they were surprised. 'What! Only $9.95 for such a coat?' The upshot was she bought 10 dozen coats. The salesman I was with—he would have quit as soon as she said she didn't buy coats for under $25. These people want to be sold. I know" (25, pp. 195–96).

the most significant discrimination that takes place may not occur on the job itself but is likely to take the form of the *prevention of learning*. Persons of minority group status may find it difficult to secure a job to begin with. But even if they should secure a job they are likely to find it difficult to learn. We are not referring here simply to the technical skills; the individual may have those already from a school which he has attended. We are referring rather to the tricks of the trade and to the social skills. It is on the basis of the latter that the worker secures recognition and acceptance within the work group, and it is these skills that are precisely the most difficult to get without having been *already* accorded at least tentative recognition. To even begin to teach a person the tricks of the trade and the social skills is by that token to admit that some day the person is to be included within one's work group and to be regarded as an occupational equal. The son of the owner of a furniture moving company may be put into a work group by his father in order that he shall learn the business from the ground up. The men with whom he will be working can do one of two things. They can be quite rough toward him, assign him the dirtier jobs, and so treat him as they would any new worker. On the other hand they can, if they choose, be very kind and prevent him from learning anything whatsoever.

We have very little knowledge of the nature of discrimination and of prejudice in the factory. A considerable body of thought in this area thinks of the phenomenon mainly in terms of *restriction of opportunity*.[10] This restriction may be explained simply by saying that "these people do not like Negroes," or else it may be regretted and referred to as "un-American." This approach to the matter does not help us in understanding it very much. It is an *individual* analysis wherein the reason for the phenomenon is attributed to the unhappy attitudes of individuals. A logical next step is psychiatric treatment to try to change those attitudes.

It is the theme of our approach to work that in order to understand the mechanism of prejudice one must look at it essentially as a status phenomenon. It will be recalled that status is to be regarded as a blend of an individual's felt conception and his interpretation of the conceptions that others have of him. The individual spends a good deal of his time attempting to reconcile these two sets of conceptions.

When a member of a minority group is introduced into a work situation this is interpreted by the other workers in terms of their self-conceptions. It is not so much that the new person may be regarded as a threat to their jobs. Often he is, but just as often, particularly in periods

[10] Cf. (10, 14, 31, 45, 48, 49, 56, 71, 79, 81, 82).

of labor shortage, he does not represent a serious threat. Rather, the worker is likely to ponder the meaning of this move on the part of management. As one worker put it when women were introduced into his shop and were doing work that was essentially like his own.

What does that mean? Does it mean that the supervisors feel that my job is so unimportant, requires so little skill or training that *anybody*, even women, can do it? If that is true then they apparently don't think as highly of me as I thought they did.

Occasionally the worker will express his self-conceptions by saying "I will not work next to those people because they are dirty." Again he regards it as beneath his dignity, as not in accord with his self-conception for the reason only that he may feel that management cannot think very highly of him if it expects him to be willing to do such a thing.

It has been a frequent comment that one is likely to meet the most violent expressions of prejudice against ethnic or minority groups from *insecure* persons.[11] An insecure person is precisely the one whose self-conception does not agree with what he conceives of to be the conception that others have of him. In industry, the insecure person is the person who for some reason feels that management's opinions of him or his fellow-workers' whose opinions he values do not accord with his own.

When we look at ethnic prejudice in this way we get a clue as to how minority groups may be introduced into the work situation. It would be desirable if such a program included some medium for the reassurance of each white person (or whatever the dominant group is) of his value to the company. Some means should be provided for indicating to him that his self-conception is to some extent at least shared by management. Unfortunately often just the opposite is done and the members of the minority group are introduced suddenly and without warning.

2. FACTORY STATUS DETERMINANTS

We consider next the extent to which the job itself confers an increment of status on the individual which he then takes with him into the community and which in turn affects his self-conceptions and the conceptions that others have of him there.

a. TYPE OF FACTORY

Type of factory is significant for the status of a worker. The heavy industries in our culture tend to have more prestige than do the light manufacturing industries such as textiles or the needle trades. Those

---

[11] Cf. (2, 11, 64, 70, 76).

activities connected with food, such as canning, processing, or the to-bacco industry (indirectly) tend to have less prestige than others.

The particular factory itself is significant. The location of the factory, its appearance, or its size may be important. The worker is often considered to have more prestige if he works for a very large company than if he works for a very small one. The name of the factory, if widely known or respected, may also be of significance (4).

b. FORMAL POSITION

The position of the individual within the factory structure is of great significance for his status. Status, a compound of self-conceptions and of conceptions that others have, is a complex phenomenon. In the factory, the most important "other" is one's formal superior.

The supervisor-subordinate relationship is perhaps the most common relationship in the structure of any bureaucratic system (20a, pp. 8–10). Every employee spends his working life in a directly subordinate position to a superior. In most other types of subordination there is some escape, but in the factory, the person is subordinate to a given superior for practically every minute of the day.

The subordinate must continually adapt himself to the demands of the superior. A failure is likely to mean loss of opportunities or perhaps even a loss of the job. Consequently, one finds in the factory a profound tendency for the worker to focus his attention on his superior. This relationship appears to be more important to the worker than any other that he has in the factory and to have more potentiality for emotional disturbances than any other.

Although the subordinate focuses his attention up, the superior normally does not focus as much of his attention down. The relations of the superior to his subordinates down the line are likely to be more or less taken for granted unless there is some difficulty. The superior does not give as much attention to what his subordinates think of him as he does to what *his* supervisor in turn is thinking of him. Throughout the authority structure one gets a focusing of attention upward.

Each subordinate tries to evaluate the effect on his superior of almost every act in which he engages. He may avoid actions unless he feels certain of approval in advance or else dodge those which might possibly bring disapproval. There is also often a hesitancy to communicate anything up which may bring criticism. This may prevent important information from moving up the line. Either the supervisor or the subordinate may initiate any discussion, but it is usually the superior who does. In addition the superior may go to the subordinate or request that he come to him. But the subordinate in general always goes to his superior.

The amount of interaction is also significant to the subordinate. In general, the worker will have a higher self-conception the more interaction he has with his superior. He then feels "close to the boss." If there is little contact then the subordinate is likely to feel distant and to feel himself in a weak position. He may then fear that his superior dislikes him or has a low opinion of his ability. To avoid this the subordinate will often *seek* contact. He will try to think up excuses for approaching his superior or else to direct his superior's attention to things that he has accomplished. When a subordinate appears to be initiating excessive interaction, especially about small matters, that can usually be interpreted as an expression of insecurity or of dissatisfaction with the relationship.

Of course it is only the person's formal relationship to his immediate superior that is significant for his job status. The person will also *assume* a certain status by virtue of his position itself (the department head will, for example, have a higher status than the foreman). Status tends to reflect formal position although not precisely. But there is a general feeling that it *should,* and when it does not there is likely to be disturbances in self-conception.

c. TYPE OF ACTIVITY

Shop workers tend to be concerned with the manipulation of things, supervisors with people, and executives with symbols. This is part of the basis for shop-office distinctions. Indeed there is sometimes a tendency for the lowliest of office workers to feel superior to a top engineer. A frequent source of conflict between job and office is not simply a feeling of superiority on the part of the office worker. Rather, the shop worker may *expect* the office worker to feel superior, and to decide in advance that any behavior on the office worker's part is indicative of typical office worker's smugness.

The distinction between things, people and symbols helps explain why such persons as those who think up new products are likely to receive the highest pay and the most august recognition. It is also part of the reason that of all the departments within an industry, the sales department is probably at the top, for it is the sales department that is concerned with ideas and promotional activities. It is interesting that it is also the sales department which is most significant in bringing new money into the company.

d. EARNINGS

The amount that a man earns is likely to be the object of status assignment. A certain increment of status attaches to the $1.20 man as compared to the $1.10 man. However this way of looking at it is putting the cart before the horse. It is earnings that reflect status rather than that status is determined by earnings. Pay indeed tends to function as a status *symbol* rather than a factor in and of itself which confers status.

Because this is the case, there is a strong feeling that earnings ought to reflect status very precisely. If a foreman receives two or three extra workers within his crew, he is likely to feel that this is a basis for a raise in pay. If a person is given a share in decision-making or in the manipulation of symbols then he is likely to feel that that change in itself warrants a raise in pay.

Sometimes management will attempt to avoid pay raises by conferring a new status. During World War II, in some factories, the attempt was made to use many of the older workers in the shop as teachers for women and others who were introduced into industry for the first time. Many of these men had been in their jobs for many years and had never been promoted. Some were then given the new teaching job *and* the title of "functional foreman." No one was fooled.

Not infrequently, a transfer to another shop is interpreted as a promotion and may be the occasion for a request for a raise in pay. In fact, almost any change will be scrutinized carefully by the worker. If he sees in it a raise in status, he is likely to expect a raise in pay.

Status is a picture which does not look well unless the frame is on the picture. The lieutenant-colonel who may do almost the work of a full colonel and who may be receiving almost as much pay is still not happy unless he has the chickens on his shoulders. It is not so much that his status must be proclaimed to others: it must also be proclaimed to himself.

3. FREEDOM

Freedom cuts across all other factors. One of the commonest manifestations turns up in the form of sentiments with reference to overly-rigid supervision. C. R. Walker (78), in a study of a steel mill, states:

In reviewing what the men said about supervisors, no characteristic of their relationship was appreciated more deeply than what might be called the light load of supervision—the absence of bossing, or drivership.

Some of Walker's subjects commented (78): [12]

They don't press you at all . . . In other plants they walk behind you and say, "Hurry up, boys, hurry!" No one has ever told me to hurry up here. We know what to do and we do it, and we're proud of what we know.

He [the foreman] knows I know my job and he lets me alone.

[12] On the importance of freedom from control and independence to the worker, see also (3, 52).

The importance of freedom is observable in another way. The more the worker is tied to his job, the more it requires his constant attention, then the lower is his status likely to be. Conversely, the more leisure the job provides for informal conversation, for coffee, for conferences, then the higher is the prestige of the job-holder likely to be.

This phenomenon turns up in a peculiar situation. The greater the extent to which the individual can leave his work in a subordinate's hands, then the higher is his prestige likely to be. He is then free for other tasks. A supervisor will sometimes make the mistake of attempting to be the *only* one who can carry out his job. He may do this because he feels that to be indispensable means that management will recognize the man's value to the company and reward him. The individual may justify close attention to his work and refusal to take time off for informal banter by saying "I get results." But his value to the company must be shown in more than "results." In addition it is necessary that the individual have the leisure to "chew the fat" with others of his own rank so that these others may become *aware* of his abilities. The importance of social skills in status must be borne in mind. A promotion to the higher ranks is likely to depend almost entirely on the social skills that the individual has. The higher up the individual moves the more likely is he to be concerned with dealing with people. It is in *informal* interaction that individuals are able to size one another up so far as social skills are concerned (26).

TEACHING AND LEARNING IN THE FACTORY

The first question, as always, is: who is permitted to learn? Factory workers may be divided into those who bring with them knowledge acquired in a special school or university, and those who received their training on the job either at the given factory or others. The first group includes professionals, such as engineers, accountants, and other staff personnel, and persons who attended vocational schools, such as some mechanics, maintenance men, and typists and stenographers.[13] The second group, by definition, has had no formal training other than that to which persons might be subjected in many public or high schools, such as manual shop training. And it is this second group that is by far the larger, at least with reference to the manufacturing process itself. Even for the persons in the first group, a great part of their learning takes place on the job, no matter how much technical training they have had. Everyone must get training—usually informal, sometimes formal—on the job

[13] Some of the latter will be college graduates who have specialized in secretarial studies. But it is likely to be their special skills—typing, shorthand operation of business machines—that were primary considerations in their getting the job.

itself. We may look upon the personnel office or hiring hall as the factory analogues of the registrar's office in a university. For if a person cannot get a job, then he is prevented from getting the learning necessary to develop competency at the job. The situation is a circular one. As a student commented to the writer:

> You know, people that do the hiring are pretty silly. You go out looking for a job and the first question they ask you is: "How much experience have you had at this kind of work?" Naturally, I haven't had any. So I say, "None," and he says, "I'm sorry, but we only hire experienced people." Well, how in the world do they expect you to *get* the experience if they won't give you a job in the first place? These "experienced" people that they want so badly— there must have been a time when *they* weren't experienced either.

The question, then, of who is permitted to learn becomes one of who is permitted to get a job.[14] The general question of discrimination will be discussed in Chapter Fifteen, but there are certain special considerations relevant to the factory which we will discuss here.

The factory in the United States occupies a paradoxical position. On the one hand, of all institutions, it is one of the greatest discriminators against particular groups. Those who are interested in minority group prejudice and fair employment practices legislation will often focus attention on factories in the community.[15] Yet, on the other hand, the factory is one of the great frontiers of race and culture contact. Many immigrant groups to the United States—Poles, Czechs, Italians, Germans, Britons, and Irishmen—formed the bulk of the laboring group who built the roads, canals, railroads, and buildings and houses. And a large proportion found employment in factories, where they—or their children —often overcame the discrimination they had to fight.

Industry has continued to discriminate against women, Jews, Catholics, and other ethnic groups, but by far the most important, in terms of numbers and significance, have been the Negroes.[16] Unlike most other groups, not only have Negroes sought entry into industry in large numbers, but they are highly visible and retain that visibility indefinitely.

Even when he succeeded in getting a job, the Negro's background made it difficult for him to succeed. Usually he came from a rural area in the South where he had been given a very poor education and was not possessed of even the most elementary factory skills. He was often alone, separated from the psychological support of family and friends,

---

[14] This is a variant of the "vicious circle" principle advanced in (48).

[15] Cf. (34, 61, 62).

[16] Approximately one-tenth of all machine workers are Negroes. See (71, pp. 362–67; 81).

and lacked a tradition of success. The hopes and best wishes of his family often went with him, but there was usually no one else in the family who had "made it" and on whom the young man could model himself. On top of these disadvantages, he was, at first, assigned to the lower, dirtier jobs—janitor, disposing of wastes, pushing or lifting heavy objects. These jobs are not only unpleasant and poorly paid; they also involve the least skill and are not related to other factory jobs. Thus he could not regard them as a type of apprenticeship wherein he was learning the skills he would need for better jobs later.

But during the two World Wars, the labor shortage and the actions of the Federal government to reduce discrimination forced changes and Negroes began to move up into regular factory jobs. In factories where Negroes had never been employed before, Negroes were introduced, often in large numbers, and often with conflict. The only persons available to train these Negroes were white employees, and the latter often refused in part because of prejudice and in part because of anxiety about their own status. Also, in many cases, Negroes were not accustomed to factory routine and had never worked as equals with whites before. When attacked or criticized, having no social routines to fall back upon, they were likely to respond in kind.[17]

The net result was that Negroes either did not learn what they needed to know to succeed and therefore were discharged or sought other jobs, or else they were largely self-taught. In the latter process, they were aided by an unintended ally—the growing simplicity of factory operations. The situation might have been very different if Negroes had been introduced into the factory a hundred or two hundred years ago when many of the activities involved hand-processes and a high degree of skill, but the modern, highly mechanized factory is committed to a policy of task-simplification and skill-breakdown.

A second group who were, and are, restricted in getting the learning needed by restriction on entry is made up of women. The major prejudices they had to fight were the general expectation that they were not career-oriented because of the traditional role of women as housewives and mothers, traditional beliefs about "men's" and "women's" work, and the lack of a tradition of success for women in factory work.

---

[17] A highly suggestive study, whose significance extends beyond the limited problem it dealt with, was concerned with authoritarianism among Negroes and whites. The authoritarianism test developed by T. W. Adorno (1) was given to a sample of Negroes and whites. The mean score for Negroes was 4.68 and for whites 3.86, a difference significant at the .001 level, and indicating markedly more authoritarianism among Negroes. The implications for the factory situation where Negroes are forced to work both under whites as foremen and with whites as equals deserve further exploration. The study is reported in (50).

An effective way to prevent a woman worker from learning is to treat her as a *woman* rather than as a fellow-worker. In many cases, particularly for women in supervisory positions, failure resulted because the women set their own standards too high.

Even if one already has the technical skills, learned elsewhere or on the job, one must still learn the tricks of the trade and the social skills, and these can only be learned on the job. Tricks of the trade, as we have pointed out in Chapter Four, are short-cuts and devices to save a person form his own mistakes. Social skills involve learning to get along with others and learning to feel at home in the factory social world. These may be grouped into two categories: those things one must learn which are imposed from above, and those things which are organized about the worker's world, and are required by fellow-workers. This is not to say that all workers learn these things, but they are expected to. As will be seen, not all of these things are consistent.

1. TRICKS OF THE TRADE AND SOCIAL SKILLS REQUIRED BY MANAGEMENT

a. WORKING BY ROUTINE

In order to operate the factory in a predictable manner, management expects that workers shall adopt a routine so that management, at any given time, will know where people are, what they are doing, and what they have yet to do. This means first, and most obviously, regularity of attendance at stated hours. When a worker is late, or absent, it is not simply that the factory loses money, but the routine is upset. Workers must be shifted, plans altered, and special arrangements made. The attitude management wishes to cultivate is one of dependability. Penalties in the form of censure or pay reductions are last resorts, or serve the purpose of setting an example. If they must be continually resorted to, then management feels, and correctly, that something is wrong. The very idea of working implies dependability and should be taken for granted by the worker. Often these matters are spoken of in terms of that catch-all, "efficiency."

A factory is a finely articulated mechanism which requires that all parts should function in a synchronous manner. It is routine that makes this smooth coordination possible. Production schedules are broken down by factory departments with each department responsible for certain parts or operations. But in addition they must produce those parts or carry on those operations at a rate *which is keyed to the rate of work of other departments.* Therefore, if one department slows down, *or* speeds up, schedules are upset, parts are scarce or not needed, and pressure is put on supervisors to explain and make changes. Consequently management cannot tell each person to go ahead and work at top speed. Individuals differ and no coordination would be possible. Instead, the worker must work at a *designated* speed, which management tries to control.

b. MEETING PRE-ESTABLISED STANDARDS

Management expects the worker to meet standards with reference to quantity of work, speed, accuracy, pace of work, and the saving of company money. The slogan "a fair day's pay for a fair day's work" is believed in and attempts are made to enforce it. But sheer quantity and speed would be meaningless if poor quality work were turned out; the worker is also expected to follow specifications and do accurate work. Accuracy is always emphasized in connection with any record-keeping activity, and usually adding-machine tapes and even waste paper will be saved for a long time.

Not only should the worker produce a lot, work at a rapid speed, and maintain quality, but it is also expected that he will keep doing these things all day long. Finally, the worker is expected to do all he can toward saving money. He must not be wasteful of materials, use tools until they are really worn out before turning them in, try to solve his own problems and only seek help from a supervisor or fellow worker as a last resort, and try to think up short cuts which should then be made known to everyone.

c. ORIENTING ONESELF TO MANAGEMENT GOALS

Management is itself a middle-class group. Very often the members of management have gotten there by striving very hard and making sacrifices. Consequently, there is a considerable tendency for them to assume that others are similarly motivated. When they discover, often with a shock, that many workers are not, they often feel that the workers *should* be so motivated. If they are not, then they are shiftless, irresponsible, and not deserving of rewards.

Management feels strongly about these matters and justifies them in moral terms. Partly this is because raises and promotions are the major incentives management has to give and if workers will not orient themselves to them, management feels it has no control over workers. But partly also the strong, moralistic feelings are a consequence of the fact that modern management is the latter-day inheritor of the Protestant ethic in which work had come to be a positive value and a means of recognizing those who were predestined for salvation. In the United States, the Puritans carried these ideas into their own work and were in part responsible for their passing into the general culture. Miller and Form state (43, p. 558):

Life on the frontier made hard work a *necessity;* the influence of Puritanism made hard work a *virtue.*

Because these ideas originated in a religious context and have become a part of cultural mores, they are interpreted by management (which is usually quite rational in other matters) in emotional terms. The worker is expected to measure up to them not simply because it is to the company's economic advantage if he does, but rather because the worker just *should*. To do otherwise is immoral.

2. TRICKS OF THE TRADE AND SOCIAL SKILLS REQUIRED BY FELLOW WORKERS

a. OBEYING THE MORES OF THE WORK SITUATION

As we have seen in the case of other work organizations, workers have certain expectations of one another which may or may not be consistent with the expectations of management. The most important has to do with restriction of output—the maintenance of an agreed-upon rate with reference to speed, quantity and pace of work. One of the first things the worker must learn is what this rate is, and he is generally introduced to it quite early in his employment.

In addition, he learns *how* the job is to be carried out. For example, in a plant that manufactured lawn chairs from aluminum tubing, there was only one inspector, who checked the chairs of different designs from several departments. It was customary for each department not to send its chairs to the inspector as each was completed, but rather to wait until it had completed twenty-five or thirty chairs, and then send them over as a group. This practice was justified by foremen in terms of efficiency but a major secondary reason was that this meant the inspector would be involved exclusively with the chairs from one department for about one hour. The foreman spent that time observing the inspector and noting his criticisms. In this manner, the work group had, in effect, an informal running assessment of how they were doing and could make appropriate modfications without waiting for criticism from on high.[18]

The worker will also be exposed to a general social-psychological orientation. He will learn which foremen are "good eggs" and which are not to be trusted, the appropriate attitudes toward top management, whether management promises on promotions are to be believed or not, union attitudes, and attitudes toward ethnic or minority groups.

b. GETTING ALONG WITH FELLOW WORKERS

The new worker is expected to orient himself toward the problems of fellow workers. The man who is instead oriented upward and identifies himself with management is likely to suffer sanctions and censure. Upward mobile persons as such are not objects of criticism, but it is expected that they will not use other workers as means to the accomplishment of their goals. One of the most important expectations in this context

[18] Description based on student term paper by Ernest E. Bishop.

is the expectation of help in difficulties. Workers help each other out, fill in for each other, and make excuses for each other. In addition, they have typical interests and subjects of conversation which the new worker is expected to engage in.

c. IDENTIFICATION WITH FELLOW WORKERS VIS-À-VIS MANAGEMENT

Closely related to the matter of getting along is that of identification. The worker is expected to recognize that he is a *member* of a work group with its own social world. He should feel himself in the same boat with other workers and recognize that, in the last analysis, his true friends at work are fellow workers rather than management. A worker in a Canadian steel mill that made steel from scrap iron spoke as follows:

Maybe in the States a guy can start at the bottom and push his way to the top, but I haven't seen it around here. I've been on this job for 11 years and I've only seen three men get promoted, and two of them were special because of war expansion. So I figure that if I spend my time trying to get ahead by licking the sup's (superintendent's) boots and saying "yes, sir" and "no, sir," I won't get anywhere and besides the other men'll treat me like dirt. It's better and makes more sense to realize that my real friends here are guys like Bill, and Tom and Jock. The sup's a nice guy but he don't give a damn about me, except what he can get out of me. And I don't resent that. That's the way a sup. should think.

Identification with fellow workers means feeling at home with them, enjoying their company, learning actively to engage in horseplay, and learning their language. As we have discussed elsewhere, every occupation with any degree of integration tends to develop an argot or specialized language. The argot does not consist of (though it usually includes) technical terms. Rather, the terms are easily translatable into perfectly good ordinary words which might have been used instead. Mencken (42) provides the following examples of garment workers' argot: "automobile" —a fast operator; "barker"—a foreman; "Brooklyn Bridge"—a garment difficult to press; "clothing"—men's clothing only; "fireman"—a presser; "honey"—the wax used in pressing; "pinochle season"—the slack season; "Professor"—a good cutter.

It is of the very nature of such words that they refer to specific objects, operations or attitudes which are inherent in the job itself. They must therefore be learned as one works. The argot identifies the experienced worker and therefore the person one can trust. It serves therefore as an almost infallible way of recognizing the outsider or the one who does not belong. Quite obviously, also, it is a very efficient means of communication in which meanings may be transmitted with little likelihood of confusion. In this sense it is akin to a technical vocabulary.

In summary, the worker learns technical skills, management-imposed tricks of the trade and social skills—working by routine, meeting pre-established standards, and orienting oneself to management goals—and worker-imposed tricks of the trade and social skills—obeying the mores of the work situation, getting along with fellow-workers, and identifying with fellow-workers.

THE TEACHERS OF FACTORY WORKERS

Technical skills may be taught by outsiders in universities, vocational or trade schools, by special trainers assigned to teach new workers, or by fellow-workers. There are few long-term status implications if the teacher is an outsider someone in the factory specially assigned to train new workers; the new worker subordinates himself to this teacher only for the period of the training. His real boss is his foreman and the worker regards the teacher as a special staff person rather than as one who has supervisory authority over him. When the teacher is a fellow-worker who has been asked to "fill this man in" on the job, there may or may not be status implications. Whether there are depends largely on how complex the technical skills are. If they are very complex and require years of experience, then the experienced person will be in a very definitely superior position, is likely to let the newcomer know it, and expect appropriate recognition. But, as we have commented repeatedly, highly complex skills are slowly disappearing from the factory and being replaced by highly complex machines which require only minor skill to operate. In a very few weeks, the new worker runs the machine quite competently. Of course there will still be a status difference between newcomer and "teacher" in terms of experience and other variables, but these relate to other matters than technical skills.

The learning of tricks of the trade and social skills is considerably more complex. Since these include such strong social psychological components, the acquisition of appropriate attitudes is often made before the worker ever takes a job. For those tricks of the trade and social skills which are imposed by management, there is considerable learning in the home, the church, and in school. The home (if it actually succeeds at all) may implant in the growing child a set of attitudes which may make it easier for him to adjust to management demands later on. The child in the home of a factory worker comes to take for granted his father's absence from home from early in the morning till dinner time. He may model himself on him and perhaps dream of himself in a similar role. The success of such role-conceiving however depends on whether other aspects of his father's personality make it easy for the child to take his father as an ego-ideal. Just as likely is a rejection of the father role and rebellion.

More crucial, perhaps, is the obvious fact of the family's dependence on his father's often meagre earnings. Through overheard arguments between his father and mother about finances, through experience of deprivation of expected gifts or rewards, and especially the experience of a layoff, the child is likely to feel keenly the lack of control of his father over his work destiny. If his father curses the foreman or expresses antagonism toward management, the child may begin to look upon management with feelings of fear or even hatred comparable to those that the child of a criminal may feel toward a policeman. These matters, however, are perhaps common to *all* occupations involving working for others, whether one works in a factory or not.

Often the father will want his son or daughter to get a better job than he has. The child will be told that he must stay in school and "make something of yourself." But such hopes must often be laid aside as the needs of the family make it necessary for the child to quit school as soon as the law permits and go to work.

The need of learning to work by routine—one of the things to be learned imposed by management—is to a limited extent learned by the child as he carries on his work duties around the home. Miller and Form (43, p. 530), drawing on the Louisiana Educational Survey, feel that the doing of household chores helps the child to adjust to unskilled, repetitive work. But it is doubtful whether there is much of a carryover to the factory situation. Chores are practically always highly meaningful (though not necessarily pleasant) tasks, in which a given job is done from start to finish. They are usually not routinized from moment to moment though they are often periodic from week to week. Quite frequently they are random and engaged in to make money for a particular goal. The home atmosphere is also so different from the factory that comparisons are dubious. On the farm, there is probably more routine, but a large part of the learning is related to the obvious process of maturation and learning *society's* work values, rather than the values associated with chores as such.

Much the same can be said about the effect of the home in preparing the growing child for the meeting of management standards with reference to quantity, speed, accuracy, and pace of work. In addition, much will depend on how strict the father or mother may be in insisting on compliance. Some children will emerge as hard, conscientious workers; others will not. But here again the social context is decisive. To speak of someone as "a hard worker" and another as "lazy" is a misleading vestige of nineteenth-century "trait" psychology. These are more properly descriptive of a person's reputation than his behavior. Probably anyone is a hard worker when he is motivated and when his work takes place in a meaningful context.[19] And the same person will be lazy on other matters. So the point is not whether a boy's parents have adequately trained him or not, but rather whether such training as he has gotten in work habits becomes meaningful and rewarding in the factory work situation.

The role of the home in orienting the child to management goals appears to be largely a class matter. The middle-class child will be so oriented because management goals are consonant and often identical with middle-class goals. But the child from the lower class is likely to be oriented toward security rather than success. To him, the most important goals are likely to be getting a job and hanging on to it, rather than pushing up to the top. This is related to the actual experience of his father and other people he meets around the home and is related to lower-class values as such.

The training the child receives in Sunday school and the church is relevant insofar as the church supports the status quo and urges the Puritanical virtues of hard work, thrift, and so on. Also, insofar as the church is a stabilizing influence it may conceivably create in some individuals an apathetic or negative attitude toward strikes and other relatively direct forms of social change. But this is doubtful and indeed the role of the church in relation to work has not been studied.

The school appears to be of considerable significance, at least potentially. The school, like the factory, requires regular attendance and employs a daily routine. It enforces standards of quantity of work,

[19] The matter was well-stated by E. C. Hughes in a symposium as follows:

"What we mean by an uninteresting or low-skilled job is a relative matter. I assume that it means the job that is the least interesting in a particular organization and is considered so by the one who does it or by other people. Certainly there are things which in history have been defined at times as dirty work, or uninteresting work, which, in other settings, become more interesting. In hospitals nowadays the nurses are making a great fuss about sweeping floors. They didn't used to make a fuss about sweeping floors. They used to do it as an initiation rite in becoming nurses, expecting to become the right-hand man of the doctor and save the doctor from mistakes. In other words, they had a role definition, not a task definition, of their job. Now they are having trouble because they are delegating the sweeping to nurses' aides, who have no hope of becoming nurses. These nurses' aides find this work uninteresting, and they don't do it with as much vigor as the people who had at least a prospect of becoming something important.

So it would seem to me that as we get into this question of uninteresting work, we are inevitably getting into the question of organization and what kind of futures and prospects people have before them. The job ceases to be a thing by itself. It becomes part of the organization and part of a man's view of himself and what he is worth. I think of the case of the surgeon, who used to be a pretty low fellow. There wasn't anybody who did such messy work as the surgeon. But surgery has risen from low to high prestige. Is any work monotonous or uninteresting in itself? Or does that depend upon the organization and the attitudes of people in general?" See (75).

speed, accuracy, and pace of work, and it tries to inculcate middle-class success standards. The school is the child's first major introduction to the competitive ideology underlying capitalism. It is there that he is continually compared with his fellows, ranked, and offered rewards for success on competitive striving. But in its very attempts to transmit middle-class success standards, the school presents a paradox. For it is for those children who *are* from middle-class homes that this approach is likely to be most meaningful. They can be counted upon to understand and what they learn at school is consistent with what they learn at home. But lower-class children will not find the system so congenial. Further, they are not so likely to be favored by their teachers and therefore will not find that orienting themselves to teacher-approved goals is so rewarding. They are not so likely, therefore, to internalize success values. Yet it is just *these* children who are the ones who will likely end up in factory jobs. Moreover, those lower-class children who do make the shift in values and become success-oriented are, by that very token, likely to stay in school longer and therefore get clerical or other non-factory jobs. The net result is likely to be that a large proportion of factory workers will not, much to the exasperation of management, respond to management-sponsored goals and rewards.

There is, finally, the learning of management-imposed tricks of the trade and social skills that takes place on the job. The learning of routines is largely transmitted indirectly by penalties for lateness or absenteeism. This does not of course mean that the worker has internalized the appropriate attitudes. Moreover, the factory is not consistent on routinization. It applies most directly to the worker at the bottom. Strangely, the higher he rises in the firm the less is routine required and the less is it rewarded. Office workers may hardly be penalized at all for occasional lateness or even absence. Many executives decide themselves what hours they should put in, and their work is anything but routine.

The standards of quantity of work, speed, accuracy and pace of work are also transmitted by reward and punishment, but here the work group is of great importance, as we shall discuss later. Finally, orienting oneself to management goals is almost wholly a work-group phenomenon. Whether the worker does orient himself or not depends on how much he values work-group fellowship and on how adequately management is able to promote workers and raise the pay of workers. In most cases, raises are relatively slow and promotions very rare indeed.

The only significant non-factory agency which is instrumental in teaching tricks of the trade and social skills imposed by fellow-workers appears to be the childhood play group and gang. It is in such play groups that the child learns values such as fair play, fellowship, getting along with others, and loyalty. But the context within which such learning takes place must be borne in mind. We cannot assume that the child who shows dog-like devotion to a gang leader will transfer that loyalty to a foreman later.

Unquestionably, the major learning of workers' mores takes place in the factory itself. Here they are taught largely through *social* rewards, such as group approval and *social* punishments such as ostracism. The nature of such rewards and punishments will be discussed below under "Systems of Control."

When the appropriate learning has taken place to a level acceptable by management or fellow-workers, there is often a process of initiation to proclaim the worker's change of status. If the worker has succeeded in learning the management-imposed skills and requirements, then there may be the very obvious change of status involved in a promotion or a new job, or a raise in pay. The learning of worker-imposed requirements is likely to be accompanied by "ribbing." (Sending a worker to look for a left-handed monkey-wrench has become a part of our general folklore as a symbol of the "green" worker.) Nell Giles tells us that her set-up man who assigned her jobs and replaced drills she broke was fond of calling her a "drill-wrecker," and worst of all, would chide her with "Helping Hitler again, huh?" Then she describes with satisfaction the happy day, when, after she had burred 1,056 pieces without breaking a drill, he said to her casually: "Hi Babe!" (22).

Such ceremonies or ritualistic phrases recognize a change of status. They mean that the worker has gained the right to regard himself as a member of the work group and is entitled the privileges of group membership, such as protection in case of criticism or attack, and group support when he gets into difficulties. They function also to give the individual a sense of group belonging and therefore a place where he feels at home. Such a worker is likely to work with the least strain and may have high morale. This does not, however, imply that that morale will be reflected in high productivity. For his morale is related to the work group rather than to management goals.

SYSTEMS OF CONTROL

Once the individual has gotten a job in a factory, he is assigned a formal status in the division of labor and in the authority structure. But he is now a participating member of an organization and finds himself confronted with a large variety of controls on his behavior. In the American factory, from the strictly formal point of view, only a segment of his behavior or personality needs to be controlled: his *work* behavior. But the paradox is that although only a segment of his personality *needs* to be controlled, the worker brings his whole personality with him to the work situation. In fact, therefore, controls of a considerably broader character are observed.

1. THE FACTORY FORMAL ORGANIZATION AS A CONTROL

As far as the worker is concerned, the entire formal organization of the factory is a giant control mechanism which is necessary to achieve predictable objectives. This control is formally limited to the individual in his role as a worker. It requires, first, specialization. Each person is assigned to and expected to carry out a particular job, but is also expected to cooperate with others. This requires from the worker something in the way of a breadth of view and interest extending beyond his own immediate job. He is expected to see where his work fits in the organization at least with reference to closely related jobs, and to take that into account. The worker who says: "I do *my* job. Let others worry about theirs" is not likely to be regarded as a desirable worker by other workers *or* by management. A worker in a small firm that manufactured insignia for fraternities and lodges spoke as follows:

The best thing about working here is it's small enough so you can see the whole thing. I know what everybody's doing and that makes for a smoother operation all around. All I have to do is look up from my bench and see what Jerry's doing and then I know if I should speed up or take it easy. But back at ———— (a large factory that made costume jewelry)—that was really a madhouse. One minute the foreman'd be jumping me to get the lead out, and then ten minutes later, he'd say: "What're you knockin' yourself out for? Inventory's bulgin' with so many rings, they're stackin' the boxes on the floor." How was I supposed to know what was goin' on in Inventory? But they expected you to find out somehow. At least if you were behind, you'd be the one that would get it in the neck.

The authority structure in the factory is by definition a control system. Supervisors in general, of course, occupy the positions in this system, but higher supervisors tend more to be concerned with general policy and planning. As far as the worker is concerned, minute-by-minute control is exerted by his immediate supervisor, and for the majority of workers this person is the foreman. The marginal position of the foreman has often been noted.[20] From management's point of view, he is the "first line of management" and is, therefore, expected to transmit orders to his men and see that they are carried out. From the workers' point

[20] See, for example (15, 36, 54, 72, 84, 89). A revealing report, in part in reaction to the NLRB's decision to recognize foremen's groups as collective bargaining units and the hubbub that followed, is provided in (19). The object of the report is stated to be: ". . . to make foremen more management conscious" (19, p. 1).

of view, he is a fellow much like themselves who has, in many cases, risen from their ranks. He is the person to whom they turn with complaints and from whom they expect help. As a consequence, he finds himself subject to pulls from above and below. And since he enjoys few of the privileges of management or the opportunities of workers (such as being able to join the union), his identification is often not clear. In order to do his job, he frequently finds he must spend as much time controlling his superiors as he does controlling his work group. A foreman in an aircraft plant at which I was employed described a fascinating instance of control from below.

You remember the trouble we had with the mouth organ [an air-scoop which fits in the assembly that surrounds the motor]. It was the last thing to go in down at final assembly. I've had plenty of experience with final assembly and I know a man's stupid to make more than one or two parts before you see if they fit or not. Prints [blueprints] don't mean a thing. They're made up by slick-haired little boys with thick glasses. The contract called for 55 airplanes. Okay—that means 110 mouth organs [there were two motors]. So Art [the department head] gives me the go ahead: "Make me 110 mouth organs," he says. Like hell I made him 110. I made *two* and then I put the men to work on something else. You were with me when I tried to put that damn mouth organ in. It didn't fit! So there was the test flight scheduled for the next day and everybody had half a day off to go out and see it [this was the first plane to come off the assembly line]. You know that airplane flew the next day, and the mouth organ was in it. You want to know the secret of my success? [He picked up a hammer.] This. I smashed the bugger into place. Of course the whole thing had to be redesigned, but meanwhile I didn't have 110 mouth organs sitting on the scrap heap. And y'know, that son of a bitch Art didn't give me no credit at all. 'Its not your job to worry about things like that," he says. "You run your shop and let me worry." Huh, *him* worry. All he worries about is trying to make Janet [a shop clerk]. Wish he'd stay out of this shop altogether.

Such a situation would probably be regarded, even by foremen, as unusual, and it is noteworthy that the airplane described was the first one to be manufactured by the company. Yet, new situations are always coming up, processes are changed, and department heads come and go. Normally, however, management tries to provide for control norms which will work in most situations. The formal authority system operates as a control by providing a work design. In it, supervision is clearly allotted and the division of labor is specified (78).

The formal system, like all control systems, has attached to it a set of sanctions for violations. These formal sanctions are, mainly, refusal of promotion, refusal of a pay raise, or occasionally actual pay reduction, and as a last resort, discharge (4, pp. 123 ff.). But the most common sanction is a reprimand by one's formal superior. When it is recalled how much the worker focuses attention on his superior, one may recognize that this sanction usually works. Further, it is often construed as a threat of more serious action, and its effectiveness may therefore depend on whether past experience suggests that the foreman "really" means it or not. Some foremen become famous as perennial grumblers and workers expect criticism from them. When such a foreman says nothing or merely grunts, this action is interpreted as a resounding accolade.

The fact that the more serious sanctions are rarely applied is not peculiar to the factory. It is of the very nature of a control system that it requires the internalization of attitudes of obedience. If sanctions must be continually applied—whether in a family, a school system, a religious system, a political system *or* a factory—then the system is unstable and is perhaps breaking down. In the case of the factory, effective functioning of the formal control system requires the worker to develop a set of *habits* such that the work design and his particular work operation become routinized and fairly automatic.

Much of factory work does become automatic, and to the extent that that is true, the formal control mechanism is controlling work behavior. On the other hand, changing processes—and processes are always changing in a rapidly changing culture—may make the development of such habits difficult, or a real hindrance if they do develop. Under such conditions, flexibility and a readiness to adjust to change may be more useful as work requirements.

2. FOLKWAYS AND MORES

The folkways and mores of workers are informal understandings revolving about expected work behavior. They deal with the quantity of work to be done in a day, the speed with which it is to be carried out, canons of accuracy, the pace at which work is to go forward, attitudes toward management-set goals, and obligations to the work group. The nature of such understandings is discussed below under "Informal Relations." Here we are concerned with the methods by which such understandings are enforced.

The major method is that of group pressure. The worker who engages in approved behavior is rewarded with inclusion in the work group and protection. That is, he is treated as if he belonged to the group, he is invited to participate in group play or recreation, such as having a drink after work, he is told the secret information the group has, such as which jobs are the tough ones and which are the easy ones, or short-cuts in work that the group knows about, and he is protected if he is attacked by other workers or by management.

The worker who violates informal understandings is not given such protection or help, and is instead subject to snubbing and ostracism. In general the group will make things tough for him. A sewing machine operator in a plastics manufacturing plant that was employed making raincoats described an instance of such coercive behavior:

She was always so high-hat. She'd be late gettin' back to work from lunch 'cause she was primpin' in front o' the mirror. Then she'd say, real mean-like: "Those of us that has got looks like to take care o' them." She made all of us mad, and the worst of it was she was a real good worker. Fast as a whip. 'Course she was jest doin' that to show up the rest of us. We fixed her good. Soon's she'd complain that her machine warn't workin' right, right away a couple of us would call for help on ours. Half the time by the time he [the maintenance man] was finished with us, he had somethin' more pressin' to do someplace else and he'd leave her high and dry. Then soon's she started runnin' short of material, the rest of us would order material so half the time she'd have to wait for hers. Guess it was sort o' cruel. But some people jest don't learn no other way.

Of course the work group may use the power of group pressure to force fast workers to slow down or slow workers to speed up.
Walker (78, p. 80) provides quotations from the men illustrating how such pressure is implemented in a steel mill: [1]

We all work together. It doesn't take very long to find out where the slowdown is. If the furnace isn't rolling down the billets, the piercer will start to razz us with his whistle, then the hi-mill will begin to razz us and then the reeler. When our boys at the furnace hear all that razzing it kinda peps them up and makes them work better . . . whoever has a whistle likes to razz the fellow who is slowing down.

Foremen in the mill were aware of this and apparently approved. One said:

A foreman doesn't need to put pressure on a slacker. I don't remember going up to anybody and telling him he should speed up his work. The system just takes care of him itself. If a man slows up I don't have to jump him. Don't worry—all the other men jump in and start blowing whistles. Sometimes, the hi-mill plugger will pound his tongs on the hi-mill trough. It isn't long before they get that man going.

The success of group pressure—whether of approval or disapproval —depends mainly on two factors. First is the presence or absence of a status escape for the individual on whom pressure is being put. If the individual has an important status other than that of worker—such as

Negro, woman, union officer, relative of the boss—then the group pressure will not hurt him much and therefore not affect his behavior. He will interpret group pressure, especially if negative, as directed at his other status, or else he will simply not consider group feelings important. The latter is especially likely for women who regard themselves as temporary workers who are helping supplement their husband's income. Second, the success of group pressure depends on how well integrated the work group is. Group pressure works less well in a new situation or in one of high turnover. It is likely to be seen in its most intense form in a group of workers who have worked together for many years on the same sort of work operation.

The importance of group integration for the successful operation of group pressure has implications for the researcher or outsider who sets out to observe such behavior. By its very nature, group pressure is informal, and is usually taken for granted and not talked about. Often, it will not be approved by management. Therefore, the researcher will not necessarily find it present, at first. Indeed, the more intensely the group is integrated and the stronger its pressures, the *less* likely is the researcher to discover it, for it is precisely well-integrated groups that offer resistance to outsiders in general. The researcher who pops in with a questionnaire and then disappears is not likely to discover it. Nor is the researcher who spends very much time with management or who is identified by the worker as on management's side likely to learn much about it. This creates a special problem for the academic scholar, who is practically always identified as a management-oriented man. His vocabulary, his peculiar interests, and the fact that his own middle-class background is likely to make it easier for him to talk with management personnel rather than workers provide obstacles for him which he does not always overcome.[21]

3. CONTROLS FROM OUTSIDE THE FACTORY

Besides controls from within the factory structure, there are outside agencies or influences. If these outside controls operate formally through management, they are likely to be manifested in the inspection process. If the factory is working on a government contract, quite commonly the government will have some special inspectors of its own in the plant. If the factory is a subcontractor for another factory, the other factory may have some of its personnel in the plant also. Within recent years, a new type of government control has appeared. Owing to the cold war and the dangers of Communist infiltration, considerable pressure has been

[21] The role of social differences between researcher and subject has been examined only recently. See (8, 9, 16) and the *American Journal of Sociology* series on interviewing special groups—Frenchmen, Negro Pentecostals, water-dowsers, and others.

brought to bear on factories with defense contracts not to even *hire* persons unless they have successfully passed a security check.

The community in which the factory is located often makes for certain controls.[22] Hours of work often reflect not so much production needs as community customs. In rural areas, where persons are accustomed to work from dawn till dusk, one may find 11- and 12-hour shifts; in other places, any attempt to extend the shift beyond 8 hours would meet with a strike. The make-up of the work force may also be determined not so much by factory needs or desires as by the availability of personnel and community customs.[23] Relevant here is whether women and children are accustomed to work or not. Wages are also much affected by local situations. A factory will usually have to meet the "going wage" in the community. If the factory requires skilled persons, standards of craftsmanship are often a matter of tradition in certain communities and not in others.[24]

The family, apart from the fact that racial and ethnic factors operate through it, acts as a major control on women. Since many women are working to supplement the family income, they do not regard themselves as full members of the factory work force and therefore do not orient themselves to management goals nor pay much attention to work group pressures.

But unquestionably the most important *outside* controls are the *internal* controls the individual brings with him to the job. Each person brings with him a self-conception and set of expectations based on his previous life and his group memberships. The expectations of men will be different from women, Negroes different from whites, Jews different from Christians, Puerto Ricans different from fourth generation Irish, Southerners different from New Englanders, "old hands" different from new workers. These expectations act as controls on behavior which may make the difference between the worker's finding in the factory a fulfillment of his hopes or a denial of his worth as a worker or even as a human being.

CHAPTER REFERENCES

1. Adorno, T. W., *et al., The Authoritarian Personality,* New York: Harper, 1950.

[22] In general on this point see (23, 27, 35, 40, 53, 73).

[23] A study of Bantu industrial workers in Durban points out that natives are attracted by machine work "because they consider that working on the machine puts them on a level with the European" (2).

[24] See (25, pp. 190–93; 80, *passim,* but esp. Chs. IV, V, IX).

2. *The African Factory Worker,* Dept. of Economics, University of Natal, New York: Oxford University Press, 1950.

3. Bakke, E. W., *Adaptive Human Behavior,* New Haven: Connecticut Labor and Management Center, Yale University, 1947.

4. ———, *Bonds of Organization,* New York: Harper, 1950.

5. *No entry.*

6. Belcher, D. W., *Wage and Salary Administration,* New York: Prentice-Hall, 1955.

7. Bendix, R. and Fisher, L. H., "The Perspectives of Elton Mayo," *Review of Economics and Statistics,* 31:312–319, 1949.

8. Benney, M. and Hughes, E. C., "Of Sociology and the Interview; Editorial Preface," *American Journal of Sociology,* 62:137–142, 1956.

9. Benney, M., Riesman, D., and Star, S. A., "Age and Sex in the Interview," *American Journal of Sociology,* 62:143–152, 1956.

10. Berger, M., *Equality by Statute,* New York: Columbia University Press, 1952.

11. Bettelheim, B. and Janowitz, M., *Dynamics of Prejudice,* New York, Harper, 1950.

12. Bishop, E. E. (a description based on this student's term paper).

13. Caplow, T., *The Sociology of Work,* Minneapolis: University of Minnesota Press, 1954.

14. *Check List of State Anti-Discrimination and Anti-Bias Laws,* The Commission on Law and Social Action, American Jewish Congress, New York, 1953.

15. Chinoy, E., "The Tradition of Opportunity and the Aspirations of Automobile Workers," *American Journal of Sociology,* 57:453–459, 1952.

16. Dexter, L. A., "Role Relationships and Conceptions of Neutrality in Interviewing," *American Journal of Sociology,* 62:153–157, 1956.

17. Dickenson, Z. G., *Collective Wage Determination,* New York: Ronald, 1941.

18. Douty, H. M., *Wages: An Introduction,* Los Angeles: Institute of Industrial Relations, University of California, Los Angeles, 1951.

19. *Experience of 132 Companies in Improving Relations with Foremen,* Chicago: The Dartnell Corporation, Report No. 527 (Section 1), Mimeo, No date.

20. Friedmann, G., "Philosophy Underlying the Hawthorne Investigation," *Social Forces,* 28:204–209, 1949.

20a. Gardner, B., *Case Materials on Human Problems in Industrial Organization,* Chicago: University of Chicago Bookstore, September 1943, 1st ed. (mimeo.).

21. Gardner, B. B. and Moore, D. G., *Human Relations in Industry,* Homewood, Ill.: Richard D. Irwin, 1952.

22. Giles, N., *Punch In, Susie! A Woman's War Factory Diary,* New York: Harper, 1943.

23. Gilfillan, L., *I Went to Pit College,* New York: Literary Guild, 1934.

24. Gouldner, A. W., *Wildcat Strike,* Yellow Springs, Ohio: Antioch Press, 1954.

25. Gross, E., "Informal Relations and the Social Organization of Work," unpublished Ph.D. Dissertation, University of Chicago, 1949.

26. ———, "Some Functional Consequences of Primary Controls in Formal Work Organizations," *American Sociological Review,* 18:368–373, 1953.

27. Hart, C. W. M., "Industrial Relations Research and Social Theory," *Canadian Journal of Economics and Political Science,* 15:53–73, 1949.

28. Heron, A. R., *Why Men Work,* Stanford: Stanford University Press, 1948.

29. Hughes, E. C., Statement in Staley, E. (ed.), *Creating an Industrial Civilization, A Report of the Corning Conference,* May 17–19, 1951, New York: Harper, 1952, p. 29.

30. *Payment by Results,* Geneva: International Labor Office, 1951.

31. Johnson, C. S., *et al., Into the Main Stream,* Chapel Hill: University of North Carolina Press, 1947.

32. Kennedy, V. D., *Union Policy and Incentive Methods,* New York: Columbia University Press, 1945.

33. Kerr, C., Brown, J. D., and Witte, E. E. (eds.), *The Aged and Society,* Champaign, Illinois: Industrial Relations Research Association, 1950.

34. Kesselman, L. C., *The Social Politics of FEPC,* Chapel Hill: University of North Carolina Press, 1948.

35. Lahne, H. J., *The Cotton Mill Worker,* New York, Farrar and Rinehart, 1944.

36. Leiter, R. D., *The Foreman in Industrial Relations,* New York: Columbia University Press, 1948.

37. Lester, R. A., "Results and Implications of Some Recent Wage Studies," in Lester, R. A. and Shister, J., *Insights into Labor Issues,* New York: Macmillan, 1948.

38. Louden, J. K., *Wage Incentives,* New York: Wiley, 1944.

39. Lytle, C. W., *Wage Incentive Methods,* New York: Ronald, 1942.

40. Macdonald, L., *Southern Mill Hills,* New York: Hillman, 1928.

41. Mayo, E., *The Social Problems of an Industrial Civilization,* Cambridge: Harvard University Press, 1945.

42. Mencken, H. L., *The American Language, Supplement II,* New York: Knopf, 1952.

43. Miller, D. C., and Form, W. H., *Industrial Sociology,* New York: Harper, 1951.

44. Mills, C. W., "The Contributions of Sociology to Studies of Industrial Relations," Proceedings Industrial Relations Research Association, Champaign, Illinois, 1949, pp. 199–222.

45. Moon, B., *The High Cost of Prejudice,* New York: Messner, 1947.

46. Moore, W. E., "The Aged in Industrial Societies," in Moore, W. E., *Industrial Relations and the Social Order,* New York, Macmillan, 1951.

47. ———, "Current Issues in Industrial Sociology," *American Sociological Review,* 12:651–657, 1947.

48. Myrdal, G.; Sterner, R.; and Rose, A., *An American Dilemma,* New York: Harper, 1944.

49. Northrup, H. R., *Organized Labor and the Negro,* New York: Harper, 1944.

50. Prothro, J. W. and Smith, C. U., "The Psychic Cost of Segregation," *Phylon,* 15:393–395, 1954.

51. Reynolds, L. G., *The Structure of Labor Markets,* New York: Harper, 1951.

52. ———, and Shister, J., *Job Horizons: A Study of Job Satisfaction and Labor Mobility,* New York: Harper, 1949.

53. Rhyne, J., *Some Southern Cotton Mill Workers and Their Villages,* Chapel Hill: University of North Carolina Press, 1930.
54. Roethlisberger, F. J., "The Foreman: Master and Victim of Doubletalk," *Harvard Business Review,* 23:283–298, 1945.
55. ———, and Dickson, W. J., *Management and the Worker,* Cambridge: Harvard University Press, 1947.
56. Rose, A., *The Negro in America,* New York: Harper, 1948.
57. Ross, A. M., "The Dynamics of Wage Determination Under Collective Bargaining," *American Economic Review,* 37:793–822, 1947.
58. ———, "The Trade Union as a Wage-Fixing Institution," *American Economic Review,* 37:566–588.
59. Rothschild, K. W., *The Theory of Wages,* New York: Macmillan, 1954.
60. Roy, D., "Work Satisfaction and Social Reward in Quota Achievement: An Analysis of Piecework Incentive," *American Sociological Review,* 18:507–514, 1953.
61. Ruchames, L., *The Main Types and Causes of Discrimination,* United Nations, Sub-commission on Prevention of Discrimination and Protection of Minorities, 1949.
62. ———, *Race, Jobs, & Politics,* New York: Columbia University Press, 1953.
63. Ryan, J. A., *A Living Wage,* New York: Macmillan, 1906.
64. Saenger, G., *The Social Psychology of Prejudice,* New York: Harper, 1953.
65. Schneider, E. V., *Industrial Sociology: The Social Relations of Industry and the Community,* New York: McGraw-Hill, 1957.
66. Schultz, G. P., "Worker Participation on Production Problems," *Personnel,* 28:201–211, 1951.
67. Sheppard, H. L., "The Treatment of Unionism in 'Managerial Sociology,'" *American Sociological Review,* 14:310–313, 1949.
68. Shister, J., "Methods of Remuneration," in Shister, J. (ed.), *Readings in Labor Economics and Industrial Relations,* Philadelphia, Lippincott, 1951, pp. 235–238.
69. Simmons, L. W., *The Role of the Aged in Primitive Society,* New Haven: Yale University Press, 1945.
70. Simpson, G. E. and Yinger, J. M., "The Changing Patterns of Race Relations," *Phylon,* 15:328–330, 1954.
71. ———, *Racial and Cultural Minorities,* New York: Harper, 1953.
72. Slichter, S.; Clakins, R. D.; and Spohn, W. H., "The Changing Position of the Foreman in American Industry," *Advanced Management,* 10:155–161, 1945.
73. *A Social Profile of Detroit: 1954,* Ann Arbor: University of Michigan Press, Institute of Social Research, 1955.
74. Spero, S. D. and Harris, A. L., *The Black Worker,* New York: Columbia University Press, 1931.
75. Staley, E. (ed.), *Creating an Industrial Civilization,* A Report of the Corning Conference, May 17–19, 1951, New York: Harper, 1952.
76. Tenenbaum, S., *Why Men Hate,* New York, Beechhurst, 1947.
77. Thompson, K. M., *Profit Sharing,* New York: Harper, 1949.

78. Walker, C. R., *Steeltown*, New York, Harper, 1950.
79. Warner, W. L. and Srole, L., *The Social Systems of American Ethnic Groups*, New York: Yale University Press, 1945.
80. ——— and Low, J. O., *The Social System of the Modern Factory*, New Haven: Yale University Press, 1947.
81. Weaver, R. C., "The Economic Status of the Negro in the United States," *Journal of Negro Education*, 19:232–243, 1950.
82. ———, *Negro Labor*, New York: Harcourt, Brace, 1946.
83. Wermel, M. T. and Gelbaum, S., "Work and Retirement in Old Age," *American Journal of Sociology*, 51:16–21, 1945.
84. Whyte, W. F. and Gardner, B. B., "The Man in the Middle," *Applied Anthropology*, 4:1–28, 1945.
85. ———, *et al.*, *Money and Motivation*, New York: Harper, 1955.
86. William, W., *What's on the Worker's Mind*, New York: Scribners Sons, 1920.
87. Wootton, B., *The Social Foundations of Wage Policy*, New York: Norton, 1955.
88. Wray, D. E., "Marginal Men of Industry: The Foremen," *American Journal of Sociology*, 54:298–301, 1949.
89. Youtsler, J. S., *Labor's Wage Policies in the Twentieth Century*, Skidmore College, New York: Twayne, 1956.

CHAPTER THIRTEEN

THE FACTORY CAREER

Although the use of the word "career"* is restricted in everyday language to the professions and the better-paid white-collar occupations, our discussion of the career in farming and in the restaurant has suggested that it may be observed in any work situation. The processes involved— social selection, mobility, career contingencies, and work and the self— appear to be present however many times a man changes jobs or how little he is paid.

The factory is, in fact, one of the best situations in which to study the career. It is a prototype—quite as much as the government—of the bureaucratic career. Of all industries it has one of the longest "lines" from bottom to top, a fact which may be discouraging or challenging depending on how long one stays at the bottom. It offers very great rewards of income, prestige, and power, and although very, very few will secure the top rewards, they *are* offered to a group of persons of very diverse backgrounds.

SOCIAL SELECTION IN THE FACTORY

Instead of asking why persons "choose" the factory as a place to work, it is useful—as we have seen [1]—to think of the work organization as being "choosy." What types of persons does the factory attract and what types does it repel?

[1] Preparatory to the following discussion is the general treatment of the role of choice and the manner in which social selection operates which was presented in Chapter Five.

The finding of a *Fortune* survey (16) [2] that 47 per cent of a representative sample of Americans called themselves "middle-class" persons often has been referred to. The middle-class is the home of upward mobile persons and thus the finding would suggest that practically half the population was motivated to strive upwards. The same survey reported another finding, which has not received the same attention: once persons reach the age of forty, there is a distinct tendency for them to stop thinking they have much chance for advancement (16, p. 133). These findings taken together suggest that the hope and the drive to move upward are particularly strong among young persons, but that a large proportion have experiences which dim their once bright hopes. The situation assumes tragic proportions when we note that forty is certainly not an old age and, with the present expectation of life, the average person still has one half or more of his working life before him. To give up hope of trying at such a point suggests that the individual's experiences must have been particularly bitter and souring. What then have been these experiences? What is the nature of the selection process to which they have been exposed, such that some have achieved their goals and others have decided it is not worth hoping any longer?

CULTURAL PERSPECTIVE

The employees of the factory represent all ranges of skill and education from the unskilled porter who quit school even before the law allowed to the research chemist with a Ph.D. Yet if we exclude specialized staffs, who are usually small in number, and management, the great body of workers on the production line have relatively few skills and little education. This makes the factory one of the most open of all work organizations. The factory can use and wants persons with relatively few skills or special training; hence, it has absorbed women as well as men, immigrants from Poland, Italy, and Puerto Rico, Negroes as well as whites, and the uneducated and the unskilled. But it has not done so without stress. Nor can one conclude that the factory is indiscriminate. For, as with the professions, the farm, and the restaurant, there are selective processes at work.

1. LOCATION

The boy who would be a medical doctor must often move. He may have to leave home to go to medical school, he may get an internship in still another city, and may practice in yet another place. By contrast, many factories, especially textile mills and those using sparsely distributed raw materials (such as aluminum ingot foundries), are set up in

---

[2] When forced to use certain terms, the per cent became 79.2.

relatively isolated areas and draw upon a local labor supply. In many cases, the factories are deliberately located in nonurban areas to take advantage of cheap, nonunion labor. The result is to place a major means of employment on the front-door-step of hundreds of thousands of adolescents and youths. In some cases, for example in the automobile industry, factories are located in large cities, but they so dominate the town (or the news) that the availability of the industry is obvious. This factor is coupled with the fact that the factory *can* absorb persons of little training.

Thus Harris (20, p. 273) says of the automobile industry:

With the mounting mechanization of the industry, about 45 per cent of its jobs can be learned within two or three days; about 35 per cent within a week; some 7 per cent within two weeks, and the remaining 13 per cent within a month to year or longer.

Thus, many are exposed to a pull which the young person, looking for quick money to help out his family or to take out his girl friend, is highly susceptible to. He may know *vaguely* of other possibilities. His father may caution him and remind him of the terrible years when the mill laid off two-thirds of the men. But there in front of his eyes is the sign: MEN WANTED. GOOD WAGES. And surely it would not hurt to find out about it and try it out for a year, maybe. He could surely use the money. Chinoy, in an outstanding study (11, p. 116), describes the problem of the youth who must choose between an immediate, and well-paying job on the line, or an apprenticeship at lower wages, which will mean a more skilled job later on.

The teen-age working-class youth is not likely to make the sacrifice of present satisfactions unless his aspirations gain support from a personally significant model or are encouraged by persons whom he respects, admires, or loves. One thirty-one-year-old skilled worker whose father had also been a skilled worker commented:

"When I was an apprentice I was torn by two desires. One was to go to work on the line like the rest of my friends and make some money. But there's no future in that. The other was to stick to the apprenticeship in hopes of getting some place. Seeing the way my dad worked through—even if he had his troubles and lost his home—I felt that it paid my father dividends anyway."

It is noteworthy that thirty-nine per cent of all apprentices registered with the Autotown Technical School in 1947 (fifty of 129) were sons of skilled workers; only eleven per cent were the sons of nonskilled workers. The rest came from urban lower-middle class or from farm families.

The majority, who do not have such a model, are likely to take the step that will bring money in the pocket now. Once such a step is taken, then other possibilities that require education are closed. Also, family responsibilities soon will force them to become security-conscious and to try to hang onto what they have rather than taking chances on what might be.

2. EDUCATION

The educational system cuts two ways. It is, of course, a major avenue of upward mobility. But also, as Caplow (9, p. 216) comments, it is a major restrictor (in the sense that once a choice is made, by the student, then other choices are eliminated. Our schools are organized in terms of curricula: "general" (terminating with high school), "academic" and "vocational." Only the academic curriculum keeps choices fairly open until the child reaches college. Yet often this curriculum involves subjects—Latin, foreign languages, history, mathematics—which are tolerated by the child only if he has psychological support from his parents. By contrast, the vocational curriculum is much shorter and its utility is patent. Shorthand may be boring, but its usefulness and the need for persons who know it are obvious from a casual perusal of the newspaper classified advertisements. The same is true of the mechanical arts. The twelve- or thirteen-year-old boy can *see* the point of learning how to operate a lathe; the point of history or of French is not so obvious.

When to this we add the fact, already discussed,[3] of the tendency of teachers to encourage middle-class children to go on to college, we see a strong tendency for lower-class children to elect the vocational or general curriculum and then find they are equipped only for jobs in a factory or related work. Hollingshead (22, p. 168), describing the high school in a Midwest corn belt community, reports as follows:

The high school curriculum is organized around three courses: college preparatory, general, and commercial. Enrollment in each course is related very significantly to class position; that is, each course acts either to attract or repel students in the different prestige classes. In 1941, the class I's (top class) and class II's concentrated on the college preparatory (64 per cent) and ignored the commercial course. Fifty-one per cent of the class III's were in the general, 27 per cent in the college preparatory, and 21 per cent in the commercial course. The class IV's entered the general (58 per cent) and commercial courses (33 per cent) and avoided the college preparatory; only 9 per cent were in it. The pattern for the class V's was similar to the class IV's, except that 38 per cent were in the commercial and 4 per cent in the college preparatory course.

[3] See above, pp. 194–196.

One of Hollingshead's subjects, a senior girl, in explanation, spoke as follows (22, pp. 169–70):

If you take a college preparatory course, you're better than those who take a general course. Those who take a general course are neither here nor there. If you take a commercial course, you don't rate. It's a funny thing, those who take college preparatory set themselves up as better than the other kids. Those that take the college preparatory course want to run the place. I remember when I was a freshman, mother wanted me to take home economics, but I didn't want to. I knew I couldn't rate. You could take typing and shorthand and still rate, but if you took a straight commercial course, you couldn't rate. You see, you're rated by the teachers according to the course you take. They rate you in the first 6 weeks. The teachers type you in a small school and you're made in classes before you get there. College preparatory kids get good grades and the others take what's left. The teachers get together and talk, and if you are not in college preparatory you haven't got a chance.

Hollingshead relates such attitudes to the fact that the majority of the middle and upper class students were in college preparatory courses. On the role of teachers in this process, he states as follows (22, p. 171):

Because the academic teachers believe that college preparatory students have more ability, are more interested, and do better work than those in the general course, they prefer to teach the former group. Although these contentions may be true, more probably teachers of the college preparatory group satisfy their desire to see the students reflect the academic values they hold. These teachers look upon students in the general course as persons who have nothing better to do with their time, are mediocre in ability, lack motivation and interest. Students in the commercial courses are believed to be lower in ability than those in the general course.

We observe, therefore, a strong tendency for lower-class children, who come from families in which their parents have relatively little education or training, and whose fathers are working as semiskilled or unskilled workers, to be effectively prevented from taking the college preparatory course which would greatly raise and widen their job possibilities. The net result is that a large proportion find themselves leaving school with training that equips them only for factory or related jobs. Such persons, therefore, are likely to respond to the "chance" remark of a friend that he heard they were taking on new men out at Western Foundry.

3. SEX

The factory has attracted women for many of the same reasons that the restaurant does. It offers many jobs which require little training or

experience, it has large labor needs which may expand or contract suddenly, and its ability to take on workers for short periods or for overtime
work makes it well-adapted to women who only work now and then to
help support their families. The lack of career involvement or identification have made women more willing to accept lower wages, and have
meant that, since they tend not to be upward oriented, they are not so
upset as men might be about being at the bottom of a giant hierarchy.
Women also gravitate toward the factory because they are restricted from
many other jobs by law, informally, or by traditional beliefs.

In view of the preference of women for marriage over/and a career
(discussed in Chapter Five), working women are seen to include a large
proportion who work part-time or occasionally. They, therefore, provide
a large reservoir on which the factory may draw as it feels the need to.
As in all situations where a large reservoir exists, this will mean that
wages can be kept low and that women will be found at the lowest ranks
in the industrial hierarchy (9, pp. 234–37; 36, pp. 320–23; 48). At the
same time, as long as women remain in the bottom ranks, the opposition to their employment by male employees is likely to be slight, since
such women are simply playing the traditional role of women—helping
their families—and are not competing directly with men.

4. SOCIAL CLASS

As we saw in Chapter Five and elsewhere, in the case of the factory,
the relative ease of entry and lack of need for education produces a selection toward the *lower* end of the social class scale. And this process works
both ways: the factory selects the lower classes, and the lower classes select
the factory.

An important type of research, discussed in Chapter Five, is that
which has been concerned with the aspirations of persons for success.
Lower-class persons, like everyone else, are exposed to the ideology of success in the movies, advertising and in the schools. Yet, Chinoy (11, pp. 112–
13) comments as follows:

But as soon as he leaves school, or even before, the working-class youth must
come to terms with a world of limited opportunity where there are few chances.
Lacking financial resources, he cannot look forward to the possibility of professional training, or even to four years of college which would widen his perspectives and increase his skills. He cannot step into a family business or acquire
easily the funds with which to launch one of his own. As soon as his education
ends, he must find some kind of job. And in Autotown even a large proportion
of high-school graduates will probably become factory workers; a third of all
employed persons in the city were engaged in factory labor of some kind, primarily in the four large automobile plants.

Many working-class boys therefore give up dreams of a rich and exciting occupational future—if they ever have such dreams—even before taking their first full-time job. In a questionnaire submitted to all boys about to graduate from Autotown's two high schools in June, 1947 and June, 1948, the question was asked: "If you could do what you wanted to what occupation would you choose?" Forty per cent of all working-class boys (forty-seven of 118) had no choice or chose occupations which carried comparatively little prestige and provided only limited rewards. (Occupations included in those with low prestige and low rewards were skilled work, clerical jobs, military service, and miscellaneous jobs which required no training. Those with high prestige and high rewards were the professions, technical and semiprofessional occupations, art and literature, scientific farming, and business.) Only twenty-three per cent of the middle-class boys, on the other hand, were without a choice or chose low-prestige, low-reward occupations, indicating a statistically significant difference. When asked about their actual intentions, forty per cent of the working-class boys said that they merely intended to "look for a job," without specifying any particular kind of job. Another twenty per cent intended to learn a skilled trade, to apply for some definite manual job which did not require previous training, or to enlist in the armed services. These figures compare with fifteen and twelve per cent respectively for boys of middle-class origin.

Some working-class boys, particularly those without academic aptitudes or interests, may quit school as soon as they are able to secure a job since they feel that they will find themselves in the factory eventually, even if they do graduate from high school. They can no longer do as their parents might have done in the past, leave school in order to learn a trade, since admission to formal apprentice training for any trade now usually requires a high-school diploma. The jobs they find, therefore, promise little for the future.

Many working-class boys only come to grips with vocational reality when they finally graduate from high school. Stimulated to a high level of aspiration by the mass media, encouraged by parents and, sometimes, by teachers, they entertain inflated ambitions until the time when they must choose a definite course of action. For example, a third of the boys whose parents were manual workers reported that they intended to go to college. While some boys with requisite academic abilities do muster the necessary financial resources and enter college, most of them in fact find themselves looking for a job after they graduate from high school. According to high school officials, less than a third of all graduates from Autotown's two high schools go to college, most of them probably from middle-class families. An even smaller proportion ever complete work for a degree. It is therefore highly probable that a very large proportion of those working-class boys who said that they intended to go to college did not do so.

Owing to such influences, the aspirations the young person develops will be closely related to his class position. Hollingshead (22, pp. 176–78) compares the aspirations of children in different social classes as follows:

The class I and II boys and girls know that high grades are necessary if they are to achieve the educational goal set for them by their family and class. Parents, friends of parents, brothers, sisters, and relatives who have been outstanding students in Elmtown High have set precedents they are urged to follow; for most, high school is merely a preparatory step for college. Then too, parents and relatives, who have achieved prominent positions in the community, expect them to be leaders. Stimulated by this interest and these examples, they generally respond by aiming for greater achievement. A by no means negligible element is a teacher's expectation that the class I and II child will "make good"; and she helps him realize this goal for, after all, his parents may "help" a teacher or cause "trouble" very easily. These factors react in subtle ways to produce high grades and leadership in extracurricular activities in Classes I and II.

Class III children tend to come from families who are either in relatively prominent, secure positions or who are insecure "climbers" who have achieved their positions within recent years after a long period of hard work. The latter group of parents normally are anxious to see their children achieve more in life than they have; consequently they place great emphasis upon grades and extra-curricular activities. They would like to see their children go to college, at the very least into nurse's training, business school, or some type of short, direct training beyond high school. The secure parents do not have such strong desires for· their children as the "climbers," but they want them to have a high school education. Approximately one-fifth of the parents in both groups realize they will not be able to send their children to college; these parents assume that the high school will give their children the last formal training they will receive. Class III children who aspire to climb the social ladder take the same courses as the class I's and class II's, groom themselves in a similar manner, join the same clubs, try to work into their cliques, and follow the same leisure time activities. Some two-thirds, however, are content to drift along, associate with other unambitious class III's or with the class IV's. They are not particularly interested in good grades, extracurricular activities, or training beyond high school. In passing, we may note that these children do not exhibit the tensions the ambitious upwardly mobile ones do.

Class IV students carry into the school situation attitudes they receive from their parents. A prevailing attitude in this class is: "No matter what you want to do or would like to do, the children from the 'rich families' and the teachers won't let you do it." The great majority of their parents did not attend high school, and a goodly segment of these people have little appreciation of the work the school is doing or what the child will get out of it. To many parents, high school is a needless drain on family finances, and they think that the boy and girl ought to be working. For a small majority the high school provides their children an opportunity to receive at relatively little expense to them some type of vocational training. The children from these families tend to enroll in the secretarial, agriculture, shop, and homemaking courses. Some of these parents have a blind, almost pathetic, faith that education will enable their children to gain something from life that was denied to them.

For instance, Mrs. Ellis Johnson, who worked as a scrub woman to supplement the family income, largely earned by her truck driver husband, spoke to us on three different occasions about her son.

Please talk to Jim, and try to get him to stay in school. His Paw had to drop out. I couldn't finish, and neither could his older brother and sister and they don't seem to be getting any place. Jim's a good boy, but he's not interested in school. He doesn't think it is doing him any good.

Jim lackadaisically walked from class to class, often without his notebooks or textbooks. He sat in study hall daily, dreamily looking out the window. When the teacher told him to get to work, he would slowly reach into his desk, take out a Western magazine or a comic book, and read it for the rest of the period. Jim thought the best thing for him to do was to join the Navy. He said he was going to do this just as soon as he was 16; after the outbreak of war, he was more convinced than ever that this was his destiny. The day he was 16, he quit school; the day after, he joined the Navy. Jim believed his mother had to work too hard for him to achieve a high school diploma; besides, "What good is it? I know a lotta guys at the Mill; they ain't finished eighth grade." His father didn't care whether he went to school or not, but he thought in a vague way that it would "be a good thing if Jim finished" high school.

A high school education is outside the experience of class V parents, and beyond the expectancy of most of their children. The principal ambition of the class V child is to grow up and escape from the authority symbolized by his parents and teachers. For him growing up means quitting school, getting a job, and doing as he pleases. Six of the 8 class V boys in school were freshmen, 2 were sophomores; none expected to finish high school, for all wanted to quit by the time they were 16. They were all enrolled in the general course, and none was actively interested in whether he passed or failed. Although the 18 class V girls in high school showed more interest in their studies than did the boys, they believed generally that they would not graduate, about 3 out of 4 girls expecting to quit at the end of the year or as soon as they were 16. Thus, there was little incentive to work for good grades. Only three class V girls were seniors; one withdrew before the second semester was over, and the other 2 graduated in the lowest quarter of the class in June, 1942.

Not only is the lower-class child prevented from going on to college and getting a high-status job, but he does not *want* even to try. Instead, he wants to leave school and wants to escape from the domination of both school and family. Yet the fact that he is poorly educated and trained means he must accept whatever job is available, and this usually means a factory or related job. Hollingshead's findings are not unusual. The evidence is quite strong that lower-class persons want and expect less and are consequently more likely to be responsive to the immediate job and money chances offered by the factory.[4] The explanations offered for this process are varied. Some place emphasis on the old idea that members

[4] See (1; 8; 14; 24, pp. 426–42; 29; 30; 33; 38; 40; 41).

of the upper classes are more intelligent, healthier, or more attractive (2, 46). Others refer to psychological factors, such as achievement motivation.[5] The Kluckhohns (26, 27) have emphasized differences in value systems in the different social classes. Whatever the explanation, however, it seems clear that a lower level of aspiration will mean that the lower class person has, in effect, a set of blinders which effectively narrow his choice of occupations. Given his low level of training, he is forced to take what he can get.

POSITIVE RESTRICTIONS

The factors we have just discussed are part of the individual's cultural perspective. They are internal to his group and give him an orientation or set of attitudes and expectations which he brings with him to the job. Their effect is to limit his choice and his hopes. Here we consider the obverse side of the coin—the actual restrictions or resistances which the work-world itself offers to the job-seeker or new employee.

The factory does restrict entry, but its voracious labor-needs make it difficult for it to do so, particularly in urban areas where it must compete with alternative employment opportunities available to the worker. The most serious restriction it offers is to the worker already employed *in* the factory, a restriction which takes the form of limitations on promotion or upward mobility. For example, the factory *will* hire women and may even promote them up one step. But Stanes, in a study of women managers in thirty-three British clothing, cocoa, chocolate, cotton, sugar confectionery, and biscuit manufacturing firms, found that women were being paid less than men doing comparable work, and had fewer privileges and opportunities to get specialized training (47, pp. 875–80, 899–900). Caplow (9, p. 234) comments that the principle of "equal pay for equal work" usually becomes officially accepted when it becomes meaningless—either because of sexual segregation of jobs (so that certain jobs are being performed only by women, who are then not doing the same work as any men), or by the policy of rapidly promoting men only.

At the same time, the factory is one of the few work organizations in which there are many persons who did not *drift* in. That is, there is a considerable tendency for a *straight career line* to exist from school to work. A high proportion of engineers will go directly from college to a factory and remain there for their working lives. Similarly, a large proportion of the products of vocational schools—typists and those with mechanical training—go directly to the factory. We have seen the strong tendency of lower-class persons to leave school as soon as possible and seek

[5] See (10, 23, 31, 32, 45).

a factory job immediately. Typically, then, the factory is likely to have, at any given time, a considerable number of young beginners. And, in spite of cultural perspective, it is such persons, as we have pointed out above, who have the highest hopes and most faith in chances for upward mobility. Yet the pyramidal structure of the factory means that most of them will be disappointed.

Important in mobility restriction is the folklore of workers about mobility chances. Every occupation and work organization develops a fund of stories about those who have gotten ahead, and it is important to the worker whether these stories suggest good or poor chances. Thus, the writer once asked a radio announcer what he and his colleagues talk about when they get together. He replied:

Talk about? Lots of things, but the guys I know (who are mostly fairly young), we talk mostly about guys who've got it made. Like _____, on the _____ show. He gets $350 for that one show. And he's not the only one. To get a show with a national hookup—just get *two* shows and you're set. You can live like a king. And it's being done every day.

This man's attitude may be contrasted with that of a repairman in the final assembly division of an automobile manufacturing company (11, p. 56):

I don't think I'll ever get to be a foreman because I won't suck the foreman's rear end. There ain't no damn chance of getting on supervision unless you make a damn fool of yourself like that. The superintendent in the X division, I used to work with him on the line, that's how he got there.

Another of Chinoy's subjects, a truck-driver, explained:

It isn't so much what you know, but it depends on who you know and what lodge you belong to. For instance, I have a friend, he belonged with some other guy who was made a foreman and then he was made a foreman. They say it wasn't that, but—. And the other guy's father-in-law was a general foreman too. A man sees those things and he doesn't figure he's got a chance.

Chinoy goes on to comment in an insightful passage:

Obviously these explanations may only be rationalizations of the failure to gain advancement or of the lack of interest in a goal sanctioned by tradition. But to the extent that these ideas have a quasi-independent existence as part of the shop folklore, are constantly repeated and reinforced in shop talk, and are transmitted to newcomers or to the children of factory workers who eventually find themselves in the plant, they may well serve to inhibit interest and stifle hope.

MOBILITY

Traditionally, the phrase "upward mobility" refers to the individual's rising within a hierarchy. Such data as we have suggest that the amount of such mobility in factories is relatively small. One stumbling block is that the sheer number of opportunities is slight. Guest (18) found that among automobile workers one foreman's job became vacant for every 120 workers per year. Chinoy (11, p. 44), in his study of automobile workers, practically rejects promotion as a type of mobility even worth discussing. Among the 6,000 workers in his factory, there occur ". . . only ten or twelve openings or workers each year as assistant foremen die, retire, quit, or are promoted."

The number of promotional opportunities will, of course, vary over time, expanding, for example, during a war or a period of accelerated production. Also, some departments of the factory are better than others. For example, departments doing skilled work are usually smaller and thus require more foremen per capita; also, in such departments, it is easier to appraise a man's skills and, if such skills are a factor in promotion, then it is easier to decide who should be promoted. But for the majority of workers, promotional opportunities are scarce.

The problem is stated very well by Chinoy, who enunciates six "disparities between tradition and reality," of which four are relevant to the present discussion (11, pp. 20–21):

1. Each job should be looked upon as a step to something better.
   But: In the factory there are few clear-cut sequences of progressively more skilled, better-paid jobs.
2. The corporation provides a "pyramid of opportunities from the bottom toward the top."
   But: Executives and technicians are increasingly recruited from well-trained college and technical school graduates rather than from the ranks of factory labor. In the factory the narrow range of wage rates sets a low ceiling on possible advancement.
3. Initiative and ability inevitably lead to promotion and advancement.
   But: Carefully laid-out time-studied jobs in a highly rationalized industry provide little opportunity to display either initiative or ability.
4. Success depends primarily upon each individual's efforts and capabilities.
   But: Advancement within the factory is increasingly collective in character.

Nor are these "disparities" peculiar to the automobile industry. Indeed it is ironical that these problems should prove so poignant in the automobile industry, an industry identified in the past with expansion, opportunity, and hope and one which gave us in Henry Ford a figure to set more men dreaming of great futures than Horatio Alger ever did.

Chinoy's second and third disparities are particularly important. The poorly educated man on the assembly line, too old to stop and get the necessary education, cannot compete. At the same time, the very make-up of factory operations places a premium on regularity and conformity. This makes it difficult for a man to attract attention to himself by outstanding initiative or originality. Even rate-busting (working faster than other workers) becomes impossible on an assembly-line, where the worker must gear his speed to the speed of movement of the belt. The worker must not slow down; but also, he must not speed up. If the worker somehow manages to preserve his interest in moving up in spite of these obstacles, he meets still other problems. In many cases, there are no clear-cut criteria toward which the individual can point himself. Management itself is not sure and often uses subjective criteria which are difficult to verbalize. There are two objective criteria which may be used: education, which we have already commented on, and seniority. But seniority conflicts with the strong tendency to promote men under forty. How, then, is a man to accumulate seniority if in the process he becomes too old to be considered for promotion?

In the face of these uncertainities and obstacles, one interesting and tragic result is a *lowering of aspirations*. Chinoy found (11, p. 49):

Despite the objective importance of foremanship as the initial step forward for factory workers and its sanction by tradition, most of the men interviewed lacked hope for or interest in the possibility of rising into the ranks of supervision. In some cases they even denied its desirability. Of the sixty-two workers interviewed, thirty-one said that they had "never thought of becoming a foreman" or failed to mention foremanship at all in discussing their hopes and plans for their future in the factory . . . Only six of the workers interviewed wanted to become foremen and felt that they had a good chance to do so.

The lack of interest, hope, and desire was so widespread among the workers interviewed that it must consider the "normal" reaction to the circumstances in which they found themselves.

Blum, describing workers in the Hormel meat packinghouse in Austin, Minnesota, says (7, p. 85):

Most workers are so busily engaged in pushing the flow of work that they do not *consciously* suffer from the inherent monotony of their work. They are well adjusted, because they have reduced their level of aspirations to the rather low level of the job. They coast along, keeping busy, visiting, talking, making time go by, and getting the work done in order to get "out of there" in order to get home! A worker to whom this passage has been read commented on it as follows: "True worker brings aspirations to level of job. That's why a new man is not so good. The first six months are the toughest. I was at the verge of quitting. After a while, you get used to it."

Guest (18) found a general lack of ambition among the automobile workers he studied. Only 7 per cent wanted to become supervisors; the largest group were those who wanted to shift to some other job in the factory. And their desires for making such a shift were in general couched in terms of the desire for security or seniority rather than the chances to get ahead. Only 12 out of 435 comments referred to positive attractions, such as the chance for advancement or liking the new work. Bakke (4, p. 52) found a similar lack of enthusiasm, and a poll of factory workers in 1947 reported that 58 per cent said they would not care to be foremen (15, p. 6).

Well, then, what do the workers want? Barred from promotion, or lacking interest in it, workers turn to other goals, of which the following are the more important.

a. MAKING MORE MONEY [6]

Here, at least, is a goal which most workers would be expected to be interested in, and most are. But where a factory becomes mechanized —and such is the trend—then the fact that much work is semiskilled tends to compress wages within narrow limits so that the maximum a worker can hope to get may not be much more than what he started at. Chinoy (11, p. 108) found:

In February, 1950, for example, 60 per cent of all workers in passenger-car plants earned between $1.50 and $1.70 per hour; the earnings of 50 per cent fell within a fourteen-cent range around the average . . . In most plants, new workers start at rates slightly below the regular job rates which they reach after a ninety-day probationary period. A substantial spread between minimum and maximum hourly rates is found only in some skilled occupations.

With such limited wage differentials, most workers can hope to earn more money primarily through general wage increases. For them, opportunity in the large plants in which they work has become to a great extent a collective affair in which the union plays a major role. Advancement is less and less an individual matter and more the collective gaining and holding of standardized agreements which provide for higher wages and for other benefits such as old-age pensions, hospitalization insurance, and life insurance.

Chinoy also states that maximum and minimum rates tended to be quite close to each other (11, p. 38):

[6] The major categories which follow are drawn from Chinoy's work, although he does not specifically list them in the manner in which we have done.

For roughly three-fifths of the job classifications in the factory, covering about 80 per cent of all workers, maximum hourly rates were ten cents above the minimum and were automatically reached ninety days after a worker was hired.

Walker and Guest (49, p. 108) report similar findings:

. . . there is little spread between the lowest and highest job classes. The wage range of our group, for example, was hardly more than twelve cents an hour. Two-thirds of the workers in the two largest departments received exactly the same wage. Thus, for most workers there was little *financial* incentive for promotion among production jobs.

They refer to a study in a steel fabricating plant which reported that the base rate wage in an average production department ran from $1.25 to $1.89 an hour, covering *more than eighteen* job classifications. The actual base pay of the men in Walker and Guest's sample is presented in Table 21 below (49, p. 84):

TABLE 21
BASE PAY (WEEKLY) FOR TYPICAL PRODUCTION WORKERS AT PLANT X (BASED ON HOURLY RATE × 40)

BASE PAY (PER WEEK)	NUMBER OF MEN
$60.40	95
61.20	16
62.00	2
62.40	20
63.20	5
64.00	41
66.00	1

That such narrow ranges are not peculiar to the automobile industry is indicated in the following passage from Walker and Guest's study (49, pp. 84–85):

This narrow wage range (between lowest and highest job classes) is a characteristic of almost all mass production industries and particularly of the automotive industry. The introduction of conveyors and machine hand tools has narrowed the wage distance between the day laborer's job and that of the skilled craftsman. Many mass production jobs, certainly jobs such as those found in automotive assembly operations, require greater skill than that of the ordinary "unskilled" worker. On the other hand, individual work operations have been either so mechanized or so fractionalized (broken down into simple tasks) that . . . craft skills have been virtually eliminated. One result of this technological development has been wage standardization.

The semiskilled worker (and this category includes an increasing number of factory workers), then, who desires to increase his income within the factory, finds few opportunities for doing so.

b. GETTING A SKILLED JOB

The only important category in which there is a considerable wage spread is that of skilled work, as in, for example, the tool-and-die shops. Since skilled work also has higher prestige, we might expect to see semiskilled or unskilled workers striving to obtain such work. What are their chances?

It is intriguing that in spite of the Census and practically every other job-classification system, Chinoy (11, pp. 29–30) reports that automobile workers hardly even recognized the category of "semiskilled." The inference is that mechanization and the general decline of skills has gone so far that the amount of "skill" required to operate a machine is not regarded as skill by the workers themselves. Instead, they broke down all jobs into skilled and nonskilled, although the nonskilled was further broken down into "production" and "off-production." In other works, the word "skill" was restricted; if the amount of skill was very slight, then workers referred to the jobs in terms of its location or type.

How, then, can such a nonskilled worker attain the skills necessary to rise to the ranks of skilled work? There are two methods: either he can become an apprentice, or he can try to pick up the skills informally.

Owing to the impact of mechanization and the consequent decline in need for skilled workers, apprenticeship, as a formal training method, has greatly declined. It reached a particularly low point during the great depression of the thirties when even skilled workers found it difficult to get jobs. But the demands of war production and the gradual aging of the already skilled produced a revival of interest in apprenticeship, and many companies started apprenticeship programs (52, 53, 54). But most workers who are already employed are unable to take advantage of such programs. In most cases, the programs cover only certain jobs, and are generally restricted to young persons and those who have a certain minimum education. More importantly, becoming an apprentice means working at a low salary for a considerable period, a step which many workers with families and debts would be unable to afford.[7]

The other procedure for learning a skilled job—informal learning— is made difficult if not impossible by the rigid job classification which modern industrial timing and production control requires. Union policies are a further obstacle (11, p. 42):

[7] Chinoy states that among his workers "at 1947 wage rates it would have taken an apprentice toolmaker approximately eighteen months to reach the wage level of assembly-line workers" (11, p. 41).

. . . rules established by collective bargaining have made it difficult for employees to acquire journeyman skills without formal training. Helpers, for example, who could once hope to learn the trades of the men under whom they worked, must now perform only those duties assigned to workers in their classifications; otherwise they would be engaged in tasks which call for higher wages and would be taking work away from skilled employees. Only in small plants, where rigid job classifications do not exist or are not adhered to closely, is it possible today for workers to become skilled via an informal and casual training process.

The net result is that the factory must fill the greater part of its need for skilled workers from the ranks of persons who have already acquired their skills elsewhere.

c. BECOMING A WHITE-COLLAR WORKER

As a goal, white-collar work does not loom very large in the thinking of factory workers. The main obstacle is their lack of training in the sort of "book" skills that office work usually requires. In most cases, the wages they would get, at least at first, are no higher and often lower than what they are getting in the factory. Further, there is the shop-office antagonism to which we have referred earlier. The status symbols, attitudes toward people who do only "paper work," and often the lack or felt lack of interpersonal skills make it difficult for a factory worker to orient himself seriously toward white-collar work. More commonly, he justifies to himself the superiority of "primary producers" like himself, but encourages his son or daughter to "stay in school, learn something, and maybe make something of yourself—don't make the mistakes your old man did."

d. GETTING A "BETTER" JOB

Here, at least, we come to a type of mobility (if it may be called that) which the worker is seriously interested in and which is often achievable. Workers will often indicate a preference for a different job in the factory, but the structure of such preference may be far from management's conceptions of desirability or even that of the average observer. Chinoy (11, p. 66) pictures the "hierarchy of desirability" his workers recognized as in Figure 18. Figure 18 demonstrates that the workers place custodial work, which includes janitors, night-watchmen, elevator operators, and clean-up men, at the very bottom. Actually, such work is regarded as marginal in most factories, and most workers in describing the "bottom jobs" might not even mention it. Customarily it is assigned to teen-agers (temporarily employed), or to old persons. When Negroes are first hired, it is usually those jobs that they get. It is Chinoy's second category—assembly-line work—which is the actual bottom. This is work which—in a real sense—is the heart of the whole operation. It is also

FIG. 18

HIERARCHY OF JOB PREFERENCE AMONG AUTOMOBILE WORKERS

TYPE OF WORK	PLANT DEPARTMENT OF DIVISION
Unskilled custodial work	No plant segment
Assembly line	Final assembly
	Paint shop
	Axle plant
	Motor division
Machine operation	Sheet metal (press room)
Miscellaneous production	Chiefly in automotive production
Off-production	Inspection
	Parts and service
	Material-handling
	Shipping
	Material control
	Maintenance (nonskilled)

the work which most often involves the conveyor belt to which the worker must adjust. Walker and Guest (49, p. 51) report the following attitudes toward conveyor work:

> The bad thing about assembly lines is that the line keeps moving. If you have a little trouble with a job, you can't take the time to do it right.
> On the line you're geared to the line. You don't dare stop. If you get behind, you have a hard time catching up.
> The line speed is too great. More men wouldn't help much. They'd just expect more work out of an individual. There's an awful lot of tension.
> I don't like rushing all the time . . . I don't mind doing a good day's work, but I don't like to run through it.
> The work isn't hard, it's the never-ending pace . . . The guys yell "hurrah" whenever the line breaks down . . . you can hear it all over the plant.

They go on to point out that while the attitudes expressed above were those of a large majority, a small minority liked the challenge and excitement of keeping up with the line.

Machine operation was preferred over assembly-line operation but the preference was not very great. Such work involves as much repetitiveness and monotony, but the worker is under somewhat less pressure than in adjusting to a moving line. Off-production jobs provide the greatest freedom of all. Chinoy comments (11, p. 72):

> They (off-production jobs) do not usually tie workers to fixed positions or require the constant repetition of a limited series of movements. Men in parts and service and in material-handling perform simple though unstandardized tasks such as packing parts for shipment, unloading materials, operating power trucks, or looking after a tool crib. Some inspectors, it is true, only operate

machines which test finished parts, but others do their work by listening to the motor, making visual or tactile examination of parts, or by manipulating various kinds of gauges. For many off-production tasks no fixed quantitative standards of performance exist against which foremen can measure the efforts of their workers, though they must obviously maintain some standards of efficiency. "That's the advantage of a job off production," said a truck-driver. "There's no set amount of work you have to do. You aren't pushed or crowded like on production."

Other values, particularly regularity of employment, were also involved in the hierarchy of preference. We shall give attention to them below.

On the whole, this structure of desirability of jobs is certainly not what the outside observer would call very ambitious; and it seems very far indeed from the tradition of starting at the bottom and fighting one's way to the top. Indeed, jobs higher up in the preference scale rarely coincided with higher wages, and in some cases involved lower wages.

e. MOVING UP IN THE UNION

Mills (37) and others (50) have seen in the labor union movement a new avenue of upward mobility for workers. And certainly some persons have risen to positions of great prestige and power in labor unions. The union offers, furthermore, very real advantages to the worker. Union stewards are often the last to be laid off and the first to be rehired. They are permitted to take time off from their work to handle union affairs, and the higher up in the union a man is, the more such time is he permitted off. However, although the outside observer may see union activity as a type of mobility comparable to rising in the factory hierarchy, it does not appear to be so to the worker himself. Mills (37) suggests three types of motivation—the "business-like men," the "political men" and the "disgruntled working men"—to which Chinoy adds a fourth —those pushed into union activity by the encouragement of friends (11, pp. 104–05). It is only among the "business-like men" that typical middle-class upward strivings seem important. These are often persons with previous white-collar work experience and with education who see in the union a means of advancing themselves. They do not appear to be very common. In none of the remaining three types do mobility drives appear to be important. "Political men" are allied with the union because of social or philosophical beliefs and see in it a major means of altering the structure of society. They are less common now than they were in the early days of union organization in the United States. (51, *passim*). "Disgruntled working men" use the union as a means of aggression toward management when they have not been able to solve their problems in other ways. And those pushed into union activity by friends often "find" themselves elected steward and take on the job because their friends clearly need their social skills to help achieve their collective objectives. Instead, then, of actively seeking union office, most union men get interested in the union for other reasons and seek union office later.

The very nature of union activity runs counter to the self-interest that individual striving for upward mobility implies. The person who wishes to rise in the factory (or any) hierarchy must look out for himself, watch for his opportunities, ingratiate himself with management, and if necessary, give up friends or associates who stand in his way. The union official, by contrast, must give up personal desires in the interest of others. His job is to *serve* others, not rise above them. Chinoy states the matter as follows (11, p. 101–02):

> The circumstances which gave rise to the ideal of the selfless, devoted leader have largely disappeared; the personal risks to which organizers and active members were once exposed are virtually gone. Indeed, workers who assume a full-time union office usually do not even lose their seniority standing in the plants from which they come; they are given leave for the duration of their union assignment and can return to their previous jobs at any time. Further, though it would be easy to overstress the point, union officials have also gained some degree of recognition as community leaders through membership on welfare councils, school boards, and other public organizations. Nevertheless, the very nature of the union official's role and of the path to office in the union sustain the frequently expressed belief that "you've got to have it in your heart to do the job."

> Full-time work for the union almost inevitably entails much more time than the eight hours each day put in by the ordinary factory worker. The union official must attend an almost endless procession of meetings of various sorts. The president of the A.B.C. local, for example, normally attends the monthly meetings of the local, the local executive board, the steward's council of the local, and the Autotown C.I.O. Council. He frequently attends the occasional meetings of workers from one or another district of the plant, of the various committees of the local, as well as occasional political caucuses. Nor is this a complete list. In addition, he may be called at any time by workers with problems or grievances.

> So strenuous are the demands on union officials' time that they are likely to prevent the pursuit of personal interests. Painting one's house, digging in one's garden, or merely having a good time must be set aside or neglected. Even one's family may be neglected in favor of union meetings or other union responsibilities. This inability to satisfy personal interests in a culture which emphasizes the personal and private rather than the social is widely looked upon as the sacrifice which union leaders must make. This sacrifice is to all intents and purposes directed to no personal ends; union officials have no direct personal interest in the goals toward which they direct their energies. They are continually giving up their time for the welfare of others. And local officers

may even spend a good part of their time on problems which have nothing to do with work in the factory. In the course of his day the local union president may perform such varied services for members as arrange for a loan from a credit union or for some service from a social agency, help the worker secure compensation for an injury suffered on the job, or even resolve a family quarrel and give advice about buying a house. Two local presidents estimated that over half of their time was taken up with personal problems of workers rather than their job problems in the plant.

The ideology of selflessness gains further support from the fact that the path to union office usually begins in the local union with positions at the bottom of the hierarchy which are widely labeled as "thankless tasks." While a few men catapulted to the top in the first chaotic years of organization, the possibility of such meteoric progress now is slight.

One may certainly exaggerate the matter. These days, as Chinoy notes, selfishness and devotion to unionism as a cause are no longer so necessary or common as they used to be. Yet it remains true that the effectiveness of a union man is measured by how well he satisfies his followers and how much of a following he has. His position is closer to that of a leader than it is to that of, say, a department head in a factory. Further, unless he is very high up indeed, his position in the union is not usually equated to comparable positions in industry. The union steward is not usually accorded any particular respect in the community, and even the president of the union local is not, by that token, likely to be accepted as an equal by factory management and invited to their homes. Indeed, the very position of the union man as an antagonist of management in union negotiations or grievances militates against his being accepted by management. His position is likely to be marginal. He may be called upon to serve on community committees and may even be a member of the Board of Regents in a large urban university. In people's minds, he is more likely to be regarded as a politician than as a "success" in the business sense of that term. Nevertheless, for a very few, the union does provide a means of "making something" of oneself, and a few men have attained national eminence through this medium.

f. LEAVING THE FACTORY

In view of the blocks and obstacles to moving up in the factory, one might expect to find a number of workers who saw better chances for success if they left the factory altogether and bought a farm or started an independent business. And certainly factory workers often talk of such ambitions. But both Guest (18) and Chinoy (11, Ch. VII, *passim*) point out that most workers will not actually try to achieve these ambitions. Major preventatives are their desire for security, the seniority they have already accumulated, and the fact that they would have to start all over again. A man in his forties with growing children and a mortgage on his home, who finds that he is spending every cent he earns, is not likely to "chuck it" and open a grocery store. In any case, he rarely has the savings necessary to buy the original capital.[8] Nevertheless, in spite of these obstacles, success as a small businessman *is* possible and some factory workers have adopted this procedure. The writer recalls a worker in an aircraft plant who started a small restaurant near the plant and immediately gained a clientele by cashing the paychecks of plant workers on payday. On those days, he appeared happy and continually joshed the workers as "wage slaves." To the writer he confided:

It's just like quitting smoking. The hardest part is the beginning. I figured if I cash their paychecks, that'll bring them in and maybe they'll buy something else and be regular customers. It brings them in alright, on payday, and they'll all buy a cup of coffee or maybe a piece of pie. But they don't come back, except once in a while. They won't bring their wives in for dinner or their girl friends after a date. It's because this place is pretty small and my furnishings ain't so fancy. But if they'd only give me some business, I could make this into the best place in town. It's a vicious circle—that's what it is.

As we have seen, those who wish to enter a new area need a tradition of success. Someone *like them* must have succeeded so that the possibility becomes real. Those who visit the restaurant of the man just referred to are likely to be depressed rather than to have their own ambitions stimulated. In any case, the success of persons *outside* the factory is hardly testimony to mobility opportunities within the factory.

All things considered then, we do not observe very great mobility opportunities within the factory. And the lack of such opportunities tends to depress such ambitions as workers may bring with them initially. But this does not mean that factory workers have "given up" and are ready to form a working class. For paradoxically, the factory worker tends still to subscribe to the ideology of success as evidenced particularly by his hopes for his children. In addition, Chinoy points out (11, pp. 94–95) that *talking* about buying a farm, or starting a motel, even though the worker will rarely go ahead and try, still serves a safety-valve function. It is a type of fantasy escape which serves to reaffirm his basic faith in the possibility of getting ahead which democracy offers. Chinoy further

[8] Should he try to become an independent businessman, his chances of success are distinctly low. The work of W. Miller and his students on the tendency of highly successful business and industrial leaders to be recruited from the middle and upper class has already been referred to (pp. 180–181, fn. 51). Nystrom points out that the failure rate of small business is and probably always has been high (39). Mayer (34) refers to the very high annual turnover in small business of from 12 to 20 per cent.

discovered that *security* itself, while traditionally regarded as the opposite
of upward striving and advancement, becomes in the worker's mind,
a type of mobility (11, p. 125):

But workers do not see security . . . as an alternative to advancement. Questions which were designed to elicit the relative importance assigned to security
and opportunities for advancement frequently proved meaningless; the respondents could see no difference between them. "If you've got security, if you've
got something you can fall back on, you're still getting ahead," said a twenty-
eight-year-old truck-driver with three children. "If you can put away a couple
of hundred dollars so you can take care of an emergency, then you're getting
ahead," declared a forty-year-old nonskilled maintenance worker with four
children. "If you work during a layoff, like back in the depression, that's my
idea of working up," commented a thirty-two-year-old fender-wrapper who had
been in the plant since 1935. And a thirty-nine-year-old oiler summed it up:
"If you're secure, then you're getting ahead."

Such statements testify to the great strength and vitality of beliefs in
opportunity in a democratic society. As long as such hopes and interpretations continue, rigid social classes are not likely, and the very hopes
themselves keep alive a strong desire to make them come true.

CAREER CONTINGENCIES

As pointed out above, the person who stays in school and later goes
on to college is continually exposed to a wider and wider variety of occupational opportunities. It is true that these opportunities are practically
all in the professions, but there are a great many of them and they offer
high rewards. When a person gets to college he may *hear* of fields he never
thought of seriously—such as social work, personnel work, interior
decoration, counseling, or research—or may hear of fields he had not
realized were professionalized and could be adopted as careers—such as
city planning, service in the U.S. State Department abroad, or the preparation of educational films. The person who goes into factory work
on the line has a very different experience. Usually he has left school at
an early age and has little training. He *then* finds that he has closed doors
behind him, and when he begins to recognize his limitations, it is usually
too late to turn back and pursue a new career.

The person who goes into the factory is usually young. If he has
left school at the earliest time the law allows (and many do) then he may
be only fourteen or fifteen years old. Such an adolescent will typically be
concerned with immediate gratifications. He is just now escaping from
the to-him onerous controls of school and parents, and he wants to
get out and have a good time. He wants to get a car, and go out on dates

with girls, stay out late, and enjoy himself free of responsibilities. Nor are these desires entirely internal in origin. Our culture now emphasizes consumption, and through the mass media and advertising the individual is continually encouraged to buy the many wonderful goods that efficient production and inventiveness have made possible. Under the impact of a new popular ideology shaped by Keynesian economics rather than the Protestant Ethic, spending, rather than thrift, becomes a positive virtue. For if people hoard their money and buy less, stores must close down and factories lay off workers. The youngster, therefore, fresh out of school and eyeing a sports roadster in a show window, finds that powerful cultural forces add urgency to his desire to buy it. But where is he to get the money to buy it?

. . . the immediate objective becomes a well-paid job, a goal most easily achieved by going to work in an automobile plant (or other factory). Within a few months the son of an automobile worker who goes to work in the factory may be earning as much as his father, who may have been there for twenty years. Despite the low status of factory work and the hope frequently expressed by automobile workers that their sons will not follow in their steps, many boys head for factory personnel offices as soon as they are old enough or as soon as they finish high school. And others find themselves seeking factory employment after having tried other, less remunerative jobs (11, p. 114).

Soon, however, they marry and have children. By then they have accumulated some seniority in the factory; but more importantly, they will likely have accumulated debts and obligations which require an uninterrupted weekly flow of money. *Now* when they begin to think seriously about the future, they find that their hands and minds are tied. They do not have the training to enter a new career, nor the savings to buy an independent business, and, owing to having stopped school so early and because of their limited experience, they do not *know* of other occupational possibilities. The net result is to place an emphasis on present and immediate needs, where just "hanging on" is considered an achievement.

The pressure of the weekly grocery bill, the rent or mortgage payment, installments on a refrigerator or a washing machine or vacuum cleaner, the need for a new pair of work pants or a pair of shoes for a child, the doctor's bill for a tonsillectomy, all keep life on a pay-day-to-pay-day basis. The future, for men in an industry known for irregular employment, bristles with threats. They are not usually prepared to cope with unemployment or with sickness and accident, the normal hazards of life. And the future is still resonant with echoes of the depression of the 1930's; men were employed by the W.P.A. in Autotown until the eve of war in 1941. Workers may conclude, therefore, that "it doesn't pay to think about the future," as a thirty-one-year-old line-tender put it (11, p. 117).

Factory workers must orient themselves to a career in the factory, making the best of such talents as they have brought with them. It is usually too late to make a change.

Promotion within the factory presents an age contingency. In general, it is the youngest workers who have the strongest mobility drives. Chinoy (11, p. 88) found a tendency for new, young workers to regard their jobs as "temporary" and to express an intention to leave unless they obtain advancement. But time passes and they do not advance. They then come up against the brute fact that if they are ever going to be promoted at all, it will be when they are in their thirties. The chances of becoming a foreman decrease rapidly after a man passes forty, so that if he does not make it by then, he probably will not make it at all. But these are also the years when children are growing up and when responsibilities are heaviest. Even should the opportunity to advance present itself, many workers will be unable to take advantage of it. Chinoy mentions a plan to offer abbreviated apprentice training to former upgraders (temporarily promoted during the war and since reduced to former ranks). The reaction was strong and negative (11, p. 63):

All eight former upgraders interviewed rejected the very idea of this proposal, even before it could gain any formal status. Seven had one or more children, the eighth a chronically ill wife. None could have managed easily, if at all, if their wages were cut to the rates paid apprentices. All were in their thirties or forties; none relished the thought of occupying a status in the plant which was normally associated with teen-agers and men in their early twenties, even if it were temporary.

In the case of these men, the drop in status was not only financially, but also psychologically, objectionable. It includes also the notion of an age-grading process.

As the worker gets older, he meets other contingencies. A man may attain considerable skill on a particular job which may then suddenly be eliminated by changing technology or consumer demands. The spectre of old age itself introduces many uncertainties. Haber and Stanchfield (19, p. 68) refer to a study made in 1929 in which 30 per cent of the concerns investigated admitted the adoption of a definite age limit for workers. They state:

The problem of the aged worker is most serious in the mass production industries, in which semi-automatic machine operations have decreased the value of skill and experience and put a premium on strength and youth. Increases in the tempo of production, synchronization of production processes, and the demand for higher output per man make it difficult for the older worker to retain his place in industry. Many firms tend to lay off the older worker earliest in a slack season and to hire him last when employment picks up, if they rehire him at all. And definite hiring limits, in many cases, make it almost impossible for the older men to compete for jobs against younger workers. Many other factors contribute to the same result; among these is the fact that, since group insurance rates are based on the average age of a firm's employees, employers prefer to keep the average age of their employees as low as possible.

They then go on to document these assertions.

Added to these uncertainties is the greater vulnerability of older persons to physical disabilities. When a man is dependent for his income on a continuous weekly paycheck, an illness which forces him off the job may be financially disastrous. Workmen's disability payments and group insurance programs have, however, reduced somewhat the hardships involved.

As the worker gets older, his chances of leaving the factory to seek improvement in independent business decrease also. Aside from the fact that his seniority now becomes precious to him and the fact that he may have contributed a great deal to a group old-age insurance policy, the sheer energy and hope that new enterprise requires may have left him. In addition, the urge to leave is likely to come at just those times when business conditions are poorest:

In the upward phase of the business cycle, when production is being maintained at a high level or is increasing and workers are regularly employed, the desire to leave the factory is at a minimum even though opportunities for small business may be at their best. When production falls off and temporary layoffs and short workweeks occur, interest in out-of-the-shop goals increases even though workers' resources are being rapidly drained away and the chances of business failure are especially high. (11, p. 119)

Such considerations create a great need for careful calculation of an uncertain future and proper timing.

THE JOB AND THE SELF

1. THE FACTORY CAREERIST

Among those who look upon factory work as a life-long career and identify themselves with the factory are a number of types. Those who live in a relatively isolated town which is dominated by a factory may so conceive of themselves from a very young age. When one's father and other male relatives are all "out at the mill," and, as one grows older, one's friends are also employed there, it is easy to fashion one's own career plans in a like mold. This is especially likely if the factory is an old one, identified with the town's history, and if ownership has remained in the hands of local residents who feel a strong sense of civic responsibility. Such cases appear to be increasingly rare. Towns grow; new, competing industries are established; the factory itself grows; and ownership passes into the hands of widely dispersed stockholders. Under such circumstances, youngsters (and oldsters too) may lose any feeling of identification and one may get instead labor-management conflict and the emigration of young people to larger cities. In larger cities, if factory workers live in a large housing project built especially for them, workers may come to feel a sense of unity with one another. One feels oneself "in the same boat" with one's neighbors, and even the grocery store owner and gas station attendant are keenly interested in factory affairs (they have a stake in continued employment and high wages also). Such living conditions may stimulate griping but they also give the individual a sense of social support to help carry him through stresses that might otherwise lead to his shifting to other employment.

A second group who see themselves as factory careerists are some professionals. These are the group whose work is, by definition, associated with manufacturing—engineers,[9] draftsmen, research chemists, and some personnel specialists. Many such persons, while still in college, expected, and looked forward to a life's work in a factory. A third group is management, particularly top management. Although managing is itself a transferable skill which may be applied to factories, wholesale houses, governmental administration, and even the armed services,[10] a man who accumulates many years of experience in the management of a factory is likely to feel a very close identification and even attachment to it, so that even should another opportunity present itself, he will find it difficult to leave. A fourth group are skilled factory workers, such as those involved in tool and die work, woodworking, jig assembling and the like.

These groups form an important core in any factory, but do not usually make up a majority of the workers in a typical, urban factory. Instead we find a considerable tendency for *most* of the workers in a

[9] Becker and Carper (5) studied the work identifications of a group of graduate students in engineering. While they emphasize the breadth of the engineers' expectations, they point out that the enginers "feel that their future lies somewhere in the country's industrial system." "For the majority, any industrial firm in the country represents a possible employer." (p. 345). It is interesting also that these men felt that in an economy becoming increasingly "technical," they could also expect to move into managerial positions.

[10] L. Reissman has suggested that army administrative experience may be a possible factor in explaining the employment of retired army generals in civilian industry. See (21, 42).

factory to feel little identification with factory work as a career at all. One of the most important factors militating against such identification is work *mechanization*. When work operations are divided, subdivided and subdivided yet again, the operation that the worker is called upon to perform may be so segmented and repetitive that a worker can hardly identify with it as a "career" and still preserve his dignity or self-respect. The challenge and meaningful content that we associate with a career are almost wholly absent. Some of Walker and Guest's (49, pp. 54–55) subjects commented:

> I dislike repetition. One of the main things wrong with this job is that there is no figuring for yourself; no chance to use my brain. It's a grind doing the same thing over and over. There is no skill necessary.
>
> I'd rather work for a small company any day. They're interested in doing good work, and they are willing to allot enough time for it. The assembly line is no place to work, I can tell you. There is nothing more discouraging than having a barrel beside you with 10,000 bolts in it and using them all up. Then you get a barrel with another 10,000 bolts, and you know every one of those 10,000 bolts has to be picked up and put in exactly the same place as the last 10,000 bolts.
>
> I'd like to do different things on this job. I get bored. It's the same thing all the time. Cars always coming down the line endlessly every time I look up.
>
> I would like to perform different operations, but I do the same thing all the time. I always know what I'm going to do when I come in.
>
> There's nothing to look forward to like there was on my old job.
>
> The job gets so sickening—day in and day out plugging in ignition wires. I get through with one motor, turn around, and there's another motor staring me in the face. It's sickening.[11]

Walker and Guest found further that the very slight skill and small learning time required was the occasion for feelings of apology and shame (49, pp. 56–57):

> Ten minutes—any junior high school kid could do it—except he wouldn't.
>
> Only took a half hour to pick it up—then it's only a question of speeding up. Some men get it in less than half an hour.
>
> Two hours—nothing to learn.
>
> A five-year-old can come in and do it now.
>
> It took approximately three days on-the-job training. No previous work experience was of any value learning this job.

---

[11] As might be expected, there was also a minority who simply did not care or who preferred repetition: "I like doing the same thing all the time. I'd rather stay right where I am. When I come in in the morning, I like to know exactly what I'll be doing" (49, p. 55).

On the other hand, when learning time was longer, a touch—but only a touch—of pride entered into comments (49, p. 57):

> At least a month to learn. It takes quite a while to get real savvy on the job. And it takes some practice to know how to tongue bolts and get them at the right tension.
>
> I'm still learning. And a new model will be coming soon. A repairman just about really learns everything about the job on one model when a new one comes in. It took me a couple of months to catch on, but I knew something about metal and maybe that helped a bit.

Identification with their work is further hindered, for factory workers, by their separation from their tools and from the goods they produce, as we have commented previously. Chinoy describes this process insightfully (11, p. 85):

> The tools and machines which workers use or operate, the visible symbols of the craftsman's identity, belong to others. Workers have no claim to the goods they produce; in that respect they are alienated from the fruits of their labor. Although automobile workers, unlike many other industrial workers, can recognize the finished product to which they have contributed, their contribution is so small because of the division of labor, and so insignificant because of the substitution of machines for manual skill, that the psychological tie between worker and product is tenuous enough to be almost meaningless.
>
> Going to work in a large mechanized plant entails the surrender of control over their own actions for those hours for which workers are paid; that they can be paid by the hour is itself evidence of external domination and separation from the product. In most jobs machines set the tempo and rhythm of work. In all jobs workers must submit to the authority of those in whom control is vested by the organization, with only the indirect influence of the union as a check upon the power of management.
>
> To a lesser degree this process of alienation affects the skilled workers as well. They too do not own most of the tools they use; they have no claim on the goods they must produce; they are subject to the authority on management. And in a large plant they too are subject to the anonymity and impersonality of a complex bureaucratic organization.
>
> These features of work in mass-production industry which alienate the worker from his labor and from himself lead to deprivations which are not easily verbalized. Yet they do show themselves in various ways: in the sad comment, "The only reason a man works is to make a living"; in the occasional overflow of resentment, "Sometimes you feel like jamming things up in the machine and saying good-bye to it"; in the cynical observation, "The things I like best about my job are quitting time, pay day, days off, and vacations"; in the complaint, "There's no interest in a job in the shop"; and in the resigned answer to questions about their work, "A job's a job."

Under these circumstances, where work identification is almost wholly absent, some workers give up all work goals and content themselves with a day-to-day philosophy, some workers talk dreamily of "getting a little farm some day," some shift to active union work, a few become active in local community affairs, and some turn to meaningful leisure-time activities.[12] But many turn from their work to an identification with the factory work-organization itself. Becker and Carper (5, pp. 342–43) comment on the significance of "occupational title" as an important part of a man's "work-based identity." What we are likely to find among factory workers is that since their occupational titles (semiskilled worker, punch press operator, assembly line operator) do not form prideful bases for "work-based identity," the title or name of the whole factory may become a more meaningful identification. When asked who he is, the factory worker is more likely to respond: "I'm out at Boeing's" than he is: "I'm an assembly line operator." Bakke (3) identified this phenomenon, "organizational charter," as one major bond of organization. Walker and Guest (49, p. 135) note that:

In the undirected part of our preliminary interviews it was found that nearly every worker expressed an opinion about the company and almost always in terms of what Plant X or Company Y was doing for him or for some other employee, whether much or little.

This experience led them to ask a general question dealing with the total company. The actual findings are not of interest at this point; what is relevant is the fact that workers did think in terms of the whole company, sometimes distinguishing it sharply from their jobs, as in the following (49, p. 136):

Under the existing conditions I would say the company was doing everything possible for the men. After all, they are running a business. It's the work that's rough, but it's a good outfit.

[12] In spite of certain sampling problems at the lower levels of occupational prestige, Clarke's study (12) of the relation between leisure and levels of occupational prestige is relevant. He found that while persons at upper occupational prestige levels were more likely to spend their leisure time at theatrical plays, concerts, lectures, conventions, and reading, persons at the lowest prestige levels spent their time working on automobiles, watching television, fishing, driving, in taverns and at baseball games. Interesting also was the fact that persons at the lowest prestige levels tended to engage very little in spectator recreation, though in this case they stand in contrast to the middle rather than the upper prestige levels. In addition, the lower prestige levels engaged most in "craftsmanlike" activities. When asked what they would do with an extra two hours in the day, upper-level groups were more inclined to read or study, while lower levels were more inclined to "relax, rest, loaf, sleep." More than twice as many of the upper level persons said they would work at their jobs as did lower level persons. Part of this is undoubtedly a matter of opportunity, but part also is likely due to interest and career-orientation.

Of course others blamed the company for unfavorable job conditions.

Such tendencies to think in terms of the whole company rather than one's own job are important for union organization. Insofar as emphasis shifts to the company, unions organized on a company or industrial basis may have more meaning to the worker than those organized on a job or craft basis—automobile workers, say, in contrast to carpenters.

2. MOBILITY ORIENTATION

Kahl (25) showed that "common-man" boys who were oriented to getting ahead had been "pushed" or stimulated by their fathers. The majority of common-man boys do not have such an experience. We have already referred to the large proportion of factory workers who do not even *want* to become foremen. Partly this phenomenon is due to the realities of the situation—a recognition of the low chances of being promoted. But part also is due to the attitude or point of view workers bring with them. Chinoy (11, p. 59) feels that workers may lack confidence in their ability to handle a foreman's job. Knupfer (28) supports this possibility in referring to the finding that lower-class persons tend to lack self-confidence and to avoid responsibility. The net result is the worker who does not *conceive* of himself as a foreman or even as a successful person.

Also, in order to move up, the worker has to *learn* how to handle authority. The average factory, with its carefully planned and timed jobs, presents little opportunity for the worker to learn how to exercise discretion and make decisions. This is especially true in assembly-line operations where the attempt is made deliberately to remove all responsibility for decision-making from the worker and "built it into" the machine. One of Chinoy's subjects, a thirty-one-year-old truck driver, said (11, p. 59):

I've never thought about the possibility of getting to be a foreman. I don't think they'd give it to anybody anyway without some sort of special training. We're not trained for leadership. We sometimes kid around—"you're trying for a foreman's job"—but we're not trained to manage men. We're trained to work together and we just do the best we can.

Chinoy himself adds (11, p. 59):

Workers at the bottom of the corporate hierarchy learn to combat authority or to accept it, not how to exercise it.

Of particular importance in this context are personality variables needed for success in the modern industrial corporation. Bendix has described brilliantly the shift in the characteristics considered essential for success in the nineteenth century with the present. In the early period (6, pp. 258–59):

> . . . the employer's authority was justified by oft-repeated references to his success, which was a sign both of his virtue and of his superior abilities. Those who failed were believed to lack the requisite qualities, and they were enjoined to obey the men whose success entitled them to command . . .
>
> This division between employers and their men was held to illustrate the survival of the fittest and most virtuous, since the one possessed the power to originate and conduct great enterprises and the other "obviously" did not. Indeed, the workers would live in squalor and want without the beneficial guidance of capital and brains.

This static view, with its emphasis on "virtue" and personal characteristics, gradually began to change in the 1920's and 1930's (6, p. 308):

> Gradually the worker came to be viewed as an embodiment of aptitudes and feelings, which had to be assessed so that his job assignment would be advantageous to him and profitable to the enterprise. From a person whose chances for success were vague but unlimited as long as he had not yet proved himself, the worker had become a person whose chances for success had become specific and restricted, depending as they did upon discretionary evaluations and promotions by management. From a person to whom hope and virtue had been preached, he had become a person whose aptitudes and attitudes had to be tested . . . The leaders of economic enterprises had been regarded as men whose success in the struggle for survival testified to their superior abilities, and these abilities consisted of such qualities as perseverance, capacity for work, prudence as well as daring, and other . . . Gradually, however, these leaders became more consciously preoccupied with the complex tasks of management. The imagery of their superior virtues changed accordingly from the praise of qualities ideally suited to the competitive struggle to a praise of qualities ideally suited to *the management of men and to the advancement of careers in a bureaucratic environment.* [Ital. mine]

The new qualities identified as necessary for success were characterized by Mayo (35) as the "organization of cooperation." That is, the successful manager had to be a man who himself had sufficient social skills to be able to secure the cooperation of his subordinates and to train them in the skills of cooperation also. Riesman, Glazer and Denney (43, pp. 130–32) have described this process as a shift from the inner-directed to the other-directed man:

> The inner-directed man has a generalized need to master resource exploitation on all the fronts of which he is conscious. He is job-minded.

The frontiers for the other-directed man are people; he is people-minded . . . Take, for example, the position of the foreman. He no longer stands alone, a straw boss in a clear hierarchy, but is surrounded with people. He is a two-way communication channel between the men under him and a host of experts above and around him: personnel men, safety director, production engineers, comptroller's representatives, and all the rest of the indirect managerial work force. The plant manager is hardly better off for emotional elbowroom: he is confronted not only with the elaborate intra-plant hierarchy but with the public outside: the trade association group, the unions, consumers, suppliers, the government, and public opinion . . .

. . . the newer industrial revolution which has reached its greatest force in America . . . is concerned with techniques of communication and control, not of tooling or factory layout. It is symbolized by the telephone, the servo-mechanism, the IBM machine, the electronic calculator, and modern statistical methods of controlling the quality of products; by the Hawthorne counseling experiment and the general preoccupation with industrial morale. The era of economic abundance and incipient population decline calls for the work of men whose tool is symbolism and whose aim is some observable response from people.

Such shifts in values suggest that the man who wants to get ahead must somehow develop social skills—the ability to work with people, to "get along." The workers themselves are well aware of this requirement in their oft-repeated complaint that getting to be foreman requires "pull" or "connections" or "bootlicking."

But here we encounter a contradiction in work values. For it is on the assembly line—the actual process of manufacturing—that social skills are *devalued* and indeed may be defined as inappropriate by management itself. The careful planning and timing of work tasks are engineered so that production planning itself shall define social relationships. The individual is supposed to interact only with those with whom he is directly connected in a division of labor relationship and in manners prescribed by job descriptions. When two men work as a riveting team—one holding a block of metal, the other driving the rivet flat against it—it is not required that these two men shall get along with each other, only that they shall work together. Production planning does not take into account the fact that if they *do* get along, it may mean simply that when one suggests taking time off for a smoke, the other is likely to agree. Nor does success as a riveter require—from management's point of view—getting along with machinists, clerks, tool-and-die men, inspectors, and time-study men. Success as a riveter refers to technical competence in the riveting job itself. At this lowest level, then, men perform and are judged according to technical criteria. Yet if they wish to advance, they must somehow develop social skills, which may even be forbidden, as in the case of the superintendent who wants the men "to stop all this horsing around and visiting and sneaking out for coffee. Let each man stick to his job and we'll have an efficient organization." But the more each man sticks to his (technical) job, then the less chance does he have either to develop social skills or demonstrate them, so that when a foreman's job comes open, he will be considered.

In this situation, where social skills become difficult to achieve, the worker's values turn to other things. We pointed out that factory workers think of jobs in terms of an informal hierarchy, with assembly-line jobs at the bottom and off-production jobs at the top. Chinoy found that the values accounting for these preferences were two: regularity of employment and relative absence of physical and psychological strain (11, p. 67):

In the long run, they feel, a steady job will provide a better income than an irregular job that pays higher hourly rates. "I can make about two thousand dollars a year on this job and I don't think the guys on the line can make that much even if they are making six cents an hour more," said a stock-picker in parts and service earning $1.35 per hour who had been transferred at his own request from an assembly-line job that brought $1.41 per hour. "I've got the best job in the shop," boasted a yard-maintenance man. "I work fifty-two weeks a year. I don't get paid as much but at the end of the year I'm better off than the guys on production."

Here we see operating a powerful motive that might lead a man to refuse an offer to be promoted to a higher-paying job, or not even to regard such a job as a promotion at all. In speaking of "physical or psychological strain," Chinoy refers to the planned rhythms and pace of work. One of his subjects stated (11, p. 71):

Now that I'm off the line I don't know how I stood it for ten years. But where I am now I like it. You're not on the same job all the time, and if you want to go missing for a while you can without a foreman running down on you and telling you to get back to work.

We note that of these two characteristics, the first—steady work—does not indicate any particular job preference as such and the second—absence of strain—is a negative characteristic in which the worker is trying to escape something he dislikes. They are therefore indicative more of general attitudinal set than they are of "job preference" as such.

3. ALTERNATIVE IDENTIFICATIONS

The worker who does not identify with the factory and see in it a challenge worthy of his best efforts may turn his attention to other identifications. We have already commented on the vague, though real interest of workers in getting out and buying a small business or farm. Where such goals become strong, work in the factory may hardly enter into a man's thoughts except as a means to another end. But the irony of such hopes, if unfulfilled, is that they serve to give a meaning to his *factory* work which it would not have otherwise. For even something that is a means to something else has more meaning than an activity with no purpose whatsoever. As the years pass and the outside goal fades as a genuine possibility, the many years the man has spent in the factory become precious, for giving up now means giving up pension rights, group insurance privileges, and any other benefits modern corporations provide to workers with long seniority.

Some men become union men. Of the types that were described above—business-like men, political men, disgruntled working men, and those pushed into it by friends—probably only the political men and some of the disgruntled see in the union an expansion of the sense of self. For such men, however, the union gives an exciting character to the factory which it has for very few. The factory becomes an arena on which noble, and worthwhile struggle may take place. Effective union action calls for qualities such as loyalty, devotion, and self-sacrifice. At a union meeting in a plastics manufacturing firm which was called to discuss a raise in union dues, considerable opposition was voiced. In defense of the raise, the vice-president of the union addressed the membership as follows (17, pp. 201–02):

A lot of blood and sweat went into our being able to sit here tonight in comfort in a democratic union. There has been a lot of talk about the "new world" that we're fighting for. I feel that we'll only get the "new world" through organized labor. I don't know what the union means to you people, but I know that I enjoy the privilege of being able to stand up on my feet and tell the boss what I think, whether I get a raise or not. (Scattered applause.) We need a strong union to talk for us.

The union has gotten us vacations with pay. We have the finest cultural program of any union in the country. We want to keep these things and get more. We simply have to stick together. We must stand together (pause) or divided we fall.

In his speech, the appeal to unity, democratic symbols and the "new world" are clearly dominant in his thinking, while reference to the factory work itself only occurs once and indirectly in the reference to vacations with pay. Such persons are, however, relatively rare. The majority of members of a typical industrial union are apathetic, rarely attend union meetings, and regard the union largely as a resource or type of insurance which should provide concrete benefits in exchange for union dues.

Another identification of great importance is one's family or circle of friends outside of work. In Chapter Five, we noted the importance of family identification for women workers who are only working temporarily to help out the family. But among lower-class persons—including a large proportion of factory workers—such an outside group comes to function as a large clan to help see *any* of their members through periods of economic distress. Davis describes this in the following case (13, pp. 87–91):

Pearl Elno, the white female worker, was born of old native stock in southern Indiana, the daughter of a coal miner. At the beginning of the great depression, her father came to Chicago to seek work, bringing his family. Here Pearl met Jim Elno, a young machinist, the son of a Polish laborer and a charwoman, and, like both his parents, extremely devoted to liquor in general and to schnapps in particular. At eighteen, Pearl married Jim Elno. Both youngsters were ambitious and smart. They were both good workers, anxious to buy a home of their own, and to get ahead in the world. Jim studied hard at his trade; and he bought a derby hat and a pair of spats—just to show his friends that he was a man who took himself seriously and intended to get somewhere in the world.

His young wife was always more practical and conscientious than Jim, and forced him to leave his mother's, set up a home of his own, and to work for goals more enduring than a derby and spats. All her efforts for a house of their own and for a decent standard of living were defeated, however, during the next 10 years, by the rapidly increasing number of their children. Jim was a Catholic, and Pearl was a very fertile woman. In 9 years, she bore seven children.

Unable to secure work during most of the thirties, and presented annually with a new baby by Pearl, Jim began to drink heavily. Any father who has had to come home to five, or six, or seven small children, and has had to try to live and sleep with them, crowded into a three-room flat, will sympathize with Jim, I imagine. During the depression, four children were born to the Elnos. They had to flee to steadily smaller and poorer apartments, and the children were reduced to half-starvation rations, which kept them sorely undernourished and chronically ill. Unemployment and their hopelessly large family wore away the determination and the morale of the parents, especially of Jim. They separated twice, and Jim deserted once but returned. He was arrested two or three times for panhandling while drunk. He beat his wife several times, when he was drunk. The Elnos and their seven little children were on the rocks and seemed headed for the bottom. But Pearl still had her own parental family. Her father and mother, and her sisters, together with their husbands, formed a closely organized and loyal clan, which repeatedly rescued her and her seven children. The sisters took them in, when Jim was violently drunk, or when they were evicted for inability to pay the rent. They bought the children clothes, and helped feed them. Pearl's mother, still able to hold a job at sixty, borrowed money on her home to lend to Jim, when he was employed by the Works Progress Administration. She came up from southern Indiana repeatedly to care for the children, so that Pearl could work as a waitress, and as a machine operator, to help feed the children while Jim was unemployed. One of Pearl's sisters opened a tavern recently and employed the mother, who in turn helped Pearl's family. Both the sisters and mother thus have continued to help Pearl.

The history of the Elno family illustrates in part how the organization, and the typical experiences of the white working-class family, control the motivation of the lower class worker. First, its size is typical of working-class families, and it is an important factor in their motivation. We found the average number of children in white *middle-class* families in Chicago to be only 2.2. In white working-class families, the average number of children is 3.3. This is a tremendous difference; along with the lower incomes that go with these much larger families, it changes the nature of family relationships in the working class, the methods of child training, the standards of nutrition, of cleanliness, of education, and of sex behavior. The actual daily pressure of 5 to 10 hungry stomachs to fill, backs to clothe, and feet to cover forces the working-class parent to reduce his ambitions to this level of subsistence; to lower his sights as far as long-term planning and studying for better jobs and for finer skills are concerned; to narrow, limit, and shorten his goals with regard to the care, nutrition, education, and careers of his children.

This terrible pressure for physical survival means that the *child* in the average working-class family usually does not learn the "ambition," the drive for high skills, and for educational achievement that the middle-class child learns in his family. The working-class individual usually does not learn to respond to these strong incentives and to seek these difficult goals, because they have been submerged in his family life by the daily battle for food, shelter, and for the preservation of the family. In this sense, ambition and the drive to attain the higher skills are a kind of luxury. They require a minimum *physical security;* only when one knows where his next week's or next month's food and shelter will come from, can he and his children afford to go in for the long-term education and training, the endless search for opportunities, and the tedious apple polishing that the attainment of higher skills and occupational status requires.

Secondly, the Elno family's history illustrates the deprivations, the shocks of fortune, the drain of illness and malnutrition, as well as the social and psychological disorganization, that reduce the efficiency of the underprivileged worker. A society that pens families into this kind of physical and social environment actually cripples both the ability and the work motivation of its workers. If there is one thing that modern psychology makes clear, it is this: men cannot be motivated successfully to work hard, or to learn well, simply by putting the screws upon them. The starvation theory of wages may or may not have been abandoned in actual industrial practice, but it is certain that other theories of social punishment, and of economic pressure, other theories that men will work hard and well *only* when they are *compelled* to by economic or legal necessity are still very popular. But the analysis of our system of economic and social prestige, as well as the findings of psychologists, make it clear to any realist that men work hard and learn well only when they have been trained to work for increasing rewards.

To improve the underprivileged worker's performance, one must help him to learn *to want* and to be anxious to attain higher social goals for himself and his children. All one can get out of methods of starvation conditions in wages, or of threat and intimidations, is more of the same inferior work and more concealed resistance, as in the case of a man whipping a poorly trained mule. The problem of changing the work habits and motivation of people who come out of families like the Elnos' is far more complex than mere supervision and pressure. It is a problem of changing the goals, the ambitions, and the level of cultural and occupational aspiration of the underprivileged worker.

This change in his cultural motivation cannot be attained by getting him into the starvation box. For, as the Elno family illustrates, the average working-class family is a large economic unit, a clan of kin. They can depend upon *each other* for shelter and food in time of unemployment, or of reduced income, or of prolonged absenteeism, or when they simply quit the job. In this working-class culture, one may usually fall back upon his brothers, or sisters, or aunts, or nieces, or cousins for a bed and meals, in a way that middle-class people cannot. The middle-class adult person is ashamed to go to his relations or friends for food and shelter. "Respectability" prohibits such dependence. To avoid this embarrassing loss of "face," he will work harder, take more punishment of a mental and emotional kind on the job, and cling to the job more desperately than will the average lower class, underprivileged worker.

That is to say, the masses of working-class people, like the Elnos, cannot be frightened and forced into better work habits, simply through having the economic squeeze put on them, or through being threatened constantly with firing. Such threats do not intimidate them, as they do the middle-class clerk or schoolteacher, because the underprivileged worker is thoroughly accustomed to those conditions of life that middle-class people call "insecurity." Most important of all, he knows he can always "bunk in" with a relative, usually on his mother's side of the family, and he is certain that an extra plate will be filled for him and his, so long as his relatives have food. The harder the economic *noose* is drawn, the tighter the *protective* circle of the average working-class family is drawn. Thus economic intimidation is much less effective than with white-collar employees. Since most working-class people do not get the rewards of social and economic prestige in our society, they do not fear the loss of the job or the attendant loss of respectability in their communities nearly so deeply as do the white-collar workers.

In our terms, the Elnos have an alternative identification to that of the job or the factory.

Davis later comments on the need to reward workers and raise their standard of living if management desires that they shall be motivated to work harder. To this it may be added that the same things must be done if it is desired to increase the worker's identification with the factory.

CHAPTER REFERENCES

1. Albrecht, R., "Social Class in Old Age," *Social Forces*, **29**:400–405, 1951.
2. Anderson, C. A., *et al.*, "Intelligence and Occupational Mobility," *Journal of Political Economy*, **60**:218–239, 1952.
3. Bakke, E. W., *Bonds of Organization*, New York: Harper, 1950.
4. ———, *The Unemployed Worker*, New Haven: Yale University Press, 1940.
5. Becker, H. S. and Carper, J., "The Elements of Identification with an Occupation," *American Sociological Review*, **21**:341–348, 1956.
6. Bendix, R., *Work and Authority in Industry*, New York: Wiley, London: Chapman and Hall, 1956.
7. Blum, F. H., *Toward a Democratic Work Process*, New York: Harper, 1953.
7a. "Boom in Apprentice Training," *Business Week*, Dec. 6, 1947.
8. Bradley, W. A., Jr., "Correlates of Vocational Preference," *Genetic Psychology Monographs*, **41**:327–408, 1950.
9. Caplow, T., *The Sociology of Work*, Minneapolis: University of Minnesota Press, 1954.
10. Centers, R., "Motivational Aspects of Occupational Stratification," *Journal of Social Psychology*, **28**:187–217, 1948.
11. Chinoy, E., *Automobile Workers and the American Dream*, Garden City, N.Y.: Doubleday, 1955.
12. Clarke, A. C., "The Use of Leisure and Its Relation to Levels of Occupational Prestige," *American Sociological Review*, **21**:301–307, 1956.
13. Davis, A., "The Motivation of the Under-Privileged Worker," in Whyte, W. F. (ed.), *Industry and Society*, New York: McGraw-Hill, 1946.
14. Dynes, R. R. *et al.*, "Levels of Occupational Aspiration: Some Aspects of Family Experience as a Variable," *American Sociological Review*, **21**:212–215, 1956.
15. "The Fortune Survey," *Fortune*, **35**:5 ff., May, 1947.
16. "The Fortune Survey," *Fortune*, **21**:14 ff., Feb., 1940.
17. Gross, E., "Informal Relations and the Social Organization of Work in an Industrial Office," unpublished Ph.D. Dissertation, University of Chicago, 1949.
18. Guest, R. H., "Work Careers and Aspirations of Automobile Workers," *American Sociological Review*, **19**:155–163, 1954.
19. Haber, W. and Stanchfield, P. L., *The Problem of Economic Insecurity in Michigan*, Lansing, Michigan: A Report to the State Emergency Welfare Relief Commission, August, 1936.

20. Harris, H., *American Labor,* New Haven: Yale University Press, 1939.
21. Herring, P., *The Impact of War,* New York: Farrar and Rinehart, 1941.
22. Hollingshead, A. B., *Elmtown's Youth,* New York, Wiley, 1949.
23. Hollingshead, A. and Redlich, F. C., "Social Stratification and Psychiatric Disorders," *American Sociological Review,* 18:163–169, 1953.
24. Hyman, H., "The Value Systems of Different Classes: A Social Psychological Contribution to the Analysis of Social Stratification," in Bendix, R. and Lipset, S. M. (eds.), *Class, Status, and Power: A Reader in Social Stratification,* Glencoe, Ill.: Free Press, 1953, pp. 426–442.
25. Kahl, J. A., "Educational and Occupational Aspirations of 'Common Man' Boys," *Harvard Educational Review,* 23:186–203, 1953.
26. Kluckhohn, C. and Kluckhohn, F., "American Culture: Generalized Orientations and Class Patterns," in Bryson, L., *et al., Conflicts of Power in Modern Culture,* New York: Harper, 1947.
27. Kluckhohn, F., "Dominant and Substitute Profiles of Cultural Orientations: Their Significance for the Analysis of Social Stratification," *Social Forces,* 28:376–393, 1950.
28. Knupfer, G., "Portrait of the Underdog," *The Public Opinion Quarterly,* 11:103–114, 1947.
29. Kroger, R. and Louttit, C. M., "The Influence of Father's Occupation on the Vocational Choices of High School Boys," *Journal of Applied Psychology,* 19:203–212, 1935.
30. Lipset, S. M., "Social Mobility and Urbanization," *Rural Sociology,* 20:220–228, 1955.
31. McArthur, C., "Personality Differences Between Middle and Upper Classes," *Journal of Abnormal and Social Psychology,* 50:247–254, 1955.
32. Maslow, A. H., "A Theory of Human Motivation," *Psychological Review,* 50:370–396, 1943.
33. Mayer, K. B., *Class and Society,* New York: Doubleday, 1955.
34. Mayer, K., "Small Business as a Social Institution," *Social Research,* 14:332–349, 1947.
35. Mayo, E., *The Social Problems of an Industrial Civilization,* Cambridge: Harvard University Press, 1945.
36. Mead, M., *Male and Female,* New York: Morrow, 1949.
37. Mills, C. W., *The New Men of Power,* New York: Harcourt, Brace, 1948.
38. Mulligan, R. A., "Socioeconomic Background and College Enrollment," *American Sociological Review,* 16:188–196, 1951.
39. Nystrom, P. H., *Economics of Retailing,* New York: Ronald Press, 1932.
40. Porter, J. R., "Predicting Vocational Plans of High School Senior Boys," *Personnel and Guidance Journal,* 33:215–218, 1954.
40a. "Recent Developments in Apprenticeship," *Monthly Labor Review,* 69:126–130, 1949.
41. Reissman, L., "Levels of Aspiration and Social Class," *American Sociological Review,* 18:233–242, 1953.
42. ———, "Life Careers, Power and the Professions: The Retired Army General," *American Sociological Review,* 21:215–221, 1956.

43. Riesman, D., Glazer, N. and Denney, R., *The Lonely Crowd,* New Haven: Yale University Press, 1950.

44. Rogoff, N., *Recent Trends in Occupational Mobility,* Glencoe, Ill.: Free Press, 1953.

45. Rosen, B. C., "The Achievement Syndrome: A Psychocultural Dimension of Social Stratification," *American Sociological Review,* 21:203–211, 1956.

46. Sorokin, P. A., *Social Mobility,* New York: Harper, 1927.

47. Stanes. D., "Women as Managers," *The Manager,* 23:875–880, 899–900, 1955.

48. Tyler, L. E., "The Measured Interests of Adolescent Girls," *Journal of Educational Psychology,* 32:561–571, 1941.

49. Walker, C. R. and Guest, R. H., *The Man on the Assembly Line,* Cambridge, Harvard Univ. Press, 1952.

50. Watson, G., "Labor Unions and Morale," in Watson, G. (ed.), *Civilian Morale,* New York: Society for the Psychological Study of Social Issues, 1942, Chap. XVIII.

51. Wilensky, H., *Intellectuals in Labor Unions,* Glencoe, Ill.: The Free Press, 1956.

52. Williams, H. J., "Apprentice Training," *American Machinist,* 91:113–128, 1947.

53. "Boom in Apprentice Training," *Business Week,* Dec. 6, 1947.

CHAPTER FOURTEEN

THE FACTORY WORK GROUP

A "work group" is a unit of the division of labor: several specialists whose specialties are related to each other in a cooperative manner by the fact that they are engaged in producing a joint product. In one sense the entire factory may be looked upon as a large work group. The term is, however, restricted to smaller units within this larger organization, such as an assembly-line team, a riveting crew, and so on. It is analogous, and in certain respects homologous to the "colleague group" among professionals.

The major tie binding workers together in the work group and defining their relationships to each other is that of symbiosis, or interdependence. One man cuts a piece of metal to certain dimensions, a second cuts another piece of metal, a third takes these two pieces and drills corresponding holes in them, a fourth bolts the two pieces together. If any one of them does not do his job, the work of the whole group is brought to a halt, or else pieces pile up, and bolted assemblies are not produced. If the group is paid according to how many bolted assemblies they produce, then individual earnings will also drop. Each member of the group is therefore dependent on every other member of the group.

Homans (24, Ch. 5) feels that small group research supports the hypothesis that if people interact with each other frequently, they are likely to come to like each other. Symbiosis is one of the forces that brings people together and forces them to interact with each other.

Consequently, it should lead to common liking. On the other hand, the very existence of symbiosis may lead to antagonistic feelings. The manufacture of steel requires iron ore and coal. Consequently a symbiotic relationship between France and Germany has existed for centuries, with the French needing German coal and the Germans needing French iron ore. But anyone who thinks that this relationship has lead to good will and mutual liking is ignoring elementary historical facts.

The question is of particular importance in the factory work group, and, indeed, is one of the reasons for studying the work group. Does the fact that men are members of the same work group mean that they will also like each other and exhibit solidarity? And conversely, if a work group exhibits high solidarity or cohesiveness, will it also function *efficiently* as a unit in the division of labor? Current personnel practice and the thinking of management gives both yes and no answers to these questions. On the one hand we see the "progressive" industry spending a great deal of money on "morale-building" devices—music in the shop, clean toilets, recreation rooms, air-conditioning and so on. It is hoped that these things will make the worker happier to be employed at the company and that they will make his job more pleasant. Company picnics, "understanding" managers whom the worker can talk to, "good-will" plant inspections by the president and like will, it is hoped, increase solidarity and a sense of belonging among workers. All these things, it is assumed, should result in a greater devotion to work and consequent higher productivity. On the other hand, when workers begin to show signs of developing a feeling of belongingness and solidarity—exhibited for example by the formation of strongly-knit informal groups which may be seen "slinging the bull" around the water-cooler, management is likely to feel that "cliques" have no place in the shop and must be resisted. The study of such informal groups is therefore vital to an understanding of the whole matter of efficiency and will lead us also to an examination of the problem of motivation.

INCLUSION AND EXCLUSION

The make-up of work groups is a function of the division of labor. The entire factory is formally divided up into a network of interrelated groups, which in turn are organized into shops and departments. The new worker—after his skills, aptitudes, and previous education or experience have been assessed by the personnel office—is assigned a formal position in one of these formal work groups where it is felt he will make the maximal contribution to factory efficiency and effectiveness. An important effect is that workers are *thrown together*. One type of research—that on sociometric preferences [1]—has been concerned with trying to show that persons are happier and possibly more efficient when they have the opportunity to choose their working associates. But the division of labor can rarely be organized on the basis of personal preferences, for such preferences will not necessarily correspond to competence or the needs of the factory. The worker typically cannot choose his working associates and finds himself surrounded by strangers.

How he shall behave toward these strangers is described carefully in his job description. He is to receive a piece of metal from one particular man, place it in a press which turns it to a particular shape, then pass it on to another particular man. That is all the formal organization requires—that these three men shall form a work group. But there grows up in addition a network of informal, friendly relationships between workers. These informal groups mirror the formal work groups, but not precisely.

Propinquity or nearness obviously is a factor in the selection of friends and in the fashioning of likes and dislikes—in the factory as elsewhere. A worker cannot become friendly with someone he has never met, and is most likely to choose his work friends from among those he usually interacts with while working. Walker and Guest (51, Ch. 5), in their study of automobile workers, found that they could classify their workers into three social categories: isolates, those doing independent work but near others, and work teams. The isolate was illustrated by a paint sprayer of wheels and small parts who works alone in a shed separated from other paint operations. Such men felt that their isolation was a strong factor in their not liking their jobs. But isolates were, and are in most factories, quite rare. Most workers are either near others or work directly with others in a joint task. Men who work near, but not with others are illustrated in Fig. 19 which shows the line for a group of polishers in the paint department (51, p. 71).

E, the central figure in this chart, polishes the doors on his side. Across from him, F polishes the doors on his side. Previously, C and D had polished the trunk; A is the trucker who helps move the unit onto the line. After E is through, G and H polish the fender and I and J polish the quarter panels. It is not clear from Walker and Guest's description what groups are present here or how cohesive they are, but they state that (51 p. 72):

There are ten men in all whom E considers as members of his work group (A to J). His closest social contact, however, is with only four of these men.

---

[1] See (26; 30, Ch. II; 33, pp. 317 ff.; 39, 61).

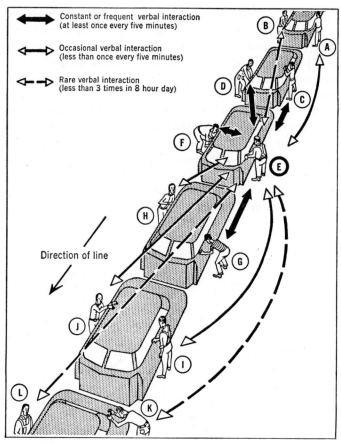

Constant or frequent verbal interaction
(at least once every five minutes)

Occasional verbal interaction
(less than once every five minutes)

Rare verbal interaction
(less than 3 times in 8 hour day)

Direction of line

FIG. 19
SOCIAL INTERACTION PATTERN OF TYPICAL MAIN
ASSEMBLY LINE WORKER-POLISHER, PAINT
DEPARTMENT *

The latter are F, C, D, and G, who are all close to him spatially. Walker
and Guest go on to insist that

The men from A to J comprise a group *only* from E's point of view. If we
looked at the relationship pattern of G, his immediate group would be E, F,
H, and I. It would not include C and D, who were clearly members of E's immediate group. Thus each man on the line has a slightly different group from
that of the man next to him.

* Reprinted by permission from Walker, C. R. and Guest, R. H., *The Man on the
Assembly Line* (Cambridge: Harvard University Press, 1952), p. 71.

While this seems logical, the language does not make it clear whether this is a deduction from E's situation or whether each member of the line in fact described a different group. Earlier the authors stated that they asked each person to describe those with whom he interacted, so the latter interpretation is probably correct. Propinquity is thus a factor in group formation.

How free are workers to move around? The polishers described above were limited by having to work with fixed equipment—a hand-polishing machine suspended above each man by wires. In other cases where location is not so fixed, workers have greater freedom to select associates over a wider area.

The other type of work relationship—the team—also involves continuous interaction within the team, and is illustrated in Figure 20 (51, p. 75).

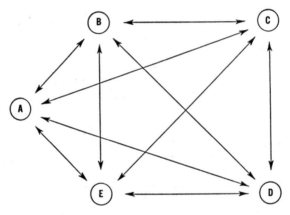

FIG. 20
SOCIAL INTERACTION PATTERN AMONG MEMBERS OF THE GRILLE AND FENDER ASSEMBLY TEAM *

Walker and Guest did not study the degree of group cohesiveness directly, but they state (51, p. 80):

In discussing the amount of talking they did, the isolates were the most vehemently negative. The largest group, those working side by side but independently, were more likely to refer to their social relations in the negative terms of how they would feel were they not able to talk, and of the effects of interaction in

* Reprinted by permission from Walker, C. R. and Guest, R. H., *The Man on the Assembly Line* (Cambridge: Harvard University Press, 1952), p. 75.

counteracting other job tensions. In marked contrast, those who were members of true teams spoke of their group interaction in positive and cheerful terms.

Generally speaking, then, informal interaction is related to work association, but not in a rigid manner. Some may restrict their association only to those with whom they work or are near, others who are freer to move about, may interact with a wider group. Then, of course, a worker may meet someone from another division of the factory altogether at lunch, on the bus going home, or in connection with factory-organized recreation, such as a bowling league, or at union meetings. But such widely dispersed groups will not have the opportunity to develop cohesion during the working day, and, most importantly, the integration does not have the same probability of being related to the *work* they do as is the case with teams or those working near each other.

Propinquity or team relationships—which are by-products of the division of labor—give a man a number of persons from whom he can *select* a group with whom to maintain close ties. Propinquity and team situations are therefore not necessarily causal, but instead may be only facilitating. *Whom* he selects (or by whom he is selected) depends on congeniality, likes and dislikes, and degree of agreement on work values, of which the last is probably the most important, at least in highly cohesive groups. A man who does not share the values of such a group is likely to be excluded or, worse, subjected to group sanctions.

In this connection we observe an ironical (and to management, exasperating) situation: the formal organization of the factory *assists* the group in applying sanctions on deviants. If a man living in a certain neighborhood discovers that his neighbors do not like him, he *can* move away; and if the man joins a club and finds its policies distasteful, he can quit. But in the factory, the worker is *forced* by the division of labor and job requirements to work with or next to certain people. Therefore if his fellows wish to apply sanctions on him, it is difficult for him to escape, except by quitting altogether or asking for a transfer. The former is usually out of the question, while the latter is often difficult to arrange and the worker himself may not wish to give up a job in which he has competence or job seniority for a new one.

A worker subjected to sanctions may discover rejected assemblies turning up inexplicably in his work pile. It is only because his fellows are near him or work with him that they are able to slip these assemblies in unobtrusively. The worker is "stuck." The division of labor—created by production planners—itself helps determine the makeup of informal groups and helps these groups to maintain themselves against those

regarded as deviants. The situation becomes ironical when the "crime" of
the deviant consists, as it often does, of orienting himself to management
goals—by, for example, producing at a very high rate of speed.

In general, who is chosen for membership depends in small part on
symbiotic factors and in large part on consensual factors. Symbiotic
factors operate in favor of including the following people: a good (that is,
fast or efficient) worker whose potential productivity may help pull the
group through when it is under pressure; the "key person" who has access
to needed information or whose work is of such a nature that he may
move freely in and out of the shop; occasionally, an "old-timer" who
knows the ropes and thus can help in a group of younger men (21, Ch. 1);
a man from another department who serves as a medium of communication for the group (19). All of these types are *useful* to the group in a
symbiotic sense. They have something to offer the group which it needs.

But of much greater importance are consensual factors. For a man
to be included, he must be liked as a person. This includes a great variety
of factors such as age, previous experience, education, race or ethnicity,
religion and all the other factors that may affect friendship relations
(20). But in addition consensus includes worker attitudes to such things
as restriction of output, promotion, the union, and even lesser matters
such as politics or baseball.

The importance of consensus is both cause and consequence of work
group solidarity. Among work groups of low solidarity, the makeup may
be variable and shifting. This is particularly likely in a new, large
factory before routines have become established and people know each
other. It is especially likely if upward mobility is relatively easy, as it is in
a period of expansion. But as the lines begin to harden and as men reach
the point where they can look back on ten or fifteen years in front of a
work bench, solidarity tends also to increase. At the same time, there is
greater emphasis on work values and resistance to newcomers or those
who do not share these values. That emphasis in turn also increases
solidarity in its own right.

Their very solidarity makes these groups difficult to study, so that
they may be missed by the outsider, the temporary worker, or even the
researcher who spends a relatively short time in the factory. On the one
hand, if such groups are weak, the observer concludes they are not
present or are not important. If they are strong, they resist study, particularly by use of direct questions. In my own research, I found that in
an office where a number of quite strong informal groups existed, the
members responded to direct questions by denying the groups' existence
or considering them of no importance. Frequently the resistance is quite
subtle, taking the form, for example, of being very nice to the outsider

but telling him or letting him see nothing. A student of mine provided the following illustration of this process:

My dad owns a fish cannery over on the coast, and last summer he put me to work. He's from the old school and he expects me to take over the business some day so I was supposed to learn the business from the ground up. It's interesting but it's pretty dangerous too. There's a sharp knife that runs automatically, popping up and down, and you take the salmon and put him into position so's the knife slices off his head. You got to keep those salmon moving and keep your fingers out of the way. Many's the man who's gotten badly hurt or lost a finger. That part of the job I never particularly cared for—I couldn't even stand to watch it. The crew that worked the knife were pretty good-natured, always kidding around, and I liked to talk to them, but I'd look the other way while they were working. The thing is they were real nice to me. Naturally I figured it was because I was the boss's son, and it didn't bother me none. One day my dad comes out because one of the men on the knife got sick and had to go home. "You work the knife," he says to me. Well, I just froze. I suddenly realized I'd never once had a chance to work with the knife! The crew never once had urged me to, and I wasn't about to do it on my own. When I blurted that out to the old man, he was plenty sore.

If such resistance may be shown to the boss's son, clearly a strongly knit group will not hesitate to resist fellow-workers or outsiders.

INFORMAL RELATIONS

As we have seen, the formal organization of the factory consists of a division of labor and a formal supervisory organization. These are called formal because they are set up formally by management. They define for the worker *minimal requirements* as to how he shall do his work and who is to judge him and his work.

This organization makes itself felt to the worker in the form of a set of definitions or norms or rules. The worker who enters the factory finds these definitions or rules already in existence. In such a situation the worker may do one or more of three things: (1) obey the formal rules directly; (2) adopt procedures which, while not constituting direct obedience, have the effect of rule compliance; or (3) reject rules.

The first alternative is called *formal behavior;* the second and third alternatives are called *informal behavior.*[2] We should note that both types of *informal* behavior are reactions to the *formal* organization and its *formal* rules (3, Ch. 10). One explains little if one attributes informal behavior to the persnicketiness of the worker—some sort of self-assertion

[2] For valuable discussions of informal organization, as contrasted with formal organization, see (3, pp. 73, 122–23; 36; 37, pp. 121–22; 48).

or a determination on the part of the worker to behave as he pleases in the manner of a negativistic little boy. Informal behavior is basically a technique by which the worker manipulates the formal organization itself.

PROCEDURES THAT HAVE THE EFFECT OF FORMAL RULE COMPLIANCE

When the worker confronts the formal rules, he will find that many of them do not seriously disturb his self-conceptions and so may be obeyed directly. These may include such rules as prohibitions against smoking in an explosives plant, the wearing of prescribed work clothes, or the taking of lunch at an hour prescribed by management. Some rules, however, he may not wish to obey directly but they may have to do with matters that are regarded as so serious by management that they cannot be ignored. The worker may then adopt certain procedures which will satisfy management without however actually obeying the rules directly. There are a variety of such procedures and they will vary depending on the particular factory. The most common are the following.

EMPLOYMENT OF TRICKS OF THE TRADE

We have given attention to tricks of the trade in previous chapters.[3] We may note here that one set of formal rules in the factory is the following: work fast, produce a large quantity, and maintain a steady pace of work. If the worker knows the tricks of the trade, then he can *appear* to be working fast and to be maintaining a steady pace when he is in fact not doing so. At the same time he will still produce a large (or acceptable) quantity of work. One of the most important tricks in every trade is that of knowing how to organize one's work efficiently. Most of us have observed this process in the speed with which experienced furniture movers operate. Yet they do not seem to get overly tired and do not *seem* to be working very rapidly.

One important trick involves "cheating" and getting away with it. Roy (40, p. 257), in a steel fabricating plant where he worked, found "cheating" elaborately developed in connection with rate-setting on piecework jobs:

. . . job timing was a "battle all the way" between operators and time-study men. The objective of the operators was good piecework prices, and that end justified any old means that would work. One cardinal principle of operator job-timing was that cutting tools be run at lower speeds and "feeds" than maximums possible on subsequent production, and there were various ways of

[3] See above, pp. 131–132, 343–346, 386–387.

encouraging the institution of adequate differentials. Also, operators deemed it essential to embellish the timing performance with movements only apparently functional in relation to the production of goods: little reachings, liftings, adjustings, dustings, and other special attentions to conscientious machine operation and good housekeeping that could be dropped instanter with the departure of the time-study man.

Elsewhere, Roy provides us with a vivid description of how this was done. Starkey, an experienced worker, is telling Tennessee the facts of life (59, pp. 15–16):

"If you expect to get any kind of a price, you got to outwit that son-of-a-bitch! You got to use your noodle while you're working, and think your work out ahead as you go along! You got to add in movements you know you ain't going to make when you're running the job! Remember, if you don't screw them, they're going to screw you! . . . Every movement counts!"

"Another thing," said Starkey, "You were running that job too damn fast before they timed you on it! I was watching you yesterday. If you don't run a job slow before you get timed, you won't get a good price. They'll look at the record of what you do before they come around and compare it with the timing speed. Those time-study men are sharp!"

"I wasn't going very fast yesterday," exclaimed Tennessee. "Hell, I was going as slow as I could without wearing myself out slowing down."

"Well, maybe it just looked fast, because you were going so steady at it," said Starkey.

"I don't see how I could of run it any slower," said Tennessee, "I stood there like I was practically paralyzed!"

"Remember those bastards are paid to screw you," said Starkey. "And that's all they got to think about. They'll stay up half the night figuring out how to beat you out of a dime. They figure you're going to try to fool them, so they make allowances for that. They set the prices low enough to allow for what you do."

"Well, then, what the hell chance have I got?" asked Tennessee.

"It's up to you to figure out how to fool them more than they allow for," said Starkey.

"The trouble with me is I get nervous with that guy standing in back of me, and I can't think," said Tennessee.

"You just haven't had enough experience yet," said Starkey. "Wait until you have been here a couple of years and you'll do your best thinking when those guys are standing behind you."

Now Starkey provides further instruction in the art of getting a slow timing for a fast job. He explains the possible adjustments of speeds and feeds on his machine.

"I was timed once on some levers like the ones you're running. I got a price of $4 a hundred, and I could make about $2 an hour! But I didn't run them the way they were timed. When the time-study man came around, I set the speed at 180. I knew damn well he would ask me to push it up, so I started low enough. He finally pushed me up to 445, and I ran the job later at 610. If I'd started out at 445, they'd have timed it at 610. Then I got him on the reaming, too. I ran the reamer for him at 130 speed and .025 feed. He asked me if I couldn't run the reamer any faster than that, and I told him I had to run the reamer slow to keep the hole size. I showed him two pieces with oversize holes that the day man ran. I picked them out for the occasion! But later on I ran the reamer as 610 speed and .018 feed, same as the drill. So I didn't have to change gears— And then there was a burring operation on the job too. For the time-study man I burred each piece after I drilled and reamed, and I ran the burring tool by automatic feed. But afterwards, I let the burring go till I drilled 25 pieces or so; and I just touched them up a little by holding them under the burring tool.—Hell, I used to make out in five hours, easy, on that job."

Of course, such short-cuts and speed-up techniques are used even where no time study men need be worried about.

Who can adopt tricks of the trade? Obviously only the experienced worker, for the novice is not yet familiar with them. Later we shall discuss what the novice does when there is no Starkey around to help him.

CHECKING ONE ANOTHER'S WORK

In every factory, workers constantly engage in a process of checking one another. Along with the formal inspection required by management there also goes on a continuous process of informal inspection. When worker B receives a part from worker A and performs some operation on the part, in describing the formal division of labor, we would say that the part passes from A to B. But observation reveals that if the part is defective, B will often return the part to A even when B could go ahead and do his own work in spite of A's error. Through this means, individual A is enabled to maintain both a higher rate of production and a better record with the inspector (25).

SHARING WORK

Work consists, formally, of *coordinated* specialties. But in addition the formal division of labor calls into existence an *informal* division of labor in which workers cross specialty lines. This occurs in large part because of the increasing simplification of much factory work. The work becomes so easily learned that workers can take over one another's "specialties" in emergencies.[4] The worker can thus "obey" the rules while

---

[4] Walker and Guest (51) suggest that advantage should be taken of simplicity of tasks in order to reduce monotony, mechanical pacing and repetitiveness. They suggest "job enlargement"—giving the individual more than one job to do. In addition, job rotation is recommended.

out having a cigarette—because meanwhile his work is being carried on by someone else.

SHIFTING RESPONSIBILITY

The individual can avoid obeying a formal rule directly by pointing out that it was someone else's responsibility to obey the rule. In order to accomplish this one will find among workers a very definite conception of what may be called an "area of concern." The worker will feel that his own responsibility extends to his own work and some of the work directly related to him. For any other activities he is likely to exhibit a profound indifference. One office worker in the Credit Department at a plastics manufacturing firm stated:

> I check ledger cards to see what a man's past credit record with the Company is. All that I want from the Accounting Department is clear, up to date posting on the card. I don't know where they get their information and I don't care. I'm paid to do a job here and how they do theirs is none of my affair.

Of four techniques described, the first involves tricks of the trade, and the last three involve social skills—the ability to deal with people and to get along with them. The novice, not yet familiar with the tricks of the trade and social work skills, can use none of these devices. What then can he do? He obviously must obey the formal rules directly. This is one of the problems of the new worker and is one of the reasons that new workers are often "management minded," and seem to be "eager beavers." The new worker may behave in that way because he simply has not learned *any other* way of satisfying the formal requirements except to do so directly.

REJECTION OF THE RULES

Under certain circumstances workers express dissatisfaction with the rules or actually disobey them. This disobedience extends all the way from ignoring the NO SMOKING signs to restriction of output. The latter, because of its importance to the production process and because it appears to be practically universal, will occupy the bulk of our attention.

By restriction of output (the old "ca'canny," and also called "soldiering") is meant producing a limited amount of work, working at a limited rate of speed, and/or maintaining a limited pace of work, and doing these things deliberately. Kennedy [5] (27, pp. 108–09) points

---

[5] Kennedy, using Veblen's phrase, defines restriction of output as ". . . varying degrees of withholding of efficiency, by individual workers on their jobs and usually acting in concert . . ." (p. 106).

out that restriction is not *always* deliberate but may be customary, either through tradition or because of resistance to change. However this type of restriction is both relatively uncommon and not of particular significance. We will restrict our discussion to deliberate restriction.

Roy (41) has described two distinct types of deliberate restriction (hereafter called simply "restriction"). His research was conducted in a plant which had a piecework incentive system. The worker was paid so much per piece, but in addition, as is usual, he was guaranteed an hourly rate. Thus a worker might have an hourly rate of $1.00, and be paid $.10 a piece. If he produced ten pieces in an hour, he received $1.00. If he produced 15, he received $1.50. But if he produced only five pieces, he still received his guaranteed base pay of $1.00 for the hour. Such guarantees are usually made since the worker might be interrupted by factors beyond his control, such as shortages of material, a breakdown of machinery, or a work stoppage in another department. In addition, labor unions usually insist on such a guarantee.

The workers divided jobs into "gravy jobs" and "stinkers." Roy describes the distinction as follows (41, p. 429):

When an operator discovers that he can earn $1.00 an hour on Job B, he will then put forth extra effort and ingenuity to make it $1.25. When, however, he finds that he can earn only 95 cents an hour on Job A, he rejects that amount and drops to a level of effort that earns only 50 cents an hour and relies on his 85-cent base-pay rate for "take home." Job B has therefore become the "gravy" job, and Job A the "stinker." Into the "stinker" bin goes A, along with 90-cent jobs, 85-cent jobs, and 60-cent jobs.

In other words, if the worker discovers that he can produce enough pieces to exceed his base rate pay without much effort, he puts on extra effort so that the job really pays him a satisfactory bonus. But if normal effort yields an amount close to his base pay, then trying to earn any more is either impossible or not worth the effort. He then drops back to a very low level of effort, content to draw his base pay per hour for the job.

Both procedures involve restriction of output. In the case of "gravy jobs," the worker pushes the rate of speed up but he still stops short of what he might produce by all-out effort. The truth of the latter statement is attested to by the records of rate-busters who manage to produce at a much higher rate and by the statements of operators themselves. The type of restriction in connection with "gravy jobs," Roy calls "quota restriction." The other type, used with "stinkers," he calls "goldbricking." When workers are paid a straight base pay with no incentive arrangements, as is true of maintenance workers and all workers in some factories, then "goldbricking" is the only type of restriction present. "Quota restriction" was, however, the first type to become the object of serious research (38, Ch. XVIII) and has received the most attention since.

It is impossible to understand restriction unless one recognizes that it is not a phenomenon characteristic of the worker but rather of the work *group*. If the lone individual were to attempt to restrict, he would simply be fired. Restriction of output is an expression of *common understandings* among the members of a work group.

Such common understandings require participation not only of the work group itself but of persons serving it: inspectors, tool crib personnel, time checkers, stockmen and setup men, etc. Roy calls this cooperation as "the fix," thereby drawing what is more than an analogy between such collusion and the practices of professional criminals in the larger community.

Restriction is, to begin with, an illegal activity from management's point of view, which states that for a day's pay a worker should give a fair day's work. But from Roy's descriptions (40, pp. 263–64) we get a picture of a vast (perhaps horrifying) network of illegal collusions to make an illegal system pay the worker money dividends. It all requires a great deal of trouble as well. An obvious way out, of course, is for the worker to stop restricting and go all out and produce as much as he can, relying on bonus earnings to keep his pay up. This, of course, is what management would like. Yet workers continue to restrict under even very strong pressures of the most punitive sort. To many members of management (and outsiders) restriction is a senseless activity. For why will men deliberately hurt themselves in an economic sense, when by merely working harder they could earn a great deal more money? Further, a perennial restrictor is not likely to be looked upon favorably by management and therefore will probably not be chosen when a promotion up the line becomes vacant. Finally, the practice itself together with the "fix" is contrary to management rules and subjects the worker to the risk of immediate discharge. Why, then, do workers do it? There appear to be a number of important reasons.

A CONTROL ON MANAGEMENT

In the factory, management is in formal control and the worker is there at management's sufferance. All of his work behavior is subject to direction and he may be discharged (allowing for union controls) at any time. But by restriction the worker gains some measure of control or sets limits on management's control.

Restriction may be used deliberately to force management to accede to some worker demand. As such it may be little different in effect from the slowdown, a device old in union history. Murray and Cooke (34, p. 63) claim that the slowdown is no longer an important tactic of organized labor, but it does persist in isolated cases.

Quite apart from its use as labor union tactic, the slowdown (goldbricking) may be used by a work group on piecework to try to force management to raise the piecework rate. Here the thought is that producing at a slow pace and making no bonus may convince management that the rate was set too low and should be raised.

Restriction of output may also be used as a device for expressing aggression against management. Such aggression is usually directed against foremen, but may also be directed in fantasy against time-study men (42).

FEAR OF A CHANGE IN THE FORMAL RULES

This is the reason that is given most commonly by the worker himself when he is asked why he restricts. He will say that if he produces at a higher rate or at top speed, then he will be expected to do it all the time. In the case of piecework, he says that if he continues to earn considerably beyond his "bogey," then a change will be made in piecework rates so that he will be earning no more than before. One group of investigators reports the following comment from industrial workers:

One man said, "Pay it by the hour or pay it by the job, that little man in the straw hat won't pay you any more than he has to." Another operator remarked, "Sure they won't cut the rate on this job, but what's to prevent them changing the casting a little and giving it another number. Then it's a different job and they'll set a lower rate on it. Piece work is like leading a goat around by a carrot. You give the goat a nibble, but you never let him have a real bite."

Nor is the worker's fear that rates will be cut entirely irrational. Kennedy (27, pp. 111–12), for example, cites the following case:

An experience of the workers in a men's shoe plant may be cited as a typical illustration of what may happen in this type of industry if workers are not on guard. The men in this shop could make approximately 125 pairs of shoes a day without over-exertion, and piece rates were set at this level. When small additional orders came in the employer would point out that the increased work did not justify the employment of additional workmen, but that the regular force could do it by increasing work-effort slightly. In this way the work load was gradually increased as new orders came in. Each worker worked harder but was being paid by the piece so felt rewarded for the effort. Suddenly the employer came to the union with proof that the earnings were out of line with the workers' "day rate" or supposed average earnings for the respective crafts. If the union refused to sanction a rate cut, the employer went to arbitration and usually won his case. In the end the workers' earnings were the same as they were prior to the increase in work load.

Even when no such occurrence has ever taken place in the plant, the fear remains. Furthermore, the worker knows that, except under very special circumstances, the market will only take so much of the plant's products. If the worker works faster, inventories are filled sooner and management may be forced, if not to lower rates, then to lay off workers.

THE PROVISION OF LEISURE TIME

One of the reasons that workers restrict, especially in the case of gold-bricking, is that they are enabled to perform what is considered a satisfactory day's work and then are free for talking, reading, coffee, or "government work." [6] Restriction, therefore, provides even the lowliest worker with some opportunity to enjoy the advantage of freedom which the members of occupations of high prestige enjoy. Roy (41, p. 432) describes the extent of such free time:

One evening Ed Sokolsky, onetime second-shift operator on Jack Starkey's drill, commented on a job that Jack was running:

"That's gravy! I worked on those, and I could turn out nine an hour. I timed myself at six minutes."

I was surprised.

"At 35 cents apiece, that's over $3.00 an hour!"

"And I got ten hours," said Ed. "I used to make out in four hours and fool around the rest of the night."

If Sokolsky reported accurately, he was "wasting" six hours per day.

Ed claimed that he could make over $3.00 an hour on the two machines he was running, but he could turn in only $1.40 an hour or, occasionally, $1.45 or $1.50 for the two machines together. Ed said that he always makes out for ten hours by eleven o'clock, that he has nothing to do from 11:00 to 3:00, and has even left early, getting someone to punch his timecard for him.

"That's the advantage of working nights," said Ed. "You can make out in a hurry and sit around, and nobody says anything. But you can't get away with it on day shift with all the big shots around. Jack has to take it easy on these housings to make them last eight hours, and that must be tough."

"Old Pete," another "Old-timer," confided in me:

"Another time when they timed me on some connecting rods, I could have made $20.00 a day, easy. I had to run them at the lowest speed on the machine

---

[6] Sometimes also called "home work" and used to refer to doing personal jobs, such as repairing the leg on the dining-room table, mending home tools, making toys for one's children, and so on.

to keep from making too much. I had a lot of trouble once when I was being
timed, and they gave me $35.00 a hundred. Later they cut it to $19.50 a hundred, and I still made $9.50 a day."

If Old Pete could have made $20.00 a day, he was "wasting" four hours a
day.

The significance of such free time must be appreciated in more than
utilitarian terms. It will be recalled that previously we referred to degree
of freedom permitted as one of the elements contributing to the prestige
level of an occupation. Besides that factor, the emphasis on freedom in
our culture general speaking provides a strong impetus for the worker
to make his job yield as much of it as possible.

Roy (42, pp. 511–12) points out that the free time gained provided for
another type of freedom, a reduction of pressure from supervisors:

. . . making out meant a reduction in the rate of interaction with supervisors.
When an operator achieved his quota, or showed signs that he was in the process
of doing so, he was left alone. Pressures from foremen and superintendents were
applied only when performance fell short of day rate.

CONTROLLING COMPETITION

By controlling competition, restriction takes on added social significance. By restricting, the worker avoids being unfavorably compared
to others. It means that the worker can relax and avoid continuing
pressure and the fear of being "shown up" by fellow-workers. It is for
this reason that restriction is always an *agreed* matter. This is not to
say that workers assemble in secret and set an upper limit. There is some
flexibility and the new worker learns informally what the agreed rate is.
Often it has been understood for years in the work group.

Not only is competition in the strictly economic sense controlled by
restriction, but status competition as well. When a rate-buster arrives,
he upsets status relations as much as economic relations. The nature of
this process is illustrated by a case supplied by Whyte (59, pp. 213–15):

The department manufactures fine glassware. The men work in teams of
from six to eight. This is a hand operation taking a high degree of skill and also
requiring close cooperation among team members. The appointed leader of
each team and the highest skilled man is known as the "gaffer." At the time we
began our study, Paul DeSantis was recognized as the top prestige gaffer of the
twelve who worked on two shifts in this department. He was a man in his mid-
fifties with more than thirty years' experience in the trade. He received the
most difficult job assignments from management because he was recognized as
the most skillful and versatile gaffer. However, he was also a rather slow worker.
This presented no problem as long as DeSantis was working on pieces which

no other work team produced. However, as management introduced new pieces into production, some of the pieces that had been done by DeSantis' team exclusively were now assigned to the work teams of Jack Carter and Ralph Orlandella, two much younger men who had only recently attained the position of gaffer. These men had risen rapidly to the top in a period when production was expanding, so that the number of teams was doubled at a time when the old-time craftsmen were retiring or dying off. The old men in the department considered Carter and Orlandella as upstarts who were not really qualified glassworkers. The young men in the department, on the other hand, were encouraged to find men like themselves moving up and tended to gather around the young gaffers.

At first Carter and Orlandella had difficulty in doing the pieces that had been assigned to them from DeSantis' team, but in time they mastered the technical problem and developed the necessary skill and coordination of their team members. When they had mastered the jobs, they built up production to the level that had been attained by DeSantis and then began to move above his previous records. This was a conscious bid by the young gaffers for management approval (and possible pay increases) and for prestige among fellow workers. The young gaffers pointed out to their friends that they were showing that they could produce just as good pieces as DeSantis had turned out and more of them. DeSantis and other old-timers reacted against this challenge. Some of the old men refused to give technical advice that the inexperienced men badly needed, or gave misleading advice. The old-timers could not fail to acknowledge that the young men were getting good production but they deprecated this record by saying that the quality was poor and would never have been accepted when management in the old days had higher standards. Furthermore, DeSantis tried through intermediaries to get the young men to slow down. The argument they were to present was "Why do you want to kill the job? Seven an hour is a fair day's work."

Why this pressure to keep down production? DeSantis and his friends were talking just as do incentive workers when they warn their fellows that management will cut the rate if they produce too much. But there was no threat of rate cutting because there were no incentive rates. The rising production of the young men, furthermore, presented no possible economic threat to DeSantis because he was at the top of the rate range for the position of gaffer. He could go no higher except through general increases negotiated between union and management. On the other hand, long-standing company policy and the union contract protected him against wage cuts or layoffs, for his seniority was among the highest in the department.

He was saying in effect to the other men: if you work faster, management will expect everybody to work faster. There may, indeed, be some physical substance to this argument quite apart from the money to be gained or lost. There are important satisfactions in maintaining a customary work pace. However, the strong feelings manifested on both sides in this situation can hardly be attributed to questions of work pace and fatigue. The rise of the young men presented a threat to the status of DeSantis. He had held the unquestioned top prestige position. He was recognized as the most skilled and most versatile man. It was he to whom people turned for advice and it was he whom people watched when he had a particularly interesting job and they could take a moment from their work.

Now Carter and Orlandella were narrowing the gap in skill between themselves and DeSantis. They equaled DeSantis or even surpassed him in speed of production on certain pieces. Their status in the department rose. Especially the younger men gathered around them and followed their progress with interest. Thus we see that even in a department where skill is on a handicraft basis the speed of production can have an important effect upon the status of workers.

AVOIDANCE OF THE SANCTIONS HEAPED UPON THE NONCONFORMIST

From the point of view of restrictors, the nonconformist is the rate-buster. Usually rate-busters are individualists who defend their behavior in economic terms, asking only to be left alone. Dalton, who made a careful study of a group of rate-busters, quotes two of them as follows (10, pp. 7, 8):

If dey let me make de bonus, I can do 400 per cent. I can beat any man in de shops. I can turn out more and better work dan anybody! Dese guys in here try to stop me, but dey don't bodder me! But I don't want to kill a good ting. De company has to have its profits you know, and if I get too much dey cut me down.

The youngest of the rate busters spoke of his plans:

I'm going to retire at fifty. I've really made the bucks since they put in this incentive. It's the best thing that ever happened in here. They may take it out one of these times. If they do while I'm working, I'll sure stop putting out. They're going to be laying off men one of these times, so I'm getting mine while the getting's good.

Rate-busters are felt to be ignoring the needs of the total group and to be defying it. As a consequence, they are practically always the object of profoundly bitter feelings. Group disapproval is expressed in various ways. The rate-buster finds that fellow-workers will not check his work and will permit it to go through to be rejected by the inspector. They will not share work with him in emergencies. They are also likely to keep secret information from him, such as knowledge of which are the "tight" jobs, and secret labor-saving devices which workers have invented. Kennedy states (27, p. 118):

In many instances groups of workers have found it effective simply to refuse to work with an individual whom they charged with "spoiling the job." Discrimination in the distribution of hard and easy work is another of the ways in which a group can bring pressure to bear on one of its members.

Three girls in a glass plant who had had to pay about $40 in back dues when the closed shop came in were resentful and thought to embarrass the union by producing well over the limit observed in the plant. A union official was able to secure the cooperation of the foreman in handling this case in the interests of maintaining unity of action and discipline within the union. The foreman began feeding the most difficult work to these three girls until they came into line.

In some cases the union imposes penalties for serious infractions, in the form of a brief suspension from work or a money fine. An interesting arrangement is the "kitty" system encountered in a few cases. A limit on production or earnings by the hour or by the day is agreed upon and workers forfeit any amount earned over the limit into a common fund or kitty. This fund is expended periodically for a group function or celebration. That less formal and more direct methods of enforcement are sometimes used is indicated by the statement of a committeeman at one plant that if a worker persisted in exceeding the limit established some of the boys would "take him out in the alley and beat hell out of him."

Of course group ostracism is itself a powerful control device (8, p. 9):

Ed: That guy (pointing to a machine) is the greatest rate buster in the shop. Give him a job he can make a nickel on and he'll bust his ass for the company.

Mike: That's no lie. He's ruined every job on that machine. They've cut him down to the point where he has to do twice the work for half the pay. A few more like him would ruin this shop. . . .

Ed: It's guys like that that spoil the shop for the rest of us. Somebody ought to take a piece of babbit and pound some sense into his thick skull. That's the only kind of treatment a guy like that understands.

Mike: We're handling him the best way as it is. The only way to handle those bastards is not to have a thing to do with them. That guy hasn't got a friend in the place and he knows it. You can bet your life he thinks about that every time he comes to work.

While the force of group disapproval is directed outward on deviants, it is also true that the force of group approval is directed inward on fellow-restrictors. Roy (42) found that earnings were a continual topic of conversation and were reported like ball-scores. If a man made out on a tough job, he reported it with pride. If a man failed to make out on an easy job, he was scorned and usually tried to offer an explanation. We observe again that restriction is not just a matter of slowing down but rather of producing at an agreed rate.

Finally, an indirect effect of sanctions against nonconformists is that the rate-buster, because of the strong feelings against him and group rejection, is likely to get a reputation for not being able to get along with people. This in turn may make management regard him as a poor risk for promotion to a supervisory position. Yet, ironically, he is the one man in the shop who is going out whole-heartedly to pursue management goals.

GIVING MEANING TO WORK

We have commented repeatedly on the dullness and routinized features of much of factory work. Mechanization and the fineness of the division of labor tend to break work up into meaningless segments involving repetitive, endless movements. Yet our description of restriction of output thus far gives a picture of work which is meaningful in the extreme. We have a "fix" by which "stinkers" are converted into "gravy jobs," we have the workers controlling and manipulating their masters, maintaining a police system against deviants and providing for themselves bountiful amounts of leisure for "government work" or for just plain loafing. Here are values indeed which make an otherwise dull job into an adventure. And more. The job becomes something of a game, with wins, losses, and scores. A worker trying to make out on a stinker is pitting his skills and ingenuity against the skills and ingenuity of time-study men and all other management minions.

An indirect, but very important by-product of making work into a meaningful activity is a reduction in fatigue. It is a fact of common experience that meaningful, challenging activity tires one out much less than dull, purposeless activity. Roy describes this effect as follows (42, p. 510):

Several months later, however, after fellow operator McCann had instructed him in the "angles on making out," the writer was finding values in the piece-work system other than economic ones. He struggled to attain quota "for the hell of it," because it was a "little game" and "keeps me from being bored." He felt that he was the only one motivated by such considerations, thinking that the other operators were being induced to work for higher pay in the manner of the horse led to pull the wagon by a carrot hanging in front of his nose.

In addition to escaping the monotony of factory labor by "playing a game," the writer found that there were physiological advantages in speeding up. He found that fast rhythmical work seemed less fatiguing, although the reduction of fatigue may have been related to the reduction of boredom. He discovered further that the same job that had bored and wearied him as a "time study," or non-piecework operation, now interested him and gave him exhilaration on piecework.

The writer made occasional diary comments on such values of piecework for the remainder of his stay in the shop. Recorded comparisons between piecework and day work experience keep telling the same story.

Dooley watched me set up for the frames, and remarked, "You can make out on that if you want to break your neck."

This "breaking my neck" was a welcome relief to the monotony of time study on the replacers. I was so sleepy I could hardly keep awake before I started on the frames, but at eleven o'clock I felt bright and wide awake. This set me to thinking in a new light about the value of the piecework system.

My legs were very tired tonight. Slow jobs like this one seem to wear me out far more than the fast ones. I mentioned this to Johnny.

He said, "That's the way with me. I've got to keep my mind occupied or I get bored, and it wears me out. I can't stand around either."

When I am going hell bent for election on a good piecework job, the evening passes very swiftly and I do not realize that I am tired until it is all over. On these day work jobs I get so bored I could stand in the aisle and yell; and my knees feel tired from standing in one spot so long.

It is interesting to note that Roy found that work lost its meaningful-game components under two conditions: when chance played too large a part, in the case, for example, where there was unpredictable tool breakage, and when the operator completely mastered the task so that he always won. In the former case, the work became frustrating whereas in the latter, it became too easy and therefore routinized.

THE WORK GROUP'S SOCIAL ETHIC

Management tends to assume that the worker is strongly oriented toward the same sort of goals that management itself is. These are, for the most part, money and success. The worker himself, however, is not likely to feel this way at all. That is, he is not a compulsive neurotic who brings with him an urge to "try, try, try" under any and all conditions. Instead, he *will* try *if the effort will yield meaningful rewards*. Therefore, if a worker is given a "stinker," he will at first try to see if it will yield a bonus. But if his best efforts fail, he would certainly be a fool if he kept producing at top speed and still made only his base pay. Instead, at some point, he gives up trying.

If the worker cannot make a bonus that makes the effort worthwhile, then even though the job carries an incentive the worker does not regard it nor treat it as an incentive job. It becomes the same as day work yielding a guaranteed hourly wage.

But what about the other rewards—the possibility of a merit raise or a promotion? Here again, the worker will strive for such goals *if* he has a decent chance of achieving them. But the range of wages on semiskilled factory jobs is extremely narrow, and a worker typically reaches the maximum a few months after initial employment. Very great effort might then produce merely a few pennies more per hour, and be hardly worth the struggle.

We have dealt with promotions in detail above. The worker's level of aspiration and the very great scarcity of actual promotions means that the average worker practically rules out promotion as an achievable goal. Collins, Dalton, and Roy state the matter well as follows (8, p. 14):

This feeling among machine operators that the paths of upward mobility are closed is strong. One operator said, "Sure, I'm a high school grad, but where does that get me. I didn't know there was such a thing as a college prep course until after I graduated. I went to ——— Tech and over there nobody was going to teach me anything to set me up in competition with the boss's son. All those guys want you to learn is how to read a blueprint and you can learn enough of that to do this work in six months. It's different with you, Slim. You got off to a good start and I wish you well for it, but if you'd come up through the depression in a trade school the way I did you'd be in the same boat I am. You make the most of it, Slim, and some day you'll be a boss. Then you can walk through here and say, "Hi there, Jack," and walk along thinking "Old Jack there never got very far," and I'll say, "Good morning, Mr. ———," and after you're gone I'll say, "I knew that so-and-so when he was a white man."

To the extent that such feelings are present—and they are widespread— the worker will be profoundly unresponsive to appeals based on promotion promises.

This leads to an important conclusion: there is an inverse relationship between upward mobility and restriction of output. It follows that one way to reduce restriction is to increase the number of promotions or the available lines of upward mobility. But of course this approach has serious limitations. There are, after all, only a limited number of available promotions; experience suggests they are normally very few indeed. Further, there is an increasing tendency to hire persons for higher positions from outside the factory—persons with appropriate educational and training backgrounds. If anything, then, the chances may be decreasing. Yet it would still be worth-while for management to give workers every chance to try for available opportunities for which they are qualified. If education is required, then that fact should be made perfectly clear to the worker and encouragement provided for the worker to get such education through night classes or by going on leave. If such a course of action is pursued, it is hardly necessary to add that management must be perfectly sincere and consistent. There will be only a few workers who will try to make the necessary effort. But if their efforts are not rewarded, if management passes over them in favor of outsiders, they will cease trying, and, more important, other workers will point to these cases as providing dramatic evidence of the fruitlessness of upward mobility as a goal.

MOTIVATION

Our discussion raises the whole question of motivation in the work situation. Restriction is in fact usually conceived of as a motivation problem. Management asks: How can we stop this practice? How can we get individuals to be motivated in the direction in which we want them to be motivated? A large part of the difficulty in providing a satisfactory answer has to do with basic misunderstandings of the nature of work motivation.

Motivation is usually regarded as a "problem." The individual is given a task or set of requirements or a goal, such as a certain desired rate of production in a factory, a minimum grade-point-average in school, or, perhaps, for the six-year-old boy, table manners. The question is then asked: How can one get the individual to exhibit maximum output toward the achievement of that goal?

This approach involves two assumptions: (1) Motivation is an individual phenomenon. The object of attention is the individual and consequently the study is a legitimate and proper one for the psychologist; it is one to which he has given much attention.[7] The role of the sociologist is obscure. (2) It involves an assumption that the individual is not motivated, and if left to himself, will not do anything, or will not perform as hoped for. This assumption follows from the point of view that motivation is a problem, like crime or divorce. With reference to the latter, in sociology, we then ask: How can one stop people from committing crimes? How can one keep men from being unfaithful to their wives? Underlying such questions in sociology is a Hobbesian conception of human nature—if nothing is done to stop them, men *will* go out and commit crimes or find paramours.

A significant part of motivation research operates on the above-stated assumptions. People are naturally lazy or lethargic or plain ornery and if let alone, will do as little as they can get away with. Therefore, the appropriate action is to offer an *incentive*—piece work, a bonus, a reward. The model is the donkey and the carrot. If incentives fail, one may then use threats or punishment—one may shout at the donkey or beat him. If that fails, one may shoot him—in industry, fire the man—and get a more spirited donkey.

But if we look closely, there is something seriously wrong with both assumptions. For we observe that men who exert a minimum of energy on their jobs will display enormous energy in the pursuit of a hobby

[7] It is hardly necessary to document this statement. For a provocative survey of the current status of motivation research in psychology, see (28).

(or, sometimes, of a woman). The research on restriction of output which we have discussed is highly revealing in this context. Two conclusions stand out: (1) Restriction is a group phenomenon. The men produce at an informally *agreed* rate, which is high enough to return them a fair wage, but far below their capabilities. The work group, rather than management, determines the standard. Further, the group enforces the standard on its members with appropriate sanctions for the deviant. Under these conditions, any prospective rewards that management offers to the individual are not responded to. (2) Restriction is not an expression of any desire to do little work. The person who produces too much— the rate-buster—is punished. But so is the slacker—the person who produces too little. If the work group is on group piecework, the slacker pulls the pay of the whole group down. In any case, he is a "free-loader" —he enjoys the benefits of group protection without himself contributing sufficiently.

Instead of the assumptions discussed above, research argues loudly for the following:

WORK IS A SOCIAL ACTIVITY

This point has been discussed freely in previous chapters. Most work that is done is done in concert, and there is almost always a division of labor, varying from a simple sexual division of labor, as found in some pre-literate societies, all the way to modern Western society, for which, in the United States, the Census of Occupations and Industries lists over 20,000 different specialties. A division of labor, by definition, implies a social organization of work. Persons may and do work alone briefly, but such cases are usually highly exceptional or temporary, and often the person only apparently works alone.

This means that any scheme of motivation for the work situation must focus itself on the group. If the scheme appeals to the lone individual, it is simply unrealistic or inapplicable, although many, perhaps most, incentive plans do operate in this manner. The individual is told: *"You* work harder and *you* will get more." As pointed out above, this appeal ignores the fact that work is a cooperative and often requires that the individual forego his own possible immediate gain or interest in favor of a fellow-worker in difficulty, either because that fellow is new, or anxious, or is a member of a group with whom he has an understanding.

The second assumption is that human beings are *normally active,* and that they are engaged in a continuing process of relating themselves to the world, of imposing meaning on it, and of attempting to control it in the light of their needs.[8] If this assumption is granted, then the prob-

_____

[8] This is the Symbolic Interactionist approach described for example in (9, 14, 31).

lem is not one of motivating people—they *are* motivated, at least in certain directions. Certainly the quotations provided above do not give us a picture of workers lying about and staring idly at the ceiling. These workers were enormously active and energetic, using all their intelligence and ingenuity, though not in the pursuit of management goals. The problem thus becomes one of *redirecting* these energies so that they become focused on goals more consistent with those of management. It is at once evident that this is a much easier, more manageable task than is that of *creating* motivation. The latter implies increasing the energy output; redirection assumes the energy is there and attempts to control it. And since work is a group activity, the problem becomes one ultimately of social control. That is, management's problem is to enlist the resources of the work group in order to redirect its energies.

Much of the difficulty in implementing incentive systems in the factory may be traced to the ignoring of these assumptions. The most common incentive system is directed at the individual and involves the use of money rewards. In line with business logics, it is felt that the worker is there as an isolated individual to make money to satisfy his needs outside the factory—needs centering about family, housing, automobiles, recreation. Also, since the worker must *be* motivated by management, the work is not in itself satisfying to the worker. The only thing giving his work meaning is the *money* it yields. Obviously, then, if you give the worker a chance to make more money, he can satisfy his non-work needs better and should respond.[9]

But, in order to work as a calculable motivating influence, incentives require a continual variation of rewards which may be wholly at variance with the industry's needs. For example, in seasonal industries, if a big effort is required in the spring, and if this happens to be the time when the worker desires money, say, for his forthcoming vacation, then one has a lucky coincidence. But if the rush season happens to be in the fall, after the vacation, then the worker would presumably be less motivated. It would be manifestly impossible to run a factory in any predictable manner on such a basis. Further, individuals differ from each other in their needs and therefore their desire to translate work into money at a given time. For example, two men may form a work team in a riveting crew. One holds the rivet in place with a jig, the other rivets it. But

[9] This approach has been examined most carefully at the theoretical level by Max Weber, who conceived of it as one of the major types of social action and which he called *Zweckrational*—the use of the expectations of others as a means for the pursuit of one's own rational goals. This he contrasted with *Wertrational* action—the pursuit of a goal for its own sake, irrespective of success or failure. Both types are rational and are in turn contrasted with affectual and traditional action. See (17, pp. 196–264; 35, pp. 640–49; 23, pp. 324–423).

one man's wife is in the hospital and he wants money and for the moment may be highly motivated to increase production, but the other has no pressing needs at the moment. If differential effort is rewarded, the result is likely to be conflict between the two men, since the nature of the job requires that the two men work at the same rate of speed.

Further, such a system places a premium on motivation which is intrinsically *unrelated* to the specific work that the man does. It hopes to get the worker to work harder, or faster, or more accurately by asking him to pay attention to something *other* than the work itself. One asks the sewing machine operator to sew more raincoat pockets because he wishes more money to make the down payment on a new car, perhaps. Now, there is no intrinsic relation between raincoat pockets and automobiles, and if such a scheme is to work, the worker must be continually jogged with a reminder of the purpose of his work—money for the car. But to work faster or do better work, he must pay attention to the *job at hand* —raincoat pockets—and not automobiles. Yet the more one emphasizes the externally related reward aspect of the work, the more meaningless the work itself becomes. Such an attitude was expressed to me by a worker in an aircraft plant:

> You take this doohickus here—I don't know what they call it. My job is to drill three holes in a triangle shape. All I do is set my pattern on the plate and drill the holes. They tell me it fits somewhere in the wing section. Morgan, the shop foreman, was giving me some bull about how the airplane would fall apart without my three holes. Well ain't that great! Look, all I want is my $1.40 per. If three holes in a triangle will do it, that's fine. If they want 'em in a straight line, just give me the pattern and I'll do it, just so long as I draw my $1.40.

Such a man manifests almost no interest in his work. He is unaware of its relation to the work of others or its importance and does not care. He does only the minimum to get his money and if he makes an error, he will only know about it when the piece is rejected by an inspector. He will then respond by making another one. If he is pressured by loss of pay for rejected pieces, he may work harder, but only to produce a required number and not one more. Moreover he will have to be continually pressured at considerable cost of administrative time. He will be quite unresponsive to appeals in emergency or rush periods. The point is that his work is *meaningless* in itself, and only becomes more so the more emphasis is placed on the reward which lies outside the work itself.[10]

[10] These criticisms do not, of course, imply that extracurricular rewards should or can be ignored. There is certainly a basic minimum required, though what this is is

But we must beware of a false lead here. Many industrial leaders, recognizing these problems, have tried to infuse meaning into work by indirect devices or propaganda. A common procedure is exposure of workers to "educational" programs describing the company's many products and emphasizing its service to the community. In large factories, tours for employees may be arranged so that workers may learn how their work fits into the whole. Company picnics, visits to the assembly-line by the president or other top executives will, it is hoped, give the worker a feeling that his work is important. An idea heard frequently is the importance of "giving the worker a sense of participation." The trouble there is that a "sense" is not enough. It usually fools no one in any case, since such a "sense" usually means very little participation or participation in minor or unimportant matters. When unions or workers take management at its word and ask for real participation in important matters, management is likely to back away sharply and begin talking about "managerial prerogatives."

Meaning cannot be imposed from above or outside. At the same time, it is equally a mistake to remove what little meaning there is in work by *forcing* the worker's attention away from his work by overemphasis on money related to goals outside his work. By contrast, we may recall Roy's discussion of how workers themselves gave their work *real* meaning by making piecework itself into a challenge and game, and how *they* determined production standards. Here is real participation. They do not merely consult in an advisory capacity with management on what "normal" productivity ought to be. They go ahead and decide this issue for themselves.

Before considering what management may do to improve the motivation situation, it is necessary to look further into the problems created by incentive systems which ignore the social nature of work and the active orientation of the worker.

RATE-SETTING PROBLEMS

The theory or individual incentives rests on the assumption that objective job standards can be determined. A "normal" productivity rate must be calculated so that it can be determined at what level the worker begins to be entitled to bonus earnings. Perhaps in a Huxleyan or Orwellian world, this standard might be determined by an analysis of

---

hard to determine. Yet the United Automobile Workers have found it profitable to recognize it in their escalator clause, and Barkin (2) seems to feel that a certain minimum attempt to keep workers "happy" or satisfied is also necessary. The criticism is of those who apparently feel that money and fringe benefits should *alone* solve the motivation problem.

the job alone, but in the world as we know it now, we must have recourse to the actual performance of human beings at work. We have seen how workers try to outwit the time-study man who sets rates. Time-study men are therefore forced to regard worker performance as no more than a very rough guide. If when he observes the worker, the time-study man finds that the worker produces ten pieces in a half an hour, he will try to get him to speed up. The time-study man may increase the speed of the worker's machine. Through such urgings, production may go up to twelve pieces in a half an hour. The time-study man tries to guess whether the worker is still restricting or not. Finally, he may decide that the worker *probably* is and guess that he is holding back about 25 per cent. Consequently, he sets the "normal" figure for the job at fifteen pieces to the half hour. If the worker was not restricting that much, the job has become a "tight" one, a stinker. If he was restricting more than that, it has become a "fat" job, yielding "gravy." Obviously, the process of rate-setting is highly subjective, resting on judgment and the success of the rate-setter in outguessing the worker. Any claim that rate-setting is "scientific" and should therefore be placed outside the area of disagreement between management and unions is untenable, at least at the present state of development of rate-setting techniques. The attempts to make rate-setting more objective by taking movies of work-movements and the compiling of "standard data" have not been particularly successful (1). Whyte (59, pp. 203–04) points out that such attempts have been marked by disagreement among the experts and by the fact that they ignore the sequential character of work-movements. At the same time, to the extent that such attempts do try to take into account this sequential character, to that extent they are back to observing actual workers at work.

More important, perhaps, than these technical considerations is the fact that the social control of rate-setters is usually vague. They seem to belong nowhere. They are staff people who spend a great deal of their time in the shop. To the worker, they are foreign elements who do not understand their problems.

CONFLICT BETWEEN INCENTIVE AND JOB EVALUATION SYSTEMS

All factories have some sort of job evaluation system. That is, an attempt is made to arrange jobs in a hierarchy according to criteria such as degree of training needed, degree of experience, amount of skill, and so on. In many places, this job evaluation is informal, having grown up gradually over the years, and is simply understood by the employees. In other places, especially large ones, it is formalized, based on careful studies, and may even be published on a bulletin board for all to see.

Such a job evaluation system has the effect of creating a status system and, as usual, it is felt that wages should reflect this status system. The higher the job in the system, the more money it should pay.

Such job evaluation systems create serious problems in themselves because they, like incentive systems, focus on the individual. Sayles (44) points out that they are often resisted by workers because the values on which they are based may be different from worker values. A particular job may be rated low in the job evaluation system; but the worker may rate it high because it allows bonus earnings or overtime. Often, too, a job evaluation system, when first instituted, upsets seniority and promotion expectations. A worker may have been planning for and preparing himself for a job which is rated high only to discover that the job evaluation system places it lower (and therefore it pays less money). Sometimes, too, a job rated low by management but high by the worker (because of incentive pay) may lead to workers wanting to "demote" themselves, which may be forbidden by management or often by the union.

But quite apart from problems intrinsic to the job evaluation system as such, Whyte (55, pp. 78–79) points out that there is a basic conflict between the job evaluation system and the incentive system. A job evaluation system orders jobs in a hierarchy. But if an incentive system is also introduced, a worker lower down in the hierarchy (and earning a lower base pay) may be able to earn more money than a man higher up. This is especially likely if the job lower down happens to be a "gravy job" and the one higher up happens to be a "stinker." The most serious conflict occurs between piecework and day workers. Usually, the former are production workers, whereas the latter are often maintenance and toolroom people. The pay of the latter is fixed, whereas the pay of the former can rise through incentive earnings. Yet maintenance and toolroom activities often involve a good deal more skill and experience than most production jobs. The result may be deep feelings of bitterness toward management as well as antagonism and tension between the two groups. The point here is that job evaluation implies a certain fixity or stability of relations between jobs, whereas an incentive system is deliberately calculated to encourage special effort and consequent interpersonal and intergroup variation.

INTERGROUP CONFLICTS

Incentive systems based on individual output by their very nature encourage intra-plant variations in income. Consequently, one common effect is severe conflicts between departments where incentive earnings make it possible for one department to earn considerably more than another department. Sayles, who has studied this phenomenon, cautions as follows (43, p. 490):

In developing incentive proposals for a particular job, . . . the entire plant must be considered a social unit.

He provides the following illustrative case. In an attempt to increase productivity in a department to meet a government contract, management put in an incentive system permitting earnings in this department above other departments. The effect was (43, p. 488):

Long service employees were bristling that young men who had been in the plant for less than a year were earning substantially more than they. One worker, a former union officer, summed up their sentiments:
> "Can you imagine how I feel walking into a bar and getting my check cashed next to some youngster who has only been in the plant a few months? He maybe gets thirty dollars more than I do and I've been around here for 15 years."

Throughout the plant there were demands that all incentive rates be renegotiated.

Even in the rare case where incentive earnings in different departments are "in line," there remains the problem of the relation between incentive workers and day workers, as we implied in our discussion above. But it is not just a matter of invidious comparisons. For day workers, such as maintenance or tool workers, are not separated from production workers. There is usually trouble between production workers and day workers who immediately precede or follow them in the manufacturing process. If incentive workers speed up, then a shop that follows them is also forced to speed up even though they get no more pay. If the day workers precede them, then the incentive workers put pressure on them to hurry so that they are supplied with enough parts to maintain high output. When production speeds up, maintenance and tool work in general must speed up also. Resistance, slowdowns, complaints, and severe conflict are the inevitable results. Such intergroup splits may become so serious as practically to wipe out the advantages of the incentive system itself.[11] George Strauss provides a striking case of such conflict: [12]

[11] Sayles' general point on intergroup conflict was recognized by V. D. Kennedy who wrote in 1945 (27, p. 113):
> "Union leaders also consider limitation an effective means of avoiding much of the friction that is caused between individuals, groups, or shifts by differences in earning rates and distribution of work under incentive payment plans."

[12] This case was written especially for Whyte (59, Ch. 10, pp. 90–96). A footnote to

This is the story of an experiment that failed because it succeeded too well.

The Hovey and Beard Company manufactured wooden toys of various kinds: wooden animals, pull toys, and the like. One part of the manufacturing process involved spraying paint on the partially assembled toys and hanging them on moving hooks which carried them through a drying oven. This operation, staffed entirely by girls, was plagued by absenteeism, turnover, and low morale.

A consultant, working with the foreman in charge, "solved" the problem. But the changes that were made in order to solve it had such repercussions in other parts of the plant that the company abandoned the new procedures, despite their obvious benefits to production in that local area.

THE PROBLEM

Let us look briefly at the painting operation in which the problem occurred.

The toys were cut, sanded, and partially assembled in the wood room. Then they were dipped into shellac, following which they were painted. The toys were predominantly two-colored; a few were made in more than two colors. Each color required an additional trip through the paint room.

Shortly before the troubles began, the painting operation had been re-engineered so that the eight girls who did the painting sat in a line by an endless chain of hooks. These hooks were in continuous motion, past the line of girls and into a long horizontal oven. Each girl sat at her own painting booth so designed as to carry away fumes and to backstop excess paint. The girl would take a toy from the tray beside her, position it in a jig inside the painting cubicle, spray on the color according to a pattern, then release the toy and hang it on the hook passing by. The rate at which the hooks moved had been calculated by the engineers so that each girl, when fully trained, would be able to hang a painted toy on each hook before it passed beyond her reach.

The girls working in the paint room were on a group bonus plan. Since the operation was new to them, they were receiving a learning bonus which decreased by regular amounts each month. The learning bonus was scheduled to vanish in six months, by which time it was expected that they would be on their own—that is, able to meet the standard and to earn a group bonus when they exceeded it.

By the second month of the training period trouble had developed. The girls learned more slowly than had been anticipated, and it began to look as though their production would stabilize far below what was planned for. Many of the hooks were going by empty. The girls complained that they were going by too fast, and that the time-study man had set the rates wrong. A few girls quit and had to be replaced with new girls, which further aggravated the learning problem. The team spirit that the management had expected to develop automatically through the group bonus was not in evidence except as an expression of what

the chapter states that the chapter was "written by George Strauss, based upon information furnished him by the consultant in the story, Alex Bavelas. The consultant also reviewed and revised the chapter" (p. 90).

the engineers called "resistance." One girl whom the group regarded as its leader (and the management regarded as the ringleader) was outspoken in making the various complaints of the group to the foreman. The complaints had all the variety customary in such instances of generalized frustration: the job was a messy one, the hooks moved too fast, the incentive pay was not being correctly calculated, and anyway it was too hot working so close to the drying oven.

INTRODUCING THE NEW APPROACH

The consultant who was brought into this picture worked entirely with and through the foreman. After many conversations with him, the foreman felt that the first step should be to get the girls together for a general discussion of the working conditions—something, incidentally, which was far from his mind originally and which in his own words would only have been "begging for trouble." He took this step with some hesitation, but he took it on his own volition.

The first meeting, held immediately after the shift was over at four o'clock in the afternoon, was attended by all eight girls. They voiced the same complaints again: the hooks went by too fast, the job was too dirty, the room was hot and poorly ventilated. For some reason it was this last item that they complained of most. The foreman promised to discuss the problem of ventilation and temperature with the engineers, and it seemed that the girls' cynical predictions about what the engineers would say were going to be borne out. They and the superintendent felt that this was really a trumped-up complaint, and that the expense of any effective corrective measure would be prohibitively high. (They were thinking of some form of air conditioning.)

The foreman came to the second meeting with some apprehensions. The girls, however, did not seem to be much put out, perhaps because they had a proposal of their own to make. They felt that if several large fans were set up so as to circulate the air around their feet, they would be much more comfortable. After some discussion the foreman agreed that the idea might be tried out. (Immediately after the meeting, he confided to the consultant that he probably shouldn't have committed himself to this expense on his own initiative; also, he felt that the fans wouldn't help much anyway.) The foreman and the consultant discussed the question of the fans with the superintendent, and three large propeller-type fans were purchased. The decision was reached without much difficulty, since it seemed that the fans could be used elsewhere after their expected failure to provide relief in the paint room.

The fans were brought in. The girls were jubilant. For several days the fans were moved about in various positions until they were placed to the satisfaction of the group. Whatever the actual efficiency of these fans, one thing was clear: the girls were completely satisfied with the results, and relations between them and the foreman improved visibly.

The foreman, after this encouraging episode, decided that further meetings might also be profitable. He asked the girls if they would like to meet and discuss other aspects of the work situation. The girls were eager to do this. The meeting was held, and the discussion quickly centered on the speed of the hooks.

The girls maintained that the time-study men had set them as an unreasonably fast speed and that they would never be able to reach the goal of filling enough of them to make a bonus.

The turning point of the discussion came when the group's leader frankly explained that the point wasn't that they couldn't work fast enough to keep up with the hooks, but that they couldn't work at that pace all day long. The foreman explored the point. The girls were unanimous in their opinion that they could keep up with the belt for short periods if they wanted to. But they didn't want to because if they showed that they could do this for short periods they would be expected to do it all day long. The meeting ended with an unprecedented request: "Let us adjust the speed of the belt faster or slower depending on how we feel." The foreman, understandably startled, agreed to discuss this with the superintendent and the engineers.

The engineers' reaction naturally was that the girls' suggestion was heresy. Only after several meetings was it granted grudgingly that there was in reality some latitude within which variations in the speed of the hooks would not affect the finished product. After considerable argument and many dire prophecies by the engineers, it was agreed to try out the girls' idea.

With great misgivings, the foreman had a control with a dial marked "low, medium, fast" installed at the booth of the group leader; she could now adjust the speed of the belt anywhere between the lower and upper limits that the engineers had set. The girls were delighted, and spent many lunch hours deciding how the speed of the belt should be varied from hour to hour throughout the day.

Within a week the pattern had settled down to one in which the first half hour of the shift was run on what the girls called medium speed (a dial setting slightly above the point marked "medium"). The next two and one-half hours were run at high speed; the half hour before lunch and the half hour after lunch were run at low speed. The rest of the afternoon was run at high speed with the exception of the last forty-five minutes of the shift, which was run at medium.

In view of the girls' reports of satisfaction and ease in their work, it is interesting to note that the constant speed at which the engineers had originally set the belt was slightly below medium on the dial of the control that had been given the girls. The average speed at which the girls were running the belt was on the high side of the dial. Few if any empty hooks entered the oven, and inspection showed no increase of rejects from the paint room.

Production increased, and within three weeks (some two months before the scheduled ending of the learning bonus) the girls were operating at 30 to 50 per cent above the level that had been expected under the original arrangement. Naturally the girls' earnings were correspondingly higher than anticipated. They were collecting their base pay, a considerable piece-rate bonus, and the learning bonus which, it will be remembered, had been set to decrease with time and not as a function of current productivity. (This arrangement, which had been selected by the management in order to prevent being taken advantage of by the girls during the learning period, now became a real embarrassment.)

The girls were earning more now than many skilled workers in other parts of the plant. Management was besieged by demands that this inequity be taken care of. With growing irritation between superintendent and foreman, engineers and foreman, superintendent and engineers, the situation came to a head when the superintendent without consultation arbitrarily revoked the learning bonus and returned the painting operation to its original status: the hooks moved again at their constant, time-studied, designated speed, production dropped again, and within a month all but two of the eight girls had quit. The foreman himself stayed on for several months, but, feeling aggrieved, then left for another job. . . .

. . . The factory is a social system, made up of mutually dependent parts. A drastic change in one part of the system—even a change that is viewed as highly successful within that part—may give rise to conflict reactions from other parts of the system. It may then be dangerous for management to try a new approach in one small part of the system unless it is prepared to extend this approach to the whole organization.

It is obvious, then, that the problems of incentive systems are massive and not easily solved. Many brilliant and well-experienced industrial executives have tried to overcome them by the use of literally hundreds of devices and approaches—some of which give partial or temporary relief, and some of which do not work at all. There are two approaches which seem appealing but which appear to be practically fruitless: trying to make everyone into a rate-buster, and the use of slogans and suggestion boxes.

POSSIBLE SOLUTIONS: 1. EVERYONE A RATE-BUSTER

In some factories, the thought has been that if all workers could *really* make a large individual bonus by extra effort, then perhaps they would do so. Yet everything that we have said above implies that sheer attractiveness of bonus will not produce extra effort. We observed that workers on quota earnings who *could* make much more money still stopped short at an agreed rate. We also discussed the reasons for such restriction.

The dubiousness of this approach shows up most clearly when we look at rate-busters themselves. For not only are they a very small proportion of the work group, they also appear to be socially and individually distinct. Dalton (10), who has made the most intensive study of rate-busters, found it difficult even to get a fairly large number of them for study. Of a total of about 300 skilled machinists, he found only 9 who exceeded the informal production ceiling of 150 per cent, and who could therefore be dubbed rate-busters. In spite of this small number, they do represent what is apparently a 100 per cent sample. Further his discovery that this group is unique in background characteristics makes it well worth-while to look closely at them. For they are the persons whom management apparently regards as prototypes that others ought to model themselves on. Dalton characterizes rate-busters as follows (10, pp. 17–18):

. . . the rate-buster is (1) likely to come from a family of higher socioeconomic level than that of other members of the work group, or, if he does not, he is trying to reach such a level. He is ambitious and his immediate goal is money. Later he may convert his savings into some form of security and/or prestige. For the present he is often content to possess middle class material symbols and to ignore present social experience of enjoyment. Often, too, the rate-buster is of rural origin, having a personality organization well-adapted to individualistic behavior at work. (2) He is much more likely to be a nominal Protestant who rarely if ever goes to church than he is to be a Catholic. (3) Ethnically he will probably be an Anglo-American or an immigrant from one of the countries of Northwestern Europe. (4) Politically the rate-buster will usually be a Republican and will read a conservative newspaper. He dislikes labor unions and regards their function as essentially immoral. He is insensible of the struggle for power between management and labor and of his role in it.

(5) The rate-buster is a "family man." He marries early and does not divorce. His marriage, however, is not of a modern equalitarian type. Instead, he practices the traditional Puritan virtues of a good provider and a home-lover and avoids the Puritan-abhorred vices of drink and gambling.

He prides himself on keeping out of debt, minding his own business, speaking forthrightly, and not being dependent on others. He is master in the home and makes all decisions of consequence. If he does not marry he is likely to show strong family attachment by living with his parents or close relatives. His preoccupation with his family is so great that he is likely to have little social activity outside it. He regards such activity as frivolous and costly, and is inclined to prefer material things like real estate, a car, and luxuries in the home. He is also likely to consider hobbies as impractical and expensive. (6) His familial devotion is accompanied by a relative indifference to the community at large, as shown by his reluctance to aid charitable organizations. In this he is unlike the civic-minded middle classes whom he apes materially. (7) Despite his restricted social life and extremely individualistic behavior, the rate-buster is not personally disorganized. He has a set of standards valid to himself. His adherence to them may make him a problem to the work group, but not to himself. He rebels against authority of the work group, but not that of the social order, the competitively derived success values of which are the same as his own. There is no uncertainty or confusion in his behavior. His impulses are channelized and guided by clear-cut images and goals. He is maladjusted only in the sense that he is a microcosm of laissez-faire thought in occupational contact with workers of a collectivistic outlook. Any disjointing he may suffer from this experience is healed by his knowledge of sympathy from groups with whom he identifies himself.

His social world has remained so small and manageable that he finds laissez-faire more workable than do its great proponents in the entangled spheres of commerce. Feeling no need of the workers about him, he ignores their demands on him. In his aspirations and mode of life the rate-buster represents one of the nearest possible approaches to the concept of an "economic man."

Low producers (goldbrickers) Dalton found to be "socialized" in background and oriented to social approval and participation with their fellows. Rate-busters, by contrast, were strongly inividualistic, tending to concentrate their attention only on their families, and isolating themselves from community participation in general. As an indication of the strong difference in point of view of these two groups, we may contrast the following two statements, the first from a low producer, the second from a rate-buster (11, pp. 326–27):

(Low producer) I'd like to have a good home and good family. I'd like to be able to take a two-week trip around some part of the country every year. I wouldn't want to run around with ritzy people because I don't like social functions. You've got to sit around and chew the fat too much. You wouldn't be free to come and go when you wanted to. I would like to live in a little better neighborhood than I do now—it's not safe to go out at night. But I wouldn't want to live among the swells.

Right now I could use a little more income, but I don't like making it under an incentive system. They're a bad thing for men. There's always fighting and injustice. I don't think they could make a system that'd be fair and please everybody. Bill over there says a group system would do it. It would help some guys, but the smart, fast guys'd be sore and lay down on the job. They wouldn't want to put out a lot and share it with guys who couldn't. Then there's the lazy guys—always trying to pull a fast one and get something for nothing. Nobody'd want to share with them.

(Rate-buster) I don't want a lot of money. I just want a nice living. I want to send my two boys and girl to college.

My oldest girl married as soon as she left high school—but she married a go-getter, a real hustler. He's here in the plant now. His dad is a boss, and they're both Masons. And between you and I, that helps. He'll get a good job out of it. I've told him that a factory is a hell of a place to work. I don't want my boys in here. But if you get up where you can hand the orders down, it's all right. It's hell when somebody's breathing them down your neck. You'll never get ahead in a spot like that.

You need more money than just what's needed to live on. You've always got to have money saved for taxes, and you've got to save for times when work will be slack. All my life I've saw layoffs and reduced time. You never know when it's coming, but you know it will come. And when it does come you've got to be ready for it. The only way to be ready is to save. That's why I work like hell. If I wasn't making this bonus, I couldn't lay anything by. Most of the boys raise hell because I work so hard. Hell! If I get laid off or start working two days a week, they won't help me out. Ain't that right?

We have here two quite distinct social types. Rate-busters have the type of background and orientation which makes them particularly susceptible to the sort of appeal that incentive systems offer. By contrast, other workers, and they form the overwhelming majority (97 per cent, if Dalton's factory is representative), have a background and orientation which places a high value on fellowship and the work group values. It is very easy for them to agree to restrict if others are doing so. Under such conditions, trying to make everyone into a rate-buster would involve a fundamental change of values. It is, in any case, an approach which involves a confusion of means and ends. Workers are obviously restricting because they have good reasons for doing so and because they feel it is right. Instead of offering a goal which directly conflicts with these reasons and feelings, it is more intelligent to try to change the social conditions so that workers do not feel the need to restrict in the first place. A direct appeal is like the oft-repeated injunction to the neophyte golfer: "Relax!" Obviously, if the golfer knew what to do and felt confident of his ability to do it, he would relax. But relaxation is the *end* product. So with productivity in the case of factory workers.

And, indeed, when we look seriously at the attempt to make everyone into a rate-buster, we see that its achievement would not be a boon but a catastrophe. Let us imagine the base rate were $1.00 an hour and everyone were to go all out producing at top speed continually. From the evidence we have of rate-buster achievement, everyone might then be making $2.50 or $3.00 an hour. If such a state of affairs could ever actually be produced, then management would certainly feel that rates were set much too low and must be revised, for the wage bill would be staggering. And with everyone producing at top speed, inventories would rapidly fill and the company would quickly run out of work. The only possible exception to the latter would be in a wartime economy in the case of a munitions or airplane factory where all production could be absorbed. Even then, there is still competition and government allotment of contracts to act as a brake on all-out production. But such conditions are highly exceptional in any case. In sum, the ideal of "everyone a rate-buster" is not only unlikely to be achieved, but if conceivably achieved, would produce a drastic lowering of wages and large-scale unemployment.

Perhaps, then, Dalton's proportion of 9 rate-busters to 300 employees is not really small. It is simply all a factory can afford.

POSSIBLE SOLUTIONS: 2. SLOGANS AND SUGGESTION BOXES

Slogans and suggestion boxes are illustrations *par excellence* of the direct appeal to the individual, while ignoring the group. Many factories make extensive use of slogans, often posted in conspicuous places, frequently presented as attractively as possible in colors and with the aid of cartoons. As the worker pushes his card into the timeclock, his glance strays up to a placard which reminds him: WHAT YOU DO TODAY WILL DE-CIDE WHAT YOU'LL BE DOING TOMORROW. As he passes into the shop, a cartoon depicting a baseball game draws the moral for him: TEAMWORK WINS. As he hangs up his coat, he discovers that Marilyn Monroe is smiling down at him from the wall and saying: I LIKE A MAN WITH GET-UP AND GO! Such devices often impress the casual visitor; they have little or no effect on the worker. They can be most aptly compared not with any scientifically tested propaganda technique but rather with primitive magic. They represent a kind of repetitive will, or fiat magic—a hope that if a formula or pattern of words is repeated enough, the event will somehow be made to happen.

Suggestion boxes are found in most factories (and other work organizations as well). The worker who has an idea that will save time or money writes out his idea and puts it in the box. If management considers the idea valuable, it pays the worker a cash award of from $5.00 up to thousands of dollars in a few, very rare cases. Most usable ideas, however, yield very modest rewards.

Such boxes do produce some suggestions and occasionally valuable ones. But usually they produce very few suggestions, and only a small proportion of these turn out to be usable. Even where suggestion boxes seem to work fairly well, they only produce a very small proportion of the potential, for there are five major limitations which Whyte states as follows (59, pp. 171–72):

1. The traditional suggestion plan puts its emphasis upon the contribution of the *individual*. He is offered an individual reward for his individual idea. In many cases a cost-saving idea will involve the readjustment of jobs and people in the department. Such changes may be looked upon by other people as a threat to their position and security. Thus the individual who makes such a suggestion may win money and yet stir up the resentment of fellow workers. Under such conditions many people would rather keep their suggestions to themselves.

2. *Foreman-worker relations*. Many foremen look upon a successful suggestion submitted by a worker in their departments as a reflection upon their

own competence. They fear that higher management might say, "Why didn't the foreman think of that himself?" Many workers recognize this and fear that the foreman will retaliate against them if they submit suggestions. Even when the worker prefers to withhold his name in the contest, the foreman is likely to have a pretty good idea as to which of his men might be putting in suggestions.

This problem can be met to some extent if management takes pains to give the foreman recognition for suggestions coming out of his department. For example, management is advised to have the foremen present the awards and with a maximum of fanfare and publicity, especially if the award is a substantial one. However, even these measures may not eliminate worker fear of retaliation if no other changes are made in the foreman-worker relations.

3. *Problems in the ownership of ideas.* The standard suggestion approach assumes that a good idea is devised by a single individual—though sometimes two individuals may sign their names to a suggestion. This assumption is contrary to experience and to research observations. We saw in examining Donald Roy's experience that the workers in his department had many production ideas that were unknown to management. No doubt some of these ideas were developed full blown by a single individual, but even in those cases the ideas had been shared with the rest of the shop. Some of these ideas had been around for a long time, so that it would be quite impossible to determine who had invented them. There were also, of course, ideas originated by one individual but modified and improved upon by one or more others. This same observation can be made in many other factory situations.

Now suppose some individualist decides to take one of these ideas and put it in the suggestion box. Then we hear from fellow workers, "It was really my idea, but that bastard stole it from me and cashed in on it," and similar expressions of resentment. Thus the individual incentive on suggestions may stimulate conflict within a department.

4. *Complex ideas and human relations.* We generally find that the most valuable ideas for the improvement of efficiency are not those limited to one machine or to one productive operation. Such ideas may involve changes in the relations of machines to each other, in the relations of worker to worker and of workers to management people. In such a situation the individual may have the initial idea but a group process may be required before the idea can be put into practical form. This calls for consultation among a number of people. However, the individual suggestion award discourages such consultations. The emphasis is upon individual ownership of the idea, and many people naturally fear to talk their idea over with other people lest they lose some claim on its ownership.

5. *Paper communication vs. social interaction.* The standard suggestion system is a depersonalized operation. It is only at the point of making the awards, especially in some of the larger cases, that a personal element enters in. The communication of the suggestion is in writing and the suggestion committee studies these written documents. Furthermore, many workers who have good ideas find it difficult to express them in writing. The writing requirement thus serves as a barrier to communication.

Particularly important is Whyte's fourth point. The really good ideas are practically always collaborative and require collaboration for their execution. Not only can the individual not appreciate this from his isolated position, but he may have just the germ of an idea which may be very valuable, when coupled with engineering or personnel theory. Schultz and Crisara present the following case (47, pp. 178–79):

Start-grind-stop-wait-"mike." And start all over again. That is the way to grind round broaches. Start the machine, grind off a little stock, press the stop button, wait for the machine to coast to a stop, then "mike" the broach. Learn to set up and operate the machine, read blueprints, dress the abrasive wheel, get the "feel" of micrometers. These skills are required of a cylindrical grinder.

Where was the problem? Production and quality were good. The foreman was satisfied. The company was satisfied. But a worker thought the job could be done better. For him there was too long a wait between pressing the stop button and being able to "mike" the broach. He had a vague idea that applying some kind of electrical brake on the machine would make it stop faster and therefore speed up production. His foreman liked the idea. But together they were unable to go any further with it.

They suggested it to management, but were told that it would cost $1,200 to buy a speed control, and that the present speed reducer which cost $450 would have to be scrapped. This was considered too expensive.

But neither the worker nor the foreman gave up. In a chat with an electrician they got further information and, in a few days, what seemed to be a practical solution. The results, as told by the electrician, were:

"This didn't require a major change in the machine, because we found a way of supplying a source of d.c. current directly to the motor windings and using a shot of d.c. current as a brake. The time saving is so great that, after we put it on the first one, they applied it to seventeen other machines. They tell me this saves one hour a day per machine. It cost only $1.25 for the fuse block, about $14.00 for a relay, plus a couple of hours for the maintenance man to install."

What would have happened with the usual suggestion box? Probably the worker would not even have submitted one, because he really had nothing to suggest except a vague notion of some kind of electrical brake. Actually, as described in the case, the worker (and his foreman) did make the suggestion to management and we know what happened. Very likely, therefore, if the worker had put his idea in a suggestion box, the same thing would have happened: management would note that the idea was too expensive to implement, and here would be just another case of an "impractical" suggestion. But by far the most remarkable feature of the case was that the usual limitations of suggestion systems that Whyte refers to above were apparently absent. The worker seemed to have no hesita-

tion in going to his foreman with his idea when elsewhere he might fear
the foreman would steal his idea or feel that it was a reflection on his
abilities. The two of them in turn did not hesitate to seek out the help
of an electrician who knew more than they did and might well steal the
idea and claim it as his own. Here, then, the group nature of work was
recognized and taken advantage of rather than ignored. It would be a
great mistake to jump from this case to some such conclusion as: "Ah! Here
is a good illustration of the value of teamwork. If only people realized that,
we'd have many more such cases." If that conclusion were drawn, we
would still be at the slogan stage and would not have learned anything
from the case. For the question is not how do we make people *realize* the
value of teamwork, but rather how do we *create the conditions* under
which teamwork becomes the natural or usual way of doing things. The
situation is analogous to measures designed to increase safety on our
highways. The sloganistic, individualistic approach is to put up lots of
signs, hire policemen and continually urge people to DRIVE SAFELY.
The alternative is to create the conditions which make accidents less
likely—to build safety into the highway itself by such devices as banking
curves, cloverleaf intersections, wider highways with speed lanes, and
so on. Similarly, we must ask how we can build teamwork into the human
structure of the factory itself.

GROUP APPROACHES TO MOTIVATION

The fundamental clue on which practically all subsequent findings rest
was provided by some experiments begun in 1924 at the Hawthorne
Works of the Western Electric Company in and near Chicago. The experiments, in the beginning at least, were quite routine and were of the
sort that were the stock-in-trade of engineers and psychometricians. It was
desired merely to discover how differences in lighting intensity affected
productivity. For this purpose, three typical departments were chosen—
one where employees inspected small parts, one where employees assembled telephone relays, and one where employees wound electric coils.
After securing data on average output before the experiment, the lighting was changed systematically in each group. In each department, the
lighting was increased in intensity four times. The results were puzzling.
In the first group, output jumped up and down without direct relation to
the amount of light; in the second group, output increased but not as a
sole function of illumination; in the third group, output was always
higher than at the beginning but not in any regular relation to the lighting changes. These strange results were attributed to the fact that other
variables besides illumination were not being controlled. Therefore a

second experiment was carried out using only coil winders and this time employing a control group. In the test group, lighting was increased; in the control group it was kept as nearly constant as possible (amount of daylight was an interfering variable). But the results were more surprising than ever, for the output of the test group went up, but so did that of the control group and to almost exactly the same amount!

It was decided to control the effects of variable daylight by designing a third experiment using only artificial light. Again test and control groups were provided, but this time the lighting in the test group was *decreased* at intervals, one foot-candle at a time. Again, output went up in both test and control groups. However, when lighting fell in the test group to a point where the operators complained that they could hardly see what they were doing, their production rate did decrease. But their efficiency was maintained up to this point.

There was much head-scratching and mutterings about "still uncontrolled variables" and it was decided to conduct further experiments. These are described as follows (38, p. 17):

. . . Two capable and willing operators were selected. They were provided with working facilities in a locker room which could be made completely dark. The illumination at the bench in this room was cut down from the original amount of light to which the girls had been accustomed to 0.06 of a foot-candle, an amount of light approximately equal to that on an ordinary moonlight night. Even with this very low intensity of light, the girls maintained their efficiency. They said that they suffered no eyestrain and that they became less tired than when working under bright lights.

The experimenter was not yet completely satisfied that it had been clearly demonstrated that the effects of the illumination secured in the previous studies were more "psychological" than real. He therefore decided to try further tests on the girls in the coil winding group. First, the amount of light was increased regularly day by day, and the girls were asked each day how they liked the change. As the light was increased, the girls told the investigator that they liked the brighter lights. Then for a day or two the investigator allowed the girls to see the electrician come and change the light bulbs. In reality, the electrician merely took out bulbs of a given size and inserted bulbs of the same size, without in any way changing the amount of light. The girls, thinking that the light was still being "stepped up" day by day, commented favorably about the increase of light. After a few days of this, the experimenter started to decrease the intensity of light, keeping the girls informed of the change and soliciting their reaction. After a period of this day-by-day decrease in illumination, he again allowed the girls to see the electrician change the bulbs without really changing the intensity of illumination. Again the girls gave answers that were to be expected, in that they said the "lesser" light was not so pleasant to work under as the brighter light. Their production did not materially change at any stage of the experiment.

The clue which was uncovered here was not actually recognized at the time. The significant variable had apparently not been the lighting but the *attitudes* of the operators. For we note in the informal experiments that even when lighting was unchanged, if the girls thought it was being changed, they expressed the same feelings as when it was in fact changed. The attitudes of the workers was in turn related in a fundamental sense to the fact that they had become the objects of special attention and concern by management. But the significance of the latter was not brought out until the next experiment was performed, involving the assembling of telephone relays. This experiment, and the work that followed it, was called by a book reviewer: "the most outstanding study of industrial relations that has been published anywhere, anytime." For its description, the best account from the point of view of lucidity, conciseness and vividness is that of Stuart Chase. A portion follows (7, pp. 15–20):

It was decided to use a group of girls assembling telephone relays. A telephone relay is a small gadget, looking something like a pocket whistle, made up of thirty-five separate parts. The task of the girls was to take these parts out of trays and put them together. It was a typical machine-age repetitive job.

Two girls were selected who were skilled at assembling relays, and they picked four companions. Five of the group were about twenty years old, three of Polish families, one of Italian, one of Czech. The sixth had been born in Norway, and was about thirty years old. They were all moved into a special room separated by a thin partition from the big relay department where 100 employees worked.

Here the six girls sit, at one long bench, trays of tiny metal parts in front of them. Their nimble fingers fly. Every minute or so a relay is finished, dropped into a chute, and carried out into a box on the floor, where it is collected. On each girl's chute is placed a little machine operating a kind of ticker tape which counts every relay coming through. For five years these tickers will click—from 1927 to 1932—giving an accurate record of hourly, daily, weekly output.

Five of the girls were assemblers, while the sixth was the "layout operator," who prepared the trays of parts so the girls could assemble them more easily. A seventh person was also in the room—the observer. He represented the research staff. His job was to record everything of significance that happened. He was to be the counselor and friend of the girls, telling them about the experiment, talking over proposed changes, inviting their comments, listening to their complaints.

The idea was to let the girls work along as they had been doing in the regular department, and count the relays coming down the chute. This would give a base rate of output. Then, following the plan, shift the payment for a few weeks, and count the relays. Then introduce rest pauses of various kinds, and count the relays. Then vary the hours in the working day, give Saturday off and what not, and count the relays. If more relays per week went through the tickers, the change of course would be proved a good one and could be extended over the plant. If fewer relays went through the ticker, the change was obviously bad, and should not be adopted. It was all as clear as A B C.

If the investigators had been disturbed by what happened in the lighting experiments, they were knocked galley west by what happened to these six girls with flying fingers in the relay room. Things didn't happen the way they were expected to happen. Assumptions as to cause and effect were found to be completely false. As the weeks grew into months and years, the mystery became deeper and deeper. What was the matter with these girls? Why didn't they do what the efficiency books said they ought to do?

Being true scientists, however, the investigators kept doggedly on, recording faithfully what happened, even if they did not know what caused it or what it meant.

Here in brief outline is the mystery story, divided into chapters:

Periods 1 and 2, lasting seven weeks. These periods were devoted to getting the base output figures. The girls were found to average about 2,400 relays a week each. They worked the regular forty-eight hours, including Saturdays.

Period 3, lasting eight weeks. A variation in wages was introduced, putting the girls on a group piecework basis. Output went up.

Period 4, lasting five weeks. Two rest pauses of five minutes each were introduced, at ten in the morning and at two in the afternoon. Output went up.

Period 5, lasting four weeks. The rest pauses were increased to ten minutes each. Output went up sharply.

Period 6, lasting four weeks. Six five-minute rest pauses were tried. The girls complained that the rhythm of their work was broken. Output fell off slightly.

Period 7, lasting eleven weeks. Rest pauses were reduced to two, one of fifteen minutes in the morning, with a hot snack provided by the company, and one of ten minutes in the afternoon. Output went up.

Period 8, lasting seven weeks. The same conditions as Period 7, except that the girls were dismissed at four-thirty instead of five o'clock. Output went up sharply.

Period 9, lasting four weeks. The same as Period 7, except that closing time was moved to four o'clock. Output remained on a level.

Period 10, lasting twelve weeks. Back to the exact conditions of Period 7, with closing time at five o'clock. Were the girls discouraged by losing an hour a day of liberty? They were not; output went up with a rush!

The research staff began to tear their hair. Their assumptions were disintegrating. Some unmeasured force was constantly pulling output up no matter how they juggled hours, wages, and rest pauses.

So after trying Saturdays off for twelve weeks, in Period 11, with output on a level, they prepared for the greatest test of all. They would throw the whole experiment back to where it started and take away everything they had given the girls over a year and a half. Surely this would crush their spirits and reduce the number of relays going through the counters. Surely every rule of common sense and factory management indicated that.

Period 12, lasting twelve weeks. The girls went back to the exact physical conditions of Period 3—no rest pauses, no company hot lunch, a full forty-eight-hour week. Output jumped to an all-time high—3,000 relays a week, a cool 25 per cent above the original Period 3!

THE UNKNOWN FACTOR

The staff swooned at their desks. They thought they were returning the girls to the original conditions of the experiment, but they found that the original conditions had gone forever. The experiment had changed under them, and the group they now had was not the group they had started with. Because of some mysterious X which had thrust itself into the experiment, this group of six girls was pouring 25 per cent more relays into the chutes, though working arrangements were precisely like those at the beginning of the test.

What was this X? The research staff pulled themselves together and began looking for it. They conferred, argued, studied, and presently they found it. It wasn't in the physical production end of the factory at all. It was in the girls themselves. It was an *attitude,* the way the girls now felt about their work and their group. By segregating them into a little world of their own, by asking their help and co-operation, the investigators had given the young women a new sense of their own value. Their whole attitude changed from that of separate cogs in a machine to that of a congenial team helping the company solve a significant problem.

They had found stability, a place where they belonged, and work whose purpose they could clearly see. And so they worked faster and better than they ever had in their lives. The two functions of a factory had joined into one harmonious whole.

With this discovery, the results of the lighting experiments became clear. Both groups in the lighting test had come to feel important. So their output went up regardless of the candle power sprayed upon them.

The relay room showed other significant results. Cumulative fatigue was not present at any time, as proved by regular medical examination of the girls. They always worked well within their physical capacity. If monotony was present, it was blotted out in group interest, as the output curves bore witness.

It was found that each girl had a definite style in her work. She placed the parts so and assembled them so. Sometimes she put little frills on the job; the higher the IQ, the more frills. This helped to give her a real interest in the task. Beware, you stop-watch men, of destroying little habits like this. You may run into the paradox of decreasing output by saving motions.

There was a visible increase in contentment, and an 80 per cent decrease in absenteeism. The girls were eager to come to work in the morning—a phenomenon as startling as a small boy eager to go to school. Early suspicions gave way to complete trust in the observer and in the integrity of the experiment. The girls came to feel that they had no boss. They moved about as they pleased, talked as they pleased. Nobody silenced them.

Two of the girls were talking together. Said one:

"The fun in the test room is what makes it worth while."

The other: "Yes, there are too many bosses in the department."

The first: "Yes, Mr. —— (the observer) is the only boss we have."

The other: "Say, he's no boss. We don't have any boss."

With this sense of freedom came a sense of responsibility, and they began to discipline themselves. They evolved into a compact social unit, working as a team, helping each other, making up each other's work when one of the group was not feeling well, giving parties for one another outside the factory. They squabbled a bit, but underneath they were members of the same gang. They had found here some of the clan unity which the machine age has stripped away from so many industrial workers. They stayed in the factory, but they came out of the cage.

This study and others that followed it have been subjected to much criticism. The experimenters have been accused of too great a faith in clinical or case methods, of a neglect of theory, of being biased in favor of management, and of concentrating too much on the shop situation and so ignoring other institutional structures, such as labor unions, which have penetrating effects on the factory.[13] In general, such criticisms are valid, but none of them is of such a character as to destroy the findings. Rather one may say that if the experimenters—Mayo, Roethlisberger, Dickson, Pennock and others—had been able to take these criticisms into account, they would have done a much more significant and better job. But the findings stand on their own, nevertheless, and—given the limited interests (and possibly backgrounds) of the experimenters—the findings are remarkable indeed. The experimenters neglected many things, but they did provide a major clue: if one wishes to change productivity and therefore motivation, one must change the *attitudes* of workers; and if one wishes to change the attitudes of workers, one must change *the pattern of social interaction*. For the experiment itself represented a fundamental change in the pattern of interaction that the workers were accustomed to. Two close friends proceeded to choose their fellow-workers. Thus was the work group formed. The purpose of the experiment was explained and their comments solicited—another unaccustomed procedure. At each point in the experiment, the central position of the workers—their reactions, their health, their criticisms—was constantly emphasized. Here for the first time the *workers* were participating actively in a management-sponsored experiment. This was no theoretical scheme dreamed up on the drawing boards in the far-off engineering offices by bright young college men, and imposed on the workers without even consulting them. The experiment was simple, the workers understood why it was being carried out, and they understood also that whatever good results might come from it depended completely on them. For these girls, this was the *first time* that

[13] For elaborations of these criticisms, see (5, 6, 18, 22, 32, 41).

management behaved as if it really was concerned about them. It is not surprising then that output went up beyond the dreams of the most optimistic of time-study men.

The Relay Assembly Test Room experiment is now a classic, but it was only the beginning. Let us shift next to the immediate present and examine a system of organizing work which elaborates on the original clue and builds it into a full-blown motivational structure. This is the so-called Scanlon Plan.[14] This is no formula which can be put into effect automatically in any plant by fiat of management or union. Rather it is essentially a system for building worker-union-management cooperation into the structure of the factory. In describing it, we shall follow Whyte's procedure (59, Ch. 14) of describing its operation at one particular plant —the Lapointe Machine Tool Company.[15]

The Scanlon Plan is first of all a plant-wide incentive system. There is no individual reward to the worker as in the case of individual piece-work. The plan at Lapointe provides that any increase in productive efficiency resulting in a saving of labor costs shall be paid back to all employees (except to management, who are covered by a plan of their own based on sales). Each employee is paid a proportion of the saving in accord with his regular pay. If the saving is one-third, the employee making $300 a month is paid an extra $100; the employee making $600 a month is paid $200. Workers who were on individual incentive before the plan went into operation are guaranteed their average bonus earnings. Provision is made for changes in case of technological changes, price changes, or product changes—to be worked out by joint consultation.

Here we see a concrete illustration of how teamwork has been built into the organization. Workers are not pitted *against* each other as they are with individual piecework. Rather, whatever any individual does redounds to the benefit of the entire organization. Under such conditions, it is not necessary to put up cartoons or appeal to workers to *please* act *as if* they were a team. They are a team, and the income earned is everybody's income in the same sense that the score in a ball game is the score of the whole team and not of one person in it.

The payment plan is, however, only one aspect of the Scanlon Plan, and indeed, by itself, it would not work at all. Many firms have cost-sharing schemes but still suffer low productivity and internal conflict. For such a scheme to work it is necessary for workers to *feel* they are part of a team, and the only way to do this is by reorganizing work relations so

[14] Named after Joseph Scanlon, formerly a labor union man, and now at the Massachusetts Institute of Technology.
[15] Whyte gives credit for part of the chapter to "Savies and Strauss." The reader should also consult (12, p. 461; 45; 46; 47).

that they operate as a team. This process is best illustrated by the remarkable system used to enlist joint participation in production suggestions.

First, and most important, there is *no* individual reward of money to the originator of a suggestion. Thus at one swoop do we remove most of the problems of the suggestion box. Interpersonal resentments at payoffs to one man "because that was really my idea" are practically eliminated, for whoever makes the suggestion, everyone benefits. But more than this the group nature of most valuable suggestion is directly anticipated in the social structure. In each department, a union production committeeman and a foreman form a production committee who meet once a month to discuss suggestions. The union grievance committeeman may sit in on these meetings to consider the possible conflict that an otherwise good suggestion might create. In addition, where ideas involve several people, the appropriate workers are called in for consultation. If this group considers an idea feasible, it may proceed at once to put it into effect. In any case, this committee sends a copy of minutes to a screening committee, consisting of three management representatives and three union representatives. They are concerned with suggestions involving several departments or requiring higher level action.

In very brief form, these are certain of the major features of the Plan. It is simple and eminently practical and cheap to operate. Its major characteristic is not the incentive plan as such, nor the suggestion plan as such, but rather that both involve and require group participation and have a structure provided for such participation. The results are almost beyond belief. The payoff has been substantial. Over a fifty-eight-month period, bonus payments ranged from 0 to 52.1 per cent, distributed as follows: sixteen months—no bonus, twenty-two months—bonus under 20 per cent; twenty months—bonus 20 per cent or over. Union-management relations have improved greatly, with grievances declining profoundly. The motivation effects have been equally striking, for restriction has declined greatly. Whyte says (59, p. 185):

On the basis of previous studies, we have been accustomed to assuming that restriction of output exists anywhere and everywhere. Apparently in some of these Scanlon cases it has been well-nigh eliminated. The union president cites an example of a grinder at Lapointe who had been averaging $76.40 a week on his incentive rate. In four days after the Plan was instituted, he turned in enough work so that it would have amounted to $184 under the preexisting incentive plan. This is only a single example and is certainly not enough to allow us to assume that no restriction remains at all. However, it does suggest that the tight ceiling on production has been eliminated. With no more individual incentive rates there is no longer any threat of rate cutting, and the worker can contribute to the goal of the total organization without incurring the enmity of fellow workers.

Whyte's comment that the fear of rate-cutting has been abolished is, however, only one explanation, for it will be recalled that there were six other reasons for restriction. But this Plan cuts much of the ground out from under these six other reasons as well. Workers restrict in order partially to control management. But the Plan builds right into the structure a continuous and real control on management with respect to the element most important to the workers—wages. Workers restrict to provide leisure time. But they do so because leisure is a greater value than working hard on "stinkers" to make just base pay, and because of the controls of fellow-workers on quota output. With no individual incentive payment, the motives for such restriction no longer exist and the worker must now balance the values of leisure against the values of bonus payments. Undoubtedly some will continue to prefer leisure, but this time they find that the pressures on them are not to restrict but to go all out. Here the person who loafs is not "one of the boys," but just the reverse. Workers restrict to control competition and avoid the sanctions heaped upon the nonconformist. Here again the situation is reversed: competition is not there to be controlled, for workers' outputs are not continually compared, and the nonconformist here is the restrictor, for *he* pulls down the earnings of the whole group. Workers restrict to help give meaning to work. But the Scanlon plan provides as much challenge and game elements as any quota system, and it has the advantage of being a group challenge as well. Finally, workers restrict because they do not feel that management rewards of higher income and promotion are really achievable. The problem of promotions remains, but certainly higher rewards are possible and are continually being achieved. Most important, in sum, is that high productivity has become a *group expectation* and the powerful resources of the group of ostracism and punishment are, for once, being focused on values that management strongly approves of.

The suggestion system has had just as striking results. Davenport provides the following illustration (12, pp. 177–78):

One of the greatest advantages of this kind of (system) from the worker's point of view, is the knowledge that it gives him of the business. When a slump is coming, he knows it. He even is given a chance to combat it, in the sense that if he can devise a cheaper way of turning out his product, perhaps the company will be able to take business from somebody else. In a number of instances the Lapointe workers have actually done this, the most spectacular example being that of an order from a big automotive concern in December, 1948. The workers had been pressing management to accept orders even at the break-even point so as to tide over a bad period. Mr. Prindiville, who sometimes sits in on the screening-committee meetings, had given in to the pressure some months previously to the extent of taking an order from this firm for 100 broaches at $83 per broach. But Lapointe had lost 10 per cent on the deal, and Mr. Prindiville now put his foot down. If this business was to be taken again the price would have to be raised. In view of new competition, it meant that Lapointe almost certainly would not get the business—and at a time when work was scarce.

The gloomy gathering that listened to Mr. Prindiville's pronouncement was then electrified by a question from Jimmie McQuade, skilled grinder and one of the most outspoken members of the screening committee. "Who says we can't make those broaches at that price for a profit?" Mr. McQuade wanted to know. "If you'd give the men in the shop the chance to go over the blueprints before production starts, and to help plan the job, there are lots of ways of cutting costs without cutting quality." The idea grew and the next day the suggestion ran around the shop like wildfire. The order was taken at the old price, this time with a *profit* of 10 per cent—a total gain in efficiency of 20 per cent.

Here is an example, again, of real participation in a tough production problem which required worker cooperation to solve. We may feel fairly sure that in the normal situation if management announced that "costs simply have to go down in making broaches," workers would have shrugged their shoulders and said, "Making a profit is your problem, not mine."

Not only is there real participation, but a very high proportion of employee suggestions are accepted. Normally, with the usual suggestion boxes, about 75 per cent of suggestions are rejected. At Lapointe, 80 per cent have been *accepted* and put into operation. Yet the workers at Lapointe are neither more intelligent nor more imaginative than workers at other factories. Rather, a structure has been provided which is more successful than the usual suggestion box. Consultation is not simply encouraged: it is the only way an idea can get past the production committee. This process also has an important screening effect, for undoubtedly one of the reasons for the high acceptance rate of ideas is that ideas are criticized before being permitted to go any further. Thus poor or genuinely impractical ideas never get to the point of being formally rejected. This suggestion approach apparently draws the same kind of individual suggestions the usual suggestion box does. But in addition, it is engineered to handle collaborative suggestions and for putting suggestions requiring collaboration into action.

It is important to emphasize that the Scalon (and similar plans) has definite limitations. It is strictly an in-plant scheme and contains within it no magic for handling problems involving a genuine difference of interest between management and labor.[16] If workers decide they want a share of profits, let us say, and are willing to go out on strike to get it, the Scanlon plan will not prevent such a strike. Nor, in spite of Davenport's illustration, can the workers in any one plant do anything about a slump. They may be able to help their own company, but this will simply mean the loss of business for some other company. Problems of slump require industry-wide and governmental action. But taken within the context of the plant and the problem of motivation, the Scanlon plan has a great deal to recommend it.

Lest some be tempted to place too much emphasis on the plant-wide incentive aspect of the Scanlon plan, it should be emphasized that the principle of cooperation and group collaboration will produce valuable effects without such an incentive system. Whyte describes a case at Inland Steel Container Corporation in which severe conflict broke out over a pail cover.[17] A punch press blanked out covers for use on the pail line. Since the covers tended to stick, a worker had installed an air hose on the assembly which blew air down to loosen the cover. When management discovered this, it put a metal hose on, operating from the bottom, and then proceeded to cut the rate for the job. A bitter conflict resulted in which the air-hose case became a symbol of management heartlessness and mistrust. Then, for various reasons, certain things happened which changed the pattern of relations between workers-union and management. When the air hose case came up for discussion at the fourth step in the grievance procedure, the explosive issue was settled amicably in less than two minutes' time. Even the much-hated rate-setters can be integrated into the cooperative system (55, pp. 78–79). At Inland Steel, rate-setters are not permitted to roam at will and pounce on unsuspecting machine operators. First a rate-setter must get the approval of the general production supervisor and then show his written authorization to the foreman and union steward. Before a rate can be put into effect, it must first have the approval of the general production supervisor and of the foreman, and the rate is discussed with the union steward. This process nips many grievances in the bud, for the time-setter knows in advance whether a rate is going to be fought over or not. Much time and money is saved if such arguments can be prevented. In this case, then, even rate-setting has been socially integrated. The broad object of group approaches to motivation has been very well stated by Whyte as follows (55, p. 73):

[16] Note, for example, Koivisto's point that concentration on the values of "cooperation" and "industrial peace" ignores the *consumers'* interest (29). In this connection see also Stone's argument (50) for the compatibility of "human relations" and "conflict of interest" approaches to labor-management studies.

[17] Described in several places by Whyte. See his (55; 58, pp. 67–69; 59, Ch. 11).

Many people are arguing the question to-day: Which is more important to work-ers, economic incentives or human relations? In that form the question is mean-ingless and unanswerable. Men are interested in money. They are also concerned about their relations with other men. Offer them a financial reward for behavior that damages their relations with other men, and you can hardly expect them to respond with enthusiasm.

The issue is not: economic incentives *or* human relations. The problem is to fit economic incentives and human relations effectively together, to *integrate* them. In other words, the pulling power of the money reward will be strongly affected by the pattern of human relations into which it is introduced.

In our emphasis on group approaches, it may be felt that we have ignored individual and personality questions. Yet such an emphasis does not represent a one-sided bias in the present state of research or indus-trial practice. For the overwhelming emphasis at present is on *individual* approaches and such cases as we have described are in a small minority. Also, one must be careful in assessing the success of any approach before it has been in operation for a long while. Many schemes are *initially* successful. They are a novelty and generate interest for that reason alone. (This is one of the important lessons of the Hawthorne experiments.) Often too the mere hope that a plan will work stimulates productivity until hopes begin to fade. Yet the Scanlon plan has been in operation at Lapointe for five years, which is perhaps long enough for us to dismiss novelty or mere hope as significant causal variables. Certainly, at least, the success of plans involving genuine participation and a direct im-plementation of the social nature of work justifies optimism that this line of attack may be fruitful.[18]

CHAPTER REFERENCES

1. Abruzzi, A., *Work Measurement,* New York: Columbia University Press, 1952.
2. Barkin, S., "An Evaluation of Personnel Philosophy," *Monthly Labor Re-view,* 77:153–155, 1954.
3. Barnard, C. I., *The Functions of the Executive,* Cambridge, Mass.: Harvard University Press, 1945.
4. *No entry.*
5. Bell, D., "Adjusting Men to Machines," *Commentary,* 3:79–88, 1947.
6. Bendix, R., "Primitivism, Authority, and 'Human Relations,'" *Research Studies of the State College of Washington,* 17:29–34, 1949.

[18] Other cases illustrative of group approaches are the following (16, 52, 56, 57, 58, 59, Ch. 12).

7. Chase, S., *Men at Work,* New York: Harcourt, Brace, 1945.
8. Collins, O.; Dalton, M.; and Roy, D., "Restriction of Output and Social Cleavage in Industry," *Applied Anthropology,* 5:1–14, 1946.
9. Cooley, C. H., *Human Nature and the Social Order,* New York: Scribners, 1922.
10. Dalton, M., "The Industrial 'Rate-Buster': A Characterization," *Applied Anthropology,* 7:5–18, 1948.
11. ———, "Worker Response and Social Background," *Journal of Political Economy,* 55:323–332, 1947.
12. Davenport, R. W., "A Case History of Union-Management Cooperation," in Pigors, P. and Myers, C., *Readings in Personnel Administration,* New York, McGraw-Hill, 1952.
13. *No entry.*
14. Dewey, J., *Human Nature and Conduct,* New York: Henry Holt, 1922.
15. *Fortune,* January 1950.
16. Friedmann, G., *Industrial Society,* Glencoe, Ill.: Free Press, 1955.
17. Gerth, H. H. and Mills, C. W., *From Max Weber: Essays in Sociology,* New York: Oxford University Press, 1946.
18. Gilson, M. B., Review of Roethlisberger and Dickson's *Management and the Worker, American Journal of Sociology,* 46:98–101, 1940.
19. Gross, E., "Characteristics of Cliques in Office Organizations," *Research Studies of the State College of Washington,* 19:131–136, 1951.
20. ———, "Informal Relations and the Social Organization of Work in an Industrial Office." Unpublished Ph.D. Dissertation, University of Chicago, 1949.
21. ———; Loether, H. J.; and Strinden, D. N., *A Study of the Small Group,* Report to Human Resources Research Institute, Maxwell Air Force Base, Ala.
22. Hart, C. W. M., "Industrial Relations Research and Social Theory," *Canadian Journal of Economics and Political Science,* 15:53–73, 1949.
23. Henderson, A. M. and Parsons, T., *Max Weber: The Theory of Social and Economic Organization,* New York: Oxford University Press, 1947.
24. Homans, G. C., *The Human Group,* New York: Harcourt, Brace, 1950.
25. Horsfall, A. B. and Arensberg, C. M., "Teamwork and Productivity in a Shoe Factory," *Human Organization,* 8:13–25, 1949.
26. Jacobs, J. H., "The Application of Sociometry to Industry," *Sociometry,* 8:181–198, 1945.
27. Kennedy, V. D., *Union Policy and Incentive Wage Methods,* New York: Columbia University Press, 1945.
28. Koch, S., "The Current Status of Motivational Psychology," *Psychological Review,* 58:147–154, 1951.
29. Koivisto, W. A., "Value, Theory, and Fact in Industrial Sociology," *American Journal of Sociology,* 58:564–572, 1953.
30. Lindzey, G. and Borgatta, E. F., "Sociometric Measurement," in Lindzey, G. (ed.), *Handbook of Social Psychology,* Cambridge: Addison-Wesley, 1954, Vol. 1.

31. Mead, G. H., *Mind, Self and Society*, Chicago: University of Chicago Press, 1934.

32. Moore, W. E., Review of Mayo's "The Social Problems of an Industrial Civilization," *American Sociological Review*, 12:123–124, 1947.

33. Moreno, J. L., *Who Shall Survive?* Washington, D. C.: Nervous and Mental Disease Publishing Co., 1934.

34. Murray, P. and Cooke, M., *Organized Labor and Production*, New York: Harper, 1946.

35. Parsons, T., *The Structure of Social Action*, New York: McGraw-Hill, 1937.

36. Reissman, L., "A Study of Role Conceptions in Bureaucracy," *Social Forces*, 27:305–310, 1949.

37. Roethlisberger, F. J., *Management and Morale*, Cambridge: Harvard University Press, 1952.

38. ——, and Dickson, W. J., *Management and the Worker*, Cambridge: Harvard University Press, 1940.

39. Rogers, M., "Problems of Human Relations in Industry," *Sociometry*, 9:350–371, 1946.

40. Roy, D., "Efficiency and 'The Fix': Informal Intergroup Relations in a Piecework Machine Shop," *American Journal of Sociology*, 60:255–266, 1954.

41. ——, "Quota Restriction and Goldbricking in a Machine Shop," *American Journal of Sociology*, 57:427–442, 1952.

42. ——, "Work Satisfaction and Social Reward in Quota Achievement: An Analysis of Piecework Incentive," *American Sociological Review*, 18:507–514, 1953.

43. Sayles, L. R., "The Impact of Incentives on Inter-Group Work Relations—A Management and Union Problem," *Personnel*, 28:483–490, 1952.

44. ——, "Worker Values in Job Evaluation," *Personnel*, 30:266–274, 1954.

45. Scanlon, J. N., "Adamson and His Profit-Sharing Plan," AMA Production Series No. 172, 1947, pp. 10–12.

46. Schultz, G. P., "Worker Participation on Production Problems," *Personnel*, 28:201–211, 1951.

47. ——, and Crisara, R. O., "The Lapointe Machine Tool Company and United Steelworkers of America," National Planning Association, Nov., 1952.

48. Selznick, P., "An Approach to a Theory of Bureaucracy," *American Sociological Review*, 8:47–54, 1943.

49. Sheppard, H. L., "The Treatment of Unionism in 'Managerial Sociology,'" *American Sociological Review*, 14:310–313, 1949.

50. Stone, R. C., "Conflicting Approaches to the Study of Worker-Manager Relations," *Social Forces*, 31:117–124, 1952.

51. Walker, C. R. and Guest, R. H., "The Man on the Assembly Line," *Harvard Business Review*, 30:71–83, May–June, 1952.

52. Whiteford, A. H. and Gardner, B. B., "From Conflict to Cooperation: A Study of Union-Management Relations," *Applied Anthropology*, 5, Special Issue, Fall, 1946.

53. Whyte, W. F., "Economic Incentives and Human Relations," *Harvard Business Review*, 30:73–80, March–April, 1952.

54. ———, "Human Relations Theory—a progress report," *Harvard Business Review*, 34:125–132, September–October, 1956.

55. ———, "Incentives for Productivity: The Bundy Tubing Company Case," *Applied Anthropology*, 7:1–16, Spring, 1948.

56. ———, *Pattern for Industrial Peace*, New York: Harper, 1951.

57. ———, "Patterns of Interaction in Union-Management Relations," *Human Organization*, 8:13–19, Fall, 1949.

58. ———, "Union-Management Cooperation: Toronto Case," *Applied Anthropology*, 6:1–9, Summer, 1947.

59. ———, et al., *Money and Motivation*, New York: Harper, 1955.

60. Wirth, L., "World Community, World Society, and World Government: An Attempt at a Clarification of Terms," in Wright, Q. (ed.), *The World Community*, Chicago: University of Chicago Press, 1948.

61. Zeleny, L. D., "Selection of Compatible Flying Partners," *American Journal of Sociology*, 52:424–431, 1947.

PART FOUR

TWO MAJOR PROBLEMS:
UNIONS AND RACES
AT WORK

INTRODUCTION

Up to this point we have been concerned with elements of work which are universal. The institutional system, status and authority system, career and work group may be observed in all cultures. The areas to which we now turn—labor unions and ethnic relations—are not.

In some places, almost every worker belongs to a labor union; in others, labor unions have not been heard of. They have reached their most complex development in Western culture and their importance there justifies our giving special attention to them. Ethnic relations are similarly of regional interest. Dobuans are (or were, until recently) not concerned with them, and the ethnic homogeneity of Eire is striking. But in some places, especially where Western conquerors or industrialists have gone in search of booty, labor, or glory, ethnic relations fairly dominate all areas of life.

Labor unions and ethnic relations deserve separate treatment for a second reason: each of these phenomena has a life of its own outside of work. Labor unions exist because work organizations exist, but the labor organization is a separate one which no one would confuse with, say, the factory organization. Ethnic relations enter work organizations, but they too have a character all their own which affects not only work but family, church, housing, recreation, and politics as well.

In other words, an examination of labor unions and ethnic relations takes us outside the world of work so that we are looking at the relation between work and the larger community—what we have called "the work complex." Yet it is important to bear in mind that we shall not be concerned with unions or ethnic relations *per se*. Throughout this volume our focus has been on *work* as a theoretical area in its own right in sociology. It is entirely consistent with our framework, then, that we should treat unions and ethnic groups in terms of their effect on work relations. The clarity that is achieved by such a limitation of focus is attained at a cost: we cannot give attention to such matters as the labor movement in the United States, the internal organization of labor unions and the many variations in tactics, the impact of racial discrimination in job assignment on Negro housing or education, or the denial of political rights to migratory laborers. It is hoped, however, that our discussion will provide leads for those interested in important questions such as those.

CHAPTER FIFTEEN

UNION WORK RELATIONS

Our concern in this chapter is with union *work* relations, that is, with the manner in which the presence of a labor union affects the social organization of work. It is helpful if we have in mind a model, and for maximal generality this model should be close to the typical situation in which a labor union is likely to be found. If one were told that the average annual membership in American labor unions was over five million in 1920 and around eight and one-half million in 1940, one might conclude that membership had been increasing. Actually, membership dropped to less than three million in 1933, and, in fact, the period of the twenties and the early thirties was one of low membership figures (50, p. 56). But since then, unions have made spectacular gains (6) and at present about one-third of organizable workers are members of unions. These persons are by no means equally distributed. They tend to be a lower-middle socioeconomic status group (46, pp. 48–51), heavily concentrated in cities and in certain industries, especially manufacturing, mining, transportation and communication, entertainment, and construction. The percentage covered by collective bargaining arrangements is around 70 for manufacturing and is over 90 in certain kinds of manufacturing such as automobiles, aircraft, basic steel, trucking, and railroading. On the other hand, the figures are very low for farming, domestic service, and many branches of trade; only one-sixth of white-collar workers are unionized.[1] The heavy concentration of membership and collective

[1] See our discussion of white-collar unionization, p. 63, esp. fn. 24. Perhaps the most insightful treatment of the resistance of white-collar workers to unionization is Mills' (45, Ch. 14). See also the excellent discussion in (26) of the hesitation of unions of en-

bargaining agreements in manufacturing, together with the fact that we have given special attention to the factory in Chapters 11 to 14 leads us to make use of the factory, as a model, in the following discussion. There will, of course, be important variations in other industries.

THE UNION AND FACTORY SOCIAL ORGANIZATION

What changes occur in the factory's social organization as a sonsequence of the present of a duly recognized union local? In Chapter 11 we described factory vertical communication: orders go down the line and information comes up. As information comes up, it may be altered or even stopped. Such changes may occur because the information is too detailed to be usable by a higher supervisor, because the supervisor himself feels the information must be related to other data he has, or because he feels the information is threatening to him. One of the most threaten-

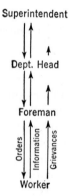

FIG. 21

MOVEMENT OF GRIEVANCES WITHOUT A UNION

ing kinds of information is the grievance. When a worker has a complaint he normally carries it to his foreman, who usually will try to deal with it on the spot. The foreman typically prefers that his supervisor should not hear about it if possible. Only as a last resort is he likely to carry it further up. This is true at each level of the organization. We may represent this in the form shown in Fig. 21.

It may be observed that there is a tendency for the grievance to peter out as one moves higher up.

gineers and scientists to make common cause with the production union and the feeling of these professionals that it was "undignified to strike." A thoughtful treatment, by an anonymous union organizer, is (75).

When a union enters, however, a totally different pattern manifests itself. This is represented in Fig. 22.

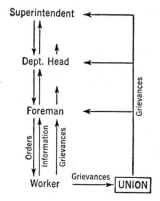

FIG. 22

GRIEVANCE MACHINERY WITH A UNION

A grievance *may* move up in the old way, but if it is frustrated at any point, or if, in the worker's or union representative's opinion, there is little point in carrying it up step-by-step, then the grievance may move out of the line structure altogether, move up several steps if necessary, and reenter the line structure at a high point. Should the union succeed in convincing the appropriate line officer or group with whom they are negotiating that the grievance should be settled, then the superintendent may issue an order to a subordinate to rectify the matter. What started out as an item of information or a request has now become an order from a superior. Supervisors at every level now find this new pressure coming to them from below and above at the same time, as it were, and the result is likely to be more sensitivity than usual to complaints.

The entry of the union also means the presence of union representatives in all shops of the factory. These men often have a privileged status: they often enjoy top seniority (50, p. 208), have relatively high wages (66), and may have the right to leave their job to take care of union business. Stewards and committeemen do not have much power themselves but they do possess the ability to call into action the resources of a national labor union which may be richer and more powerful than management in a particular factory. The need to meet management on equal terms has led national unions to add to their staffs experts in law,[2] race relations,

---

* This chart is modelled on one provided in (23).

[2] The varied legislative controls and legal rulings over the years has increased the need for the labor lawyer, as Joseph Kovner indicates in the following: "There was the

economics, public relations, housing, insurance and many other areas (76). Management will not lightly take up arms against such an organization. And this organization does not suddenly make its appearance at contract-renegotiation time: it is inside the gates camped continually on company property.

ATTITUDES OF TOP MANAGEMENT TO A NEW UNION

There are three typical ways in which management reacts to the first entry of a union in the factory.

REJECT THE UNION

Management may do everything possible to overthrow the union and look upon it as a temporary thing soon to be removed. It may even instruct foremen to ignore the union steward or put him off. Under such conditions, any rapprochement between management and the union is made extremely difficult, and there is antagonism, conflict, and perhaps strikes.

ACCEPT UNION BUT ATTEMPT TO CONDUCT BUSINESS AS IF THE UNION WERE NOT THERE

Occasionally the union will be tolerated but an attempt will be made to carry on as if the union were in fact not present. This occurs particularly with reference to discharging employees. Such independence of action may not represent an attempt to ignore the union, but rather a feeling that hiring and firing employees is part of the normal course of running the business and therefore a matter in which the union may have no legitimate interest.

It is often difficult to draw a sharp line between union and business interests, in part because of the nature of the union contract. A contract is a result of negiotations and compromise; it tends to contain a considerable amount of vague language which represents that compromise. The following quotations are from a union contract of steelworkers (1, pp. 17, 53, 55):

Management will develop an appropriate hourly, tonnage, incentive or piece-work rate.

---

development of the labor injunction in the 1890's; application of the antitrust laws in the 1900's; the exempting provision of the Clayton Act in 1914; the anti-injunction act of 1932; and the accelerating innovations since 1935. In 1914, upon the eve of the Clayton Act's passage, the AFL relied upon its counsel to approve the proposed language exempting unions from the antitrust laws. In 1949, William Green withheld comment on the government's bill to repeal the Taft-Hartley Act until he had consulted counsel" (28a). See also (62).

The proposed rates will be explained to the grievance committee with the objective of obtaining agreement to the installation of the proposed rates, or, to the installation of the proposed rate for an agreed upon period which will serve as a trial period.

The management of the work and the direction of the working forces, including the right to hire, suspend or discharge for proper cause, or transfer, and the right to relieve employees from duty because of lack of work or for other legitimate reasons, is vested exclusively in the company, provided that this will not be used for purposes of discrimination against any member of the union.

The company shall continue to make reasonable provisions for the safety and health of its employees at the plant during the hours of their employment. Protective devices, wearing apparel and other equipment necessary to properly protect employees from injury shall be provided by the Company in accordance with the practices now prevailing in each separate plant. Proper heating and ventilating systems shall be installed where needed.

Note the use of vague, undefined terms. The contract speaks of "appropriate" hourly incentives. Provision is made only for future discussions to discuss proposed rates. Responsibility for management is lodged with the company. However, it is provided that the company shall not use its power to "discriminate" against any member of the union, without specifying how discrimination shall be proven or demonstrated to be not present. The safety and health provisions provide for "reasonable" provision and for "proper" heating and ventilating systems. These are loopholes which can provide the subject for future conflict and disagreement; they represent the result of compromise.

RECOGNIZE THAT THE UNION MEANS A GENUINE CHANGE IN THE SOCIAL STRUCTURE OF THE FACTORY

Management may recognize that the union is not simply an addition to the situation but represents a profound transformation. Management will then calculate how the new element will affect relations with their subordinates (9) and will be concerned not to take unilateral action. How far it may be necessary to go in such thinking is not always clear. It may be obvious that the union will be upset by a wage cut, but not so obvious that it will be upset by a wage increase—if the increase is made by management on its own initiative. For if management will freely grant wage increases, then one important benefit of labor union membership has vanished. Most unions will wish to be notified in advance of such an increase and have the opportunity to discuss it with management. Nor is this simply a matter of wanting to take credit where none is due. An increase in one shop may produce a rush of grievances in a different shop. Or consider the following case (59, pp. 45–46):

Management told the girls in a large office to go home at midday because there was insufficient work for them. They complained to the union, which eventually won them a full day's pay. Immediately a flood of abuse was poured on the officers (of the union local) by the girls who had actually worked the entire period for the same pay.

That case is remarkable because it was management's *acquiescence* to the union demand that resulted in the new grievances. One may be sure that the union leadership will now be looking for ways of "rewarding" the girls who had worked the entire period. Cases such as these lead Sayles and Strauss to speak of the grievance procedure as being one of mutual "problem-solving" except in armed-truce situations (58). One great advantage to management in consulting continuously with the union is that the union may then help back an unpopular measure. For example, the establishment of seniority rules which will satisfy everyone seems to be a near impossibility. If management can get the union to agree on a provision for handling seniority, then the union will be forced to share the criticism that will be directed against the provision. And, speaking generally, a labor economist, Chamberlain, has written (10, p. 315):

While property rights carry with them a power of disposition of goods, they do not carry an equal power to use those goods *if* the cooperation of others is necessary to that use. Cooperation, without which the property right is reduced to a power of disposition, cannot be commanded. It can only be won by consent . . . And there is no legal compulsion upon the workers to cooperate . . . Thus the management and direction of others do not flow out of legal rights but must be granted by those very people who are managed and directed. And the price of the grant may be that management yields its independence in certain matters of business operation. What matters? *Potentially* none would seem to be excluded —whatever matters are deemed important to those whose cooperation is being sought.

Of course the union is not the only medium through which such consent may be secured but it is a highly convenient one which involves negotiation with responsible officials. There are, then, advantages in consultation for both management and union. It does not, of course, follow that they will agree.

LOWER LEVELS OF MANAGEMENT AND THE UNION

After a union contract has been signed, special problems may arise in connection with foremen and sub-foremen in the implementation of the contract. Often, when top management negotiates a contract, the lower ranks are not consulted. They simply have the existence of the contract announced to them one day. Because of the suddenness of the change, the foremen may feel that top management actually does not want the union. Consequently they decide not to cooperate with the union steward and to resist the union.

One way to reduce such conflict is the employment of a ceremony. In most societies great changes are solemnized by a public ceremony, which directs attention to the change and also indicates social approval. The signing of a union contract may be done through a company ceremony. A banquet may be arranged in which all workers, or at least the lower ranks of management, are included, and the contract may be signed with a flourish in the presence of all. Of course, for such a ceremony to be effective, management must be perfectly sincere: the ceremony must be followed by day-by-day confirmation, through behavior, that management intends to accept the union in the plant.

Sayles and Strauss (59, Ch. 4) call attention to an important change which has reduced the significance of the role of the foreman in the grievance process. The steward is, theoretically, the first man a worker with a grievance turns to; the steward then will attempt to negotiate directly with the worker's foreman. But increasingly the steward is by-passed by both worker and the steward's own superiors in the union structure. The worker does not go to the steward but to whomever he thinks can get him what he wants—often someone much higher in the union organization. This man—perhaps a committeeman or union officer —goes directly to the head of the personnel department or the plant manager, a decision is made, and the foreman is ordered to take care of the problem. Even if a worker goes to his steward, the latter, recognizing his very limited power and knowledge, and perhaps reluctant to do battle with a man who may be his own foreman, passes the grievance right on to someone higher up in the union hierarchy. When grievances are settled higher up, the foreman as well as the steward come to play minor roles in the grievance procedure. Striking confirmation of relative weakness of the foreman *vis-à-vis* persons high in the union organization is provided by cases in which the union indirectly assists foremen to attain their own ends (59, p. 37):

An assistant department head had been promoted to department head and naturally requested a promotion for his secretary. When his request was rejected, the secretary's chief steward (committeeman and one step above the steward) immediately contacted the local president and both made a strong oral protest to the industrial relations manager. Several days later the secretary was upgraded— and the department head thanked the chief steward.

When a first-line supervisor is presented with such clear evidence of his own powerlessness as compared to that of a chief steward, he is not likely to participate actively in the settlement of grievances unless he feels very sure of himself or has been criticized for "bucking" too many grievances. As union contracts become more complex, bargaining becomes, increasingly, an activity for experts high in their respective organizations.

DYNAMICS OF UNION-MANAGEMENT RELATIONS

Union-management relations are often peaceful; many organized firms have never had a strike. Yet the character of union-management contacts is always conditioned by the fact that union leaders and factory management both represent power organizations which can put pressure on each other to force a desired outcome. Consequently, we shall focus our attention on two major types of areas in which the power of each may be brought to bear on the other: union recognition and collective bargaining.

UNION RECOGNITION

When a union is struggling for recognition, there may be marked conflict. The union is attempting to secure as many expressions of confidence in itself as possible from the workers. Resistance may come from the workers themselves, from management, from a company union, or even from another union trying to organize the same plant (18). But the strongest opposition is likely to come from management because of its resources, because it may feel it has a great deal to lose, and because of powerful beliefs in managerial prerogatives.

The more important management tactics have included the following. *Physical force*. Strike-breakers, the militia, or the police may be called in, if possible. This tactic is relatively rare today (though most old-line unionists can recall its use in the near past) because of legal restrictions, the strength of present-day unions, and the rejection of the use of violence by a more sympathetic public. *Discharge or threat of discharge*. Persons regarded as strongly pro-union may be discharged, often with much fanfare so that others may take warning. Again, this tactic was commoner in the past, especially before the passage of the Wagner act. *Increased liberality*. The long-awaited recreation room in the plant will now make its appearance, rest periods may be instituted and there may be pay raises. Through these means, it is hoped to convince the worker that he has nothing to gain by joining the union. *Anti-union propaganda and the injunction*. These last-mentioned procedures are among the most commonly used tactics today. Though severely restricted by the Wagner act, they have been made legal—under certain conditions—by the Taft-Hartley act. Workers may be told that those joining the union are expressing disloyalty to management, that unionism is a foreign importation from a decadent Europe, that it is Communistic, and that it violates the fundamental American emphasis on bettering oneself by one's own efforts. Injunctions may be used to prevent picketing or intended strikes.

Against such formidable obstacles the union musters all of its strength. Schneider points out that (61, p. 275):

. . . the first stage in every successful organizing drive is always the same: the development of a body of workers who feel either consciously or unconsciously bored, frustrated, resentful, and deprived.

These persons may become the core of the movement to organize the plant. The organizer seeks to discover them and to enlist their aid. Although an organizer cannot create much dissatisfaction unless the workers already feel it, he must channel this feeling and prove that the union is the only way of solving the problem. Karsh, Seidman, and Lilienthal, in a detailed report of how a small Midwestern knitting mill was organized by the International Ladies Garment Workers Union (32), point out the importance of the *personality* of the organizer. She probed for dissatisfactions and then placed responsibility for them on the employer: but in addition, she was liked and admired by workers as a person. The organizer will initiate a propaganda campaign to counter that being employed by management (63, pp. 14–17). The campaign will be directed both at the workers and at "neutral" members of the community, and will encourage workers to place pressure on management through slowdowns, boycotts, and most important, the threat of a strike.[3] If all fails, a strike may actually be called. When the early history of union-management relations are characterized by conflict as intense as this, then—should the union secure recognition—subsequent bargaining relations may take the form of what Harbison and Coleman call an "armed truce" (28, p. 20). The nature of these early relations will also affect the worker's attachment to his union, as Dunlop suggests in the following (18, p. 149):

Members organized by a vote in a Government-conducted election or by the application of the union-security provision of an agreement, whose dues are checked off by the employer to the union, can hardly be expected to hold the same attachments to the union that arose when men were organized on the picket line.

[3] Valuable studies of strikes are (24, pp. 87–170; 30; 35; 73; 74).

The nature of these attachments will affect the willingness of the worker to back up his union in future conflicts, and, in turn, management's conception of its power position will include an assessment of the amount of worker support the union enjoys.

When a union has been in a plant for some time and has successfully weathered several bargaining sessions, its position often comes to be regarded as legitimate. This does not mean that management grants immediately any and all demands or that it works hand-in-glove with union leaders; rather the union comes to be regarded as one of the facts of life with which management must deal or face consequences it wishes to avoid. In such a situation, there may arise serious problems for the union in controlling its membership. In the early period was one of conflict, the union made continuous use of the agitator or fighter. Now that the union is accepted, it requires, instead, persons skilled in negotiation and administration. What then shall it do with its agitators and fighters? Many of them have probably become stewards or committeemen. They often feel, from their previous experience, that it is still necessary to fight, may continually remind men in their shop of how management resisted recognition, and warn the men to keep their guard up at all times. This makes the development of mutual confidence very difficult and seriously hampers collective bargaining efforts.[4]

Usually, unions are loathe to discipline these persons, for they owe them a great deal and the feeling of mistrust of management may even be shared by persons high up in the national union. Yet, the union leadership will wish to control them and employs various devices to do so. One is to shift some of these persons into the Deep South or other areas not yet unionized.

The problems unions face in controlling their membership are often irritating to management. Having signed a contract in good faith, management upholds its end of the contract and expects the union leadership to hold its members in line. The very term "contract" implies a negotiated settlement between responsible parties. Yet the president of a company and the president of a union do not play comparable roles. The company president is a head of a business. The contrasting position of the union leader is well-stated by Mills (44):

The labor union is an army; the labor leader is a generalissimo. The union is a democratic town meeting; the leader is a parliamentary debater. The union is a

---

[4] For discussions of this problem, see (25, pp. 48–81; 31, pp. 288 ff.). Particularly interesting is the report by Herberg (29) of leadership problems faced by the two major locals of the New York City dressmakers' union as Italians and Jews leave that industry and are replaced by Latin Americans, Negroes, and others. See also (20, Ch. 9, 47).

political machine; the leader is a political boss. The union is a business enterprise, supplying a labor force; the labor leader is an entrepreneur, a contractor of labor.

In the performance of all of these functions, even the quasi-business one of labor-contractor, the effectiveness of the labor leader rests, ultimately, upon how favorable union members feel towards him. Even in highly corrupt unions, a leader who loses the confidence of his members is not likely to stay in power long. Consequently, as G. Popiel (52) points out, although a union is a bureaucracy, unlike the factory bureaucracy, it must consult its clients (members) on important decisions. Particularly exasperating to management is the wildcat strike where workers may reject their own leadership. Gouldner (27) discovered the dynamics of a wildcat strike in the fact that worker dissatisfaction revolved about "complaints" rather than "grievances." A grievance could be settled by reference to the contract. But a complaint was something outside the contract and was not therefore a matter which the *union* leadership had agreed upon. That leadership could not, therefore, legitimately turn to management and demand a settlement. It was left for the workers to take matters into their own hands. But what shall a leadership that has promised management there will be no strikes do? If it tries to fulfil its part of the contract by telling the members to return to work, it may easily forfeit its leadership. Yet Mills has pointed out that union leaders who behave in a businesslike manner—where the union leader becomes a dependable labor contractor who can assure fulfilment of agreements—may turn out, ironically, to be labor racketeers; that is, those who use the union for their personal economic betterment (44, pp. 122–32). A union leader, for a consideration, calls a strike against a competitor of the company's, or talks his own union into accepting a lower wage increase than what was desired. Such racketeers, Mills says, are the robber barons of labor. Of course other factors are involved, especially the internal organization of the union local, the establishment of "the fix" with local law officers, regularized relations with criminals, and an uninterested or powerless union membership.

GRIEVANCES

When a union has been recognized, the likelihood of industrial peace depends largely on the success of collective bargaining. The contract will itself describe how changes are to be made in the contract and, increasingly, governmental and legal controls delimit the conditions of bargaining. But within these limits, there is much room for maneuvering and for each side use its power to secure an advantage from the other. We may examine collective bargaining at two levels: the process or machinery for carrying it out, and the issues with which it deals. We shall limit ourselves, further, to situations in which a contract has been signed, and is in force, and in which disputes arise over the application of the contract to particular problems; that is, we are concerned with grievances.

1. THE GRIEVANCE PROCESS

The contract will usually specify a set of procedures for handling grievances. Typically, these involve a step-by-step process (39, pp. 219–313; 71, pp. 555–616). When a worker has a complaint which he feels is legitimate under the contract, he is expected first to seek redress at the hands of his immediate supervisor. If that fails, the union steward is called in and he discusses the matter with the worker's supervisor; or else he will carry the dispute to a higher official in the factory structure. If that fails, then higher representatives of both parties enter into discussions with one another. If meetings between representatives of the union international and the company manager or industrial relations department also fail, the dispute may be referred to arbitration. Some contracts specify which disputes may be submitted to arbitration; others permit any grievance to be submitted. Arbitration itself is a legalistic matter. The arbitrator (or a panel of them) gathers data, hears witnesses, and renders a decision which often has quasi-legal force (64, pp. 217–346). The use of a mutually agreed-upon arbitrator is to be distinguished from the use of a government-sponsored service such as the Federal Mediation and Conciliation Service. The representative of the latter (or any mediator [5]) is not bound by the limits usually imposed on the arbitrator but instead seeks to secure a compromise acceptable to both of the contending parties. In the process, the mediator may meet privately with each side to try to find out if he will budge, engage in horse-trading, provide a means whereby a loser can save face, and so forth (49). By contrast, an arbitrator may decide that, in a particular case, management is wholly correct or wholly wrong. Speaking of arbitration, Updegraff and McCoy insist (72, pp. 132–33):

The practice, unfortunately rather prevalent, of rendering a decision that represents a compromise, should be avoided. Compromise has its place in negotiation

---

[5] Further distinctions are often made between "mediation" and "conciliation." For example, Kerr (34) speaks of mediation as "guidance by a third party to an acceptable accommodation" and conciliation as "adjustment of a dispute by the parties themselves." In the latter case, the conciliator occupies the role of contactmaker and seeks to keep the discussions going without himself actively entering into them. However, in practice both processes go on at once whether the negotiator be called mediator or conciliator.

and conciliation. But when the parties have exhausted those means, and resort to arbitration, they want an honest decision, not a compromise. If the facts disclose a case justifying discharge, to change the discharge to a two-week lay-off in an effort partially to satisfy one party without offending the other too greatly, is not honest arbitration. And if the facts disclose that no penalty was called for, to "save face" for management by a similar compromise is equally improper. A penalty should be modified only where the facts justify it—never for the purpose of compromise.

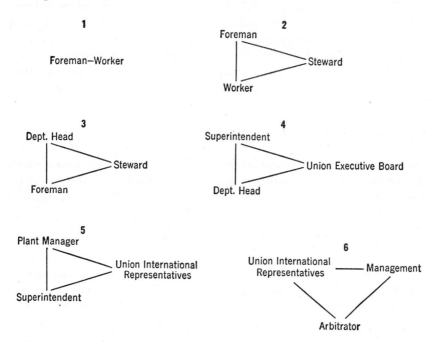

FIG. 23

GRIEVANCE PROCESS AS FREQUENTLY SPECIFIED IN UNION CONTRACTS

In actuality, arbitrators are likely to engage in some mediation as well (15).

The majority of arbitrators tend to be lawyers. Yet a considerable variety of persons are found including economists, sociologists, other social scientists (5, p. 309), and clergymen. This variety is a consequence of two facts: the lack of professional status for arbitrators, and the tendency for union and management to shop around for an arbitrator who, each feels, may render a decision favorable to it.

The above procedure is in fact used and a high proportion of cases are settled through it. But there are many variations in particular plants. Sayles and Strauss (59, Chs. 3, 4–7) found a strong tendency for workers to shop around and select whomever they thought could meet their grievance. This person might be the foreman or a steward, but it could also be a department head, or someone high up in the union who could be contacted at lunch or at home. Further, a grievance might be initiated by almost *anyone* however high he might stand in factory or union. A worker at the bottom might not wish to initiate a grievance but the union grievance committee might do so in any case, if it felt an important principle was involved or if it wished to harass management in order to attain some quite different objective. The fact that top management often uses the number of grievances a foreman receives as a measure of his efficiency makes it possible for a union official to get action on a desired matter by a threat such as was made to a foreman by one of Sayles and Strauss' subjects (59, p. 31):

I've got thirteen grievances in my pocket. If you don't wise up, then you get all thirteen in the morning. Understand?

On the other hand, the union itself may frustrate a grievance which it does not regard as worth fighting for or which it may feel interferes with other matters it is more interested in. In his excellent study of Local 28 of the United Packinghouse Workers at Swift and Co. in Chicago, Purcell (54, p. 224) reported also on the tendency to deviate from the grievance procedure specified by the contract:

. . . the foreman will sometimes defer giving any decision on a grievance or even handling it until he has presented the whole matter to his general foreman or division superintendent or even to the plant Labor Relations man. In this way, the foreman seeks to avoid mistakes and also to sew up a water-tight case.

All of these variations,[6] however, operate within the framework of a set of rules laid down in the contract and, if any of these informal procedures will not work, the formal procedures are still there to be used when needed. On the other hand, should these procedures fall into disuse to the point where the individual worker was forced to depend only on his own ingenuity and ability to buttonhole higher members of the union, then one would conclude that contract amendments would be desirable to increase the ease of communication and efficiency of the grievance system. Chamberlain has pointed out (10, pp. 113–19) that certain conditions appear to

---

[6] It is worth noting that the Taft-Hartley act specifically authorizes a worker and lower supervisor to by-pass the formal grievance procedure and carry their disagreement to higher plant officials, though the union is permitted to have an official present also.

be necessary for the efficient operation of a grievance system. Among those he mentions, the following are the more important: workers at all levels must be well-informed on how the grievance system works and what problems constitute proper grievances; there must be acceptance of it as the proper means of handling grievances, as opposed to unilateral action; there must be acceptance of the authority of union and supervisory officials and of their right to the positions the grievance system assigns them; persons must continue working while a grievance is being processed; to protect workers' rights, management must agree to grant union officials a kind of superseniority so that they will not be laid off and the workers left without their elected representative; there must be prompt action; the grievance system will not work well if glutted with grievances; participants in the grievance process must be assured of protection against personal loss; and there must be high probability of a fair consideration for a grievance and willingness to accept the final decision (including, of course, the possibility of arbitration).

2. SUBJECTS OF GRIEVANCES

If a union is powerful enough, theoretically almost anything can become a subject of grievance. If the matter is not mentioned in the contract, or even specifically excluded, then, if it comes to be regarded as important, it will become a matter for consideration at the time of contract renegotiation and may then be covered in the contract. But whatever the relative strength of the union, what subjects, in fact, are workers likely to consider legitimate grievances?

There is no simple answer. Some students have sought an answer in general or theoretical terms. For example, Bakke (2) suggests that the question must be answered in terms of a theory of motivation in which particular wants are explained in terms of broader needs or goals. He includes such needs as creature sufficiency (food, shelter, etc.), control over one's own affairs, integrity, and understanding. Ellsworth (19) used Bakke's approach in an institutional analysis of a manufacturing company in a New England community, but found it necessary to supplement Bakke's list with two other needs: security and satisfactory working conditions (3, 11, pp. 110–111).

Others have sought for a general answer by inquiring into factors associated with unionization. In oversimplified form some of the more important of these theories are the following. Commons (12) advanced the theory that unions arose in the United States when expanding markets forced a difference of interest on employers and journeymen—the former toward lower prices to enable them to compete with other employers, and the latter toward higher wages. Perlman (48a) laid emphasis

on the desire of the worker for a type of job proprietorship or security.[7]
Tannenbaum (67, 68) directs attention to the attempt to regain the
values of fellowship, dignity, and a sense of personal worth which were
destroyed by the growth of large-scale industry.

Such theories have drawn heavily on analyses of the history of labor
organization in the United States (13, 16, 48). Often, those who survey that
history end by characterizing the goals of union members in terms of a
cleavage which is described picturesquely by Lens as follows (41, p. 4):

Labor, a progressive social force, is led, by and large, by conservative officials
whose chariots are tied to the status quo.

And certainly United States labor history shows elements of both. There
were powerful groups desiring the wholesale reconstruction of society in
the Knights of Labor and the International Workers of the World, and
the occurrence of bloody combats such as the Haymarket riot of 1886, and
the Homestead strike of 1892, suggest that management and the general
public was far from willing to grant labor unions the right to bargain
collectively. The first major accusation of Communist backing was directed
at the leaders of the steel strike of 1919, and that factor, together with
labor's failure to organize the mass production industries and the pressures of both prosperity and depression, dealt labor organization a blow
from which it did not recover until 1935 (50, pp. 18–20). The passage of
the Wagner act in that year signaled an important change in labor union
tactics, for it was demonstrated how valuable a weapon legislation and
the courts might be when used to support labor demands, and it helped
labor throw off the reputation it had with many for being radical. Present-
day labor unionism has, in general, tended to follow the direction given it
by Samuel Gompers who helped turn it away from revolutionary objectives
to the pursuit of limited goals within the context of capitalism.[8] Taft, in
a valuable discussion of radicalism in the American labor movement (65),
points out that the major form radicalism takes now is infiltration by
Communists of existing unions (rather than dual unionism or the formation of One Big Union). Such influence does not appear to be great, and
for those unions where it is, Taft argues, Communist success is (65, p. 238):

---

[7] On the importance of the union as a general defense against job insecurity see (4, p.
99; 56). It has also been used as an argument for foremen's joining workers' unions, for,
should the foreman be demoted, he would lack seniority and other guarantees the workers have. See (40, p. 52).

[8] This does not, of course, imply acceptance of the other aspects of what is sometimes
called: "Gompersism—craft unionism, no politics in the unions, and community of
est between labor and capital" (21, p. 11).

. . . traceable to the policies of industry which have refused to allow unions to function and for many years denied their workers a voice in affairs of vital importance to them. As a consequence, neither effective trade unions, official cadres, or a nucleus of an experienced membership existed, and it was therefore easy for Communists to entrench themselves.

Without agreeing with Taft—for there were many other factors beside management opposition to labor unions that account for Communist influence in the labor movement—one may still accept his general argument that workers do not, in the main, look to their unions to change the structure of American society.

In contrast to such general approaches toward understanding workers' interest in unions, other students of union-management relations have gone to particular factories or unions and asked the workers themselves what they want from their unions. Rose, in his study of a teamsters' local in St. Louis, Missouri (55), found that workers felt the main function of their union to be the betterment of wages and working conditions, but there was a strong interest in other matters, such as health benefits and security; for example, the workers strongly favored seniority provisions for handling promotions and layoffs. While he gave little evidence of a "class struggle mentality," Rose reports there was strong support of the policy of using union funds for political activity (but the members themselves do not wish to be told how to vote).[9] Purcell's (54, pp. 150–51) packinghouse workers, however, gave as their most important reason for union allegiance the "job-protection and status" that the union offered; "decent wages" took second place as a motive for union membership. By "job-protection and status" was meant:

The workers talk of "not being pushed around," being "able to go over the boss' head," "having seniority," "protection for our people" (colored), having "someone to talk for you." For one, it is protection against discrimination in layoff or advancement. For another, it is insurance that his foreman will not overstep himself. For another, it is the enforcement of seniority rules . . . The worker wants recognition, respect, dignity; he wants to be listened to; he wants some say about conditions in the work life of the plant community; he wants to express the feeling of solidarity he has, in greater or less degree, with his fellow workers.

Rosen and Rosen (57, pp. 36–42) report that only about one-half of the members of District No. 9, International Association of Machinists, that were sampled supported the union policy of taking an active part in pol-

[9] See (55, pp. 3–15) for an excellent summary of the multiple functions of trade union membership.

itics. However, like A. M. Rose's subjects, the machinists strongly favored union support of political candidates who back pro-labor legislation. Another important finding of the Rosens' was the strong desire of the machinists to be kept informed of what the union leadership was doing, not only at the local level, but at the District level as well. Sayles and Strauss found that almost every person they interviewed in their sample of a number of union locals felt strongly that the union was necessary for economic security and protection against arbitrary management action (59, pp. 222–23).

Another way to shed light on dynamics of union-management relations is to examine the specific matters that form the subject of grievances, and which are likely to be carried on up the line until they are submitted to mediation or arbitration. Among the more important of such grievances are those dealing with seniority, safety and health, vacations, discharges, and wages.[10]

a. SENIORITY

Within industry, seniority may be of several types (7). One may have plant seniority, division seniority or job seniority. Disputes tend to fall into two areas: (1) Determination of the period of continuing service of the contending parties; that is the arbitrator will have to make a factual determination of when service began, and (2) The determination of the ability of rival candidates to perform a given job.

Most contracts provide that "continuous service" shall govern providing that there is no appreciable difference between the contending parties. Ordinarily, the question of when a worker started to work is not a severe problem unless it occurred far back in the past and the company has not maintained adequate records.

Serious problems are likely to arise when workers are *shifted*. For example, if there is division seniority and a person is shifted to a different division then he may lose his division seniority; or he may lose seniority if he is suspended from his work for a given period of time. In the case of the second type of conflict, problems may arise because usually the union is committed to a policy of seniority, and management wishes to exercise some degree of discretion based upon the ability of the worker. The significance of this conflict is brought out in the United Steel Workers contract of 1945 with Carnegie–Illinois Steel Corporation; its seniority provision states in part as follows:

---

[10] The following discussion is based on these sources (10, Ch. 14; 17; 33, pp. 280–91); a series of lectures given by Herbert Blumer after serving as a labor arbitrator for Carnegie-Illinois Steel and the United Steelworkers of America (CIO); and the writer's own experience as employee and researcher in two factories.

The parties recognize that promotional opportunity and job security in event of promotion, decrease of forces and rehiring after layoff should increase in proportion to length in continuous service, and that in the administration of this Section the intent will be that wherever practicable full consideration shall be given continuous service in such cases.

In recognition, however, of the responsibility of the Management for the efficient operation of the works, it is understood and agreed that in all cases of:

1. Promotion . . . The following factors as listed below shall be considered; however only where factors "a" and "b" are relatively equal shall length of continuous service be the determining factor:

a. Ability to perform the work;

b. Physical fitness;

c. Continuous service.

2. Increase or Decrease in Forces . . . The following factors as listed below shall be considered; however only where both factors "a" and "b" are relatively equal shall continuous service be the determining factor:

a. Ability to perform the work;

b. Physical fitness;

c. Continuous service.

The arbitrator under such an agreement may be called upon to decide whether the difference in ability between two workers is sufficient to warrant by-passing the seniority provision. For this purpose the arbitrator will make use of production records, the opinions of foremen and superintendents and any other information he is able to gather. An important question here will revolve about the ability of the worker not at *present* but his ability at the time the change was made. Also normally the arbitrator will be interested in the man's ability to do a *given job* and not necessarily in his general abilities. It is indeed in connection with the latter that problems may arise. Management may feel that while individual A can do the job better than individual B, nevertheless individual B shows broader knowledge and ability which will be useful in the higher realms of supervision and consequently it is desired to give preference to individual B.

b. SAFETY AND HEALTH

The contractual agreement with reference to safety and health is fairly standardized. It usually provides simply that the company shall exercise care in safety and health provisions (71, pp. 728–38). Where there is disagreement, usually the company doctor will be called upon to settle the matter.

The important point here is that the union may use the safety and health clause in the contract in order to get something else done which they are unable to secure in any other way. Blumer referred to the prob-

lem of the reduction of crews in the changeover to diesel locomotives.
When the steel companies began to use diesels for switching purposes the
need for a fireman in the locomotive was removed. The union claimed
that to remove the fireman would be to violate the safety and health provision of the contract: when a locomotive goes down the track in a yard,
the engineer can only observe out of one window on one side of the train;
[meanwhile there] someone might be crossing the tracks on the left-hand
side, whom the engineer would not see; thus (it was claimed) the fireman
should be retained so that he could watch simultaneously out of the left-
hand window.

Here is another example. In rooms where the coke ovens were
located the temperature often rose to 85°F or 90°F. It was therefore
customary to have reliefs or spell crews for one half hour out of every
hour. A dispute arose in connection with how the men should be paid
for this stand-by time. The union claimed that the men should be paid
at the regular wage since it was not their fault that they were required to
be relieved, and that it was simply a matter of carrying out the provisions
of the safety and health clause in the contract.

c. VACATION

Most contracts specify a vacation period for the worker after a certain length of service, but certain problems arise. For example, a person
may be discharged before his vacation is due. Or a returning serviceman
may claim that time accumulated before he went into the service should
be counted.

d. DISCHARGE CASES

These are often difficult to handle because the matter of discharge
is surrounded with emotions. There is, therefore, a tendency to hunt
for technicalities in the contract. Most contracts merely say that management shall have "proper cause" for discharge. Usually the company presents some evidence but it is often a borderline case.

These cases are also difficult because of two conflicting philosophies
with reference to discharge that are invoked by union on the one hand
and by management on the other. The union usually stands on the Anglo-
Saxon principle of law that a man is innocent until proven guilty; consequently (it is maintained) the burden of proof is on management to
show why a person should be discharged. Management takes the view
that it is running the company and has the right to do as it pleases except
where the contract specifically says that it does not have that right; therefore the burden of proof is on the union to show that the company did not
have the right to discharge a man. The arbitrator's problem then is to
determine if there is "proper cause" for the discharge. That may necessitate examining the employee's record, securing testimony, etc.

e. WAGES

In a sense, most grievances are wage grievances of one sort or another and the wage section of the contract is therefore probably the most important. Wage problems usually revolve about the question of a *change* in the rates or a change in the pay. A contract is usually much clearer on this than on other matters. It will say that whatever rates are in effect at the beginning of the contract period shall remain in effect for the balance of the contract period. One is likely to get severe disputes before the contract period begins. Management will usually desire rates that are satisfactory to them because they will then be stuck with these rates for the duration of the contract. Therefore it is just at such times that the attempt will be made to lower the rate. The claim may be made that a rate was set by mistake for example at five cents higher than was really intended. The arbitrator will then have to institute an inquiry. The first question perhaps will be: How long has the rate been in effect? If it has been in effect a long time then the company might have conceivably be said to have endorsed this by having taken no previous action, or perhaps because of the complexity of the accounting system a change might go undetected for a long period of time.

This type of problem is not so common, however, as those centering about changes in the work load. When this happens the employee may claim that the rate has been changed. Tied up in such disputes is the old question of what constitutes a "fair day's work." Some industrial engineers have tried to define it by some such measure as the rate of work done in walking three miles per hour over level ground, carrying no load (36, Ch. 2, pp. 342 ff.; 54). Such definitions are rarely acceptable to either union or management.

Copelof (14) describes a case of a work load dispute in a cotton finishing firm, involving the elimination of the jobs of one man from the starch department and one man from the bleach house. The remaining work crews in each department sought an increase in their rate of pay on the grounds that they now had to do the work of the men who had been discharged. Management, however, insisted that both changes were the result of mechanical improvements which had been introduced gradually over the years, and that there had been no substantial increase in the work load of the remaining crews. Copelof describes the result (14, p. 156):

At the arbitrator's request and with the approval of both parties, the United States Bureau of Labor Statistics made a survey of the work loads of groups of employees in other textile mills doing this same general type of work. The results of this survey were inconclusive and the arbitrator therefore based his findings on his own factual determination as to the extent, if any, of the changes in duties of the employees of the starch department and the bleach house. In each instance he found that the changes in equipment had indeed made it practicable to eliminate a job without placing any undue burden on the remaining employees. He did find, however, that the work load of each group had increased by approximately 5 per cent. Thus he ordered an increase of 5 per cent in the rates of the employees affected.

Our discussion of the content of grievances has suggested the great *diversity* of subjects which union members consider to be appropriate concerns of union leaders. There appear, in sum, to be three major matters which workers clearly expect from their unions: wage improvement (including fringe benefits), job security, and protection from arbitrary management actions (which may, of course, include actions with reference to wages and jobs but which includes many other matters as well). Some of the dispute among students of union-management relations revolves about the question of which of these is "first," but clearly they are all important.

Further, all are dynamic and do not, by definition, admit of permanent settlement. Wages can always move up or down, no job can be perfectly secure, and a management whose action is restricted in one area can always increase its pressure in another. Though dealing mainly with wages, the following interchange between old-unionist Samuel Gompers and Morris Hillquist, a Socialist attorney, before a governmental industrial inquiry, makes the point dramatically (70, pp. 587–88):

Mr. Gompers (Interrupting): Just a moment. I have not stipulated $4.00 a day or $8.00 a day or any number of dollars a day or 8 hours a day or 7 hours a day or any number of hours a day. The aim is to secure the best conditions obtainable for the workers.

Mr. Hillquist: Yes; and when these conditions are obtained—

Mr. Gompers (Interrupting): Why, then we want better—

Mr. Hillquist (Continuing): You will still strive for better?

Mr. Gompers: Yes.

Mr. Hillquist: Now, my question is, will this effort on the part of organized labor ever stop before the workers receive the full reward for their labor?

Mr. Gompers: It won't ,stop at all at any particular point, whether it be that towards which you have just stated, or anything else. The working people will never stop in their effort to obtain a better life for themselves, and for their wives and for their children and for humanity.

Mr. Hillquist: Then the object of the organized workmen is to obtain complete social justice for themselves and for their wives and for their children?

Mr. Gompers: It is the effort to obtain a better life every day.

Mr. Hillquist: Every day, and always—

Mr. Gompers (Interrupting): Every day. That does not limit it.

Mr. Hillquist: Until such time—

Mr. Gompers (Interrupting): Not until any time.

Mr. Hillquist: In other words—

Mr. Gompers (Interrupting): In other words, we go farther than you. (Laughter and applause in the audience.) You have an end (Socialism); we have not.

WORKER INVOLVEMENT IN LABOR UNIONS

The growth of union in the United States has created a new channel of upward mobility, new men of power, and a new status. For some, especially in certain industries such as garment making, their membership in the labor union is of supreme importance, giving their behavior meaning and their life a purpose. But data on rank-and-file attitudes indicate that such strong involvement is rare. Miller and Young (43) in a study of six union locals in Columbus, Ohio, characterize the feeling of most workers as one of "disinterested allegiance." Sayles and Strauss (59, pp. 224–25) found that, while their sample strongly accepted the economic function of their unions, only a minority showed "emotional identification" with the unions' organizational goals. They write:

Participation is relatively high in matters which concern the union's *collective bargaining* function. However, participation in *internal* activities is much lower unless these are directly tied in to collective bargaining. As has been discussed, attendance at union meetings averages 2 to 8 per cent of the total membership, but extraordinary events, such as strike votes or contract negotiations, may bring out 40 to 80 per cent.

The apparent apathy of union members toward internal union activities has been noted by many. Schneider (61, pp. 265–67) offers a number of possible reasons including wages and such "practical" matters are not "burning issues," workers feel they have little control over their unions, and the union itself becomes an oppressive control. Sayles and Strauss' results are especially valuable because they are based on actual research and because they made use of projective techniques. The latter uncovered attitudes and anxieties which workers rarely would express in words; namely, a feeling of shame or humiliation at having to accept union help in securing their goals, doubts about attacking the company, and fear of management reprisal (59, pp. 225–30).

Others, however, have raised the question as to whether the lack of "emotional identification" is a problem worth being concerned about, for it is certainly not the only measure of loyalty or participation. Kovner and Lahne (38) point out the importance of not ignoring the great deal of union talk that takes place in the shop and the fact that many questions are settled at the shop level by the union steward. Rose (55, pp. 46–54) found a good deal of participation in Teamsters Local 688, if one included in "participation" not only attendance at union meetings but also support of the union negotiating during periods of contract negotiation, reading and understanding the union contract, and serving on picket lines. And Sayles and Strauss, while noting that participation is high when it has to do with collective bargaining only, nevertheless are careful to point out that such participation may reach very great heights (59, p. 223):

Even in new unions the picket line is almost sacred. Most members will refuse to cross one even when they think the strike is unjustified. Perhaps the most striking demonstration of loyalty was shown by the union-shop elections under the Taft-Hartley Act where over 90 per cent of the workers voted to accept a union shop.

These data strongly suggest that labor union members are selective in their participation and apparently do not support any and all union activities. Rosen and Rosen (57, pp. 66–69) found that the machinists they studied could be divided into four groups: "Pickers and Choosers" who selectively decide on their areas of satisfaction and dissatisfaction and do not generalize from one issue to all others; "Patriots" who seem to be satisfied with almost anything the union does; "Gripers" who answer "dissatisfied" to all questions about union activities; and "Fence-Sitters" who are undecided. The Rosens found that most members were "Pickers and Choosers" with "Patriots" in second place. Form and Dansereau (22), in a study of an amalgamated industrial local in the United Automobile Workers, found they could classify workers according to their orientations toward union functions and that participation reflected those orientations. Persons with "social" orientations (the union as a fraternal and social organization) have the highest participation rates, those with "economic" orientations were second, and those with "political" orientations saw the union as a device to protect them from arbitrary management rules. Lipset, Trow and Coleman (42, Ch. 5), in their study of the International Typographical Union, found a relationship between amount of informal interaction of printers with one another in the occupational community and interest in and participation in union politics and affairs.

There is then a good deal of participation in certain activities. The important question appears to be: what is the significance of various types of participation for union interest and loyalty? Informal participation, such as attending union picnics or going to union dances, may be very important to these who engage in it and those who engage in such activities may also be interested in union affairs. But one cannot conclude that those who do not so participate are uninterested in union affairs. Rose reports the generalization (55, p. 51):

The more a member participates in his union, the more favorable is his attitude toward it.

But it does not follow that favorable attitudes always result in participation. It is quite possible, then, for there to be poor attendance at meetings, poor turnouts at minor elections, and poor response to union-sponsored recreational affairs, and yet most of the membership may be solidly behind the leadership in a crisis.

THE UNION AS A POWER ORGANIZATION

Although our primary interest has been on the relation between the union and work organization, such a limitation does not preclude a recognition that the labor union is a major institution in its own right whose independent development affects seriously the character of union-management relations. From a sporadic, semi-revolutionary activity, American unionism has not only become respectable but has become one of the major centers of power in the larger society. While the general strike has never been as significant a tactic in the United States as it has in Great Britain and France, American labor unions are able to accomplish almost as much because of the fact that national unions may contain hundreds of thousands of workers and can bring key industries, such as coal-mining and the automobile industry, to a virtual standstill. While about two-thirds of collective bargaining relationships are between a single union and a single firm, there has been a trend toward multiple bargaining (51). Employers have usually opposed such bargaining because it forces a small firm often to deal with a large union, and because it forces "marginal" firms to pay the same wages as more prosperous firms. On the other hand, often the only way a small firm *can* oppose a large union is by joining forces with other firms. Although unions may wish to "pick off" one firm at a time and so set up a "generating pattern" throughout an industry, most of the time unions have preferred multiple bargaining in order to prevent wage differentials between firms.

Where one, or a few national unions can bargain with a far-flung industry, unions become very powerful indeed, a fact which has led some to write of a "labor monopoly" which should be restrained (78). Yet even the Taft-Hartley act did not forbid multiple-bargaining, in part because not only unions but many employers favored it.

Another important concern has been about the degree to which unions are democratically organized. As unions get larger, they become large scale bureaucracies within which the membership may have little power. Yet Taft, in a careful discussion of "opposition in union elections," points to the fact the effectiveness of a union is decided not only by how much participation or control the members have of it, but also by whether the union accomplishes its goals, such as higher wages and union security (65, Ch. II). A membership may elect a person to office again and again, even though he be as dictatorial as John L. Lewis, provided he satisfies their job wants. Nor are all unions monocratically controlled, though it is true that the two-party system that Lipset, Trow, and Coleman describe in the typographers is a rarity. Nevertheless, there seems to be no question that some labor union leaders have used the union for their own, rather than their followers', benefit. One should not, however, conclude that all labor leaders are of this sort. Most are honest and highly responsive to member attitudes.[11]

The large, powerful union is relatively new in the United States. This very novelty has meant that many efforts to establish standards or develop a set of expectations which may be used as guides in the settlement of disputes have proved abortive. Some, noting the relative decline in the use of violence in union-management disputes, have felt that disputes have declined, but the evidence does not support such a belief. Union-management relations are, in the last analysis, power relations, and of these Blumer writes (8, p. 235):

Since action is neither held to an application of a code nor guided by a consideration for the other's welfare, a premium is placed on the successful pursuit of *one's own goal,* thus inevitably introducing egotism and possibilities of ruthlessness that have always made power action morally suspect.

When an industrial giant and a union giant meet in such a power context, the only factor which can force a compromise in the public interest is a power stronger than both combined—public opinion, legislation, and the state. The latter have been able to force the settlement of disputes in some cases, and assist their settlement in others (69, Ch. 6; 77). However, even as the role of the state in labor-management relations increases, one should not expect to see a decline in labor-management disputes. We should rather hope for the development of more harmonious and efficient techniques for handling disputes when they arise.

[11] Good studies of labor union leaders are (24; 44; 59, Chs. 8, 9; 60).

CHAPTER REFERENCES

1. *Agreement Between Carnegie-Illinois Steel Corporation and the United Steelworkers of America, CIO,* March 13, 1945, Pittsburgh.
2. Bakke, E. W., *Principles of Adaptive Human Behavior,* New Haven: Labor Management Center, Yale University, July 1946.
3. ———, "Why Workers Join Unions," *Personnel,* **22:**37–46, 1945.
4. Barbash, J., *Labor Unions in Action,* New York: Harper, 1948.
5. Bernstein, I., "Arbitration," in Kornhauser, A., Dubin, R., and Ross, A. M., *Industrial Conflict,* New York: McGraw-Hill, 1954.
6. ———, "The Growth of American Unions," *American Economic Review,* 44:301–318, June 1954.
7. Bloch, J. W. and Platt, R., "Seniority and Bumping Practices," *Monthly Labor Review,* 80:177–185, 1957.
8. Blumer, H., "Social Structure and Power Conflict," in Kornhauser, A., Dubin, R., and Ross, A. M. (eds.), *Industrial Conflict,* New York: McGraw-Hill, 1954.
9. Brooks, G. W., "Observations on the Changing Nature of American Unions," *Monthly Labor Review,* 80:151–154, 1957.
10. Chamberlain, N. W., *Collective Bargaining,* New York: McGraw-Hill, 1951.
11. ———, *The Union Challenge to Management Control,* New York: Harper, 1948.
12. Commons, J. R., "American Shoemakers, 1648–1895, A Sketch of Industrial Evolution," *Quarterly Journal of Economics,* 24:39–84, 1910.
13. ———, *et al., History of Labour in the United States,* New York: Macmillan, 1926–35.
14. Copelof, M., *Management-Union Arbitration,* New York, Harper, 1948.
15. Davey, H. W., "Hazards in Labor Arbitration," *Industrial and Labor Relations Review,* 1:386–405, 1948.
16. Dulles, F. R., *Labor in America,* New York: Crowell, 1949.
17. Dunlop, J. T., *Collective Bargaining,* Homewood, Illinois: Irwin, 1949.
18. ———, "Structural Changes in the American Labor Movement," *Monthly Labor Review,* 80:146–150, 1957.
19. Ellsworth, J. S., *Factory Folkways,* New Haven: Yale University Press, 1952.
20. Fisher, L. H. and McConnell, G., "Internal Conflict and Labor Union Solidarity," in Kornhauser, A., Dubin, R. and Ross, A. M. (eds.), *Industrial Conflict,* New York: McGraw-Hill, 1954.
21. Foner, P. S., *History of the Labor Movement in the United States,* New York: International Publishers, 1947.
22. Form, W. H. and Dansereau, H. K., "Union Member Orientations and Patterns of Social Integration," *Industrial and Labor Relations Review,* 11:3–12, 1957.

23. Gardner, B. B. and Moore, D. G., *Human Relations in Industry,* Homewood, Ill.: R. D. Irwin, 1952.

24. Ginzberg, E., *The Labor Leader,* New York: Macmillan, 1948.

25. Golden, C. S. and Ruttenberg, H. J., *The Dynamics of Industrial Democracy,* New York: Harper, 1942.

26. Goldstein, B., "Some Aspects of the Nature of Unionism Among Salaried Professionals in Industry," *American Sociological Review,* **20**:199–205, 1955.

27. Gouldner, A. W., *Wildcat Strike,* Yellow Springs, Ohio: Antioch, 1954.

28. Harbison, F. H. and Coleman, J. R., *Goals and Strategy in Collective Bargaining,* New York: Harper, 1951.

28a. Hardman, J. B. S. and Neufeld, M. F. (eds.), "The Labor Lawyer," in *The House of Labor,* New York: Prentice-Hall, 1951.

29. Herberg, W., "The Old-Timers and the Newcomers," *Journal of Social Issues,* **9**, No. 1:12–19, 1953.

30. Hiller, E. T., *The Strike,* Chicago: University of Chicago Press, 1928.

31. Howe, I. and Widdick, B. J., *The UAW and Walter Reuther,* New York: Random House, 1949.

32. Karsh, B., Seidman, J. and Lilienthal, D. M., "The Union Organizer and His Tactics, A Case Study," *American Journal of Sociology,* **59**:113–122, 1953.

33. Kennedy, V. D., "Grievance Negotiation," in Kornhauser, A., Dubin, R., and Ross, A. M. (eds.), *Industrial Conflict,* New York: McGraw-Hill, 1954.

34. Kerr, C., "Industrial Conflict and Its Mediation," *American Journal of Sociology,* **60**:230–245, 1954.

35. Knowles, K. G. J. C., *Strikes—A Study in Industrial Conflict,* Oxford: B. Blackwell, 1952.

36. Knowles, W. H., *Personnel Management,* New York: American Book Co., 1955.

37. Kovner, Joseph, "The Labor Lawyer," in Hardman, J. B. S., and Newfeld, M. F. (eds.), *The House of Labor,* New York: Prentice-Hall, 1951.

38. ―――― and Lahne, H. J., "Shop Society and the Union," *Industrial and Labor Relations Review,* **7**:3–14, 1953.

39. Lapp, J. A., *Labor Arbitration,* New York: National Foremen's Institute, 1946.

40. Leiter, R. D., *The Foreman in Industrial Relations,* New York: Columbia University Press, 1948.

41. Lens, S., *Left, Right & Center,* Hinsdale, Ill.: H. Regnery, 1949.

42. Lipset, S. M., Trow, M. A. and Coleman, J. S., *Union Democracy,* Glencoe, Ill.: Free Press, 1956.

43. Miller, G. W. and Young, J. E., "Member Participation in the Trade Union Local," *American Journal of Economics and Sociology,* **15**:31–47, 1955.

44. Mills, C. W., *The New Men of Power,* New York: Harcourt, Brace, 1948.

45. ――――, *White Collar,* New York: Oxford Univ. Press, 1951.

46. ―――― and Anderson, T. E., "People in the Unions," in Hardman, J. B. S. and Neufeld (eds.), *The House of Labor,* New York: Prentice-Hall, 1951.

47. Muste, A. J., "Factional Fights in Trade Unions," in Hardman, J. B. S. (ed.), *American Labor Dynamics,* New York: Harcourt, Brace, 1928.

48. Perlman, S., *A History of Trade Unionism in the United States,* New York: Macmillan, 1937.

48a. ——, *A Theory of the Labor Movement,* New York: Kelley, 1949.

49. Peters, E., *Conciliation in Action,* New London, Connecticut: National Foremen's Institute, 1952.

50. Peterson, F., *American Labor Unions,* New York, Harper's, 1945.

51. Pierson, F. C., "Prospects for Industry-Wide Bargaining," *Industrial and Labor Relations Review,* 3:341–361, 1950.

52. Popiel, G., "Bureaucracy in the Mass Industrial Union," *American Journal of Economics and Sociology,* 15:49–58, 1955.

53. Presgrave, R., *The Dynamics of Time Study,* Toronto: University of Toronto Press, 1944.

54. Purcell, T. V., *The Worker Speaks His Mind on Company and Union,* Cambridge, Massachusetts: Harvard University Press, 1953.

55. Rose, A. M., *Union Solidarity,* Minneapolis: University of Minnesota Press, 1952.

56. Rose, C. B., "Morale in a Trade Union," *American Journal of Sociology,* 56:167–174, 1950.

57. Rosen, H. and Rosen, R. A. Hudson, *The Union Member Speaks,* New York: Prentice-Hall, 1955.

58. Sayles, L. R., "The Impact of Incentives on Inter-Group Work Relations," *Personnel,* 28:483–490, 1952.

59. —— and Strauss, G., *The Local Union,* New York: Harper, 1953.

60. —— ——, "Occupation and the Selection of Local Union Officers," *American Journal of Sociology,* 58:585–591, 1953.

61. Schneider, E. V., *Industrial Sociology,* New York: McGraw-Hill. 1957.

62. Segal, R. M., "Labor Union Lawyers: Professional Services of Lawyers to Organized Labor," *Industrial and Labor Relations Review,* 5:343–364, 1952.

63. Selekman, B. M., *Labor Relations and Human Relations,* New York: McGraw-Hill, 1947.

64. Sturges, W. A., "Summary of the Statutes Governing Arbitration," in Kellor, F., *Arbitration in Action,* New York: Harper, 1941.

65. Taft, P., *The Structure and Government of Labor Unions,* Cambridge, Massachusetts: Harvard University Press, 1954.

66. ——, "Understanding Union Administration," *Harvard Business Review,* 24:245–257, 1946.

67. Tannenbaum, F., *Philosophy of Labor,* New York: Knopf, 1951.

68. ——, "The Social Function of Trade Unionism," *Political Science Quarterly,* 62:161–194, 1947.

69. Taylor, G. W., *Government Regulation of Industrial Relations,* New York: Prentice-Hall, 1948.

70. Ulman, L., *The Rise of the National Trade Union,* Cambridge: Harvard University Press, 1955.

71. *Union Contract Clauses,* Chicago: Commerce Clearing House, 1954.

72. Updegraff, C. M., and McCoy, W. P., *Arbitration of Labor Disputes,* Chicago: Commerce Clearing House, 1946.

73. Warner, W. L. and Low, J. O., *The Social System of the Modern Factory*, New Haven: Yale University Press, 1947.
74. Wellisz, S., "Strikes in Coal-Mining," *British Journal of Sociology*, 4:346–366, 1953.
75. "Why White Collar Workers Can't Be Organized," *Harper's*, 215:44–50, Aug., 1957.
76. Wilensky, H. L., *Intellectuals in Labor Unions*, Glencoe, Ill.: Free Press, 1956.
77. Witney, F., *Government and Collective Bargaining*, Chicago: Lippincott, 1951.
78. Wolman, L., *Industry-Wide Bargaining*, New York: Foundation for Economic Education, 1948.

CHAPTER SIXTEEN

ETHNIC RELATIONS IN THE WORK SITUATION

CONCEPTS AND EPITHETS

FOLK TERMS AND SCIENCE

When we approach the area of ethnic relations, we approach a subject that quivers with emotion. The feelings that people have are expressed overtly in the words that they use to refer to each other: "bloody Jew," "uppity Nigger," "Damyankee," "beef-eater," "frog," "gook," "greaser," "dago," "bohunk," "proster Goy." [1] Because such terms are not pleasant, the group that uses them often seeks to justify them in various ways. There may be appeal to the needs of one's own group: "We Germans must keep our stock pure." Reference may be made to an economic threat which the other group is supposed to represent. Or there may be an appeal to reason or "facts": the epithet may be justified by referring to the other group's laziness, irresponsibility, adaptability, ability, character and habits.

Science enters the picture in this last type situation. When a group seeks to justify its attitudes by an appeal to reason or "facts" then the way is open for the scientist to try to prove or to disprove the justification that is offered. Such proofs are often beside the point and do not reckon with the emotional or sentimental content of the justification. Thus, Mayer in a series of articles describing a stay in Germany mentions the effect of the Nazi race theories on the common folk that he interviewed and came to know very well. In one article he says as follows (33):

[1] For a representative list of what the author calls ethnophaulisms, see (42).

None of my friends was in the least interested in Nazi race theory as such, not even the tailor or the bill-collector. Five of the ten of them laughed when they spoke of it, including the cabinet maker: "That was nonsense, for the SS and the universities. Look at the shape of my head. Look at my brunette wife. Do you suppose *we're* not Germans? No; that they could teach to the SS and the university students. The SS Flott—"cream" sarcastically—would believe anything that made them great, and the university students would believe anything complicated. The professors too. Have you seen the "race purity" chart? "Yes," I said. "Well, then you know. A whole system. We Germans like systems, you know. It all fitted together, so it was science, system and science. If only you looked at the circles, black, white, and shaded, and not at real people. Such *dummheit* they couldn't teach to us little men. They didn't even try."

And Hughes calls attention to the danger of allowing the direction of scientific research to be dictated by the defenders of racial and ethnic injustice (21):

Those opposed to racial prejudices and inequalities have shown a tendency to slight or even to deny the existence of any differences at all. Fishberg's book on the Jews has long served as a text to prove that no one can tell a Jew when he sees him—a very dubious compliment to Jewish parents who have put forth great effort so to bring up their children so that they will respect and practice conduct which their parents consider rooted in their Jewish faith and culture.

The question then is not only whether assumed differences actually exist or not but also, *are* those differences of significance? If, for example, it is claimed that Negroes should be denied the right to vote because they do not have enough education to exercise it intelligently, the question that should be settled is not simply whether Negroes are well-educated or not but whether the franchise should depend on how much education a man has. Although a major function of science remains that of the assessment of alleged facts, the study of prejudice is essentially a study of attitudes.

This raises the question of what should be the relation of scientific concepts to folk concepts—those used by laymen—especially when the scientist is discussing those very folk concepts themselves. It is often stated that the physicist, for example, does not have to worry about audience misunderstanding of the words he uses. Since he talks about inanimate things, he can assign them any names he wishes in order to avoid misunderstandings and so that each term will have a clear, definite meaning. The social scientist, however, worries a good deal about his terms being taken into popular language and suffering "corruption." Actually, the physicist has little hesitation in using terms like "work," "energy," or even "suction." He does, however, give these terms operational definitions and uses them in his own way. He does not worry very much about whether they will be interpreted correctly by a lay audience or not. The social scientist however often feels a concern because he is talking *to* people *about* people. Thus, Hughes (23, p. 136) notes that Arnold and Caroline Rose justify their avoidance of the term "prejudice" by saying that the term has come to assume too much respectability in people's eyes and thus a stronger term—hate—is preferable. Hughes (23, pp. 132–33) also comments that the anthropologists, like the physicists, escape the need to worry a great deal about communicating since the peoples they study are not likely to read their reports. The sociologist defines his terms so as to communicate with his colleagues; but he is also concerned with communicating with lay persons, and with them he feels the terms may be misunderstood.

The situation is particularly serious in an emotional context. There are some persons who cannot carry on a rational conversation if certain terms are used. For example, this is true of many Arabs with reference to the state of Israel. Because of Arab feelings that the state is not justified, there is a tendency to avoid the use of the term Israel and to refer instead to "Palestine." Any person, therefore, who uses the term "Israel" is touching a sore point and is suggesting by implication where his own sympathies lie. One can often get around this problem by statements such as "so-called" or "what the Jews call Israel." On the other hand, while such circumlocutions serve the purpose of enabling discussion to go forward, they do not of themselves remove the need for terms of some sort on which there is agreement.[2]

Nothing much is gained by forbidding terms completely. Nor is a great deal gained by continually shifting terms or adding new ones in accord with popular shifts in interest and attitude. The important thing would be to *stick* to the terms that we make use of in science as long as they are useful and carefully defined. We need not worry a great deal about folk meanings attached to the words that we use: folk meanings change and lay persons soon invent new terms, so that the scientist may continue to use the term that he is using when it has been divested of its emotional connotations by its falling out of popular favor. This may mean that in communication a translation process is necessary since what we are talking about when we speak, let us say, of prejudice, may not correspond precisely to what a southern gentleman is talking about when he refers to prejudice. However, our difficulties here are not very much greater than that of the physicist who will use the term "work" to

[2] Compare George Bernard Shaw's comments on the difficulty of discussing sex because of an absence of an adequate vocabulary in (47, pp. 234–35).

refer to the movement of a mass through distance rather than follow the layman who thinks of work in terms of what he does for a living.

ETHNIC RELATIONS

We define the term "ethnic group" as follows: *any group which is recognized as distinctive by others and by themselves, and whose distinctive marks are the occasion for expression of feelings.* The term "ethnic" is adopted because it is very general and almost devoid of emotion in common usage (23, p. 7).

The distinguishing mark that sets off an ethnic group can be almost anything—color of skin, language, religion, clothes, eating habits, or color of hair. In the last case, for example, we would probably not feel that the redheads in the world formed an ethnic group. On the other hand, Hitler attempted to set off the blonds in the world and make them into the core of a super-race.

One of the most important distinctive ethnic marks is provided by race. The salient facts are well stated (18, pp. 3–6) by Hart: [3]

The human species is held by science to have developed from a single line of ancestry, just as all dogs, to mention another species for comparison, go back to a single type of dog. . . .

As population increased in the world, groups of early men moved away from the center of man's origin into other regions, where they became (a) isolated, (b) inbred with each other, (c) adapted to their new environment. After long periods of isolation, inbreeding and local adaptation, distinct types of humans were produced, each distinct type confined to a distinct locality. The same thing was true of dogs; in isolated areas distinct breeds were produced, as can still be seen from their names—Irish terriers, spaniels, danes, afghans and the like, each species named from the geographical region where it developed as a distinct type or breed. In the case of humans, how distinct any one group became from the rest of mankind depended upon how completely and how long they were cut off from contact with the other groups. The Australian aborigines who appear to have been isolated in their remote continent from early times until about two hundred years ago, are strikingly different in physical appearance from the rest of mankind. They therefore have some claim to be regarded as the only pure race still in existence. On the other hand groups living in less isolated areas, near the centres of world population like Asia or Europe, could not retain any isolation and hence had little or no chance to develop a distinct physical type.

There was a point in time, though we shall probably never be able to fix it, when the factors making for isolation (sparse world population, tribal conditions of living, lack of means of transportation, lack of trade between tribes)

---

[3] No single author cited.

began to be over-taken by the factors making for contact and mingling of peoples (increasing world population, roads, ships, wars of conquest, migrations into already occupied areas). When this happened the tendency to produce and perpetuate distinct breeds was checked and reversed by the opposite tendency, that is the tendency towards race mixture, or as it is technically called hybridization. This had to be so since any social mingling of different peoples due to war, trade, etc., always leads inevitably to intermarriage between them, as we can see in historical times, for example, when the Norman-French settled in Saxon England, or when the Europeans settled among the Indians of North and South America. The point in time at which the tendency towards race-mixture overtook the tendency towards distinct breeds may be impossible to fix, but we can be sure that, for the centres of world population like Europe, Asia and Africa, it was a very long time ago indeed, and that in those areas at least, hybridization has increased in geometrical ratio ever since. The parallel with dogs still holds good. As long as the spaniels were confined to Spain, the danes to Denmark, the pomeranian to Pomerania and the Pekinese to Peking, "pure breeds" were developed. As the pure breeds moved out into the wider dog world, they began to lose their distinct characters and to be replaced by mixtures (hybrids) of all kinds which can only be labelled as just plain dog.

Thus both dogs and men as species have gone through five phases of development: (1) a single line of ancestry; (2) isolation of small groups; (3) development of local types with distinct characteristics (breeds of dogs, "races" of men); (4) breakdown of isolation, mingling of types; (5) further mingling of all types, complete mixture so that no "pure" type is distinguishable. At present, it would seem, human beings are somewhere between phase 4 and phase 5, and much further advanced towards phase 5 than the species dog, since not even the Gestapo can possibly be as effective in keeping human breeds apart as the snobbery of dog-fanciers has been in keeping pure the pure breeds of dog.

The human species has not yet got to the point of being just plain human. Though it is unquestionably getting fairly close to that point there are still in existence a few survivals of clear-cut breeds. These are few in number, however, and refer only to broad general classes of mankind whose physical differences from each other are unmistakable. The so-called white, yellow and black races (or as they are often called, the Caucasian, Mongoloid and Negroid stocks) together with the Australian aborigines, make four groups which are still distinguishable enough from one another to be regarded as distinct stocks. But these four are the only clearly differentiated groups in the present world population. Within these four stocks all attempts to separate out smaller groups as distinct "races" invariably end in failure, since no two attempts to list the "racial subdivisions" of the white race or the yellow race ever agree. Put another way, such words as Negro, white man, yellow race, are meaningful words because they refer to certain physical characters (hair form and skin colour in particular) which mark off each of those groups from the rest of the human species; such words as Nordic, Alpine, Hindu, Aryan, Celtic, etc., are quite meaningless as racial terms, since no two specialists agree as to what a typical

Nordic or a typical Alpine looks like, or indeed what they once looked like when the world was far less mixed than it is now. Recent attempts by illustrated newspapers to inform their readers how Chinese and Japanese may be distinguished from one another, are an excellent example of this. These attempts succeed only in making the readers more confused than they were to start with; because apart from language or food-habits or costume there is no way of telling Chinese and Japanese apart, just as there is no way, on physical grounds alone, of telling Englishmen from Scotsmen or New Yorkers from Torontonians.

It is necessary to put this emphasis upon physical traits because it is physical traits and physical traits only that are inherited in the germ plasm and hence are fixed at birth. The Ethiopian cannot change his skin. But he can change his food-habits or his language or his clothing. These latter are not matters of inheritance at all but are learned behaviours which can be acquired after birth by any infant, irrespective of his skin colour. If it were clearly recognized by all who talk about race, that a racial trait is one fixed at birth, much misuse of the term would be avoided.

Race distinctions, then, are biological distinctions and are inherited. The point that must be emphasized, however, is that it is not the biological differences as such that are significant in the understanding of racial attitudes. The biological differences become a *symbol* in people's minds of assumed social or psychological differences. When a person sees a Negro, he immediately assumes that that person has certain psychological or social characteristics which are associated with the Negroes as a group. Any other kind of distinction such as a British accent or an Italian accent, may function as a symbol. But the Negro is in a special position because his badge is easily visible, inherited, and, above all, *cannot be changed.*

One does not get far in the area of race relations in attempting to attach any meaning to the race differences as such. Certainly, the feeling of American whites toward color or hair-form is not involved in their feelings toward the Negroes. Otherwise we would not have the millions of people who every year stretch themselves out on the sand with as little clothes on as possible in order to make themselves as brown as possible, nor would we have the millions of dollars that are spent by American white women on permanent waves and pin curls. However, race differences assume particular importance because they are unable to be changed easily. That fact plus the large number of Negroes in this country has meant that for many writers a discussion of ethnic relations is simply a discussion of race relations.

Another term frequently used to refer to ethnic differences is that of "minority group." Wirth defined a minority group as a people ". . .

who, because of racial or cultural differences, are treated as a people apart or regard themselves as aliens in the country in which they live and are, by virtue of this fact, held in lower esteem and debarred from certain opportunities open to the dominant group." [4] The fact that minority groups exist in our society means that our society has not as yet been knit into a single ethnic community through intermarriage, interbreeding, and free communication and social intercourse. Because such groups are held in lower esteem, they are likely to develop attitudes and sentiments of inferiority and sometimes of persecution. But what really matters is not so much their actual exclusion from privileges or high status in our society, as such, but rather the conception that such a group has of itself and of others, particularly the attitude of the dominant society to them. A minority group is one which, whether or not it suffers from discrimination and exclusion, conceives of itself as an object of such differential treatment, and is regarded by others as such. [5]

We shall use the term "minority group" where necessary. However, it has the disadvantage that studies of minority groups focus only on one-half of the scientific problem. If we are interested in ethnic relations we must, as Hughes (23, pp. 8 ff.) points out, give attention both to minority and dominant groups and to the relations between them. The concept of the ethnic group does not carry the same limited connotation. Both whites and Negroes are ethnic groups, and every person is in some ethnic group.

We stated that the differences between ethnic groups are the occasion for feelings. The question that arises is, What *sorts* of differences are likely to be the occasion for feelings? The most inclusive answer we can give is *cultural* differences. Culture, in general terms, may be regarded as a set of traditional ways of thinking and acting which are not biologically inherited. Since the ways of culture are traditional, they take time to develop, and in the process of developing, culture tends to spread out and becomes enmeshed in all areas of life. We see cultural distinctions in food tastes, child-rearing, art, technology, work, and techniques of expression (13). Differences in intellectual activities—ways of thinking about the world and people—may also become culturally colored. Some might speak of Western culture as being characterized by a scientific outlook. Ruth Benedict (3, p. 220) speaks of the "aggressive, paranoid tendencies" of the Dobuans. Wirth found a strong orientation among Jews toward success,

[4] Louis Wirth. In lectures, University of Chicago, 1946.
[5] It is important also not to think of a minority group as one necessarily small in numbers. The Negroes in some towns in the deep South outnumber the whites. The French Canadians in Canada make up from one-fourth to one-third of the whole population and are indeed the largest single group in Canada. The significant point is the feeling of the group that is an object of distinctive or differential treatment.

particularly with reference to relations with the Gentile world (53, pp. 106–12). Drake and Cayton (10) have pointed out how white attitudes toward Negroes have found their way into everyday language. Persons speak of something as being "black as sin," of "giving a disliked person a black look"; when one gets out of some difficulty one speaks of "emerging from darkness to light"; we say "that's 'damn white' of you," or we speak of a person as being "free, white, and twenty-one" to indicate maximal freedom and maturity.

When we meet anything new we discover that how we should behave towards this thing or this person has to some extent been decided by the culture in which we have been brought up. We arrive with an already made set of evaluations or definitions which tell us what to think or how to feel. Culture is concerned not only with right and wrong but with the good and the valued. Culture makes for people internal judgments on their possessions and orders people in terms of them, assigning to them higher or lower positions in a social structure. The ordering or valuational aspects of culture may be expressed in the form of caste and class systems.

Castes and classes are important in our discussion because ethnic groups may themselves have class or caste structures and because if the differences between the castes or classes within a society become the object of sufficient feeling, and if the classes or castes are sufficiently distinct, then they may themselves become cultural or ethnic groups. This is particularly likely to happen when one culture moves into the land of another and sets up an industrial enterprise there.

Culture, then, gives the individual a ready made set of definitions and therefore organizes his life. It gives him fixed stars to navigate by. But, to continue the metaphor, there may occur a storm which blocks out the stars or else the person may move to another part of the world where the stars are all shifted around (29, p. 170–73). This situation, where the culture does not work, is referred to variously as cultural disorganization, *anomie,* or social unrest (11, pp. 353–73). The contacts of ethnic groups, particularly where they involve profound cultural differences, are especially likely to reproduce social unrest which may lead to native revolts, nationalistic movements and revolutions.

Dewey (9, pp. 12–15) maintained that thought arises when the individual's routine is interrupted. As long as the individual meets nothing out of the ordinary his behavior is likely to be governed by habit or established patterns. When, however, something occurs which is not specifically provided for in the individual's habit structure or in the culture in which he lives, then the individual is thrown on to his own resources and begins to think. It is under these conditions that the *individual* emerges.

One of the most important occasions for the breaking up of cultures is, therefore, the meeting of ethnic groups. (It is not the only one— natural catastrophes, disease, or warfare may also break up cultures.) The tampering with culture that is involved in significant interpenetrations of ethnic groups is never taken lightly and tends always to occasion strong expressions of feelings. That is why we have included in our definition of ethnic group the idea that the distinctions must be the occasion for the expression of feelings.

ETHNIC CONTACTS

As mentioned above, it is common to look upon Negroes, Jews, Catholics, or other ethnic groups as minority groups: they are faced with a dominant group and suffer discrimination and expressions of prejudice. When this point of view is taken, it leads naturally to a plea for tolerance and is accompanied by recriminations and counter-recriminations.

It must be recognized, however, that ethnic groups, if they are of any significance at all, are also likely to be cultural groups and this of course is true both of dominant and minority groups. As we have pointed out a culture is a set of channels or patterns by which certain behavior is encouraged and other behavior is frowned upon. It is, in addition, true that all cultures tend to be ethnocentric. The culture tends to develop in the person a feeling that it is best, that its behavior is right. This means, then, that when ethnic groups meet we get a clash of ethnocentrisms. The concept of the "frontier" which Park and Hughes (38, pp. 57–85) make use of in their analysis of the meeting of peoples does not quite state this condition (23, p. 19). A frontier implies a situation in which peoples who know very little about each other meet. They are also likely to meet under conditions of an absence of a common law or of common understandings. However, the meeting of ethnic groups in the modern world usually has been preceded by stories, reports and the like so that when the groups meet they have already formed a set of more or less definite attitudes or conceptions of each other, and their early behavior is likely to be carried out in terms of these conceptions.

When peoples meet, they meet as bearers of cultures, that is, as bearers of a certain conception of themselves which includes the idea of themselves as superior or more able and as entitled to certain *rights*. But the rights or available opportunities are always scarce. Consequently, one gets competition for them. The competition may be for raw materials, or may be for the survival of dearly valued practices. But one of the most important rights that any ethnic group claims for itself is the right to a "living,"—the right to a certain level of comforts, prestige, and life

chances. And the place where this battle is fought is in the work situation
—on the plantation or in industry. There is certainly nothing unusual in
the fact that the Bible records that it was a work-task—the building of
the tower of Babel—that was the first important Biblical occasion for the
meeting of peoples of different languages. Everywhere, industry has
provided a stage where different peoples meet.

In this context, ethnic contacts have taken place in a variety of
social situations. These may be classified into two major types: those
where the culture of the industrial owners is different from that of the
people of the area in which the industry is located, and those in which
the culture of the industrial owners is the same as that of the people in
the area. The culture of owner and employees may be different when
industry goes out from a mother country, e.g., as it has done from western
Europe to South Africa, Indonesia, South America, and French Canada,
or when foreign groups come into a mother country, e.g., in the case
of the United States, particularly in the early years of railway building
and industrial growth, when large numbers of European immigrants
entered the country. It is also illustrated in the United States by the
growth of the plantation system with the importation of Negroes and
by the role of coolie labor in the building of railroads.

Where the culture of the industrial owners is the same as that of
the employees we may observe again two sub-types. The first is provided
by the case where the workers come to the industry to stay. In the United
States this is illustrated by the movement of Negroes out of the deep
South into Northern industry, by the movement of Puerto Ricans into
New York City, and by the great migrations of those uprooted from the
dust bowls of the southwest who moved into California. Besides those
who come to stay, there are those who come and go. Here the most
important category is provided by the migratory workers in many countries. We proceed next to discuss the effects of these types of contacts.

TYPES OF INDUSTRIAL SITUATIONS WHERE ETHNIC GROUPS MEET

WHERE MANAGEMENT AND WORKER ARE CULTURALLY DISTINCT

This type of situation arises where there is movement that brings ethnic
groups together. It may occur when industry searches for raw materials,
cheap labor, non-union labor, or lower taxes. Or it may take place when
people from far away (in distance or culture) come to the industry. They
may be searching for freedom, for comforts or may be uprooted by
changes at home. Miner mentions that a considerable proportion of the
early settlers in the corn belt areas of Iowa were motivated not so much

by the dream of security and a desire to found a home but rather were seeking advancement or upward mobility (34, p. 8).

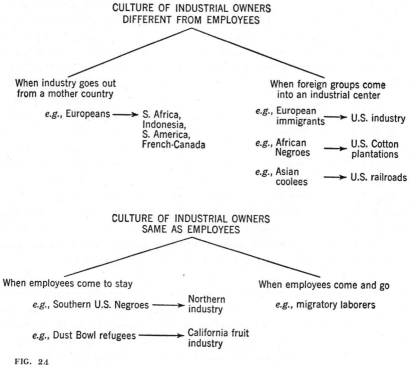

FIG. 24

TYPES OF WORK SITUATIONS WHERE ETHNIC GROUPS MEET

1. WHEN INDUSTRY MOVES

Modern industry arose within the complex of events that ushered in the industrial and agricultural revolutions, the exploration of the new world, the Renaissance, the discovery of new raw materials, and the emergence of modern capitalism and Protestantism. In some cases raw materials were shipped to the mother countries for manufacturing operations there. This was true for example of rubber from Malaya and Brazil, jute from India, cotton from the American colonies, wool from Australia, and tin and bauxite from Central and South America. That, however, in turn meant the rubber and cotton plantation, or the jute mill in the country in which the raw material was found. Later in some places it proved cheaper to ship the entire industry to the site of the raw materials and to produce a completed product. This condition was the norm from the very beginning when heavy construction work went on as in the case of dam-building, road-building, and the construction of docks and railroads.

The mother countries of industry tended to be Protestant and were derived mostly from Western culture with the one important exception of Japan. Western industry tended to operate with certain precepts; there was the notion of freedom from government controls as advanced by Adam Smith and John Stuart Mill, and the notion of the free movement of labor. Yet when industry has moved into an alien culture it has exercised whatever legal or political controls it might find necessary in order to force people to work. The labor compound and indenture system or even slavery make their appearance (16, Ch. VI). We have then a contrast between the avowed objectives or principles of industry and its behavior when it moves to foreign lands. How then is this contrast to be explained?

When industry moves it is likely to find an already existing and vital society. That society is usually based on land and the professions although there may be some local commerce. The persons concerned with the professions and commerce are likely to form an established middle class and those whose wealth is based on land are likely to form an upper class. To the members of the society the new industry is likely to be an object of ambivalent feelings. On the one hand, it means more trade for the area, it increases the value of land, and increases the need for professional services. On the other hand, the industry also provides new lines of upward mobility which may compete with existing lines. For example, the coming of industry to the French-Canadian countryside created the French-Canadian foreman who might then compete for prestige and power with the French-Canadian shopkeeper.

If the new avenues of upward mobility actually work and natives do rise in the work hierarchy, then some type of accommodative relationship may be worked out [6] and the new occupations fitted into the existing society. More commonly, however, in part because of lack of training, language, and other cultural barriers, and in part because of conceptions that the industrial owners may bring with them, the natives are assigned a position at the bottom of the hierarchy and kept there. Under those conditions, there may arise profound ethnic antagonisms and the conflict between management and labor may be expressed in ethnic terms. The fact of differential advantages and possessions may make for class differences and class hatreds.

Under certain conditions, for example, strong resistance from a native

[6] A striking case of a fairly close approach to relatively free job competition, though accompanied by an elaborate racial division of labor, is presented by Bahia, Brazil. See (40, p. 177 ff.).

population (17, pp. 200–53), industrial owners may import labor from elsewhere, particularly from areas of landless persons who are willing to come for money.[7] This has been true of the Chinese in the East Indies, the East Indians in South Africa, and the Chinese and Japanese in Hawaii and the Western United States. Later, when the indenture period was over most remained to become a middle class of traders.

But native tribal peoples are often unwilling to work in the industries at all, particularly if their culture is a well-integrated, functioning one. They have their own prestige systems and goals and the new industry does not help them reach those goals. Nor do they have need for the money the industry has to offer. Under those conditions the natives may be coerced into working or the need for money may be deliberately created as Frazier (16, pp. 102–03) shows for the case of Haiti:

According to European political theories that were current when the Spaniards entered the New World, they did not come as conquerors but as pacifiers of a region which had been granted to the Spanish crown by the Pope. Therefore, it was only necessary to inform the Indians that they were the subjects of the Spanish crown, and if they refused to acknowledge the Spaniards as their overlords, they were guilty of treason. Within two years after the arrival of Columbus, the island of Haiti was pacified and each adult Indian was required to pay a stipulated head tax to the crown. Indians who could not pay the tax in goods were required to work for the Spanish colonists who paid the tax. In the face of the growing demand for Indian labor, the colonists were not satisfied with this arrangement and soon the Indians were organized into labor gangs.

When Western capitalism came to Indonesia it created what Boeke calls a "dualistic economy," that is (3a, pp. 3, 4):

. . . A distinct cleavage of two synchronic and full grown social styles which in the normal historical evolution of homogeneous societies are separated from each other by transitional forms, as for instance, pre-capitalism and high capitalism by early capitalism, and which there do not coincide as contemporary dominating feature . . . Without doubt the most frequent form of social dualism is to be found there where an important Western capitalism has penetrated into a precapitalistic agrarian community . . .

In Indonesia, the economy of the area before the coming of the Westerners is described as involving the following elements: (1) a local economy extending little farther than the village. The village in turn is

[7] Nor should one ignore the active connivance of the leadership of these peoples, in some cases at least. See (7, pp. 65–7).

bound together by religious and genealogical ties and engages in the farming of a food crop. (2) Communal disposal of wealth and service. There is an assumption of prior village rights rather than individual rights. (3) Limited needs (3a, p. 40):

> Anyone expecting Western reactions will meet with frequent surprises. When the price of cocoanuts is high, the chances are that less of the commodities will be offered. When wages are raised the manager of the estate risks that less work will be done; if three acres are enough to supply the needs of the household, a cultivator will not till six; when rubber prices fall the owner of a grove may decide to tap more intensively, whereas high prices may mean that he leaves a larger or smaller portion of his capital trees untapped. Examples may be multiplied indefinitely. This inverse elasticity of supply should be noted as one of the essential differences between western and eastern economies.

The motives here are analogous to those we described earlier for "gold-bricking" in the factories. (4) Individual self sufficiency at least so far as the village is concerned. (5) Absence of income or a money economy. (6) An absence of profit-seeking as a regular full-time activity (it may be engaged in occasionally for excitement). (7) Industry is only *supplementary* agriculture. Industries exist, such as weaving, the making of earthen pots, *batik* work, and the manufacture of hats and cigarettes, but are considered and are secondary to the major job of agriculture. They become important only in times of stress when the crop fails.

With the entry of Western industry and the introduction of a money economy, all seven of these characteristics are contradicted. Through a money economy, trade is extended over a wide area, considerably beyond the confines of the village. With money there comes also an emphasis on individual wealth accumulation, a great expansion of needs, the entering into world markets, and industrial work and profit-seeking as professional, full-time activities.

Boeke points out that under the circumstances there emerge a number of types who form classes and ethnic groups (3a, pp. 79 ff.): (1) *Trekkers.* The term means transients and refers to the original Europeans who set up the industry. (2) *Blijvers,* a term which means stayers. These are persons of European ancestry who were born and grew up in Indonesia. They tend to perform the managing tasks and skilled work in the industry. (3) *Native Indonesians.* These are found at the bottom of the industrial hierarchy. They perform the labor and unskilled work on the sugar estates and the rubber plantations. (4) *Chinese.* These persons form a middle class of traders and shopkeepers.

Thus, the Indonesians have become integrated into the industrial structure at the bottom. One gets, then, an ethnic and racial contrast between owners at the top and workers at the bottom of the organization. Those natives who are not willing to work are taxed and, thus, are forced to accept employment in order to get the money to pay the taxes. Such a situation gives birth to profound hatreds which, after some generations, may be converted into deep-rooted prejudices. Under these conditions there are two major types of effects: (1) Changes in social organization. These involve the breakup of the native social organization and the making of the natives into a lower class or caste in the new society which is a blend of the European and native elements. (2) Cultural disorganization.

The extent to which both social and cultural disorganization may go is well illustrated in a striking case history supplied by Sharp (46, pp. 69–90). He describes the effects of the introduction of the steel axe to an Australian aboriginal group, the Yir Yoront, who live at the mouth of the Coleman River on the west coast of tropical Cape York Peninsula. Before the coming of the steel axe, the natives used polished stone axes. Axes were considered men's property, and associated with masculinity as well. Women actually did more axe-work than men—particularly cutting firewood—but would be forced to borrow an axe from a man for this purpose, as would any children. The stone for axes had to be obtained from quarries 400 miles to the south, by exchanging spears. This was accomplished through a long chain of regularly established trading partners, and most of the exchanges took place at the time of the great aboriginal fiestas, which center about initiation and totemic ceremonials and rites and are occasions of great excitement. In lay affairs, the axe had no religious significance. But in religious terms, the stone axe was the totem of the Sunlit Cloud Iguana clan, and was associated with the clan's mythical ancestors.

Such, in brief, was the function of the stone axe. Then missionaries arrived with steel axes, which they began to give out as gifts to persons showing progress in being converted or who did some odd job around the mission station. The effects were far-reaching:

Having acquired an axe head through regular trading partners of whom he knew what to expect, a man wanting a stone axe was then dependent solely upon a known and adequate nature and upon his own skills or easily acquired techniques. A man wanting a steel axe, however, was in no such self-reliant position. While he might acquire one through trade, he now had the new alternative of dispensing with technological behavior in relation with a predictable nature and conduct in relation with a predictable trading partner and of turning instead to conduct alone in relation with a highly erratic missionary. If he attended one of the mission festivals when steel axes were handed out as gifts, he might receive one simply by chance or if he had happened somehow to impress upon the mission staff that he was one of the "better" bush aboriginals (their definition of "better" being quite different from that of his bush fellows). Or he might—but again almost by pure chance—be given some brief job in connection with the mission which would enable him to earn a steel axe. In either case, for older men a preference for the steel axe helped create a situation of dependence in place of a situation of self-reliance and a behavior shift from situations in technology or conduct which were well structured or defined to situations in conduct alone which were ill defined. It was particularly the older ones among the men, whose earlier experience or knowledge of the white man's harshness in any event made them suspicious, who would avoid having any relations with the mission at all, and who thus excluded themselves from acquiring steel axes directly from that source.

The steel axe was the root of psychological stress among the Yir Yoront even more significantly in other aspects of social relations. This was the result of new factors which the missionary considered all to the good: the simple numerical increase in axes per capita as a result of mission distribution; and distribution from the mission directly to younger men, women, and even children. By winning the favor of the mission staff, a woman might be given a steel axe. This was clearly intended to be hers. The situation was quite different from that involved in borrowing an axe from a male relative, with the result that a woman called such an axe "my" steel axe, a possessive form she never used for a stone axe. . . . Furthermore, young men or even boys might also obtain steel axes directly from the mission. A result was that the older men no longer had a complete monopoly of all the axes in the bush community. Indeed, an old man might have only a stone axe, while his wives and sons had steel axes which they considered their own and which he might even desire to borrow. All this led to a revolutionary confusion of sex, age, and kinship roles, with a major gain in independence and loss of subordination on the part of those able now to acquire steel axes when they had been unable to possess stone axes before.

The trading partner relationship was also affected by the new situation. A Yir Yoront might have a trading partner in a tribe to the south whom he defined as a younger brother, and on whom as an older brother he would therefore have an edge. But if the partner were in contact with the mission or had other easier access to steel axes, his subordination to his bush colleague was obviously decreased. Indeed, under the new dispensation he might prefer to give his axe to a bush "sweetheart" in return for favors or otherwise dispose of it outside regular trade channels, since many steel axes were so distributed between natives in new ways. Among other things, this took some of the excitement away from the fiesta-like tribal gatherings centering around initiations during the dry season. These had traditionally been the climactic annual occasions for exchanges between trading partners, when a man might seek to acquire a whole year's supply of stone axe heads. Now he might find himself prostituting his wife to almost total strangers in return for steel axes or other white men's goods. With trading partnerships weakened, there was less reason to attend the fiestas, and less fun for those who did. A decline in one of the important social activities which had symbolized these great gatherings created a lessening of interest in other social aspects of these events.

Not only did an increase in steel axes and their distribution to women change the character of the relations between individual and individual, the paired relationships that have been noted, but a new type of relationship, hitherto practically unknown among the Yir Yoront, was created in their axe-acquiring conduct with whites. In the aboriginal society there were almost no occasions outside the immediate family when one individual would initiate action to several other people at once. For in any average group, while a person in accordance with the kinship system might be superordinate to several people to whom he could suggest or command action, at the same time he was also subordinated to several others, in relation with whom such behavior would be tabu. There was thus no overall chieftainship or authoritarian leadership of any kind. Such complicated operations as grass-burning, animal drives, or totemic ceremonies could be carried out smoothly because each person knew his roles both in technology and conduct.

On both mission and cattle stations, however, the whites imposed upon the aboriginals their conception of leadership roles, with one person in a controlling relationship with a subordinate group. Aboriginals called together to receive gifts, including axes, at a mission Christmas party found themselves facing one or two whites who sought to control their behavior for the occasion, who disregarded the age, sex, and kinship variable among them of which they were so conscious, and who considered them all at one subordinate level. Or the white might impose similar patterns on a working party. (But if he placed an aboriginal in charge of a mixed group of post hole diggers, for example, half of the group, those subordinate to the "boss" would work while the other half, who were superordinate to him, would sleep.) The steel axe, together, of course, with other European goods, came to symbolize for the aboriginal this new and uncomfortable form of social organization, the leader-group relationship.

The most disturbing effects of the steel axe, operating in conjunction with other elements also being introduced from the white man's several subcultures, developed in the realm of traditional ideas, sentiments, and values. These were undermined at a rapidly mounting rate, without new conceptions being defined to replace them. The result was a mental and moral void which foreshadowed the collapse and destruction of all Yir Yiront culture, if not, indeed, the extinction of the biological group itself.

From what has been said it should be clear how changes in overt behavior, in technology and conduct, weakened the values inherent in a reliance on nature, in androcentrism or the prestige of masculinity, in age prestige, and in the various kinship relations. A scene was set in which a wife or young son, his initiation perhaps not even yet completed, need no longer bow to the husband or father, who was left confused and insecure as he asked to borrow a steel axe from them. For the woman and boy the steel axe helped establish a new degree of freedom which was readily accepted as an escape from the unconscious stress of the old patterns, but which left them also confused and insecure. Ownership became less well defined, so that stealing and trespass were introduced into technology and conduct. Some of the excitement surrounding the great ceremonies evaporated, so that the only fiestas the people had became less festive, less interesting. Indeed, life itself had become less interesting, although this did not lead the Yir Yoront to invent suicide, a concept foreign to them . . .

All ghosts are totems of the Head-to-the-East Corpse clan. They are thought of as white, and are, of course, closely associated with death. The white man, too, is white and was closely associated with death, so that he and all things pertaining to him are naturally assigned to the Corpse clan as totems. The steel axe, as a totem, was thus associated with the Corpse clan. But it is an "axe," and is clearly linked with the stone axe, which is a totem of the Sunlit Cloud Iguana clan. Moreover, the steel axe, like most European goods, has no distinctive origin myth, nor are mythical ancestors associated with it. Can anyone, sitting of an afternoon in the shade of a ti tree, create a myth to resolve this confusion? No one has, and the horrid suspicion arises that perhaps the origin myths are wrong, which took into account so little of this vast new universe of the white man. The steel axe, shifting hopelessly between one clan and the other, is not only replacing the stone axe physically, but is hacking at the supports of the entire cultural system.

. . . we note one further devious result of the introduction of European artifacts. During a wet season stay at the mission, the anthropologist discovered that his supply of tooth paste was being depleted at an alarming rate. Investigation showed that it was being taken by old men for use in a new tooth paste cult. Old materials of magic having failed, new materials were being tried out in a malevolent magic directed toward the mission staff and some of the younger aboriginal men. Old males, largely ignored by the missionaries, were seeking to regain some of their lost power and prestige. This mild aggression proved hardly effective, but perhaps only because confidence in any kind of magic on the mission was by this time at a low ebb (46, pp. 83–89).

The quotation above illustrates the far-reaching effects of even what might be regarded as a relatively minor change in the technology of a native people. It gives, therefore, a hint of the effects of much more far-reaching changes such as are represented in the introduction of whole factories, docks, or railways.

2. WHEN PEOPLES COME TO INDUSTRY

While Western Industry has ranged all over the globe, it has also grown at home. In this case it attempts to attract workers from elsewhere. In early United States history, industry grew up in the industrialized North and in the feudal South and attracted or pressed Negroes, Chinese and northern and southern Europeans into work. The industries in the Ruhr and the Saar have attracted Frenchmen, Germans, Poles, Czechs, and other peoples.

What is remarkable about industry on its own home ground is that it behaves quite differently from the way it behaves when it finds itself in an alien land. First, it normally does not attempt to make its own laws in the attempt to force workers to remain at work in the industry.[8] Second, industry at home is forced to be sensitive to public opinion and to the notions of justice and right which have grown up within the context of western Christianity. Third, the workers, though they may at first be different culturally from the owners, precisely because they are now living in a Western land, are likely to learn Western ways quickly and to demand the right to move up, more money and the other rights which are enjoyed by the natives of the country at large.

Under these conditions, the cultural disorganization that takes place is primarily confined to those cases where large numbers of immigrants have come in from a far land and have attempted to bring with them as much of their cultural baggage as they could. Disorganization is more likely to take place at an individual level than is the case where industry moves to foreign lands. This is not to understate the cultural disorganization that may take place. Still, when the Irish, for example, moved to America the social structure of rural Ireland remained intact, and indeed its stability was to some extent insured by the migration.

Hughes has described the manner in which a middle class arises when an immigrant group comes, in order to provide for the needs of the new group (23, pp. 85–7):

As a general rule the peasants who joined the American industrial labor force were not accompanied by a middle-class people from their own country. Perhaps a few priests came to save their souls in their own peculiar way. Even when the immigrants were Catholic they wanted priests of their own vernacular; it is well enough to have the Mass in a universal language, but people prefer to confess their sins in the language in which they conceived and committed them. This was but one of many wants so peculiar to their own culture that they could not be met by American professional people in institutions. Indeed, a culture is, seen from one angle, a peculiar set of consumers' wants; and perhaps when people want nothing that cannot be easily supplied by strangers they have no peculiar culture left. Jews want special food, rabbis to circumcise their infant boys, and to teach them things Jewish. Immigrant Sicilians want special food, maybe a special kind of midwife, and someone to ward off the evil eye, as well as priests who appreciate their favorite saints and ways of celebrating great days.

Besides these traditional wants of spirit and body which strangers cannot

---

[8] One might regard the plantation in the antebellum U.S. south as an exception, although this was a regional phenomenon and involved the importation of forced labor. In addition, special laws, such as the Taft-Hartley law, may protect certain industries in cases which are felt to be in the public interest.

supply there are others which are new: the wants that arise from the very fact of being so far from home. At home one is surrounded by kin who will look after one in sickness and death. Here some substitute for kin and village must be found; so in the new land burial and sickness insurance societies burgeon. Things that seem to get done without conscious effort in the peasant village here require thought, enterprise, and an organization got up for the purpose.

There was paper work to be done. Letters had to be written home; money saved and sent home to support parents, or to bring wife, fiancee, or kinsmen to America. Passports and steamship tickets had to be got to old people in the Old Country. It was said cynically in the old Russian empire that you could tell a peasant from a pig because he had a soul and a passport. But the passport wasn't for him to read; it was just to show when he went on journeys or when the Tsar's officers came to see who had done military service and who had not. The New World required more paper work. A Mexican lawyer on Halstead Street in Chicago still includes letter writing and the reading of government notices among his services to immigrant clients.

In addition to the need for such paper work there is the desire for news. The immigrant could not read the big American newspapers; they did not tell anything about his own people, either here or at home, anyway. So he was ready to spell out what a little newspaper in his own language had to say about the things that really interested him.

Some among the immigrants began to satisfy, each for their own people, these two kinds of peculiar wants, the traditional ones and the ones created by being away from home. The list of special services in surprisingly alike in the varied groups: food, clothing (but not for long as they must and soon do take up the clothing of their new country and their new work), religion, medicine—both folk and professional—paper work, insurance and other devices to meet crises, news, sociability, preservation of home traditions, and protection against the exigencies of the new life.

Since professional and business people from home did not come hither in any number, the supplying of these many wants was undertaken by peasant immigrants themselves. Thus there grew up a compliment of service institutions. They furnished opportunity for a few of the group to rise in the new world on the backs of their fellows. Italians imported and sold to their compatriots spaghetti, olives, olive oil; they grew zucchini and broccoli to sell to them. Some then sold them to others. Irish men learned to corral votes and trade them for jobs on city streets, and in city ditches and later in city hall offices, handling papers, or on the police force. Bohemians and Poles wanted to buy houses; men of their own group founded savings and loan banks and real estate agencies. Other immigrants founded newspapers in their mother tongues, burial and sickness societies, protective associations. Some women served as midwives to fellow peasant women who had never thought of going to male physicians. Some immigrants or immigrant sons got into the medical profession—although that takes time and money—and found a natural clientele among their own people. In short, the beginnings of a middle class rose by giving services to the immigrants. (23, pp. 90–91)

Hughes, however, also points out (23, pp. 90–91) that the fate of this middle class is subject to various contingencies. While its members feel that any increase in the welfare or standing of their people will mean more business and advancement for themselves, nevertheless they recognize that advancement may also mean alienation from their own ways and therefore the lack of a need for a peculiarly ethnic middle class.

Such a middle class may for long periods monopolize certain activities, particularly those centering around religion, but the monopoly may fade rapidly with reference to food, clothing and other matters which the children soon learn to reject in favor of "American" food and clothing. If the cultural distinctions between the immigrant group and the surrounding people are not great, then the monopoly decreases generally and the people move into the mainstream of western culture.[9] But this ethnic distinction may continue to be made and to affect marriage and religious affiliation for long periods. Vogt (50, p. 241) comments that among the corn farmers near Jonesville the distinctions between the Old Yankee stock and the Norwegians are still maintained even after several generations.

WHERE MANAGEMENT AND WORKERS ARE OF THE SAME CULTURE

We have discussed the case where there are profound cultural differences and differences in accustomed economy between management and workers. But ethnic groups may meet where cultural differences are slight or hardly present at all. Thus, the American Negro in present-day Chicago industry illustrates the case of an ethnic group that has come in where there are almost no cultural differences between management and worker. We have here an almost pure case of race difference. But once race becomes identified as a distinguishing ethnic mark, there may later develop cultural differences as those are organized about low income, segregation and the like. Similarly, the Okies from Oklahoma, Texas and elsewhere were a group who were very similar to their fellow Americans, as American as straw hats and blue overalls, with the main distinction being one of income difference.

Both of the above illustrate groups who have *come to stay.* Besides them there are groups who *come and go,* of which the most common as well as the most important are migratory workers. These may be of different race, as in the case of some Mexicans, or else they may be old stock Norwegians and Swedes.

[9] A recent problem of importance has been that of middle-class persons uprooted from Germany and Eastern Europe who have not always been able to maintain their former status. See (24, pp. 74–82).

1. THOSE WHO COME TO STAY

The most important group among those who exhibit relatively slight cultural differences between management and worker in the United States have been those whites and Negroes who have come out of the deep South. The American Negro brings with him profound disadvantages: he is usually poor; he has had little or no training in skilled work; his education is likely to have been poor; he was often uprooted from the land tenure system of the South because of low income, debt, or mechanization; and—as important as any of these factors—he has come with a lack of a tradition of success so that his hopes and aspirations themselves limit his ability to rise.

These limitations are not much different from those which confront the poor white Southerner who comes North, but his is the advantage of a lack of visibility, at least after one generation. The Negro enters an area in which the higher positions are already preempted; that is, he enters at the bottom. His earliest entry into Northern industry in the United States was as a strikebreaker (49, pp. 128–46). This was facilitated by the fact that the Negro's freedom to enter labor unions has been severely restricted. The AFL discriminated against Negroes, in part as a consequence of its policy of exclusiveness toward all semiskilled and unskilled workers, and in part because of its policy of trying to keep a monopoly on highly skilled jobs by keeping *out* potential competitors. As a consequence, a significant change occurred with the formation of the CIO which adopted the opposite policy of trying to control the price and rights of labor by encouraging all workers to join. Yet in spite of important gains, a book published as recently as 1953 [10] listed twenty-two labor unions which exclude Negroes either by provisions in the ritual, by provisions in the constitution, or by tacit consent. Nine other unions listed admit Negroes but only into specially segregated locals.

Yet it would be a mistake to conclude that American unionism is anti-Negro. When the AFL and CIO merged in 1955, an anti-discrimination resolution was adopted. Although Kornhauser (27) cautions against expecting too much from labor unions since race relations programs are marginal to their "central" functions, others have described how labor unions could and have functioned as agents to break down race barriers in employment. Sexton (45) suggests that if a labor union will *act* first (by insisting whites and Negroes work together) and conduct educational programs afterwards to explain the accomplished fact, it can accomplish a great deal (30). John Hope (19) reported that in three southern plants of the International Harvester Company, a policy of

---

[10] See (8; 36; 48, pp. 368–69).

nondiscrimination (even including Negroes' "bumping" whites out of jobs) worked successfully because union and management cooperated in its implementation. Similarly, a survey (20) of a packinghouse workers union which had a high proportion of minority group members in it (Negroes, Mexican-Americans, and women) revealed that discrimination could be attacked through the union contract and grievance machinery (5, 52).

An important question is whether such efforts to reduce discrimination and prejudice at work carry over into non-work situations. Such research as we have tends to fit Myrdal's description of the "rank order of discriminations." [11] Rose (42a) found that a sample of St. Louis, Mo., Teamsters union members exhibited the following attitudes toward Negroes: in social settings, largely negative; on the job, equally divided; in the union, largely favorable.[12] Reitzes (41a) reports a similar lack of carryover: Negroes were accepted in the work situation but rejected in the residential neighborhood. He suggests that this implies that organized groups offer the individual ready-made definitions of the situation; these groups are the union in the work situation and the property-owners association in the residential situation. This point of view leads Reitzes to suggest that a labor union might be able to change neighborhood racial attitudes by indicating to its members that non-discrimination practices might serve their interests as *property-owners* better.[13] Such a suggestion is worth testing. The role that labor unions play in racial programs is of great potential importance for Negroes do not loom as large in white-collar occupations, where unionization is low, as they do in such areas as construction and manufacturing, where unionization is common.

As with the case, discussed above, of the middle-class dependent upon the immigrant, segregation offers certain at least temporary bene-

[11] That is the ranking of certain forms of discrimination as much more important than others from the high rank given to intermarriage and sexual intercourse with white women, through informal contacts, use of public facilities, the franchise, discrimination at law, and discrimination in land acquisition, jobs and public relief. See (36, pp. 60–67).

[12] Rose (43, p. 138) states: "For example, 83.7 per cent do not think that Negroes should be allowed to live in the same block as whites; 44.2 per cent think it is a bad idea for the union to try to get jobs for Negroes when there are vacancies; but only 33.8 per cent think it is a bad idea to have Negroes on the union staff."

[13] A. M. Rose makes a related suggestion: "Although evidence is not complete from this survey, it would seem that emphasis on the economic and legal *rights* of Negro members is one of the most effective ways in which the union can change the ethnic attitudes of its white members" (43, p. 187). Further, Rose points out, the union can take advantage of the opportunities it has to create situations in which Negroes meet as equals in friendly interaction as on the picket line or at union social affairs.

fits to the Negro middle class. To a considerable extent, this middle class is made up of persons who supply personal services to the Negro. Simpson and Yinger make the following notes (48, p. 378):

Negroes as a group are poor, but 15 million people constitute a sizeable market. Negro business enterprise, however, is concentrated in fields which are not subject to the full competition of white business. A recent study showed that more than 70 per cent of Negro business establishments in twelve cities were in such personal service fields as beauty shops, undertaking establishments, taverns, and filling stations, and in food stores and eating and drinking places.

Negro businesses are small businesses as may be seen, both in the volume of transactions and in the number of employees involved. Pierce's survey of 3866 retail stores, service establishments, and miscellaneous businesses showed that almost 70 per cent of these concerns had a volume of less than $10,000 during 1944. Actually, the proportion is probably higher because 17 per cent of the businesses included in the study did not specify their volume. Less than five per cent of these establishments reported a volume of $25,000 or more. The latter establishments fall in the miscellaneous business category, and specifically life insurance companies and casket factories. The same study found that the average number of employees per retail store is 2.8, 2.3 for the service establishment, and 9.1 for the miscellaneous business.

These facts lead Frazier (15, p. 173) to describe Negro businessmen as a "lumpen-bourgeoisie," and to deplore the tendency to exaggerate the purchasing power of Negroes:

The myth that Negroes were spending 15 billion dollars in 1951 was widely circulated by whites as well as Negroes since it served to exaggerate the economic well-being of Negroes in the United States and to whet the appetites of the black bourgeoisie, both *Negro* businessmen and Negroes employed by American corporations, in their efforts to reap benefits from the increased earnings of Negroes.

Nor do Negro businesses and service establishments have anything approaching a monopoly of the Negro market. Pierce (39, p. 32) showed that in the cities which he studied the entire Negro population spent less than two dollars per person in Negro stores in 1939 (26, Chs. V, VI). The reasons that Negroes do not necessarily shop at Negro establishments are related to their desire for good quality, style, low prices and courteous service. There is apparently profoundly lacking in any significance or strength a racist attitude towards the supplying of personal needs. To a considerable exent this is a reflection of the lack of important cultural differences between the Negroes and whites in cities.

We have already discussed in earlier chapters the Negro in the professions. Here we may merely add that the Negroes enter the professions only to a slight extent. In medicine, their ability to practice is restricted by the fact that they are unable to enter most hospitals. For example, no Negro doctor could treat a patient at any accredited hospital in San Francisco until as recently as 1947. Williams (51) has shown that Negro doctors, like Negro businessmen, do not enjoy anything approaching a monopoly of Negro trade. The Negro patient exhibits a preference for the white male doctor. However, the Negro doctor is likely to get the cases of certain whites, particularly those suffering from venereal diseases or other diseases which they wish to keep secret from members of their own community.

On the Negro lawyer, Hughes (23, pp. 96–97) makes the following statements:

The Negro lawyer gets practically no white practice, and far from all of the Negro practice. The white lawyer enjoys partial dominance, having all the white practice and a share of Negro clients. Mr. William Hale found that a white lawyer often gets the cases of poor Negroes, rarely of the Negro middle class. To the poor, the law is trouble to be got out of. A lower class Negro wants to win an insurance case against an utility or an employer. A Negro woman has a son in jail and wants to get him out. They often believe that a white lawyer can manipulate all these institutions better than a Negro lawyer could: it is, after all, a white man's world. They may get the white lawyer through a store front preacher or a ward heeler of their own race. On the other hand, the middle class Negro wants a divorce which has already been agreed upon; he wants a deed, articles of partnership or incorporation, or advice concerning a contract. It is "friendly" law. He goes to the Negro lawyer and feels very loyal to his race. He and the lawyer are both part of that relatively small group, successful middle class Negroes who got there by serving Negroes.

The most common professions for the Negro are teaching and the ministry. In the former they are found largely in the South, where a segregated school system creates a need for Negro teachers, and in the latter they are in a profession which does not compete with the whites.

2. THOSE WHO COME AND GO

Americans have been profound movers. There have been approximately 35 million immigrants who have come to the United States; and this movement goes on still: to the Northeast, to the Midwest, and to the far West. Usually the movers have eventually settled down and, where they have entered industry, have tried to move up in the industrial hierarchy. But there remain some who continue to move and some to whom it is a way of life. Under modern conditions of transportation and communication, migratory workers may range over enormous distances. For example, in the eighteenth and nineteenth centuries, Irish

laborers were accustomed to move to the hop yards of England; since the
1870's, Poles have migrated to the sugar-beet fields of Saxony; each year,
workers move from Italy and Spain to the fields of Argentina; and large
numbers of Chinese laborers move in and out of Manchuria every year.

In the United States, the migratory laborers have been associated
with agricultural work. They follow the harvests and fruit picking, beginning in the South and tending to move North. The Social Science Research Council reported that there are five major seasonal migrations.
These are summarized by Barnes as follows (1, p. 302):

1. The Southern migration of winter and spring to pick citrus and truck
crops, all the way from Florida to New Jersey;
2. The berry-crop migration, in which workers migrate all over the Eastern
United States, from the Gulf states to the Great Lakes;
3. The Western cotton migration, involving about 50,000 workers who pick
cotton from Texas to California;
4. The Sugar beet migration, mainly restricted to Western States; and
5. The Pacific coast migration, embracing everything from fruit picking
to lumbering, and involving several races and 150,000 migratory workers in
California alone.

In composition migratory laborers represent a wide variety. The
following distinctions may be made:
1. Immigrants attracted by prospects of high wages, or uprooted
from native lands. Here are included Italians, Scandinavians, Irish, and
persons from the Far East.
2. Races. Included are Chinese, Japanese, Negroes, Filipinos, and
whites.
3. Depression products. These are dust-bowl refugees and persons
left by the decline of the aircraft industry in California after the war.
4. Low income groups in or out of argiculture. For these people the
whole family is likely to work in order to try to provide a living income.
5. Transients, who may only want temporary work.
6. Professional hoboes, bums, and home guard.
7. Students and others seeking pocket money.
As may be seen from the list, migratory laborers represent a considerable variety of ethnic groups. The races represented among the
migratory laborers come to be regarded ethnically. The Chinese and
Japanese were originally recruited for work on the railroad and in the
construction industry. Later they went into agricultural work as their
only alternative. They were considered to be industrious and desirable
although not necessarily by the white labor unions. Later, when the
Japanese began to develop solidarity and to demand rights, they came to

be regarded as "troublemakers" and the fear of the "Yellow Peril" was induced. Owing to immigration restrictions and to the effects of displacement during the Second World War and to the fact that many became owners rather than laborers, the Chinese and Japanese at present form only a very minor group in the ranks of the migratory laborers.

In the case of Mexicans, Puerto Ricans, Filipinos, and Negroes, racial or cultural differences are great enough for ethnic distinctions to be made. Indeed we observe a kind of discrimination in reverse. The agricultural growers of peas, California cotton, grapes, etc., are likely to *prefer* ethnically different groups because they are forced to work for lower wages, since they are excluded from factory and other work owing to prejudice or union restrictions.

In order to understand the social makeup of the migratory worker and his special work problems, it is necessary to look at the economic base that provides the need for migratory labor. Lloyd H. Fisher (14, p. 9), in his excellent study of the harvest labor market in California, has described what he calls "the structureless market." He conceives of it as involving five conditions:

(1) No mechanism for restricting the number of laborers. This means no unions or quota systems; (2) Anonymity of worker to employer: that is, an impersonal relation so that no informal obligations develop or any kind of moral tenure; (3) Unskilled work; (4) Compensation by unit of product, and not by time; and (5) An operation requiring little or no capital or machinery. These five conditions are exemplified by agriculture in California.

1. Unions are virtually absent. This is due to the great diversity of people who enter the migratory labor market and therefore to the difficulty that they experience in building up *esprit de corps*,[14] to the transiency, to low wages, such that migratory workers can rarely afford to pay union dues, and to the opposition of growers and to the political power of growers who are able to enlist the aid of police and the powers of the state government when the laborer showed interest in forming combinations.

2. Anonymity was early established because of race and cultural differences. The Chinese, who were the earliest group to appear, were of a different race, a different language, and culture. Consequently the grower did not feel the presence of any tie with them. It was further claimed that these were precisely the kind of workers that were wanted. The grower said that Americans would not accept field work, they needed "stoop labor" or "squat labor" (referring to the needs of the vegetable

---

[14] But see (2) where it is suggested that a unifying factor may be provided by the grower himself who may function symbolically as a "common enemy."

crops). Later people came to believe these things, and the persistence of Chinese in the migratory market tended to make of them a people apart and ethnically different.

Further accentuating the barrier between growers and employees was the emergence of the labor contractor or boss. The use of such a middle man, with his gang of workers, is an old device appearing among the Italians in construction and railroad work in the form of the *padrone*, and in the garment trades in the form of the "sweater." [15]

In the early years, the labor contractor was needed because he could act as a go-between. He was himself a Chinese or Japanese, knew the habits and language of the workers, and could transmit the employers' instructions to his men. In exchange, he was likely to receive a bonus from the grower. It was among the Japanese that the bargaining potentialities of the gang system were first realized. The first thing the Japanese did was to drive out the Chinese from the labor market by the simple device of underbidding them, a process which stopped when it was no longer necessary. They then developed solidarity. Ichihashi (14, pp. 26–27) has described the camp or bunkhouse that developed among the Japanese:

A few typical cases of these Japanese labor organizations may be sketched. In 1892, one Kimura took with him a dozen of his countrymen to Watsonville, California and worked on a farm in the district, he acting as their "boss." His employer gave him a "bunkhouse" in which to lodge his men. But soon other Japanese appeared in the district and their number kept on growing. Whereupon Kimura effected in 1893 what he called a "club" for these Japanese by renting a house and having each man pay annual dues of three dollars, for which he was allowed to cook his meals or lodge at the club or both whenever he was out of work. In time this club became a general rendezvous for the Japanese in the district, and when employers needed extra hands they went to the club and secured the men they wanted. Advantages of the club were soon recognized by Japanese leaders. Thus another came into being in 1899. When the writer visited the town in 1908, there were four of these clubs with a total membership of 650 in this district roughly embracing 100 square miles . . .

To assist these migratory members, the secretary studied the situation in the neighboring districts, if he did not know them already; in fact, he often arranged with employers of such districts for the employment of his men before the members were allowed to move, and in this case he collected the five cent

---

[15] See also the discussion of the role of the *sardar* in the recruitment and overseeing of labor for the coal mines of Bengal and Bihar in Mukerjee (35, pp. 25–26). A similar situation prevails for factories where the jobber (*sardar, mukaddam,* or *maistry*) ". . . is the mechanic, the fitter, and the overseer, . . . *de facto* recruiter, and largely exercises in practice the powers of dismissal, punishment and grant of leave to the workers" (35, pp. 35–36, Ch. III, *passim*).

commission. More often, however, in order to obtain accurate information from the latter he communicated with the bosses of such localities. . . . When the men secured their jobs through the bosses they paid the five cent commission to the bosses and not to the secretary. Thus the club members kept going from industry to industry and from place to place until there were no more jobs; then they returned to their clubs to spend the winter, doing such casual jobs as they could pick up in their residential district.

With the boss and camp as a social base, the Japanese began to develop labor union tactics such as the "quickie strike" when a crop would be hurt by any delay, a refusal to scab against fellow nationals, restriction of numbers, the boycott, and so on. For once the labor unions and the owners found themselves on the same side of the fence and the resulting anti-Japanese sentiment led to the "Gentlemen's Agreement" of 1905 and consequent restrictions on immigration. Further, a considerable number of Japanese became proprietors themselves and left the migratory labor ranks.

Subsequently, with the coming of the Mexicans an attempt was made to try to control the labor contracting system through the introduction of the labor contract itself, which limited the freedom of the contractor, and by trying to encourage culturally heterogeneous gangs so as to reduce the chance for the development of consensus.

But the role persisted, and the contractor became a power because of his intermediate position. He performed essential functions for both grower and worker. For the grower, he assured a labor supply when needed; and he supervised the work itself, often going as far as actually planting the crop, weeding it, harvesting it, and delivering it to the warehouse or the cannery for the grower. The labor contractor also kept records and paid the workers. For the worker, the labor contractor also had invaluable services to offer. He was first of all a medium of communication. He knew where work could be obtained, he knew what wages would be like, and he knew the state of the crop, the good or bad pickings. Second, he provided for the needs of the worker. He provided a living place (though it might be only a tent or only some space on which a tent could be pitched), he provided food, transportation, and even recreation, including gambling and brothels in some cases. The labor contractor did not necessarily engage in these activities gratuitously. Generally it was a means by which he made additional money by operating a commissary or in other ways. But third, the labor contractor was the one "understood" the worker. And being more sophisticated or eloquent he could present the worker's demands to the grower more effectively.

As a consequence, in spite of racketeering, absconding with funds, short-weighting, and other malpractices, he remained even when cultural differences between worker and grower disappeared, and his power became entrenched. Indeed, after a long period of the absence of any strikes (1921–1928), the first strike, by the cantaloupe pickers in the Imperial Valley, was a strike against the labor contractors and not against the growers.

The alternative to the labor contractor would be a state employment service and/or unionization, neither of which have gotten very far in California. The contractors are a diverse group who change from year to year and who may possess only a truck for transporting workers. Attempts to force labor contractors to register have met with only moderate success. It should be noted that the labor contractor acts as an employer of labor in effect but without the responsibilities of the employer. The worker is not working for the grower, he is working for the contractor. The contractor supervises his work, weighs the boxes or sacks and pays the men. Any attempts to control or to make changes in this system would involve some means for drawing the grower and the worker closer together, a highly unlikely occurrence.

3. Agricultural work which employs migratory laborers is on the whole unskilled. It requires relatively little learning or judgment. It is necessary to know which bolls of cotton are fully developed or which fruit is ripe for picking, but this is easily learned. There is considerable skill involved in harvesting of asparagus or lettuce; however, these are the prerogatives of those—chiefly Filipinos—who have this skill and and therefore this does not affect the demand of labor for other crops.

The total situation is one of an almost complete absence of restrictions on freedom of entry into the ranks of migratory workers so that almost anyone can become one. This helps to keep wages down, to keep the group fluctuating, and to keep it heterogeneous.

4. The ability of California agriculture to absorb a heterogeneous labor force is further facilitated by the almost universal use of the piece-work system. Payment is either by volume, as tends to be the case with tomatoes, apricots, grapes, potatoes, oranges, olives, and carrots, or else by weight, as in the case of cotton and peas. Only rarely, as with lettuce and asparagus, is payment made on a time or hourly basis. However, as already mentioned, the latter vegetables are a virtual monopoly of the Filipinos, and skill is of some significance. We do find time rates occasionally in the case of highly perishable and easily bruised fruits, such as apricots, where it is desired that the worker shall take extra care in handling.

The whole field, therefore, is controlled overwhelmingly by piece rates. If time rates were used, then it would be necessary to distinguish between individuals as to their competence. But with piece rates, labor costs are relatively equalized.

5. The absence of the need for much capital and of mechanization tends to be an overwhelming characteristic of the harvest. When mechanization is present in any industry, it creates the need for a number of workers who must be usually at least semiskilled. However, if the work is non-mechanized, then it is possible to absorb an almost indefinite number of workers. Indeed, employers will often prefer to have a large number of workers so that the harvest may be taken in before the weather changes. One of the biggest problems faced by the state government is the attempt to control indiscriminate handbills, which may have the effect of pulling into an area thousands of workers where only hundreds are required. Although the employers will probably be able to offer employment to every one of them, the employment may last for an extremely short period. The piece-work system again makes this possible. It makes little difference to the employer whether a hundred men or five hundred men are working in his fields, always provided he is able to pay by volume or by weight of produce. It of course makes a great deal of difference to the workers themselves, since the more workers there are, then the shorter the period of employment. When fields are picked over rapidly by large numbers of employees, the workers are soon likely to become a relief problem to the local authorities and to face severe hardships themselves.

The five characteristics of the structureless market that we have just discussed add up to a combination of economic, social and political forces that make the migratory worker into a relatively permanent class of worker. From the exigencies of the market, he has little recourse. The government is sensitive to his problems, but most migratory laborers are not in a position to influence political policy. Many of them are not citizens, and a great proportion of them are transients who do not stay in one place long enough to establish voting rights. Consequently they are almost totally without political power.

The migratory workers are a group who have almost no control of their numbers, who are excluded from factory or alternative employment (particularly in the case of those exhibiting race differences from the whites), with a piece-work system which operates to keep wages low, forced to move from one place to another, and with income spread thinly over a large family (the majority are Catholics and all of low income). The problem of the migratory laborer is brought out vividly in the following case which Lowry supplies (31, p. 16–18):

The father and mother, age 54 and 53 respectively, both came from pioneer stock, their people having crossed the plains in early days to Utah, where they were reared. Their seven surviving children were living with them.

In the early years of their married life there were a few moves to better their condition, but in 1929 there was a series of catastrophes, illness, death, financial loss. The parents and seven children, ranging in age from six to seventeen, packed themselves into a Ford truck, and in May 1929, really set out on their travels. The seven years since that time have been quite a long journey with frequent layovers.

Forty-four headquarters were established by this family in the twenty-six years of their married life; but this does not include a number of places where the family group camped for so short a period that they did not count them. There were forty-one locations in the last ten years, and twenty-eight in the last five years, including stops in 13 different counties in California. During this time they journeyed some 7,700 miles—about 6,000 of these in the last five years. They have worked in the following 13 crops: apples, apricots, cotton, figs, grapes, hay, hops, lettuce, olives, oranges, peaches, peas, and young berries. The father of the family has also done some sheepherding and trapping, and he has worked as a barber.

For the most part they have lived in tents. Year after year Boards of Health have been investigating and threatening camp inhabitants, but it was not until the sheriff drove the campers out of their location during the period of this study that this family had ever known a health officer to carry out a threat.

When driven out, the family paid two dollars a month for the privilege of camping on a vacant lot, water and the use of an outdoor toilet being included in the arrangement. The living quarters consisted of two tents (12 by 14 feet) facing each other across a four foot aisle. One tent, used as a bedroom, dressing room, and bathhouse, was filled with four beds made of old car cushions picked up in the neighboring junk yards. These were to be discarded when the family moved on, as they take up too much bulk when traveling. The boys said that they had been able to find automobile cushions in any fair sized junk yard of the state. Iron beds had long been the dream of the mother. "Every year," she explained, "the boys will say, 'now we'll get iron beds when we get on the next job,' but we don't have any yet." The other tents served as a kitchen, dining room and living room. A small two wheeled trailer, covered with a canvas tent, provided a storeroom. Over the sod in the kitchen tent were strips of well-worn linoleum, which served as a wavy floor. A stove with an oven had been constructed by the father from the car-backs found in the dumps. The only "chairs" the family has used in years were half a dozen benches made out of boards so built that they could be torn apart quickly for traveling. An apple box served as a cupboard for groceries and the girls' cosmetics which were kept in a coffee can. There was also a collapsible table and an improvised lounge covered with a soiled quilt. Everything was neatly arranged. The wash tubs and water pail were kept outside with the wood pile.

The routine of moving, practiced so many times, was a matter of a few hours' work. The men first dispose of the bed springs and other articles too bulky and too heavy for the journey. The bedding is placed on top of the sedan, some articles are tied on the side, and the tents are packed on the trailer. The family of nine crowds into the automobile. Each journey means a transfer of all their worldly possessions, with the exception of one trunk which for years has been stored with a friend. When the car can no longer be repaired by the father and the boys—who never think of going to a garage—they use all their available cash for the first payment on another second hand car. By the time that is paid for, it is ready to be junked.

The family would like to settle down on a farm somewhere but have little hope of doing so.

The case, while drawn from the period of the great depression, is, nevertheless, fairly typical. The important differences one might find from that described is the tendency within recent years for migratory laborers to move without their families, and the very diverse racial makeup of the working force.

SOCIAL AND ECONOMIC COSTS

Hughes makes what he calls "three sweeping statements" which are as follows (22, pp. 211–12):

INDUSTRY IS A GRAND MIXER OF PEOPLES

Industry appears to exhibit an insatiable demand for population. We have seen this well illustrated in the case of the fruit harvest, but it is also true in the case of the factory, the office and other work organizations. Nor are we likely to see in the near future any greatly reduced overall demand for labor. In spite of mechanization, we have observed in this country a continuously expanding labor force. The only times of labor surplus are those of the depression, and there of course we do not see the effect of mechanization but instead of disturbances in distribution and in confidence. There is perhaps a tendency to place an exaggerated emphasis on the great increase in leisure time that has been produced by mechanization. Only a small part of the world's population has been thus affected—agriculture perhaps more drastically than the factory. With the exception of children and possibly women, mechanization does not appear to free persons from labor as such; it means instead the reduction of working hours from, say, fourteen hours to eight hours a day. Also concomitantly with the increase in leisure one gets the rise of industries devoted to recreation, with their great needs for workers.

Mechanization also creates its own changes and demands for labor in the form of the rise of new industries as in the case of the automobile, the telephone, radio, television, and the expansion of the white-collar industries. As a consequence, it is in industry that we observe one of the great occasions for the meeting of peoples of different races, different religions, and different cultures.

INDUSTRY SEGREGATES

Hughes (22, p. 212) defines segregation as "deviation from chance in the distribution of people of various ethnic groups among the positions in industry." As we have seen, it is customary in colonial areas for invading Europeans to occupy the top positions, and for the natives to occupy the bottom.

INDUSTRY DISCRIMINATES

That is, segregation is not due always to differences in skill and managerial talents. Rather, industry deliberately discriminates on the basis of imagined differences in ability between ethnic groups, and continues to do so even if the differences are known not to be directly related to work ability.

This then raises for consideration a paradox created by the fact that business logics imply the following principles:

(1) Rationality. This means the use of only the most efficient technique and the most efficient worker and the rewarding of that efficiency.

(2) The Pursuit of Self-Interest. This is the doctrine of the economic man. He is the one who seeks only to maximize profit and therefore to keep costs down.

(3) Free Competition. All industries and concerns are to have equal access to the market and to have equal freedom to bid for workers. The worker in turn is expected to go where he can obtain the highest price for his labor.

Industry, as a grand mixer of peoples, has tended to smash old cultures. It has helped to break up castes in India, race relations in the United States, and has broken up culture after culture in different parts of the world. Whereas the Greeks spoke of the "Barbarians" and the late nineteenth-century prophets of progress spoke of "the savages" and "lesser peoples without the law," we use the term "underdeveloped areas," and publish maps in which these are indicated. The underdeveloped areas include much of the entire world outside of Western Europe, North America, and small portions of Australia, New Zealand, and South America.

Scientific or nutritional standards are used to define such areas but they are all Western standards. Whereas the Crusaders went to free the Holy Land from the Saracen, and the British assumed "the white man's burden," the present-day invader goes to uplift people in the name of science. But the earlier uplifters at least were limited by transportation and communication inadequacies. Now, the whole globe is laid bare, and the whole process is enormously accelerated. Earlier, the missionary or trader provided what little knowledge he could for the benefit of industries that were planning to move to native areas. Now the *survey* goes forth first, in which skilled agricultural experts, anthropologists, and home economists present a thorough picture of the culture and of the people before industry moves.

Yet industry may justify all this if for no other reason than the economic principles cited earlier, namely, rationality, self-interest, and free competition. However, the fact that industry also segregates and discriminates does not square with these economic logics. The industrialist at home will respect the imagined community sentiments about Negroes and Jews,[16] and abroad will carry those ideas with him. The result may be highly uneconomic, and involve the cost of segregated toilets, dining halls, living quarters, etc. Free competition may be ruled out with military assistance and by the introduction of indenture, compounds, or slavery.

The paradox suggests again the value of looking upon work structures as control or power structures, rather than as exclusively economic organisms. As stated earlier, the authority structure in industry exists to *coordinate* the activities of the workers so as to attain the goal of the owner or manager. The goal *may* be making money. However, it also may be supplying raw materials needed for war or for national prestige, or helping other peoples to become effective military allies. The point that is distinctive is the presence of a goal in the service of which control is required. At home, segmented controls are enough to insure the reaching of these goals and the continuation of the work process; industry is here an integral part of the culture. But abroad, should such limited controls prove inadequate, whatever other controls that are thought necessary may be used. One of the clearest cases is described by Marchant (32). The earliest Portuguese traders in Brazil bartered trinkets and tools for a wood used for dye-making and for food. Then the Indians began growing food especially for the traders. Finally, when the Indians refused to work on the Portuguese plantations or quit work after they had secured the trinkets they wanted, the Portuguese tried forcing them into labor. Owing to resistance from both the Indians and Jesuits, the traders began to import Negroes from Africa. Here, as elsewhere, Frazier (16, p. 108) comments:

[16] The question of whether such practices reflect the industrialist's own prejudices or whether they are matters of personnel administration are discussed in (6).

. . . Negro slavery . . . was the result of the failure of Europeans to reduce the native population to slavery.

It is no paradox but a case in point to note that management may use its power—at home—to break *down* ethnic barriers for it can force persons to work together. Reed (41) describes how the management of a large aircraft plant was able to introduce Negroes in the face of considerable anti-Negro feeling by threatening to dismiss those whites who became "troublemakers." [17] When it is recalled that employment is at the bottom of the white man's rank-order of discriminations, such cases are not so surprising and such policies might work more often than many realize.

The meeting of peoples and the creation of ethnic groups, while a destructive and costly process, is also a creative one. One of the most remarkable of the products of the meeting of ethnic groups has been the *marginal man* whom Park (37, p. 892) described as:

. . . a cultural hybrid, a man living and sharing intimately in the cultural life and traditions of two distinct peoples; never quite willing to break, even if he were willing to do so, with his past, and his traditions, and not quite accepted because of racial prejudice, in the new society in which he now (has) sought to find a place. He was a man on the margin of two cultures and two societies, which never completely interpenetrated and fused.

Park saw him in the emancipated Jew, and in the racial hybrid—the mulatto, the Mestizo, the bastaard.

The true marginal man is not simply a product of diverse traditions or a mixed blood. If the individual casts his lot completely with one or the other of his ancestral groups and succeeds in doing so, then he may be an apostate or a renegade, or simply a somewhat odd member of a group. If he and fellows like him retire to isolation, as have some of the mixed bloods in the foothills of the Blue Ridge Mountains of Virginia, then they are not marginal either. The marginal man is the one who *continues* to live on the margin; he continues to straddle two cultures.

Park pointed out that because he is in the culture but not of it, he can then gain greater objectivity, and if he has at least normal intelligence, he will see more than his culturally inbred fellows will see. With this comes sophistication, individuality, and cosmopolitanism. Park saw a close relation between marginality and the emergence of the metropolis, as has Simmel before him in his discussion of "the stranger" (54, pp. 402–08).

[17] Also important were other factors, especially the war emergency. See (25).

Industry, by bringing cultures together, has been a prolific mother of marginal men. In the early contact of races, when the sex ratio of the immigrants is high, then intermarriage and miscegenation are likely to occur. We then get a generation or more of hybrids.

These persons, detribalized but not accepted into the guest society, have often been the centers of leadership of nationalistic and anti-Colonial movements. But they have also occupied middle positions in the new industrial structures. They have become the clerks and bookkeepers, the shopkeepers (4) and the mediators between the old and the new. Boeke tells us that the Malay word for "trader" is *orang dagang,* which is also the Malay word for "foreigner."

Within industry itself, the marginal man may become a "straw boss," as Hughes has used the term (22, p. 218). The Negro personnel man or the female supervisor are brought in to handle the "race situation" or the "female problems." This leads to the important research question that Hughes raises as to where their loyalties lie. They may wish to identify with staff organizations. But if the company should drop their Negro workers or women workers from the working force then the Negro or female supervisor would probably be let go also (28). Furthermore, the Negro or woman is probably not accepted into the colleagueship of other personnel employees. Consequently, they are likely to be pushed into identification with their own people and to become racists or feminists.

The labor boss in the fruit harvest shares a different fate. He is usually drawn or self-appointed from the labor group itself. He was or is a Chinese, a Japanese, a Negro, a Mexican, or a Filipino. He then leans to use his position in the middle in order to enhance his own power. The worker needs him because of his knowledge and because of his ability to provide for the worker's needs; the employer needs him because he provides an assured supply of workers and supervises them. The labor boss cements his power through striking, through threats of withdrawal of the working force, or blacklisting.

But we find here a major difference between this straw boss and the one typically found in the factory. In the factory, the Negro personnel man or straw boss throws in his lot with the Negro workers because he realizes his fate is tied up with theirs. In pea picking, the labor boss's position is also dependent on that of his workers. *But* the employer cannot stop using Negroes, Mexicans, and so on, as a factory owner might. The employer is therefore hoisted by his own petard. He is the one who has taken every step to insure that the migratory worker *cannot* enter the other non-agricultural employment. He is the one who has asked for Mexican labor. He is the one who wants a cheap, unskilled labor force in large numbers. He has asked for these people and is *stuck* with them. The entire industry is based on the existence of a poorly paid, piece-work rated, heterogeneous, large labor force unable to secure employment elsewhere. This in turn affects prices, the organization of work, and the political power of the growers and the entire structure of the economy. The labor contractor therefore need have no fear, as does the Negro straw boss in the factory, that the growers will drop his Negroes, Filipinos, or Puerto Ricans. His position is entrenched and he can afford to maintain a relatively free-floating role.

The future of ethnic relations in work is a matter for speculation. The present immigration laws in the United States have the effect of reducing new immigration to a trickle. Yet there are still large groups of Mexicans, Puerto Ricans, and Canadians who enter the United States. The Deep South continues to pour out Negroes and whites into other areas of the country, although as industry moves into the upper and Deep South, that process may slow down.

The evidence does not support the statement that intergroup conflict in the work situation is greatly declining. But we can forecast that the work situation will continue to be a major place where divergent peoples are brought together. Whether relations among them will be harmonious or not will depend on the efforts of the groups themselves, management, unions, government and other organizations which link the work situation to the larger society.

CHAPTER REFERENCES

1. Barnes, H. E., *Society in Transition,* New York: Prentice-Hall, 1946.
2. Becker, W., "Conflict as a Source of Solidarity," *Journal of Social Issues,* **9**:25–27, 1953.
3. Benedict, R., *Patterns of Culture,* New York: Penguin, 1946.
3a. Boeke, J. H., *Economics and Economic Policy of Dual Societies,* New York: International Secretariat, Institute of Pacific Relations, 1953.
4. Broom, L., "The Social Differentiation of Jamaica," *American Sociological Review,* **19**:115–125, 1954.
5. Brophy, I. N., "The Luxury of Anti-Negro Prejudice," *Public Opinion Quarterly,* **9**:456–466, 1945.
6. Bullock, H. A., "Racial Attitudes and the Employment of Negroes," *American Journal of Sociology,* **56**:448–457, 1951.
7. Burns, A., *History of Nigeria,* London: Allen and Unwin, 1951.
8. Cayton, H. R. and Mitchell, G. S., *Black Workers and the New Unions,* Chapel Hill: University of North Carolina Press, 1939.

9. Dewey, J., *How We Think,* Boston: Heath, 1933.
10. Drake, St. C., and Cayton, H. R., *Black Metropolis,* New York: Harcourt, Brace, 1945.
11. Durkheim, E., *The Division of Labor in Society,* trans. Geo. Simpson, Glencoe, Ill.: Free Press, 1949. First published in 1893.
13. Efron, D., *Gesture and Environment,* New York: King's Crown Press, 1941.
14. Fisher, L. H., *The Harvest Labor Market in California,* Cambridge, Mass.: Harvard University Press, 1953.
15. Frazier, E. F., *Black Bourgeoisie,* Glencoe, Ill.: Free Press and Falcon's Wing Press, 1957.
16. ———, *Race and Culture Contacts in the Modern World,* New York: Knopf, 1957.
17. Freyre, G., *The Masters and the Slaves,* New York: Knopf, 1946.
18. Hart, C. W. M., *The Problem of Race,* Ottawa: The Canadian Council of Education for Citizenship and the Canadian Association for Adult Education, March, 1944.
19. Hope, J., "The Self-Survey of the Packinghouse Union," *Journal of Social Issues,* 9:28–36, 1953.
20. ———, "Industrial Integration of Negroes: The Upgrading Process," *Human Organization,* 11:5–14, 1952.
21. Hughes, E. C., "Principles and Rationalizations in Race Relations," *American Catholic Sociological Review,* 8:3–11, 1947.
22. ———, "Queries Concerning Industry and Society Growing Out of Study of Ethnic Relations in Industry," *American Sociological Review,* 14:211–220, 1949.
23. ———, and Hughes, H. M., *Where Peoples Meet,* Glencoe, Ill.: Free Press, 1952.
24. Kent, D. P., *The Refugee Intellectual,* New York: Columbia University Press, 1953.
25. Killian, L. M., "The Effects of Southern White Workers on Race Relations in Northern Plants," *American Sociological Review,* 17:327–331, 1952.
26. Kinzer, R. H. and Sagarin, E., *The Negro in American Business,* New York: Greenberg, 1950.
27. Kornhauser, W., "Ideology and Interests," *Journal of Social Issues,* 9:49–60, 1953.
28. ———, "The Negro Union Official: A Study of Sponsorship and Control," *American Journal of Sociology,* 57:443–452, 1952.
29. Lee, A. M. (ed.), *New Outlines of the Principles of Sociology,* New York: Barnes and Noble, 1946.
30. London, J. and Hammett, R., "Impact of Company Policy Upon Discrimination," *Sociology and Social Research,* 39:88–91, 1954.
31. Lowry, E. E., *Migrants of the Crops,* New York, Council of Women for Home Missions and Missionary Education Movement, 1938.
32. Marchant, A., *From Barter to Slavery,* Baltimore: Johns Hopkins University Press, 1942.
33. Mayer, M., "My Ten Anti-Semitic Friends," *Harper's,* 208:77, January 1954.

34. Miner, H., *Culture and Agriculture; An Anthropological Study of a Corn Belt County,* Occasional Contributions from the Museum of Anthropology of the University of Michigan, No. 14, Ann Arbor: University of Michigan Press, 1949.

35. Mukerjee, R., *The Indian Working Class,* Bombay: Hind Kitabs, 1951.

36. Myrdal, G., with the assistance of R. Sterner and A. Rose, *An American Dilemma,* New York: Harper, 1944.

36a. Northrup, H. H., *Organized Labor and the Negro,* New York: Harper, 1944.

37. Park, R. E., "Human Migration and the Marginal Man," *American Journal of Sociology,* 33:881–893, 1928.

38. ———, "Race Relations and Certain Frontiers," in Reuter, E. B. (ed.), *Race and Culture Contacts,* New York, McGraw-Hill, 1934.

39. Pierce, J. A., *Negro Business and Business Education,* New York: Harper, 1947.

40. Pierson, D., *Negroes in Brazil,* Chicago: University of Chicago Press, 1942.

41. Reed, B. A., "Accommodation Between Negro and White Employees in a West Coast Aircraft Industry, 1942–1944," *Social Forces,* 26:76–84, 1947.

41a. Reitzes, D. C., "The Role of Organizational Structures," *Journal of Social Issues,* 9:37–44, 1953.

42. Roback, A. A., *A Dictionary of International Slurs,* Cambridge: Scri-Art, 1944.

42a. Rose, A. M., "The Influence of a Border City Union on the Race Attitudes of Its Members," *Journal of Social Issues,* 9, No. 1:20–24, 1953.

43. ———, *Union Solidarity,* Minneapolis, Univ. of Minnesota Press, 1952.

44. ———, and Rose, C., *America Divided,* New York: Knopf, 1948.

45. Sexton, B., "The Intervention of the Union in the Plant," *Journal of Social Issues,* 9:7–11, 1953.

46. Sharp, L., "Steel Axes for Stone Age Australians," in Spicer, E. H. (ed.), *Human Problems in Technological Change,* New York: Russell Sage, 1952.

47. Shaw, George Bernard, *Man and Superman,* Baltimore: Penguin, 1952.

48. Simpson, G. E. and Yinger, J. M., *Racial and Cultural Minorities,* New York: Harper, 1953.

49. Spero, S. D. and Harris, A. L., *The Black Worker,* New York: Columbia University Press, 1931.

50. Vogt, E. Z., "Town and Country: The Structure of Rural Life," in Warner, W. L. *et al., Democracy in Jonesville,* New York: Harper, 1949.

51. Williams, J. J., "Patients and Prejudiced: Lay Attitudes Toward Women Physicians," *American Journal of Sociology,* 51:283–287, 1946.

52. Winn, F., "Labor Tackles the Race Question," *Antioch Review,* 3:341–360, 1943.

53. Wirth, L., "Some Jewish Types of Personality," in Burgess, E. W. (ed.), *The Urban Community,* Chicago: University of Chicago Press, 1926.

54. Wolff, K. H. (trans. and ed.), *The Sociology of Georg Simmel,* Glencoe, Ill.: Free Press, 1950.

NAME INDEX

Throughout the text, sources are cited by authors' names and/or by chapter-reference numbers. Many pages contain more than one citation, often as numbers only. This index, then, refers, wherever necessary, both to page and chapter-reference numbers. For example, the D. F. Aberle study mentioned on page 196 is cited on that page as (1), the first entry in the chapter-reference list. Hence, the index entry reads: Aberle, D. F., 196(1) . . . .

SUBJECT INDEX

Absenteeism, 66-67
"Absolute" occupational mobility, 169-170
Acceptance, job, 133
Administration: business; *see* Work, economists' approach to; personnel; *see* Work, economists' approach to
Advancement, in occupations; *see* Career contingencies in occupations
Age, as a status symbol, 11, 129-130
Age grading, in occupations, 199-200: education as a factor in, 199-200; point-of-crucial-decision in career, 201; rate of movement as a factor of, 200; rate of technological change in, 200
Agitator, union, 576
"Agricultural ladder" in agricultural mobility, 355-356
Agricultural products, types of, 293-295
Agriculture, trends in, 69
American Society of Equity; *see* Farm, work group
Anomie and the division of labor, 53, 604
Anti-nepotism, 156
Apprenticeship, 57, 232, 480
Arbitration, role in grievance process; *see* Grievances, analysis of
Argots, 238-241
"Armed truce," in labor-management relations, 575-576
Aspirations, lowering of, in factory workers; *see* Career, factory
Associations, informal; *see* Informal groups, in occupations
Atmospheres and traditions, influence upon occupational inheritance, 155-156
Attitudes: of work performance, internalization of, 134-135; of workers, importance of group motivation; *see* Factory work group, analysis of
Authority, 24, 38, 82-86, 102, 122-123
Automation, 8, 57-58
Avocations; *see* Hobbies

Barbering, 73
Bargaining, collective; *see* Collective bargaining process
Bias, of researcher, 14-15
Birth rate; *see* Differential fertility
Births and deaths, role in farming; *see* Farming, institutional system
Blue-collar workers, 49-51
Boredom, 58
Boycotts, use of in union organization, 575-576
Bureaucracy, 84-86
"Bureaucratic personality"; *see* Personality types, occupational, role of, in occupation and self
Business administration; *see* Work, economists' approach to
"Business-like men" in labor union movement, 483-485

"Calling," conception of as an occupation, 202-208
Career, as analytic category, 40
Career contingencies, 43: in occupations, 196-201; factor of recruitment upon, 197-198; occupational advancement a factor of, 198-199; role of age grading in, 199-201; role of job changing in, 196-197
Career, factory, 464-502: career contingencies in, 487-490; mobility in, 476-487; social selection in, 465-475; work and self in, 490-502
Career, mobility, 179-180
Career, occupational, 143-212
Career, in restaurant industry, 390-391
Cash farming; *see* Farming, organization of
Caste, social; *see* Social caste
Casual laborers; *see* Farming, economic complex
Chain of command; *see* Factory
Changes in opportunity structure; *see* Classes, rigidity of